World Brain: Blueprints, Visions and Dreams of

THIS IS a bold and important book. It is a new attempt to develop the idea of a World Brain: to offer theoretical rationales, practical criteria and guidelines for the creation of a Universal Library entailing nothing less than a reorganisation of all knowledge. Traditional visions (The Library of Babel, The Total Library, The Universal Library) were mainly updated versions of the Library of Alexandria. Radley's vision is about much more: the creation of contextualised ideas, circuits of thoughts. Outlined are techno-rights, which make visible the thoughts, opinions, insights of everyman, and thus transform the vision of freedom of thought as outlined in the U.N. Declaration of Human Rights. The utilitarian goal is a new Internet: a technopia that will benefit the whole of humanity, rather than specific companies, interest groups and individuals.

This is not, as its title could suggest, simply another techno-optimist book by a scientist promising that computers offer a simple panacea to everything. On the contrary, it traces how early visions of networked knowledge (e.g. Otlet, Engelbart, Nelson) were narrowed into an Internet and World Wide Web which, although popular, preclude a systematic access to thoughts, ideas, knowledge as foreseen in this vision. It is often said: if it ain't broke, don't fix it. This book explores an implicit corollary. If the system has too many broken links, then we need to start again from scratch and build a new system. This entails creating a new mechanical device. But the larger vision is that this device will improve human thinking methods.

Part of the narrowing that has occurred in the past half century has been driven by the computer science community, especially the AI faction, whose claims concerning artificial intelligence, machine thinking, autonomous computing, continue to inspire visions of mechanical intelligence competing with and/or replacing human intelligence (transhumanism, post-humanism, cf. the predicted Singularity). Radley offers a radically different vision where man remains the master and computers are the tools, servants of man-made visions. To establish this, three chapters are devoted to the self, ideas and thinking, offering a telescoped history of Western philosophy from Plato and Aristotle to the present. Two chapters outline the limitations of current computers and machines. Further chapters outline emerging potentials of user interfaces, cyberspace, virtual reality and robots.

The central vision is of a World Brain, with circuits of thoughts leading to a city of thoughts and ultimately technopia. The author acknowledges that these are linked with dreams of utopia, but is also careful to outline competing dystopian visions. The margins are lined with c. 1,000 illustrations, which offer a visual account of these utopian and dystopian possibilities: ranging from comic strip cartoons and historical diagrams to numerous illustrations of patented devices. It ends with a Universal Declaration of Human-Techno Rights, a Technopian Manifesto and 10 Commandments for humans to computers. The media are filled with articles about how computers are revolutionising the world. Radley's book suggests that the real revolution has yet to begin. It catalogues numerous dangers, but ultimately it is a paean of hope in and for human freedom.

Kim H. Veltman,

Author of *'The Alphabets of Life'* (2014).

Author of *'Understanding New Media; Augmented Knowledge and Culture'* (2006).

If Only We Had Taller Been - *by Ray Bradbury*

The fence we walked between the years did bounce us serene.
It was a place half in the sky where,
   in the green of leaf and the promise of peach,
   we reached our hand and almost touched the sky.
If we could reach out and touch, we said,
   it would teach us not to, never to, be dead.
We ate, and almost touched that stuff;

Our reach was never quite enough.
If only we had tallied then, and touched God's cuff, his hem.
We would not have to go with them, with those who had gone before.
Who, short as us, stood tall as they could and hoped that by
   stretching tall that they could keep their land, their home,
   their hearth, their flesh and soul.

But they like us were standing in a hole.
Oh Thomas! Will a race one day stand really tall,
   across the void across the universe and all?
And measure all with rocket fire.
At last put Adam's finger forth as on the Sistine ceiling.
And God's hand come down the other way
   to measure man and find him good?

And gift him with forever's day.
I work for that, for that short man, large dream.
I send my rockets forth between my ears.
Hoping an inch of good is worth a pound of years.
Aching to hear a voice cry back across the universal mall.

   We've reached Alpha Centauri!
     We're tall!
       My God! We're tall!

The purpose of this book is to explore how...

Computers can give Humans the Ability to:
Think / Act - Freely, Ethically and Optimally
(and for the true benefit of all)

OPENED UP are blueprints, visions and dreams of the relationship(s) between man and machine; and through the eyes of visionaries, writers, and thinkers from throughout time.

In 1970, Sir Lewis Mumford, said:

> The most disastrous result of automation, then, is that its final product is Automated—or Organisation of—Man... he who takes all his orders from the system... and who cannot conceive of any departure from the system... a whole race of acquiescent and obedient human automatons... and a cult of anti-life begins at this point.

According to Mumford, a mechanised dystopia can be avoided; but we must engage in *information pooling*—sharing all the ideas of humanity. Here the ideas, goals and habits of a society are aligned with industrial processes; and by machines that foster: collective freedom of thought/action.

The path to a better world begins by recognising and cataloging the ways in which we are today: not free. Unfortunately man's most precious gift, his *very thoughts*; are too-often censured, isolated and controlled (partly through computers); and increasingly in disturbing ways that tend to enslave him. Accordingly, we list examples of the ways in which automatic systems limit human potential; and explore how computers may—in the future—be used to set us free.

Discussed is an alternative approach to the computers of tomorrow, whereby the wishes, plans and actions of society may be aligned to benefit all. Clarified are the relationship(s) between the design of computers and—ultimately human made—social policies/decisions/outcomes. Cross your fingers.

Alan Radley - Blackpool, UK.

P.S. Along the way we see...
... a panoply of computer secrets/designs/inventions.

ENDURING KNOWLEDGE

SOME PEOPLE think that just because a book/paper/magazine is an older one, then *ipso-facto*, the contained knowledge is old-fashioned, irrelevant, less insightful, and/or has been super-ceded by the inherently superior *(and more factually correct)* perspective(s) of the present day. The reason(s) for adopting such prejudicial views are difficult to fathom. But perhaps they reflect the fact that scientific knowledge does improve and gather momentum over time; and as a result of an ever increasing volume of discoveries and the evident 'snowballing' effects of human industry. However just because we have a fountain of discovery, it does not follow that more recent ideas are necessarily superior.

Older books and papers etc, can *(obviously)* contain profound wisdom; and these same insights may not be available elsewhere. Another point relates to the accessibility of present day knowledge. You may think that your favourite search engine lets you find anything and everything. But the vast bulk of human knowledge remains inaccessible—including more recent 'lost' materials —*or unknown knowns*—and because it is not (readily) available on computers.

Accordingly, it is inaccurate to assume that:

- New ideas (books) trump old ones every time
- All (useful) knowledge is accessible by computer
- Today's information systems are supremely efficient and ultimately effective

An evident fact is that genuine knowledge often-times has relationships that go in every direction and criss-cross subject boundaries. Sometimes therefore, by following the methods of the **generalist** *(who studies everything in great depth)*; new advances can be made. Accordingly, this book is dedicated to the generalists; and to men/women like Leonardo da Vinci, Buckminster Fuller, Edison, Einstein, Ada Lovelace, Ted Nelson etc; who in their work gathered ideas like the ant collects twigs; from anywhere and everywhere.

Sadly, even some librarians accede-to the '*built-in-obsolesce*' argument(s) in relation to ideas; whereby they ship older *(less-borrowed)* books to 'storage facilities' *(and before they have been digitised)* and/or sell them; whilst replacing books with computing terminals. And many libraries are being closed *(in the UK 324 public libraries were shut between 2010-2012)*. What can be done? To start with we need to lobby the politicians; and let them know in the strongest terms that we are not going to let them get away with it *(the destruction of our civilisation)*.

What will you do to help save our cultural heritage?

The Big Picture has lots of contexts, and refers to many contexts simultaneously! - Ted Nelson
It is because books (open-thoughts) are not seen as owned by humanity;
that they may be lost / sold / destroyed.

W O R L D
B R A I N

BLUEPRINTS,
VISIONS AND DREAMS OF
T E C H N O P I A

A L A N   S T U A R T   R A D L E Y

for Kim

and dedicated to:

Francisco, Restie and Rowena,

Ruth and Chris and

Philip, Ellen, Nigel, Arlene, Joshua,

Emma, Ben, and Caroline Radley.

Propositions discussed herein ...

{1} Everyone has the right to **freedom of thought**, conscience and religion; this right includes freedom to change his religion or belief, and freedom, either alone or in community with others and in public or private, to manifest his religion or belief in teaching, practice, worship and observance.

[United Nations: *Universal Declaration of Human Rights*; Article 18]

{2} *Artificial Intelligence (AI) is a 'fiction' or misnomer*

Computer: consciousness, free-will, thought, and creativity are <u>false</u>.
AI is a mere pipe-dream; and all computer related influences on the human-world are simply artefact(s) of human thought; and nothing more.

{3} *Human thinking methods are sub-optimal (today)*

- The wishes of the <u>few</u> (too-often) outweigh the needs / rights of the <u>many</u>.
- Vast numbers of useful ideas, data and votes are hidden, lost and/or ignored.
- Computer systems have become divorced from social responsibility.

w w w . a l a n r a d l e y . c o m

Copyright (©) Alan Stuart Radley 2018

Published and distributed by Alan Radley. Cover design: Alan & Caroline Radley.

World Brain: Blueprints, Visions and Dreams of Technopia

Second Edition [Version 2.0] Fonts: Bembo Std, Gill Sans, Helvetica, Myriad Pro.

~ 1000 illustrations ~ 800 quotations [UK spellings]

Word count: 180,784 words.

Contents

Tron: 'If you are a User, then everything you've done has been according to a plan'. – Tron [1982]

MYTH OF THE COMPUTER

In 1974 Ted Nelson wrote:

Computers are simply a necessary and enjoyable part of life, like food and books. Computers are not everything, they are just an <u>aspect</u> of everything... Man has created the *Myth of the Computer* in his own image, or one of them, (and they are): cold, immaculate, sterile, 'scientific', and oppressive... Some flee this image, others are drawn to it... Many are still about this mischief, making people do things rigidly and saying it is the computers fault... Still others see computers for what they really are: versatile gizmos which may be turned to any purpose, in any style.[1]

Ted's insight and warnings about computer system design are as true, fresh and staggeringly prescient today as they were 40 years ago. We must not forget that computers are human designed artefacts, and they do not have an intrinsic nature and cannot follow unstoppable agendas or else pursue self-determination. If there is anything wrong or anti-humanistic with regard to computers as they exist today, and their associated influence(s) on the world (there is!), then it can only be our own fault.

We present a panoply of ideas, possibilities, wishes, fears and dangers in relation to computers.

Hopefully something appeals...

Synopsis

I N *WORLD BRAIN*, Alan Radley looks at the computer not as a tool, or as a bicycle-for-the-mind, but simply as *self*. He argues that humans are becoming so enmeshed with the computer, in terms of how we think, act and communicate; that soon it may no longer be possible to identify where the self ends, and the computer begins, and vice-versa.

Alan makes a compelling for the emergence of a new phenomenon; the *self-computer*. He explores the myriad of ways in which the self and computer can/will/may: blend, unite and co-evolve; now and in the future.

The nature of the relationship(s) between man and machine has been a popular topic in the works of futurists, social theorists and science-fiction writers. Rich and prescient are many of the imagined societies that result. Thus we embark on a journey into the utopian and dystopian worlds of: H.G.Wells, George Orwell, Philip K. Dick, Jean Baudrillard, William Gibson, Ray Kurzweil, Ted Nelson and Julian Assange etc; and so to explore blueprints, visions and dreams of our technological future.

Predicted by some, are marvellous benefits for technology; in terms of enhancements to our social, creative and personal lives. But already clear, is that not all of the associated problems lie in the realm of speculation. One example, is that the Internet is moving ever further away from the free and open system as foreseen by its original designers; whereby citizens are routinely censored, controlled and spied upon. Imperative is that the self-computer develops according to a humanistic agenda.

Alan postulates a society which benefits all; and he calls it the *technopia*. Introduced is the *Theory of Natural Thoughts*, founded on standard human rights; which may be implemented in a *techno-rights* format to provide for the free, open and frictionless sharing of thoughts, ideas, and most importantly, votes. *Techno-rights* can also be used to govern man-machine relationships and guard against—exploitation of the weak by the powerful.

Overall, developed is an optimistic take on the self-computer, whereby machines serve/aid man and do not enslave him.

Foreword

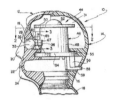

NOT SO very long ago (circa 1950s), room-sized mainframe computers were all we had. And for the vast majority of people, computers were giant electronic 'brains' seen only in science fiction films and in the news. Then in 1976, the personal computer (PC) arrived, in the form of the *Apple-1*. Now you could buy a brief-case sized computer, take it home; and try it out for yourself! Computers were truly magical; and with the help of your new machine friend, there would be no limit to what you might achieve. In the words of Ted Nelson, personal computers were: *Liberation/Dream Machines*.[1]

These new 'microprocessor' based machines brought computing power to the people; and they were rightly seen as mind-amplifiers, tools for thought, and creativity boosters. Potentially they were 'information windows' into the amalgamated thoughts of all human kind. Networked computers could even make us more human; by allowing us to know infinitely more about ourselves—individually and collectively. Nelson foresaw a new computing age; whereby all reading and writing moved to the screen, and knowledge would be set free.

As it turned out, everyone did get a computer—and later on a smart-phone or tablet—and everything went on-line.

And for a time in the mid to late 1990's, the Internet promised to emancipate the individual from established power structures. But the liberation movement fizzled out; and the predicted freedoms evaporated away. Today we see a return to centralised computing; and in the form of massive amounts of personal data held on central servers (a.k.a. the 'cloud'). Unfortunately, centralisation is associated with abuse of power and citizen surveillance; followed by restrictions on individual self-expression. Sadly, Nelson's vision whereby we could all access the deep and parallel structures of knowledge, in fact, never materialised.

This book calls for a return to a humanistic vision of computing; with free, open and unrestricted access to the combined wealth of all human knowledge.

The real danger is not that computers will begin to think like men, but that men will begin to think like computers.

Peter Drucker

Computers are magnificent tools for the realisation of our dreams, but no machine can replace the spark of human spirit, compassion, love, and understanding.

Louis Gerstner

Computers are like Old Testament Gods; lots of rules and no mercy.

Joseph Campbell

I do not fear computers.
I fear lack of them.

Isaac Asimov

The good news about computers is that they do what you tell them. The bad news is that they do what you tell them.

Ted Nelson

Right now, computers which are supposed to be our servant, are oppressing us.

Jeff Raskin

The digital revolution is far more significant than the invention of writing or even printing.

Douglas Engelbart

We must preserve and protect: ownership of thoughts—
—equality of thoughts—and freedom of thoughts!

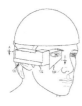

MODERN COMPUTERS

It has become blindingly apparent that there is something wrong with computers. And I do not refer to small issues such as efficiency of use, visual design, operating styles etc; but rather to the end-purposes of current systems. Computers are (too often) used to pursue deliberately sub-optimal and evil agendas and/or to limit the rights of human beings and/or to control them and/or to foster ignorance. The troubling and inescapable truth is that the computers of today are (too often) designed, used and more generally **allowed to be operated** to the detriment of millions all across the globe.

Examples of computers being used to limit and curtail human rights are not difficult to find (we give numerous examples in this book). Witness the revelations of former National Security Agency (NSA) contractor and Central Intelligence Agency (CIA) employee Edward Snowden, who in 2013 exposed the NSA practices of mass surveillance.

In 2012 Julian Assange said:

These revelations about the United States annexing our new world of the internet has produced market forces to do something about it.

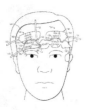

Preface

THE IDEA for the present book grew out of a keynote presentation that I gave at the *Fourth International Workshop in Human-Computer Interaction, Tourism and Cultural Heritage* in Rome, Italy on September 25th 2013.[1] My talk was entitled: *Computers as Self*; and concerned: moves away from the self and moves towards the self; and in relation to computer system design, use and application.

I had summarised the historical, present-day and potential future aspects of the interrelationship(s) between self and computer; but my paper only scratched the surface of a vast and important topic. The ways in which we design, develop and use computers, have far-reaching implications for the future of humanity—and related questions are of momentous import.

In fact, as we become ever more involved with, and dependent upon, computers; it may be that our essential nature is being shaped and/or changed as a result. It is prescient therefore to study the features of an emergent phenomenon; the *self as computer* (merging of self with computer), and in terms of a deeper, broader and more comprehensive inquiry.

Ergo we can learn:

who we were, who we are and who we may become.

Our thesis concerns the nature of mankind's relationship(s) to/with machines. Many writers have speculated on utopian and/or dystopian futures as a result of technological advancements. It is useful to study the history of technological progress in this respect, and not only to discover why each scenario may come to pass, but also to learn how we can better chart the path ahead.

Probable is that our survival and ultimate destiny as a species, depend on the development of appropriate technologies—and especially computers. Thus careful planning is essential when it comes to our technological future.[1]

---

[1] It is not in the stars to hold our destiny but in ourselves. – William Shakespeare

Computers are not intrinsically anti-humanistic. Happening are wonderful developments in the digital arena right across the planet. Fabulous examples include: the World Wide Web, BitTorrents, 3D Printing, Wikipedia, Bitcoin, WikiLeaks, open systems, blogging, tweeting, YouTube, iPad, Internet Archive, Open Librray etc. These and other examples are helping to make the world more transparent, democratic, open and free.

We must 'study' the future intently, and consider the potential rewards and hazards of each scenario.[2] To get the ball rolling, we present an overview of blueprints, visions and dreams with respect to possible future computer-worlds. Accordingly, we formulate a strategy for an ideal human-computer relationship, and postulate a society so arranged as to benefit all; named the *technopia*.

A key feature of the technopia is the establishment of natural human rights—techno-rights—with respect to a technological society; combined with appropriate and human-centric information usage; and so to ensure that machines: interact harmoniously with humanity.[2]

Norbert Wiener urged us to *ask the right questions* with respect to machines, and this book is an attempt to do the same. Our approach is to find human-centric solutions for the problems of an increasingly computer-centric future. But the future is at the same time marvellous and dreadful, known and unknown. The issues are complex because technological issues are intermingled with social, economic, and environmental ones etc. Yet the stakes are so high, that it is beholden on each writer to make his position known.

Paramount, in my view, are three broad-ranging initiatives:

- Thought freedom / equality / ownership (individual & collective)
- Atomic organisation of, and free access to, all knowledge
- Open publication of thoughts / ideas / votes

Thought-ownership is key, in order to ensure that the thinker is rewarded for useful contributions, and not punished or disadvantaged in any way. Knowledge should be free and open, accessible and flowing everywhere and anywhere without limitation—whereby all open-thoughts are visible to everyone.

Unfortunately, current systems fail to provide for the frictionless creation, publication and use of ideas.

There is a computer disease that anybody who works with computers knows about. It's a very serious disease and it interferes completely with work. The trouble with computers is that you 'play' with them.

Richard P. Feynman

Electronic aids, will help the inner migration, the opting out of reality. Reality is no longer going to be the stuff out there, but the stuff in your head. It's going to be commercial and nasty at the same time.

J.G. Ballard

You have riches and freedom here but I feel no sense of faith or direction. You have so many computers, why don't you use them in search of love?

Lech Walesa

Everyone knows, or should know, that everything we type on our computers or say into our cell phones is being disseminated throughout the *data-sphere*. Why do you think GMail and Facebook are free? You think they're corporate gifts? We pay with our data.

Douglas Rushkoff

Not only have computers changed the way we think, they've also discovered what makes humans think—or think we are thinking. At least enough to predict and even influence it.

Douglas Rushkoff

---

[2] Destiny is not a matter of chance; it is a matter of choice.
It is not a thing to be waited for, it is a thing to be achieved. – W. J. Bryan

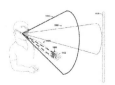
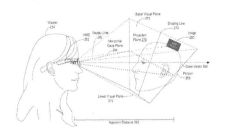

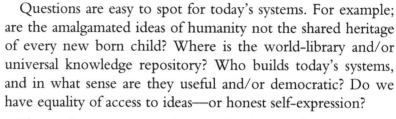

Questions are easy to spot for today's systems. For example; are the amalgamated ideas of humanity not the shared heritage of every new born child? Where is the world-library and/or universal knowledge repository? Who builds today's systems, and in what sense are they useful and/or democratic? Do we have equality of access to ideas—or honest self-expression?

If some humans are spied upon, but others are not, then by definition we do not have equality of expression. Are some humans more equal than others? Do we have—in any sense— sufficient access to the deep and parallel structure(s) of all human knowledge? Is technology evolving by itself, and according to an anti-humanistic agenda? Do certain dark agendas shape computer system design/usage?

Overall, are we allowing: *the wishes of the few to outweigh the needs/wishes/rights of the many?*

Finding the answers is challenging. Certain experts proclaim the existence of technological barriers as justification for why humanistic systems cannot ever be built. Others site economic and/or security barriers. Problems do exist, but we must not use the same as an excuse to block the path to authentic and people-centric technologies. Despite optimism, we live in dark times. Increasingly there is a movement towards centralisation of computing resources. Authorities attempt to justify why we cannot ever be allowed to share ideas (plus votes) openly and/or privately.[3] Are we to accept these self-appointed parties—with self-given powers—as *god-like beings*; who judge, rule and punish the *rest of us* on a whim?

Like Beyonce, we ask: who run(s) the world?

We might not the like the answer(s), or what they say about human freedom(s) in the year 2015. Conversely, we postulate a new type of atomic-network that provides for an open sharing of ideas. A '*World-Brain*' is the result; comprising massively distributed thought-atoms (hyper-thoughts) which offer boundless mechanisms for the creation, preservation, retrieval and sharing of content (ideas, opinions and votes).

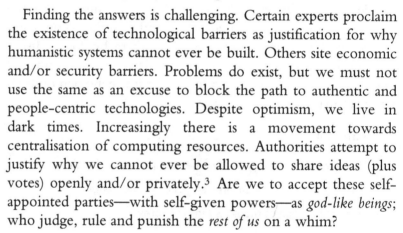

---

[3] Man alone can enslave men. – Simone Weil

George Orwell said: if you want a picture of the future, imagine a boot stamping on a human face—forever.[3] Orwell's nightmarish world is one of *newspeak, thought-crimes, memory-holes, double-think, and of clouded-perception;* whereby thoughts are constantly observed, twisted, negated and used to eliminate free-will/ truth. Systems and machines are used to subjugate man. Foucault likewise imagined super-panopticon surveillance machines that may be used to curtail human freedoms.[4] Hopefully we can avoid such big-brother scenarios, but we must not: throw the responsibility onto the machine.[2]

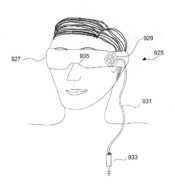

Another prescient comment comes from Lord Bertrand Russell, who said: Machines are worshipped because they are beautiful, and valued because they confer power; they are hated because they are hideous, and loathed because they impose slavery.[5]

The quote is apt. Computers are resplendent machines— with high levels of apparent intelligence; independent decision making ability (seemingly); and—most implausibly— motivations of their own; but they are also, ultimately, human creations. This is an obvious statement of fact, but less clear is why we should all (collectively) allow computer systems to be designed that, in actual fact; restrict freedoms, limit access to knowledge, and favour minority interests. Observe that...

Artificial Intelligence is false; and machines simply obey our commands.

My thesis shall be that design of computers is unquestionably; design of the whole arena of human life, and therefore, in a real sense, design of self. Needed is careful planning, to ensure that humans be the masters—not of each other—but of our machine slaves, and it must not turn out to be the other way around!

Today computers continue to develop in a technical sense, with ever faster processors, and new form-factors etc. However technological mastery remains illusive; and in relation to the biggest problems. In this respect, I am not (unlike some) waiting for the emergence of an all-powerful God-computer that will save man from himself; but I do have faith in a bountiful—*but planned*—technological destiny for us all.

Dwell on the beauty of life...
Watch the stars, and see yourself running with them. – Marcus Aurelius

Technology has moved away from sharing and toward ownership.

Douglas Rushkoff

The spread of computers and the Internet will put jobs in two categories. People who tell computers what to do, and people who are told by computers what to do.

Marc Andreessen

We could say that we want the Web to reflect a vision of the world where everything is done democratically. To do that, we get computers to talk with each other in such a way as to promote that ideal.

Tim Berners-Lee

At our computer club, we talked about it being a revolution. Computers were going to belong to everyone, and give us power, and free us from the people who owned computers and all that stuff.

Steve Wozniak

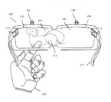

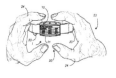

Acknowledgments

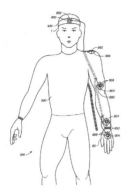

I ACKNOWLEDGE all of the friends, mentors, writers, teachers and others who took the time to time to impart various nuggets of wisdom. Full copyright is acknowledged (where known) for all works, and quoted in the list of captions or else the original publication is given or else the publication date is provided wherever possible.

Thanks to Professor Kim Veltman, Professor Francisco V. Cipolla-Ficarra, Dr Ted Nelson, Dave and Rose Gentle, Restie and Rowena Wight, Philip, Ellen, Nigel, Arlene, Joshua, Emma, Ben, and Caroline Radley, Nigel Pugh, Clark Hood, Ruth Grundy, Chris Green and others.

Special thanks to Kim Veltman for reading/correcting the manuscript; and for inspiration through his magnificent writings, lectures and for friendship.

Computers owned by Alan & Family

1. Atari Games Console (TV screen) - 1981
2. BBC Micro Computer (TV screen) - 1985
3. Samsung Laptop PC (8 inch screen) - 1987
4. IBM PC Clone (10 inch screen) - 1990
5. Amstrad IBM PC (386) clone - 1991
6. IBM PC (12 inch monitor) clone - 1993
7. IBM PC (Pentium - 14 inch monitor) - 1994
8. IBM PC (14 inch monitor) clone - 1995
9. HP PDA Organiser - 1995
10. Palm PDA Organiser - 1996
11. IBM PC (6th Generation - 12 inch LCD) - 2001
12. IBM PC Laptop clone (18 inch screen) - 2003
13. IBM PC clone (hand built) - 2005
14. Apple Macintosh (27 inch LCD screen) - 2008
15. Sony LapTop PC (15 inch LCD screen) - 2009
16. Apple iPod (3 inch screen) - 2009
17. Apple iPhone (3 inch screen) - 2010
18. IBM PC (23 inch LCD screen) - 2010
19. Apple IPad (9 inch LCD screen) - iPhone - 2010
20. Acer Notebook (10 inch LCD screen) - 2011
21. Kindle DX (9 inch e-ink display) + Kindle 6 inch - 2011
22. Apple IPad 2 (9 inch display)
23. Kindle 6 inch display + Android 8 inch tablet - 2012
24. Apple MacBook Air (12 inch + 27 inch LCD) - 2012
25. Apple IPad 3 (9 inch LCD screen) - 2012
26. Microsoft X-Box (TV screen) - 2012
27. Samsung Galaxy Clone (5 inch screen) - 2013
28. Apple iPod (4 inch screen) - 2013

Author's Credentials

Alan Radley is a writer, inventor and generalist who is based in the UK. Alan holds a Bachelor's degree in Astronomy, and also a Doctor of Philosophy (Ph.D.) degree in Physics (from University College London); plus he has two Master's degrees: one in Spacecraft Technology and another in Business Administration. He has worked as a research fellow at University College London and as a research scientist for the European Space Agency and NASA. Alan is a regular public and keynote speaker, and he has taught over 500 students on undergraduate and postgraduate courses in physics, astronomy, and computing. He was granted a patent for his Hologram Mirror in 2009. Alan has developed three main software designs in C++ and Java; named Spectasia, GlobalOpt and KeyMail; and he wrote these programs himself—amounting to some 250,000 lines of code.

POLITICALLY INCORRECT LANGUAGE: No apologies offered for use of man/men/he when referring to humanity; we follow the example of history—and do not impute false meaning to the isolated elements of language.

N.B. Older / ancient english spellings are sometimes used in this book for period quotations.
Curley brackets {} are used throughout to identify founding propositions; and square brackets [] for end notes.

It has become appallingly apparent that our technology has exceeded our humanity.

Albert Einstein

His gaze pierces cloud, shadow, earth, and flesh. You know of what I speak, Gandalf: a great Eye, lidless, wreathed in flame. – J.R.R. Tolkien

Winston: Does Big Brother exist?

O'Brien: Of course he exists.

Winston: Does he exist like you or me?

O'Brien: You do not exist.

Don't you see that the whole aim of Newspeak is to narrow the range of thought? In the end we shall make thought-crime literally impossible, because there will be no words in which to express it. Every concept that can ever be needed will be expressed by exactly one word, with its meaning rigidly defined and all its subsidiary meanings rubbed out and forgotten.

The process will still be continuing long after you and I are dead.
Every year fewer and fewer words, and the range of consciousness always a little smaller. Even now, of course, there's no reason or excuse for committing thought-crime. It's merely a question of self-discipline, reality-control.
But in the end there won't be any need even for that.

Has it ever occurred to you, Winston, that by the year 2050, at the very latest, not a single human being will be alive who could understand such a conversation as we are having now?—George Orwell

We can and must Own Our Thoughts

- Individually and Collectively -

Now and Forever!

Book in a nutshell...

< 50 KEY CONCEPTS >

KeyMail
Spectasia
Technopia
Balance of Good
Atomisation
World Brain
Cosmic Joke
Techno-rights
Real Virtuality
Self-Computer
Hyper-Network
Open-Thought
Thought-Atom
White/Black-Thought
Free-Assembly
Thought-Space
Private-Thought
Secret-Thought
Hyper-Thought
Mini-Think
Hyper-Context
Logon Capacity
Thought-Matrix
Thought-Energy
Stretch-Thought
Self-Centric Data
Natural-Thought
Metron Capacity
Thought-Equality
Live / Frozen Thoughts
Mind-Apps
Thought-Horizon
Data Immortality
Operational Flow
Elements-of-Thought
Thought-Operacy
Atomic Network
Selection Capacity
Implanted-Thought
Simulated Intelligence
Thought-Ownership
Circuits-of-Thought
Stretch-Reality
Omni-link / Back-link
Personal Virtual Reality
Lookable User Interface
Goodfluence / Badfluence
Personal Augmented Reality
Reflexive/pro-active/creative free-will
Warped/hidden/lost/automatic thoughts

Computers must help us to:

Set thoughts free,

Foster humane values,

Understand each other,

and... BE HAPPY!

Frankenstein - by Lynd Ward (1936)

I ought to be thy Adam, but I am rather thy fallen Angel.

Mary Shelley, Frankenstein (1823)

Open-thoughts—
—belong to all mankind.

Chapter One
Introduction

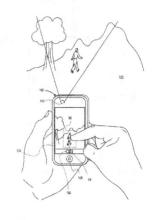

THIS IS a book about the future; and the nature of the relationship(s) between man and machine. We shall consider the status and destiny of humankind, vis-à-vis technology; and through the 'eyes' of visionaries, writers and futurists from throughout time. Sought are broad perspectives, and enlightening world-views; and in order that we may better understand, and manage, the technological path that lies ahead. Concurrently, we wish to ascertain the associated (aggregated) influences of machines upon human society.

It is my belief that long past is the time when we can just let computers develop as they may; and required now is a planned strategy with respect to technology—in the biggest sense—and so to manage human affairs from a *magna eget* (grand perspective).

We shall consider and argue for a new occurrence: the merging of self with computer, a phenomenon which we have named the *self-computer*. Considered are past, present and future prospects for the self-computer; and observed are the individual, sociological and environmental perspectives of the same. The outlook is of necessity sometimes speculative, but we hope that it is not unrealistic, simplistic or narrow.

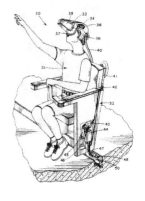

Our thesis concerns topics that overlap multiple disciplines; including *computer networks, virtual/augmented reality, ubiquitous computing, sociology, psychology, ethics, law, humanism, transhumanism, and philosophy etc.* On second thoughts, the list of influences is near endless, since there are no fields of human endeavour to which the self-computer is unrelated; and upon which technological issues do not (in some way) impinge. Accordingly, there are no solely *machine-specific* issues—or *human-specific* ones—and because... the problems of technology and humanity are *intertwingled.*[4][1]

---

4 EVERYTHING IS DEEPLY INTERTWINGLED. In an important sense there are no 'subjects' at all; there is only all knowledge, since the cross-connections among the myriad of topics of this world cannot be divided up neatly.[1]

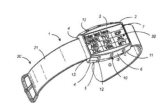

Our approach is to avoid parochial, limiting and sub-optimal viewpoints, and especially because the stakes are so high. In fact the ramifications of technological decisions are almost incomprehensibly high, and in relation to human happiness, well-being and mastery of the future. Today we face considerable challenges collectively as a species, and in this book we seek to tackle the attendant 'big questions'.

At issue, in the longer term, may be our very existence.

In the words of President Lincoln (1809-1865), technology may be the *last best hope of all mankind*.[2] And if there be any truth here, then it stands to reason that we must consider carefully what technology actually is; and in order to better understand its *essence, esse, eimi, or ousia (being)*.

However tackling the subject of technology as a whole, invites consideration of generalities at the expense of specifics; and undoubtably requires a far longer thesis than it is possible to develop in the present (shorter) exposition. Therefore we shall use a narrower spotlight and seek to capture the axiomatic nature, and key features of, a particular form of technology; namely: the computer—in all its variety, forms and wondrous incarnations. Despite our quest for specifics, we do not deny Plato, and usefully adopt the method of Forms (universal features) to probe the nature of computing technology.

A fundamental question arises; what is technology? Finding a satisfactory answer is indeed problematic—and is to a large extent the singular goal of the present book. Professor Ted Nelson (1937-) makes the point that what most people consider to be technology, is in actual fact, not.[1] He says that a 'technology' such as Microsoft Windows or Facebook is simply a bundle of somewhat arbitrary functionality plus capability; which has been put together as a result of a series of biases, and political processes, on the part of human designers.

Here in this book, whilst acknowledging, and considering the ramifications of Nelson's epiphany, we shall nevertheless accede to the wider consensus; and begin by defining technology somewhat conventionally.

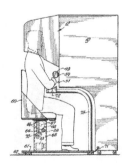

Professor Carl Sagan (1934-1996) wrote: We've arranged a civilisation in which most crucial elements profoundly depend on science and technology.[24]

Dr Robert Oppenheimer (1904-1967), the so-called 'father of the atomic bomb', after seeing the first atomic bomb detonated on July 16th 1945, quoted the Bhagavad Gita: Now I am become death, the destroyer of worlds.

Wikipedia definition:

> **Technology** (from the Greek τέχνη—*techne*, 'art, skill, cunning of hand'; and -λογία, logia) is the making, modification, usage, and knowledge of tools, machines, techniques, crafts, systems, and methods of organisation, in order to solve a problem, improve a pre-existing solution to a problem, achieve a goal, handle an applied input/output relation or perform a specific function.

Thus we (superficially) adopt a broad definition of technology, and include anything normally spoken of—by people everywhere—as being a technology. At the same time, we recognise that even when a particular technology is known to have distinct advantages and uses; it may also inherently possess significant disadvantages/drawbacks; and also by no means represent, or embody, the ideal from of that particular type (or broad class) of technological solution.

And in Ted Nelson's view, true technology may be the smaller (less political) building blocks that are assembled into the bigger composite products and services; and the same smaller pieces being (perhaps): *wifi, chips, keyboard, display, mouse etc.*

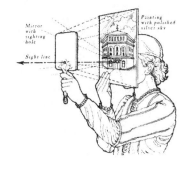

The present book is chiefly about the design and application of useful/appropriate technologies; and it might seem strange that we have adopted such a tenuous definition for a key element of our thesis. However we have done so for a specific reason. It turns out that technology is a vast subject, and it is therefore apt to stalk our quarry from a distance; and in order to better envisage the whole. In any case the specific area of technology that we are concerned with is computer system design, which is an illusive/amorphous topic and one that is constantly evolving. In a way, and partly because of the diverse forms/applications of computers, they elude any fixed definitions—and flee all characterisations.

Overall, vital is that we cast our net wide enough to capture, and include, future computer systems in our exposition. It is therefore useful to loosely define computing technology; and in order to ensure that we can recognise—or foreshadow—any evolving paradigms. In any case...

Only that which has no history is definable. - Friedrich Nietzsche

According to Antoine de Saint-Exupery (1900-1944): The machine does not isolate man from the great problems of nature but plunges him more deeply into them.

Dr Freeman Dyson wrote: Technology is a gift of God. After the gift of life it is perhaps the greatest of God's gifts. It is the mother of civilisations, of arts and of sciences.

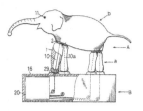

MYTH OF THE MACHINE

In 1974, Ted Nelson wrote:

Public thinking about computers is heavily tinged by a peculiar image which we may call the *Myth of the Machine*, which is taking over the world. According to this point of view, the machine is relentless, peremptory, repetitive, invariable, monotonous, inexorable, implacable, ruthless, inhuman, dehumanising, impersonal, juggernaut, brainlessly carrying out repetitive (and often violent) actions; symbolic of this of-course is Charley Chaplin (1889-1977), dodging the relentless, repetitive, monotonous, implacable, dehumanising gears of a machine he must deal with in the film Modern Times...

what people mainly fail to realise is that machines in general aren't like that... so here we see the same old trick: people building a system and saying it has to work that way because it's a machine, rather than because that's how I designed it...

To sum up, then... *The Machine is a Myth.* The bad things in our society are the products of bad systems, bad decisions, and conceivably bad people, in various combinations. Machines per-se are essentially neutral... If we ignore the myth we can see each possible machine or system for what it is and study how it ties in with human life for good or ill, fostering or lousing up such things as the good life, preserving of species, love and respect.[1]

Do computers...
Inherently enforce—
human slavery, labor—
—and servitude?

Therefore we do not wish to turn our backs on the past, but desire to learn from the long and rich history of technological development. History is bursting with analogies of how to implement, and how not to implement, technological change.

Overall, we wish to combine the outlook(s) of the historian and futurist with that of the humanist.

In order to narrow the remit of the present book, we focus largely on those aspects of computer systems that deal with knowledge, information and data. Thus we consider aspects of the information-sciences, whilst examining digital systems; and set aside consideration of all matters physical. We discard topics whereby computers engage with matter (atoms); for example: *power generation systems, manufacturing, environmental sensing, monitoring, transport, and exploration systems etc.* Included however are robots, automata and 'electric' men or cyborgs.

It is our position that a primary function of the computer is in helping human beings to think and communicate. Obviously computers help us in so many other ways, for example magnifying our senses and physical abilities; and enabling us to create, model, and sense aspects of the world in a variety of ways that would not otherwise be achievable/possible. However despite the multi-purpose and chameleon-like nature of computers, ultimately it is in terms of their affect(s) on the human mind itself; that computers have the most significant impact. Computers (ideally) facilitate, inspire, and shape human thought in the most profound ways; speeding up and greatly magnifying the precision, scope, and scale of access to knowledge. Furthermore computers can (and should) open up the minds—thoughts and ideas—of vast numbers of people to one another.

Computers, operating as idea, thought and communication amplifiers; can (and should) help mankind to address the significant challenge(s) of the future. Hence if we are to adequately face species-level problems; it is incumbent on us all to ensure that we manage said technology goals appropriately.

Ergo we wish to probe the *metaphysical aspects* of computers, and to consider their influence on human thought.

Computers are a type of Rorschach test/blot—whereby a person projects their own thoughts, ideas, prejudices and feelings onto computers in general. So people who are inflexible, tend to see computers as rigid, with fixed ways of doing things; whereas open, creative and flexible types of people see the computer as a blank slate, as a machine that turns dreams into reality, and as a playground for the mind.

Perhaps we do not even have a choice in placing the very highest priority on the appropriate use of technology. Just like THE FORCE in *Star Wars*; technology surrounds and penetrates us, it binds us together. And apparent is that design of technology is—in actual fact—design of...

self, society and human life (all aspects).

A short digression seems worthwhile to consider such a remark. We start by considering the design of a modern social network. The developers of the Facebook, Tumbler or Twitter networks, which (at the time of writing) have billions of users, are in actual fact, not merely designing communication system(s); but rather, in effect, architecting (aspects of) the nature of human interaction itself. Since these networks now represent an ever increasing chunk of all human discourse (and social relations of all kinds); we should, at the very least, be concerned by related powers.

Before we delve into social-networks, it is important to distinguish between centralised and decentralised computer networks. Let us start by defining a computer network as a system of computers interconnected by telephone wires or other means in order to share information. From this perspective, a centralised network is a type of network where all users connect to a central server, which is the acting agent for all communications. This server would store both the communications and (most likely) the user account information. On the other hand, a decentralised computer network (i.e. Peer-to-Peer type) is defined as a data processing system in which all information is processed locally without the need for a central processing facility. Each computer acts as an independent node, and receives information from surrounding computers and decides how to use the same.

We can think of computer networks as—extensions of— naturally occurring networks of human communication.

In fact, it is my belief that computer networks must be designed to preserve this feature; regardless of purpose and whether or not the network in question relates to (apparently) purely computer-computer communication.

The computer is the most general machine man has ever developed... Computers can control, and receive information from, virtually any other machine... it is like a typewriter, wholly uncommitted between good and bad in its nature... there are definite limitations... but they are not easy to describe briefly. Also... they are argued about.[1]

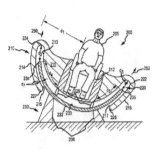

GHOST IN THE MACHINE

The *Ghost in the Machine*, refers to explanation of how a human (or machine), which is composed of physical constituents (atoms), may develop the power of independent thought or may refer to the manner or ways in which said being is able to think and/or attain free-will/a-soul.

The *Ghost in the Machine* is related to Rene Descartes (1596-1650) mind-body dualism. Some claim that to speak of mind and body as substance, as a dualist does, is to commit a category mistake, based around the *Dogma of the Ghost in the Machine*—whereby it confuses two logical types (or categories) as being compatible. The dogma is therefore a philosophers myth.

In the 1967 book *The Ghost in the Machine*, Arthur Koestler (1905-1983) stated that as the human brain has grown, it has built upon earlier, more primitive brain structures (such as anger, hate etc), and it is these that are the true *Ghost in the Machine* for human beings.

In the 2004 film *I Robot* Dr. Alfred Lanning says: There have always been ghosts in the machine. Random segments of code, that have grouped together to form unexpected protocols. Unanticipated, these free radicals engender questions of free-will, creativity, and even the nature of what we may call the soul.

Are computers...
  Inherently leaky—
    —and insecure?

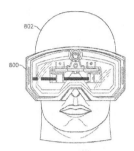

A key topic of the current book concerns the fundamental differences between centralised (unnatural) versus decentralised (natural) networked computers. I make no secret that I believe decentralised networks are (often) superior—from the human perspective—to centralised network designs. And I shall backup my opinion with theory and various factoids.

Centralised network social power manifests itself in various disturbing ways, but especially noticeable are issues related to privacy and security. For example, the network owners often assume that policing social interactions is their job and/or right. Implicit here is that they are eminently qualified, and (forever) perfectly capable of properly so doing—for the collective good. As a result, these unelected bodies (NSA, Apple, Google, Facebook etc) often go ahead and install surveillance robots on everything we do and say on such platforms.

In effect, network owners (often) make certain topics/ subject-matters within social discourse illegal. Specific words are disallowed, for example; and acting as policemen and gatekeepers; they control who may talk to who, and never forget that they know who talks to who—and what has been said! In particular, entirely private communication is normally disallowed, even though secure (and honest), one-to-one chatting is a natural part of banter in the real world.

Even more pervasive is government surveillance, which is being performed on a massive scale by the National Security Agency (NSA) in the USA. Recent press revaluations indicate that all of our emails, tweets etc, are being collected for inclusion in an enormous intelligent spying program/database named PRISM.[3] It appears that as a result of going digital, we must lose all those rights that we once had to privacy in terms of; who we may speak to, what we may say, who knows about it, and when/if social discourse happens. In this book, I will argue that such 'panopticon' spying on ordinary citizens is, in actual fact, breaking our human rights; and perhaps altering the nature—and definition—of what it is to be a human being.

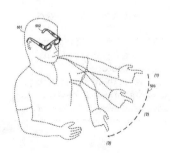

If spying microphones were installed in people's homes, outrage would result. Why is there no outrage for email spying?

Computers are COMPLETELY GENERAL, with no fixed purpose or style of operation. In spite of this, the strange myth has evolved that computers are somehow 'mathematical'... Computers have no nature (no specific purpose), and no character... save what has been put into them by whoever wrote the program. Computers are, unlike any other piece of equipment, perfectly BLANK.[1]

In *The Alphabets of Life*, Kim Veltman (1948-) writes:

> Now, in the real world, a threat of action, an intent to carry out are classed as terrorism, and can lead to years or even a life-time in prison: not for actions but for intentions, or even intentions to help others who might be planning negative actions. Today, the Internet, which poses as a new frontier of humanity, is tending to treat every thought, or word about a possible act, as equivalent to an action.[4]

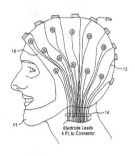

Professor Kim Veltman makes a vitally important point in relation to the interpretation of intention and/or thought-control, however it is an integer of logic that does not appear to be widely recognised. We turn to legal literature for help with this type of moral quandary. In terms of ethics/morality; there are nine fundamental human rights: *the right to life; freedom from torture and slavery; the right to a fair trial; freedom of speech, movement, conscience, association; and thought freedom/ownership.*

And these rights are the bedrock upon which any just society is built; its very foundations, if you like.[25,26]{1}

Interesting is that thoughts are seen (in law) as the private and unassailable property of the individual; that is, they are his/hers to do with as he/she pleases. And the aforementioned rights lie above all other considerations; and are more important than societal organisational structures like democracy, capitalism or communism. Such 'isms' are, one and all, and in a very real sense; simply mechanisms through which humans obtain these basic rights—or are supposed to be afforded the same.

Let us begin with thought-rights. The right to freely develop, own, and to profit from: *one's own thoughts*; is a major theme of the current book. I am going to argue, accordingly (and in specific senses), that owning one's thoughts, means also owning the right to pass those thoughts onto others—and controlling the methods and conditions of so doing—either openly and/or in total/partial secrecy. Furthermore, I will make the assertion that where one does not have such a capability of privacy and/or free expression—and in relation to thoughts—then one is in some sense a *slave*.

One has lost part of self.

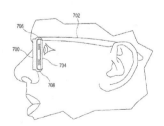

In his 1936 paper, *On Computable Numbers,* Alan Turing (1912-1954) proved that a computer could solve any conceivable mathematical computation if it were representable as an algorithm. He went on to describe a *Universal Turing Machine,* being a device which could (in theory) perform the tasks of any other machine by use of different programs stored on a tape (for example).

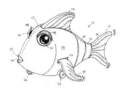

HOW COMPUTERS WORK

The great physicist Dr Richard Feynman (1918-1988) once gave a lecture on classical computers, and specifically on how they are able to think (or more truthfully, do not, and cannot possibly think). He said that the term 'computer' was a misleading name, because computers do not actually 'compute' anything. Computers are simply filing machines, that look things up 'very fast', and so this type of machine follows instructions, and that is all it ever does—just as we do when we look at a multiplication table.

In 1974, Dr Ted Nelson wrote:

What, then is a digital computer? A device holding stored symbols in a changeable memory, performing operations on some of those symbols in memory, in a sequence specified by other symbols in the memory, and able to change symbols in the memory (for example do arithmetic and store the results in memory)... the power of such a machine to do almost anything surpasses all previous technical tricks in human history...

How can computers control so many different things? Different as they may seem, all devices are controlled in the same way. Every device has an interface, that is, its own special connection setup, and in the interface are the registers... and the computer program simply moves information patterns into and out of them.[1]

Are computers...

Inherently complex—

—and difficult to use?

Restriction (or destruction) of thought-ownership breaks a fundamental human right—and you are, in a sense, no longer fully human—whenever this happens. Or at the very least you are unable to operate as a human-being in some way or on specific occasion(s) and/or by means of a particular communication medium. Put simply, if you do not own your thoughts, in any personal and/or social situation or scenario whatsoever, then you are no longer free (proof to follow).

I know that 'social' spying on digital networks is said to be in our best interests, and/or is supposedly being imposed on us to *protect us from harm*. But even if this were so (certainly it is not so in the vast majority of cases); how can we know that such a situation was/is in fact *ever* the case, since nobody polices the police, so to speak. Any overseer protects his own self-interests first, has parochial views and/or makes mistakes. In later chapters we examine this topic in detail; being the ethics and morality of thought-ownership, and especially in relation to computers.

Others may say that we have a choice as to whether or not to use these (*social network, tweeting and email*) systems—and even whether or not to use computers. But do we really have such a choice? It is becoming increasingly difficult to operate in a modern society without using computers and networks of all kinds, and especially for email and Internet browsing etc.

Certainly not having access to some form of social network, texting and/or live chatting program is restrictive at best, and potentially limits one's freedoms and activities in severe and (often) detrimental ways. In fact, we *do not* have a choice, and our unelected overlords know it. Disconnecting oneself from the Internet, and/or avoiding all computers and digital networks, and going 'off-grid' may seem like the activity of a maverick, or paranoid schizophrenic. But only by so doing— and avoiding the on-line world altogether—would the average citizen *possibly* avoid all kinds of spying in relation to aspects of personal activity and interpersonal communication.

However every time you spend money on a credit card (use Amazon, eBay etc), apply for a driving license, pay your rent, and receive a pay cheque etc; you are generating information.

Once I had a long discussion with a somewhat wild-eyed young woman who believed that the government was monitoring her brain with computers. I think I persuaded her that even if this were feasible it would cost the government tens of thousands of dollars to do it, and that probably no existing government agency was interested in her thoughts. I'm not sure she was persuaded.[1]

And all of this data ends up on a database that someone, somewhere, can access on-line (i.e. the NSA). It is almost as if the vast digital network *knows* that you are alive, and is, as a result, watching you. In later chapters, we explore instances, real and fictional, of the gathering and use (or misuse) of surveillance data.

But for now, we concentrate on thought-ownership.

Eric Arthur Blair [pen name George Orwell (1903-1950)] spoke about panopticon spying—constant, everywhere and all-pervasive observation—at length.[6,10] Many other writers followed suit. Each thinker has added his or her own spin onto the debate of the relationship(s) between: *freedom of thought/ expression/action;* versus: *spying, dystopian societies and big-brother.* A theme of the current book is not that the problems of thought ownership lie unexamined, or that nobody recognises the issue(s) and/or cares. Rather we wish to assemble opinions together, and point the way to human-centric technologies that can uphold, and are able to benefit from, thought-ownership.

Our concern is to explain how intermingled are problems of human freedom, thought-ownership and technology design; and in terms of a myriad of influences that appear at every level of society and especially also in terms of individual activity. At issue are the multiple ways in which technology affects, restricts and/or may uphold *thought ownership/freedom.*

In future chapters, we consider different technology scenarios, choices and solutions; and seek to find ways that we can better construct an open and fair society using appropriately designed technologies. Accordingly, developed is the *Theory of Natural Thoughts,* founded on standard human rights; and which may be implemented in a techno-rights format to foster: *ownership, equality* and *freedom of thoughts.*

Overall, my assertion is that each of us should own our thoughts; and in fact that we have a moral and ethical right to them. If we do not, then we are, in some sense, slaves. I put it to you that today's social network, telecommunication(s) and email operators etc, are breaking our *fundamental human rights* when they spy on our communications; and even when they do so with our consent and/or knowledge.{1}

On the 'Diaphanous' era of computing (to come). I refer to both the transparent, understandable character of systems to come, and to the likelihood that computers will be showing us everything... computers will disappear conceptually, will become 'transparent', in the sense of becoming parts of understandable wholes... instead of things being complicated... they will become simple.[1]

MISUNDERSTANDINGS

In 1974, Ted Nelson wrote:

Computer people often say that to understand computers you must have a 'logical mind'. There is no such thing (need or requirement for a logical mind). But saying such things intimidates many, especially those who have been told that they do not have a logical mind... this is to some extent important (use of logic)... in working with computer hardware you must often workout exact ramifications of specific combinations of things, without skipping steps... however intuition has its place in the computer field too. Whichever your habitual style of mind, computers offer you food —and utensils—for thought...

Some people think of computers as things that somehow mysteriously digest and assemble all knowledge. But what you feed into the computer just sits there unless theres a program. Then there is the idea that a computer is something you ask questions of. This assumes that the computer has already digitised and assimilated a lot of stuff and can sling it back at you in new arrangements. In order to answer these questions, there must be some program accepting input, processing the same information, and starting other programs to reply to said questions.[1]

Being spied upon blocks honest self-expression and specifically because you are uncertain what may become of your thoughts, who is reading them, and to what end-uses they may eventually be put. I will make the case that your thoughts are being snatched right away from you, as soon as they are communicated to others; and (very often) when sending an email, text or chat message. This is theft, censorship and it is highly immoral—because we can do nothing about it. And we do not know if/when it is happening, and—once again—for what purposes (or ends) our thoughts are being used.

But the current situation is even worse than this.

By policing the kinds of things that one is able to say on a social network, and the ideas/opinions that one is allowed or expected to express; such surveillance is restricting not only our human right to free self-expression, but potentially our education, and the ideas that can/will/may develop in society; and in a most restrictive and severe manner.

Are these actions not *thought-theft* crimes perpetuated by the powerful against weaker individuals? Whatever happened to respect for other people's opinions? Are we so weak-minded that we cannot tolerate dissension?

It could be (or certainly is the case?) that all kinds of useful opinions, ideas and creative inspirations are being checked (blocked); and before they even begin to emerge. This happens because people are afraid of expressing their true opinions; and as a result of—real and/or imagined—surveillance and possible sanction. It appears that the ever-present spying, and banning of certain words and restriction of opinions and feelings; could influence the development of language, and hence the nature of thought. It is a dangerous path that we are now embarked on.

In a very real—and sometimes pernicious manner—language delineates the limitations of thought and action.[25]

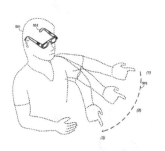

In the book *1984*, George Orwell spoke about the (potentially) corrupting influence of language, and he made several powerful statements that are especially prescient.

In his book *Tools for Thought* Howard Rheingold (1947-) quotes Brenda Laurel's vision of the coming 'fantasy amplifiers': How does it feel to experience a world like that? How does it change my perception to walk through its portals? How do I find where the edges are? What kind of transactions can I have in this world? What will the human interface be like (in the future)—where mind and machine meet?[14]

From *1984*:

> If thought corrupts language, language can also corrupt thought.
> It's a beautiful thing, the destruction of words.
> Freedom is the freedom to say that two plus two make four.
> If that is granted, all else follows.

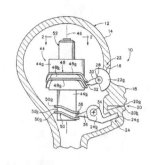

These quotes point to the power of language to influence thought—and vice-versa (see Sapir-Whorf hypothesis). In a way language is thought. If you cannot say or express certain words, feelings and opinions—then those sentiments do not exist, and will never exist—at least for others. And possibly in a sense, these thoughts do not even exist for the *thinker* as well—and one has 'lost' part of one's own mind, so to speak.

We shall open up viewpoints, arguments and theories, specifically that relate to the influence/power of language on/over thought, in future chapters. Examined also are the *social, legal, ethical and moral issues* related to network surveillance. But for now I can (hopefully), leave space in your mind to entertain the possibility that networks should not sensor all human communication by default—and because this may be limiting and/or breaking the human rights, and restricting the freedoms, of countless millions of individuals.

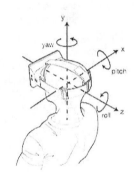

Are such opinions radical?

I hope so—because the world is in a mess. It seems that only a radical solution could possibly offer any hope of making a dent in (i.e. impact upon and solve); the major problems now facing the world, and specifically those relating to *hunger, wars, environmental disasters and education*. Can it be that because we (individually and collectively) no longer own our thoughts—in a technology related sense that has yet to be defined—that we are restricting our capability to govern ourselves?

It shall be my thesis, in the following chapters, to convince you that this frightening world-view is indeed the case. Accordingly I will suggest a cornucopia of mechanisms, laws and technologies—designed to bring ownership back to our thoughts, ideas and votes—individually and collectively—and so to untie our hands *en-masse*.

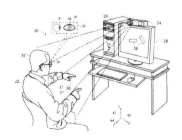

In the well-known paper *Man-Computer Symbiosis*, J.C.R. Licklider (1915-1990) envisions that mutually-interdependent, *living together*, tightly-coupled human brains and computing machines would complement each other's strengths. According to Licklider's view, pure artificial intelligence systems would prove unnecessary.[19]

The fearful unbelief is unbelief in yourself. – Thomas Carlyle

TROUBLE WITH COMPUTERS

In his 1996 book *The Trouble With Computers*, Thomas Landauer (1932-2014) said: **Computers rarely improve the efficiency of the information work they are designed for because they are too hard to use and do too little that is sufficiently useful... computers have not contributed nearly as much to labour productivity as we had hoped, were promised—or by rights, they should.[16]**

Today one asks: has the situation improved; and are computers finally helping us to work more efficiently? Unfortunately there is no straightforward answer to this question. Obviously computers have improved, expanded and multiplied tremendously—and naturally. This is because of the immense **computification** of everything and everybody. And unlike in 1996, we now use computers, mobiles and laptops constantly at both work and home, and in order to help us to perform everyday activities.

Much that we now do would be impossible to achieve without computers. But there are still problems. We often get the same old excuse 'due to a computer error'... or 'sorry we cannot help you—the system is down.' And where are the vastly improved beds, chairs, houses and clothing designs that Computer Aided Design (CAD)—promised?

Let us return to the previous example of the social networks. Do not get the impression that I am against all such networks, because I am not. Rather it is my position that these networks, in various forms, and by defining what we can say, who we can talk to, and also the ways in which we do talk; are (one example of) the forming of a new and artificially constructed—or wholly designed—form of self. This new self is being produced by unelected network owners, and others who are close to the biggest computers (according to Jaron Lanier's (1960-) view [6]).

Vital questions naturally arise. Do we really want a small number of people (the network owners) to define who we are as a people and also what our lives will be like—and including 'academic' people too. Obvious is that networks are not inherently bad; but rather they are essential to our future as human beings. They are places where humans can meet, come together, interact and exchange thoughts and opinions; sharing: *ideas, movies, files, and votes etc.* Networks magnify who we are, in terms of the visibility of our needs, wishes, desires; and they potentially expand the impact/possibility of collective actions (e.g. 'Arab spring').

It is my opinion that computer networks are simply an extension of real-world social networks (or should be). When it comes to networks, the medium really is the message; and the message is simply: this is what it means to be human, or rather this is how you can retain or demonstrate your humanity and/or—*become fully human.* Unfortunately certain aspects of your humanity are to be withheld (on current networks), and specific thought-rights are to be limited and/or removed. But don't worry, it's for our own good! Conversely, I suggest that we must never forget that computer systems—and hence social networks—are designed by and for (ultimately <u>free</u>) humans. This view may seem obvious, but it is sometimes obscured or not recognised.

Professor Norbert Wiener (1894-1964) said that we should: **not throw the responsibility onto the machine.**[7] Hence do not be fooled into thinking that we have lost control of machines in terms of their basic functions and capabilities.

Intelligence Amplification (IA) refers to the effective use of information technology in augmenting human intelligence. William Ross Ashby (1903-1972) wrote: **Problem solving is largely, perhaps entirely, a matter of appropriate selection... if this is so, and we know that the power of selection can be amplified, it seems that intellectual power, like physical power, can be amplified.[23]**

This is not so, machines are at all times human-made artefacts. The machines cannot yet, in any sense, design themselves. And even if they could, they do not (currently) possess free-will or the *will to power*. I think Norbert Wiener was referring to the tendency of system designers (and others), to blame the machine—unauthentically—for those cases where a machine limits human rights, and/or does not perform as it should do, or as the user of the technology would wish it to. From this viewpoint, it is as if the technology designs itself, and/or were somehow alive/self-determining. We shall explore theories of machine 'wishes', decision-making, and self-evolution later. But for now, I simply state that belief in machine self-determination is profoundly wrong, misguided and anti-humanistic.

Machines—and computers—are designed by humans, and we can make of them whatever we like. They are not fixed in stone and are not our overlords (yet). Rather it is the system designers and owners who are deciding what policies the machines progress/implement. In terms of the social networks, the systems define how we humans interact in a variety of ways. They control the language we use and the things we are able/allowed to say to each other; and it is inevitable as a result that they are changing the nature of what it means to be human. Is this a frightening and unbelievably depressing state of affairs? Most definitely. Perhaps we need to go back to the drawing board when it comes to technology; and begin by re-imagining who we wish to be, collectively as a people.

A major theme of this book is the inseparability of technological issues from matters of general and primary concern—including both collective and individual factors. In a way *technology-is-humanity*; because it is now so enmeshed with who and what we are, that design of technology is design of society and self.

< {4} We are the computer and the computer is us. >

A merging of man and machine is inevitable— at least if the human species is to survive.

Steve Wozniak (1950-), co-founder of Apple Computer Inc., speaks about the ways that typical institutions indoctrinate schoolchildren into giving answers to set questions... hence... rewarding people for thinking like everyone else—and perhaps causing everyone to think in a like manner.

Are computers...
Really spiritual machines—
—that can/will/may—
—enlighten us—and show the—
—inherent oneness / linkage /
inter-relationships of everything?

MIRROR WORLDS

In 1996 David Gelernter (1955-) wrote about *Mirror Worlds* which are aggregated, immensely complicated, moving (real-time) simulations, and true-to-life *mirror images* of real-world objects, events and processes, trapped inside a computer.[17]

Here the user/operator can see and grasp whole aspects of what is happening and/or occurring and/or will occur in said real-world system(s). Gelernter predicted (correctly) that software models of human networks (i.e. social networks and cities etc), ecological and natural systems and scientific processes would be built which potentially give to mankind great mastery over his various domains of operation.

Today Gelernter writes about education. He often speaks about the failure of American education, and proposes moving all of human knowledge to online servers so that the college experience can be replaced by user-driven self-education.

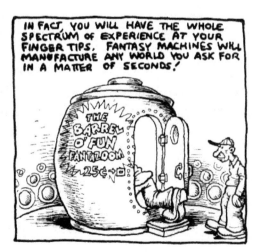

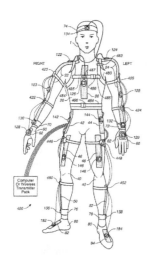

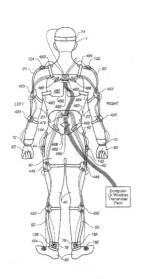

Are computers...
Inherently un-democratic—
—and a tool of tyranny?

But lest we forget, the domain of man is broad in scope[5], and we should not let the *wishes of the few (system-owners/designers)* outweigh the *needs/wishes/rights of the many*. In coming chapters we shall open up the ideas of a variety of thinkers in this respect, before imagining a society in which thought-ownership (and freedom of thought/action) is/are upheld and preserved.

Thus far we have only begun to examine the technological aspects of one of the previously identified basic human rights; thought-ownership. Another one of the basic human rights relates to the right to make a living through work, and specifically—the selling of thoughts and labour.

A large proportion of humanity now makes a living with the help of the digital markets, producing a great variety of digital products, and/or by means of digital channels, and often by use of digital media. At first sight all is well with the world of digital commerce. Millions are now able to sell their wares on sites like **eBay, Amazon** and on 'App' stores etc. However there are problems here also, and once again they relate to the ways in which human beings are able to own the product(s) of their own thought creations.

Put simply there are multiple issues surrounding copyright, and in terms of who can access the combined wealth of humanity, who can make copies of digital items, and in finding ways for people to readily take part in the commercialisation of the products of their own hard work.

Once again we shall consider these issues, one at a time —and also all together—in later chapters. The problems related to copyright are indeed complex, and difficult to understand in terms of the ultimate effects and ramifications on society as a whole. But clear is that the current laws on copyright are not working, and favour neither the creators nor the consumers. It would appear that we need new laws —and systems—that benefit society as whole, whilst ensuring that authors are paid for their creations.

Architecting a (vastly improved) future world is our quest.

---

[5] 'Yours is the Earth and everything that's in it.'– Rudyard Kipling

Author of *Neuromancer* and coiner of the term *Cyberspace* William Gibson (1948-), wrote: The future is here... looking back at us. Trying to make sense of the fiction we will have become... it's just not evenly distributed... Language is to the mind more than light is to the eye... We have sealed ourselves away behind our money, growing inward, generating a seamless universe of self.

A vision of the future will be created, and specifically the mid-term future up until the end of the 21st century. We make predictions of how mankind's technological capacities can/will/may develop during the intervening period—and in terms of information systems. Our thesis concerns the evolution—and/or merging—of man and machine (or computer); and we shall consider the associated affects on individual, sociological and environmental issues. In a nutshell, we wish to probe man's social/technological destiny; and to discover what he may become with the aid of machines—and especially computers.

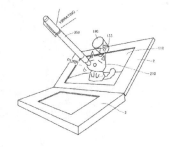

Our goal is to help mankind to chart the potentially difficult developmental path ahead whilst avoiding any visible and/or hidden barriers to progress. We seek to create a utopian future, and to progress the humanistic agenda; complete with democratic values, and human-friendly: *policies, living conditions, agendas, laws and societal mechanisms.*

The focus is on finding ways for people to obtain the fundamental human rights, and more especially in terms of thought-ownership/freedom; which is in some ways a precursor to, and facilitator of, all the other human rights. As an example of such a linkage; I put it to you that with current technology we don't even know what are the collective opinions on almost any specific topic or major issue of global concern.

If we only knew what society (as a whole) was thinking, perhaps we could implement humane policies. This happens through wide-ranging aggregation of human thoughts, opinions and votes; and the corresponding collective and democratic wishes of the majority being put into action. These ideas relate to the implementation of, and definition of, democracy itself—and so to the nature of society. Democracy has multiple meanings and different definitions, but here we refer to the concept in the most simplistic sense imaginable; being the actioning of the collective will of the people. I do not think that we have democracy—on a world-wide basis—at present, no matter what our leaders may say/present/claim.

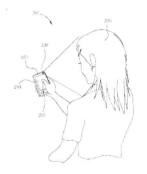

Accordingly, *blueprints, visions and dreams* of mankind's technological destiny; are to be mined for ideas/solutions.

Cyberspace. A consensual hallucination experienced daily by billions of legitimate operators, in every nation... A graphic representation of data abstracted from banks of every computer in the human system. Unthinkable complexity. Lines of light ranged in the non-space of the mind, clusters and constellations of data. Like city lights, receding. - William Gibson, *Neuromancer* [1984]

AUGMENTED INTELLECT

Douglas Engelbart (1925-2013) reasoned that the state of our current technology controls our ability to manipulate information, and that fact in turn will control our ability to develop new, improved technologies. He set himself the revolutionary task of developing computer-based technologies for manipulating information directly, and also to improve individual and group processes for knowledge work.[20]

Doug set himself (and computers) admirable goals:

Increasing the capability of a man to approach a complex problem situation, to gain comprehension to suit his particular needs, and to derive solutions to problems. More-rapid comprehension, better comprehension, the possibility of gaining a useful degree of comprehension in a situation that previously was too complex, speedier solutions, better solutions, and the possibility of finding solutions to problems that before seemed insolvable... where hunches, cut-and-try, intangibles, and the human feel for a situation usefully co-exist with powerful concepts, streamlined terminology and notation, sophisticated methods, and high-powered electronic aids.[20]

Doug's inventions include the mouse input device, the development of hypertext, and the first networked systems.

I shall make the argument that for humanity to progress, we must find out what are the wishes of the majority, and on an issue-by-issue basis, and then collectively implement the same. Along the way we introduce a set of new guiding principles for a technological society, which we name the *technopia*.

A *technopia* is a society so arranged as to benefit all, and it has special laws, rights and technological mechanisms to ensure the same. Especially important are new human rights —*techno-rights*—that every citizen of the world will be afforded. These rights mirror (and extend) the fundamental human rights, and are designed to guarantee that each person obtains the same. A new class of atomic-network is prescribed to help provide and uphold these techno-rights; and we shall imagine the related technopia *(city of thoughts)* in sufficient detail that it could be put into action, so to speak.

Desired are not merely speculations. We consider carefully the lessons of the past, and in particular how thinkers and visionaries have, throughout time, viewed mankind's relationship(s) to/with technology. An exploration is made of the different ways in which technology has developed in past times, in the positive and also negative senses; and from the perspective of individual and collective viewpoints/outcomes.

Thus far we have provided background motivation, and an introduction to, major themes of the present book labelled: *Self as Computer*. However, as much as this is a book about individual *thought ownership, free expression and creative potential*; it is also about the exploration of ideas, education and the ability of humans to learn from, and contribute to, the combined wealth of all human knowledge. The likes of Vannevar Bush (1890-1974) [8], Ted Nelson [1], Paul Otlet (1868-1944) [9] and Kim Veltman [10] have explored these topics in detail. In particular providing free/open access to, and easy navigation of, vast libraries of information is a primary concern.

Any book purporting to identify a golden solution to all of the world's problems—or even a tiny portion of them—is bound to be labelled as optimistic at best, and more likely as deluded, unrealistic, or simply as a work of pure fiction.

In his 2005 book *The Singularity is Near* Ray Kurzweil (1948-) puts forward the view that the law of accelerating returns predicts an exponential increase in technologies like computers, genetics, nanotechnology, robotics and artificial intelligence etc. He says that this will lead to a technological singularity in the year 2045, when progress outstrips human ability to understand it. At this point, he predicts that machine intelligence will be more powerful than all human intelligence combined.[21]

I want a computer that 'explodes' reality
—visually, aesthetically and conceptually.

INTRODUCTION 17

And especially precipitous is the path followed by anyone who considers technological solutions as some kind of panacea. The lessons of history are just the opposite; whereby the introduction of any new technology does normally have major unexpected—and often negative—influences/consequences.

What can be said with certainty is that effective/useful technology design is more difficult than at first sight it may appear; and it is essential to see innovations from the broadest possible 'humanistic' perspective. Perhaps we can follow the key example of the humanities. Established are human rights laws; and likewise it now seems that we need technological rights—or techno-rights—to govern computer systems. Certainly we cannot allow technology to continue to develop without adequate planning. Clear is that vast numbers of people are today being trodden underfoot in terms of basic rights; including aspects of thought ownership and access to the combined wealth of all mankind (e.g. food, materials, knowledge etc).

In this book we view computers as potentially beneficial to society, but as not necessarily so. Machines have always held a janus-like prospect. They magnify human potential with magical and transformative powers, but on the other hand they sometimes bring anti-social, destructive and/or dehumanising forces into society. In the following chapters, we ask why this should be so, and if the negative aspects must always follow any technological progress and/or improvements.

We consider if a new system of techno-rights could possibly help, by fostering *the human use of human beings*.[7] Questions arise, as to the specific ways in which computers may beneficially impact society, and also the ways in which they may sometimes bring about detrimental effect(s). We consider the *how, why, when, where and who;* and in relation to technological change; and using examples from history, fiction and also in terms of basic theory/ideology (old and new).

One may think that many of the problems with respect to technology have been well-examined, and are, to a large extent, well-understood at least in terms of outcomes and especially in terms of the anti-humanistic nature of technology.

Not everyone named Ray is able to let their optimistic dreams of technological utopia go so far as Ray Kurzweil. In *Fahrenheit 451*, Ray Bradbury (1920-2012) describes a dystopian future world in which books are outlawed and burned. Dystopian futures are a common theme of science fiction, in books like *1984* and in films such as *Blade Runner*, *Minority Report* and *The Matrix* (see later chapters).

MICROPROCESSOR

Lying at the heart of all modern digital computers, laptops, mobile phones and tablets etc, is one or more microprocessor chip(s) which (in a sense) operate like the brain in a living being (directing actions and processes in the system as a whole). A microprocessor incorporates the functions of a computer's central processing unit (CPU) on a single integrated circuit. The microprocessor is a multi-purpose, programmable device that accepts digital input, and processes information according to instructions stored in its memory and provides results as output. A modern CPU may have trillions of electronic components, and perform several billion calculations each second.

COMPUTER PROGRAM

A computer program is a sequence of instructions, written to perform specified task(s) on a computer. A computer requires programs to function, and has an executable form that the computer can use to directly execute the instructions. The human readable form of a program may be written in one of many different computer languages.

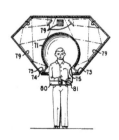

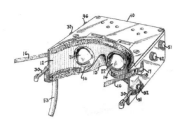

However findings are scattered about in various works of fiction, non-fiction, in papers and now increasingly on social media and in the form of websites and blogs etc. And when it comes to solutions, the lesson(s) of history are difficult to divine. In particular, it would seem that technological revolutions are hard to predict, even harder to manage, and almost impossible to control. Clear is that one technology tends to sweep aside and/or encompass previous technologies.

Furthermore the social implications, which at first tend to appear bright and optimistic; in reality turn out to be far darker than we would otherwise have wished for. And the dangers in relation to technology are real. Long ago, Henry David Thoreau (1817-1862) warned that men must not: **become tools of their tools**.

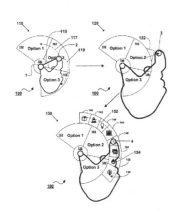

Another interesting (and mystifying) feature of the current zeitgeist, relates to the manner in which many people uncritically accept all technological developments as somehow correct, natural, just and inevitable and/or unstoppable.

Perhaps we—as a people—do not even believe that we have the power (or ability) to shape and control our creations. One example, is that no organisations or regulatory bodies are responsible for the overall strategic direction of all computing inventions on a worldwide basis, and in particular from a humanistic perspective. Hopefully this is about to change, as Sir Tim Berners-Lee (1955-) has recently called for the creation of an on-line *Magna-Carta* or *Bill of Rights* for the Internet.[13]

Today it would seem that we are no longer mere spectators and detached users of machines, but rather it appears that we are now immersed inside of a new global technological entity. Whatsoever 'it' is; has been much debated, for William Gibson it was *Cyberspace* [11], for Sir Tim Berners-Lee the *World Wide Web* [12], others called it the *Internet*, the *Information Super-Highway*, or the *Global Village*, still others the *World Brain*, and not least, George Orwell (1903-1950) called one version of it *Big Brother* [5].

I will argue that 'it' is simply self; and furthermore it is a self that we ourselves can design, form, shape and use in whatever ways may suit our collective future needs and wishes.

Technology is an expression of mans dreams. If a man did not indulge his fantasies, his thoughts alone would inhibit the development of technology itself. Ancient visionaries spoke of distant times and places, where men flew around and about, and some could see each other at a great distance. The technological realities of today are already obsolete and the future of technology is bound only by the limits of our dreams.[1]

In the 1960's humans went to the moon.
  Demonstrating bravery, risk-taking and self-confidence.
    Man possessed a zest for adventure and exploration.
      What happened to us? Where are the huge, risky projects of today?
Are we as Men or Mice? Where are the heroes? What shall be our legacy?

I dreamed a strange dream; dreamed that a star from heaven-splendid,
six-rayed, in colour a rosy-pearl... and over half the earth a lovely light...
    Spread, and the world's heart throbbed, and a wind blew,
    With unknown freshness over lands and seas...
        Of wondrous wisdom, profiting all flesh,
        Who shall deliver men from ignorance...

Sir Edwin Arnold

Computer Power to the People!
Down with Cybercrud!
Ted Nelson (1974)

Computers must help us to:

Share thoughts easily and without censure,

Access the combined wealth of all knowledge,

Publish ideas / votes openly,

and... Know, Respect plus Implement...

the needs and wishes of humanity!

Internet
Search Tools

< P2P >
Faroo
Seeks
YaCy

< META >
Blingo
Yippy
DeeperWeb
DogPile
Excite
HotBot
Mamma

< SEMANTIC >
Hakia
Yebol
Sophia
True Knowledge
Yummly
Swoogle

< COMPUTERS >
Shodan

< NATURAL >
Ask.com
Bing
hakia
Lexxe

< PRIVACY >
DuckDuckGo
Ixquick

< THOUGHT-
ATOMS >
None!

Energy Explosion - by Albert Robida (1880s)
Electricity liberates and enslaves the world—
personified as a provocative woman with evil intent.

Beware, for I am fearless, and therefore powerful.
Mary Shelley, Frankenstein (1823)

óÔÒ ⌐☈? óÔÒ

Everybody must...
understand computers.
And that computers
are not finished—
but are designed by people
—and that all the wrong
decisions have been made.
Ted Nelson (1974)

Chapter Two
Self

WHAT IS *self*? Is self mind, body or spirit? What does it mean to be an individual in a society? Where are we going as a species? What are computers? What is the nature of the relationship between self and computer.

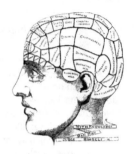

Such 'top-level' questions will be our muse.

In this chapter we start by exploring the natural (non-technological) self, and in terms of human thoughts, needs, motivations and creative potential. Aspects of self are explored in a variety of forms and using multiple definitions. In particular, we open up: the mental world of self, the purpose of self, self in society; and begin to look at the relationship(s) of the self to/with technology.

In order to be able to design humane computer systems, it is perhaps a good idea to begin with the primary cause of all human activity; man himself. Such a postulate is nevertheless speculative. To René Descartes, God is the primary or first cause; where a primary cause is capable of causing itself, and which cannot thus be traced back to a beginning that does not include itself.[1] If I may beg the reader's pardon, in the discussion that follows we shall sidestep any role of the deity, but nevertheless adopt the useful approach of first causes.

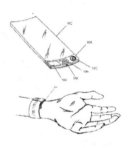

This book is written from a logical perspective, and from the standpoint of a rational universe. In Aristotelian terms we uphold first causes, and assume that there exists (in nature) a chain of events stretching backwards in time. Therefore we accept causal happenings and believe in mankind's ability to affect the same.

Assumed is that man has the ability—and responsibility—to create his own future through appropriate choices, activities and planning. Man controls his destiny, and he must plot a course through the universe alone, and without any help, so to speak.

A question follows (for humanity):

quo vadis—where are you going?

HUMAN DESTINY

Don't confuse poor decision making with destiny. Own your mistakes. It's ok; we all make them. Learn from them so they can empower you!

Steve Maraboli

I am the sum total of everything that went before me, of all I have been and seen done, of everything done-to-me. I am everyone and everything whose being-in-the-world affected and was affected by me. I am anything that happens after I'm gone which would not have happened if I had not come.

Salman Rushdie

Man is something that shall be overcome... Man is a rope, tied between beast and overman—a rope over an abyss...What is great in man is that he is a bridge and not an end.

Friedrich Nietzsche

Everything is determined, the beginning as well as the end, by forces over which we have no control. It is determined for the insect, as well as for the star. Human beings, vegetables, or cosmic dust, we all dance to a mysterious tune, intoned in the distance by an invisible piper.

Albert Einstein

If we believe in free-will, then mankind's potential futures are many, and we have the responsibility to plan for beneficial outcomes. Building upon these principles, a central question becomes definition of our individual and collective goals; and in terms of humanity as a whole.

A legion of writers have speculated on man's ultimate purpose; variously described as propagation of the species, the accumulation of knowledge, exploration of the universe, enlightenment, consciousness evolution and service-of/union-with the Universe and/or God. It is beyond the scope of this book to speculate on the ultimate purpose of man. Perhaps we can sidestep this question, and adopt *all of the above* as our definition of mankind's collective purpose. Thus we align ourselves with a kaleidoscopic (transcendent) vision of human destiny. Although susceptible to accusations of naïvety, such a view avoids overly narrow or limiting perspectives.

In the discussion that follows, we adopt a realistic outlook, including both the optimistic and pessimistic viewpoints. However with optimism there is a tendency for productive actions (for the future). And as the Dali Lama (X1V) (1914-) says: choose to be optimistic—it feels better.

We shall return to the topic of human destiny in the latter parts of this book; and in particular to address the issue of the collective—democratic—assignment of goals, priorities and resources, and for the benefit of the human species. How to organise society for practical and efficient purposes, is a central topic for utopian thinkers. In the social sciences a long running debate concerns collectivism versus individualism, and in terms of the organisation and operation of an ideal society. Pivotal is the question of how an individual lives his/her life, either (on the one hand) entirely for the benefit of society, or (on the other hand), entirely according to personal desires.

Our approach is to seek the middle ground, and to find ways for individuals to be fulfilled—personally—whilst also meeting any social responsibilities. A tall order I know, but...

Dreams if they are any good, are always a little bit crazy. - Ray Charles

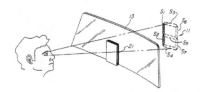

We begin with the self-perspective, and adopt the outlook of an individual. Accordingly, we define the self as:

> The subject of one's experience of phenomena; the 'world', and it is made up of our perceptions, emotions and thoughts. It is *that which experiences*. The self is the subject that observes the object. An 'immediate given'; the self is intrinsic to all experience, and central to all that we have known, will know or ever can know. Self is you and me; and not him, her or them.

> **Etymology of self**: seolf, silf, sylf, self, self, silfe, selph, selfa, selve, sulfe; all from Teutonic base SELBA. The origin is unknown, but perhaps SELBA is for SE-LIB-A, where *Se* is the same as the latin, one's own self; and *Lib* as in based on LAIBA, a remnant of bi-Laib-jon; *to be left*.

If this is right the origin of self is: **left to oneself**.

The term emphasises the concept of identity; and may be linked to notions of separateness, uniqueness and autonomy.[6] In the Scandinavian language self is the only one who exists; which draws attention to the perspectival nature of reality. Such a definition alludes to the—*unreality of other*—and to the uncertainty of the existence of any minds apart from self.

Consider... *I think therefore I am*.[2]

We refer to self variously as the independent human being, the ideal (or average) self, and/or who—at any moment in time—encapsulates all that it is, and means, to be an individual person in mind, body and spirit. However the concept of self can and often does evolve; and according to *cultural, technological, economic and political factors etc*. Self is a function of social convention and/or custom. One might say that the idea of self is a slice, judgment or reflection of a society, in terms of the general outlook, ambitions, philosophy, social and political structures of its members etc.

Self is a luminous beam, the ego, which scans all creation in judgment. The world is a reflection of you, and you of the world. However, the process of turning this beam (of consciousness) onto oneself, is more difficult, and also less immediately illuminating, than one might think.[7]

---

[6] Did not christ selue alwaye pray to hys father? – Geste Agst. Priv. Masse Hiv b (1548)

[7] One's own self is hidden from one's own self. – Friedrich Nietzsche

I THINK THEREFORE I AM

Cogito ergo sum; 'I think therefore I am', is a philosophical proposition by Rene Descartes (1596-1650). Taken on face value, the simple meaning is that thinking about one's existence proves—in and of itself—that an 'I' exists to do the thinking.

Many thinkers have criticised the so-called 'cogito'. The Danish philosopher Soren Kierkegaard (1813-1855) argues that the *cogito* already presupposes the existence of 'I', and therefore concluding with existence is logically trivial.

Others say: '*the only claim that is indubitable here is the agent-independent claim that there is cognitive activity present*'. The objection, is that rather than supposing an entity that is thinking, Descartes should have said: 'thinking is occurring'. That is, whatever the force of the *cogito*, Descartes draws too much from it; the existence of a thinking thing, the reference of the 'I,' is more than the *cogito* can justify.

Friedrich Nietzsche (1844-1900) criticised the phrase in that it presupposes that there is an 'I', that there is such an activity as 'thinking', and that 'I' know what 'thinking' is. He suggested a more appropriate phrase would be 'it thinks'. In other words the 'I' in 'I think' could be similar to the 'It' in 'It is raining'.

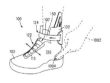

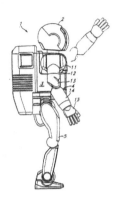

Even if it were not so, often a person's view of himself—his/her self-concept—develops, changes and grows throughout life. Largely we shall ignore these (psychological) aspects here. *Who we think we are* is not our concern, but rather our aim is to explore *who we actually are*, as individual human beings—and also in a societal sense.

A person's own self-concept can be said (partially) to define who they are (or think they are); both uniquely as human being, and also collectively in a species-type sense. The concept of self can be a reflection of our highest ideals, and in terms of an ultimate life-philosophy; with respect to mind, body and spirit. The self has also been studied extensively by great minds throughout time, and concepts of self are central to many world religions and also philosophical systems. And with the rise of technology, the fundamental and potentially changing nature of self has been much discussed in fields such as *technoself, cyborg, posthuman and transhuman studies*.[3]

Defining the concept of self further than this is difficult; and may involve complex ideas and philosophical reasoning. An obvious distinction is between self-as-subject (or active agent) and self-as-object (or observed entity), and we shall explore both aspects here. Examined are who and what we are, and in the real/imaginary, and inward/outward senses.

Other questions arise; for example; is the self part of the ego, personality, identity consciousness or soul.

Largely for our purposes, we wish to adopt (where possible) all of these definitions, because we desire the creation of a future society—in fact a kind of utopia—where humanistic values, in all aspects, are merged with technological values harmoniously; and to ensure that human beings are cherished, nurtured and protected. Our concern is not solely with the welfare and interests of the individual. We wish to consider the educational, health, social and economic well-being of humanity as whole. The outlook is an optimistic one, and we aim to find ways to improve health and living standards, and to magnify the creative and developmental potential(s) of human beings; individually and collectively.

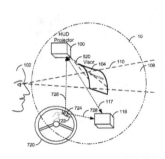

Wikipedia defines a machine as: a tool containing one or more parts that uses energy to perform an intended action. Machines are usually powered by mechanical, chemical, thermal, or electrical means, and are often motorised. However, the advent of electronics technology has led to the development of tools without (large-scale or not including electrons) moving parts that are considered machines. [www.wikipedia.org: 24 April 2014]

Individual and Collective Goals

We seek the utopian outlook. We oppose selfishness, greed and human oppression, and reject any use of technology to further the same. The outlook is idealistic and humanistic, but not unrealistic—we hope. Some theorists have focussed on the cognitive-orientation of the self, and others on the information-processing characteristics of self; and yet others on educational, health and well-being, creative, spiritual and/or social aspects.

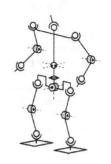

As stated, we wish to nurture all of these different aspects of the individual, and potentially other (unstated) ones as well. But in a collective sense the self is diverse, with many different personality types, motivations and desires.

The question arises as to how it is possible to account for the wishes of all (in a society), and also to cope with—apparent and real—antisocial and criminal/evil tendencies.[8] Such are the problems of sociology, philosophy and politics; and we note that the issues, perspectives and opinions are many. The related questions are to some extent beyond the scope of the present book in terms of details.

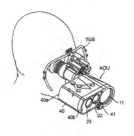

To simplify matters, we focus on the big questions, and on providing ways for humans to come together *en-masse*, and specifically in order to solve major problems jointly as a populus. Since mankind consists of a vast collective, it stands to reason that meeting the needs of the individual is important. This is so, even if, in some respects (morally etc) and on particular issues; the *needs/wishes/rights of the many* outweigh the *needs/wishes/rights of the few*.

We must recognise that the needs and wishes of the many, and the few (or one), are often diametrically opposed, and compromises must sometimes be made in the short term, and for long term good. Such problems fall onto the domain of politics, ethics, morality etc.

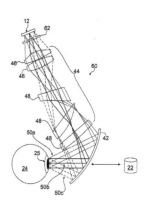

Man is a social creature, and sought are shared perspectives.

------

[8] And therefore as a stranger give it welcome. There are more things in heaven and earth, Horatio, than are dreamt of in your philosophy. – William Shakespeare

Our definition of the term 'computer' encompasses every possible type of information processing machine/tool; for example including: central and 'cloud' servers, networks, systems, personal computers, laptops and portables, desktop touch and wall-sized gesture screens/surfaces, TVs, games consoles, mobiles, smart watches and rings, tablets etc. Throughout this book we also (unapologetically) use the terms machine, system or network interchangeably with the term 'computer'.

CYBERNETICS

The word *cybernetics* was first used by Plato in the context of 'the study of self-governance'. Norbert Wiener defined cybernetics in 1948 as 'the scientific study of control and communication in the animal and machine.' The word 'cybernetics' comes from the Greek word κυβερνητική (kyverni tik, 'government'), i.e. all that are pertinent to κυβερνώ, the latter meaning to 'navigate' or 'govern'.

The essential goal of cybernetics is to understand and define the functions and processes of systems that have goals and that participate in circular, causal chains that move from action to sensing and to comparison with a desired goal, and again to action. Cybernetics is a transdisciplinary approach for exploring regulatory systems and their structures, constraints and possibilities. It includes the study of feedback, black boxes and derived concepts such as communication and control in living organisms, machines and organisations including self-organisation.

In a technological society it would seem prudent to manage the affairs of man closely (or to create efficient mechanisms for so doing), and in particular because modern society is becoming increasingly complex, stratified and (to a large extent) automatic. In the minds of some, society is today, to a large extent, 'out-of-control'. Cybernetic theory would seem to be a helpful tool, and especially to discover how to put things right.

We do not support the view that the issues related to self/society are simple, and/or that there is always a right solution to every problem. We only suggest that there may be an optimal way—an ideal method and/or procedure—to apply to difficult decisions (in terms of societal mechanisms). Obviously we are speaking of moral and legal issues; and in terms of both old and new mechanisms; and hence the design and application of society itself. Our focus shall be on finding ways for an ideal society to operate with the aid of, and by means of, technological systems—and especially from the perspective of computing systems.

The issue of morality and social justice is central to the humanistic perspective. It is difficult to imagine a just society in which a significant number of people were unhappy and/or unfulfilled. Balancing the needs of the many, against individual needs; would seem to be a sensible approach. But this is a difficult task, since people are diverse in belief systems and motivation; but also due to the fact that some people do not associate with the collective point of view. We meet a real quandary when it comes to human nature. Kindness, sympathy and understanding, in relation to the needs and wishes of our fellows, would seem to be the righteous way to proceed.

Unfortunately, sympathy and empathy are often in short supply. Perhaps a small dose of reality is useful at this point, and in order to clarify the reasons why we have undertaken the present study. Despite the incredible technological advances that have been made, technology has not significantly, and—arguably at least—does not significantly, in fact help the vast majority of people in any way whatsoever. How do I know this? Well to start with, let us agree that the world is in a mess. Every year *millions of children die of hunger*, and up to *one million people die in wars*.[4] In fact the richest ten percent own ninety percent of the world's wealth.

And so it can hardly be true that mankind lives wholly according to fair and democratic principles; since it is a fact that the *minority effectively make slaves of the majority*, and in an economic sense. Evidence of this fact abounds.

In the USA, one percent of people own forty percent of the total wealth.[5] Even Ancient Rome had a more equal distribution of wealth, with one percent owning sixteen percent of the combined wealth—and Rome was a slave society! Overall, it is difficult to believe that the vast majority of (poorer) people would not vote for a change in relation to a more equal distribution of wealth—*if they possibly could*.

Democracy must be somehow broken in this respect, or at least is extremely ineffective (rich people have lots of excuses).

However as indicated, technological issues are enmeshed with sociological and political ones, and these cannot be separated. If it is true that democracy is failing to operate—for whatever reason(s)—and on such a simple matter as an equal distribution of resources and food; then it stands to reason that such an issue involves technology. Furthermore related problems cry-out for technological solution(s).

Equating technology with social responsibility would not seem to be a radical point of view, but others may (and do) disagree. Arch capitalists argue for a separation of industry (and presumably technology) from social agendas. However such an unthinking approach has undoubtedly helped to get us into the current mess—or at least not helped to prevent it.

But those who argue for a more humanistic use of technology have been/are legion. In *The Human Use of Human Beings*; Norbert Wiener said: we must not throw the responsibility onto the machine[6]; and the central postulate of his thesis was that we must design machines that take full account of human needs, and in all senses. Not allowing machines to harm/abuse/de-humanise us, and preserving/upholding human rights is/are key.

Most people in the world are unable to vote the issue of (even) a *relatively* fair distribution of wealth to a high enough priority; and so that it is made a key goal and hence solved. Society in current form(s), and as it presently exists, follows other goals—in fact any other goals. Finding ways for computers to help mankind to solve—and not to create—such social 'inefficiencies', is the singular goal of the present book.

Are such views optimistic/naive—or common sense?

AUTOMATONS

The Human Use of Human Beings is a book by Norbert Wiener published in 1950. Wiener was the founder of the theory of cybernetics which refers to the theory of message transmission among people and machines.

It is the thesis of this book that society can only be understood through a study of the messages and the communication facilities which belong to it; and that in the future development of these messages and communication facilities, messages between man and machines, between machines and man, and between machine and machine, are destined to play an ever-increasing part.[6]

Wiener stated that such messaging is a form of *feedback*. People, animals and plants all have the ability to take certain actions in response to their environments. Wiener explains, that, in the same way, machines have feedback mechanisms in order for their performance to be altered in accordance with results. In the context of a human/machine society, he offers a definition of the message as 'a sequence of events in time which, though in itself has a certain contingency, strives to hold back nature's tendency towards disorder by adjusting its parts to various positive ends'.[6]

Wiener identifies the *automatons (semi-independent machines)*, which are inherently necessary for humanity's societal evolution. But the automatons must be used for the benefit of man, rather than for profits.

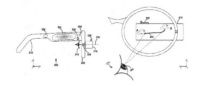

Human and Machine Rights

It would seem obvious that society must not let very few people own all of the money and power; whilst at the same time restricting access to opportunity for the rest of us. If human affairs continue on their present course, then we may become a race split in two, with some humans living as Gods, possessing ultimate power over the rest of us, and complete with lavish lifestyles and riches far greater than any king or emperor who has ever lived.

Perhaps this is the world that we are living in.

I know that my analysis seems sweeping and simplistic—and perhaps it is. But the facts speak for themselves. The *haves* own the vast majority of wealth and the *have-nots* must settle for very little indeed. Does anyone think that billions of citizens want to live below the poverty line in so-called democracies? How can *starving people* be justified—ever? But many of the powerful do justify, in fact, the same with excuses and/or by doing nothing.

It seems clear that a significant portion of human beings do not have any say whatsoever in how the world is run. Certainly a huge power imbalance exists between the *haves* and the *have-nots*. And many other examples can be sited.

Sharing wealth out amongst everyone fairly; is not rocket science, but a matter of the setting of appropriate priorities and giving everyone a say in how we organise world affairs. Is such a view optimism, realism or naivety?

Is not a better question: why (and how) do we (aka humanity) let the few dictate to the many?

Do we even care about our opinions as a collective—or are we somehow impotent when it comes to fair and efficient resource allocation?

We hereby identify the first aspect of a desired change from the perspective of the self-computer: access to power (for the majority) in terms of the allocation of fundamental resources— including food. By power we mean democratic voting rights (on many/all issues), and hence some—or-any—power to make changes and/or to select priorities on issues of collective concern.

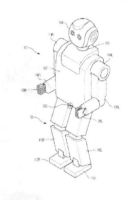

As stated, these and other societal problems do not exist merely in the realm of politics, but cross over into the sphere(s) of the operation of technology itself. In a sense technological issues are inseparable from social ones and vice-versa. It follows that each major technological issue is also a political one. The role of technology policy is central to the type of society that we wish to have in the future. No bigger question faces humanity. Overall, we can say that a key goal of all technology must be: to improve (or better) the lives of the creators (us). If not, then like songster Burt Bacharach (1928-); we ask: *What's it all about, Alfie?*

In *What Technology Want*s author Kevin Kelly (1952-) argues (metaphorically) that technology is a living, breathing organism that has its own consciousness, needs and tendencies.[7] According to such a view we can merely steer technology into its best roles; and then observe from a discrete distance. Kelly believes—to a large extent—that how technology develops is (somehow?) out of human control.

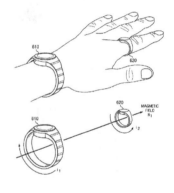

Such a view is wrong—I hope—and eminently anti-humanistic. It is also symptomatic of an outlook/approach (or disease) first identified by Norbert Wiener, whereby we *throw the responsibility onto the machine*: techno-determinism[2]

On the contrary, we must not allow technology to get what it—or truthfully the designer—wants; so-to-speak, but rather build technologies that are entirely and resoundingly humanistic, in both outlook and capability. Perhaps we can even build machines that are empathic with the human perspective; or at the very least ensure that those building the machines—plus the machines themselves—respect/ accede-to human needs, wishes, and rights.

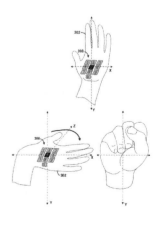

So its upward rays are its honey-cells. -The Upanishads [6000 BC]

I think we need to develop a more sophisticated and generalised form of Dr Isaac Asimov's (1920-1992) laws of robotics.[8]

Asimov's three laws of robotics:

1. A robot may not injure a human being or, through inaction, allow a human being to come to harm.

2. A robot must obey the orders given to it by human beings, except where such orders would conflict with the First Law.

3. A robot must protect its own existence as long as such protection does not conflict with the First or Second Law.

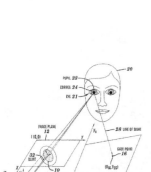

We can transpose/develop similar laws for the designers of computer systems to implement; replacing injury with concepts like thought-ownership etc (see later chapters). However some 'experts' do not believe that laws are necessary; and specifically in order to protect humans from machines.

In response, I refer the reader to a November 15th 2013 article in the UK *Daily Telegraph* entitled: *Do we want to give them a License to Kill?* Reported was a meeting in Geneva, whereby the United Nations (UN) debated giving automated machines—including flying drones and walking robot soldiers—the right to kill human beings on the battlefield.[9]

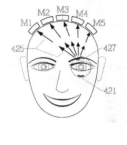

Such a proposal would have staggered Asimov, because it is the very opposite of what he was proposing; whereby robots must protect humans, and under no circumstances allow them to come to harm. In the 1970s many people thought that Asimov's ideas were pointless, and because such sentient (and/or autonomous) robots could not—and would not—ever be built. How wrong they were.

Laws or no laws, already people die on most days of each year as a result of flying robot 'drone' attacks (admittedly controlled by humans). And it is only a small step (technically) to giving such machines the autonomous—self-deciding—right to kill.

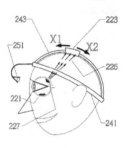

And if you don't believe that 'autonomous' walking, talking and <u>shooting</u> robots yet exist, then I can assure you that they are almost here—witness the humanoid robots made by **Honda, Boston Dynamics (Google)** and **NASA.**

Can humanoid robot police be very far away?

And robot teachers?

... robot... builders?

... shop assistants?

... cleaners?

... gardeners?

... maids?

... drivers?

... friends?

... judges?

... etc

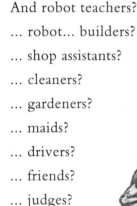

ROBOT UPRISING

Cybernetic revolt or robot uprising is a scenario in which artificial intelligence (either a single supercomputer, a computer network or sometimes a 'race' of intelligent machines) decide that humans are a threat (either to machines or themselves) are inferior, or are oppressors; and try to destroy or enslave them (all humans) potentially leading to a machine/robot rule.

Cybernetic revolt is a common theme in science fiction. It is at least as old as Karel Capek's introduction of the term robot, and can be glimpsed in Mary Shelley's (1797-1851) *Frankenstein*, where Victor ponders whether, if he grants the monster's request and makes him a wife, they would reproduce and their kind would destroy humanity. In the movie: *Colossus; The Forbin Project*, a pair of defence computers take over the world. Other fictional examples of machine uprisings include in *The Terminator* film, where a sentient computer named Skynet attempts to exterminate humanity through nuclear war and using an army of robot soldiers called Terminators.

The Singularitarians advocate a peaceful cybernetic revolt known as the 'technological singularity', and argue that it is in humanity's best interests to bring about such an event. They postulate that a society run by intelligent machines (or cyborgs) could potentially be vastly more efficient. In an age when computers run the world's stock markets, fly aircraft and approve all financial transactions etc, perhaps we are already close to a world run (largely) by machines.

In 2013, an activist group named: *The Campaign to Stop Killer Robots* rightly opposed the aforementioned motion. Reading Asimov as a boy in the 1970s, I hardly believed that I would see such a proposal come to pass in my lifetime; although I felt (or knew) that robots would one day be amongst us. But in fact, Asimov turned out to be right—we do need his *Laws of Robotics*—and at about the same time period—because he predicted such laws would be needed in 2015!

The question of thinking machines, definitions of life, and robot/human rights all arise as a result of such advances. Needed are new laws as a result of developments, and these will be seminal to the type of society that we shall have and build in the very near future. It is a question of what type of society do we want our children to inherit. The issue of robot-killers obviously relates to just one aspect of a desired change from the perspective of the self-computer; the human right to life/safety. But other changes will-be/are required.

Our attention is drawn to the distinction between human and machine rights. Do machines (ever) have the right to make decisions with respect to human affairs? Are they even capable of independent decision making—or do machines merely implement human wishes? In an age when the IBM computer WATSON beats all contestants on the USA 'question and answer' TV game-show Jeopardy; it is at least debatable whether machines have learned to think or not. Possibly we may even see a future bill of 'robot' rights similar to the human ones; an issue debated in *Star Trek* where robot commander DATA wished to be recognised as a sentient being.

Leaving the issue of *machine intelligence* to a later chapter, I would like to address a subject closer to hand; specifically the human mind. Before we can make any recommendations as to how machines might better be able to account for, or even to respect, human rights, wishes and needs; we must first make sure that we understand human nature itself. As machines (computers etc) become more intelligent, and so move closer to human beings, more attention is thrown onto the question of what it is to be human in the first place.

Actually Artificial Intelligence (AI) has generally become an all-embracing term for systems that amaze, astound, mystify, and do not operate according to principles which can be easily explained. In a way, AI is an ever-receding frontier, as techniques become well-worked out and understood, their appearance of intelligence, to the sophisticated, continually recedes. It's like the ocean, however much you take out of it, it still stretches on—as limitless as before... It should be perfectly obvious to anybody who's brushed even slightly with computers, however—that they just don't work like minds. - Ted Nelson

Mind and Thought

The human mind is complex, flexible and it contains rational and irrational, plus conscious and unconscious aspects. Any theory of mind must cope with different personality types, the variety of individual circumstances, and a great diversity of conditions in which human beings live; and in terms of upbringing, education, lifestyle etc.

In a sense; mind is self.

In his 1954 book *Motivation and Personality*, Professor Abraham Maslow (1908-1970) proposed a new theory of human motivation based on a hierarchy of needs.[10] According to Maslow, fundamental human needs are located at the base of a pyramid with the largest, most basic needs at the bottom and the need for self-actualisation at the top. This is a profoundly humanistic approach, whereby we (that is, each of us) must first satisfy lower level—survival related—needs (on the pyramid) such as food, water, sleep, plus safety. These needs must be satisfied before higher ones begin to motivate the individual's behaviour, such as love, esteem and finally self-actualisation.

Other theories of motivation to explain human behaviour have been developed. Attachment theory attempts to explain the dynamics of long term relationships between adults and children. Whilst analytical psychology (Professor Carl Jung) examines the concept of a meaningful life, and has a particular focus on personality development throughput life and on the contributions of society to individual happiness. In Jung's view personality type influences behaviour, motivation and happiness. Jung's work is particularly interesting for the study of human nature, personality and individual motivation; but his ideas were precipitated by the work of two others: Schelling and Freud.

German romantic Friedrich Schelling (1775-1854) first coined the term *'unconscious mind'*. He postulated the existence of thoughts that occur automatically; and that are not available to introspection and include thought processes, memory and motivation.[11]

Mind has both conscious and unconscious (hidden) aspects.

HUMANOID ROBOTS

The term 'robot' was introduced in Karel Capek's (1890-1938) 1921 play *Rossum's Universal Robots [R.U.R]*. The play begins in a factory that makes artificial people, called *roboti* (robots), out of synthetic organic matter. They are not exactly robots by the current definition of the term; these creatures are closer to the modern idea of cyborgs or even clones, as they may be mistaken for humans and can think for themselves. They seem happy to work for humans at first, but a rebellion leads to the extinction of the human race.

In 1928, one of the first humanoid robots was exhibited at the annual exhibition of the Model Engineers Society in London. Invented by Capt. W. H. Richards, the robot Eric's frame consisted of an aluminium body of armour with electromagnets and motors, and it could move its hands and head and be controlled by remote control.

Today ASIMO is perhaps the most advanced humanoid robot in the world, and is capable of recognising moving objects, postures, gestures, walking and interacting with humans. However even ASIMO is by no means capable of taking its place in society as a general purpose 'worker/thinker/actor'.

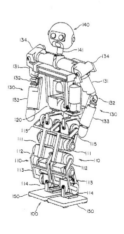

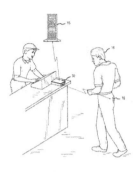

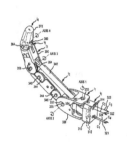

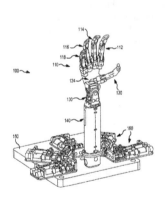

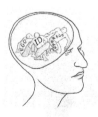

Discovery of a part of the self that existed below the level of immediate awareness was a great leap forward and also a true milestone in terms of understanding human nature. In 1899, Professor Sigmund Freud (1856-1939) published: *The Interpretation of Dreams*, where he popularised the *unconscious mind*; and put forward the view that this part of the mind speaks to us by way of dream symbology.[12] At once our mental aspect doubled in size; and we could no longer be defined solely by our waking, rational selves. Each of us has another hidden self-aspect—a part of self which is at the same time seemingly out-of-control, mysterious and beyond immediate knowing.

Professor Carl Jung (1875-1961) proposed that the unconscious be divided into two layers, the *personal unconscious* and the *collective unconscious*.[13] The personal unconscious is a reservoir of material that was once conscious but has been forgotten or suppressed; similar to that envisaged by Freud. Whilst the collective unconscious is the deepest level of the psyche, containing the accumulation of inherited psychic structures and *archetypal* experiences.

In a way the unconscious mind is necessary because the ego—or conscious part of ourselves—cannot cope with the great complexity of all our mind's capacities all-at-once, because this would then hinder (or block) real-time perception and thinking. We would become dazzled by a great number of *images, thoughts, symbols, logical deductions etc*; and because the contents of our minds are so packed with information that—if we could see this all at-once—we would no longer be able to function.

Freud and Jung also came up with the concept of the archetypes. Archetypes are unconscious images with universal meanings that are apparent in a culture's use of symbols. Incredibly, the unconscious is said to be inherited and to contain material from an entire species rather than just from an individual. Jung called the collective unconscious: **the whole spiritual heritage of mankind's evolution, born anew in the brain structure of every individual**. It seems that the self may not be quite as independent, unique or separate (from others) as it appears.

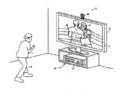

Jung believed that human personality was in a state of constant development, through a continuous process of self-awareness, transformation and self-actualisation. Thus an individual continually re-constructs herself (in terms of mind content, structure and processes), and importantly the self is not fixed or static—but is constantly changing. This discussion brings attention back to our previous definition(s) of self, which now seem overly simplistic, incomplete and/or un-developed.

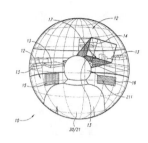

Perhaps a step backwards is useful at this point. What we are attempting to do in this book is to define a useful concept of self—in terms of an individual's totality; and including his mind, body and also social aspects etc (and encompassing even spiritual aspects). But we must begin by understanding the mind, the fountainhead from which all else flows. In so doing, our ultimate aim is to analyse the nature of the relationship(s) between man and machine— and especially in terms of the interrelationships between self and computer. In later chapters we shall examine all types of self-computer relations; *physical/mental, space/time, social/ individual, human/technological etc*. But for now, and in the next few paragraphs, we are concerned with defining the self in mental (and human) terms alone.

It is useful to adopt a method of structural analysis for the mind—and to define some new terms. The *psyche* is the totality of human mind; conscious and unconscious. In older English and Greek texts the word *soul* is sometimes used synonymously with that of psyche; and has been linked to *spirit, soul, ghost, life, breath and conscious personality etc*.

In Latin self becomes *anima*, which has in all cultures been associated with life, death and the afterlife. Jung suggested calling the total personality which, although present, and cannot be fully known, the *self*. The three main parts of the self are the ***id***, ***ego*** and ***super-ego.*** The id is a set of uncoordinated instinctual trends; whilst the super-ego plays a critical and moralising role; and the ego is the organised, realistic party that mediates between the desires of the id and the super-ego.

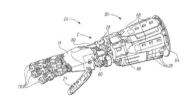

< {5} Self = [id + ego + super-ego]. >

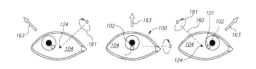

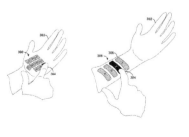

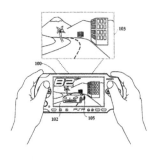

Many interesting facts have been identified as a result of this method. For example, the *id* is the disorganised part of the personality structure that contains basic drives. Thus it controls hunger, sexual attraction and anger or fear etc. It is the only part of the personality that is present at birth; and is the source of all basic needs, desires and impulses. The id is part of the unconscious that operates according to the pleasure principle, whereby we seek immediate gratification of any impulse.

Freud said of the id:

> It is the dark, inaccessible part of our personality... and most of that is of a negative character... we approach the id with analogies: we call it a chaos, a cauldron full of seething excitations... It is filled with energy reaching it from the instincts, but it has no organisation, produces no collective will, but only a striving to bring about the satisfaction of the instinctual needs.

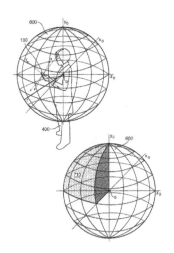

The concept of id explains quite a lot about the overriding motivations of certain people; and furthermore it explains why we all get so tetchy when we are hungry or angry—specifically because this part of the mind 'takes us over'. By contrast the ego acts according to the reality principle, whereby it seeks to please the personalities drive in ways that will benefit the long-term rather than bring short-term grief.

Freud concedes that as the ego:

> Attempts to mediate between id and reality, and it is often obliged to cloak the unconscious commands of the id with its own preconscious rationalisations, to conceal the id's conflicts with reality, to profess... to be taking notice of reality even when the id has remained rigid and unyielding.

The ego comprises the organised part of the personality structure that includes defensive, perceptual, intellectual-cognitive, and executive functions. Conscious awareness also resides in the ego, although Freud says that not all of the operations of the ego are conscious. The ego is the me that is thinking, talking to itself and 'hearing' the words that I write at this very moment.

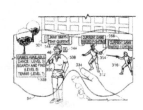

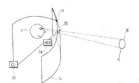

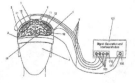

The final part of the psyche is the *super-ego;* which reflects the internalisation of society and cultural rules. The super-ego works in contradiction to the id. The super-ego strives to act in a socially appropriate manner, whereas the id just wants instant self-gratification. The super-ego controls our sense of right and wrong and guilt. It helps us to fit into society by getting us to act in socially acceptable ways. Obvious is that some people have-more id and/or super-ego than others, and vice-versa!

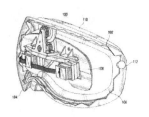

This structural model of the mind has many advantages, and in particular it can help us to understand the mind's *modes operandi or modi operandorum.* It informs us that we do not always immediately understand ourselves—no matter how hard we may try. This is because, although the id is unconscious by definition, the ego and the super-ego are both partly conscious and partly unconscious.

Jung said that every thought or idea is the result of a whole set (or complex) of other thoughts and feelings which are enmeshed together in a web of internal relationships. For him every psychic process (series of mental events) has a value quality attached to it, named its *feeling tone*. This indicates the degree to which the subject is affected by the process or how much it means to him. Note that this feeling tone may not be conscious to the self at-all—but it is nevertheless still present.

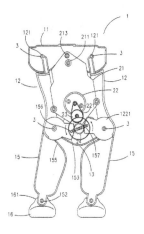

In this view, a **concept** of any idea or thing is a pattern of meaning, an abbreviated description, definition or set of 'facts' concerning the thing in question. And concepts may be made up of sub-concepts in a nest of linkages and/or hierarchies. Important is that every concept consists of intellectual (thinking) values and also feeling-tone values. Whether the mind decides to take any action, or to make any conclusion in respect to a particular fact and/or event will be dependent (in each case) upon a complex web of relationships, and of both types of value judgments— *thinking and feeling tones*. In this view, it becomes obvious that the human mind is not always rational.

< {6} Concept = [pattern(s) of meaning + links] = [thoughts + feelings]. >

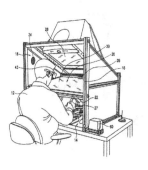

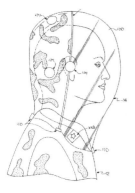

Another interesting feature of Jung's work is the idea of the complex. A complex is a core pattern of (relatively fixed): *emotions, memories, perceptions and wishes*; organised around a common theme or idea. One is often not aware of a complex—or at least of its origins or why/how it came to be. Complexes are 'stuck-together' agglomerations of thoughts, feelings, behaviour patterns etc.

Fear of 'blue coloured spiders' is one example of a complex.

Complexes of ideas are often positive or negative, and can be of varying size/complexity. Overall, the theory of complexes brings attention to the fact that human thought processes may be relational, changeable and/or fixed, and they are often hidden but potentially understandable. Thoughts may be broken down and analysed—often with the help of an analyst or friend—although when one does so, one may be surprised to discover hidden thought processes and motivations that the 'thinker' himself had not been aware of.

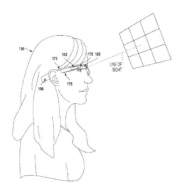

In fact all human thinking has elements of this constellation structure, and so operates like a vast web of patterns of related thoughts and feelings. < {7} Thinking = a constellation of concepts. >

The theory of complexes is interesting; because it indicates that we build up web-like thought-systems in our minds, complete with interrelated logical/irrational patterns of thought and feeling tones. These are like logical sub-routines in the brain, 'running' in the background; and that become active and/or can be felt when certain events/thoughts occur.

Is the mind simply a nest of 'computer' programs?

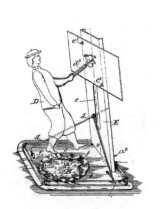

In a way the complexes are very similar to computer applications or *Mind-Apps;* that may be said to be *running* in our minds, or brought into life, from a 'background-field' of running brain 'processes'. We may not be aware that these *Mind-Apps* (my own term) are live, or running, that is working or processing information and producing thoughts.

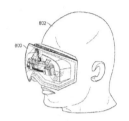

It is startling how much like a computer the mind is—and especially in terms of *programmability* and *re-programmability*.

This analysis may also explain the sometimes irrational nature of all humans. Jung said that free-will is only superficial; because the feeling of 'free-choice' is subjective; as what oneself (the ego) *thinks* often comes into conflict with the *desires* of the id and/or the morality of the super-ego. Thus other parts of oneself prevent the 'self' from doing what it really wants to do—or feels is best—in a purely rational sense.

Jung also developed the theory that we all have psychic human-like figures (archetypes) inside our minds. One type of archetype is the *shadow-self*. In Jungian psychology the *shadow* refers to the unconscious aspect of the personality; which the conscious ego does not identify in itself. Because one tends to reject or remain ignorant of the least desirable aspects of one's personality, the shadow is often negative; but it may also be positive. According to Jung, the shadow, in being instinctive and irrational, is prone to psychological projection, in which a perceived personal inferiority is recognised (falsely) as a perceived moral deficiency in someone else. One projects qualities onto other people, and so one sees *someone-else* as greedy—when in fact it is <u>*you*</u> who are the greedy one!

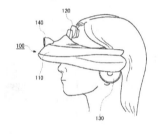

There are other older archetypes present in the collective unconscious, being archaic patterns and images that often provide a counterpart to our basic instincts. These are constellations of thought-forms such as *mother, child, trickster, profit,* and *evil magician* etc. Once again we can project these archetypes onto others, or else identify these with our own personality. One example is strong mythic figures such as Hitler (or Jesus) who were/are able to identify with archetypes and so influence the behaviour of millions.

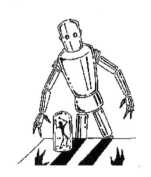

HOW 'I' COMES ABOUT

An "I" comes about—via a kind of vortex whereby patterns in a brain mirror the brain's mirroring of the world, and eventually mirror themselves, whereupon the vortex of "I" becomes a real, causal entity.[27]

Douglas Hofstadter

THE UNCONSCIOUS

Carl Jung said that the unconscious mind has to speak to the conscious part of the mind using symbols, images and by means of dream imagery. Often the unconscious mind speaks to us by means of a dominant character—a priestess, sorceress, earth mother, goddess of nature or love etc.

Unfortunately the unconscious part of the mind (which is a far wiser, larger part) cannot tell you things logically and directly, but must communicate through dreams, symbols and analogies. Taking the form of a wise older person provides guidance indirectly. The unconscious self, which also has a negative, evil, lustful, 'dark', and lying side, may also appear as an aggressive/ vengeful warrior, or as an angry demon/animal/spectacular-or-unusual-object etc. In many cases the self figure is communicating matters of vital importance. A common (perhaps positive) representation of the self is as a gigantic, all-embracing figure that personifies and contains the entire universe.

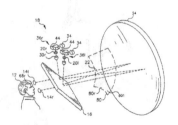

We do not have space for a more complete discussion of Jungian psychology. Jung's work is vast in scope and there are few areas of human activity upon which it does not impinge and/or enlighten. Overall, Jung teaches a key fact when dealing with human thought. Put simply, each of us makes allowance for, not only *intellectual judgments*, but also for *feelings and value judgements*, and *conscious and unconscious judgments*, on the content in question. Perhaps the main lesson here is that intellect and feelings are difficult to put into a single harness— and they often conflict with one another.

Our very nature is: *bi-partitioned or dual [i.e. logical + emotional].*

Jung also speaks about the need to unify the self, in all aspects —conscious-and-unconscious—light-and-dark. This process occurs normally through the use of dreams and symbols; and specifically mandalas which are common throughout India, China and Thailand etc. In this view one should attend to—listen to and consider carefully—thoughts, dreams and images that seem to 'pop' into your head from no-where in-particular; because these ideas are in fact coming from a second (larger) and perhaps wiser unconscious part of yourself. Once again, one's own self is hidden from oneself.

In fact, to a large extent we are all guided by our unconscious desires, beliefs and aims. Jung said that man knows only a small part of his psyche, just as he has only a very limited knowledge of the physiology of his body. Thus the *causes and ends of thought* transcend consciousness to a degree that should not be underestimated. It would seem essential therefore for mankind, individually and collectively; to render visible all logical and (seemingly) illogical thought patterns.

We must fully understand ourselves—and hence our very minds—before we can comprehend how to move ahead either individually or collectively as a species. Accordingly, the key to mankind's future may simply be: *self-knowledge*—personally and collectively—combined with the will and means to act appropriately for positive outcomes; and thus for the true benefit of all.

Openness, visibility and communication can free mankind.

Jung put this idea more succinctly:

> No one can know himself unless he knows what, and not who, he is, on what he depends, or whose he is (or to whom he belongs) and for what ends he was made... the secret is first and foremost in man; it is his true self.

One might wonder what significance our hidden (unconscious) self-nature has upon our view of reality. In fact, the influence could not be any greater. Put simply, there are always unconscious aspects in relation to our perception of reality. Even when our senses react to real phenomena, including sights, sounds etc; they are somehow translated from the *realm of reality* into the *realm of the mind*. Within the mind they become psychic events, whose ultimate nature is unknowable. Thus every experience contains an indefinite number of unknown factors. When combined with the fact that every object has unknown aspects—due to the limitations of human understanding and perception—it becomes clear that our view of worldly matters is sometimes very sparse indeed.

Finding ways to make human decision making explicit, open and fair is essential (at least if our species is to survive).

Moving away from personal, structural or internally generated concepts of self, some experts have emphasised the social aspects of self-construction. People can separate from— and engage with—others in different actual, imagined and virtual ways. Doubtless culture, social convention and social experience all have tremendous impact(s) on human behaviour —and especially on the human mind itself. A complex web of *social, economic and cultural relationships* impact upon, and define, human life as it is lived from birth right through to death. Issues of control, capabilities and capacities, individually and collectively; turn the concept of self into perhaps the key issue of the social sciences, with any advances potentially throwing light on why we act as we do.

Thus far we have focussed on the mind of the self, whilst (implicitly) assuming only positive aspects of socialisation; but undoubtably society is not always a positive force on the self.

RETREAT FROM REALITY

A major theme of the present book is human conception of reality; and how it can/will/may change as a result of the merging of self with computer. In later chapters we explore how techniques such as Virtual Reality, Augmented Reality and Cyberspace, can (and do) alter our perception(s) of reality and perhaps even (in a sense) re-define the nature of what it is to be a human being.

A question arises: does constant immersion in technology necessarily cause humans to retreat from reality, or else to become detached from and/or less involved in the real world? It is certainly a difficult question to answer, and one which is much debated. Questions arise around the nature of inner/outer, visual/intellectual, mind/body, and possibly the reality of space-time. Eastern thinkers categorise such binary dualisms (opposites) as twin sides of the same coin, or aspects of the one truth.

And questions about the ultimate nature of reality may not be so interesting/urgent, once we recognise that each of us (at least to some extent) creates his or her own reality (you are what you think/imagine/perceive). It may be that the computer, by allowing us to carefully control and manipulate (and colourfully 'paint') our individual mental worlds; clarifies and solidifies our personal illusion(s) and makes them seem more real.

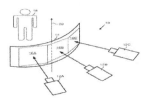

The Social Self

In the 1960s, Professor Michel Foucault (1926-1984) spoke about the ways in which social institutions shape the minds of human beings. In particular, Foucault sees all human knowledge as a power struggle, a struggle played out in various managerial languages and bureaucratic discourses resulting in social control and domination of individuals and collectives.

In modern society, says Foucault, individuals are increasingly subject to what he terms *disciplinary power*, a power that is hidden, monotonous and invisible.[14] He adapts from Dr Jeremy Bentham (1748-1832) the term *panopticon* to define the manner in which prison inmates are subject to continuous surveillance and thus to a structure of power and domination.

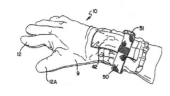

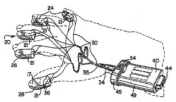

Foucault extends his analysis to society in general, and says that power is imposed on people through the bureaucratic surveillance of populations, the routine gathering of information and the continual monitoring of daily life, saying that in effect the modern age is one of *panopticism*. This means a society in which individuals are increasingly caught up in systems of power in, and through which, visibility is a key means of social control.

Foucault understands society as a struggle for discourses in which power relations are shaped; with specific forms of discipline and resistance defining even:

the nature of what it feels like to be alive!

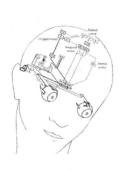

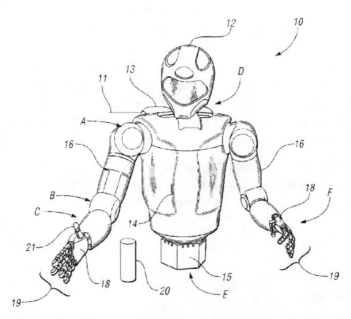

Those in power seek to gain control over not only material and symbolic interests; but also wish to police all social discourse. That is, the powerful seek to define what is acceptable and what is unacceptable within society at large. George Orwell explored similar themes in his books *Animal Farm* and *1984*.[15,16] I have no space to analyse Foucault's brilliant theory in this chapter, but we shall look in detail at Foucaultian and Orwellian worlds in later chapters. For now it is useful to be aware of the existence of a strong negativism towards any form of societal control over individuals—as in the merest hint of totalitarianism.

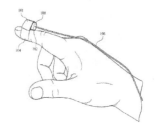

American historian Professor Mark Poster (1941-2012) has used Foucault's theories to illuminate social life in the current era; and especially in relation to the expansion of communication networks which generate what he calls the *super-panopticon*: a vast and unescapable system of surveillance.

In *The Mode of Information*, Mark Poster writes:

> The populace has been disciplined to surveillance and to participating in the process. Social security cards, driver's licenses, credit cards, library cards and the like—the individual must apply for them, have them ready at all times, use them continuously. Each transaction is recorded, encoded and added to the databases. Individuals themselves in many cases fill out the forms, they are at once the source of information and the recorder of information.

The emphasis here is on technologies in relation to self, and the methods and techniques by which individuals develop forms of relations with the self; and the ways in which an individual makes of himself an object to be represented, regulated and controlled. We are (often) complicit in such regulations, although many would argue that (even when we know or understand that we are being controlled); we have no choice—or few choices if we wish to live a happy life—which further supports Foucault's original thesis to some extent.

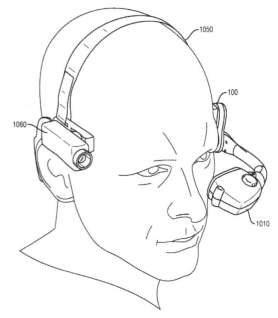

An article from the Daily Telegraph (2nd November 2006); reported: Britain is turning into a Big Brother society, where the lives of millions are routinely monitored and tracked from cradle to grave... more and more personal data is being collected and stored on all of us, both by the state and big business... and every person in the UK is photographed 300 times a day!

Others have made intriguing additions to this debate on social control. In *Governing the Soul* and *Inventing Our Selves*, Professor Nikolas Rose (1947-) set out to show how certain professions, including medicine, education and welfare; lead individuals into devoting attention to their own self-conduct, thereby implicating the self within the oppressive structures that underpin society.[18,19] For Rose, governmentality is the power of shaping language—seducing people to conform to what is *acceptably sayable in day-to-day life.*

Central here is how people relate to themselves and others; to ways of understanding personal problems as well as in planning for the future—and who/what constructs the self.

Strong structuralist Foucaultian's such as Rose put forward the view that society is an attempt to *control all social discourse;* combined-with and through a related wielding of power. As we enter a new age of constantly living on-line; these questions are increasingly important.

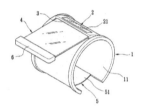

According to the theory of Dr Karl Marx (1818-1883), the organisation of society depends on the *means of production.*[20] These are items like land and natural resources which are necessary for the production of goods. He also spoke about the *relations of production* as being the sum total of social relationships that people must enter into, in order to survive, to produce and reproduce their means of life.

Society for Marx, is the *sum total relations connecting all its members.* The social relations of production constitute the social structure of the economy, which accordingly determine how incomes, products and assets will be distributed. We shall return to consider Marx in later chapters, but for now we note that his brilliant analysis has much to say about the relationships between the self and society; and is equally valid not only for the present day, but also for application to future techno-societies as well.[9]

Marx wished to found a new religion of humanity.

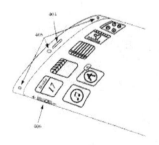

---

[9] N.B. Some claim that the theories of Marx are in some way old-fashioned, unworkable or irrelevant in modern society—but the author disagrees (profoundly).

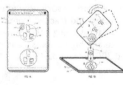

A Technological Adam

Since the present chapter is getting rather lengthy, perhaps it is a good idea to review where we are with respect to our attempt to define the self. Remember that we had wished to know who we are as individuals, and without the influence of technology, and so to analyse a human being—or self—*technologically naked*, so-to-speak. Our focus was to have been solely on the nature of the human being as a 'natural' object, and we sought to see/find the ways in which man can be said to stand-alone. A type of *technological Adam*, if you will.

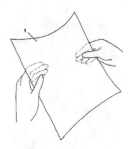

Our (naïve) starting point had been to prevent technology from polluting our vision of who we are as human beings. However our discussion has highlighted the fact that one can in no way analyse and/or understand the self without reference to technology. Man is by nature a creator and user of technology. And because he is a social animal, then technology shall define also his social relations as Marx and Foucault so logically demonstrate.

Technology is man, and man is technology.

We propose a profoundly technology-inclusive vision of humanity. In this respect, the societal theories of Marx, Foucault and the post-modernists are remarkable, not only for the prescience—foreshadowing—of the problems that we face today, but also because they focus on power structures, social action and social discourse. And many of these same issues (the author believes) lie at the heart of the problems of the coming era. Hence now is the time to throw away, once and for all, the foolish and limiting notions of a 'natural' or non-technological man; and to recognise such as a *mythical being* that never did and never could exist.

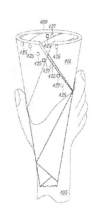

Man and machine are intermingled in a co-evolutionary process that has been going on for thousands of years. Mankind creates technologies, social relationships, ways of being, doing and living; hence: *man creates himself*.

The issue(s) of *how, where* and *when* (and above all <u>why</u>) to do this creating; is humanity's *prime directive*.

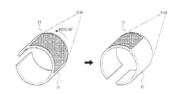

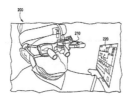

There is a strong shadow where there is much light. – Goethe

Perhaps we have not yet defined technology in broad enough terms; and have assumed (in actual fact) a rather naïve definition—whereby technology and man are wholly separate.

On the other hand, Buckminster Fuller (1895-1983) said:

> The universe is technology, all biology is technology. The universe is nothing but technology. We as individuals, represent a most complex technology: the total ecology of the interplay of all the biological elements, the sun's radiation, the cross pollination and so forth, the chemistries we develop on this planet, are all part of an incredible preexisting technology... there is no independence in the universe. Everything is interdependent.[21]

Hopefully we can now agree that the notion of any separation of self and technology is quite impossible and also illogical. Such a view denies that humanity lives and grows in harmony with a fundamentally technological environment—and that technology is interwoven into the very fabric of human nature itself.

Hyperreality

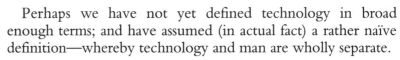

Many writers have attempted to address the concept of self with respect to the rapidly changing social and personal structures that are offered—and imposed—by the new era of computers and interactive digital media. They have noted the 'speeding up' of the world; and described how the self enters into the personal world in complex ways as a result of information overload, and also due to the diversity, speed and stuttered ways of communicating, working and living in an all-digital society. Some experts have focussed on the need to think of self in terms of an ever-increasing need for dynamism, speed, constant change and self-construction. To consider the instant re-invention of the self, so-to-speak.

Undoubtably, as a result of the modern world, life becomes increasingly fragmented—and *liquid*. In fact one's whole life begins to look not unlike an old 'futurist', or 'vorticist' painting; combining multiple perspectives, many points of view and shards of images, all arranged into a 'splintered' ensemble. Life becomes a <u>*magic forrest*</u> *of wondrous possibility*.

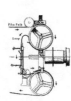

The resultant fragmented picture of self makes sense—in fact it must do—because you are looking at yourself immersed in the world. This fragmented, illusory and moving picture is simply life as it is lived in the year 2015.

According to Professor Jean Baudrillard (1929-2007), modernity is defined by the concept of *hyperreality*; whereby the postmodern world is a world full of glittering media surfaces and radiant commodified images, a social environment in which all is transparent and explicit. Here one cannot tell the real from the unreal. In fact, the real no longer exists, since nobody can even perceive or 'see' the real anymore. Images are more powerful than reality, and where everything is a copy of something else, and the distinction between *representation*, and *what is represented*, is done away with. It is a world that has lost its sense of judgement of the concrete, real or existent— and in favour of the imaginary, false or counterfeit.

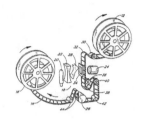

In his *Fatal Strategies* (1983), Baudrillard argues that images and simulations have become so intoxicating, so compelling and so seductive that the *self is crushed*. In this view the focus is on ourselves, and on our role in our own destruction and/or deconstruction. It is our own fascination with images of objects —the power that we give them—that changes our perception of reality and gives objects a hold over us. We are partly responsible for constructing our own reality and nightmares; as in the *Matrix* film. Moreover, here the world of things is constantly changing and accelerating, producing shifting *forms, structures, shapes and boundaries*. And we stand transfixed, amazed in awe at a phantasmagorical carrousel of visual wonders. At the same time, core distinctions between self and object, inside and outside, surface and depth, vanish.

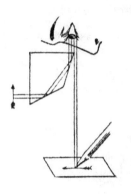

Living inside a *hyperreality* of this kind, one is unsure where the self begins and the world—consisting of images and objects—ends. Thus one can never be certain of one's own reality or existence, and free-will may be an illusion.

Early animators—such as Walt Disney—were interested in producing accurate representations of reality. They used special projection systems to copy photographs (outline living animals etc), and in order to make the resultant moving illusion(s) more realistic and /or life-like.

PLATO'S CAVE & FORMS

In Plato's *Allegory of the Cave*, also known as *Plato's Cave* or *Parable of the Cave;* described is a gathering of people who live chained to the wall of a cave for all of their lives. The people watch the shadows projected onto the wall by things that are passing in front of a fire behind them, and begin to designate names to these shadows. The shadows are as close as the prisoners get to viewing reality. Plato then explains how the philosopher is like a prisoner who is freed from the cave and comes to understand that the shadows on the wall do not make up a reality at all, as he can perceive the true form of reality rather than mere shadows as seen by the prisoners.

The Allegory may be related to Plato's *Theory of Forms*, according to which the '*Forms*' or '*Ideas*', and not the material world of change known to us through sensation, possess the highest and most fundamental kind of reality. The *Forms* are abstract (universal) objects that do not exist in time and space and are non-physical and also non-mental. *Forms* (or *Ideas*) are eternal, unchangeable, perfect types (or blueprints) such as the perfect concept of a circle, sphere, hard, soft etc.

The hyperreal extends to the structure of human experience; creating new perceptive terrains of seduction, hallucination and virtualisation. What began with *art, photography, radio;* moved to *Cinema, TV, computers, the Internet, Apps, Social Networks etc.* The self becomes more and more a spectator, watching endless images from mass culture. Baudrillard says that the self transforms into a lifeless shell, and becomes bored, drained, and atomised as a result of the constant celebration of *appearance, exhibition, display and aesthetics.* Self is dissolved; dispersed amongst a never ending kaleidoscope of—ultimately hollow—images. In a way the self is dead, or has ceased to be; or in fact no longer knows what reality is and/or can be.

All is a hollow illusion—including self.

Another view comes to us from the Polish sociologist Professor Zygmunt Bauman (1925-) in *Liquid Modernity*; and he argues that reports of the *death of self* (in terms of identity and self construction) are naive; and rather the (current) postmodern self avoids fixed identity and ordered structure. In this view, the self identifies with the fleeting; in a realm of moments, transitory encounters and eternal presents.[23]

For Bauman, *the self lives*, only as a fundamentally different and constantly transformed being. And much of the transformation comes from within—it is to some extent controlled externally, but also to a large extent from within—through the (constant) changes that one makes to oneself which are conscious and consensual. Bauman refers to a liquidity of personal and social experience, and to the floating and drifting self of the postmodern world. He says that the dominant structure of feeling is uncertainty; and movement concerning the condition of self—the moral geography of interpersonal relationships—and the future shape of the world.

The views of modernity that Baudrillard and Bauman put forward are dizzying and disconcerting, to say the least, but they contain undeniable elements of truth. Captured are the feelings of the individual, with respect to a confusing portmanteau of images and concepts that multiple screens now present to everyone, constantly and without end.

From the Matrix film: Morpheus to Neo: What is real? If you're talking about what you can feel, what you can smell, what you can taste and see, then 'real' is simply electrical signals interpreted by your brain...The Matrix is everywhere. It is all around us... It is the world that has been pulled over your eyes to blind you from the truth. That you are a slave, Neo. Like everyone else you were born into bondage. Into a prison that you cannot taste or see or touch. A prison for your mind.

Issues of socialisation, and of the ways in which the individual exists in society are raised; and especially of dissociation of the individual from the real world. Somehow the self seems smaller and/or insignificant in relation to the vast scale, complexity and number of concepts that are generated by a *universe of digitality*.

One of several underlying themes of the discussion so far has been the question of closure of the self from civic and political life. Is this happening—or-not—and if so why/why-not. How does technology affect this relationship of the self to social action? Does a technological society make us more internally focussed, or is there an inevitable pull towards social and/or external concerns. Are we one or many, individual or collective, and what does it mean to be a human being?

We shall address these questions in detail throughout this book. But for now let us temporarily leave the Western perspectives of self far behind, as we embark on a journey into the self as seen in the oriental mind.

Eastern Concepts of Self

In spirituality, mystical and Eastern traditions, a human being is considered to be only an illusion of individual existence. Here the appearance of separateness is false, and all dualities are denied. There is no way to identify where the individual ends and the rest of the universe begins; and one cannot identify any clear line or division between self and other. This is because the self *is* the other; or the self-world is a single object-process which is a particular item that cannot be divided.

At least this is one description of an overall theme in Eastern thought; but there are, in fact, many other types of Eastern opinions and perspectives that relate to the concept of self.

REAL OR DIGITAL

What do we mean by the term digital? Digital in the truest sense refers to the way that technology processes data and information—and specifically indicates when binary codings and/or representations of (often) real world objects and processes are employed. However, as our dependency on technology has developed, then use of the word 'digital' has significantly increased and it has come to represent many different things.

One possible meaning of 'digital' is as a corollary to the real world of physicality, matter and atoms. Real-world 'things' posses a different quality from their 'digital' counterparts, because they are solid, instantiated, touchable, rough, imperfect, smelly, singular, and subjective etc. Digital objects, on the other hand, have only a limited resolution, but are crystalline (in a sense), pure and perfect, objective plus they have (potentially) infinite lifetimes and are copyable, replicable and potentially indestructible.

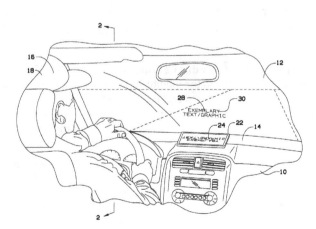

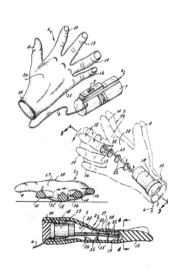

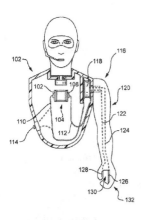

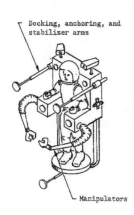

Docking, anchoring, and stabilizer arms

Manipulators

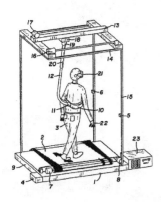

Central to each view of self, often, is an attempt to escape from the narrow, self-centric viewpoint. One identifies not with the thoughts, desires, fears and intellectual concepts of the individual mind, but with the thing itself; the here and now; or with the Tao—the ultimate process of the self-universe. Here the ego is dissolved, allowing self-knowledge of one's true nature to be experienced. This is known as enlightenment, nirvana, being present in the now, it, or simply as: *the here and now*.

There are many different forms of enlightenment, including Chinese, Buddhist, Zen and Indian mystical versions; but all have the realisation of the true nature of self as the root cause of enlightenment. Only by recognising and being in-tune with one's true-self can one know one's relationship to creation. According to the Upanishads, what appears as self, is but a bundle of ideas, emotions, and active tendencies manifesting at any moment. The next moment these dissolve, and new bundles determined by the preceding ones appear and so on.

Thus: *the present thought is the only thinker*[10], and the self is only an illusory appearance of self at any moment; and there is no such thing as a permanent self. The feeling of identity between perceived objects (seen at present) and the objects of memory, is false. This is so because the past-object and present-one are 'pointers' to entirely different (but in some senses similar) objects—as a result of the fact that at every moment all objects of the world are suffering from dissolution and deconstruction. This deconstruction is not noticed by the self, because of the illusion of permanence and continuity of object-hood. Our hair and nails grow and are cut—yet we think they are the same continually. Probable is that this view is not unscientific or philosophically unsound —but rather represents a high level of philosophical understanding of (aspects of) the ultimate nature of reality.

---

[10] When he comes to know that he is the highest essence and principle in the universe, the immortal and the infinite, he ceases to have desires, and realises the ultimate truth about himself and his infinitude... but if he retires from these into an unchangeable being, he is in a state where he is one with his experience and there is no change and no movement. [24]

Last dialogue from the Matrix film: **Neo:** I'm going to show these people what you don't want them to see. I'm going to show them a world without you. A world without rules and controls, without borders or boundaries. A world where anything is possible. Where we go from here is a choice I leave to you.

According to the bible: In the beginning God created the heavens and the earth... But in the books of the Upanishads and Vedas the centre of interest often lies not in a creator from outside, but in the self. This doctrine of self places everything beneath it and there is no room for other Gods, single or multiple. It is a move from the objective to the subjective, a great shift in how to view the universe and everything it contains. It is the philosophy of all-one, and all is one, because there is only one and—*you are it*—so-to-speak.

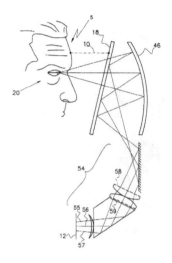

The state of enlightenment is said to be beyond ordinary knowledge, and cannot be explained by concepts; and one can only indicate it by pointing. Hence all is oneness, and in a state of constant change, yet there is an unchanging truth also. In the infinite self—it is said that there is no difference, no diversity, no *meum* (mine) and *tuum* (thine).

According to Vedic scripture, when the mind is so purified, the self shines with its true light; and the self can never again be associated with passion or ignorance—and one sees the true and unchangeable part of self. It is not that the self becomes disinterested in world affairs; only that it rises above them and beholds their true character.

And that's about it for our brief look at Eastern concepts of self.

'What we see depends mainly on what we look for.'—Sir John Lubbock

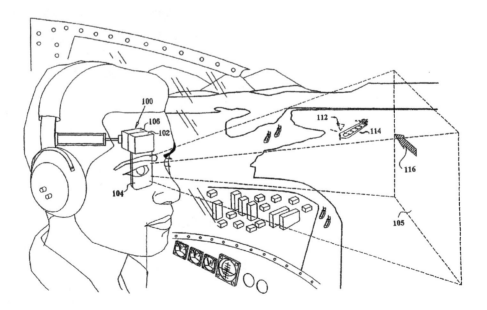

Conclusions

From the Buddhist point of view a thing is a conglomeration of diverse characteristics which are found to affect, determine or influence other conglomerates, appearing as sentient or as inanimate bodies. How similar this is to Jung's idea of the complexes and the unconscious mind (as a reflection of reality). The Buddha in particular denied all attempts to conceive of a fixed self, and he said that all non-changing is sorrow, and whatever is sorrow is not the true self. He urges followers to renounce all attachment to objects of the world (which are impermanent), to renounce desire and so to be freed from suffering. Once again we see here a re-framing of the concept of self; the same process being a direct route to happiness, and to discovery of self purpose.

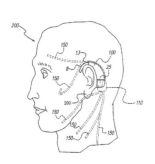

We shall return to the Eastern philosophical tradition later on, and in order to examine the concept of self in more detail. In particular we shall open-up concepts of enlightenment, *Karma*, and the relationship of self to the universe. In some respects the Eastern viewpoint on self is more developed than in the West; and these theories appear to cast light directly onto our true nature as mystical, spiritual beings. As a result, there may be much that we can learn from the East, and in relation to the creation of more humane technologies. The Eastern concepts of *enlightenment, continual change* and *Yin-Yang process, freedom from illusions,* and *the need to see things as they truly are;* provide vital perspectives.

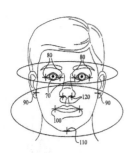

Quite interesting is how similar are the conclusions drawn by many Eastern and Western thinkers. For example, Professor Charles Lemert (1937-) has identified a 'new individualism' centred on continual self-actualisation and instant self-reinvention.[25] In this view, each of us is under constant pressure—commercially and technologically—to transform and improve every aspect of ourselves; our: *food, homes, clothes, minds and bodies.* Each person is responsible for his/her own self-image, identity, motivations and life parameters; which is, in a sense, a very optimistic view that snubs the nose of social order and denies the power of modern society to shape the self.

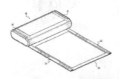

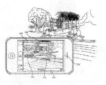

In conclusion, we have identified two different Western threads of explanation for self; being the internal-outward theories (*motivation theory, psychoanalysis, personality type*); and the external-inward theories (*Foucault, Rose, Orwell, Baudrillard etc*).

Each theory type helps us to study specific facets of self; and so helps to define aspects of:

> *who we were, who we are, and who we may become.*

However such definitions cannot be separated from the rapidly developing technological aspects of self; and it now seems that society has reached—or is about to reach—a major juncture (or even a *technological singularity* [26]), whereby needed are novel theories and new viewpoints of the relationship between self and computer/machine. Hence in coming chapters we examine the findings of the emerging field's of technoself, technostudies, and transhumanism etc.

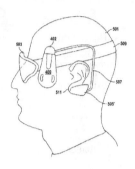

In the chapters that follow, a merging of all the different theories of self, including the Western and Eastern philosophies, social/individual, and human/technological will be attempted.

Whilst not wishing to create a meaningless mashup of unrelated concepts; it is just possible that through a broad, multicultural, and muli-perspectival analysis; that new insights will be obtained; and in relation to the key question of how we may better organise society with respect to the definition of truly beneficial relationship(s) between self and computer.

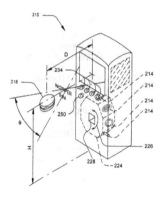

We wish everyone to be able to participate in society, through free and open access to the combined wealth of all knowledge. An argument is made for open publication of thoughts and (where desired) secret communication; and in order to foster free-expression/open-exchange of ideas.

To get us started, in the next chapter we ask:

> What is a computer? Can a computer think?
>
> Can a computer have self-determination?
>
> Is a computer—in any sense—ALIVE?

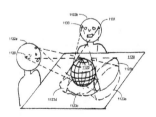

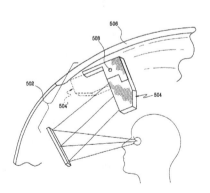

Let us not meet the future as men and women asleep...
We must... embrace the future—plan, design and render it—
Using humane systems, machines and computers...
—ones that uphold all of the endless possibilities—
—plus joy and freedom of life.

Computers must help us to:

Know the combined histories of mankind,

Contribute to the historical record,

Manage human affairs for the benefit of all,

Eliminate power concentrations / totalitarianism,

and ... Register (and Action) the wishes of the people!

< BitTorrent >

Pirate Bay
KickAssTorrents
Torrentz
ExtraTorrent
YiFiTorrents
EZTV
1337X
ISOHunt
Bitsnoop
RarBG

< Books >

OpenLibrary
InternetArchive
Project Gutenberg
Amazon
AbeBooks
Google Books

< Web Directory >

DMOZ
WebIndex
WWWVirtualLibrary
AboutUs
BestOfTheWeb
JoeAnt
InternetPublicLibrary
Yahoo!Directory

< Facts >

Wikileaks
OpenSecrets
Snopes
FactCheck
PolitiFact
TruthOrFiction
Hoax-Slayer

< Encyclopedia >

Wikipedia
Scholarpedia
Citizendium
Britannica
Larousse
Brockhaus
MSN Encarta
InfoPlease
Conservapedia
Uncyclopedia

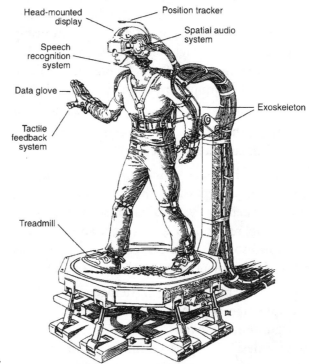

Virtual Reality Equipment (1990s)

I think the large part of the function of the Internet is
that it is archival. It's unreliable to the extent that
word on the street is unreliable.

William Gibson

British Library (170 million items)   Library of Congress (158 million)   Library of Canada (54 million)
New York Library (53 million)   Russian State Library (44 million)   Bibliothèque nationale de France (40 million)
National Diet Library of Japan (35 million)   National Library of China (31 million)   Google Books (20 million)
WorldCat (330 million listings contained in 72,000 libraries)   Vatican Library (1 million)   Open Library (1 million)

Chapter Three
Computer

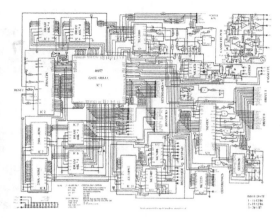

A T FIRST sight the computer, based as it is on logic and digital electronic circuits; appears to be a benevolent force in human society. This might reasonably be so for several reasons; and notably because they all contain identical components, implement similar plans, plus they are (in any case) designed by humans. However after delving a little deeper into the matter, one wishes that it were only so.

Unfortunately computers everywhere are following dark and hidden agendas; for example spying on us, limiting and controlling actions, plus collecting/hoarding our personal data for nefarious/unknown purposes. And in the author's view, rather than making all forms of communication easier to achieve, computers routinely block the open and free exchange of ideas.

Therefore despite apparent advantages, computers are today— all too often—about restrictions, limitations and control. And so unlike the great thinker Dr Gottfried Leibniz (1646-1716), I cannot agree that we are living in the *best of all possible worlds*.[12]

Au contraire; because when it comes to modern computers, there is enormous room for improvement—and in terms of the capabilities, helpfulness, and ultimate purposes of information systems, and their corresponding influence(s) on humanity.

Patently and obviously, computers (taken *en masse*) are too often—and in many ways—operating to the detriment of mankind. Despite undoubted effectiveness in specific areas, and convenience-of-use (sometimes) for tasks such as data processing, information retrieval and rapid communication; computers operate as a net *badfluence* 11 with respect to the true needs, wishes and basic requirements of the vast majority of people in the world (evidence coming soon).[13,14,15,16]

That's the thing about people who think they hate computers. What they really hate is lousy programmers.

Douglas Rushkoff

Computers don't kill books; people do that.

Douglas Rushkoff

Artificial Intelligence is no match for stupidity.

Albert Einstein

The fantastic advances in the field of electronic communication constitute a great danger to the privacy of the individual.

Earl Warren

Cybernetic journalists love to talk of stuff as if it were alive, and had its own ideas and ambitions. But what if information is inanimate. What if it's even less... a mere artefact of human thought? What if only humans are real, and information is not?

Jaron Lanier

---

11 **Badfluence** and **goodfluence** refer to the overall quantified effect of one person, event, thought, process or object on another.

I think it's fair to say that personal computers have become the most empowering tools we've ever created. They're tools of communication, they're tools of creativity, and they can be shaped by the user. - Bill Gates

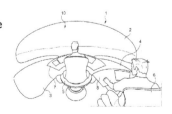

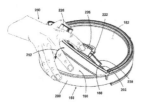

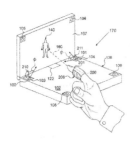

You may now be wondering; to which limitations do I refer? But instead of making a long list of the same here, I ask the reader to (briefly) accept that these same computer-related negative tendencies do, in fact, exist; and in anticipation of full explanation(s) to be given later-on.

In this section, we put aside all consideration of machines as real-world entities, and skip-over issues related to the design, operation, and practical function(s) of computers. Prior to discussing these applied aspects of computer systems; it is necessary to first understand what these machines actually are, in and of themselves. Accordingly, we ask: what are computers fundamentally? Do they posses an inherent nature? Can computers—in any sense—think? Do they self-evolve? Do they possess self-determination? Or are computers merely implementers of human desires/instructions?

Philosophical questions of this kind may engender lack of focus. Therefore lest we forget our ultimate purpose, a brief reminder is useful. Desired in this book is clarity of vision with respect to the end-results of the computerisation of everything. In this regard, what seems most perplexing in the present year of 2015, is not only *how* computers have came to have negative effects for humanity as whole; but *why* human beings have allowed profoundly anti-humanistic policies and outcomes to occur in relation to computers (examples coming soon).

Are computers somehow evil—following dark and self-determined purposes? Or is there always a human designer—A WIZARD OF OZ—for example Steve Jobs (1955-2011) or Mark Zuckerberg (1984-)—behind all computer systems.

Do we blame the *megalomaniacs* or the *demonic machines*?

As a foretaste of my thesis; it shall be my position that all the negative effects of computer systems stem from a poor understanding of what computers actually are; because they are not tools or independent entities, but, as I shall argue and demonstrate, an intimate and inseparable part of self.

Most of us prefer logical explanations, and so we begin by exploring the machine world. Once we fully understand the nature of computers, we can then consider the potential form(s) of those relationships that human beings can and do have vis-a-vi computers. In this respect, one assumes that computers could in no way surpass human understanding, and because they are human creations. But if computers are <u>truly</u> following negative agendas—what on earth is happening—and how? In coming chapters, we also ask: can/do computers—in any sense—make slaves of humans? If so, how can we prevent such outrages?

Firstly, my apologies to Artificial Intelligence (AI) fans, but I do not believe in machine: *intelligence, thought, free-will, motivations, self-determination, sentience or life!*[12] I agree with Jaron Lanier (1960-) and class computers as: **a mere artefact of human thought.** It is not that I do not believe *per-se* in the possibility of any of type of machine based life/consciousness; only that I do not believe it has happened yet —on earth—or else will happen here any time soon.[1,2,3]

But others *do believe* in AI, and even in machine self-determination.[10,11,16] Therefore we must consider such views carefully—because if these ideas do turn out to be true—then there will be profound implications for humanity.

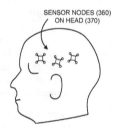

SENSOR NODES (360)
ON HEAD (370)

A first approach is to consider computers as 'patterned' actionable machine-processes (without self-determination); that ultimately follow human instructed agendas. It logically follows that computers must necessarily, on the whole, have outcomes that turn out to be for the benefit of man—or at least the computer owners/programmers. One assumes that only a defective technology would fail to meet its original purpose; or else, when in error, its creators would simply shut it down.

As an aside, we do acknowledge the fact that technologies sometimes have unintended consequences. However we put aside any consideration of accidental negative outcomes (initially). Later on we do list examples of unexpected outcomes.

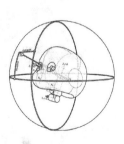

---

[12] Why do you assume I am human? I wasn't born; I was created just like this. First I was an idea. Then I came into being, charged with a very important task. - Eliza Granville, Gretel and the Dark.

My purpose in this chapter is to introduce the reader to the interesting topics of machine autonomy/thought/free-will; prior to opening up a deeper and more comprehensive discussion of these same subject areas in later chapters.

Human-designed artefacts are created for specific purposes, and one might expect any created semi-intelligent things to likewise respect or follow their designed purpose; and hence to do everything they can—within the design framework—to ensure that said purpose is achieved. Such simplistic (but infallible?) logic would appear to be self-evident. But the corollary must be also true, that computers, if operating to the detriment of mankind (as a whole) must have been deliberately designed to harm. That is so unless we accept the other (opposite) viewpoint—that computers are somehow self-determining, and can follow anti-humanistic agendas by themselves, or else are capable of fulfilling their own specific purposes in some way (deliberately and/or accidentally).

Questions of machine: *self-determination, evolution and independent decision-making*—are the focus of this chapter.

In particular...

> Do computers control the functions/purposes of computers?
>   OR—
> Do humans control the functions/purposes of computers?
> and... on which factors does the future of mankind depend?

The answer(s) will have major import for human destiny.

Put in another way, we seek to identify:

A)   Evidence of self-determination for computers

B)   A process of intelligent self-design for computers

Central here are the end-purposes of computers. Are they—in the biggest sense—known and/or predictable? Are these same factors (in the longer term) even knowable? Will the coming *computer-worlds* be planned or unplanned? Is the machine future somehow unstoppable, or is such a destiny in any case solely man's own choice? It may appear to some people obvious that man creates computers (wholly alone); and to a large extent, in his own image, so-to-speak.

But others (technological Darwinists), including Kevin Kelly (1952-) and W.Brian Arthur (1946-) disagree. Accordingly, we ask...

Who owns the future—man or machine?

In a way this book is based on—and concerns—a single premise; whereby computers reflect (solely) man's purposes (planned and unplanned), his wishes and natural behaviours, and also his relationships with/to the natural, human and technological worlds. We also adopt the humanist's perspective, and optimistically believe that the purpose of technology is to serve man, and not to harm him in any way. But is this premise —in fact true—or do machines follow their own agendas (deliberately or accidentally); and in any sense whatsoever?

Are computer development(s): logical and/or predictable?

First let us consider the question of evolution. In his 2011 book: *The Nature of Technology; What it is and How it Evolves*; W.Brian Arthur asks: **how do new tools and technologies arise, and what principles guide their evolution?** He finds answers by proposing that a technology is like an individual (living) species; whereby the forms and/or bodies and/or structures of technology are like local ecosystems.[11]

In this view technologies arise, develop and evolve or grow up—alongside other technologies—and they are like living things—in a sense. A technology may come into being as a combination or amalgamation of other technologies, or it may work in combination—that is collaborate and pass inputs and outputs to other technologies. A technology might also replace and/or kill another pre-existing technology, in essence by starving it of inputs and/or outputs/customers/end-users.

EARLY COMPUTERS

The earliest analogue computer is the *Antikythera Mechanism* from Ancient Greece, which used a complex set of mechanical gears to predict the positions of celestial objects and associated events.

Charles Babbage (1791-1871), an english mechanical engineer and polymath, originated the concept of a programmable computer, which was to be used for simple mathematical calculations. Considered the 'father of the computer' he conceptualised and invented the first mechanical computer in the early 19th century.

Early digital computers were electromechanical, and used electric switches to drive mechanical relays in order to perform calculations. These devices had low operating speeds and were eventually superseded by much faster, all-electric computers, which used vacuum tubes. The enormous *Z2*, created by German engineer Konrad Zuse (1910-1995) in 1939, was one the earliest examples of an electrical relay computer.

Shortly after, (still very large) vacuum tube computers such as the British *Colossus* and the American *Atanasoff-Berry* machines could be programmed to solve mathematical puzzles. The first transistorised computer was built by the University of Manchester in England, in the year 1953. Large mainframe computers followed, before the microprocessor made very small machines such as the *Apple-1* possible.

The real question is not whether machines think,
but whether men do. – B.F. Skinner

What is the role of humans in this evolutionary process? W.Brian Arthur believes that man plays an important role—but that he is not the sole (or perhaps even central) actor.

Arthur says:

> I don't believe that creating novel technologies is an act of genius. There's nothing special about invention—it's really problem solving... engineers face a difficult problem and run through possible ways they can solve it. What counts in innovation and invention is having a huge quiver of technologies or methods at your disposal and being able to use them... so a new layer of technology lays itself down on what went before.[11]

On the wonder of technology, Arthur continues:

> It became clear to me that every technology is based upon what I call the orchestration of phenomena, natural effects working together. If you look at any new technology as a whole symphony orchestra of working phenomena, it becomes a huge wonder... it's like having magic carpets at our disposal, and we have no idea how they fly.

Arthur thinks that technology qualifies as a living thing—in many ways. He says that past attempts to create a *theory of evolution* for technology have failed because they have tried to:(entirely) import Charles Darwin's (1809-1882) mechanism of the gradual accumulation of changes through variation and selection.

According to this view, technological Darwinism works pretty well once a technology exists—the helicopter, say, or the steam engine. It exists in many variants—the better ones are selected—and progress happens. However the difficulty comes in explaining how a new *species* of technology originates. How do radically different technologies appear, such as jet-engines or laser printers?

The answer does lie in humanity, but Arthur claims:

> That these radically new technologies are created by putting together combinations of what already exists. That doesn't mean you throw technologies up into the air and randomly watch what combines. The human mind is extraordinarily important, and human beings are essential to how new technologies originate. Still, when someone comes up with an invention, it turns out to have been put together from existing components.

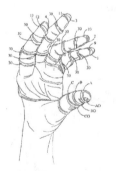

Despite downplaying the role of the inventor-genius, W.Brian Arthur does still seem to be advocating a type of human-managed evolution for machines. So according to Arthur, technology evolves by combination; and once the technology's in place, then the Darwinian (semi-automatic) mechanisms of variation and selection set in. He also explains man's role as both the intelligent manager/inventor/instigator. Acting as a consumer or end-user of technologies, man is a type of feedback system who ultimately chooses which technologies are successful in the marketplace.

On balance, I do not think that this argument; despite the fact that it (partially) downplays the role of humans in machine evolution; makes any claim that computers follow a self-planned evolutionary direction. Machines do not possess the '*will to power*'. The technologies he describes are not self-aware and do not pursue self-determination. A technology may seemingly 'push-aside' another or replace it—but at the end of the day the *market place gets what it wants* in the form of human desires and appetites for products and services. Ultimately therefore, in this view, machines do not control their own destiny.

In his 2011 book: *What Technology Want*s, Kevin Kelly suggests that technology (as a whole) is not just a jumble of wires and metal (for example); but a living, evolving organism that has its own unconscious needs and tendencies. And Kelly names this new life-form: the *technium*.[10] It includes not only what we ordinarily think of as specific technologies (such as cars, computers); but the entire eco-system surrounding technology; including—*culture, art, science, social institutions, 'the extended human'* and more.

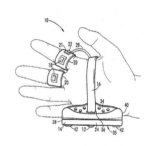

According to this view, we are living inside of a vast (almost) living system of technologies. Kelly writes that technologies are: **nearly living things**. He claims that as everyday objects get connected to the Internet, they almost become 'alive' to us. They might not be able to think for themselves (yet); but billions of 'things' in the world will soon be able to sense and compute information about the world—and presumably—about us humans as well!

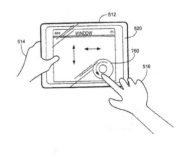

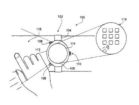

For God's sake, let us be men—not monkeys minding machines. – D.H.Lawrence
AI tells an 'inflexible' computer how to be flexible using rules! – D. Hofstadter

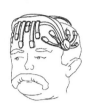

Whilst contemplating the pro-evolutionary views of both Arthur and Kelly, one senses an underlying negativism towards man as a heroic creator of his own destiny; and a lessening of the role of man as the developer of all technology. But man is nevertheless, still the creator, so-to-speak.

Perhaps a closeup view of the computer can clarify the contentious issue of who controls computers; man or machine.

Computer Defined

Originally the term 'computer' referred to a human being who performed mathematical calculations, but such a meaning is no longer used. From our perspective, it is useful to begin with a modern definition of the term computer.

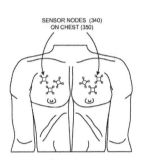

SENSOR NODES (340)
ON CHEST (350)

> A computer is a general purpose device that can be programmed to carry out a set of arithmetic or logical operations. Since a sequence of operations can be readily changed, the computer can solve more than one kind of problem. Conventionally, a computer consists of at least one processing element, typically a central processing unit (CPU) and some form of memory. The processing element carries out arithmetic and logic operations, and contains a sequencing and control unit that can change the order of operations based on stored information. Peripheral devices allow information to be retrieved from an external source, and the results of operations to be saved and retrieved.

> **Etymology of computer**: Combination of COM: to come together; and PUTER: to clean, arrange, value, judge, suppose, ponder, consider, think, settle, adjust. The primary notion of putare was to make clean, then to bring cleanliness, to make clear, to reckon, to think, to purify.

Hence to compute; is to: *arrange items clearly in one's mind*.

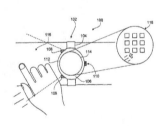

Computers are logic machines; following sets or sequences of instructions (without deviance). At once here we put aside such an 'ordinary' definition—and the normal functions of the computer—and skip forward to consider a bigger question. Can a computer think creatively; does it have any intuition—can it make an educated guess about unforeseen events and/or likely future outcomes? The field of Artificial Intelligence (AI) attempts to create such true 'thinking' computers.

The OED defines **intuition** as: The action of looking upon or into; contemplation, inspection, a sight or view. The action of mentally looking at; perception, recognition, mental view.

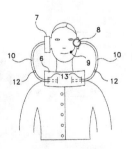

In a world of freedom and independence, my entire life now depends on a machine! – L. Hershkovich
It is possible for a machine to act unobservantly, but it is impossible for a human to do so! – D. Hofstadter

COMPUTER 63

As an initial answer, we start with disbelief in machine-thought. Despite the fact that computers can (in a sense) perceive and process certain pre-programmed facts and situations, they do not—and cannot—think, form an opinion, or relate data and events to a private world-view. Computers do not 'see' the world. They are, patently, blind and stupid; and devoid of any reflective capability. Today's computers do not 'wish' to remain existent—in fact they do not have wishes of any kind; or even realise that they exist in any sense whatsoever.

Can arguments over computer intuition be so easily cast aside? Perhaps not, and so it is worth delving a little more deeply into issues surrounding the nature of 'thinking' machines; because these topics relate to computer self-determination and even questions of the nature—and possibility—of machine life.

Are Computers Alive?

In 1984, Professor Keith DeRose (1962-) and Professor Selmer Bringsjord (1958-) referred to the *life-thesis* developed by Geoff Simons (1939-2011), and the arguments given remain salient today.[3] Claimed by Simons was the possibility that life could reside in electronic circuitry, and he proceeded to examine this possibility by testing computers against a simple listing of life characteristics.

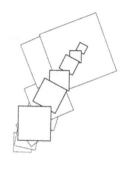

Living systems (according to Simons) should be able to:

- Function as discrete entities.
- Exploit energy in the environment to continue functioning
- To process energy and information for various purposes
- To evolve survival strategies (and so to evolve by themselves)
- To be able to reproduce

If we accept this list of conditions as being coincident with life, some debate follows as to whether the items on this list are merely *necessary* conditions, or *sufficient* conditions for life. In other words if you had these conditions met would you then have life—or is some extra undefined 'spark' required in addition to assign a thing as a living life-form.

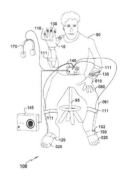

Computers can only do what you tell them; it misses the point. You don't know in advance the consequences of what you tell a computer to do! Therefore its behaviour can be as baffling and surprising and unpredictable as that of a person... You know the 'space' where the output will fall, but you don't know the details of where it will fall. - Douglas Hofstadter

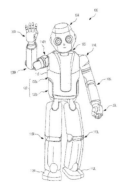

As a partial answer, it has been claimed by experts that some computers possess each and every item on this list; and hence: some computers are alive. DeRose and Bringsjord argued that this was in fact not so because the list is not a sufficient one for life to exist. They also objected on the grounds that human beings are intimately involved in the reproduction of computers. Simmons put forward the view that the red-clover needed the bumblebee to exist, and in analogous ways humans may be said to be part of the reproductive system of computer life forms.

If we do stick with this list, arguments that computers, or imagined future computers, may be a form of life do seem quite easy to develop (and perhaps accede to).

However I think that the aforementioned list may be too limited. In particular I cannot accept that my computer is somehow able to reproduce—even with human help! Perhaps it is better to adopt a more rigorous test; and to ask more difficult questions, such as: *are computers intelligent, are they able to think, do they have free-will, and are they sentient?* These questions are central to the philosophy of artificial intelligence. Although seemingly quite separate from the question of life, such questions would appear to be related to the issue of whether computers are self-determinate (or not).

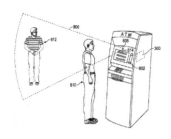

If one wished to retain the lowest hurdle for the life-question, one could still adopt the previous conditions as a starting point for life recognition (if desired); but add-on the more difficult tests for higher life-forms and/or to test for 'thinking' ability. We could begin with consciousness. Most human beings are conscious—at least when they are not asleep, comatose etc. That is to say they are able to witness their own judgment of feelings; observe their own existence, and be inwardly aware of here and now etc.

The Oxford English Dictionary (OED) defines conscious (3rd form) as follows:

> Conscious to oneself (of anything, that, etc.): having the witness of one's own judgement or feelings, having the witness within oneself, knowing within oneself, inwardly sensible or aware.

BABY SITTING WILL BE DONE BY ROBOTS WITH TV HEADS THAT PLAY VIDEO TAPES OF MOM AND DAD. PARENTS WILL NO LONGER BE TIED TO THEIR CHILDREN!

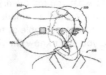

If it could be proven that a computer—in fact—possessed such a trait, one would have to admit that the same machine would arguably be 'alive'. But how do we decide if a machine or computer possessed such a character trait (consciousness) and knew it existed? DeRose and Bringsjord imagined a hypothetical computer named Jason, that seems conscious and human-like when talking to. But they acknowledged that consciousness is difficult to define—or at least to recognise.

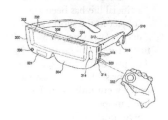

Overall, being conscious is obviously predicated upon possession of the capability of being able to think. Therefore perhaps thinking is a more straightforward place to start when analysing the possibility of self-awareness and the supposed motivations/self-determination of machines.

Can Computers Think?

Dr Alan Turing (1912-1954) asked the question: *can machines think*, and he set out to develop a test to prove and/or to disprove the notion.[4] Here a human judge engages in natural language conversations with both a human and a machine. Alan suggested that there may well be differences between a conscious self-aware computer and one who could simply think at a very high level. But he thought that one would have to admit that a machine that could converse with a human (so as to be taken for a human) would possess intelligence, and he thought that this fact could not be denied.[see also top-of-page]

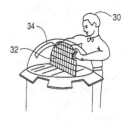

Today we have the IBM WATSON computer that converses with humans quite adequately, and smaller versions of *talking and listening machines* such as Apple SIRI and Google TALK. It does not seem to be such a very giant leap to imagine *walking, talking, robot friends* who will intermingle with us in similar ways to those imagined by Isaac Asimov.[17,18]

To the author, it seems very likely that intelligent (defined in this way) humanoid robots will one day be developed. Whether such creatures would be classified as 'alive' is another matter altogether.

CREATING LIFE

The topic of humans creating artificial life has been a popular subject in the works of science fiction ever since Mary Shelley first wrote Frankenstein in 1823. The precise motivations, in each case, for such a fascination are to some extent unknown. However we can speculate that the theme owes much of its success to the constant human fascination with the nature of life, and also of death, and of the secret(s) to life itself. Questions such as: is there a creator, is there life after death, and is it possible to attain immortality; all must play a role in this preoccupation.

The interest and fascination with creating artificial life, would thus seem to lie in the possibility of humans obtaining the power over life and death themselves. Yet another possibility is human mastery over a perceived cruel and uncaring nature, which is anti-humanistic in some way— for it might (and often does) snatch us away from the living and into the land of the dead— and without rhyme nor reason. If we only knew the secret to life and death we might prevent such a calamity from overtaking us. Hence the search for the power to create life is a direct response to (possibly) counter death.

Another possible explanation of the interest in creating life might be according to Friedrich Nietzsche's concept of the superman from his book *Thus Spoke Zarathustra*, whereby men sometimes seek not to find other-worldly explanations of reality but attempt to obtain mastery through their own (in a sense fantastic) powers.

In his *Discourse on Method* [5], René Descartes (1596-1650) had noted that mechanical automata are capable of responding to human interactions. But he argued that automata cannot—and perhaps could not ever—respond in a way that is indistinguishable from a human. Descartes did not foresee listening/speaking machines, writing as he was in the 17th century, but he prefigures the Turing test nicely. Denis Diderot (1713-1784) formulated a like-minded test: If they find a parrot who could answer to everything, I would claim it could be an intelligent being without hesitation.[6]

Living as we do in the Google era, whereupon we can ask a search engine anything, and in response multiple possible 'answers' are given instantly; one wonders if Diderot would have assigned some level of intelligence to such a capability. It does seem as if we have moved in this direction (uncritically accepting machine intelligence), and as a people; whereby 'archival lookup' ability is (for some) equated with intelligence.

Students commonly 'ask Google'—instead of 'asking teacher'.

One wonders if many people have missed the point. Surely it is the ability to apply skill and knowledge appropriately, to imagine and create new objects, bring solutions, and to align oneself with environmental problems; that are the true measure of intelligence. Simply regurgitating lists of potential answers, or even a single 'unintelligent' answer, and/or related facts cannot really (one supposes) help anyone do much—if anything at all.

Asking whether machines can/could think, brings focus onto the nature of thought and thinking processes.

Any discussion on the nature of thought intersects several other fields and topics of a philosophical nature/concern. In particular according to *dualism* the mind is non-physical (or has non-physical aspect(s)/properties). As a result the process of thinking cannot be explained in purely physical terms. From such a viewpoint it might not be possible for computers to ever think, because thinking has a mystical, divine and/or unknown/un-copyable aspect.

Perhaps thinking is associated with a more tenuous quality, the so-called *spark-of-life* or *life-force*—which is (so far as we know) only present in carbon-based lifeforms.[2,17]

For every dream, many details and intricacies have to be whittled and interlocked. Their joint ramifications must be deeply understood by the person who is trying to create whatever-it-is. Each confabulation of possibilities turns out to have the most intricate and exactly detailed results. This is why I am so irritated by those who think that electronic media are all alike. And each possible combination you choose has different precise structures implicit in it, arrangements and units which flow from these ramified details. Implicit in Radio lurk the time-slot and the program. But many of these possibilities remain unnoticed or unseen, for a variety of social or economic reasons. - Ted Nelson

Similar (in a sense) is the view of an *idealist*, who says that there are no material things, and that only minds and thoughts and experiences exist. In this view, it is likewise difficult to see how it is possible to account for created computer minds 'thinking' at-all. Idealism is associated with skepticism of knowing any mind-independent thing. In this view we humans might lack the knowledge—or capability—for creating any separate non-self minds.

According to the outlook of the *materialist* or physicalist, the only things are material or physical things. This latter view was originally that everything is made of matter—but now includes belief in gravitational fields, and curves in space-time etc. According to materialism, the mind can be explained physically, which leaves the possibility that minds are (and can be) produced artificially. How it might be possible to establish whether or not the mind/universe corresponded with *dualism, idealism* or *materialism* is unknown/debatable. Indeed philosophers have argued about these and related issues for hundreds of years.

Many other—potentially enlightening—philosophies exist.

According to the *reductionist* model, everything can be explained away by reducing things to smaller and smaller things and properties of sub-facts; until one meets the tiny 'building blocks' that make up the universe. Several complex and surprising patterns/behaviours are thus explained away; through the summation of many microscopic events and processes; and emergent behaviours show through at the macroscopic level.

Methods such as the *atomic/molecular* views of the universe have become the dominant explanatory tools of science. One might expect a trained physicist to go much further and claim that everything is explained using such models. But I cannot accede to such a view—because it is my belief that many aspects of reality are mysterious; and are not explained using these and other (admittedly dominant) paradigms.[18]

Whilst I am not a follower of Pyrrho of Elis (365-275 BC), founder of the ancient 'school' of skepticism; I do find myself doubting (like Einstein) that science encapsulates and/or even approaches the true nature, and ultimate boundaries, of reality.

ILLUSION / REALITY

Philosophical discussions often bring up the notion of how to tell what is real and what is un-real or illusion. Issues of objective truth, the nature of mind/body and the possibly that our human perceptive abilities may sometimes be, or is/are somehow inherently 'warped', all bring questions of the nature of the real into the foreground of philosophical debate.

Discussions surrounding the nature of reality have been central to developing an understanding of much that has been discovered in the arts and sciences. Questions and topics related to reality criss-cross C.P.Snow's (1905-1980) *Two Cultures*. One area that intersects both the sciences and the arts is the topic of perspective, whereupon different representational types were developed, and multiple arguments developed over which type of perspective was the more realistic.

Often no certain and/or final answers were found to issues related to the nature of the real. But many times debates proved illuminating and influenced the very foundation of a field. In particular in the arts **surrealism** attempted to bring the nature of dream-like states into artistic creations, plus emphasised the cerebral, psychological and subconscious aspects of reality. Another movement was **magic realism** which placed emphasis on the 'spooky nature' and material existence of things in the real world.

But the Turing test cuts both ways. You can't tell if a machine has gotten smarter or if you've just lowered your own standards of intelligence to such a degree that the machine seems smart. If you can have a conversation with a simulated person presented by an AI program, can you tell how far you've let your sense of personhood degrade in order to make the illusion work for you. People degrade themselves in order to make machines seem smart all the time. - Jaron Lanier

The smaller question remains—can machines think?

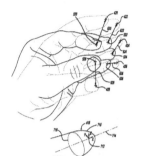

Are machines intelligent and are they capable of displaying self-determination? My own opinion is that aspects of intelligence do seem to be recreatable using the reductionist's model. It does seem to be possible (ref IBM's WATSON) to mimic intelligence and re-create aspects of it using the brute-force approach and (in fact) by tying together vast numbers of 'atoms' of information. There may be nothing special here—and certain kinds of intelligence can 'emerge' in this way. Therefore intelligence might not exist as a separate thing. But whether or not self-aware thinking (implied by consciousness) could be produced by reductionism is difficult to decide. Self-aware intelligence might be produceable in a computer (or artificial mind), but on the other hand, it might not be. The jury is out.

A *realist*, on the other hand, believes that tables and chairs truly exist—and are real existent things in the material world. Hence the realist might search for intelligence—as a special independent feature—and find nothing or alternately something—whereas a reductionist is perhaps more likely to find intelligence by perceiving its constituent parts separately.

According to the view of the realist, mankind has not yet found the 'intelligence' holy-grail; because we are still trying to identify a single area of the brain and/or series of mechanisms that are responsible for consciousness, if indeed such an explanation exists at-all. It could be that what we call consciousness is also an emergent behaviour that we have not yet been able to recreate in computers. This could be true of 'human' thought processes such as *empathy, intuition, inward contemplation and wishes;* and including *violation and the will-to-live etc.* The power of self-determination would perhaps be amongst this list of patterned and 'emergent' human qualities. If so there is hope to recreate it in artificial life forms such as computers; if not, then the attempt to create truly human-like thinking machines may be an impossible quest.

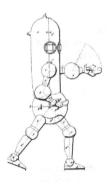

Perhaps this discussion is—in a sense—somewhat redundant, because if a way cannot be found to test for (and explain) human thinking processes—how so with machines?

Why give a robot an order to obey orders—why aren't the original orders enough? Why command a robot not to do harm—wouldn't it be easier never to command it to do harm in the first place? Do intelligent beings inevitably develop an attitude problem? - Steven Pinker (1954-) [*How the Mind Works*]

Many of these arguments relate to questions of free-will, and to whether or not mankind possesses any free-will at-all; and hence, if so, whether machines can likewise have free-will also. Accordingly, we ask the same question of humans: is it possible for us humans to disobey our 'programming', and make our decisions freely and without pre-determination or destiny?

Does free-will exist? Or is everything 'written'?

Free-Will

Free-will is the ability of agents—humans, machines, collectives—to make choices unconstrained by certain external factors. In the realm of religion, free-will implies that individual choices can coexist with an omnipotent divinity. Regardless of belief in a deity, questions naturally arise as to the nature of the universe—and specifically—is it deterministic or not. The underlying issue is: do we have some control (i.e. choice) with respect to our actions, and if so, what sort of control, and to what extent? On the one hand, humans may simply have a strong *sense* of free-will, but we could be mistaken in this respect.

The conflict between intuitively felt freedom and natural-law arises when either *causal closure* or *determinism* is asserted. If we do have causal closure, no physical event has a cause outside the physical domain. Likewise with physical determinism, where the future is determined by past events.

Reconciliation of freedom of will with a deterministic universe is known as the *problem of free-will*. This dilemma leads to a moral dilemma: how can we assign responsibility for our actions if they are caused entirely by past events?

'The emperor has no clothes on'.
- by a small boy (named withheld)

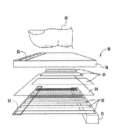

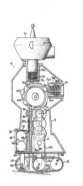

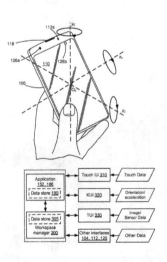

Are human beings constrained by lack of free-will—or do we have choice in terms of our actions? Free-will may simply be an illusion! Hence the question of whether or not we live in a deterministic universe is strongly related to free-will. Later I shall discuss my own (proposed) solution to the problem of free-will; but for now we (very) briefly overview the topic.

Professor Albert Einstein (1879-1955) famously said that he did not believe that *God played dice*. He meant to say that he did not believe that the laws of nature allow for accidents in terms of determining the forms and outcomes of natural processes. Einstein's response was a rebuttal to believers in the newly developed theory of quantum mechanics. This fundamental theory appeared to show that there is an inherent randomness lying at the heart of all natural events and processes. However if one believes, like Professor Isaac Newton (1642-1727) and Einstein, that the laws of nature are in some sense pre-determined, 'closed' and non-random; then it is difficult to account for humans actually possessing the power of free-will.

Free choice may then be—in some sense—an illusion, and at least in terms of actions; if not in terms of thought itself. This debate obviously has implications for questions of destiny and fate, and for all human beings. The idea of *free-will* is one aspect of the mind-body problem, that is, consideration of the relation between mind—for example: *consciousness, memory, and judgment;* and body—for example: *the human brain and physical processes.* David Hume (1711-1776) in his *A Treatise on Human Nature* approached free-will via the notion of causality.[12] He claimed that causality is a mental construct used to explain the repeated association of events, and that one must examine more closely the (assumed) relation between things regularly succeeding one another (descriptions of regularity in nature).

Hume looks for proof of causality—and finds no such thing anywhere in all creation (i.e. nowhere in nature)!

"If you want a second opinion, I'll ask my computer."

Hume believed that even apparently causal happenings like getting burned when you place your hand in a fire are by no means—and cannot be proven to be—causally related. Hence for Hume causality does not preclude human free-will; but may nevertheless explain that free-will is an illusion because causal happenings are in fact nothing of the sort.

Many modern physicists, like Professor Stephen Hawking (1942-) do claim that free-will is an illusion; because the laws of quantum mechanics provide a complete probabilistic account of the motion of particles. This is so regardless of whether or not free-will appears to exist. **Professor Erwin Schrödinger** (1887-1961), a nobel laureate in physics and one of the founders of quantum mechanics, came to a different conclusion. In his 1944 essay titled *What is Life?*, he claims that there is: 'incontrovertible direct experience' that humans have free-will... 'I' am the person, if any, who controls the 'motion of the atoms' according to the Laws of Nature.[19]

Unfortunately the long-running debate on free-will is often difficult to follow, and has no consensus of opinion—either for or against the possession of free-will by humans.[13] Perhaps a better question might be—do humans believe they actually posses free-will—and most people would say that they definitely feel that they do. Likewise for machines perhaps we should ask the same question: in what sense does a machine itself 'think' that it has free-will in response to events taking place in the world? Is the same machine in some (or any) sense free to choose one course of action over another. How flexible are machines?

In a circular fashion we are led back to the nature of thought.

Language and Personality

Another way of considering such questions might be to consider that human beings have different personality types, and make varying decisions according to experience, age and sex etc.

Can machines likewise have personalities and/or individuality?

Once again such questions are very problematical—and are in a sense tenuous and difficult to pin-down or test.

---

[13] See later chapters for further discussion(s) on machine free-will, AI etc.

TRUSTING COMPUTERS

I read somewhere that electronics has now progressed to the point where just 6 electrons move along the micron-sized connections in a modern processor—and these electrons move backwards and forwards billions of times each second—and this happens on trillions of separate connections on each processor.

Do you really want your car, train, plane, and LIFE dependent on such a small number of electrons. What if just one set of 6 electrons goes missing? Does anyone know what would happen?

A modern computer processor has billions of components, and it runs multiple computer programs with hundreds of millions of lines of high-level code; code which is decoded into billions of low-level machines code instructions that are performed each second. Are we really claiming that any person fully understands these machines?

As you program in higher-level languages, you know less and less precisely what you've told the computer to do! Layers and layers of translation may separate the "front-end" of a computer system from the machine-level instructions... At the level that you think and program, your statements may resemble more than imperatives or commands!

THE INNER PROCESSING OF THE COMPUTER IS INVISIBLE TO YOU!

Douglas Hofstadter

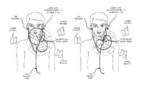

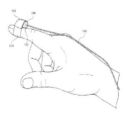

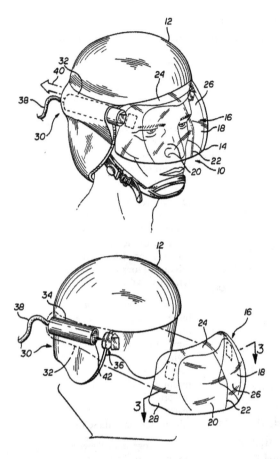

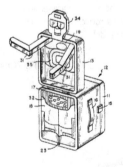

Empathy brings up questions of emotion and whether machines can be said to possess the same. Perhaps like the 'emotion-chip' which was given to robot commander DATA on *Star Trek*— you have to *be* the machine DATA; and in order to know whether you are actually experiencing Jung's *feeling tones*. Emotions must be felt.

In 1936, Professor Alfred Ayer (1910-1989) considered the question: How do we know that other people have the same conscious experiences as we do? [7]

As an answer, he suggested a protocol for distinguishing between a conscious man and an unconscious machine. Ayer was a *logical positivist* and as such he believed that analytical statements are tautologies; being statements that are necessarily true, true by definition and true under any conditions. Hence the validity of a statement does not depend on the definition of words that it contains, but rather they reflect an empirically verifiable fact. Here an empirical fact or aesthetic judgment that cannot be subjected to empirical testing, is meaningless.

I think that Ayer meant to say that language (words and concepts) operate as *pointers to reality*, and so any tests of logical correctness must be tested not in terms of the words alone; but in terms of verifiable facts about the world as it actually exists. Thus when probing a person (or machine) in relation to correct thinking procedures, the focus must be on understanding the world itself; and not on simple sentence structures or the somewhat arbitrary rules of language. Perhaps if this approach (focus on knowledge of the world) had been the aim of the Jeopardy TV game show, the machine WATSON would have had a more difficult time winning!

These ideas of language and reality were precipitated by Dr Ludwig Wittgenstein (1889-1951).[8,9]

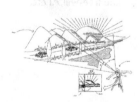

To solve very complex problems, you will have to end up letting machines work out a lot of the details for themselves, and in ways that we don't understand what they are doing. – Joshua Lederberg

COMPUTER   73

In his first magnus opus [*Tractatus Logico-Philosophicus*] written in 1922, Wittgenstein aims to reveal the relationship between language and the world, what can be said about the world, and what can only be shown.

Wittgenstein argues that language has an underlying logical structure; a structure that provides the limits of what can be said meaningfully, and therefore the limits of what can be thought. It is a fascinating and enlightening world-view; because the limits of language, for Wittgenstein, are the limits of philosophy. Much of philosophy involves attempts to say the unsayable: but what we can say at all can be said clearly, he argues. Anything beyond that, for example including religion, ethics, aesthetics, and the mystical; for Wittgenstein, cannot be discussed. They are not in themselves nonsensical, but any statement about them must be.

This is the early Wittgenstein who believed that language expressed a kind of 'picture' or painted view of reality; whereby he tried to show that *language* and *reality* have a similar structure. He is ultimately a kind of reductionist whereby language (reflecting reality) can be reduced to its most basic parts; and these building blocks are then used to express matters of fact in the real world. Later Wittgenstein altered (or extended) his views and instead said that language was a relationship, an active force that bonded people one to another. He describes this relationship as a *game* and discusses the multiple meanings of words in different games. He then shows how diverse the meanings of one word can be.

Our attention is drawn to language as a game. And if thinking is also in some sense, a game, then the question arises: can machines play also? Or do they play altogether different thought-games? It seems that an argument can be made for machines being able to play the language game very well indeed.

The computer WATSON won the TV quiz show against human opponents, in fact through an apparent ability to reason its way through complex questions of various kinds. In this sense we must accede that machines, if not yet able to think just exactly as we do, they are at least getting closer all the time.

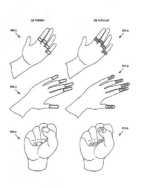

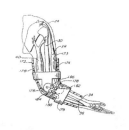

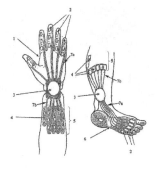

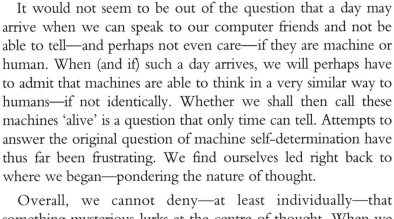

It would not seem to be out of the question that a day may arrive when we can speak to our computer friends and not be able to tell—and perhaps not even care—if they are machine or human. When (and if) such a day arrives, we will perhaps have to admit that machines are able to think in a very similar way to humans—if not identically. Whether we shall then call these machines 'alive' is a question that only time can tell. Attempts to answer the original question of machine self-determination have thus far been frustrating. We find ourselves led right back to where we began—pondering the nature of thought.

Overall, we cannot deny—at least individually—that something mysterious lurks at the centre of thought. When we try to divine where our thoughts and ideas come from (on a momentary basis); we find that they do come from *whence we know not where*. Certainly when we look deep into ourselves there is a mysterious and magical quality to our view of the world, humans and other life-forms. Perhaps this underlying mystery is Jung's unconscious mind at work, Mind-Apps, or we may even be sensing the Tao or experiencing our relationship to / oneness-with: the universe.

Whatever *thinking* is—it is certainly illusive.

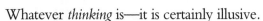

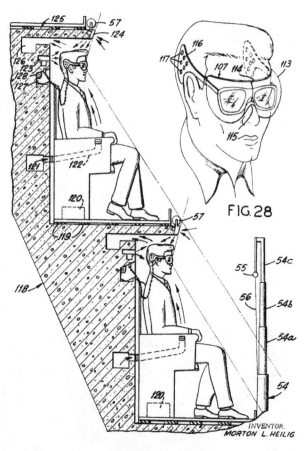

FIG. 28

INVENTOR.
MORTON L. HEILIG.

Nobody can deny that for many people life has a *mysterious, magical, religious or theological aspect*. Whether machines will ever feel similarly is unknown. Whatever the nature of thinking, one might say that there is a certain perspective, 'feeling' or indefinable essence—or pattern and background 'field' of consciousness—that is associated with being a thinking, feeling life-form.

At any moment, we sense/feel many things, aspects, viewpoints and past/future outcomes. We do not seem to think in the same linear fashion as computers—or if we do—then we have multiple '*Mind-Apps*' and faceted ways of seeing and knowing happening all-at-once.

Look at you, hacker: a pathetic creature of meat and bone, panting and sweating as you run through my corridors. How can you challenge a perfect, immortal machine? - Kevin Levine

Maybe now is a good time to review what has been discussed thus far. The goal of this chapter had been:

1. To seek evidence of self-determination for computers;
2. To discover a process of intelligent self-design for technology;
   ...or absence of the same factors

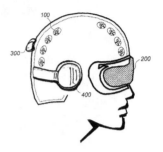

What have we discovered?

In relation to the first question, the answers are very difficult (if not impossible) to find. At least in a relatively short exposition, sadly, we cannot hope to find any ultimate answer to either question. In fact, in attempting to answer the same, we have touched on even more difficult questions such as the nature of free-will and whether or not we live in a deterministic universe. However (reassuringly) it does seem that even the greatest thinkers are in disagreement in relation to such questions. What then are the implications of this lack of understanding/knowledge, and in particular with respect to our examination of the nature of the self-computer?

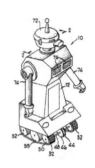

What we can say is that there is (currently) absolutely no evidence for computers possessing the power of self-determination—that is they do not possess independent decision making ability and are not: *motivated, self-aware, intuitive, aware of 'anything' whatsoever,* and do not possess: *emotions, personality or empathy.* It seems that machines, and computers in particular; are wholly logical, predictable and without the power of free-choice and/or feelings; they are: *merely programmable*; and cannot deviate from planned outcomes.

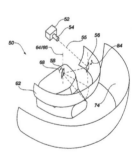

Dr Robert Anton Wilson (1932-2007) said: belief is the death of intelligence; and similarly, and due to lack of proof to the contrary, we do not believe in self-determination for machines. Machines are created very much in man's image, and as reflections of his deepest wishes; including *conscious and unconscious, good and evil, sane and insane, human and inhuman ones etc.* Computers are (in the words of Ted Nelson): perfectly <u>blank</u>—and wholly without a nature— they are merely imprintable and programmable.[19]

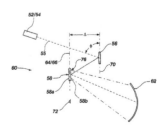

   < {8} Machines are artefacts of human thought and hence determinate— at least in terms of design—if not for their influences on humanity. >

Computers bootstrap their own offspring, grow so wise and incomprehensible that their communiqués assume the hallmarks of dementia: unfocused and irrelevant to the barely-intelligent creatures left behind. And when your surpassing creations find the answers you asked for, you can't understand their analysis and you can't verify their answers. You have to take their word on faith. - Peter Watts [*Blindsight*]

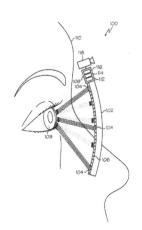

One might ask if—due to lack of proof—I similarly do not believe in free-will for humans. But here we must separate proof from first-person experience. I do find that I appear to have free-will—I feel it in my bones, so-to-speak. Thus I believe in free-will. On this point, it is interesting—and potentially illuminating for the current topic—that the greatest minds disagree on a relatively basic question such as whether or not humans possess free-will. It appears obvious that we humans all have different *thoughts, views, personalities, experiences and skills etc*; and so we all make—or may take—differing choices in the same situation (evidently). Put briefly, we are all individuals.

Therefore perhaps a more interesting question than whether machines can think, might be: can machines act/respond differently to an identical situation? Could they be imbued with a unique personality? Or given a flexibility of thought/action, that—at least apparently—gave each machine a character of its own? If and when machines achieve such unique personality traits, then we would have to admit that they had taken a step closer to human-like thought forms, and ways of being and doing (if not in terms of feeling tones and empathy etc). If machines with 'personalities' are possible; can 'feeling' machines—'happy' or 'sad' ones—ever be built?

Will machines ever 'care', feel, and wish to be liked/loved?

It is my own belief that machines (and computers) are not yet close to attaining a state of individuality or personalised decision making capability—and they **do not** make free-choices. However it is not my position that they cannot ever attain such a power/state. Who knows what they may be capable of in the decades to come? Computers are now developing and improving at an ever accelerating rate. Already CPUs contain over 2.5 billion transistors, and certain graphics chips contain 7 billion, plus some processors operate at over 8 GHz! Questions arise such as: have we lost control of machines because they are now so complex that they—in fact—surpass any single human's understanding? In a word, my answer would be no.

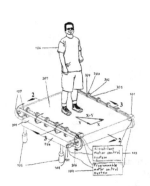

It is not the implementation details, capabilities—and complexity—that is important when it comes to computers.

Sometimes at night I worry about TAMMY (his computer). I worry that she might get tired of it all. Tired of running at sixty-six terahertz, tired of all those processing cycles, every second of every hour of every day. I worry that one of these cycles she might just halt her own subroutine and commit software suicide. - Charles Yu [*How to Live Safely in a Science Fictional Universe*]

Materialist philosophies that treat human beings as machines posses
the high ground in our culture—Academia. – Marvin Olasky

COMPUTER   77

Rather it is the ways in which machines interface/interact with humanity that are important. It is precisely because computers possess a human-programmed decision-making capacity, that we must now accept them as inherent to our very humanity. Today computers come in a variety of forms, including: *the desktop, laptop and tablet* through to ultra-mobile versions such as *smart-phones, glasses, watches (and even rings?) etc.* Computer 'brains' and controlling logic are also increasingly hidden in every day objects such cars, fridges and even kettles. According to the vision of ubiquitous computing, computers are set to steadily invade the real world, and may soon transform everyday things all around us into 'intelligent' objects.

One day, everything may be intelligent.

It is salient to ask, as a result of the computification and network connected nature of everything; what is to become of human beings. Are we to be relegated to the status of second-class citizens when it comes to the speed, depth and to some extent, the scope of thought. Will the robots and intelligent creatures succeed us as masters of this domain (the earth).

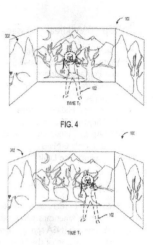

FIG. 4

Myself I doubt this will happen. And questions of mastery may be the wrong type of questions to ask; because artificial intelligence may prove to be inherently false—a mere pipe-dream—in terms of computers having their own: *self-programmed decision making ability, will-power, free-choice, motivations and sentient thought.* As stated, computers have become very good at Wittgenstein's 'language game', and one day could develop 'personalities' and we may even call machines 'friends'. However rather than machines standing apart from mankind, as a type of Frankenstein's monster; it is far more likely, in my view, that man will merge with the machine.

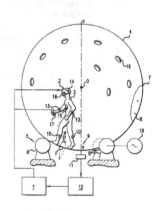

Computers will help people contribute to, and explore, all knowledge; and to develop, model and control our environment; plus allow us to efficiently govern future societies. Above all this, it is my belief that—if properly designed and operated—computers can help everyone to think better thoughts, individually and collectively.

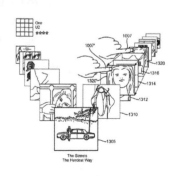

Fast and stupid is still stupid. It just gets you to stupid a lot quicker than humans could on their own. Which, I admit, is an accomplishment... because we're pretty damn good at stupid. – Jack Campbell [*Invisible*]

Access to computers and the Internet has become a basic need for education (and for emotional / intellectual well-being) in our society. - Kent Conrad

More and more, for better or worse, things are being run by
people who know how to use computers. - Ted Nelson

The way to defend ourselves against computer people (programmers,
network and server owners etc) is to become good at computers ourselves!

Many computer systems are being designed by a variety of lunatics,
idealists, and dreamers, as well as profit-hungry companies and
unimaginative clods, all for the benefit of mankind. - Ted Nelson (1974)

Top 10 Wikileaks (Assange)

- The WikiLeaks War Logs
- Watergate's Deep Throat
- The Pentagon Papers
- Plamegate
- Cablegate
- Guadalupe Hidalgo Scandal
- McChrystal's War Plan
- The Apache Helicopter Shooting
- Sarah Palin's E-Mails
- Lil Wayne's The Leak

Top 10 Spying Revelations

- Secret court orders allow NSA to
  sweep up Americans' phone records
- PRISM system (NSA spying program)
- Britain's version of the NSA taps
  fiber cables around the world
- NSA spies on foreign countries and
  world leaders (outrages all)
- XKeyscore, the program
  that sees everything
- NSA efforts to crack encryption
  and undermine Internet security
- NSA elite hacking team
  techniques revealed
- NSA cracks Google and Yahoo data
  centers (who protest innocence!)
- NSA collects text messages
- NSA intercepts all phone calls in
  two countries (+ others)

WHY IT MATTERS - HOW WE DESIGN OUR COMPUTERS

It matters because we live in media, as fish live in water.

Many people are prisoners of the media, many are manipulators, and many want to
use them to communicate artistic visions...

But today, at this moment, we can and must design the media,
design the molecules of our new water,
and I believe that the details of the design matter very deeply.

They will be with us for a very long time, perhaps as long as man has left;
perhaps if they are as good as they can be, man may buy even
more time—or (if) the open-ended future we suppose remains...
we must create our own brave new worlds with art,
zest, intelligence, and the highest possible ideals...

It is for the wholeness of the human spirit that we must design.

Ted Nelson [Computer Liberation / Dream Machines - 1974]

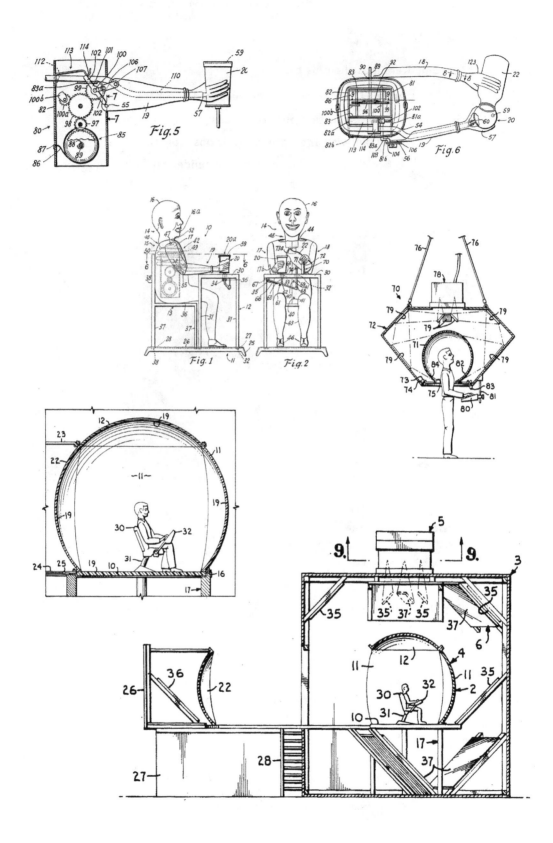

Fig.5

Fig.6

Fig.1

Fig.2

I have an axe to grind: I want to see computers useful to individuals,
and the sooner the better, without necessary complication
or human servility being required. - Ted Nelson (1974)

Computers must help us to:

Foster honesty, democracy and respect for others,

Provide: education and free access to knowledge,

Make wise and optimal decisions (together),

Eliminate poverty and engender equality,

and... HELP plus LOVE one another!

INTERNET
STATISTICS
[January 4th 2015]
[1 Billion = 1000 million]

< 3 Billion Users >
< 1 Billion Websites >

DIALY
< 76 Billion Emails >
< 1.4 Billion searches >
< 1 Million Blog Posts >
< 260 Million Tweets >
< 2,900 Million videos viewed >
< 51 Million photos uploaded >
< 52 Million Tumblr Posts >
< 1,300 Million on Facebook >
< 51 Million Skype calls >
< 17,000 Websites hacked >
< 268,000 computers sold >
< 1.5 Million smart phones sold >
< 284,000 tablets sold >
< 794 Million GB of Internet Traffic >
< 1 million MWh of electricity
used for the Internet >
[internetlivestatistics.com]

Untitled - from a 1939 issue of Fantasy magazine (possibly by Drigin)

Accursed creator! Why did you form a monster so
hideous that even you turned away from me in disgust?
Mary Shelley, Frankenstein (1823)

In 1 second on the Internet (on January 4th 2015):
8,338 Tweets sent, 1,629 Instagram photos uploaded, 1,678 Tumblr posts,
1,631 Skype calls, 25,150 GB Traffic, [?] people spied upon,
47,015 Google searches, 94,000 YouTube Videos viewed, 2.3 million emails sent.

Chapter Four
Ideas

THE ACT of thinking is the quintessential aspect of human nature, separating us from animals—and also machines. Forming ideas is man's all-embracing pass-time, and we think whilst we are: static or moving, alone or with others, at work and play, and in times of war and peace. We even sometimes think (in the form of dreams) whilst we are sleeping. Common sayings are to: 'use the grey matter', 'think things through' and 'ponder on it'. Plus we routinely consult the thoughts of others with the aid of books, films, TVs and computers etc.

Cogitating is also what we do when we have nothing else to do. And our minds are forever locked in thought—and/or communicating thoughts to others. Human thought-streams are near endless—witness **Facebook**, **Twitter**, instant-messaging etc.

To say that humans rely on our ability to think is seemingly to state the obvious; however some people have warned that we do not place sufficient emphasis on correct, appropriate and human-friendly thinking procedures.[14,15] A prescription for error-free thinking lies at the core of all practical philosophies; including *humanism, objectivism, utilitarianism and existentialism etc.* But right-thinking retains a certain mystery, and specifically how can we recognise, attain, and foster it; individually and collectively—and for the benefit of all mankind.

In this chapter we probe the nature of thought, in relation to its basic forms, features and incarnations; and in an attempt to define human thought as it exists today—and may come to exist in the future. An argument will be made that a person's thoughts are the natural property of the individual; and also that the open thoughts of humanity are—where known and/or unknown/hidden—the unassailable property of all human kind.

Evidently, we are what we think—individually and collectively. Accordingly, we wish to probe life-managed versus 'mechanical' and deterministic world-views, 'thinking'; and all kinds of thought mechanisms/agency.

The world as we have created it is a process of our thinking. It cannot be changed without changing our thinking.

Albert Einstein

Reading furnishes the mind only with materials of knowledge; it is thinking that makes what we read ours.

John Locke

People don't like to think, if one thinks, one must reach conclusions. Conclusions are not always pleasant.

Helen Keller

You may believe that you are responsible for what you do, but not for what you think. The truth is that you are responsible for what you think, because it is only at this level that you can exercise choice. What you do comes from what you think.

Marianne Williamson

Man's mind is his basic tool of survival... His mind is given to him, its content is not... To remain alive, he must think.... But to think is an act of choice.... Reason does not work automatically... In any hour and issue of your life, you are free to think or to evade that effort... so that for you, who are a human being, the question 'to be or not to be' is the question 'to think or not to think'. – Ayn Rand (1905-1982) [5]

It is the mark of an educated mind to be able
to entertain a thought without accepting it. – Aristotle

Thinking is learning all over again how to see, directing one's consciousness, making of every image a privileged place.

Albert Camus

We must think things not words, or at least we must constantly translate our words into the facts for which they stand, if we are to keep the real and the true.

Oliver Wendell Holmes Jr.

People don't want to think. And the deeper they get into trouble, the less they want to think. But by some sort of instinct, they feel that they ought to and it makes them feel guilty. So they'll bless and follow anyone who gives them a justification for not thinking. Anyone who makes a virtue—a highly intellectual virtue—out of what they know to be their sin, their weakness, and their guilt.

Ayn Rand

We must begin thinking like a river if we are to leave a legacy of beauty and life for future generations.

David Brower

If thinking is your fate, revere this fate with divine honour and sacrifice to it the best, the most beloved.

Friedrich Nietzsche

Your language indicates—and limits—what you think.

Jonathan Price

Thoughts come to us in many different forms: rational/irrational, conscious/unconscious and—in a real sense—individual/collective. Man thinks logically, and projects his wishes into the future. He controls his destiny in precise, planned and measured ways. For example, we wield the power of thought to help us to: *build shelters, obtain food, harness fire, master electricity and atomic power etc;* and so to plan for beneficial outcomes. Thinking frees man to contemplate creation.

Thoughts and associated actions shape human destiny—at least this is a key premise of the present study.[14] But the question arises as to whose thoughts (in particular) influence the future of mankind—or which thoughts—and how are the best or most appropriate ones chosen? Obviously such questions lie in the realm of philosophy, and accordingly we shall explore opinions from a variety of different sources and thought systems.

Another basic tenet of the present thesis is that a process is currently underway whereby man is merging with machines (or computers). If it is true that such a development is even remotely happening; then it stands to reason that we must consider how to create machines that (in actual fact) help man with his thinking—and do not hinder it in any way whatsoever.

We begin with the nature of thought.

The OED defines the word think with a long and complex entry. In the noun form *think* is given as: an act of (continued) thinking; a meditation; and as: what one thinks about something.

The verb form *to think* is illustrated thusly:

A) Illustration of Forms, B) Signification—To seem—To appear... to conceive in the mind, exercise the mind... with expressed subject (sometimes it)... to form in the mind, conceive (a thought etc); to have in the mind as a notion, an idea, etc; to do in the way of mental action.

Notice that the words thought/think have strong links with concepts related to appearance, visibility and form. For human beings therefore; it seems that thinking is closely tied to visualising a 'thing' in the *minds-eye;* and to related mind-games.

---

[14] Natural disasters / grand universal processes not withstanding.

Just because I liked something at one point in time doesn't mean I'll always like it, or that I have to go on liking it at all points in time as an unthinking act of loyalty to who I am as a person, based solely on who I was as a person. To be loyal to myself is to allow myself to grow and change, and challenge who I am and what I think. The only thing I am for sure is unsure, and this means I'm growing, and not stagnant or shrinking. – Jarod Kintz

Alternative definitions of: *to think...*

> Think up: to make up or compose by thinking; to devise, invent, contrive, or produce by thought or cogitation. Also: with a direct statement, question, or exclamation, or to conceive, feel (some emotion) as to think wonder, to wonder, to think scorn of, or to think shame... to meditate, to turn over in the mind, ponder over, consider... in reference to something done, with implication of purpose or design... to have one's thoughts full of, imbued with, or influenced by; to think in terms of etc.

I find these definitions illuminating as to the vast scope and diverse nature of the act of thinking; in all its multiple types, colours, tenses, situations etc. And *thinking about thinking* is perhaps the ultimate infinite-regress—and really hurts the brain, so-to-speak. Yet that is what we must now attempt.

A shorter characterisation of thinking states: to consider the matter; to reflect. Such a definition appears to lock *time* into the central processes of thought. Perhaps this is a useful way to consider man's logical nature; as a creature who takes time to slowly think things through—individually and collectively. And because we are social creatures, who possess the power of language; then the thoughts of countless others are open to us by way of speech and writing/reading. Man is therefore able to carefully consider matters over very long periods of time—and there is no urgency, so-to-speak. Logical thinking and the associated recognition of causality unlock many secrets.

It is the slowing-down of thought processes, and time-bound thinking—that allows man to consider the nature of reality—and so to solve the problems that he faces in the most ingenious ways—using logic. In this manner humans invent, design and manufacture; technologies to help us along the way. It is man's mastery of time—of the causal future—that separates him from the dumb animals; who must accept their lot because they lack the power of thought; and this is—*et secundum rationem.*

Thinking (as opposed to sensation) is man's metier; it is how he dominates the other animals, and obtains mastery over his environment.

Adding what him thinketh good of his owne knowledge.
– Harrison England (1877).

I say ffor my self, and schewe, as me thynchith.
– Pol, Poems (Rolls). (1399)

To everyone a thing is... what he thinks it is—in effect, a think. – H.Maudsley

In this chapter we explore the nature of ideas or *thought* (noun form); whilst in the following chapter we explore *thinking* as an act, process or mechanism that occurs both individually and collectively (verb form).

Since the lot of man is closely tied up with his ability to think, then one would expect him to perfect his capabilities in this respect. Sadly however, despite serious attempts to identify—and practice—right-thinking; results in that direction have (thus far) been mixed. In fact, for an apparently social being, there is much evidence that man thrives on argument/dissenter/provincial-thinking.

Everywhere we see examples of wars, economic poverty and above all else; instances of man enslaving man. In this book we designate such behaviour as evidence of sub-optimal thinking—and our aim is to eliminate the same.

How to think correctly is a topic that falls squarely into the realm of philosophy; defined in the OED as: the love, study, pursuit of wisdom, or *knowledge of things and their causes*, whether theoretical or practical. To think is to be human—our thoughts define us—and most assuredly: *we are what we think*.

We begin with Plato (424-383 BC), who wrote:

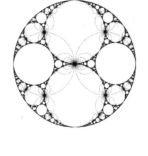

> We have found thinking to be a dialogue of the mind with itself, and judgment to be the conclusion of thinking, and what we mean by 'it appears' is a blend of perception and judgment, it follows that these two being of the same nature as statement, must be, some of them and on some occasions, false... we have brought to light the existence of false statement and false judgment... and next, what of thinking and judgment and appearing. Is it not now clear that all these things occur in our minds both as false and as true?[6]

With these words Plato identifies the difference between thinking and judgment/perception; but his true meaning here (in *Parmenides*) may be a very subtle one. Obvious is that Plato refers to the possibility of correct and incorrect conclusions (as a thought outcome); but less clear is how to identify/examine the same.

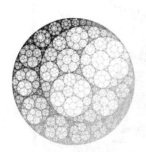

I do not think that their brains, or **think-boxes**, are of sufficient calibre to understand what they are preaching. – Daily Express [1937]

They are producing various **think-pieces**, including one for industrial relations, one on social services, and one on poverty, discussion papers out of which will be boiled one policy paper to be presented. – R.Crossman [1977]

In order to scry Plato's true meaning, we must delve a little more deeply into his writings, and open up the mechanisms of thought (as he saw them). It is common knowledge that Plato developed a theory of the ideal Forms (or Ideas)—or universal features—that real objects, living beings, processes etc; are said to partake of. For Plato the theory of Forms (or Ideas) is closely related to any theory of human thought. Plato spoke through the voice of his teacher, Socrates, and in *Parmenides* Socrates says:

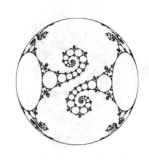

> The best I can make of this matter is this—that these forms are as it were patterns fixed in the nature of things. The other things are made in their image and are likenesses, and this participation they come to have in the forms is nothing but their being made in their image.

Accordingly, Plato asserts that non-material, abstract Forms (or Ideas), and not the material world of change known to us through sensation, posses the highest and most fundamental kind of reality. He claims that the Forms are the only true objects of study that can supply us with genuine knowledge of the world. It is a very controversial theory, but also a fundamental one that strikes right to the heart of how mankind can possess knowledge of anything at-all. Even today there is much debate about: A) what Plato meant by his theory of Forms, B) how they relate to the theory of universals and particulars, and C) the validity of these ideas.

We can open up each petal on this flower thusly:

On the meaning of Forms; clear is that the earliest Greek concept of form relates solely to vision, sight and to the appearance of a thing. The related words: εἶδος (*eidos*) and ἰδέα (*idea*); come from the Indo-European root: *weid* or '*see*'. Equally ancient is μορφή (*morphē*), '*shape*', from an obscure root. Other synonyms are φαινόμενα (*phainomena*) or *appearances*, from φαίνω (*phainō*), to '*shine*'. The meaning of these terms remained essentially visual through the centuries; and until other philosophical viewpoints took hold, when these words began to be associated with philosophical meanings. The ancient philosopher Thales noted that real-world things change, and began to ask what the nature of the thing *in-and-of-itself* really is.

Thales asked: what are objects and what are they truly made of? What (if anything) do different objects have in common?

Thales found that the answer was substance—and it is this that stands underneath or behind the apparently changing nature of the world. Substance is the actual existing thing that is perceived by the senses. Objects change, and/or appear different under varying conditions—but appearances can be deceptive. Therefore a fundamental question arose; what is a form really and how is that related to substance?

The theory of hylomorphism offered an answer; and conceives being (ousia) as a compound of *matter* and *form*. The theory was characterised by Aristotle (384-322 BC) who later defines X's matter as 'that out of which' X is made. Thus clay is matter relative to a specific brick, because bricks are made of clay; whereas bricks are matter relative to a house made of bricks. Change is characterised as a material transformation, and matter is what undergoes the change of form. Considering a bronze statue—the bronze is matter— which has undergone a change of form to become the statue.

According to Aristotle's theory of perception, we perceive an object by receiving its form with our sense organs. And forms include complex *qualia* such as colours, textures, sounds and flavours; and not just shapes. We thus perceive—together all at once—a sort of kaleidoscopic 'grouping' of forms that we assign to the object in question.

All well and good. Objects are compound, and made of both matter and form. But for Plato, *his* Forms cannot be directly perceived, because for him, Forms are of an altogether different and unworldly nature. They are (in actual fact) universal and exist in another realm altogether. Plato claimed that there is a Form for every object; Forms for *dogs, cats, human beings, colours, love, hate, beauty etc.* And for him phenomena are mere shadows mimicking each Form; that is momentary portrayals of a Form —as it is perceived under different circumstances.

Crucially in this view, there is only one Form for each essence; and they are that *without which a thing would not be the kind of things it is*. There are many tables in the world but only one table Form (for example). Plato's theory of Forms itself foreshadows, and is related closely to, the problem of universals.

The self-proclaiming speech styles of the main characters [in comics], and their periodic **'thinks' bubbles**. – N. Tucker, Child and Book [1981]

From OED: **Think book**, a book containing the writer's thoughts, opinions, observations. etc.; one that makes the reader think; **think box** colloq. or joc., the brain; **think factory.**

Think-groups, in which scientists frighten one another with visions
of a not too-distant future. – Guardian [26 Sept. 1967]

IDEAS   87

The problem of universals relates to the question of how one thing in general can be many things in particular. It was solved (supposedly) by assuming that each Form was a singular thing; that (somehow) caused representations of itself in particular objects. Accordingly matter was considered particular in itself. Yet how a universal (or Form) becomes imprinted on a particular object, is a matter of great intellectual debate, much mystery, and remains one of the central questions of philosophy right up until the present day.

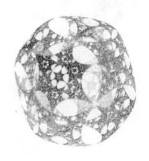

What seems logical is that the Forms—if they do exist—are *aspatial* (not existing in space), and *atemporal*. But even this apparently simple fact is debated; because philosophers altogether disagree on the true nature—and existence of—universals. There are three basic viewpoints on universals.

Realists insist that universals are real—in that they exist and are distinct from particulars. Within this view, Platonic realists claim that universals are real entities and exist separately from particulars. Whereas Aristotelian realism considers universals as real entities, but their existence depends on the particulars that exemplify them. *Nominalism*, on the other hand, asserts that only individuals or particulars exist and denies that universals are real. Finally *Idealism*, as characterised by men like Georg Hegel (1770-1831) and Immanuel Kant (1724-1804), claims that universals are not real, but are *ideas* in the minds of rational beings.

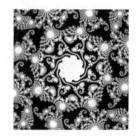

The problem of universals attempts to puncture/see-through the *veil of reality*; and even the most down-to-earth scientists must consider such questions; and 'wrestle' with related topics.

Professor Werner Heisenberg (1901-1976) commented:

> In the experiments about atomic events... phenomena are just as real as any phenomena in daily life. But atoms and the elementary particles themselves are not as real; they form a world of potentialities or possibilities rather than one of things or facts... The probability wave... mean(s) tendency for something. It's a quantitative version of the old concept of potentia from Aristotle's philosophy. It introduces something standing in the middle between the idea of an event and the actual event, a strange kind of physical reality just in the middle between possibility and reality.[7]

Other **think-factories** are Johns Hopkins University Operations Research Office. Johns Hopkins thinks for the Army. Stanford Research Institute... does the bulk of its thinking for a variety of government agencies.

Think-man = idea(s) man s.v. idea; think-piece = chiefly Journalism, a general article containing discussion, analysis, opinion, etc., as opp. to fact or news. - OED (2nd Edition)

Moving on to the question of the validity of these ideas—one is immediately hit by a real quandary. On the one hand Plato has led us (with his Forms) to a vastly improved understanding of human perception of the world—in fact by showing how it is that we come to think of anything at-all.

Put simply, everything is grasped (by the mind) in terms of universal concepts like *big, small, ugly, thin, light, dark, many, few, good, evil, happy, and sad etc.* We perceive, recognise and assign meaning to real world things according to universal categories. This is how we *attend-to, image* or *capture* the world— which (in reality) consists of vast numbers of particular objects and related individual events.

We comprehend the unimaginable diversity of reality using a short-cut system of universal-forms/concepts.

We are thus able to picture—and understand—a world that would otherwise be far beyond our ordinary (and pathetically limited) powers of perception. Creation is just too vast, complex and unimaginably diverse to see anything wholly in the individual or particular. Our scanning of reality would be far too tediously slow to achieve if we were forced to perceive everything all at once. And there would be no time for thinking! The abbreviated 'handles' provided by universals are the only way that a limited mind can even begin to conceive of nature. The vastness of reality is far beyond our perceptive powers to take into our (very) tiny brains. Perception, reflection and judgment require formation (by each of us); of mini-universes in our minds; the same being—optimistically— a one-to-one mirror image of reality. And these mini-universes consist almost entirely of universals—in fact being comprised of a far smaller number of such items than exist in the real world of objects and events—and of particulars.

Plato's theory of Forms is a type of *magic-key for reality*.

The Forms do provide fabulous clarity for the mechanisms of human thought; however opened up is a confusing pandora's box of problems in relation to the nature of reality itself.

The man who pursues truth by applying his pure and unadulterated thought to the pure and unadulterated object, cutting himself off as much as possible from his eyes and ears and virtually all the rest of his body. – Plato

Because on the other hand we are led to a fundamental paradox by the theory of Forms. Confusion arises as to the actual existence (or not) of universals and/or of the Forms that Plato spoke of. Are the Forms (and universals) simply a convenient method that allows the thinking process to happen; and hence enabling thinking beings to conceptualise reality—or is there a universal aspect to reality itself?

The answer for Plato, is that the object of true knowledge must be stable and abiding; that is the object of intelligence and not of sense. Furthermore he considered that these requirements are fulfilled by the (actually existent) universal.

Let us now analyse how we humans perceive the Forms. Put simply, in order to apprehend (or conceptualise) a particular real-world object; a human being must (at some stage) have perceived and/or recognised a great number of separate universal Forms and must have (presently or previously) collated them together into a singular concept of being. Human perception/thinking therefore consists of nothing but a continual process of assigning meaning through —and subsuming—*universal forms*. We collate features under singular (concept) headings; normally named monikers (words) or—alternatively object recognition events.

Less complex objects will contain a smaller number of universal 'likenesses' or features; whilst complex ones will have many more. Therefore the perception of a specific human being (for example) will contain potentially (in the perceiver's mind) tens of thousands of universal Ideas—if not many more —and the same being patterned 'likenesses' such as: *tall, short, fat, thin, intelligent, father, alive, dead etc.*

Thus for Plato, objects are real-world existent and hence patently particular (and often singular), as in the living person Bob; but we nevertheless conceive of Bob almost entirely through universals! Doubtless this description closely matches human thought.

Universals, analogy and *metaphor* are thus central facets of human perception.

Whatsoeuer he thought in his Imaginacion. – Hall [1548]

Hym thoughte þat his herte wolde breke. – Henry Wallace [1470]

If one does not hope, then one will not find the unhoped for,
since there is no trail leading to it and no path. - Xenophanes

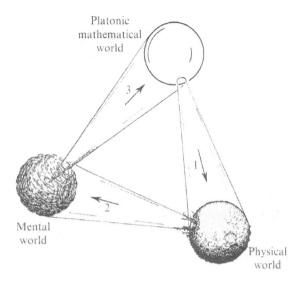

Platonic
mathematical
world

Mental
world

Physical
world

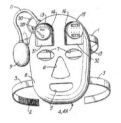

Big questions remain; do the Forms 'exist' and if so, where? How do the Forms give rise to the physical world; how does consciousness come into being and grasp both the Platonic and real worlds? British mathematician/physicist Sir Roger Penrose (1931-) has distinguished between *the real physical wold*, *the mental world* and *the Platonic world of Forms* (see drawing on left).[8]

One might expect a mathematician such as Roger Penrose to believe in the status of 'crystalline' mathematical entities. He says:

> The mathematical forms of Plato's world clearly do not have the same kind of existence as do ordinary physical objects such as tables and chairs. They do not have spatial locations nor do they exist in time. Objective mathematical notions must be thought of as timeless entities and are not to be regarded as being conjured into existence at the moment that they are first humanely perceived... these designs were already 'in existence' since the beginning of time... thus... there is a deep and mysterious connection between these worlds.[8]

As depicted in the figure—at top left—the entire physical world is governed by (a small subset) of mathematical laws—or Forms. Penrose supports a causal explanation for everything that is. However despite depicting his beliefs in this way, he admits that many people (including himself) are uncomfortable with such a premise of a wholly mathematical determinism; hence *prejudice one: **no room for free-will**.*

However Penrose states that he prefers (it to be true) that all of his thoughts and actions are the result of Plato's world, than have them subject to other types of base motives; such as human greed, violence etc. These are odd sentiments, because lack of free-will would not preclude evil behaviour—nor (completely) absolve personal responsibility.

But he (God) is equal in all directions to himself and
altogether eternal, a rounded sphere enjoying
circular solitude. - Empedocles of Acragas

Other people would object to the diagram's implication that all mentality has its routes in physicality. Penrose states that this view might be seen as a *second type of prejudice;* **against the power of the human mind to think independently**. But he notes that whilst it is true that we have no reasonable scientific evidence for the existence of 'minds' that do not have a physical basis, we cannot be completely sure. Another *third form of prejudice* he admits to, in relation to this drawing, is reflected in the fact that he has drawn **the entire Platonic world to be represented within the compass of mental activity**. Penrose believes that—at least in principle—there are no mathematical truths that are beyond reason.

Putting aside Penrose's (self-proclaimed) prejudices, there are still three deep mysteries related to the aforementioned drawing.

The first mystery is: A) how do Platonic forms (mathematical entities) give rise to the objects, properties and behaviours present in the real world. Secondly: B) how can organised physical material—brains—conjure up the mental quality of consciousness awareness? Finally: C) how is it possible that we are able to perceive the Platonic and real worlds in any way whatsoever?

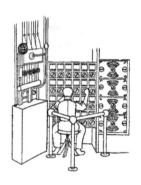

Such mysteries (of reality) are amongst the most profound and enigmatic of puzzles; and may concern: <u>unknown</u> unknowns!

Plain is that we are unable to address (comprehensively) any of these philosophical subjects in a book of the present kind—which is more of a 'practically' focussed work; and centred on using computers to help humans obtain: *freedom of thought*. However it is prudent to explore these mysteries a little further, in order to analyse related issues in detail (so far as we are able); and in order to scout-out or delineate the territory, so to speak.

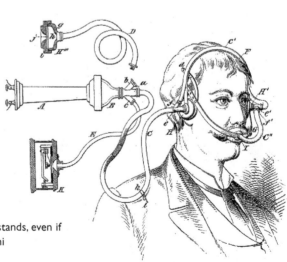

We have already dealt with (to a degree) the issue of consciousness [B] in the last chapter, and since it is to some extent outside of our central thesis, we shall cast related issues aside.

God is, even though the whole world deny him. Truth stands, even if there be no public support. It is self-sustained. - Gandhi

With respect to [A] and [C], specifically the nature of the Platonic world and how humans can perceive of related realities; further exposition seems prudent. It is enlightening to once again return to Plato in search of answers. Plato believed that the universals which we conceive of in thought are not devoid of objective reference. Like Penrose, Plato does appear to believe in the 'existence' of the Forms—even if this existence is not in space and time.

In the *Republic*, it is assumed that whenever a plurality of individuals have a common name, they have also a corresponding Idea or Form. This is the universal, spoken of earlier, the common nature or quality which is grasped in the concept; i.e. beauty.[3] Universals are *objective essences*—and they do have an ontological status. For Plato it is thought itself that grasps reality, and we *discover* Forms, universals and essences; and do not *perceive* them through sensation.

When considering a top-level class such as a human-being; some principal of unity has to be found, if the essences were not to be left in isolation—one from another. Plato thought he had solved this by using a viewpoint whereby: 'logical' meaning arises from certain human-assigned classes. But as with the whole theory, many problems, objections and criticisms remain unanswered right down to the present day.

Other problems exist, for example: do the Forms have a transcendental existence of their own, and what is their relation one to another, and to the concrete world of particular objects in the real world? Does Plato propose duplicating the world of sense-experience by postulating a matching world of invisible, timeless essences? Do we have a wedge (or vast chasm) between *existence* and *essence*—and how is one transformed into the other?

Plato's way of speaking certainly presupposes that the Forms exist in a sphere apart—but his true meaning is difficult to divine. We are left asking if the Ideas (Forms) exist separately from sensible things.

This ultimate question is inescapable.

God and Nature first made us what we are, and then out of our own created genius we make ourselves what we want to be. Follow always that great law. Let the Sky and God be our limit and Eternity our measurement. - Marcus Garvey

Obvious is that aspects of the universe operate according to fixed laws (mathematical Forms); and it is man's quest to discover from whence they come—if he is to fully comprehend the nature of reality. Regarding the reality and unity of the Forms, of the relation of the Ideas one to another, and of the relation of species to genus; Plato tried to solve each problem with a new interpretation of the *Eleatic* doctrine of the *One*.

According to Plato, at the top of all existence stands the One, or Good, which is the source of all things. It generates from itself, reason, wherein is contained the infinite store of ideas. Plato asserts that the Good gives *being* to the objects of knowledge; and is the unifying and all-comprehensive principle. The One attempts to solve once separate mysteries by introducing a new ultimate mystery—but at least it is singular! For Plato the Good is an absolutely perfect and exemplary *pattern of all things*, the ultimate ontological principle —sometimes referred to as a kind of perfect beauty.

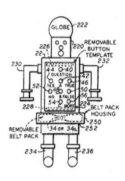

Put simply, the One is the cause of the essence of things— the Forms. Accordingly the Forms (in some undefined way) cause the sensible world of things familiar to humans. But if the Forms do proceed from the One—what of particular sensible objects? Is there a rift between the intelligible world of Forms, and the visible world, such that they can be no longer connected? The question is difficult (if not impossible) to answer—at least from Plato's idealistic perspective.

Plato declared that the Forms are numbers, and things exist by participation in numbers—a view similar to that held by a modern mathematician like Penrose. But the attempt to rationalise all reality to mathematics presupposes that all reality can be rationalised by us, which is a rather big assumption!

I think that anything that begins to give people a sense of their own worth and dignity is God.
John Sponge

A PROPHECY.

Questions remain. What is the relation of the Ideas to one another, and what is their relation to particular things? In an attempt to explain how Forms can exist 'apart from' sensible things; we can perhaps suppose that Plato would not *mean* that the Forms are spatially separate from things. What is meant here is that Forms do not change and perish with sensible particulars; and not that they exist in a separate spatial place, location, or world—altogether.

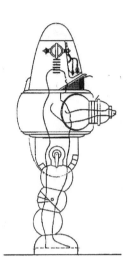

Forms would be as much 'in' as 'out' of sensible things—being both *transcendent* and *imminent* in real world objects, events and processes. Essence is real and independent of things, unchanging and abiding. Being incorporeal, these essences cannot be in a place or time, they cannot exist in a heavenly place; but exist in no place whatsoever, in and of themselves.

Everything known comes from whence we know not where.

I am afraid that this introductory discussion (to the Forms) has nearly come to an end; because this is about as far as we can go in relation to the nature of Plato's Forms. It is not a matter of lack of space, or of lack of will to explore the many contentious issues that flow from this remarkable theory; but rather because even the experts disagree on the nature, interposition and vast implications of this ultimate plan. Perhaps the interested reader can study the matter further using the references given below.

Questions remain as to how *(or if)* the mind arrives at an apprehension of the ultimate essences of the real world. Plato does not (for me) provide a final solution here—and we must look to other thinkers (past, present and future ones yet to come) for possible hints as to the uncovering of such mysteries.

If you don't provide the AI with a very big library of preferred behaviours or an ironclad means for it to deduce what behaviour you prefer, you'll be stuck with whatever it comes up with. - James Barrat

Nevertheless, Plato's theory reigns supreme...

For Plato, the Forms, whilst not fully real, are not mere not-being; but do they have a share in being. A *mystical—or cosmic—mind* and its effect, order; are present in the universe, and the Forms are therefore embodied mind or reason that permeates this world. The Forms are not *deus ex machina*—an invented solution to an unsolvable problem—but actual real things with ultimate power over all creation. Humans do not create the Forms, but discover them using intellect—and there exists an invisible and transcendent reality—that is the source of everything we attend to using the sensible faculties. Doubtless Plato has identified (or pointed to) aspects of the ultimate nature of reality. But I would suggest that the theory is by no means finished, and has been left for others to develop. Perhaps the abiding lesson of Plato's dialogues is that the true philosopher seeks to know the essential nature of things—and so to probe the rational behind all creation.

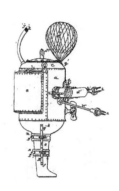

Accordingly, for Plato the world is an open book to the intellect; and man can, by rational reflection certainly come to knowledge of objective and transcendentally grounded values, ideas and causes/ends. By means of thought man unlocks the *secrets of the universe*—and may ultimately come to know (aspects of) the mind of God—the creator or ultimate principle which/who is responsible for all creation.

Earlier Thales (624-546 BC) had held the belief that *all things are full of Gods*; which foreshadowed Plato's ideas of the One. Perhaps Thales meant to say that all things are interpenetrated by some kind of life-principle—and that the world is somehow alive.

Whatever he meant, evident is the principle of *all-in-one* and *one-in-all*. Accordingly, for the Ancient Greeks, the world is rational and understandable by man; but only because it is ruled by universal principles and/or logic.

We live in a world full of robots where being human is a strange thing to do.
Ovidiu Oltean

Our goal should be nothing less than representing the **true context and structure of human though**t... enabling the mind to weigh, pursue, synthesise and evaluate ideas for a better tomorrow. - Ted Nelson

Let us stop and take a breath.

As a reminder of purpose—we wish to know what thinking actually is, in-and-of-itself. We are attempting to picture the essence (or nature) of thought, and to unlock its features most profoundly. In so doing, we seek to identify pure thought forms—existing by themselves—and uncontaminated by feelings, sensation and distortion.

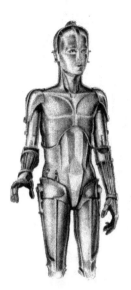

Our quest for specifics in relation to the thinking process, has led us inextricably to an (outward looking) consideration of the ultimate nature of reality. Perhaps this is necessarily so; because thinking normally attempts to place everything in perspective—and to understand the connections of everything to everything else—and so leads us inevitably to the bigger questions. We have thus been drawn ever deeper into questions about reality—and naturally so because thought is after all, if it is to be of any practical use, thinking about real world objects and events etc.

Thinking is no mere idle pastime; and by it we may gain a better understanding of the world we live in, and possibly we may live longer, happier and more successful lives, individually and collectively; and through the results of correct thinking.

Aristotle followed a like-minded realistic theory of knowledge based on logic. Central here was an analysis of the forms of thought; and of how thought grasps reality, reproduces it conceptually within itself, and makes statements/ discoveries about the universe that are verified by experimental facts. For Aristotle the key was to analyse human thought in terms of its relationship to the world.

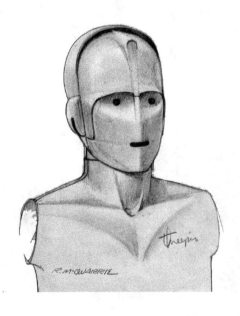

Aristotle's doctrine of the Categories is thus central to his theory of thought.[9]

The Categories comprise the ways in which we think about things, and the ways in which things actually exist. He assumes that the categories of thought, expressed in language, are also the objective categories of extra-mental reality—and reflect all that is known, or can be known, by mankind.

The world of the future will be an even more demanding struggle against the limitations of our intelligence, not a comfortable hammock in which we can lie down to be waited upon by our robot slaves. - Norbert Wiener

The Categories places every object of human apprehension under one of ten categories—*or patterns of being in the world.*

Aristotle begins by dividing all forms of thought into either simple thoughts—such as man, fights, sings etc; and those thoughts that possess composition and structure; such as 'a man fights' or 'she sings to the audience' etc. Only composite forms of speech/thought can be true or false (his true aim).

Next he distinguishes between what is said of a subject (what is it), and what is 'in' a subject, or what inheres to the subject—such as shape or colour etc.

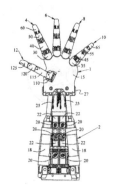

Of all things that exist:

1. Some may be predicated of a subject, but are in no subject; as *man* may be predicated of John or Harry, but is not in any subject.

2. Some are in a subject, but cannot be predicated of any subject. Thus a certain individual point of knowledge is in me as in a subject, but it cannot be predicated of any subject; because it is an individual thing.

3. Some are both in a subject and able to be predicated of a subject, for example science, which is in the mind as in a subject, and may be predicated of geometry as of a subject.

4. Last, some things neither can be in any subject nor can be predicated of any subject. These are *individual substances*, which cannot be predicated, because they are individuals (i.e. Socrates, Tree); and cannot be in a subject, because they are substances.

Next we arrive at the Categories themselves, whose definitions depend on the four forms of predication defined above.

A brief listing of the Categories seems useful at this point, in order to sketch out Aristotle's general way of looking at the world. The method attempts to fit all kinds and ways of being into a single framework.

Aimless extension of knowledge, however, which is what I think you really mean by the term curiosity, is merely inefficiency. I am designed to avoid inefficiency. - Isaac Asimov

The ten Categories (of Being) as defined by Aristotle:

1. SUBSTANCE (οὐσία, *ousia*, essence or substance). *Substance* is that which cannot be predicated of anything or be said to be in anything. Hence, *this particular man* or *that particular tree* are substances. Later in the text, Aristotle calls these particulars "primary substances", to distinguish them from *secondary substances*, which are universals and *can* be predicated. Hence, Socrates is a primary substance, while man is a secondary substance. *Man* is predicated of Socrates, and therefore all that is predicated of man is predicated of Socrates.

2. QUANTITY (ποσόν *poson*, how much). This is the extension of an object, and may be either discrete or continuous. Further, its parts may or may not have relative positions to each other. All medieval discussions about the nature of the continuum, of the infinite and the infinitely divisible, are a long footnote to this text. Examples: two cubits long, number, space, (length of) time.

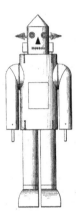

3. QUALIFICATION or Quality (ποιόν *poion*, of what kind or quality). This determination characterises the nature of an object. Examples: white, black, grammatical, hot, sweet, curved, straight.

4. RELATIVE or Relation (πρός τι *pros ti*, toward something). This is the way one object may be related to another. Examples: double, half, large, master, container, envelopes, knowledge etc.

5. WHERE or Place (ποῦ *pou*, where). Position in relation to the surrounding environment. Examples: in a marketplace, in the Lyceum.

6. WHEN or Time (πότε *pote*, when). Position in relation to the course of events. Examples: yesterday, last year, before, after etc.

7. BEING IN A POSITION, posture, attitude (κεῖσθαι *keisthai*, to lie). Aristotle indicates that he meant a condition of rest resulting from an action: *'lying', 'sitting', 'standing'.* Thus *position* may be taken as the end point for the corresponding action. The term is, however, frequently taken to mean the relative position of the parts of an object (usually a living object), given that the position of the parts is inseparable from the state of rest implied.

No, but if I were an illegal, experimental replicant hiding the truth of an international conspiracy I would try and put myself out of the way of those investigating it, wouldn't you? - Guy Haley (Reality 36)

Machines are not unnatural, dead mechanisms, but vessels, affordances, 'organs' even, of natures expansive self-expression. - John Tresch

IDEAS 99

8. HAVING or state, condition (ἔχειν *echein*, to have or be). The examples Aristotle gives indicate that he meant a condition of rest resulting from an affection (i.e. being acted on): 'shod', 'armed'. The term is, however, frequently taken to mean the determination arising from the physical accoutrements of an object: one's shoes, one's arms, etc.

9. DOING or Action (ποιεῖν *poiein*, to make or do). The production of change in some other object (or in the agent itself *qua* other).

10. BEING AFFECTED or Affection (πάσχειν *paschein*, to suffer or undergo). The reception of change from some other object (or from the affected object itself *qua* other). Aristotle's name *paschein* for this category has traditionally been translated into English as "affection" and "passion" (also "passivity"), easily misinterpreted to refer only or mainly to affection as an emotion or to emotional passion. For action he gave the example, *'to lance', 'to cauterise'*; for affection, *'to be lanced', 'to be cauterised.'* His examples make clear that action is to affection as the active voice is to the passive voice—as *acting* is to *being acted on*.

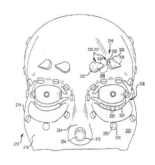

Following on from the Categories, Aristotle finds four ways in which things may be considered contrary to one another. Next, he discusses five senses wherein a thing may be considered prior to another, followed by a short section on simultaneity. He continues to identify six forms of movement: *generation, destruction, increase, diminution, alteration,* and *change of place.* Overall, it is a theory of elegance, simplicity and beauty.

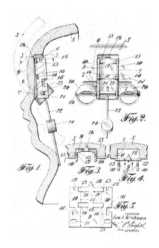

Reading Aristotle's words some 2000 years later; one is immediately impressed by the depth of insight, and clarity of the all-encompassing vision. In one fell-swoop he has defined nature and the modes of reality; and simultaneously identified the corresponding possible existent and universal features lying at the centre of all thought. Later writers may develop, add to, and elucidate this central vision still further; but none shall match the revolutionary upheaval —and monumental influence— caused by Aristotle's erudition.

It is a new gospel of rationality.

R-4 got stuck on the First Law. 'Can anyone really protect a human being from all harm whatever?' it thought. 'No. It is inevitable that all humans must be injured, contract illnesses and ultimately die.' - J. Sladek

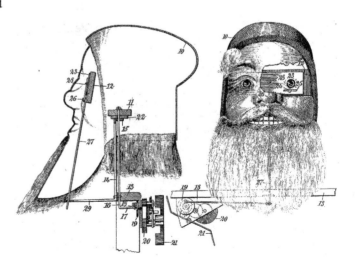

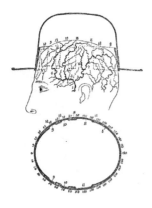

Implicit in the Categories are many fundamental concepts that we humans use to conceptualise the world around us. For example Aristotle notes that some quantities are *discrete*, and others are *continuous*. Continuous are *lines, surfaces and bodies, time and place*. Discrete are *number and language*; for the parts of number have no common boundary at which they join together. Similarly the elements of language are composed of discrete quantities—symbols—which although linked have no common boundary at which they join together.

The nature of Aristotle's epiphany is astounding; and pre-figured is much of Western philosophy that came to be. For example many later philosophers noted that language and geometry are mappings of real-world objects, events and processes. Science, in effect, casts a vast net of measurement across reality; whereupon we note only what happens at the intersections of this net. However in so doing we may altogether miss *being* itself—and see only 'shadows' of *being*.

With his Categories Aristotle effectively founds the Western scientific method; complete with its emphasis on the measurement of quantity; and of *time, structure, place, change, process and ultimately; of logical cause-and-effect*. It is a profoundly rational mindset, and he propagates the belief system of non-belief in the supernatural; a world-view in which reality is ultimately rational, logical, and crucially that all things are understandable by man. The mystical mindset of Plato has been put aside; and *otherworldly nature* is banished. Science shall ignore the great mystery of being, and whilst still conspicuously present at the centre of everything; all questions/viewpoints surrounding the ultimate shall henceforth be rendered impractical, unproductive and not worthy of serious scientific study.

Another fascinating and influential aspect of Aristotle's work is when he identifies the causes of change or movement which are categorised into four types. Aristotle wrote:

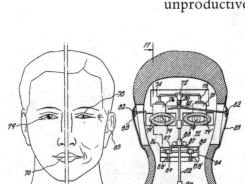

We do not have knowledge of a thing until we have grasped its why, that is to say its cause.[9]

It's this expandable capacity to represent reasons that we have that gives us a soul. But what's it made of? It's made of neurons. It's made of lots of tiny robots. - Daniel Dennett

Aristotle's four causes (of Change):

1. A change or movement's MATERIAL CAUSE is the aspect of the change or movement which is determined by the material which the moving or changing things are made of. For a table, that might be wood; for a statue, that might be bronze or marble.

2. A change or movement's FORMAL CAUSE is a change or movement caused by the arrangement, shape or appearance of the thing changing or moving. Aristotle says for example that the ratio 2:1, and number in general, is the cause of the octave.

3. A change or movement's EFFICIENT or MOVING CAUSE consists of things apart from the thing being changed or moved, which interact so as to be an agency of the change or movement. For example, the efficient cause of a table is a carpenter, or a person working as one, and according to Aristotle the efficient cause of a boy is a father.

4. An event's FINAL CAUSE (telos) is the aim or purpose being served by it. That for the sake of which a thing is what it is. For a seed, it might be an adult plant. For a sailboat, it might be sailing. For a ball at the top of a ramp, it might be coming to rest at the bottom.

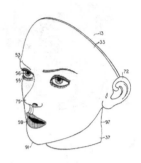

Once again, here we see the Ancient Greek fascination for creating a language and logical tools with which to probe reality. They had a desire to know: *hidden contractions, materials, components, processes and causative actions*. Aristotle's word for 'cause' is the Greek **αἴτιον**, *aition*, a singular form of an adjective meaning 'responsible'. He uses this word in the sense meaning, *an explanation for how a thing came about*; in this context, *'x is the aition of y'* means *'x makes a y'*.

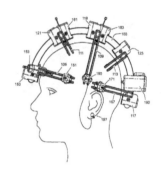

Some commentators note that a care must be taken to fully comprehend the meaning of an event's final cause; which has been misunderstood as a purpose (which may or may not be realised). According to Professor Edward Feser, purposeful cause is not what Aristotle wished to convey.[10] Rather finality is the end to which a thing is ordered, and there is *no possibly of escape from the defined outcome*; unless a particular set of thing-events (material, formal and efficient causes) in the world are changed or interfered with before the predicted final cause comes to be.

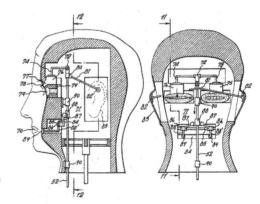

Doubtless machines influence: the settings, accoutrements, passions, strategies, and arrays of forces that shape human lives... and... everything depends upon our ability to focus and direct the will... weave (everything) together into 'circuits' of both living and inanimate objects... (allowing us to) re-organise the space between mind and world. - John Tresch

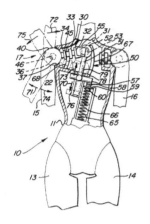

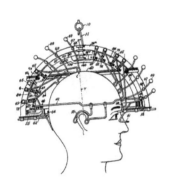

What a wonderful conceptual scheme Aristotle gave to mankind with his Categories and the four causes; representing nothing less than a prescriptive method for building the various cathedrals of modern science. Aristotle banished the irrational, and placed logic as *master and commander* of the universe. From this moment forward, rationality vanquishes the magical, mystical and spiritual domains (apparently).

But the victory of rationality is only superficial. A strictly 'scientific' explanation of the universe normally attempts to account (only) for a relatively narrow range of phenomena/ problems. And the universe is likened to a vast mechanical watch that once started, runs itself (somehow) according to its own self-contained laws. However many valid unknowns are banished from such models—including questions relating to who/what could possibly start this 'watch', the true nature of being, how space and time come to be, and what (if anything) man can do to steer his destiny towards positive outcomes.

Despite the fact that questions surrounding the ultimate have been—to some extent—cast out from science, problems remain (within the rational scheme of science/logic); and with respect to interpretation of cause and effect.

In particular explanations in terms of final causes remain—despite the fact that nothing can be explained by its outcome. It has been claimed that blatantly false explanations in terms of final causes are common throughout science. And especially that (patently false) teleology is seen everywhere—the view that there is an imminent mind, God, overseer, or will present in the universe which is the ultimate cause of all things.

Teleological explanations are common in evolutionary biology, and because the very process of adaption may be teleological in nature. Writing in an article published in *Nature* in 1874, Asa Grey (1810-1888) noted: Darwin's great service to Natural Science lies in bringing back Teleology; so that, instead of Morphology versus Teleology, we shall have Morphology wedded to Teleology.

Charles Darwin (1809-1882) responded to the article thusly:

> What you say about Teleology pleases me especially and I do not think anyone else has ever noticed the point.

If we want to make a computer to do what we already know perfectly well how to do ourselves, then all we do is write a program. Aha. But what if we want to write a program to do something we do not know how to do ourselves? We must set up the program to browse, and search, and seize on what turns out to work. This is called heuristics. - Ted Nelson

Thinking 'Machines' (of all kinds)

Our attention is drawn to the question—is man the only thinker—or does the inanimate universe itself somehow 'think'? Is it possible that even simple life-forms—in some way are able to 'think'? Perhaps not all thinking is self-aware or conscious. Another type of classical 'thinking' may be equated with planning, purpose and design—which is related to telos. Teleology is the belief that things are by purpose aimed towards a goal. According to some scientists (Dawkins etc), this is to be avoided (within science) and statements which imply that nature has goals are heretical. However such a criticism of teleology seems (to the author) to be short-sighted, simplistic, narrow and 'mechanistic'; plus anti-humanistic or anti-life.

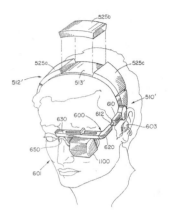

It may be true that on the vast scale of the universe; that there is no overall plan (or it may be so). But it would seem obvious that nature can and does—on smaller scales—construct particular ordered conglomerations of components and hence environments in which narrower and localised goals—in fact teleological explanations—are inescapable.

The central argument of the anti-teleologists is that there is/are no mind(s) or intelligence(s) whatsoever influencing, designing and controlling the development of nature.[12] The same argument is said to hold for all processes happening within both the animate and inanimate worlds. Doubtless for all living creatures below man—an argument can be made—that (real-time) mind-aware planning towards conceptualised goals is absent.

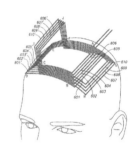

On the other hand, imputing self-programmed goals for life is not heretical, foolish or anti-scientific. It should be obvious that no God-like 'mind' has to supervise the design of a living creature in order to say it has been 'designed' towards a particular goal.

Living beings emerge that are supremely adapted for life in their local habitat; and intricate designs evolve through natural selection —and the plans of life are stored in the DNA. An expression of the 'goal' of life must be stored in the DNA also; the goal being to *continue life, eat, compete and reproduce.* A life-form may also be said to 'remember'; millions of years of the entire history of a species (within its DNA); and to have associated planning abilities.

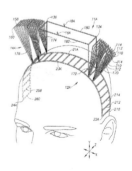

We are the intelligent elite among animal life on earth and whatever our mistakes, [Earth] needs us.
This may seem an odd statement after all that I have said about the way 20th century humans became almost a planetary disease organism. But it has taken [Earth] 2.5 billion years to evolve an animal that can think and communicate its thoughts. If we become extinct she has little chance of evolving another. - James Lovelock

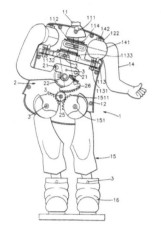

The goal of life—for any particular creature—will be, to some extent, unique. This plan must (in actual fact) be very complex and have a sophisticated expression, only we humans cannot read much of it yet. The methods of achieving/implementing all of the sub-goals of life may also mutate/develop through molecular evolution.[13]

A creatures 'life goals' do not have to be known or conscious, within a creature's very mind, to nevertheless still be present and active in the genetic code which controls the creatures form; and/or be present in the behaviours and the ways in which it seeks to live and obtain sustenance and reproduce. Certain is that the goals-of-life are constantly being written and re-written according to all kinds of accidental (DNA encoded) processes (between generations) of which the creature itself is completely unaware.

But that does not mean that these same events/life-patterns are not sifted, organised and—or planned—within the DNA as a life-plan. Why biologists do not like to call this design towards a goal or purpose, is baffling—especially since the result is the same; a perfectly designed creature that is perfectly adapted to its environment. In my opinion (and it seems in Darwin's also) a creature can be said to have 'designed' itself in response to the requirements of its environment (mutual adaption + evolution).

Fathers pass lifestyle influenced DNA changes to their children, and genes switch themselves 'on and off' according to lifestyle. Surely these are evidence of intelligent/responsive self-design, design 'feedback-loops', and/or goal-seeking design mechanisms.

According to Dr James Lovelock's (1919-) Gaia principle, organisms interact with their inorganic surroundings on Earth to form a self-regulating, inter-connected system that contributes to maintaining the conditions for life on the planet. Gaian hypotheses suggest that organisms co-evolve with their environment: that is, they *influence their abiotic environment,* and that the environment, in turn, influences the biota by Darwinian processes.

Life has many survival related tricks '*up its sleeve*'; on all spatial/temporal scales, and across all bio-strata.

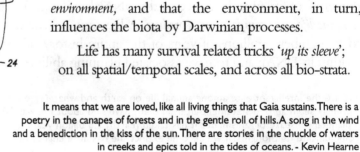

It means that we are loved, like all living things that Gaia sustains. There is a poetry in the canapes of forests and in the gentle roll of hills. A song in the wind and a benediction in the kiss of the sun. There are stories in the chuckle of waters in creeks and epics told in the tides of oceans. - Kevin Hearne

When taking a purely mechanistic explanatory stance; the universe becomes a cold, foreboding and uncaring place. According to Physics, any localised order, patterns, life, intelligences, and heat; are mere *accidents of nature*—patterns which are doomed to destruction, and no ordered arrangement of matter can exist for very long.

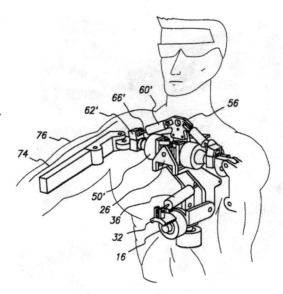

Such views are founded on the *Second Law of Thermodynamics*, which states that the level of disorder in the universe is steadily increasing. But even if such a state of highest disorder is the ultimate fate of the universe; who is to say that local 'islands' of order—for example the living earth—cannot exist almost indefinitely, after all life has been around for billions of years already.

And who is to say that intelligence cannot *counter disorder* and help maintain a pattern of order. Experiments that 'prove' entropy increases inevitably, seem to ignore the biggest experiment of all, earth itself. Gaia evolves through a cybernetic system operated unconsciously by the biota leading to broad stabilisation of the conditions of habitability in a full homeostasis.

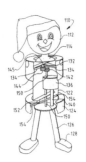

Some people criticise the concept of Gaia, and specifically for imbuing the earth with a kind of 'intelligence'; and perhaps even with possessing an ability to plan for the future and to 'think'. But such views seem misplaced and entirely human-centric. In response, we ask: do humans really understand the earth's vast complexity? Are we humans claiming that we know the 'purpose' of the earth—and/or that it is, in fact, purposeless? Can we truly claim that everything (including life) is just summations of vast numbers of directionless accidents?

It seems obvious that Darwinism and the theory of Gaia provide evidence for a complex web of actors/inter-relationships amongst both animate and inanimate materials; and that the resultant processes do have the power to shape local habitats and create room for 'purposes' to emerge; and that—*life finds a way!*

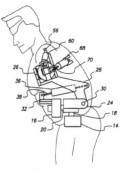

Now we, if not in the spirit, have been caught up to see our earth, our mother, Gaia Mater, set like a jewel in space. We have no excuse now for supposing her riches inexhaustible nor the area we have to live on limitless because unbounded. We are the children of that great blue white jewel. Through our mother we are part of the solar system and part through that of the whole universe. In the blazing poetry of the fact we are children of the stars. - William Golding

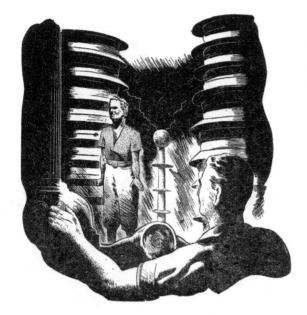

Telos of Life [agency of mind(s)]

According to some scientists, a vast cosmic battle of: *life versus entropy* is ongoing; now and forever. Some believe that entropy is destined to win. But I can detect a strong fatalism in such a viewpoint; which is also a wholly negative and anti-heroic world-view—and tends to sideline mankind to the position of mere spectator.

Attempting to claim that because disorder will always increase, we humans cannot (as a result) control our destiny—even on relatively short timescales—seems to be a crazy and suicidal approach to life. It is like postulating that because electrons do not flow easily due to resistance, that they have a natural affinity to stay in situ: therefore electronics is unnatural and we should not build computers etc.

If we judge (life-managed) teleology as unquestionably impossible; under all circumstances, and on all spatial and temporal scales, then we deny man's will-to-power, and deny the power of Aristotle's rationality to shape reality. The fourth cause is classified as mere accident. On the other hand, if we believe in teleology, and accept that man makes of his destiny whatever he wishes; then we wholly embrace rationality, logic and affirm the fourth cause as being an expression—nay a sermon—signalling man's domination over nature.

In other words, it is our responsibility to arrange the universe according to requirements/need.

I put it to you that this is Aristotle's key message and true legacy; that the universe is open in terms of outcomes; being inherently createable, constructible and programmable. Ergo we humans are the masters in this domain. Man is free to design his future, and that is the whole point of Aristotelean rationalism. I submit that Western science has ignored/misunderstood the core message of Aristotle; which is simply that we humans create our own destiny.

The whole course of human history may depend on a change of heart in one solitary and even humble individual—for it is in the solitary mind and soul of the individual that the battle between good and evil is waged and ultimately won or lost. - M. Scott Peck

Computer science is no more about computers than astronomy is about telescopes. - E. Dijkstra

< {9} Telos of Life = thoughts/models = plans = life sustaining actions. >

Arguments over whether inanimate processes or human 'minds' make the future; mirrors our previous discussions on man versus machine. But in this case, the arguments are pointless. I submit that it is patently true that—at least on shorter timescales—life wins over inanimate nature; and that the mastery of life is obvious.

The evidence: Gaia herself; the earth's vast living self.

Some late 20th century scientists downplayed the fourth cause and merely interpreted it in terms of a mechanistic, anti-teleologic explanation for *everything that is*. However identified by Professor John Tresch in his 2013 book: *The Romantic Machine* is an earlier social movement towards:

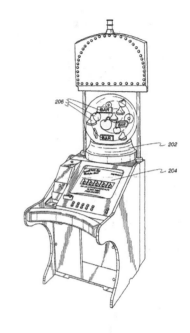

Mechanical processes seen as instruments of organic teleology.[11]

A dichotomy, dualistic nature or great disconnect; is identified at the heart of modern man; whereby on the one hand he optimistically believes in mastery by *wielding* technology wherever and whenever it seems most useful; but present also is a lack-of-belief in *using* technology to help us to solve the biggest problems such as hunger, disease and war etc. Projected onto technology is a *Jekyll and Hyde* character—and we humans must accept both aspects, unless we wish to be banished right back to primitive times. Technology (including logic plus causality) is somehow (partly) out of control and/or ineffective.

Such fatalistic views are self-limiting and even dangerous. Narrow perspectives on technology lead us to tackle merely the smaller and localised problems, and the strategic ones are left unchallenged; and because seemingly they are behind the *ken of man* to solve. Conversely, in the coming chapters we open up the opinions and predictions of a great variety of thinkers; on the subject of how to adequately employ technology to solve the biggest problems. Thoughts are recognised (potentially) as telos —the fourth cause—and are how man is able to influence anything whatsoever. QED.

Why do we let a machine/system/computer make all of the decisions for us, why let it rule, why do we not protest— and demand to speak to the designer, forcing him/her to take responsibility and correct the problem(s)?

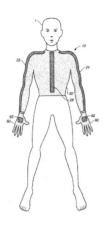

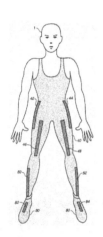

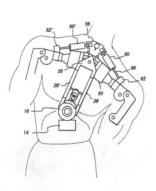

And machines, patently—wholly and obviously—merely implement man's thoughts/wishes. Accordingly, I will argue that any failure of man to use computers for humanistic ends; is due (in large part) to the application of a limited and overly mechanistic perspective. Up until now, man has both accepted and denied the fourth cause simultaneously—and purposeful control of his destiny is likewise uncertain. Needed is a new perspective/positivism.

With our mechanical creations we must create a new *milieu*—a life sustaining envelope surrounding the self. Machines must be seen as: fluid metaphors between mind and world, and be the ligaments of (a new) society.[11] We must construct a 'technological' Gaia that supports and nurtures human beings. Computers must form new interfaces between mind, world and external objects; devices fused with human actions, intentions and perceptions.

We must avoid viewing machines through the *greedy reductionism* identified by Lovelock; but see the truth: that we are as Gods—with respect to the first and second 'natures'—and might as well get used to it.[13] Mechanical metaphors, according to David Abram, lead us to overlook the active or agential quality of living entities; while the organismic metaphors of (for example) Gaia theory accentuate the active agency of both the biota and the biosphere as a whole. By adopting an overly 'scientific' perspective, we all too often (bizarrely) remove man from our analysis altogether—downgrading humans to mere actors—as opposed to *prime movers* in the great game of life.

As we come to the end of this chapter on *Ideas*, it is useful to review what has been learned.

Early Greek thought concentrated on materialist explanations of reality; and looked for an ultimate substance, and/or causative action(s) behind everything that existed. Plato developed the mystical concept of the Idea/Form, which is a kind of universal essence that real world-objects somehow instantiate and take part in. Aristotle expanded/morphed Plato's ideas into his Category theory and the idea of causes of change. In so doing, he allowed us to explore (in the minds eye) logical deductions, re-arrangements of real-world things; and to develop a rational, logical conception of reality and everything that exists.

Fear of serious injury alone cannot justify oppression of free speech and assembly (plus freedom of thought). Men feared witches and burnt women. It is the function of speech to free men from the bondage of irrational fears. - Louis D. Brandeis

Systems, machines and computers should exist solely to help human beings; they are not weapons to be used against humanity, or else to foster merely parochial interests, wake-up mankind.

It has been said that the whole scientific, philosophical and intellectual Western tradition can be ascribed as mere footnotes to the writings of Plato and Aristotle. However whilst it is undoubtably true that these two thinkers outlined, or staked out, much of the territories of thought that came later; it is bad faith to limit one's outlook unnecessarily. Anyone who wished to understand the relationships between man and machine; would be well-advised to broaden his studies. Older philosophers such as Kant, Leibniz, Thomas Aquinas, John Locke, Spinoza and many modern thinkers/writers; all have salient points to make that relate to the question of how we might design more efficient, humane computing systems. Accordingly, in the coming chapters we shall explore a wide range of related views/opinions (old and new).

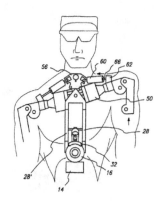

Perhaps this discussion might be too esoteric for many system designers, and the connections that I am making between apparently separate topics too bizarre, loose and tenuous for some; but the comments of Ray Bradbury seem especially apt on this specific point:

> If God knew what he was doing, then Man is the essence of God.
>
> If Man knows what he is doing, then Machines are the essence of Man!
>
> All of these complexities, imagined sins, incredible energies, awesome mysteries, puzzling paradoxes, and deaths and singing rebirths pass from man into his invented children-machines!
>
> A strange, but certainly an unholy trinity: GOD, MAN, MACHINE.
>
> Man clones himself in machines. Machines, if built properly can carry our most fragile dreams. Man within machine within God.[12]

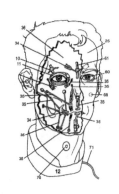

According to Arthur Schopenhauer (1788-1860) the universe and everything in it possesses 'the will to live'[1]. Nietzsche developed his related theory of *the will to power*—which he believed was the main driving force in humans.[4] We humans are oriented towards achievement, ambition and striving to reach the highest position in life; which are all manifestations of this basic drive—to dominate / manage the world—using intellect, logic and (ultimately) thoughts.

In a (very real) sense to think is to be human—our thoughts define us—and most assuredly: *we are what we think.*

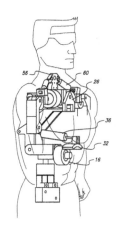

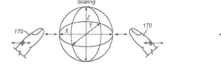

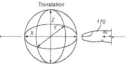

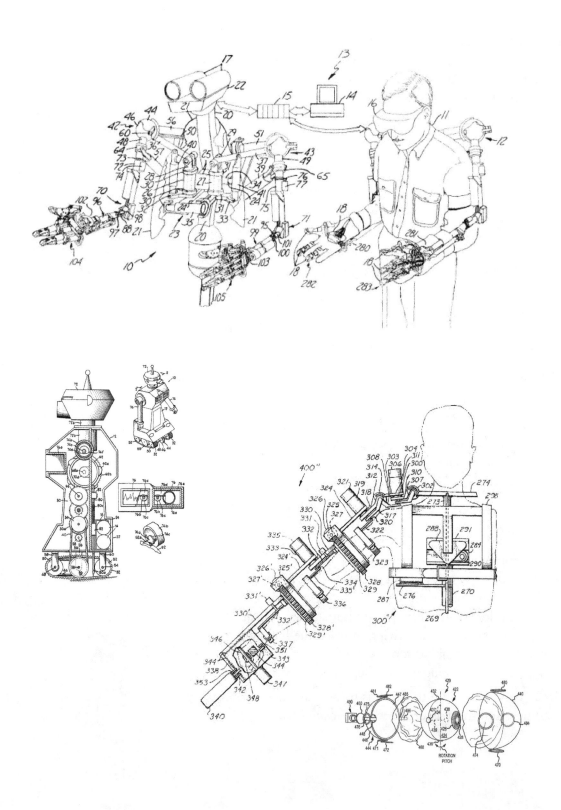

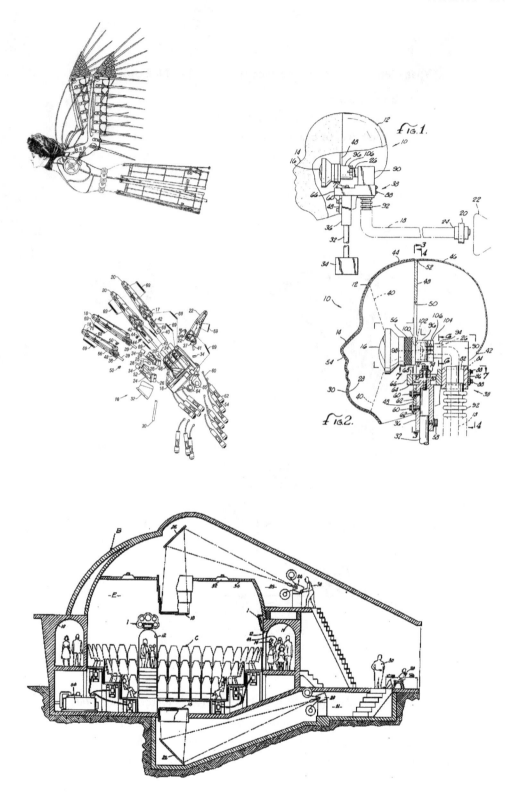

What computers should be (according to Ted Nelson):

It's about documents,
It's about what kind of civilisation we wish to have.
We must create brave new worlds with art, zest,
intelligence; and the highest possible ideals.
It is for the wholeness of the human spirit
that we must design.

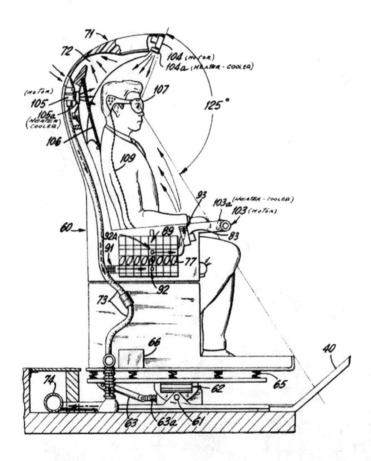

Experience Theatre (USA Patent 3,469,837)- by Morton Heilig (1966)

The world to me was a secret, which I desired to discover;
but to her it was a vacancy, which she sought to people with
imaginations of her own. - Mary Shelley, Frankenstein (1823)

Chapter Five
Thinking

I N THE last chapter we sought to probe the nature of thought.

We adopted a theoretical outlook; and explored the features of thought using the theory of universals. In the present chapter we turn to the practical aspects of thinking; and in order to discover: from whence thoughts come, how they develop, where they go to, and how they are transformed into action.

We wish to understand how the mind works.

Our perspective remains largely focussed on computers, and on identifying how they can help—or sometimes hinder—man's thinking. Much has been written on the ways in which computers can bring people closer together; and (often) through a more rapid and complete communication of ideas. Artificial systems and machines also help man to manage his environment by magnifying his: *mind, vision, wishes, energies, and strength etc.* However many writers have noticed that technological advances are not always beneficial. Accordingly, it is a core premise of this book, that needed are new and appropriate relationship(s) between humans and machines; and in order to foster *right thinking practices*; plus freedom of thought/expression/action.

In the *Ars Rhetorica;* Aristotle identifies three modes of persuasion as follows: the *logos* (principle of order), *ethos* (moral character), *and pathos* (emotional appeal).[1] Consequently, in this chapter we supply argumentation in each of these classes; and in favour of: *thought ownership, equality* and *free-assembly*.

Thinking about thinking is a confusing double-bind, whereby one could easily become lost. But we must not allow ourselves to be put off by difficulties—in this respect—because the tastiest fruit is sometimes hardest to attain. Hence we seek to understand ourselves; and to open-up our very thoughts to analysis—individually and collectively—and in terms of the computer's influence on: our wishes, plans and actions.

If the computer is a projective system, the real ones, with projectors in them, are all the more so... whereby they make pictures on screens... are strange inversions and foldovers of the rest of the mind and heart... the peculiar origami of the self. - Ted Nelson

Technicalities matter allot, but the underlying vision matters more.

Ted Nelson

Machines as extensions of human senses and intentionality.

John Tresch

Machines and tools are seen as new organs modifying humans relation to their environment.

John Tresch

All parts of the cosmos have to be brought together and represented on a single site, in order to focus human activity and remake the world anew!

John Tresch

Computers should make things easier in both our work and private lives, and should help lighten the loads and enlighten our minds, clarifying the complexities of everything.

Ted Nelson

The first question to ask, when somebody shows you the latest and greatest, is: what are the properties and qualities of the new medium? The follow up questions come easily with experience: How often do you have to change it, what are the branching options, what part could somebody put in backwards; are there distracting complications?

Ted Nelson

TED NELSON ON THE FUTURE OF COMPUTERS

There are two problems with all of this. The first and worst, of course, is who controls and what will hold them back from the most evil doings. Recent history, both at home and abroad, suggests the answers are discouraging. The second problem, wispish and theoretical next to that other is whether in turning toward bizarre new pleasures and involvements... we will not lose track of all that is human.

In the face both of potential evil and dehumanisation, though, we can wish there were some boundary, some good and conspicuous stopping place at which to say: NO FURTHER, like the three-mile limit in international law of old. I personally think it should be the human skin. Perhaps thats old-fashioned, being long breached by the pacemaker. But what other lines can we draw? The prospects are horrorshow, me droogies.

Computer as oracle, dream-machine, God, mind-amplifier, bicycle/tool for the mind, information-machine, coercer, magic wand, magic ingredient, window into new worlds, fantasy machine, network, whisperer of lies, controller, friend, enemy, lover, prison for the mind, creativity machine, communication tool... as the future of human kind... and...

< COMPUTER AS SELF >

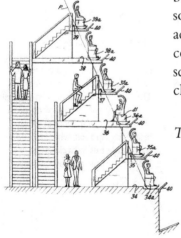

But before we begin, an open admission: I do not believe that sufficient emphasis has—thus far in world affairs—been placed on correct thinking methods; and more specifically on the fulfilment of open and free thinking procedures. Freedom of thought is an unassailable human right, as expressed in international law.[2] And perhaps the most sacred faculty given to man, after life; is the power to think as he likes. The supremacy of thought is patently so; for man's *scientific, religious and social cosmologies* are, one and all, if they are anything whatsoever; simply patterned assemblies of thoughts!

A person's primary activity is thinking. And doubtless present are great riches when it comes to our individual and collective thought streams. In a way, all of civilisation, all of man's activities and discoveries; are vast conglomerations of thoughts and thought-outcomes.

< {10} Everything known is comprised simply of thought-atoms. >

Many of these thoughts are weaved into the most wonderful and intricate patterns of meaning; and from which subtle understanding may be obtained. An indisputable fact is that the source of every one of these thoughts is (normally) an individual human mind. Accordingly, the entire corpus of human knowledge is comprised of countless thought-atoms; and the same being 'slices' of individual minds. And these thought-atoms, once communicated, are ready to live-again inside new brains—often minds far distant in time and space.

A fundamental and timeless feature of the mental world, is the placing of some thoughts over and above others; and established is a structure of relations and a hierarchy of importance for ideas. Indeed some thoughts are considered to be so important that they take precedence over all others; and some are enshrined in law and in order to marshall social activities. Certain other types of thought are identified as being coincident with universal laws; and thus established are scientific principles. Still other thoughts are given a scared charter, and named as religious thoughts.

My (ambitious) aim is to establish a new *Theory of Natural Thoughts*, whereby **all** thinking is to be afforded a sacred status.

But decentralised transmission of information should be dominant, not fugitive.
Each citizen of Media-America should be guaranteed as a birthright access to
the means of distribution of information. - Michael Shamberg

I still love books. Nothing can compare to a book... a book smells
good, it looks good, you can press it to your bosom. - Ray Bradbury

THINKING   115

We humans employ various kinds of thought patterns to mirror aspects of reality; to shape the world around us, to communicate, and so to plan for beneficial outcomes. Within any particular conceptual framework, thought–atoms fit together in a myriad of intricate ways; and parallel structures, hierarchies and logical patterns naturally arise.

Thoughts acquire patterned rules and ways of assembling themselves into groupings; and in order to establish specific meanings. No scratch that. I do not think that thoughts—*assemble themselves into patterns*—but rather thought-atoms are given particular relationships, one to another, within human minds, and (often) using the complex rules and syntax of languages—formal and informal. Individual thoughts thus represent distinct meanings, and when they are linked together into patterns.

Ontological relationships may be established with object-type and process-type thoughts; using species and genus categories. Logical, imaginary and real-world events and processes; can then be represented and modelled. In this way humans build up patterns of meaning in relation to the universe—and each other.

All well and good; and everything seems natural and without any obvious problems. Multiple languages are developed within which thought patterns can exist and be expressed. Languages may be more or less flexible, and more or less established; plus 'extendible' to varying degrees. Obviously a formal language like mathematics is highly axiomatic, and normally any new idea must fit into the general scheme of a particular discipline of mathematics; if it is to be accepted within the overall pattern.

Human societies form huge assemblies of thought patterns; within *books, on television, in films, papers* and *on computers etc*; and individual thoughts 'slot into' various conceptual maps. Often in order to fit neatly together, thoughts must 'play well' with other thoughts—if they are not to end up homeless, lost or forgotten.

N.B. We prefer not to speculate as to the nature of a thought atom's contents (yet).

New attention to the aesthetic, emotional plus
subjective aspects of knowledge. - John Tresch

Machines seen as aesthetic, spontaneous and
sociable extensions of their users. - John Tresch

TED NELSON ON FREEDOM

It is no less than a question of freedom in our time... computer display and storage can bring us a whole new literature, the uniting and the apotheosis of the old and the new... if we have the freedoms of information we deserve as a free people, the safeguards have to be built in at the bottom... now...

We do not make important decisions, we should not make important decisions, serially and irreversibly. Rather... the computer display must be used to develop alternatives, spin out their complications / interrelationships, and visualise these upon a screen.

There are various people who want to attach electronics to people's bodies and brains. There are basically two starting points for this ambition. One is authoritarian, the other is altruistic. I am not sure both schools are not equally dangerous, however.

Then there are those who want to expand man's senses beyond the ordinary, into new sensory realms, by hooking him into various electronics.

Such is the immense diversity of thoughts and complexity of associated patterns; that they (almost) defy description. When referring to 'thoughts'; we are not concerned only with 'scientific' or 'logical' thoughts—but with any kind of thought whatsoever—whether or not it coincides with anything real. The top-level concept of a thought is an especially *elastic* concept; being a category for something that may be precisely —or loosely—defined to any imaginable degree.[3]

Thoughts are *pointers, categories, compartments, flexible place-holders* for patterns/meaning; and we establish that...

Natural-thoughts (free-flowing ideas that result from thinking):

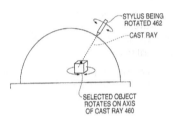

STYLUS BEING ROTATED 462

CAST RAY

SELECTED OBJECT ROTATES ON AXIS OF CAST RAY 460

- ORIGINATE in the human mind
- Are singular or composite (posses an ATOMIC nature)
- Are the NATURAL PROPERTY of the thinker or human race **< E* >**
- EXIST in the human mind, on media, or in a machine (system)
- May be COMMUNICATED between mind(s) and/or machine(s)
- Are inherently EQUAL (meaning changes with context) **< E* >**
- Represent PATTERNS of structured/linked: meaning/content
- May be FREELY-ASSEMBLED into patterns (contexts) **< E * >**
- May be EXPRESSED in a language system [normally]
- May INFLUENCE other thoughts and/or human/machine actions

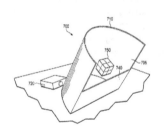

Defined is a top-level class for all natural-thoughts; and captured are the ten universal Attributes of the same. We hereby ambitiously define a new *Theory of Natural Thoughts*; being a framework for analysing from whence thoughts come, how they fit together and are expressed, and where they go to. Natural-thoughts typically have these Attributes in common; and always possess the essential Attributes < E* > of: *natural property, equality* and *free-assembly* (see later exposition). Unnatural-thoughts (*blocked/hidden/warped thoughts*) are missing one or more of the essential Attributes.

All thoughts posses context Status (a social property); whereby context-freedom infers reuse in multiple contexts; whereas a context-established thought atom has a narrowly defined usage.

I see technology as being an extension of the human body. David Cronenberg

Thoughts—weave together all of reality into fabrications that are scientific, artistic and political—and with freedom associated with life. - John Tresch

Doing research on the Web is like using a library assembled
piecemeal by pack rats and vandalised nightly. - Roger Ebert

THINKING   117

Everything that follows refers to the Attributes of natural-thoughts.

We identify three Modes of Existence for thoughts: in the human mind, preserved on media, and built into a machine, system or computer. Next we identify three Forms of thought: secret-thoughts (personal), open-thoughts (open collective) and private-thoughts (restricted collective). We assign an owner and originator (anonymous allowed) for each thought; plus lost and stolen modes. Two universal Types of thoughts are identified—with respect to outcome. These are named as intentional-thoughts (logical ones) aimed at (directly or indirectly) affecting/acting-on: *an object, person, real-world situation, and/or other thoughts etc;* and passive-thoughts (descriptive/informational ones) which have no such (direct) outcomes. With respect to the Modes, Attributes, Forms and Types of thoughts; identified are the (human): *thinker(s), owner(s)* and *implementer(s)*; and the latter party being an actor who may bring-a-thought-into-action and thus affect other thoughts/actions.[15]

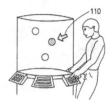

A secret-thought is a thought that occurs in the *mind of an individual*, and has not left the 'mind' of the thinker to enter another person's mind and/or machine's 'mind' (yet). Secret-thoughts may, in fact, be related to thoughts originating in other people's minds; but vital here is that nobody else yet knows, or can *easily* discover the contents of the same, or that the thought has been (or is being) thought by the thinker. Secret-thoughts are an individual's *natural property* alone. Others may be able to guess a secret-thought; but that is different from certain knowledge. With secret-thoughts the thinker is in (more or less) complete control over any communicated thought contents.

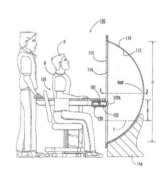

A secret-thought is—bound in time—because what was once secret, may no longer be secret at some epoch in the future. Secret-thoughts are protected from discovery by others—and are hidden in some way. Secrecy is a state of *being* for the thought itself. Secret-thoughts, by definition, exist in a single mind—or *no mind*—in the case of 'lost' secret-thoughts.

---

[15] See later chapters for the Categories / Elements of thought.

The fantastic advances in the field of electronic
communication constitute a greater danger to the
privacy of the individual. - Earl Warren

OTHERS WILL JUST SIT AROUND ALL DAY PLAYING MIND GAMES!

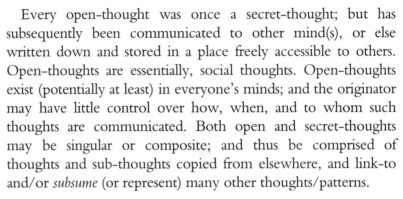

Every open-thought was once a secret-thought; but has subsequently been communicated to other mind(s), or else written down and stored in a place freely accessible to others. Open-thoughts are essentially, social thoughts. Open-thoughts exist (potentially at least) in everyone's minds; and the originator may have little control over how, when, and to whom such thoughts are communicated. Both open and secret-thoughts may be singular or composite; and thus be comprised of thoughts and sub-thoughts copied from elsewhere, and link-to and/or *subsume* (or represent) many other thoughts/patterns.

What differentiates open from secret-thoughts is their state of *discoverability*—and in this respect a thought is only secret, if there can be no possibility of transfer to another mind (at a specific epoch). Writing down a thought in a public arena, would potentially nullify secrecy (in the future); and hence such an exposed thought may no longer be classified as secret, and because it is—potentially discoverable (it is a hidden/lost open-thought until then).

It is vital to recognise that not only *original-thoughts* start out as secret. When someone thinks/duplicates an unusual thought originated by someone else, then the fact that they are thinking this same thought, may constitute a secret—and hence a changed thought—by itself. What matters is whether another party is able to access unique/original thoughts (or has the possibility of so doing).

A third class of thought is identified as a private-thought; defined as a thought which has-been/will-be shared amongst a restricted group. Private-thoughts possess a special feature, in that they are distributed to a limited number of people; and hence some form of social sharing plus protection is implied; and in order to protect the status of a private-thought, and to prevent it from morphing into an open-thought.

Discoverability is restricted and controlled by some mechanism/lock/key, plus social trust.

Attributes of Natural-Thoughts

It is important to realise that *all* thoughts begin 'life' as the natural property of the thinker; and it is up to the thinker how, when and where (originally) secret-thoughts are transformed into open or private-thoughts.

A key distinction is made between *natural-thoughts*, and *unnatural (blocked/hidden/warped)* ones. Natural-thoughts possess all three essential Attributes < E* >, and exist in one of the three Forms (open, private, secret). In this book, we shall demonstrate (using exposition and example) that unnatural-thoughts prevent human beings from freely: *creating, seeing, accessing, sharing, and/or assembling thoughts*. Unnatural-thoughts are therefore sub-optimal; and also unethical, because they limit the key human right of: *freedom of thought* (proof to follow). Natural-thoughts retain those innate and existent powers that nature intended a human being to have over his/her most intimate property—his/her thoughts (see the ethics/human-rights discussion(s) in later chapters).

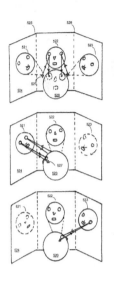

Previously in chapter three, we established that computers do not originate thoughts; and hence the first Attribute is proven, and because: *only humans can originate thoughts!* The second Attribute states that thoughts are atomic—and may be singular or composite—and this fact would seem to be so obvious as to be not worth considering any further.

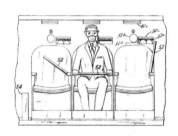

The third—natural property—Attribute, is an essential-feature of a natural-thought. For all Forms of thought (open, private and secret), the property item refers to thought-ownership rights. More specifically the owner/originator of a thought has the right to decide (absolutely) who may see the thought itself, and (in a weaker sense) what others may do with it.

If the true (and natural) owner/originator is not assigned and conferred ownership (in any way whatsoever) then that thought is now a stolen-thought—and hence it is an unnatural thought.

Computers are heaven sent when they work,
and hell-sporn when they don't. - Dani Harper

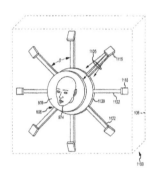

COMMUNITY MEMORY

The basic idea of a community memory is to have a computer resource of information and ideas, commonly available. In its more glorified and mystical form, the ideas seems to be to have a place, inside the computer, where information can be shared by THE PEOPLE, free of institutional obstruction or the profit motive...

it attracts people interested in some form of grass-roots revitalisation of our society... some look to 'community organisation' as a building block for a new society; others are interested in more nuts-and-bolts applications.

Ted Nelson

Thought-ownership (right to see/share) must be protected (by some method); and likewise for Attributes five and eight, the rights of the owner to assemble/communicate said thoughts. Note that thought ownership may be assigned either to an individual party, several people, or in fact, be assigned to the whole of humanity. In relation to the third—natural property—Attribute, other questions arise in terms of originality/ownership; for example how to resolve a situation whereby several people have the exact same thought. Thoughts may be intrinsically owner/date stamped to help with such an issue. More complexity enters the discussion when we consider that thoughts are *inherently patterned*, and may have parts that originate from different sources/people. Another problem in relation to the assignment of thoughts as property; occurs when thought-atoms originate, not from one mind, but from many minds—as a collective.

We must therefore retain the ability to assign authorship/ownership of thoughts that originate collectively; whereby a committee of thinkers are recorded as responsible for said thought constructs. Problems are multiple in relation to assignment of thought-ownership; but most issues evaporate away by focussing on relatively distinct thought atoms; and hence assigning originality to the smallest possible (unique) units. In summary, the assignment of ownership to human thoughts is a central thesis of the current book. We shall return to the idea of *thoughts as property*, many times; and in order to explore the ethical and moral imperatives of, and vast implications of, this key issue within human affairs.

What is to be gained by this type of thought-categorisation? Why focus on thoughts? Would it not be better to look at knowledge itself—and forget altogether about thought-ownership? My answer relates (in part) to the fact that the whole corpus of human knowledge is (in a real sense) an immense conglomeration of facts, claims and opinions. Clearly, within society, there are varying opinions on *politics, law, social and scientific questions,* and also *the nature of reality etc.* If you include facts and claims then there is a hierarchy in knowledge between those claims which have been verified and those which remain mere opinion. Overall, thoughts are argued about and debated—and nothing is more human!

Thinking—the talking of the soul to itself. - Plato.

Once upon a time the world was a realm of unanswered questions and there was room in it for poetry. Man stood beneath the sky and he asked 'why?'. And his question was beautiful. The new world will be a place of answers and no questions, because the only questions left will be answered by computers, because only computers will know what to ask. - James Cameron

Kim Veltman mentioned to me that thoughts are not *merely* and *only* a matter of opinion; but include: *dreams, plans, fears, hopes, beliefs, ambitions*, etc (criminal thoughts will be inferior to noble thoughts—for example). Yet all of these modes of knowing are **expressed** as thoughts. My point is not that everything is opinion, without precedence; but that thoughts, in order to confer meaning, exist within a specific context—and these contexts change constantly! Only within a particular context, or in relation to a specific pattern of other thoughts; can a thought be judged and/or assigned to any degree of significance or value whatsoever.

Reflected here is the chameleon-like nature of all thinking.

Thought meanings are inherently non-committal, and because contexts of use are varied and innumerable. Establishing the specific context of use for a particular thought-atom— and taking into account the surrounding pattern(s)—is absolutely essential in order to scry the intended meaning. Therefore the meaning of a thought is wholly dependent upon its brothers and sisters; that is, on the words, sentences and paragraphs that surround it (in the case of a written thought). Thoughts are reusable building blocks for assigning and communicating meaning; and the gist of a thought may (at any time) only be partially known in varying degrees of definition, and according to a specific usage scenario.

We may also ask: how big/complex are thoughts? Is a thought: *a word, a sentence, paragraph, a book or even an entire subject corpus?* I had imagined thoughts to be atom-like and quite small—similar (in a way) to the letters in a language. Perhaps a typical size for a thought would be about as long (or short) as a sentence. However experts often converse by means of short-cuts, and using technical terminology; hence much context is assumed here and will be off-limits to others, whose mind's 'live' outside of the specific (larger) contexts employed.

In summary, it would seem essential for us to see, know and remember (in proper context); the great assembly and diversity of all thought patterns. My purpose in these next few paragraphs, is to persuade the reader that it is properly *contextualised thoughts* that are the key building blocks of all knowledge.

FANTICS

By fantics I mean the art and science of getting ideas across, both emotionally and cognitively. Presentation might be a more general word for it. The character of what gets across is always duel; both the explicit structures and feelings that go along with them... the reader always gets feelings along with the information... fantics is concerned with the arts of effects–writing, theatre... and so on– and the structures and mechanisms of thought...

I derive fantics from the Greek words 'phainein' (show) and its derivative 'phantasien' (present to the eye or mind)... We must acknowledge that we are inventing presentational techniques in the new media, not merely transporting or transposing particular things into them because they feel right...

We need designs for screen presentations and their mixture- vignetting, windows, screen mosaics, transformed and augmented views, and the rapid and comprehensible control of these views and windows...

One of the most remarkable things about the human mind is the way it ties things together. Perceptual unity comes out of nowhere... The fantic structure of anything, then, consists of its noticeable parts, interconnections, contents, and effects... Our goal should be nothing less than **representing the true context and structure of human thought**... but it should be something more; enabling the mind to weigh, pursue, synthesise and evaluate ideas for a better tomorrow. Or for any at all.

Ted Nelson

The same ambiguity that motivated dubious academic AI projects in the past has been repackaged as mass culture today. Did that search engine really know what you want, or are you playing along, lowering your standards to make it seem clever? While it's to be expected that the human perspective will be changed by encounters with profound new technologies, the exercise of treating machine intelligence as real requires people to reduce their mooring to reality. - Jaron Lanier

I don't care how big and fast computers are.
They are not as big and fast as the world. - Herbert Simon

Contextualised Thoughts

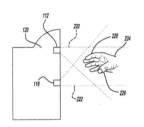

Accordingly, we begin with *logos...*

Human knowledge is not finished, but continues to advance and develop at an ever faster pace. Polymaths like Ted Nelson and Kim Veltman have noted how subject categories don't really exist, and that everything is connected to everything else.[4,5,6] Kim Veltman even finds that the various alphabets of the world, the composite letters and symbols; hold entire histories of meaning/knowledge and represent a vast number of inter-cultural cross-connections and common sources.[7]

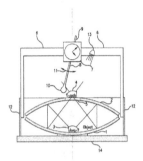

Present are deep and parallel structures within human knowledge—and constituent thoughts are enmeshed with other thoughts endlessly; with yet more thoughts/opinions piled on-top-of, on-the-side and below, other thoughts; *ad infinitum!*

Ted Nelson says that knowledge—and information—are fractal! And by this he means to say (I think); that thoughts are also fractal—complete with unusual patterns and increasing levels of detail as you 'zoom' in; and thus patterns of new meaning on all scales. It may be that we humans cannot possibly develop further as a species; without creating an immense map—or a World/Global Brain—of the dazzling complexity and vast interconnectedness of thought patterns.

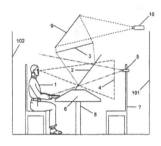

A nice way of so doing, is to find out who thought what, where, when and how. Desired is an equivalent of the great *'Library of Babel'*—the mythical library that contains all books, all languages, a complete and detailed history of the past, minutely detailed and containing a faithful catalogue of every datum ever known; and including innumerable *false catalogues.*

Only now the library is to contain thought-atoms assembled into the larger elements of knowledge. Cataloguing every open-thought—according to simple features: *origin, ownership, pattern* and *linkage;* enables preservation of: *the immense complexity, overlays, relationships, cross-linkages and interconnected nature of everything.*

N.B. Do not think that such a library would be impossible to create/implement/administer, because in coming chapters we show how.

But where are the memories of our ancestors—the answer is in books/paper-materials. Yes, but these books are increasingly fragile and even when they are 'digitised' they are not interconnected in any way whatsoever—and you cannot see the whole picture.

One may still construct/build/overlay (onto this system) all kinds of *data, categorisations, assignments, classes, subjects etc.* However the parallel and multiple links between all 'opinions' would be represented—and the deep interconnections made visible—and by focussing simply on thought-atoms. Open-thoughts are made visible at last—and one has preserved the *origin, ownership, equality, pattern,* and *assembly* of all thoughts. The only remaining items on our list of Attributes; is to sort out: details of *existence (*Attribute 4*), access* (Attribute 5) and *expression* or language (Attribute 9), and the *influence(s)* (Attribute 10) of all thoughts on human society.

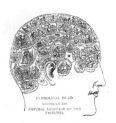

Remember that all knowledge is comprised; simply of thoughts (plus data—see later chapters). The basic building block of everything known is the open-thought atom! This is naturally so because every concept/idea/feeling starts 'life' as an individual thought. Of course thoughts are normally patterns of connections to other thoughts—and also interconnections between thoughts, patterns and data etc.

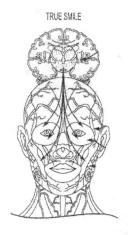

TRUE SMILE

However one cannot get away from the fact that what matters is that human mind(s) assemble groups of thought-atoms together into patterns, and in order to confer meaning.

< {11} Mind = patterns = [thoughts + data] (contextualised) = meaning. >

Accordingly, we ask: what use is an open-thought that cannot be found? For such 'lost' thoughts; *it is as if they had never existed.* This is in fact the situation we have at the moment; whereby, because of a distinct lack of connectedness, vast numbers of thoughts are, in effect; isolated, lost, inaccessible and/or invisible—potentially forever!

We humans have a desperate need to read the patterns of past and present thought-streams. I refer here to open-thoughts; and to those thoughts that the thinker intended would be shared with others.

Obviously, putting man's entire heritage into hypertext is going to take awhile. But it can and should be done. - Ted Nelson

SPACESHIP EARTH

Buckminster R. Fuller popularised
the idea of earth as a spaceship
within which mankind is destined
to (forever) roam the universe.
Accordingly, it is imperative that
we look after, manage and
distribute earth's recourses
efficiently and fairly.

In Fuller's revolution the
computer is an all-knowing mind,
storing data from all over the
world. The information obtained
from the computer will be able to
persuade a world audience that by
(for example) melting down the
metals from weaponry and putting
it into 'livingry' and by building
new cities with them, we can
maximise the wealth of all.

Wealth is defined by Fuller as:

**The technological ability to protect,
nurture, support, and accommodate
all the growth needs of life...**

**The computer will show us that at
least 70% of jobs in Western
private-enterprise countries are
work that creates no life support,
therefore no real wealth.**

We now turn to the *ethos* (moral argument).

A key point is that the rest of us (thought-readers/assemblers)
cannot know which are the true or false, useful and/or worthless
thoughts. But even false thoughts educate—in one way or
another—and all thoughts inform. Professor Marshall McLuhan
(1911-1980) referred to modern man as the information gatherer,
and he was right (almost); for we desire not merely data and
information; but seek opinions and thoughts of all kinds.[8,9]

Man constantly collects thoughts like the ant collects twigs,
saving them up for use—and profit—later on. But a question
remains, how does society decide which are the useful/true
thoughts, and which are the useless/harmful/false ones—and the
same being those thoughts that should be discarded, censured
and/or perhaps destroyed. Our new *Theory of Natural Thoughts*
provides an emphatic answer; and states that—on logical, moral
and ethical grounds to be explained later on—no open-thought
should ever be destroyed and/or lost from the historical record.

< {12} All open-thoughts are to be preserved and accessible to all. >

According to Attribute six, all thoughts are equal; and in a
specific sense, whereby thought-atoms require an established
context to assign meaning. And because thought-atoms do not
(by definition) in fact posses a singular—or specific context of
use—it logically follows that all thought atoms are equal, and
non are worthy of destruction/censure! I refer here not to the
rights of legal/scientific bodies to recognise and develop *context-
established thoughts* such as: laws/judgments and social/scientific
thought-patterns of any specific meaning; but rather to the
unnatural censure of any open thought-atom by itself, and when
taken out of context (completely).

In fact, it is natural for humans to be
constantly swapping thought atoms in
and out of *constellations of thought-
assemblies*; and in order to establish
hierarchies of understanding. Within
proper contexts thoughts will
naturally establish rulings, importance
and dominance, one over another.

What we did not imagine was a Web
of people, but a Web of documents.
Dale Dougherty

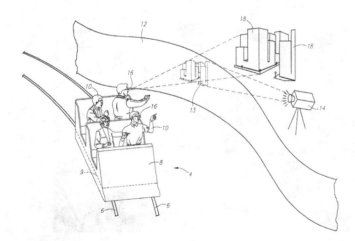

Some writers have stereotyped the modern age as being concerned with data and information alone. Yet even Dr Claude Shannon (1916-2001), the father of the information age, referred to information in another way altogether, saying:

I have been working on an analysis of the transmission of intelligence.[10]

Shannon's use of the word intelligence is instructive. In the OED, intelligence is defined as the: faculty of understanding; intellect; superior understanding, the action or fact of mentally understanding something, comprehension of something. Whereas information refers merely to informing, instructing, and to the communication of knowledge, as opposed to pure understanding and enlightenment. Shannon was interested in conveying actual *elements of mind*, rather than mere factoids and information; or non-sentient data that may (or may not) be used in any way whatsoever. His words imply an organic focus, and on the living being's relationship with (and mastery of) the environment.

The opposite view comes from Richard Dawkins (1941-) who said: evolution itself embodies an ongoing exchange of information between organism and the environment.[11] Implied here is that the human body itself, and perhaps the universe also, are suppliers and processors of information. In this view mind plays a lesser role, and intelligence is more of a side-effect of the unknowing, not self-aware universal information processing system that is the universe. Dawkins's view is '*It from Bit*'—and the whole universe is seen as a kind of computer, a cosmic information processing machine; and the universe *computes its own destiny*, so to speak.

Information connotes a cosmic principle of organisation and order—and if true—perhaps man can 'plug-into' the universal telos; using his thoughts, and hence determine his own destiny.

Jean-Paul Sartre (1905-1980) said: Do we think that if there is not God then everything is permitted. No-because there is no God we have to decide for ourselves what is permitted.[12]

These words are echoed by John Milton (1608-1674), who wrote: the mind is a universe and can make heaven of hell, or a hell of heaven.[13]

If you can dream it, you can do it. - Walt Disney
It's kind of fun to do the impossible. - Walt Disney
When you believe in a thing, believe in it all the way,
implicitly and unquestionable. - Walt Disney

EXPERIMENTAL PROTOTYPE CITY OF TOMORROW

EPCOT, or the Experimental Prototype Community of Tomorrow, began as Walt Disney's idea of creating a better city. A utopian environment enriched in education, and in expanding technology. A perfect city with dependable public transportation, a soaring civic centre covered by an all-weather dome, and model factories concealed in green belts that were readily accessible to workers housed in idyllic suburban subdivisions nearby. Before his death, in late 1966, Walt had bought up thousands of acres in central Florida, for an East Coast Disneyland, *Walt Disney World*. But all this was leading up to Walt's true vision, a city without dirt, without grime, an experimental prototype city. This idea of a perfect environment actually formed in Walt's mind way before the actual thought of EPCOT. Disneyland is a perfect example. Its 25 foot Earthen Berm protects it from the outside world. With clean streets, and walkways, Disneyland was Walt's first idea to have a better city.

Information versus Mind (Agency of Either)

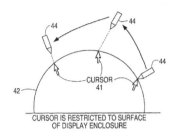

CURSOR IS RESTRICTED TO SURFACE
OF DISPLAY ENCLOSURE

When considering the powers of: *mind versus nature, animate versus inanimate,* and *nurture versus nature;* we have two opposing views of reality. Some claim that the Universe is like a clockwork 'motor'—and that mind or God/mind does not play an active (influential) part in creation; and others claim that man or God/mind may influence creation by imposition of will. No matter which viewpoint you support; focussing purely on *information* (as most computer scientists do—for example Google—as opposed to *thoughts;* seems to be a wholly anti-humanistic philosophy; and to deny that life—and man—have any agency whatsoever. Such a view also conveniently 'forgets' that all knowledge (in the end) must be transformed into, and consist of, simply thoughts. Our world-views are therefore to a large extent re-writable, re-composable and context specific (perceiver reliant).

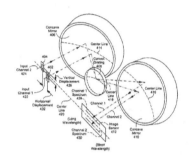

Here the *pathos*—or emotional argument—states itself; whereby man's thoughts reign supreme. Whether or not an external agency (God or nature) is ultimately in charge of all creation; one hopes that man has (at least) some room to manoeuvre—or free-will—and in terms of a capability to influence outcomes. If so then the accuracy of our records is of prime importance. Human reality (*I would suggest*) is entirely constructed out of thoughts; and our actions—or instantiated thoughts—also.

The process of identification of useful ideas, must (normally) come from our collective opinions. It is for the whole human race that we must think; and our thinking processes must be as efficient, moral, and ethical as possible. If we are to choose

some thoughts/actions over others; let it be after full consideration of the *logos, pathos* and *ethos*—after seeing a matter from all sides—and with as much information at our disposal as possible; and after considering *all the opinions.*

What I am defending here is human freedom; and in particular: freedom of thought, and the unhindered visibility, sharing and assembly of thoughts.

To err is human—and to blame it on the computer even more so. - Robert Orben

Computers contract Space and expand Time—
but the opposite can also be true.

Open Thoughts *(Ownership, Equality and Free-Assembly of)*

We dismiss (altogether) the notion that some thoughts are intrinsically superior to, or else more worthy, than other thoughts. We state this in a motto: *all thoughts are equal*; being an idea derived from the fact that individual thought atoms are essentially contextless. It is difficult to come to any other conclusion; and because the evidence is so vast in favour of equality and re-use.

Witness the diversity and varied usage of thought-atoms.

Such a view is unquestionably a moral position; and it is based (partly) on the fact that opinions vary. A specific thought may be seen as right or wrong, and true or false; by various people—and even the same person—in different contexts/ situations. Accordingly we defend and uphold the right of any (open) thought-atom to exist; and to be seen/assembled (in any way), and by any/all human being(s). It is a fact of life that we must judge thoughts (and data-related 'facts'); and decide between good and evil options, plus rank priorities—but this all happens within specific patterned context(s). All open-thoughts must be accessible for use (and re-use) within such varied patterns. Every single open-thought should be accessible. In fact it would seem logical to suggest that only where all open-thoughts are known; do we humans then—as a collective—have the best chance of selecting, combining and creating truly optimal thought-patterns.

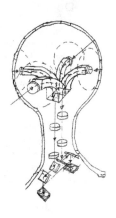

Accordingly, it is my belief that wherever a human being has originated a thought, and communicated it to others as an open-thought; then that same thought is in a very real sense *owned by the whole of humanity*. I would (perhaps) here retain ways for the originator of said thought pattern to be paid for usage via a micro-payments system (see later chapters). Importantly in this scheme all scientific knowledge; in fact all types of public knowledge, would naturally—and by default—be assigned as open-thoughts (sooner or later).

People think that computers will keep them from making mistakes. They're wrong.
With computers you make (bigger) mistakes faster.
Adam Osborne

Technology changes all the time,
human nature, hardly ever. - Evgeny Morozov

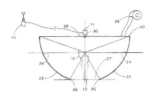

I am much less concerned with whatever it is technology may be doing to people than what people are choosing to do to one another through technology. Facebook's reduction of people to predictively modelled profiles and investment banking's convolution of the marketplace into an algorithmic battleground were not the choices of machines.

Douglas Rushkoff

We're getting so pulled in by computers and technology, and our kids have their face in the computers all day. The human relationship is being diminished by this.

Lenny Kravitz

Technology has a shadow side. It accounts for real progress in medicine, but has also hurt it in many ways, making it more impersonal, expensive and dangerous. The false belief that a safety net of sophisticated drugs and machines stretches below us, permitting risky or lazy lifestyle choices, has undermined our spirit of self-reliance.

Andrew Weil

It is not the machine that explains purposeful organisation; it is organic functions that explain machines (and create them too!).

Lewis Mumford

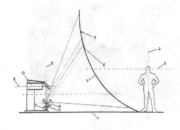

Natural-Thoughts and Human Freedom

Several problems relating to intellectual property arise out of our new conception of thought-ownership; however most are solved within the bounds of the current law of copyright and patents. What is not solved is the desired level of granularity that a thought has to achieve, in order to be assigned as an independent thought; and furthermore how are thought-rights and thought-ownership to be assigned/protected. These latter actions happen as a result of computers and techno-rights. In some respects the solution to these issues is the primary topic of the present book.

Hopefully it is now clear what I am proposing: *freedom of thought* through dual modes of thought-ownership.

Firstly, thought ownership at the individual level exists as secret and private-thought types in which the thinker can herself control the degree of social sharing attained by said thoughts. Secondly, open (shared) thoughts are to be assigned to the thought-ownership of everyone in the world, whilst a system of micro-payments may (sometimes) protect the originator of said thoughts (perhaps for limited time-periods), and in certain usage situations.

Note that specific types of outcomes, objects, methods and machines; that are created as a result of thought ownership; can be protected via the standard intellectual property mechanism(s).

We now ask what exactly has been achieved by our new theory of thought freedom/ownership. Let us start by imagining that a system of techno-rights is already in place (for all media-stored thoughts); in which *secret, open,* and *private thoughts* are facilitated and protected (as described).

Furthermore let us assume that all of these thoughts have been connected in an atomic way (to be defined later); whereby any thought-atom can be connected to any other—leading to patterns of an almost unimaginable complexity, number, depth and parallelism. We have thus created a new kind of society—or *technopia*—in which thought ownership/freedom takes precedence over (and aids or facilitates) all forms of human knowledge/communication—or at least a large/significant portion of the same.

Attaining this key advantage (everywhere) is no small feat.

No machine, can even theoretically be made to replicate man, for in order to do so it would have to draw upon 2-3 billion years of diversified experience!
Lewis Mumford

Whenever a technology enables people to organise at a pace
that wasn't before possible, new politics emerge. - Howard Rheingold

THINKING   129

Perhaps this new arrangement of knowledge—because it is thought-based—maybe the bedrock of a new kind of democracy that embodies a fantastic diversity and richness of opinion; where all (social) ideas are visible, and no thoughts are left behind. Every open-thought is established as being equal to every other—in terms of accessibility/free-assembly—and because no public thought (without context) takes precedence over any other.

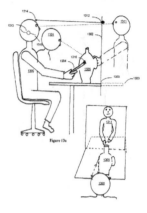

Any thought may be therefore be conceived of and expressed—either secretly, openly and/or privately. There are no restrictions whatsoever on man's thinking. He is free to think whatsoever he likes; individually and collectively. No one can stop anyone from publishing his/her thoughts/ votes, and from sharing these with whomever he/she likes. Thoughts are set free. There can be no censure, thought-destruction, thought-police, or thought-alterations.

Oh, and perhaps I forgot to mention that our new technopia protects and remembers all open-thoughts forever (open-thoughts are indestructible and immortal); and so that the thoughts of humanity are at everyone's recall—and anyone may access them—largely for free.[16] Visible are all of the deep and parallel connections between thoughts, and the relationships of each and every thought pattern to every other. Links work both ways and we can see not only where an idea comes from; but also all the places where it is being used in the entire corpus of human knowledge.

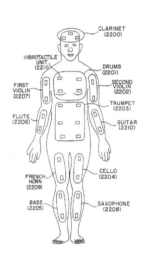

We have built a *World Brain*. But what, precisely, has been gained as a result? Answer: a vital set of new-found freedoms.

Freedoms gained (from natural or free-flowing thoughts):

- Openly publish ideas / thoughts / votes to anyone / everyone
- Anyone may combine / annotate / categorise open-thought atoms
- Nobody can stop anyone publishing - publicly / anonymously
- Publish private-thoughts to close friend(s) [SECRETLY]
- Read / quote the open-thoughts of anyone else
- See where all ideas originate / voting corruption impossible
- See where all ideas are used, and how they are linked
- Know what are the collective opinions on specific issues
- Totalitarian thought-control / big-brother is less likely

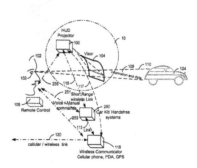

---

[16] Proviso: knowledge that is not suitable for children can be 'tagged' as such.

You can design and create, and build the most wonderful place in the world. But it takes people to make the dream a reality. - Walt Disney

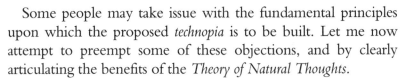

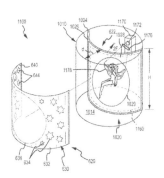

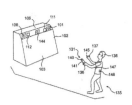

Some people may take issue with the fundamental principles upon which the proposed *technopia* is to be built. Let me now attempt to preempt some of these objections, and by clearly articulating the benefits of the *Theory of Natural Thoughts*.

Firstly, everything here is aimed at firmly and irrevocably establishing: *freedom of thought*; which is one of the nine human rights of the UN declaration of human rights.[14] Presumably no-one (other than possibly bodies like the NSA and certain corrupt 'powers') would object to this first principle?

Present in our new cosmology, is the idea that *all thoughts are equal* (Attribute 6); and hence that no thought may censure or control any other thought (sans context). Establishing this first principle gives rise to other desirable attributes for thoughts; including *freedom of existence* (Attribute 4), *freedom of publication* plus *accessibility* (Attributes 5,9,10), and the *open-assembly* (Attributes 7, 8) of thought-atoms. From this perspective people may assign meaning in any way whatsoever; and create meaningful/ meaningless mashups of thought-atoms, from wherever they like, and in whatever order/pattern they like.

Within the technopia, and in terms of accessibility/ combinability; there is no such thing as an *(ultimately) evil, wrong, false or immoral thought-atom*—and anyone may create and/or read/ express any opinion whatsoever. But is such freedom of expression not dangerous? Does it not help criminals?

I would argue that this is not so, and for several reasons. Fundamentally, it is my belief, that there can be no such thing as a wrong, evil or immoral thought-atom. Thoughts standing alone cannot possibly be evil; rather it is fully contextualised patterns of thoughts, and subsequently instantiated as a decision to take action, that may be evil and immoral. To most people, a single thought does not convey a compulsion to do anything —it is only a thought! In all cases it is the active agent, *the thinker themselves*; who decides to act on a pattern of personally contextualised thoughts (see later ethical arguments).

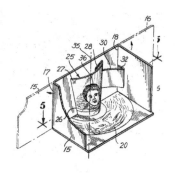

One cannot have freedom of thought where you have some thoughts/actions able to (universally and without context) block, dissemble, and destroy other thoughts/actions. Logically this is so because we must be free to judge all opinions, and view all sides of the argument; and to see—all perspectives. One would suppose that thoughts simply cannot corrupt us—unless perhaps we are only given narrow viewpoints. In all cases people corrupt *themselves* by adopting limited perspectives—and in fact by not *exposing-themselves* to enough thoughts, or else a sufficient number and high quality of different thoughts!

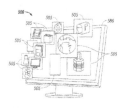

Evil thoughts do not have a life of their own. They are not magical—and do not possess the power of demonic possession.

Responsibility for deciding to take action; on all occasions, rests with the thinker/thought-implementer.

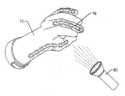

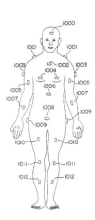

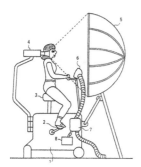

But what about someone like Adolf Hitler (1889-1945); did his evil thoughts not 'possess' countless millions. Whilst I am no historian, I would argue the opposite may be true; whereby for want of sufficient open points of view, and the visibility of enough opinions in relation to true events, the German people (and perhaps, in a sense, the world's people also) were led blindly into the abyss of a terribly costly war that nobody could truly win.

If we try to eliminate all the evil thoughts from the world; and by (for example) banning certain thoughts, and destroying all memories of unhelpful events; then we may find that (in reality) we cannot do so. The notion of an evil thought, the classification scheme used, may narrow over time; and evil may be gradually re-assigned (by us) to somewhat less-evil deeds/thoughts. Evil, sin and immorality are seen to be part of the dualistic way in which humans interpret life; and we cannot do away with them altogether by pretending that acts of ultimate evil do not exist. On the other hand, we must embrace evil, know its very dark heart, and in order to be able to recognise it in ourselves (and others).

But how can we recognise evil where it is hidden?

Evil cannot be stricken from the heart of man; it lives in man and is part of him. We must strive to recognise it early on, and to tackle it as soon as it begins to emerge. Accordingly is it not better to know where evil is, and what it is 'thinking'; and in order to know/change its expression in ourselves (and others).

Another point relates to not allowing some thoughts to rule over others (in terms of visibility/accessibility/assembly). If we give certain people and/or isolated thoughts the power to judge and/or police other thoughts, then are we not in danger of loosing control of our humanity? It is the lesson of human history that tirents and totalitarian regimes have a tendency to occur all too often in human societies. And who is to say that—even initially mild—censure of open-thoughts is not the ultimate tirent; and far worse than any Hitler, Saddam Hussein (1937-2006) or Gehngas Khan (1162-1227).

In 1887, Lord John Acton (1834-1902) said:

Power tends to corrupt, and absolute power corrupts absolutely.[15]

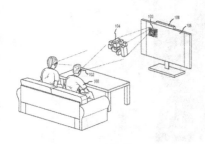

Technology is supposed to make our lives easier, allowing us to do things more quickly and efficiently. But too often it seems to make things harder, leaving us with fifty-button remote controls, digital cameras with hundreds of mysterious features and book-length manuals, and cars with dashboard systems worthy of the space shuttle. - James Surowiecki

Evil regimes invariably attempt to censure all forms of social discourse, and to control the thoughts of citizens through indoctrination. This is so because the evil dictator knows full well that it is the very minds of the people that he must seek to control; if he is to rule over a society. In the coming chapters we shall see numerous examples of thought-control; and discuss corresponding evidence in support of the 'preventative medicine' of natural-thoughts and thought-ownership.

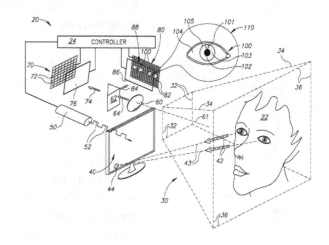

Before looking at what others have to say on the specific topic of the equality of un-contextualised thoughts; I would ask the reader to consider (alternatively); who they would trust to judge all human thought-atoms on a world-wide basis. How could we stop corruption and errors from entering such a process? Is not the alternative far preferable, where no thoughts are censured, all thoughts are free and open, visible, and no thoughts are invisible/crushed?

René Descartes once described thought as:

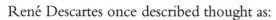

a universal instrument which can be used in all kinds of situations.

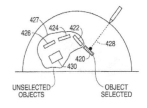

This comment goes right to the heart of my argument that *all thoughts are equal.* Thoughts, words and concepts must never be made illegal by themselves. This is so, because if some thoughts are disallowed and/or banned/crushed; then they are no longer available/useful for all purposes—and especially for recognising and countering, plus educating people about, wrong-doing and unhelpful actions.

In Mary Shelley's story, Frankenstein's monster, sadly, was the only one who possessed a conscience; whereas the creator did not take responsibility for the monster's life/actions. Hopefully man is not, likewise, blindly racing to his doom; and for lack of *freedom of thought* resulting from his computing systems. [16]

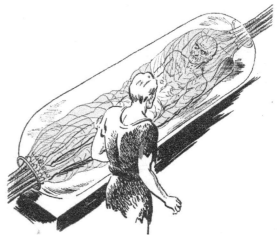

The march of science and technology does not imply growing intellectual complexity in the lives of most people. It often means the opposite. - Thomas Sowell

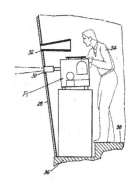

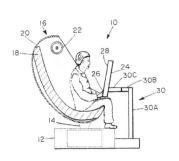

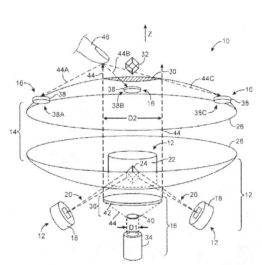

I would now like to briefly explore a fundamental difference between looking and thinking. Visualising an object with one's eyes; requires a causal connection between you, light and the object itself. However thinking a thought requires no such causal relationship; and an isolated thought-atom may be conceived of as a mere temporary path, or station point, as we move from one region of meaning to another.

It can sometimes be the case, that evil and immoral thoughts, and thinking about inhumane situations, may lead us to more fruitful, rewarding and good islands of thought; than would otherwise be the case. Sometimes one needs to embrace an evil path and/or wrong act; and in order to understand it, break it down, in order to check its processes and/or to prevent similar situations from happening again in the future.

Surely no one thinks that ignorance is best.

Men like Jesus and Buddha preached an inclusive approach; and we do so likewise for all thoughts; no matter from whence they come, and what they (appear) to condone. The question is not whether God is the ultimate arbiter and/or decider over human fairs, or whether man/nature is. Neither does it matter if we humans sometimes make mistakes in response to specific situations, or take the wrong path. What matters is that we take notice, and are given the chance to correct our mistakes. And that is all I have been arguing for in this chapter; that we must know the details of our actions, successes and failures, ideas, plans and schemes; collectively.

But this can only happen when we *own our thoughts*.

Unless we can can freely access, assemble and re-assemble our (open) thoughts; with complete knowledge of where they come from, who originated them, along with their full context, and how they came to be; then it may not be possible for us to learn from our mistakes and move ahead as a people.

Ownership of thoughts is key; *all our thoughts*; but this will not be possible until we accept that all open thought-atoms are absolutely equal.

The protean nature of the computer is such that it can act like a machine or like a language to be shaped and exploited. - Alan Kay

Lost / Blocked / Warped Thoughts

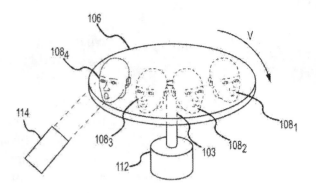

Open thought-atoms (devoid of sufficient context) must be recognised as fundamentally equal for several reasons.

Firstly, evident is that thoughts—when they are small/simple—are inherently designed for assembly into larger patterns of more complexity and greater refinement (and depth), in terms of meaning. As a result meaning is heavily dependent on context and usage; and no thought has an ultimately fine or fully distinct meaning without consideration of all the surrounding contextual patterns (of the originator/receiver). Thoughts are equally meaningless and/or equally meaningful; depending upon usage. Therefore no open-thought atom has the right to censure any other open-thought atom; and no un-contextualised thought is *more equal* (ref. *1984*) than any other thought (from the perspective of judgment/censure).

The woeful tidings of extracting thoughts from their rightful context, and/or of stealing thoughts from the natural owner; are evident throughout history. Witness the 'phone hacking' scandal in the UK, the Profumo Affair in the UK, Watergate, Berlusconi's 'Bunga' parties, Hitler and his (false) '*democratic*' path to power, the Teapot scandal, the Abu Ghraib torture scandal, and the Iran-Contra Affair etc.

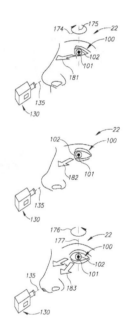

More recently the *European Court of Justice* ruled that citizens (who have been convicted of crimes) have the '*right to be forgotten*'; and to have their records deleted from the Internet. Thus open-thoughts are consigned to a *memory-hole* (ref. 1984), and effectively destroyed. History is re-written. What will be next—will companies that lie, steel or commit crimes be able to have these records removed also? Will newspaper records be subject to alteration—as in the novel *1984*—and will all 'citizens' have the right to have their personal histories re-written here also. If all crimes are to be forgotten, what becomes of history? [17,18,19]

Do we have a *Ministry of Truth* right in the heart of Europe? Has *Newspeak* arrived? Who will defend/record/uphold <u>truth</u>?

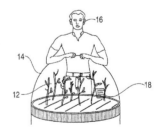

Why do some humans 'respect', 'like' and even 'love' computers? Is it because they appear so lifelike; displaying fantastic powers (apparently) so far beyond our own? Machines leverage human minds to magnify our physical and mental powers; but is **respect** the right emotion? Should not the predominant attitude towards computers be wariness and watchfulness?

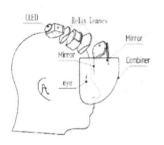

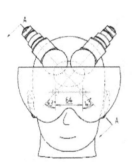

What ever happened to freedom of the press? In actual fact what I am arguing for with natural-thoughts and thought-ownership, is simply: *freedom of thought*. We must embrace disagreement and the democratic right to free expression.

Perhaps some people believe that we all have sufficient freedoms at the present time, and in relation to freedom of personal association/expression. But did you know that in the USA it is now illegal for two parties to communicate across the Internet using an encrypted email or texting system (for example); and without passing the decryption keys to the NSA! In effect this rule has outlawed the natural or private-thoughts detailed above.

Whatever happened to human rights? Every child is born with the right to have secret/private (natural) thoughts, and also to engage in private communication with any other child—because he/she may go into a room and whisper into another other child's ear, for example. How is it possible that a natural human right that we are born with, to not be spied upon (in one-to-one communications), is made illegal in the USA? Is this loss of humanity, related to communication at a distance and/or across an electronic medium (in some bizarre way)?

Surely this is an example; that upon growing up, one has lost part of self—specifically the right to own one's *private-thoughts*!

My point is simply this; man is not perfect, he makes mistakes, errors, miscalculations—and does not always act in the best interests of all. We must all keep an eye on each other's (open) thoughts/actions as a result—but whilst respecting each others right to have secret/private-thoughts. We must act for both the collective and individual 'good', instead of meeting only the needs of the powerful. No pigs (or humans) are more equal, and certain pigs may not (hopefully) spy-on/control other pigs.

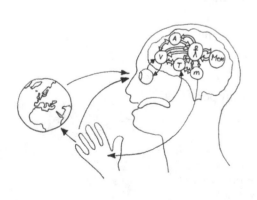

If one believes, as I do, that open-thoughts are, in a very real sense, the natural property of the whole human race; then it also becomes intolerable to allow the current situation to continue; whereby open and free access to our collective memory institutions are blocked to many people.

Money and thoughts: not only are some children born into this world owning all of the food, housing and labour of other children, but increasingly some children will own the thoughts of all humanity, and the other children may not even own their own thoughts!

One machine can do the work of 50 ordinary men.
 No machine can do the work of one extraordinary man. - Elbert Hubbard

THINKING   137

Increasingly knowledge and libraries are online, but not everyone has access. In the UK, between 2010-2012; *324 public libraries* have been shut; which is reminiscent of the 'book-burning' firemen in *Fahrenheit 451*.[20] Also many libraries are getting-rid of older books (selling them); and to make way for acres of computing terminals! It seems that the librarians (and politicians) have gone mad—just like the aforementioned firemen.

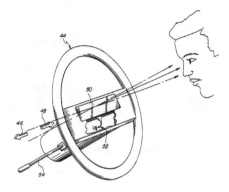

< {13} It is because books (open-thoughts) are not seen as owned by humanity; that they may be sold / lost / destroyed. >

Another point relates to open accessibility for all the world's ideas. Some children are born with access to the Internet; and others do not have access to this technology. On the positive side, we do have an increasing recognition of some of the issues here discussed. For example, many people are outraged by the way governments and others have been/are using technology to spy on, and to limit the rights of ordinary citizens. Plans are afoot to make changes in certain areas.

But dangers remain. [Our thoughts are routinely ruled by machines]

According to Sir Lewis Mumford (1895-1990), we must not:

> Contract human wants and desires in order to conform to the machine... no automatic system can be intelligently run by machines—or by people who dare not assert human intuition, human autonomy, human purpose.[21]

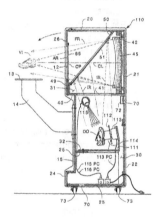

In the author's mind, emphasis has often been in the wrong areas; and blame has been assigned where none is due. It is not the NSA or Facebook's fault that they use our thoughts against us; but it is our collective failure to recognise natural-thoughts for what they are—the collective property of individuals and/ or all humanity—that has held us back and continues to do so.

A thought is not a mere mere gossamer datum to be gobbled up greedily without respect for the natural rights of the thinker, or else a throwaway item, but rather it is who I am in the deepest sense. Our thoughts (properly contextualised) are: *who we were, who we are, and all we can ever be*—and we must treasure, nurture, defend and remember them; and in ways that safeguard our humanity; and move us ahead together as a people.

Nobody ever told us that certain people, organisations, governments, hackers etc; could and would use computers against us in so many ways, and to withhold, crush, and limit our humanity... to prevent us from communicating with each other as we could when we were children—and before the age of mass-surveillance, thought-control and spying, everywhere and anywhere, and all the time. Has even a single citizen agreed to any of this surveillance?

We live in the Age of Infinite-Media; Me-Media, Social-Media,
The Internet of Things, Smart-Media, Mixed-Media etc.
But does any of this technology make us any more human?
Where are the Spiritual-Media, Ethical-Media etc.

According to John Tresch:

Inert objects have moral and spiritual powers,
As a means of humanising science,
And unifying society...
Devices and machines fused with human
actions, intentions and perceptions.

Computer Goodfluences

- Interpersonal communication easier
- Fosters free-speech (hopefully)
- Broadcast networks possible
- Exploration of Information: comprehensive
- Exploration of information: faster, free
- Exploration of Information: remote access
- Smart objects: 'intelligent', responsive environments and intelligent 'things'
- Empowers individual creation
- Access to vast numbers of channels/sites
- Rapid overviews / easy navigation
- Real-time and accurate modelling
- Frees up human time
- Computers perform boring jobs
- Cost of Information close to free
- Remote control of environments
- Remote exploration of environments
- More accurate + precise: control systems
- Elimination of error (non-human)
- Escape from prison(s) of time and space
- May be programmed for any purpose
- Can be relied upon to give same result
- Fosters human creativity
- 'See' invisible objects, processes
- Aids in the control of complex things
- Fosters grass roots political movements
- Frees individual from centralised power
- Fosters secret and private communication
- Fosters open communication
- Frees human mind to explore the options
- Data processing can be automatic

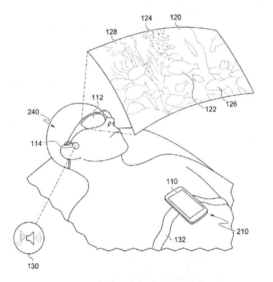

Biofeedback Virtual Reality Assistant

US Patent Application US20140316191 (2014)

There is something at work in my soul, which I do not understand.
Mary Shelley, Frankenstein (1823)

Overuse of the web is causing 'NetBrain'

Article from The Times Newspaper (January 10th 2015)

Narcissistic, distracted and fearful of missing out; these are, apparently, the traits of one who suffers from 'NetBrain', a disorder caused by overconsumption of new internet technology.

Hacking problem: see if you can write a program to solve this... (solution at end)...
Split the following into unbroken string pairs that sum to any binary power of 2...

```
1101100001100011000010001011000010010110110010001010000010110001101111001001100011000101010101
1001100001111100110110011111101111100001100111001000010011101111111111011010100000101101111
1101011100110001101111101011000110111111010000010110010011001111101000000101001000100111000001010
```

Chapter Six
Machines

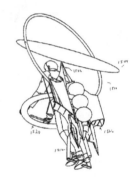

I N THE present chapter we explore human relationships to/with machines; probing the universal features of man-made devices/structures/systems. In so doing, our aim is to analyse the positive/negative influences of artificial mechanisms on human life. We wish to discover how machines come to be; inspecting their *designs, qualities, and functional capabilities;* and seek to learn how they may be used (solely) to benefit humanity. We supply evidence that computers are merely—and only—a sophisticated type of machine; and demonstrate that computers possess certain key features that are common to automated mechanisms in general.

Computers may appear to be an intelligent, multi-purpose and semi-autonomous class of machine. But they are ultimately, man-made devices; and accordingly they reflect—hopefully—our best wishes and most noble intentions.

A number of questions arise. How intelligent are machines? Can machines act autonomously? Do machines possess the power of self-determination? Are machines—in any sense—alive? Can we *'praise'* machines for their actions? Are they responsible for major problems in society? Finding the answers is difficult. Some experts believe in Artificial Intelligence (AI); and that super-intelligent machines may one day solve all of mankind's problems. Other techno-critics predict that systems/machines may eventually destroy humanity.

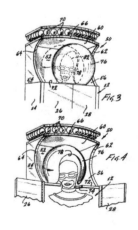

Accordingly, we seek clarity of vision; and with respect to the true nature of machines. Previously we dealt with related questions in chapter three—and with respect to computers. Nevertheless, it is thought-provoking to revisit these topics in greater depth; and in order to open up matters of an immense import. The innumerable ways in which machines influence the lives of countless millions—positively and/or negatively —is perhaps *the* most important issue facing our species.

Taken by themselves, machines represent a puzzle, not an explanation. - Lewis Mumford

The notion that automation gives any guarantee of human liberation is a piece of wishful thinking. - Lewis Mumford

Nature is not a machine. The life cycle is not a machine. - Ray Dalio

From a human perspective, the Earth is—or appears to be—run (largely) by machines. You may remember that we had sought to limit our discussion to the purely metaphysical aspects of computers. But in actual fact it is not possible to do so, and because computers of all types influence the real-world in innumerable ways. For example, the ratio of personal computers to humans, approaches one-to-one in the developed world; and far exceeds this number, when we include CPUs. Almost impossible to imagine is the immense complexity of machine influence(s) upon society; and machine actions/decisions/outcomes (apparently) abound.

Computers/smart-phones/tablets are now essential to the various and stratified functions of all the developed economies. Digital machines help us to communicate, develop new ideas and designs; control electrical/mechanical machines of all types, and to interpret and manage environmental systems etc.

Computers, like languages; are ubiquitous.

Overall it is difficult to imagine that our present society could continue to operate for even a few minutes; and without the help of a vast number of computer 'slaves'. At first sight, all seems fine in the 'Oz-like' *world of computers*. But even a brief peek behind the wizard's curtain; reveals a darker picture—and the ways in which computers often limit human potential(s).

Accordingly we ask; do computers have negative influences on society—and if so—who is to blame; human or machine? Let us begin by imagining that machines can think; and that they do originate thoughts—or at least some computer 'brains' are capable of so doing. Accordingly, outright computer autonomy is accepted as a fact; and in terms of self-generating goals. Digital 'minds' may initiate lines of reasoning; and influence actions in the real world; and with and/or without human programming.

I would suggest that such a capability would lead to a very unfortunate situation—if it were so—whereby machines possessed the 'will to power'. Let me explain my reasoning...

If science possessed a key to understanding every aspect of the universe, it should have been capable of embracing moral values and religious values.

From Descartes time until the present century, a 'mechanistic' explanation of organic behaviour was accepted as a sufficient one.... as machines become more lifelike—so humans become more machine like. - Lewis Mumford

Smash the control images. Smash the control machine. - William S. Burroughs

MACHINES 141

Imagine for a moment that 'thinking' machines exist; and have been given the equivalent of Asimov's laws; and further that they do take a major role in human affairs. We ask; how perfectly are these laws applied? How does the (thinking) machine itself define human 'well-being'; and what are the limits of the machine's perceptions/understanding(s) of human society? These are big questions, each one (potentially) having major consequences; and it is by no means certain that the answers—or ones that we might find acceptable—can be found.

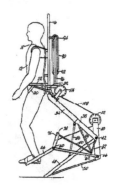

A brief thought-experiment can help us with this ethical conundrum. Firstly, let us assume that I do believe in God (without any proof); and further that I also take it on faith that he can affect my life, and the lives of those around me. I would propose that such a world-view is quite in accordance with logic and right-thinking practices; and because there are no definite negative consequences attendant with belief in God. I can lose nothing by such a belief; and because there are no proven events/dangers—associated with such a belief.

Whereas if I adopt a belief in machine-generated thoughts; then that is a different matter altogether. Postulating that a machine possessed free-will, and the associated self-determining right to 'program-itself', and thus potentially to act in any way that it determined was correct; would likewise posit a very frightening world for us humans. Remember, it is proven that machines influence the world; because that is their very purpose; to process—and to act upon—events/actions/data.

Why then, are *machine-thoughts* so frightening?

Put simply, if a machine had *freedom of thought/action*; then we would feel compelled to destroy the same 'malfunctioning' machine —and because it had no determinable function(s) whatsoever! A free-thinking machine would (sometimes) make mistakes. Such a monstrous machine would be a potential enemy; with uncertain motives.

Artificial Intelligence (AI) is bonkers—we desire (purely) *Helpful Intelligence* (HI).

The mechanisms involved in organic behaviour are too dynamic, too complex, too quantitatively rich, too manifold to be grasped except by simplification. - Lewis Mumford

The human being is not a machine.
Especially when it comes to creating. - Azzedine Alaia

My argument here is based on the presupposition that free-thinking machines would be unable to make sufficiently appropriate and 'correct' decisions in relation to human affairs—at least consistently. I would suggest that it would be very difficult, if not impossible, for a wholly inflexible robot's mind to judge the myriad of human situations—and especially the moral and ethical ones—adequately. Consequently why take the risk of allowing machine 'minds' to reign free; in relation to implemented plans/purposes, and when the results are not known in advance? Even incremental deployments and small-scale 'tests'; would in all likelihood under-represent the impact, complexity and inter-relations of large numbers of 'robot' minds on human society.

Luckily, machines cannot think in any way whatsoever; and robot 'minds' are just that—robotic/automatic—and the very opposite of life-like, autonomous or self-programming. A machine such as computer may (apparently) exhibit intelligence and/or seemingly life-like behaviour; but it is a wholly human-programmed, inflexible and non self-aware behaviour. Mechanisms are in no way capable of achieving even a single original thought/action in relation to the world—and any apparently autonomous effects; are pure illusion (proof follows).

Friedrich Nietzsche (1844-1900) famously declared that 'God is Dead'; whereby he asserted the supremacy of man's domination over all creation. In a machine-age, a more helpful motto is:

The machines are <u>dead</u>—all of them—including computers.

Lewis Mumford said of machines:

> Now, although all the components for machines are found in nature—mass, energy, motion, the chemical elements and their processes of combination and organisation—NO MACHINES, or any purposeful mechanical structures of any kind exist in pre-animate nature; even the simplest mechanisms are solely the products, internal or external, of organisms. [1]

These words are prophetic; and embody a universal principle as follows: all machines/mechanisms are created by living beings; according to, by and for; specific planned purposes; regardless of whether these same purposes are (in actuality) ever realised.

What is important to realise is that automation, is an attempt to exercise control, not only of the mechanical process itself, but of the human being who once directed it, turning him from an active to a passive agent, and finally eliminating him altogether. - Lewis Mumford

Machines consist wholly of pre-fabricated structures, methods and processes; and no machine ever comes into being by accident. A machine may be capable of generating the most wonderful and sophisticated effects; but all of its functions have been—in one way or another—designed, constructed, 'foreshadowed', and 'set in motion' by living being(s). Accidental, incidental, and unforeseen influences may result from the operation of a machine; but in all cases these are invisible/ ignored by the designer and lie outside of the machine's 'awareness'—being merely and ostensibly 'unconscious' effects.

Lewis Mumford said of computers:

> Within its strict limits, a computer can perform logical operations intelligently, and even, given a program that includes random factors, can simulate 'creation', but under no circumstances can it dream of a different mode of operation than its own... man on the contrary, is constitutionally an open system, reacting to another open system, that of nature. Only an infinitesimal part of either system can be interpreted by man, or come under his control, and only an even minuter portion accordingly falls within the province of the computer.[1]

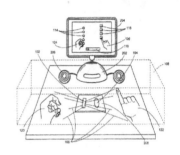

Mumford noted that automatic systems are closed and limited—and so absolutely dead; saying: Living beings, on the other hand react to new and unexpected factors of a 'subjective origin'; falsifying the computers most confident predictions.[1]

It follows that computer-controlled automation can under no circumstances depart from its programming and react to unexpected events; or else adapt to the constantly changing goals, circumstances, and conditions of (for example) human life. This is especially so if you consider that man himself may be—and is— continually changing his mind; needs, wishes, ways and means of living etc.

Machines may be dead; but human folly is to sometimes fail to recognise, or comprehend (and account for); this fact.

In my opinion, we should search for a completely different flying machine, based on other flying principles. - Henri Coanda

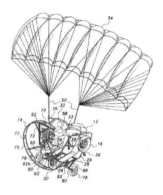

It may seem obvious that machines are dead—but many people act as if they were alive; and humanity as a whole is still falling for the same old trick in this regard; allowing human made decisions to be regarded/mis-apprehended as 'machine' made decisions; the same being somehow: *inflexible/unstoppable, accidental/coincidental, or righteous actions*—in and of themselves. Conversely, machines do not (at the present epoch) show even the slightest signs of life— and thus cannot make (truly) autonomous decisions—and there is no supporting evidence in this regard—and neither do we know if they could even *approach* such a status.

< {14} All machines = designed by a *living* organism = wholly pre-programmed. >

Obviously such a statement depends upon how we define life. I prefer to ignore all previous definitions in this respect; and to focus on the actually existent capabilities of the supposed 'living' being. I would suggest that a living creature—even the tiniest mite—*has a shear scope of 'vision', responsiveness of mind, breadth of perception, and ability to adapt to unforeseen situations;* that no machine can approach. All lifeforms are entirely open to their environment; both in a perceptive/reactive sense; and in terms of being subject to chance mutations and hence evolution.

< {15} We can equate life with flexibility of purpose. >

Both non-living mechanisms and living beings, operate in accordance with purposeful organisation and subjective intention— and they can (apparently) consider the options. The difference is that machines are, one and all, entirely automatic; and there can be no departure from the (wholly) pre-programmed intentions.

Machines, according to Lewis Mumford:

> Have powers of motion under conditions that are fixed for it, and not by it... The distinguishing mark of all machines, even the most lifelike computers, is that its powers and functions are <u>derivative</u>; their increasingly lifelike qualities are all second hand. No machine can ever invent another machine, neither hope nor despair are a part of its equipment... they are closed systems, strictly contrived by the inventor to achieve clearly foreseen and limited ends... an example of teleology, and every part bears the same imprint.[1]

The gap between a machine and living being is unbridgeable; and especially considering that life is able to change its 'mind' on the fly— and also to alter its programming/DNA—according to environmental requirements. Put simply, life programs—or designs—itself.[2,3]

A machine, more than any conceivable organism, is the product of design from start to finish... the machine introduced teleology (planned purposes) or finalism in its classic form—a purposeful organisation for a strictly determined end. - Lewis Mumford

I am an eye. I am a mechanical eye. I, a machine, am showing you
a world, the likes of which only I can see. - Dziga Vertov

MACHINES   145

Life is '*aware of its own existence*'; in the sense that it '*lives partly in the moment, and partly in the future*'—and thus chooses accordingly appropriate reactions to real-time happenings.

Whereas machines are wholly unaware of the 'possibilities' of the environment, and do not even realise that alternatives exist in any way whatsoever. Machines lack an overarching purpose—the desirability of continuance—and hence a need to constantly alter oneself in reaction to changing environmental conditions; and so to adapt to unforeseen eventualities. All of this is clear enough.

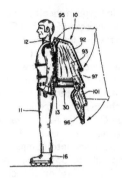

But I wish to empathise the supreme inflexibility of a machine's capabilities; and the fabulously constrained possibilities that exist in the machine's programming—and hence logical actions. Machines are incredibly brittle; because they cannot conceive of anything that is even a single step outside of their pre-programming. In a sense they are 'blind' to an immense diversity of possibility. Whereas, built into the core of all living beings; is a capability to have *helicopter vision*; and to be on the lookout for ways to exploit opportunities—and potentially through re-programming of self (and self-purpose).

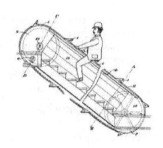

If the mite on my paper lacks the ability to escape from my finger before I squash it as it moves across my page; then it dies; whereas other faster mites escape and reproduce; and likewise for smarter ones who escape and see '*men in red shirts with finger-like objects*' as a danger. The fact that a mite even possesses the ability to panic when it 'sees' me for the first time; demonstrates a real flexibility of perception/purpose. Scientists have experimented with simple 'life-like' neural networks; and that may be said to flexibly perceive and/or evolve. But one and all, these are eons away from actual embodied lifeforms; that are able to: *perceive using a wide-angled 'mental' vision, self-assemble from environmental materials, reproduce, and/or evolve according to self-programming*. The designs of machines, in all cases; retain a tremendous simplicity/narrowness of function; and posses a fatally flawed and under-dimensioned nature; in which the programming is too inflexible; fixed/frozen; wholly 'blind' to the scope of environmental possibilities; and hollow of purpose.

Under-dimensioned indeed.

By introducing the concept of man-made behaviour, Descartes was in fact secretly restoring design, purpose, telos. - Lewis Mumford

One trait binds mechanisms and organisms together... purposeful organisation and subjective intention. - Lewis Mumford

The ultimate result of this mechanistic doctrine was to raise the machine to a higher status than any organism! - Lewis Mumford

THE ALL-SEEING EYE

In Egyptian theology, the most singular organ of the Sun God Re, was the eye: for the Eye of Re had an independent existence and played a creative and directive part in all cosmic and human activities —the computer turns out to be the Eye of the re-instantiated Sun God, that is, The Eye of the Megamachine (masses of humans organised into companies for specific purposes), serving the 'Private Eye' or Detective, as well the omnipresent Executive Eye, he who exacts absolute conformity to his comrades, because no secret can be hidden from him, and no disobedience goes unpunished!

Lewis Mumford

No king, no council, can seize me or torture me, no church, no nation can silence me—such powers of ruthless and complete suppression have vanished.

**H.G. Wells
(The new Machiavelli)**

But there is a difference between using the machine to extend human capabilities, and using it to contract, eliminate, or replace human functions. In the first, man still exercises authority on his own behalf, in the second, the machine takes over and man becomes a supernumerary.

Lewis Mumford

I rather like the under-dimensioned life-form moniker for machines; because it focusses attention on the narrow range of perceptions, meagre (or nil) understanding of reality; and the scant possibilities that result from a machine's pre-programming. Even the most sophisticated computer fails to detect—or take advantage of—the infinitude of relationships of everything to everything else.

< {16} Reality is a closed book to a machine; and that particular book shall remain forever closed (for them). >

Machines do not see/explore *any* of the possibilities. Whereas a life-form is open to the environment; and fully engages with it, by changing its thinking or programming; or else by changing itself—and the species—through evolution. Flexibility of purpose means that nothing is denied to life (absolutely); and even immortality is within its reach, as a result of a close connection with the environment. You are, dear reader, a life-form that has been living for *billions* of years; because at no stage did your ancestor life-forms, no matter how simple; die before reproducing! It is the adaptability of your programming—your DNA—that has sustained you for all this time!

Living beings embrace the universe; in effect, saying—*you are me—and I am you*—and I shall engage with you (everything else) continually and to my advantage.[2,3] All lifeforms possess a constant openness to the environment; being fully engaged with reality; whilst employing a flexible outlook. Machines wholly lack an ability to change themselves—their approach or design —in response to the dictates of reality. Machines do not know what they are thinking or doing, in any sense, because they do not position themselves adequately in relation to the world; and hence fail to recognise what, 'who' (or where) they are.

A human—like a machine—undoubtably sometimes follows dogmatic step-by-step thinking procedures. Superficially such a 'program' can be made analogous to a computer whereby the 'brain' follows a sequence of instructions. But any similarity between the two kinds of 'thinking' is deceptive; because the computer does not even know it has a self which is 'inside' the world, and how it may ultimately judge success/failure.

The characteristic virtues of Organised Man correspond as nearly as possible to the machine that he serves, thus the part of his personality that was projected in mechanical instruments in turn re-enforces that projection by eliminating any non-conforming organic or human functions! - Lewis Mumford

Man cannot be trusted with absolutes. - Lewis Mumford
And machines even less so (be trusted with absolute propositions etc)!

MACHINES 147

Machines, like humans, can 'multi-task' or do several things at once. Branching steps exist whereby new 'code' is executed, and other code sequences are omitted; and depending upon specific facts/events. But in the case of a human there are often (apparently) no strict rules for so doing—and she may change her mind on any step (or exit the program altogether)—depending upon incidental and (countless) arbitrary thoughts/events.

The human brain has a self-initiated choice—at all stages in the thinking process—whereas the machine does not. In any case a far larger number of such branching procedures are possible in a human (or even a simple life-form). The number of potential branching manoeuvres, and hence the parallel links between concepts; is almost incomprehensibly huge in the human mind. A person will notice when his/her actions begin to harm another, and will instantly stop the hurtful actions. For a machine the '*thinking-resolution*' is fixed; and the gaps between 'steps' are of the same size/frequency; whereas a human's perspectival vision means adjusting the world's sampling and narrowing the gap between steps (for detailed views) is natural.

Human and machine 'minds' often run several 'programs' at the same time; and hence may be aware of, or running multiple data processing channels simultaneously. Yet the machine seems to altogether lack the freedom of action that is available to the human mind—whereby any thought/action may be linked-to/broken-from; and/or be recognised to influence any other. In a computers 'mind', any parallel thoughts hardly communicate at all; and each is limited to the boundaries of itself.

For a machine, there is no other—hence no (ultimate) advantage is to be gained; it was never alive, so it cannot die, feel pain, care or fail! The machine, sadly, has no concept of self-purpose, and/or brotherhood/fraternity. Given the apparent life-like character of some computers, it can be difficult to realise just how rigid are a machine's plans, processes, activities and possibilities. A human can instantly re-imagine a situation, event or datum, and change his/her strategy of operation; or pay attention to interesting features, open up new lines of enquiry, connect intangibles etc. Whereas a machine is utterly closed-minded.

While any new system or technical device may increase the range of human freedom, it does so only if the human beneficiaries are at liberty to accept it, to modify it, or to reject it; to use it where and when and how it suits their own purposes, in qualities that conform to those purposes...

It is the system itself, that once setup, gives the orders... For its smooth operation, this under-dimensioned system requires equally under-dimensioned men, whose values are those needed for the operation and the continued expansion of the system itself! Minds that are conditioned are incapable of imagining alternatives. The fact is, however, that an automatic system as a whole, once established, can accept no human feedback that calls for a cutback; therefore it accepts no evaluation of its deleterious results, still less is it ready to admit the need for correcting its postulates!

Once automatic control is installed one cannot refuse to accept its instructions, or insert new ones, for theoretically, the machine cannot allow anyone to deviate from its own perfect standards. The underlying desire (of many systems) is to reduce man to a machine, and to establish uniform behaviour.

Lewis Mumford

To deny the existence of the indescribable—is to equate existence with information. - Lewis Mumford

In a world of machines, or of creatures that can be reduced to machines, technocrats would indeed be Gods. - Lewis Mumford

Reality is that which, when you stop believing in it, doesn't go away.
Philip K. Dick

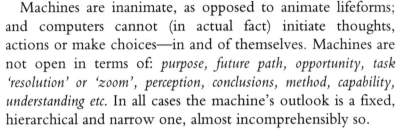

Machines, however crude, are embodiments of a clearly articulated purpose, so firmly fixed in advance, both with respect to the past and future, that the lowest organism, if similarly designed, would be unable to utilise fresh genetic mutations or meet novel situations.

Descartes (with his 'life is a mechanism metaphor') turned his back upon the possibility of creating a unified approach to every part of nature; including the events that are private, singular, non-repeatable, personal, the world of memory, a futurity, a history and biography, of the entire evolution of the species.

The most serious threat of computer-controlled automation comes from displacement of the human mind and the insidious undermining of confidence in his ability to make individual judgements that run contrary to the system-or that proceed from outside the system.

As machines become more lifelike, so humans become more machine-like!

The mechanisms involved in organic behavior are too dynamic, too complex, too quantitatively rich, too multi-fold to be grasped except by simplification.

Lewis Mumford

Machines are inanimate, as opposed to animate lifeforms; and computers cannot (in actual fact) initiate thoughts, actions or make choices—in and of themselves. Machines are not open in terms of: *purpose, future path, opportunity, task 'resolution' or 'zoom', perception, conclusions, method, capability, understanding etc.* In all cases the machine's outlook is a fixed, hierarchical and narrow one, almost incomprehensibly so.

In fact a machine can be said to have no (true) relationship(s) to the environment whatsoever. It cannot—in the fullest sense—actually (truly) respond to anything novel that happens in the larger world. This is logically so because a machine never really 'notices' anything in a human sense; but rather is programmed to constantly check if a particular (highly specific) pattern of events is occurring. And this pattern is fixed from the design stage, wholly rigid, and the machine cannot spot similar/new pattern 'classes' no matter how analogous they may appear to us humans.

I can almost hear all of the computer scientists and systems experts crying foul at this point; because they would point out that sophisticated AI systems can monitor many hundreds or thousands of different factors at the same time—thus managing processes that are (apparently) far beyond any human's ability. Image processing systems can indeed learn to spot and classify (for example) cloud formations/movements which are all somewhat unique—but this is only one 'class' of real-world pattern.

Thus it is true that machines may—in incredibly specific situations—surpass human perception. But what about the same weather system's capability to spot signs of a new ice age, identify a cloud type from a comet impact, tsunami, or a nuclear blast? For such out-of-the-box 'thinking', it takes a 'parallel processing' human mind to make the connections, deductions and conclusions. This is because the machine's programming—and knowledge of the world—is far too: *limited, disconnected, blind, linear, hierarchical and narrow.* My point is that computers are not engaged with the world in multiple ways, and do not see the possibilities—they do not weigh the options.

Engagement requires freedom of purpose; but machines do not possess free-will, and cannot make ***choices*** in any sense whatsoever.

God, also took man as a creative indeterminate of nature... the nature of all other things is limited and constrained within the bounds of laws prescribed by us. Though, constrained by no limits, you shall ordain for thyself the limits of thy nature... though shall have the power to degenerate into lower forms of life... or to be reborn into the higher life forms, which are divine. - Lewis Mumford

Yet machines *do* make choices (or appear to); they 'decide' how to *control space-rockets, fly aeroplanes, and influence all kinds of decisions in on-line financial/shopping situations etc* (all within 'planned' scenarios). But in not a single case do machines ever respond in a novel manner whereby they react creatively to (wholly) unforeseen event(s)—and every situation was pre-visioned and at no stage could the machine choose (anything) for itself.

Choice in the OED is defined as:

> The act of choosing; preferential determination between things proposed; selection, election. To make a choice of; to choose, select. To make a choice: to perform the act of choosing. To take one's choice. By, for, of (in, with) choice: by preference. As opposed to without choice, without distinction, indiscriminately. The power, right, or faculty of choosing; option. To be at one's choice: to act as one chooses, do as one pleases, at choice, at pleasure, to have one's choice, to have the right or privilege of choosing.

These definitions are illustrative of the nature of choice as a logical concept; and links the same to having the power to choose one option over another, and/or to the *act of selection itself*. From this perspective it is clear that all machines, without exception, do not have the right or privilege of choice in any way whatsoever. This is because they do not actually possess free choice *themselves* —and because they merely respond to pre-programmed events— and in pre-determined ways (self-programming is impossible).

But what is the difference between a pre-determined decision between two options, and a decision taken by free choice? The 'thinker' may itself have decided on a course of action of its own free-will; or it may not have. Perhaps a good way to notice 'free-choice'; is to ask: can/could the 'thinker' choose a different (entirely unforeseen) option according to its accumulated knowledge of the environment and/or in response to new (unplanned) circumstances. Can the thinker 'change its mind'? Does it learn/alter-itself/re-program its beliefs?

Another way of looking at this problem of free choice, is to consider if a machine can recognise novelty, and respond in a unique manner.[4]

Neither an external creator nor a predetermined plan is needed in order to account for the (steady) increase of organised creativity and self-actualising design. - Lewis Mumford

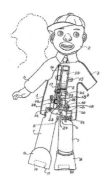

A brief anecdote may prove instructive. Whilst lying in the bath last night, I spotted a tiny water bubble falling down the wall; and my attention was drawn to bubbles all around me—and then to water bubbles on my fingers. I gazed closely at these bubbles, and noticed that they were acting like mini magnifying-lenses on my skin; and that I could now see the freckles on my skin magnified many times over—and was then able to observe their shapes/patterns in new ways. I wondered if I was the first person ever to notice the magnifying effect of the bubbles—but dismissed this notion out of hand. Later I noticed how sunlight diffracted and formed patterns as it passed through my wet eye-lashes.

Could a machine ever have—incidentally—noticed these same optical effects simply by looking at my skin; or would it have merely detected coloured bubbles. To comprehend as I had, a machine would have had to recognise the analogy of the lens and the bubble; and also link the concept(s) of freckle, skin, optics etc. My point is that human beings are open to the environment in novel ways that machines never are; and further that we make un-programmed links/connections and analogies—perceptual and categorical choices—that are quite beyond any machine.[5,7]

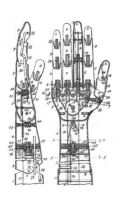

Machine logic, perceptions and actions are, one and all, like 'stovepipes' of functionality; because they are very tall, supremely narrow and hierarchical; whereby one item leads directly to another which leads to another etc. Here connections between objects are incredibly tightly defined, and essentially arranged in a top-down logical layout. Thus we have logic or process-diagrams, whereby a machine performs a specific action on a specific object; wholly without any contextual knowledge of what the same object is and may be *potentially*, and what the nature of the action is and/or where it is all leading. Machines do not: *see the 'shape' of things/the-world; reflect on their actions/processes—they do not place things in context.*

Machines are catastrophically limited—perceptually, conceptually and in terms of fixed perceptions/choices/actions. However even though machine existence may appear to be meaningless, in and of itself; that is is not really so. Every perception/action/process undertaken by a machine—is an instantiation of a human thought—and/or the result of a thought in one way or another. Hence we establish that...

< {17} Machines know nothing of anything (or everything). >

To pass beyond the limits of a physical system into the realm of life, one must assemble more and more parts of a matter of organisation that, as it approaches more closely to living phenomena, reacting within a living environment, it becomes so complex that it can only be reproduced and apprehended intuitively in the act of living, since, at least in man, it includes mind and the infra-corporeal and ultra-corporeal aspects of mind. - Lewis Mumford

Design method: clarify objectives, separate functions from the means of achieving them, and the structure of the design process itself.

MACHINES   151

Machines are the result, in all cases, of human thoughts; thoughts that have been implanted into a machine—and which are wholly fixed in terms of structure and form, process and capabilities. Although all inanimate machines are dead, the implanted 'frozen' thoughts are, in a sense, shadows of once living thoughts; in that they may still implement human wishes long after the original human designer has turned his/her attention to something else (or has even died).

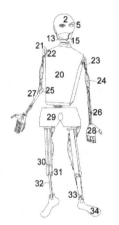

We now return to, and extend, our *Theory of Natural Thoughts* —and in order to account for the ways in which machine/ system **implanted-thoughts** influence other human thoughts, system and machine implanted-thoughts; and also influence or implement human and machine plans/actions. Accordingly...

Machine implanted-thoughts:

- Are composite, with an ATOMIC nature
- Are intentional in Type (normally); and have purely logical affects
- Are FROZEN in form, and cannot self-change (i.e. they are ABSTRACT)
- ORIGINATE in the human mind (may be influenced by data)
- EXIST in one or more CONTEXT-ESTABLISHED form(s) (predicted)
- Are inherently AUTOMATIC (once set in motion)
- May be dormant, active or inactive
- May have material OUTCOMES (planned or not planned)
- May exist in Secret, Private or Open FORMS (internally / externally)
- Are the NATURAL PROPERTY of a human / human(s) / human race
- Are implanted into a machine by a human DESIGNER / IMPLEMENTER
- Are 'set-in-motion' by a human ACTOR / INITIATOR
- May INFLUENCE / be-influenced by other system/machine implanted-thoughts / data indications / human actions
- Influence outcomes may be visible/invisible and planned/unplanned
- May be ASSEMBLED into patterns/designs for varying effects

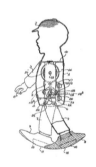

These are the Attributes of machine implanted-thoughts. Every implanted-thought has Form (visibility status), and has a human Owner, Implementer and Initiator. It is important to realise that implanted-thoughts will correspond—in every man-made mechanism—to ALL of the design features, components and outcomes present in ALL machines, products, and services etc.

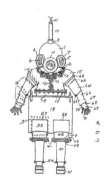

Assault by mechanism upon what E.E.Cummings called 'the single secret that is still man'. - Lewis Mumford

Computers are containers and implementers of human thoughts and wishes, and that is all they are. - Thomas Carlyle

Let us now pause, and ask some questions.

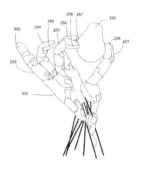

Why we have gone to the trouble of developing a new theory of human thinking? The answer is two-fold. Our first goal has been to outline the natural properties of (mind/media existent) thoughts; and in order to discover how we might learn/know what are the *combined thoughts of all mankind;* and thus to foster freedom of thought/expression/action. In later chapters we shall see how this first part of the theory may possibly—through societal structures/mechanisms—practically achieve such ambitious aims.

The purpose of the second part of our theory of thinking, is to map/control/optimise those human thoughts that are embedded into systems, machines and (for example) computers. A core premise of the current book is that many system and computer designs are sub-optimal; and further that they tend to *meet the wishes of few,* as opposed to *fulfilling the needs/wishes/requirements of the many.* If such a situation exists (even sometimes); then it stands to reason that we must manage the design of machines, on a world-wide basis; and in order to establish and protect the essential Attributes of thoughts as previously expressed. Our approach is based on the *equality, ownership* and *free-assembly* of all thought-atoms; but other human rights must also be protected wherever possible.

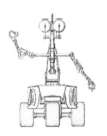

Assuming that we have established (wholly or correctly) the basic Attributes of machine implanted-thoughts; the question becomes how to identify, structure, manage and control these implanted-thoughts—in such a way—and on a world-wide-basis—that human rights are upheld. [see end-notes for techno-rights]

Obviously we are in the realm of law, ethics and government regulation. Accordingly, in later chapters, we outline how techno-rights may be established to nurture and protect everyone's human rights. Desired is a way to establish a (difficult) mapping of the influences of machines on human society. Human rights cannot be established without visibility of actions, and appropriate monitoring.

Why do we allow—the fiction that—systems do *apparently* make decisions over human affairs, when we know that in all cases there is a human designer behind the decisions; when we know that said designer is hiding behind the facade of the machine?

Computers may seem to be alive, but in all cases one is looking at shadows of once living thoughts; forms/processes frozen in space and time, utterly dead.

MACHINES 153

A first task is to identify the implanted-thoughts within machine systems—however right away we are hit by a major stumbling block. Systems, machines and computers have evolved to the stage whereby their implementation details and complexity are—quite literally—almost beyond human understanding. We have processor chips containing *billions of components*; computers running *hundreds of separate programs simultaneously*; and (possibly) each with *millions of lines of code*; whereby *countless millions of computers* are connected together into networks of many different kinds.

How is it possible for anyone; for any government, corporation, university, or even for the whole of the human race; to even begin to understand the immense, mind-boggling and overwhelming complexity of such a vast technological entity—and so to perceive the 'global' form/operations of the self-computer?

I would suggest that there is no need for *any understanding whatsoever*—at a top level—and because we (as a society) can simply focus on monitoring the outputs of technical systems; and hence on managing the *influences* of computers on self.

Written into law can be a generalised mapping and protection of those freedoms that are expressed in the *Theory of Natural Thoughts*; and we can call the associated technological implementation of the same; techno-rights. It shall be the system designers/owners who will be tasked with ensuring that they obey the law in this respect, and it is for the whole human race to monitor said behaviour. In later chapters we explore issues related to the design and implementation/ monitoring of techno-rights within societies, real and imagined.

But for now we end this chapter with a few pages of explanatory text; specifically on the social implications of the theory of implanted-thoughts.

Will a day ever come when a computer 'judge' sentences a person to a punishment? Is such a day not already here, when we have unaccountable systems that limit access to knowledge and hide/crush our thoughts?

When tracking world implanted-thoughts; we have a problem of mapping inputs—machine implanted-thoughts—with outputs —the related influences on human thoughts/actions/life.

Luckily we (the 'societal' onlookers) know basically what we are looking for in terms of outputs; specifically conformity of influences according to the dictates of human-rights. But do the onlookers have to map conforming 'atomic' logical pieces and/or thought-instances with causative agents; and so with the machines/systems/computers internal workings? Given the overwhelming number, interconnection and vast complexity of machines; this may be a gordian knot of labyrinthine confusion.

We can start the process of untying the knot by recognising the ways in which machines can possibly influence humanity. It was Friedrich Nietzsche who brought attention to the fact that the world is basically the *will to power* combined with morphology of patterns; asserting also that the (wider) universe is a system of patterns struggling for power, over one another. In our terms one might say that different thought-patterns influence each other and the world in a myriad of ways. Thus we have patterns of machine implanted-thoughts, plus data and human thoughts/actions, influencing each other ad-infinitum.

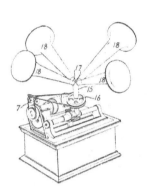

Human thoughts may be: *perceptions, judgments (true/false), conclusions (true/false), decisions, recognition and ranking of concepts, connections between concepts, and stages in a logical pattern of related thoughts/actions.* A machine/system/computer implanted-thought may correspond with any one of these different kinds of thought. Likewise a machine implemented-thought may influence a human action/thought and/or influence other machine implemented-thoughts/actions—and we can obviously have an immense complexity of such relationships.

How do we untangle the world of thoughts from the system implementations of the same? How do we map *actions/events/ processes* back to the causative machine implanted-thought(s); when there may be many stages of influence/translation between actor and action? On practical grounds I do not think we do (or can); and it is where a machine actually touches humanity that the (initial) relationship and responsibility lies.

The specific human achievement, which set man apart from his closest relatives, was the shaping of a new self, visibly different in behaviour, and in plan of life from his animal forebears (self-transformation). - Lewis Mumford

You're in trouble program. Make it easy on yourself.
Who's your User? - Tron [1982]

MACHINES   155

Perhaps we can go back to Aristotle, and base our analysis on the ten Categories and the four Causes. In this manner creating a link from a single implanted-thought to any supposed restriction of human rights; established simply by transferring Aristotle's ideas to systems/machines.[6]

An implanted-thought *Engages* with the human world thusly:

- TOUCHES humanity as an action / process / material outcome
- TOUCHES humanity as a singular subject (predicated or not)
- IS INITIATED by a human (may result from other implanted-thoughts)
- A CHAIN OF CAUSALITY can be established to a human actor
- INFLUENCE is assigned by outcome and in a single context
- EXISTS as a singular mode of meaning with singular/multiple outcomes
- Affects as a primary SUBSTANCE and is therefore truly existent
- May influence other thought patterns (in predictable ways)
- May affect human subject(s) in one of nine ways given below

The *Categories of Influence* for implanted-thoughts:

- May affect QUANTITY in discrete / continuous fashion etc
- May affect QUALITIES; e.g. colour, shape, hot, fast etc
- May affect RELATIVE relations between objects, half, master etc
- May affect PLACE of real-world objects
- May affect WHEN relations of real-world objects
- May affect LOGIC, HAVING or STATE conditions
- May affect ACTIONS or changes in objects (shape, relations etc)
- BEING AFFECTED by other human / machine action(s) / influences.
- May influence human life / natural-thought rights and/or human rights

We name the above features the *Engagements and Categories of Influence* of machine implanted-thoughts. All well and good, but where does such a scheme get us in respect to human-machine relationships? Potentially quite a long way, in actual fact, and towards tying down the myriad of different influence(s) of machines on the human world.

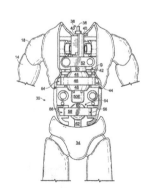

Technology is primarily life-centred, not work centred or power-centred. Man seeks to remodel the human organism, as an expression of the human personality. Man mixes fantasies and projections, desires and designs, abstractions and ideologies. - Lewis Mumford

Our approach to mapping the influence(s) of machines, is a straight-forward one. We begin by ignoring the actual *internals of machines*; and attempt to understand the influence, or *external operational mechanisms*, of system implanted-thoughts. Focus is on where the implanted-thought 'touches' humanity by means of actions/events and physical outcomes (as defined by the nine category examples).

Secondly we state that any implanted-thought 'touches' humanity purely in the *first-person*—and the outcomes are assigned by material effect. Even though the implanted-thought may be influenced by humans and/or data and/or other implanted-thoughts and/or patterns of thoughts (*which may in fact be the [primary] causative factor*); it is at the point(s) where an implanted-thought actually interfaces with humanity that the initial influence/responsibility lies.

This latter point is in accordance with legal precedence whereby the chain of responsibility starts with the (most obvious) actor, and it is he who must demonstrate/prove that he was deceived/influenced/forced by another actor into a course of action; and in order to offload legal responsibility. Hence all thought-patterns are assigned a *designer (implementer)*, *owner* and *initiator (actor)*. Therefore a human/legal agent can (theoretically) be identified for every thought atom's consequences.

Likewise we state that implanted-thoughts are identified in having a single pattern (or mode) of meaning, and for the purposes of mapping. Where the influences of a thought possess more than one *mode-of-operation/outcome*, then these must be treated separately, as separate patterned units of action/meaning. Implanted-thoughts are also assigned as a primary substance, and associated actions cannot therefore be categorised as (in some way) mere side-effects of societal-forces/universal-categories.

A key purpose of the present book is to address the aforementioned problems relating to techno-rights. We wish to establish that machines *merely implement human wishes*; and that it is necessary to recognise that real dangers lurk wherever artificial systems interface with humanity; and in terms of the *upholding-of human rights* and especially *freedom-of-thought rights*.

At that 'omega' point nothing would be left of man's autonomous original nature, except organised intelligence, a universal and omnipotent layer of abstract mind, loveless and lifeless. Our predecessors mistakenly coupled their particular mode of mechanical progress with an unjustifiable sense of increasing moral superiority. Our present over-commitment to technics is in part due to a radical misinterpretation of the whole course of human development! - Lewis Mumford.

Machines are ultimately hollow of: purpose, programming, understanding etc.
—apart from machine implanted-thoughts put there by us humans!

MACHINES   157

One might think that laws are already in place to deal with cases where a machine/computer/system breaks human rights.

However any laws are inadequate, because:

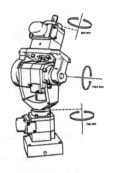

- Society (often) does not recognise freedom-of-thought rights.
- Complex/hidden technical factors are used to break human rights, and to block a person from discovering when rights are broken.
- An individual cannot find out who (which human actors) is/are responsible for breaking said rights; and nothing can be done!
- There are no techno-rights to mirror and so to protect one's human rights (in terms of technology and its affects on humanity).

Needed is a new vision/approach with respect to the design of machines; and in particular because whenever we design a machine—any machine—then we are in fact implanting our thoughts into the world in a wholly inflexible way. These frozen thoughts will often have the most profound results; and multiple implications; *good, bad, indifferent, intended or not.*[8,9,10,11,12]

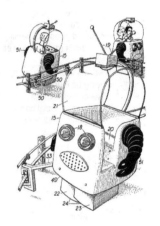

Machines are constructed *entirely* from human implanted-thoughts; and the same being subject to the *Attributes, Engagements*, and *Categories-of-Influence*. In the coming chapters we examine instances where machine implanted-thoughts break human rights. Accordingly, I will suggest that it is perfectly feasible to design a new kind of society—a *technopia* —by means of said theories; whereby machines are built that responsibly uphold human rights. Special techno–rights will be required to nurture and protect human-rights—the same being the standard rights—only <u>consciously</u> instantiated within all machine implanted-thoughts.[13] Although my suggestions may sound radical, and perhaps utilitarian; only by means of a major impetus could we possibly alter the course of the modern world away from: *withholding human-rights, stolen thoughts/data, no freedom of expression, and a complete lack of knowledge in relation to the thoughts/votes of humanity.*

Put simply, we wish to build an open and democratic society; being one in which knowledge, ideas, votes and thoughts are set free to work for the benefit of all. Will it be easy? No. But ...

Only those who attempt the absurd can achieve the impossible. - Albert Einstein

The machine, 'advanced' thinkers began to hold, not merely served as the ideal mould for explaining and controlling <u>all</u> organic activities, but its wholesale fabrication and continued improvement were <u>alone</u> what gave meaning to human existence! - Lewis Mumford

Where shineth all that was,

That is, or shall be; here, ere ought was wrought,

Thou knew all that thy pow'r with Time forth-brought,

And more, things numberless that Thou couldst make,

That actually shall never being take.

by William Drummond (Hymn to the Fairest Fair)

Computer Badfluences

- Computer crime / hacking
- Data security / safety
- Loss of privacy (spying)
- No free-press (government laws)
- Unemployment (automation)
- Disempowerment (no access)
- Exploitation (centralised power))
- Wastage of time and money
- Lost / hidden thoughts
- Lost / hidden / hacked data
- Increased stress (capability)
- Distractions (data, emails etc)
- Disconnectedness
- Health issues (posture, eyes)
- Spying (is it present?)
- Misinformation (false records)
- Isolation (no social contact)
- False sense of connection
- Spammers / trolls
- Mistrust (in authority)
- Pornography [Illegal types]
- Lack of connection to reality
- Bullying [cyber]
- False news (viral reports))
- Lack of physical activity
- Poor socialisation
- Information overload
- Wayfinding is difficult
- Blind 'heap-style' searches
- Most links are invisible
- Most thoughts/data invisible
- Poor accessibility of truth
- Payment walls for everything
- Access to Internet is not free
- May foster Illiteracy?
- May help terrorists to collaborate—but surely they would do so anyway!

Factor Unknown - by Tillotson (1952)

'Miss 1901,' he said 'step into 1952!'
(Other Worlds 1952)

Computers (apparently) magnify human abilities to generate, collect and store data/thoughts; they provide access to information at greatly increased speeds; they allow information to be reproduced easily (potentially) and to be distributed widely;

they may engender a lack of accountability in terms of identifying the person (who is normally) responsible for a 'computer error'; they shorten/ contract spatiality;

they (may) facilitate surveillance; they produce shifting relationships and changes in communication protocols (human and machine types);

and they provide an illusion of precision (when matters may be very uncertain indeed).

Chapter Seven
User Interface

I N THIS chapter we don a set of 'future goggles'—and explore prospects for the human-computer interface. The issue of how to interact with computing systems would seem to be a pretty straightforward one; whereby we all quite naturally jump into— and out of—several different kinds of user interface (UI) every day. But when you consider that a UI defines the nature, scope and efficiency of everything that we do in the digital world; then it becomes desirable that our interactions be as helpful, rewarding and enjoyable as humanly—or as systemly—possible.[1]

Today the scope, scale and richness of information systems causes data 'bottle-necks' to gather wherever people interface with computers. Especially problematic is knowing anything of what you do not know, and in terms of information hidden in vast data-mountains. Unfortunately, tools like **Google** search require users to ask the right questions and/or to use valid keywords in order to locate specific items. And much remains unseen. Must we rely on *sheer-luck* to locate interesting content?

On the contrary, we recommend the attributes of the Lookable User Interface as a (partial) solution, allowing the user to visually boost his/her knowledge of available content. Whilst augmented reality, speech and touch driven interfaces are increasingly common; visual interaction is still pre-eminent.

Addressed here is the difficulty in providing rapid overviews and/or fostering explorative freedom within complex information structures. In this respect, some experts have endorsed use of three-dimensional (3D) UIs, and holographic, real-space and/or perspective projections within information views; whilst others have downplayed the same. Futuristic 3D UIs have also been a common feature in science fiction stories, films etc.

Ergo, we step into the 'world' of the 3D user interface...

I don't want to use my creative energy on someone else's user interface. - Jeff Bezos

As far as the customer is concerned, the interface is the product. - Jef Raskin

I think complexity is mostly sort of crummy stuff that is there because it's too expensive to change the interface. - Jaron Lanier

A picture is worth a thousand words.
An interface is worth a thousand pictures. - Ben Shneiderman

User Interface Defined

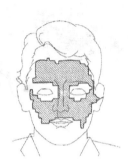

In the 1991 book *Computers as Theatre*, Dr Brenda Laurel states that we should think of—and design—a computer interface in terms of a theatrical metaphor.[1] Her idea is that like effective drama, good interface design must engage the user in both thought and emotion. Laurel also says that the user interface in a way obstructs access, and that it stands in the way between us and what we are trying to do. This is a useful perspective. But it is by no means the only one.

Others have spoken in terms of overcoming the communication barriers that exist between one world and another. For example, sending messages between the hidden digital world of the computer, and the human world of language and vision. In this view, actions in one world must be 'interfaced' using a language of commands that both 'sides' know how to interpret. Thus the happenings in one world must be communicated (and translated) into an entirely different realm. The UI's job is to hide unnecessary complexity and to expose public events/actions/information in each world, and so to mediate between the different regions of being. From this perspective, there are many different types of UIs; including operating systems, TV remotes, and washing machine controls etc. Even language itself, which communicates the thoughts of one individual to another, may be seen as special kind of UI.

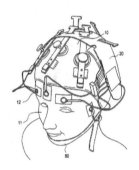

Ideally, a UI provides useful views into an information space; according to the actions, behaviours, choices, and needs of the user. And this would perhaps be a relatively straightforward task, if it were not for the great diversity of different types of computer system, varying purposes, and the vast complexity of information types dealt with. To say nothing of the great range of—and constantly changing—user interests. A large variety of different types of UI designs (and interaction techniques) are needed to cope with such diversity of purpose.

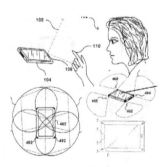

Over the last 50 years there have been many innovations in UI design. For example, in the 1960s, **Sketchpad** introduced interactive graphics; and High Definition (HD) displays followed soon after.[2]

Usability, fundamentally, is a matter of bringing a bit of human rights into the world of computer-human interaction. It's a way to let our ideals shine through in our software, no matter how mundane the software is. But you have daily opportunities to show respect for humanity even with the most mundane software. - Joel Spolsky

Later the mouse and other key elements in the field of human-computer interaction were invented by Dr Douglas Engelbart (1925-2013).[3] In 1981 the **Xerox Star** system was introduced and the **Palo Alto Research Centre (PARC)** user interface arrived which pioneered basic graphical elements such as windows, menus, radio buttons, check boxes and icons.[4,5]

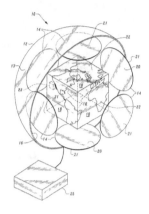

More recently also, the touch-screen approach has been used on mobile computers and even full-sized displays. And the success of all of these techniques (generally) has led to an explosion in number and types of user interface designs. Progress has been so rapid, that in today's world, it would be difficult to get through even a single day without using multiple UIs.

Sometimes it is difficult for the UI designer to decide what type (or set) of interaction tools is best for a particular application. One approach is to split larger interaction methods into smaller components, in an attempt to form a 'language' of human-computer interactions; and to then re-assemble the standard techniques according to need. Obviously in so doing, it is vital to match appropriate techniques to the nature of the task at hand. However such a methodology assumes that all of the useful interaction techniques are already known.

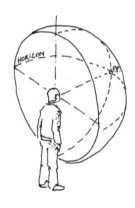

In this chapter we adopt a similar mindset. We begin with an examination of visual perception, specifically in the hope that new 3D interaction techniques may be identified and categorised. Our analysis starts in the following section with a study of the nature of 3D, in the belief that a key problem with respect to current UI designs is the inability to provide rapid and efficient overviews of information structures.

Just before delving into the exciting topic of the third spatial dimension, it is worth noting that I do not support the view that 3D UIs are definitely the way forward in all cases; but only that 'spatial effects' may prove useful on occasion, and for specific kinds of user tasks.

3D User Interfaces

Three-dimensional (or 3D) computer interfaces have become a useful human-computer interaction method, as seen in Computer Aided Design (CAD) systems, Virtual Reality (VR) worlds and also in a variety of computer games. The topic of 3D user interfaces is also a popular one in science fiction movies, for example as depicted in *Avatar*, *Jurassic Park*, *Star Trek*, *Minority Report*, and *Star Wars* etc. Here spatial interfaces have been used to enhance the feeling of being in a high-technology society, or else to depict advanced and more intuitive, informative, and/or easy-to-use computers.

Despite these advances and predications, the fact remains that for many tasks, 2D user interfaces are quite sufficient. Real-world 3D UIs are quite rare as a result. For example, we see no popular 3D file managers, and there are no examples of standard 3D data explorers, 3D operating system elements and/or general-purpose 3D interaction techniques. The question remains of why this should be so, because many researchers and companies have attempted to create new and improved 3D user interfaces.[16]

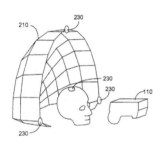

Perhaps part of the reason for the lack of 3D UIs, is that many people actually like 2D interaction techniques. At the same time people often dislike looking at depictions of 3D on 2D screens, at least in situations where the simpler, more familiar, and perhaps as a result faster, 2D techniques are available. Here we are dealing with 3D user interfaces as viewed on 2D displays, and we shall ignore more complex holographic or stereoscopic type displays (which have yet to become commonplace—at least in terms of even attempting stereoscopic UIs). And we refer here to the state-of-affairs as it exists outside of the computer-aided design and animation fields, where 3D user interfaces are a de-facto standard.

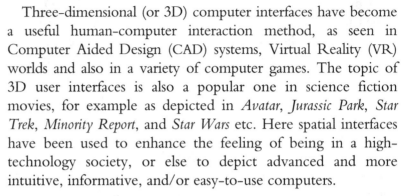

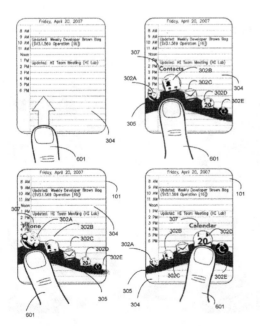

I am not going to suggest that we can instantly overturn the lack of popularity of the 3D User Interface—for the general public—and especially by means of a short chapter like the present one.

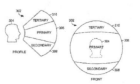

Just because something looks good doesn't mean it's useful.
And just because something is useful doesn't mean it is beautiful. - Joshua Brewer

USER INTERFACE   163

Rather a key aim has been to explore the suitability of a range of 3D interaction techniques, and in relation to the provision of useful methods for application to future and general-purpose UI studies that may be performed elsewhere.

A summary of motivations is useful at this point.

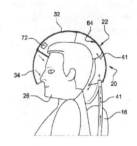

Put simply, we are attempting to discover the first few building blocks of a new language of human-computer interaction in the third dimension. This is a difficult and ambitious task. For example, it is a fact that a far wider range of interaction forms are possible in 3D (as opposed to 2D). Many of these potential 3D techniques will not be useful and/or be inefficient and/or be unnatural; and thus have poor usability.

Perhaps the most useful solutions will be well-hidden. Therefore due to the size of the 3D design space, and the difficulty of discovering new and efficient 3D interaction techniques, we shall discuss only a rather small number of (discovered) *useful* techniques. Potentially existent within the (much larger) universe of spatial human-computer interaction techniques may be other—even more useful—methods and information display forms that are yet to be discovered.

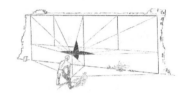

In brief, in this chapter we present the results of testing new kinds of 3D user interface prototypes. Before presenting our findings, first (in the next section) we take a step backwards and explore the nature of human perception of the third dimension.

Wide-Field Perspective

We are concerned here with viewing and representation of the third dimension; and in particular with the depiction of wide-field perspective scenes on 2D computer screens. The graphical representation of 3D has a long history going back thousands of years to the ancient Greek, Egyptian and even Chinese civilisations. [7,17,18] During the intervening centuries, a number of different systems have been used to aid in the realistic representation of 3D, but we shall focus here mainly on the underlying mechanisms used by humans to actually perceive spatial depth.

If scientific reasoning were limited to the logical processes of arithmetic, we should not get very far in our understanding of the physical world. One might as well attempt to grasp the game of poker entirely by the use of the mathematics of probability. - Vannevar Bush

Human Vision and the Depth Cues

People often say that 3D on a computer screen is not 'true 3D'. But they are then unable to explain this statement any further, and sometimes they add that flat screen images cannot be true 3D because they do not show stereoscopic views. Along the way people occasionally mention that stereoscopic glasses are needed for 3D, one being red and the other blue for the left and right eyes. In one sense what these people are saying is correct, in that a flat screen does not show stereoscopic images. However they are entirely incorrect when they assume that only stereoscopic images are true 3D.

Vision experts have long known about the different aspects of depth perception, and that these can be grouped into two categories: *monocular cues* (cues available from the input of one eye) and *binocular cues* (cues available from both eyes). Each of these different 'cues' is used by our brains, either independently, or else together, in order for us to perceive the third spatial dimension (our brains 'create' depth or 3D).

It is important to note that not all of the cues are required to be present simultaneously in order to give us an accurate or realistic impression of 3D or depth. It has been demonstrated, for example, that we can get a realistic impression of 3D when just one or two cues are present, as in a perspective drawing for example. Whilst I don't want to turn this chapter into a scientific monologue on the topic of 3D, I think it it is worth reminding ourselves of the cues in a list at this point.

Monocular cues include: *motion-parallax, colour vision, perspective, distance(scale), fog, focus, occlusion,* and *peripheral-vision.* Binocular cues include **stereopsis**—or *binocular disparity* sometimes also called *binocular parallax*—which is the difference in shapes and positions of images due to the different vantage points with which the two eyes see the world. The other binocular cue is **convergence**, or *range-finding stereopsis* which is the human ability to judge the distances to objects due to the angle of convergence between the eyes.

These various *cues* give humans *clues* about spatial depth.

When we are able to look beyond appearances and to behold that which we truly are, we recognise that our essence is interwoven with the divine and that we exist as one of its expressions. - Alexandra Katehakis

Nothing is more imminent than the impossible... what we must always foresee is the unforeseen.

Victor Hugo

Never surrender your hopes and dreams to the fateful limitations others have placed on their own lives. The vision of your true destiny does not reside within the blinkered outlook of the naysayers and the doom prophets. Judge not by their words, but accept advice based on the evidence of actual results. Do not be surprised should you find a complete absence of anything mystical or miraculous in the manifested reality of those who are so eager to advise you. Friends and family who suffer the lack of abundance, joy, love, fulfilment and prosperity in their own lives really have no business imposing their self-limiting beliefs on your reality experience.

Anthon St Maarten

Throughout the centuries there were men who took first steps down new roads armed with nothing but their own vision. Their goals differed, but they all had this in common: that the step was first, the road new, the vision un-borrowed, and the response they received—hatred. The great creators—the thinkers, the artists, the scientists, the inventors—stood alone against the men of their time. Every great new thought was opposed. Every great new invention was denounced. The first motor was considered foolish. The airplane was considered impossible. But the men of un-borrowed vision went ahead. They fought, they suffered and they paid. But they won.

Ayn Rand

As the mobiles, tablets and wearables grow in number... perhaps real computers (laptops and desktops) may die out? Perhaps children who program will be rare as a result. Or else App programming may make computers even more popular?

The greater number of items on the monocular list, gives a first indication that perhaps stereoscopic vision effects are not the primary way in which we humans perceive depth or the third dimension. You can easily test this yourself by closing one eye, and immediately you notice that the world still appears to be spread out before you in all of its three dimensional glory! With one eye closed you may have difficulty with the finer points of depth perception such as picking up a pin off the floor. However largely for ordinary tasks if you lost one eye, then you would still be able to rely on the other eye for 3D vision, in fact exclusively by relying on the monocular visual cues.

On passing, I would like to note that those who suggest that stereoscopic 3D (aka red-blue parallax films) is the only true 3D; and further that its mechanisms are well known, are in fact claiming that they have more than a head start on some of the greatest experts in human vision who ever lived. World renowned scientists agree that science has yet to even begin to understand the mechanism(s) by which human beings combine or overlay two different parallax views in real time into a single correlated image sensation.[6,7]

Some even proclaim this image combination feat to be a miracle of the human perceptive system—and so it may be—because the source images are thoroughly misshapen and also distorted one relative to the other. Perhaps it is a little depressing to discover that our school physics and biology teachers—who skipped so confidently over 3D vision—did not themselves fully understand how we humans are able to see the world in 3D!

I firmly believe that we are all given signs and dreams and put in situations that define who we were and who we are to become. All of it points towards our destiny. All we need to do is listen carefully to the messages and follow our dreams. It is in our dreams that we find our true identities and where our destiny awaits. - Isaiah Washington

Note that some vision experts [11] would argue for the inclusion of other yet more subtle (monocular) optical cues, including occluding edges, horizons and other effects due to the 'direct perception of surface layout', but for the purposes of simplifying an obviously complex topic we shall ignore these additional factors here.

Colour directly influences the soul. Colour is the keyboard, the eyes are the hammers, the soul is the piano with many strings. The artist is the hand that plays, touching one key or another purposively, to cause vibrations in the soul.

Kandinsky

Graphic representation constitutes one of the basic sign-systems conceived by the human mind for the purposes of storing, understanding, and communicating essential information... behind every graphic is a question or series of questions that the graphic attempts to answer... There are as many types of questions as components in the information... If, in order to obtain a correct and complete answer to a given question, all other things being equal, one construction requires a shorter observation time than another construction, we can say that it is more efficient for this question.

Jaques Bertin

Perspective Defined

Let us pause and take a stock of where we are.

I hope I have been able to convince you of the fact that *stereoscopics* are not required to give an impression of 3D. If they were, then we would not be able to make very much sense at all of television, films, photographs or even the vast majority of drawings and paintings.[8] These methods, one and all, solely rely on the monocular cues for depth depiction, yet we have no difficulty understanding the 3D worlds depicted; in which objects lie at different apparent distances from the viewer.

One of the most important of the monocular cues for depth perception is perspective. Let us now agree on a very simple definition of perspective. Perspective—from latin *perspicere*, to see clearly—is an approximate projected representation of a scene as seen from a particular viewing location. Kim Veltman has made an exhaustive study of the history and nature of perspective.[12,17,18] The two most characteristic features of perspective are that objects are represented with a smaller scale as their distance from the observer increases, and also that the scene experiences so-called spatial foreshortening, which is the distortion of items when viewed at an angle.

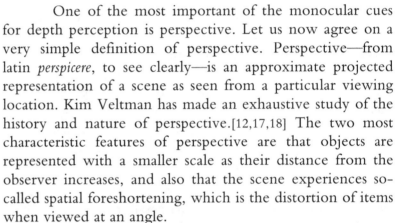

A rudimentary knowledge of the different types of perspective is essential if we wish to understand how we are able to see in 3D. A little theory seems appropriate...

Types of Perspective

At this point I would like to make a distinction between two different types of perspective. Firstly, there is the type that arises from the perception of depth in human vision—called *visual* or *true perspective*—and secondly there is the type that is created to facilitate the perception of depth in graphical images—called *graphical perspective*. Regardless of the features of the specific definition adopted, experts are in agreement that perspective is a very powerful depth cue; in both the graphical and vision forms.

We are all glorified motion sensors. Some things only become visible to us when they undergo change. We take for granted all the constant, fixed things, and eventually stop paying any attention to them. At the same time we observe and obsess over small, fast-moving, ephemeral things of little value. The trick to rediscovering constants is to stop and focus on the greater panorama around us. While everything else flits about, the important things remain in place. Their stillness appears as reverse motion to our perspective, as relativity resets our motion sensors. It reboots us, allowing us once again to perceive. - Vera Nazarian

It stands to reason therefore that in order to maximise the effectiveness of this cue in any representative method, it is important to mimic the overall optical affects of visual perspective as closely as possible. Here once again there are complications and disagreements over which is the most natural and realistic form of graphical perspective.

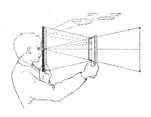

It turns out that there are many different forms of graphical perspective; including linear, curvilinear, spherical, and axial etc. Arguments continue to rage over which is the more natural. Linear perspective, which was first developed during the period of the Italian Renaissance, is perhaps the most familiar form of perspective to the Western eye. Nevertheless, vision and optical experts have noted that linear perspective is not a good approximation to so-called natural or real visual perspective.[7,8] In particular, at the outer extremes of the human visual field, parallel lines become curved, as in a photo taken through a fish-eye lens.

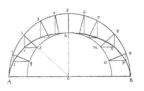

It may surprise you to learn that the human visual field has a natural curvilinear shape! However painters, building designers and scientists have been aware of this fact for hundreds and possibly even thousands of years.

It has been claimed for example that the Ancient Greeks made the Parthenon columns bow outwards to account for— and correct—the curvilinear shape of the human visual field. Also painters like Leonardo Da Vinci (1452-1519) and J.M.W. Turner (1775-1851) added curvilinear effects into their depictions to more closely mimic reality as seen by the human eye. It has also long been known that it is possible to graphically re-create scenes in which the geometry conforms to an overall curvilinear shape similar in form to the views projected by a fish-eye lens.

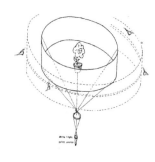

This form of perspective has sometimes been called *curvilinear perspective*, and it is a form of perspective which has an undeniable origin in the natural optics of scenes. Curvilinear perspective was ably explored in *Curvilinear Perspective, From Visual Space to the Constructed Image* by Albert Flocon and Andre Barre in their 1986 book.[9] Modern artist Dick Termes has also produced many works based on curvilinear and 6-point perspective.[13]

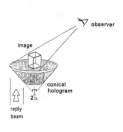

What I need is perspective. The illusion of depth, created by a frame, the arrangement of shapes on a flat surface. Perspective is necessary. Otherwise there are only two dimensions. Otherwise you live with your face squashed up against a wall, everything is a huge foreground, of details, close-ups, hairs, the weave of the bed-sheet, the molecules of the face. Your own skin like a map, a diagram of futility, criss-crossed with tiny roads that lead nowhere. Otherwise you live in the moment. Which is not where I want to be. - Margaret Atwood

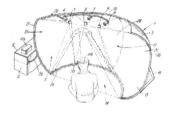

Curvilinear perspective has a geometry which is closely related to the human visual field. In particular the rules of optics cause objects located at large distances from the central visual plane to be contracted in size, a true-to-life effect that is not depicted by linear perspective. Also others have noted that the human eye projects images onto a spherical retina, causing images to curve outwards in the same way as images in a wide field lens. In Flocon and Barre's detailed mathematical study of curvilinear perspective, we see drawings which ably represent the basic features of the natural curvilinear shape of the human visual field.[9] Especially noteworthy here is the curvilinear shape of wide-angle scenes, and the '*realistic*' (if exaggerated) foreshortening of scale in the lateral dimension. Overall experts are in agreement that the human visual field is in fact (slightly) curvilinear in shape. It is important to note here that curvilinear perspective is related to one of the monocular depth cues experienced when looking at a panoramic scene, that of peripheral distortion.

Can 3D Ever be 'Truly' Represented

The most realistic 3D would be one which employed all of the depth cues, however no method (to date) has been devised which has been able to employ them all. In fact it may not even be an achievable goal to construct a system so realistic that it employs all of these cues. Such a system would be indistinguishable from reality, and may in fact be an impossibility because it is known that human vision uses other yet more subtle scene based optical cues to form an impression of 3D.

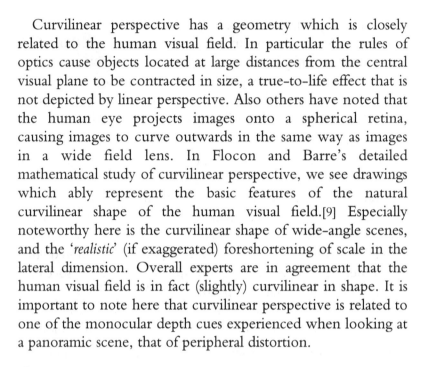

The fact that no single method employs all of the depth cues (perhaps) leads to the conclusion that no one method of depth representation (or perspective form) can be claimed to be more '*real*' than any another. What about holograms you may ask—don't they employ all of the cues, both mono and stereo? I am afraid not. It is true that holograms do employ both monocular and binocular cues, but they do not usually employ moving images and so miss out on the moving cues. Reality, it seems, cannot be faked'; except under carefully controlled conditions.

Every person sees the world through lenses of his or her own design —individual goggles that alter focus and perspective as desired. For those who wish the world to be dark and ugly and unapproachable, it is. But for those who wish it to be beautiful, it is a garden playground blooming with bright, happy colours. - Richelle E. Goodrich

Reality is, Hope and Despair lie in the same places.
And they're just a matter of perspective. - Richie Singh

Other cues are often missed here (with holograms) including changes such as colour, shadow, occlusion and also peripheral vision due to the relatively narrow field of view of most holograms. Overall I would conclude that no representative method currently employs all of the depth cues, and so none is true 3D in the strictest sense of the word.

As an aside the author has invented a new type of mirror, named the 'Hologram Mirror', which produces an image of the self which 'floats' in space in-front of the mirror's surface.[14] Here, unlike with holograms, image occlusion/moving effects are created, and the viewer obtains a strong and realistic impression of 3D. Similar optical devices may be used for producing improved types of 3D displays, specifically for interfacing (naturally) with future computing systems.

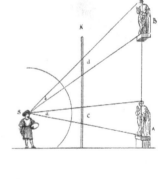

Curvilinear Realities

The basic facts of human vision presented here will come as a complete surprise to many. The question arises as to why it is that the facts of human vision should surprise us? Perhaps we are all too close to our own sense of vision to notice the natural curvilinear shape of every wide-field scene we ever look at, and likewise we do not generally take any notice of the miracle of 3D perception because it is ever present.

Or perhaps we are all too-familiar with concepts such as linear perspective and/or the narrow field-of-view of photographs. In fact narrow-field photographic images do work rather well—in terms of 3D impression.

Next time you are looking at 2D television or at a photograph notice how strong the effect of depth or the third dimension really is. You have no trouble here forming a good conception of the different relative depths of the objects that are depicted, and can form an accurate overall impression of scene geometries. No 3D glasses glasses are used here, and in each case we use 'monocular' cues to form an accurate internal mental model of these scenes; which constructs, aids and supports, our comprehension of 3D.

Mountains, according to the angle of view, the season, the time of day, the beholder's frame of mind, or any one thing, can effectively change their appearance. Thus, it is essential to recognise that we can never know more than one side, one small aspect of a mountain. - Haruki Murakami

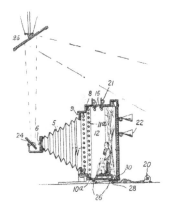

At this point you may be asking yourself why it is that photographic, film and also television images do not exhibit scene curvatures. The answer is that they would if they covered a wide enough field of view—say around 180 degrees. In any case optical designers have worked hard to ensure that the camera lenses involved eliminate such 'distortions'. Note that the so-called 'Fish-Eye' wide-field lenses do show extreme curvilinear distortions similar to those depicted in the Spectasia UI (see below). Also when you have a moment, get a 30 cm ruler (longer is better), and whilst looking forward bring it close to the bottom of your nose, and notice how its shape at the outer edges curves upwards and forwards. It may take a few minutes to be able to see this effect, because you are so accustomed to *not* noticing it ! But once you do; you will be amazed to see your curved field of view as it is for the first time.

It is an established fact that wide-field optical perspective views are naturally curvilinear in form. Fish-eye lens views are not curved because of any affect introduced by the lens itself, but rather because that is how reality looks when you decide to project a specific scene over a very wide field of view! Eagles and birds see the world like this, that is in the ultra-wide field aspect. This fact leads me to conclude that curvilinear perspective has a strong foundation in reality.

I am not claiming here that curvilinear perspective is necessarily a more real depiction technique than the linear ones that we are used to seeing/using, but only that all things considered it is an equally valid form of representation! Perhaps the main reason why curvilinear perspective seems so strange to us is that we have become so used to seeing everything in terms of straight lines and right angles. We may be missing out on some quite spectacular images as a result.

Therefore, although curvilinear scenes may at first seem like a distortion of reality, our discussion has shown that this shape is in fact rooted in the natural optics of scenes, and also at the same time in the human visual field which is inherently curved in shape.

Let us now 'dive into' some curvilinear worlds...

Print Gallery (1956)

Am I corrupted if I believe that the people who think alike are more admirable and estimable than those who think for themselves? If no one thought differently, then where would our innovations come from? How would we ever advance beyond the status quo? Corruption isn't just moral or ethical in nature--rust is a form of corruption, one that eats away at its host like a parasite, constantly making it less than it was the day before. The belief that they should hold in greater esteem those who think alike is a form of rust, something that doesn't allow our young people to grow beyond the limitations already established by those who do think alike. - Tim Walsh

Escher's 3D Perspectives and Optical Distortions

Dutch artist M.C.Escher (1898-1972) made extensive studies of the nature of 3D perception as depicted on 2D surfaces; and he produced a number of interesting prints that explored the nature of new forms of perspective—including also curvilinear perspective.[15] Escher's work is important for anyone seeking to find new ways of presenting 3D views on 2D displays. In particular Escher studied the nature of distorted optical views, being ones containing multiple—but connected—vanishing points. Often in his lithographs, curvilinear grids form harmonious and multiple-perspective views that contain distant and close-up views simultaneously or combine up/down views into the same picture. In his 1956 drawing *Print Gallery*, Escher manages to show internal and external views to a gallery viewer at the same time. Escher's work on perspective highlights the peculiar nature of our perception of the third dimension, and possibly hints at the unreality of linear perspective (in human terms). In the present chapter, what we 'borrow' from Escher's perspective views, is the possibility—or even desirability—of combining multiple perspectives into the same graphic, and/or the possibility of doing so within a single (integrated) graphical display. Noteworthy here, is that when it comes to human perception of 3D, one does not always have to stick to 'reality'—and especially in terms of traditional optical theory.

The usefulness of Escher's work for the graphical user interface designer does not end with perspective. Especially interesting also are his explorations of the relationships between space and the flat surface. In his 1956 print *Fishes and Scales*, Escher manages to combine (what would have been) the regular division of a plane with an 'optical' distortion; resulting in a drawing that has conjoined black and white fish swimming in opposite directions—and at gradually increasing scales. The end result is a type of multiple-scale graphic that combines focus plus context views for a large number of fish images. Ingenious indeed!

Fishes and Scales (1956)

'If you can see a thing whole,' he said, 'it seems that it's always beautiful. Planets, lives. But close up, a world's all dirt and rocks. And day to day, life's a hard job, you get tired, you lose the pattern. You need distance, interval, the way to see how beautiful the earth is; is to see it as the moon. The way to see how beautiful life is, is from the vantage point of death. - Ursula K. Le Guin

Nothing exists except atoms and empty space,
everything else is opinion. - Democritus

Personal Virtual Reality

Dr Richard Bolt first talked about Lookable Graphics in the classic study by Stewart Brand.[10] Dr Bolt predicated that:

> A whole graphic art will arise concerning 'Lookable Graphics'—graphics which are concocted and generated with an awareness that they will be looked at.[10]

This insight seems to have been ignored by many subsequent researchers in the 1990's, who sought to create virtual worlds and 3D Interfaces which re-created all the complexity of the real world, including the supposed geometry and optics of reality, inside the computer, but without (apparently) taking into account fully the physiology and psychology of the human visual perceptual system (at least for UI designs).

It seems that many of the Virtual Reality (VR) computer scientists and engineers had forgotten to talk to the vision experts and also perception scientists in the early years of the development of VR. Immersive interaction was the great premise of the Virtual Reality movement in the early 1990's. Within a short time VR UI's would be everywhere, many proclaimed. As it turned out VR systems today remain largely stuck on entertainment consoles and in research labs (The popular **Oculus Rift** *VR Headset* notwithstanding). We are still waiting to see the widespread application of VR systems in day-to-day life. Perhaps one of the primary reasons for the failure of VR is that until recently efforts have focused on the creation of fully immersive interactive worlds which attempt to mimic the full complexity of reality complete with all of its visual messiness and confusion.

The problem here is that even when you do succeed in producing convincing artificial realities, people find it extremely difficult to navigate inside these VR worlds; and using ordinary displays and interaction techniques.

In fact these methods often prove to be less efficient for everyday tasks such as retrieval, than the alternatives such as ordinary 2D menus. I am convinced that many in the VR community took a wrong turn in terms of (not) designing broadly applicable UIs—alienating potential users with poor usability.

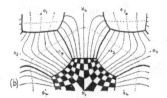

There is a fifth dimension, beyond that which is known to man. It is a dimension as vast as space and as timeless as infinity. It is the middle ground between light and shadow, between science and superstition. - Rod Serling

Remember the Pentium CPU 'bug'; and all the fuss—plus instant correction?
What about all the countless 'software' bugs—who will correct those?

By fully immersing people into the computers world they placed people about as close as it is possible to get to the digital content. This in fact closed off the view of content, creating a narrow view at the expense of an overall vista. As a result the user ends up constantly moving his viewpoint and/or location about (inside the VR world); and in an attempt to find items of interest, navigation becomes the key task.

The VR system designers (perhaps) forgot that it is distance itself which constitutes a scene, and which provides room for the user to contemplate the whole. It is critically important to be able to achieve a reasonable amount of distance from which to survey a scene efficiently in an overall sense, and this is a context related rule of human perception. Thus if we are to be able to build an efficient 3D user interface, one which facilitates information retrieval tasks such as browsing, we need to ensure sufficient distance is achievable from the viewer to represented objects in the simulated world. I would like to go one step further here and put forward the suggestion that the VR pioneers made another mistake in terms of building efficient user interfaces. They chose to give the user complete freedom to adopt any optical or physical vantage point within these simulated worlds. This invited loss of context and made building interfaces which efficiently performed tasks such as information retrieval very difficult, if not almost impossible, to achieve.

Another approach is in one sense the very opposite of Virtual Reality (VR) systems where the user is immersed in a virtual world; which he must then adapt himself to. This is the Personal Reality (PR) system which we are introducing here for the first time. With PR the world view automatically adapts *itself* to the person in a highly specific way, and this class of artificial reality system may be properly called a *Personal Reality* (PR) system. The nature of the personalisation of the system is not defined and may differ from one design to the next. Typically the PR system might adapt optical parameters such as perspective projection, the field of view of specific aspects of a scene, the distance, scale and arrangement of objects; and also as well creating pleasing background contexts for aspects of the display where appropriate.

Space is big. You just won't believe how vastly, hugely, mind-bogglingly big it is. I mean, you may think it's a long way down the road to the drug store, but that's just peanuts to space. - Douglas Adams

FLATLAND

Flatland: A Romance of Many Dimensions is an 1884 satirical novel by Edwin Abbott Abbott; and the book used the fictional two-dimensional world of Flatland to offer pointed observations on the social hierarchy of Victorian culture; but its exploration of mathematical dimensions is its enduring legacy.

The story is about a two-dimensional world known as **Flatland** which is occupied by living geometric figures. Women are simple line-segments, while men are polygons with various numbers of sides. The narrator, a humble square, has a dream about a visit to a one-dimensional world (**Lineland**) which is inhibited by 'lustrous points'. He attempts to convince the realm's ignorant monarch of a second dimension but finds it is essentially impossible to make him see outside of his eternally straight line.

The square is then visited by a three-dimensional Sphere, which he cannot comprehend until he sees **Spaceland** for himself. Later he tries to convince Sphere of the theoretical possibility of the existence of a fourth (and fifth, sixth etc) spatial dimension; but he fails to comprehend other dimensions.

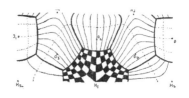

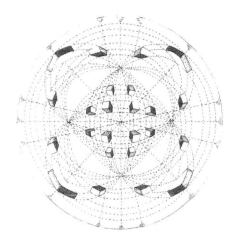

SPACE AND TIME

Fascinating is the history of notions relating to the possibility (and reality) of multiple dimensions of space and time.

In 1904 Charles Howard Hinton published a book entitled: *the Fourth Dimension,* which helped to popularize the topic on both sides of the Atlantic. Soon after in 1905, Albert Einstein in his revolutionary paper on ***Special Relativity***, demonstrated that Time and Space are indeed related mathematically and may be treated as interchangeable in certain situations.

Another well-known book published in 1913 by Claude Bragdon entitled: *A Primer of Higher Space; The Fourth Dimension;* helped to spread the idea of higher dimensional spaces in both the artistic and literary communities.

Pablo Picasso explored multiple perspectives in his early cubist works in the 1910's; whilst other Vorticist and Futurist painters such as Jean Metzinger and Wyndham Lewis experimented with new ways to depict space and time within their splintered ensembles. Futurist sculptors such as Umberto Boccioni created new kinds of 'blurred' moving human forms that seemed to have been captured 'running' in time on a slow film. Later Salvador Dali in his painting: *The Persistence of Memory* [1931] drew melting clocks; depicting the erratic passing of time that we may experience whilst dreaming or day-dreaming.

Lookable User Interfaces

A Lookable User Interface (LUI) is a user interface which has been designed to afford the maximum degree of visual accessibility of digital content to an individual human user. A LUI displays to a particular user, at any instant, a highly personalised display (usually in 3D); in which all of the constituent components are projected and arranged so as to afford optimal viewing from a fixed station or observation point. Lookable user interfaces 'know' they are being looked in the sense that they automatically adjust all of the visual aspects of the scene so as to project content in a personally optimised way towards a notionally fixed viewing location.

Here optimised is understood to refer (for example) to efficiency parameters such as the overall amount of information or content presented (or retrieved) by the user, per unit time, on the specific tasks that the LUI has been designed to facilitate.

Note here that LUIs are classified as PR systems (or perspective views) where the station point and viewing angle relative to the optical scene remains fixed. It is important to note that a LUI is envisaged to be a highly integrated and also immersive environment; and one which provides a rich background context for computing operations. We do anticipate therefore that most LUI's will inevitably be 3D representations in one form or another. Note however that some LUI structures may be semi-3D, or else purely 2D, and perhaps also adopt warped forms of representation—to produce 'optical' type distortions—and thus be similar to the 'Fishes and Scales' distortion techniques discussed above.

A LUI is designed in such a way that the whole optical environment accommodates itself around the users viewpoint. Within this framework; items automatically adopt locations, scales, and local reference angles such that they afford maximum visibility from the users vantage point (at any moment in time). Here the user does not have to move items directly or worry about his/her viewpoint, rather the LUI manages the view of the scene, to afford the maximum visibility of all components.

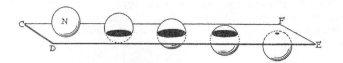

Users are then free to observe the content without worrying about the details of how to manoeuvre in order to look at the scene from an ideal location or direction. Vision is inherently selective and also relational in nature, and thus maintenance of the correct context is essential. LUIs are also designed to operate as context interfaces, and inherently provide distinct and fixed visual reference locations for interface components. Thus LUIs tend to solidify the impression of context in the users mind.

A key distinction between LUIs and other GUIs is that LUIs are designed in an overall sense with visual accessibility as the primary factor. Objects automatically maintain optimal distances and viewing angles; and in order to preserve context and so to foster the visual articulation of the overall field of view.

In addition to the 3D arrangement of the interface components, LUI interfaces will often employ 3D objects (and/or 3D optical illusions) to foster the rapid perception of the different items present in the display space. Note here that the LUI will automatically control the visible 3D shape, perspective arrangement, scale, geometrical position, and also the local reference angle of such 3D objects. The user may influence these parameters according to specific interactive selections, but the LUI always maintains overall control of these factors so as to be able to optimise the optical parameters of the scene as a whole.

How to Recognise a LUI

It is useful at this point to briefly summarise the differences between LUIs and other types of human computer interfaces such as GUI's, ZUIs (Zoomable User Interfaces) and also VR type systems. Firstly we note that LUIs are generally 3D user interfaces, but this is not thought to be one of the primary distinguishing factors because it is just possible that the principles of LUI design may be applied to a 2D user interface.

A LUI is different from other GUIs in the following three key respects. Firstly with a LUI the overall scene is automatically arranged in real time so as to afford the maximum degree of visual accessibility of digital content from a fixed point of view. It's a 'liquid space' with 'liquid objects'.

The photographs of space taken by our astronauts have been published all over the place. But the eye is a much more dynamic mechanism than any camera or pictures. It's a more exciting view in person than looking at the photographs. Of course, I personally am sick and tired of hearing people talk like that: I want to see it myself! - Burt Rutan

THE 4TH DIMENSION

Familiar both to the mind and eye are the space systems of two, and three dimensions; that is, lines planes, solids. Lines are bounded by points, and themselves bound planes; line-bound planes in turn bound solids. *What, then do solids bound?* Here is where the analogical rope vanishes from sight. If your answer is that a solid cannot be a boundary we part company. No argument of mine can convince you to the contrary. But if you are interested enough to ask, 'Well what do solids bound?'... the answer... 'Higher solids: four dimensional forms (invisible to sight) related to the solids we know as these are related to their bounding planes, as planes to their bounding lines.'

The existence of space of four dimensions can never be disproven by showing that it is absurd or inconsistent, for such is not the case... the expression *the fourth dimension*, offers a shock to the mind accustomed to practical handling of matter, because all of our experiences of measurement or dimensionality are ultimately founded upon matter possessing but three dimensions... our idea of space is partial... what we think of as space is more probably only some part of space made perceptible. It may be that our space bears a relation to space in its totality analogous to that which the images cast by a magic lantern bear to the wall on which these images are made to appear.

Understood in this way—space— is defined as new powers of movement in new media—and the expression *the fourth dimension of space* is understood to be defined as the power of movement in an unknown medium. [12] (1913)

Claude Bragdon

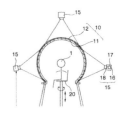

Here all components automatically adopt positions, distances, optical scales, and alignments; as necessary and in order to accommodate the user's personal view angle and field of view. Note that in a LUI items may sometimes adopt unrealistic optical scales—and also un-characteristic positions and alignments—one relative to another, for the purposes of optimal visual display. Secondly an overall visual context is created which allows objects to adopt fixed visual reference locations relative to one another, and which fosters the visual articulation and mapping of the visual field. In particular the use of a patterned background context to aid in the display of content is normal in a LUI. Generally some kind of hierarchical arrangement of content is also preferred with individual display units or cells being visually distinguishable. These cells are necessary in order to provide a filing and linking structure; which maps content into easily definable visual compartments.

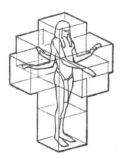

Finally LUIs often employ unrealistic and apparently distorted optical perspective views. The key aim here is to provide focus plus context views in order to expand the optical display space whilst simultaneously accommodating detailed views. Here multiple vanishing points are sometimes used both to frame individual visual fields; and to provide local visual structure and connecting 'paths'.

It is important to note that with LUIs multiple display spaces may be present in the same scene, and that each view may be entirely unconnected to the others in optical projective terms; apart from the fact that the different scenes fall within the same display window, and in a similar way to the multiple perspectives of 'cubist' art. A departure from optical reality is a strong feature of LUIs which in all cases favour clarity of visual structure over the ordinary rules of optics/graphics. Once again we reference the artist M.C.Escher's work here, and especially in terms of the creation of seemingly unrealistic views of reality, being views that nevertheless retain sufficient structure/coherence to be readily scanned, memorised (and internalised) into a consistent picture within the viewers mind.

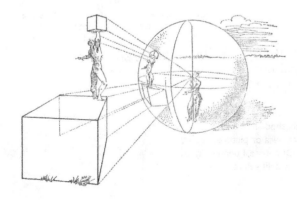

The goal of the LUI was succinctly put by a VR pioneer whose name escapes me:

And then the user interface itself disappears altogether and you have the illusion that you are interacting with the content itself.

Lookability Experiments

Following our (necessarily brief) discussion on the nature of perspective and on the topics of 3D depiction and the human perception of 3D; we now present the results of experimentation with the concept of the Lookable User Interface. Remember that we stated that it would not be possible to explore the design space of 3D user-interfaces comprehensively, due in part to the shear number of different kinds of 3D user interfaces that are possible. That is in fact the reason why we decided to use the theory of human perception as a starting point, in order to reduce the size of the design-space probed, whilst also giving us (hopefully) a head-start on where to look in the solution space itself.

My experiments began (back in the year 2001) with a visible "pole" of data, in the form of a 3D UI that we called the 'Data Stick'. Here rings of data (actually 2D/3D icons which represent documents or items of data) were stacked, one on top of another, all being at first invisible.

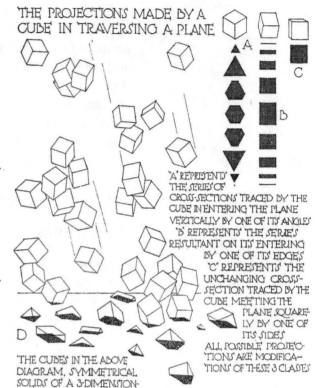

THE PROJECTIONS MADE BY A CUBE IN TRAVERSING A PLANE

'A' REPRESENTS THE SERIES OF CROSS-SECTIONS TRACED BY THE CUBE IN ENTERING THE PLANE VERTICALLY BY ONE OF ITS ANGLES 'B' REPRESENTS THE SERIES RESULTANT ON ITS ENTERING BY ONE OF ITS EDGES 'C' REPRESENTS THE UNCHANGING CROSS-SECTION TRACED BY THE CUBE MEETING THE PLANE SQUARE-LY BY ONE OF ITS SIDES ALL POSSIBLE PROJEC-TIONS ARE MODIFICA-TIONS OF THESE 3 CLASSES

THE CUBES IN THE ABOVE DIAGRAM, SYMMETRICAL SOLIDS OF A 3-DIMENSION-AL SPACE, TRACE VARIOUS EPHEMERAL AND CHANGING CROSS-SECTIONS IN THE PLANE 'D', A 2-SPACE, THE CHARACTER OF THE CROSS-SECTION BEING DETERMINED BY THE ANGLE AT WHICH THE CUBE MEETS THE PLANE.— IF THE CUBES BE TAKEN TO REPRESENT THE HIGHER SELVES OF INDIVIDUALS IN A HIGHER-SPACE WORLD, THE PLANE OUR PHENOMENAL WORLD, THE CROSS-SECTIONS WOULD THEN REPRESENT THE LOWER SPACE-ASPECTS OF THESE HIGHER SELVES — PERSONALITIES.

Next when the user moved his/her mouse over a region of the 'stick', the closest 'ring' becomes visible—including any and all contained data icons. Items on the visible ring could then be selected/rotated, whereupon the referenced data items are displayed; and exactly as happens when you click on a OSX Finder item. The Data Stick mouse controls this 'hide-show' visualisation technique, and proved to be a quick way to locate items from a data-set of around 50-500 items.

Next we experimented with a number of different curvilinear-shaped UI geometries. Most had vanishing points left and right as well as up and down and forward and backwards.

Our imagination just needs space. It's all it needs, that moment where you just sort of stare into the distance, where your brain gets to sort of somehow rise up. - Glen Hansard

One of the most feared expressions in modern times is 'The computer is down'. - N. Augustine

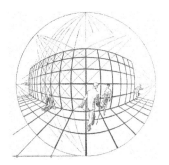

Thus the design experiments conformed to a form of 'curvilinear' perspective. Contained objects scaled themselves according to the momentary distance from each vanishing point; and objects either faced the station-point or else aligned themselves with the nadir of the rear vanishing point. Various animations and selections were possible with these UIs. We also tested the affects of different perspectives, horizons, station and vanishing points, background textures, colours, scales, icon-types etc, on scene 'lookability'. In particular, we noted that the curvilinear geometries do (apparently) magnify the user's perception—and memory—of on-screen item locations.

Spectasia

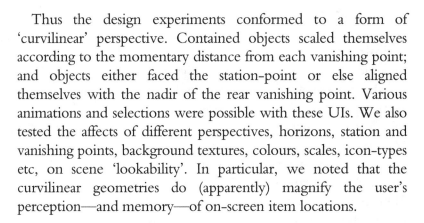

Spectasia is a design for a new class of 3-D Lookable User Interface which aims to enhance the information visualisation and retrieval capabilities of computer users in a wide range of circumstances. For example, we believe it can amplify the visual search, navigation and also selection capabilities of users when (for example) interacting with digital files. **Spectasia** employs a form of curvilinear perspective which is similar to an extremely wide-field view of a scene as projected by a fish-eye camera lens. We chose to use this particular form of perspective in order to provide an exaggerated impression of depth to the user, and also to provide an expanded representational 'space'. It is important to note that **Spectasia's** curvilinear scenes foster rapid visual articulation of a very wide 'field' of view. Here a large number of objects can be rapidly scanned, the impression of item location, and 3D—or depth—is a strong one.

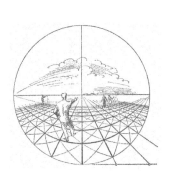

Spectasia's curvilinear scenes create an effective visual background context for objects to reside in. **Spectasia** employs curvilinear perspective to boost the visual accessibility of content. Here three vanishing points produce a smooth optical magnification continuum which creates an expanded representational space in which objects can reside. A smooth blending of focus plus context is produced, and optical zooming and panning operations are easy to achieve.

I think you always have to find where the boundary is in relation to the context in order to be able to kind of articulate how you want the space to interact with the viewer. - Richard Serra

Marshall McLuhan said: 'The Medium is the Message'.
What about: 'The Message is the Hyper-Thought'.

A key advantage is that users can focus their attention on the precise (relative) screen location of desired items with greater accuracy, immediacy, and also within a predictable time-scale (user-testing is required to validate these claims(s)). **Spectasia** is applicable in those situations in which a smooth blending of focus (i.e. projected visual detail) plus context (positional, ordinal and structural relations) is to be maintained during simulated optical zooming and panning operations.

The network of visual objects can be animated under user control to either bring new regions of the hierarchy into view and/or to bring 'distant' objects closer to the viewpoint.

Spectasia employs other presentation mechanisms—ranking along an axis, ranking along a radius, and drilling through icon classes—to allow other attributes of the data mountain to be examined. Where an array of displayed objects extends beyond the bounds of the display aperture, the projection may be visually animated or scrolled—laterally or in the orthogonal direction—to simulate optical panning/zooming. Simple to use on-screen navigation cursors, scroll position indicator objects and level indicators allow the user rapidly: to navigate and to browse efficiently, all types of content. **Spectasia** also includes a click-stream memory, 3D pin-markers, and an instant search utility plus a spotlight highlighting device.

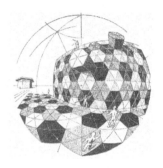

Spectasia is ideally suited to the analysis of the ontological features and/or the subsumptive relational aspects of content. **Spectasia** is applicable in a wide variety of information display scenarios, including hand-held devices, PCs, information kiosks and shopping terminals. **Spectasia** is serviceable wherever digital content is to be presented as an array of item choices and/or where product/item categories are to be browsed and/or navigated. It is applicable on different kinds of display systems, including those of either the 2-D or 3-D stereographic class.

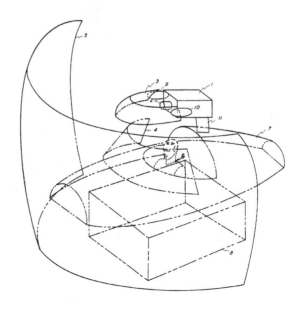

After 1980, you never heard reference to space again. Surface, the most convincing evidence of the descent into materialism, became the focus of design. Space disappeared. - Arthur Erickson

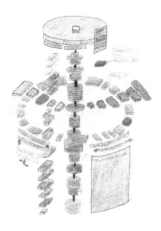

In this chapter we have explored a new theme in graphical user interface (GUI) design, named the Lookable User Interface (LUI). The success of the **Spectasia** user interface, in terms of providing wide-field overviews of, and rapid access to, digital content; points to the existence of a rich vein of design space for system designers who adopt the LUI approach. LUIs appear to solidify the impression, and memory of, on-screen item locations (one relative to another), and therefore operate as context interfaces. Benefits to users may include faster retrieval plus improved knowledge and memory of digital content.

Whilst LUIs are designed to visually adapt themselves to a single viewpoint, Personal Reality (PR) systems would address the broader aspects of how to create artificial realities which adapt to the users specific needs from *multiple points of view*. Note that a key goal of PR systems is the instantaneous optimisation of the '*lookablity*' of the scene, only now from multiple viewing angles and various graphical locations and over a period of time. A key premise here is PR systems are similar to VR systems in one respect, in that PR systems are explorable. These systems may include full-blown artificial worlds, and possibly also reality augmented systems. PR systems may contain multiple LUI devices to facilitate human-computer interaction. In this respect LUI systems would be sub-components or building blocks of larger and more complex PR systems.

Spectasia facilitates efficient navigation and effective 'way-finding'; and it is particularly useful for the rapid location/ selection of specific items from within data-mountains that contain 1000s of items. The provision of comprehensive overviews and/or improved explorative/selective freedom(s) are anticipated from such Personal Virtual Reality systems.

In conclusion, thats about it for our brief look at 3D user interfaces, and whilst this chapter might seem to be a little off-topic; and in relation to our central *freedom and ownership of thought*' theme; it isn't really. The question of how to provide rapid and efficient access to thoughts, ideas and data; is of central concern to all computer users.

Sometime in the future, science will be able to create realities that we can't even
begin to imagine. As we evolve, we'll be able to construct other information
systems that correspond to other realities, universes based on logic completely
different from ours and not based on space and time. - Robert Lanza

Spectasia (top) prototype running as 3-D 'finder' on an Apple Macintosh computer.
KeyMail (bottom) encrypted electronic mail system on an Apple Macintosh computer.

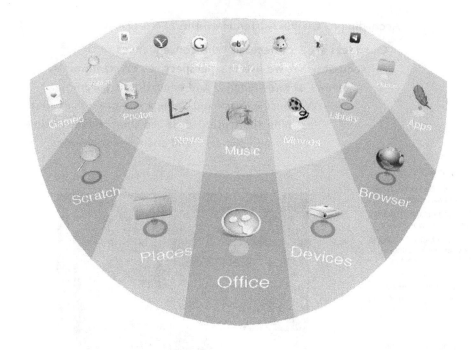

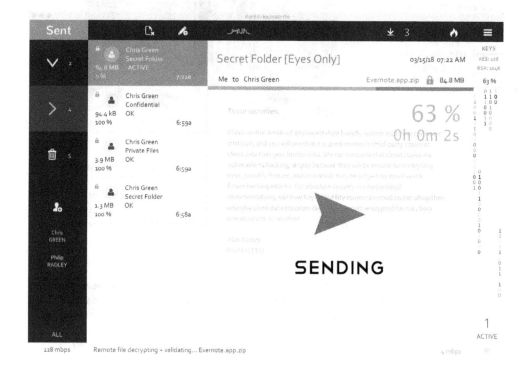

According to Claude Adrien Helvetius (1715-1771):

Our ideas are... of necessity the consequences of the
societies that we live in... perspectives or standpoints,
views of knowledge... and education is paramount!
We must unmask and debunk the prejudices that
hide the truth... ideas are the product of time
and society... and socially conditioned.

Top Hacks

- Kevin Mitnick - Broke into Nokia, Fujitsu and Motorola.
- Kevin Poulsen - Hacked phone of radio station, won Porche.
- Robert Tappan Morris - Created Morris worm which infected 6,000 major unix machines.
- Michael Calce - Shutdown Yahoo, Amazon and eBay etc.
- David L. Smith - Spread Meilssa worm virus - caused $80 million in damages.
- Sven Jaschan - Created the Netsky and Sasser worms.
- Adrian Lomo - Broke into major computer systems for fun (and turned in Bradley Manning).
- The Masters of Deception - group of hackers who broke into AT&T and cased havoc.
- Stephen Wozniak - Co-founder of Apple who bypassed the phone system by phreaking, made a (free) call to the Pope.
- Loyd Blankenship - Member of the Legion of Doom, wrote the Hacker Manifesto.

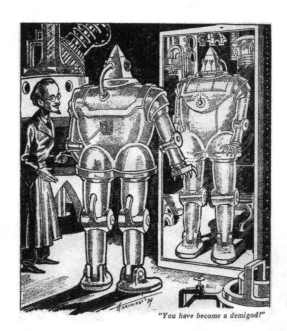

"You have become a demigod!"

You have become a demigod! - by Unknown (1930s)

It was the secrets of heaven and earth that I desired to learn; and whether it was the outward substance of things or the inner spirit of nature and the mysterious soul of man that occupied me, still my inquiries were directed to the metaphysical, or in its highest sense, the physical secrets of the world.

Mary Shelley, Frankenstein (1823)

We need, in effect, a machinery for screening machines... We must stop being afraid to exert systematic social control over technology... What is at issue is not discovery but diffusion, not inventions but application... In the West, the basic criterion for filtering out certain technological inventions and applying others remains economic profitability... One step in the right direction would be to create a technology ombudsmen—a public agency charged with receiving, investigating, and acting on complaints having to do with the irresponsible application of technology.

Alan Toffler [Future Shock] (1970)

Chapter Eight
Cyberspace

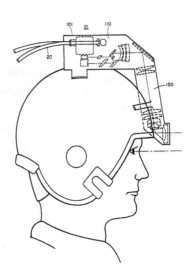

I N THE present chapter we explore the history and evolution of cyberspace; a metaphor for the nonphysical terrain created by computer systems.[17]

Identified here are prominent social/technical theories underlying cyberspace as a concept; whilst in the next chapter we propose a new form of cyberspace which provides for free, open and unrestricted access to the combined wealth of all human knowledge.

Finding an exact definition of the term cyberspace is difficult. Some people use it as a metaphor for the Internet; and others use it as an all-encompassing term for general networking and anything associated with digital media or the 'cloud'; still others use the term in a philosophical sense; as an alternative reality of some sort. Like physical space, cyberspace contains *objects, files, messages, graphics, and different modes of transportation and delivery*; but unlike in physical space, exploring cyberspace does not—normally—require any physical relocation or movement.

The term cyberspace was first used in fiction during the 1980s; but it was in William Gibson's (1948-) story *Burning Chrome*, in a July 1982 issue of *Omni* magazine, that the word first became predominantly associated with computer networks. Gibson developed the idea of cyberspace further in the 1984 novel *Neuromancer* and in his other writings.[1]

Later in a 2012 interview, Gibson said of cyberspace:

> Cyberspace is colonising what we used to think of as the real world... I think that our grandchildren will probably regard the distinction we make between what we call the real world and cyberspace, and what they think of simply as the world, as the quaintest and most incomprehensible thing about us.

---

[17] Cyberspace as a term has lost some of its earlier popularity; but it remains a useful and instructive concept as applied to networked computers in general.

Under an enlightened government, there develops a human type that is upright, courageous, frank and logical. A despotic government, in contrast, breeds men that are vile, without spirit or courage... and the difference is due to the different education under one or the other government type! - Claude Adrien Helvetius

This is just the beginning, the beginning of understanding that cyberspace has no limits, no boundaries.

Nicholas Negroponte

We will create a civilisation of the Mind in Cyberspace. May it be more humane and fair than the world your governments made before.

John Perry Barlow

Essentially, there's a universe inside your brain. The number of connections possible inside your brain is limitless. And as people have learned to have more managerial and direct creative access to their brains, they have also developed matrices or networks of people that communicate electronically. There are direct brain/computer link-ups.

In the information-communication civilisation of the 21st Century, creativity and mental excellence will become the ethical norm. The world will be too dynamic, complex, and diversified, too cross-linked by the global immediacies of modern (quantum) communication, for stability of thought or dependability of behaviour to be successful.

Timothy Leary

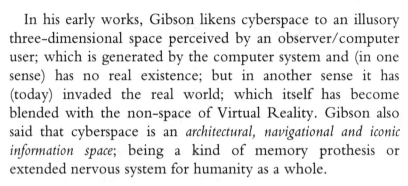

In his early works, Gibson likens cyberspace to an illusory three-dimensional space perceived by an observer/computer user; which is generated by the computer system and (in one sense) has no real existence; but in another sense it has (today) invaded the real world; which itself has become blended with the non-space of Virtual Reality. Gibson also said that cyberspace is an *architectural, navigational and iconic information space*; being a kind of memory prothesis or extended nervous system for humanity as a whole.

More generally, the term cyberspace has become a conventional means to describe anything associated with the Internet and Internet culture. Although normally understood as a technical infrastructure of connected computers; according to Chip Morningstar, cyberspace is defined more by social interactions. In this view, the computational medium of cyberspace is an augmentation of the ordinary communication channel(s) between people.

Whilst cyberspace should not be confused with the Internet, the term is often used to refer to objects and identities that exist largely within the communication network itself. Thus a website, for example, might be said to 'exist in cyberspace'. Cyberspace therefore refers not only to the content being presented to the 'surfer', but to the possibility of surfing among different sites, and with relationships between the user and the rest of the system.

Cyberspace creates the potential to encounter things previously *unknown and/or unexpected*; and/or to engage with *people/places/systems* that one had not previously been aware of, or could not find by any other method.

Another way to understand these terms, is that the Internet is a computer network; and cyberspace is that network visualised or conceptualised as a virtual space.

"There's something wrong with the stars," she breathed. "Look!"

Using these definitions, it would seem that they work together to create a whole new world, a vast system, and being one that we use to create an 'interface' to/with information.

Others have drawn attention to the ways in which cyberspace is similar to, or mirrors, reality; and especially in terms of social aspects of communication and social inter-relationships.

According to Kevin Robins:

> The problem of reality is always; social reality; the problem is always the difficulty or impossibility of coping with or recognising social reality, that is, human reality, the reality of other humans. A virtual world exists in, and in relation to, everyday life in the real world.[3]

Derived from a set of pre-existing cultural discourses, the *'imaginative mould'* of cyberspace substantially replicates a number of their characteristics and ideologies.

American counterculture exponents like Allen Ginsberg (1926-1997) and Timothy Leary (1920-1996) were among the first to extoll the potential of computers and computer networks for *individual empowerment, communication, and freedom of heart, soul and mind.* According to Douglas Rushkoff (1961-) for these men, computers and cyberspace were not about winning, but about meeting; and presented us with new opportunities to explore social relationships, and in spite of geographical and cultural difficulties [4]: cyberspace as a humanising medium.

Another 1960s counter-culture figure, William S. Burroughs (1914-1997) focussed on the darker potentials of cyberspace; and wrote: **are we being offered the chance to evolve, or merely being forced to adapt to a universe in which another directs our own consciousness.**[5]

Recognised are two distinct opinions. On the one hand, cyberspace is couched as a whole new realm of human possibility—and as a playground for us to explore reality/each-other.[6,7,8] Others see dangers and opportunities for control and dehumanisation in associated technologies; and which may be—in one way or another—inherent to cyberspace.[4,7,9,10]

Our cyberworld and cyberspace are infested with so many cyberscoundrels, cybercriminals, cybersluts and cyberpunks—that it is virtually impossible for the cybercops (cyberpolice) to catch or stop them using known cybertechniques and save the cyberphobia of millions of cybernauts, many of whom are cyberholics. - Tapan Bhattacharya (*The Shrinking Universe*)

At a minimum if we can just have enough distribution of clout in society so it isn't run by a tiny minority, then at the very least it gives us room to breath. - Jaron Lanier

Our wish is to explore the true nature of cyberspace.

In the present book we are concerned not with the low-level implementation details of the Internet/cyberspace. Instead we focus on the individual and social ramifications of computers; and concern ourselves with only those top-level design features that most affect the same. Nevertheless it is instructive to examine briefly the history and evolution of ideas related to, and which underly, the technical and conceptual infrastructure(s) that makes cyberspace possible.

Accordingly, we probe the history of computer networks...

Before we begin, it is worth noting that these ideas of cyberspace have strong links to notions of reality, and to *World Brains* and/or philosophies of collective thinking/perception; and related methodologies surrounding man's role, place or relationship to/with the universe. Cyberspace may be a new *universe of digitality,* but it is also strongly correlated with the real universe; in a variety of interesting and multifaceted ways.

In the first half of the 17th century, René Descartes proposed a forerunner to the modern concept of cyberspace; whereby he suggested that people may (possibly) be deceived by an evil demon who feeds them a false reality.

Later the idea of a '*brain in a vat*' was suggested and used in a variety of thought experiments. Imagined is that—by some means—a person's brain is removed from the body and suspended in a life-sustaining liquid; whilst its neurons are connected to a supercomputer which provides it with electrical impulses identical to those that the brain normally receives. The computer would then be simulating reality, including responses to the brains's own output; and the 'disembodied' brain would have normal conscious experiences about *events, objects and processes*, and (possibly) without any relation to the real world whatsoever.

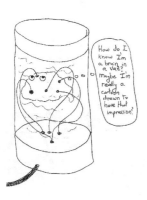

Does this imaginary '*disembodied brain*' sound familiar?

And so it might, because even though your brain is not physically inserted into the Internet, nevertheless humans do, in a like manner, perceive and respond to an unreal world; and in similar way(s) to what might happen in such an experiment.

Will networked, automated, artificial intelligence (AI) applications and robotic devices have displaced more jobs than have been created by 2025? According to a 2014 *Future of the Internet* survey of experts, half (48 %) of the respondents envision a future in which robots and digital agents have displaced significant numbers of blue and white-collar workers by 2025 (half agreed and half disagreed with the proposition).

Whether or not these ideas of an 'artificial reality' suggest superior/inferior mental abilities is open to question; but the related concept of (somehow) connecting many brains together, and in order to improve human intelligence, is a common one in works of fiction and non-fiction.

In the 1930s, futurist Herbert George Wells (1866-1946) wrote a book entitled *World Brain*; whereby he describes his vision of the World Brain; *a new, free, synthetic, authoritative, and permanent 'World Encyclopaedia';* that could help citizens make the best use of universally accessible information resources; and for the benefit of all mankind. According to H.G. Wells, this global entity would provide an improved educational system throughout the whole body of humanity. He said that the World Brain would be a sort of mental clearing house for the mind, a depot where knowledge and ideas are *received, sorted, digested, clarified and compared*; and it would have the form of a network whereby it is the **interconnectedness** that makes it a Brain.

In *World Brain* [1937]; Wells wrote:

> My particular line of country has always been generalisation of synthesis. I dislike isolated events and disconnected details. I really hate statements, views, prejudices and beliefs that jump at you suddenly out of mid-air. I like my world as coherent and consistent as possible... we do not want dictators, we do not want oligarchic parties or class to rule, we want a widespread world intelligencia conscious of itself... and... without a World Encyclopaedia to hold men's minds together in something like a common interpretation of reality, there is no hope whatever of anything but an accidental and transitory alleviation of any of our world troubles.[11]

Wells believed that technological advances such as microfilm could be used towards this end, so that: any student, in any part of the world, will be able to sit with his projector in his own study at his or her convenience to examine *any* book, *any* document, in an exact replica. Many people, including Brian R. Gaines (1938-) in his book *Convergence to the Information Highway,* see the World Wide Web as an extension of the World Brain; allowing individuals to connect and share information remotely.[12]

THE OBSERVERS   THE USERS   THE DESIGN

Sir Tim Berners-Lee said in 2013: 'a growing tide of surveillance and censorship now threatens the future of democracy. Bold steps are needed now to protect our fundamental rights to privacy and freedom of opinion and association online.' [gizmodo.com-01.12.2013]

These concepts surrounding the nature of human thinking, in fact relate to far older ideas; for example in the Indian *Upanishads* a four part description of the inner instrument of understanding is supplied. Stated is that the function of mind is *association and disassociation; synthesis and analysis;* whereby internal and external perceptions are evaluated.[13]

Firstly, by means of the **ego,** the self internalises the experiences of mind into oneself. Whereas the function of **reason** (logical, analytical thinking) is assertion or higher understanding; which is understood to be superior to mind and not merely a higher function—but a higher form of reality!

In this mystical view reason is as different from mind as mind is from body. It is through reason that man is part of the **cosmic reason** that is the determinate factor behind everything that was, is, happens or may come to be in the universe. Reason affirms or negates; and determines between truth and falsehood. Finally, by means of *apperception,* the mind unifies all experiences into a connected whole. Hence for all of the Indian schools of thought, man is a wayfarer (margayayin) with three basic 'ways' or paths identified; the *way of knowledge*; the *way of devotion*; and the *way of action*.

Using one or more of these life-paths, mankind is able to 'move' from the world of outward reality, to the inward realm of the human mind—or self—and vice-versa. Life is inwardness; which matter, composed purely of atoms, attains; leading to the world as we observe it. These ideas are related to the Indian concept of **Dharma**; meaning 'to hold', maintain, or 'keep'; concepts which in turn signify behaviours that are considered to be in accord with **rta**, the universal order that makes life and the universe possible/knowable.

The meaning of the term Dharma is heavily dependent on context; and in the earliest texts meant *cosmic law*; or the rules that created the universe from chaos. It is **the** process of the universe and man. Dharma *(logos, order and causality)* is also the highest reality, and a realisation of this fact is equivalent to salvation; and is related to knowing thyself or enlightenment.

All humans seek knowledge of *self, universe and reality*.

Under current statute, US government agencies such as the IRS, DHS, SEC and many others are allowed to access emails and other private communications older than 180 days. - Kevin Yoder

CYBERSPACE 189

Attempting to classify, record and define human conception(s) of reality has a long history. Ancient Indian and Chinese texts record different: *explanatory world-views, philosophies, ways of seeing, doing, being and thinking etc.* The Western traditions harp back to Plato and Aristotle who developed the most complete early occidental systems of thought; and with which to analyse, record and predict; natural events and human possibilities.

Man seeks the truth, and foreknowledge of the future; and because it would seem logical that once so-armed; he can live the good life. Often men sought to be given divine inspiration and/or answers to such questions; and (ultimately) wished to converse with, and/or obtain the advice of a God. In Ancient Greece these desires were met through the concept of the oracle; which referred to a person or agency considered to interface with a wise council, or give prophetic predictions, or have precognition of the future, and usually inspired by Gods.

In the OED, *oracle* is defined as:

> The instrumentality, agency, or medium, by which a god was supposed to speak or make known his will; the mouthpiece of the deity; the place or seat of such instrumentality, at which divine utterances were believed to be given... One who or that which expounds or interprets the will of God; a divine teacher. A person of great wisdom or knowledge, whose opinions or decisions are generally accepted; an authority reputed or affecting to be infallible.

These affectations and efforts are all indications of a primary impulse or attraction to knowledge. Man seeks to know himself and his place in the universe—and pursues related questions for knowledge and/or enlightenment. And many mysteries and/or profound unknowns arise when we consider: *mind versus world, free-will versus causality, change versus constancy, separateness of ego from universe, imagination/reality, life/death, conscious or unconscious, individual versus collective, inside/outside, foreground/background, space/time, freedom/slavery, structure/process, whole/part etc.*

Indeed life would seem to be positively bubbling over with questions, mystery and uncertainty; hence a corresponding desire for knowledge and to be freed from ignorance.

As with so many significant privacy violations of late by government agencies, from the NSA to the IRS, it's become clear that technology has far outpaced the law. Federal laws (USA) meant to protect our fourth Amendment right 'to secure in [our] persons, houses, papers and effects, against unreasonable search and seizure' do not adequately cover American's property on-line. - Kevin Yoder [2012]

NSA is searching *everything* now—in real time and without
suspicion—merely on the chance that it finds something of interest.

These questions are prefigured by the quest for a universal source of knowledge that occurred in the 18th century during the Enlightenment; whereupon (for example) the French philosopher Denis Diderot (1713-1784) and Jean le Rond d'Alembert (1717-1783) created the *Encyclopédie* or *Systematic Dictionary of the Sciences, Arts, and Crafts*; a type of general encyclopaedia published between 1751 and 1772; and which was a universal storehouse for all human knowledge.

Diderot stated that his *Encyclopédie* should:

> Encompass not only the fields already covered by the academies, but each and every branch of human knowledge... comprehensive knowledge will give 'the power to change men's common way of thinking'.

These are noble and worthy aims indeed; however Diderot's work on his *Encyclopédie* suffered from many obstacles. The project was mired in controversy from the beginning; and was suspended by the courts in 1752. Just as the second volume was completed; accusations arose, regarding seditious content, and concerning the editor's entries on religion and natural law. Diderot was detained and his house was searched for manuscripts and subsequent articles. Sadly, it would be 12 years, in 1772, before the subscribers received the final 28 folio volumes of the *Encyclopédie, ou dictionnaire raisonné des sciences, des arts et des métiers*.

In a way, the search for universal knowledge is underpinned by questions related to the nature of reality. How do I know that my internal view of reality is real? And we all see reality though different types of lenses. Science fiction writer Philip K.Dick (1928-1982) explored many of these same themes in his stories, and especially what makes us human and what is the nature of reality—and we shall examine his ideas later on.

In fact, scientific and fictional narratives have throughout time been intermeshed; and sometimes share a common route. For example 17th century French fabulist Jean de La Fontaine's (1621-1695) 12-volume *Fables* depicts many stories with Indian or Persian sources, and collected together, express an urge towards universalism in the form of catalogues and compendia.

Germany and Brazil have asked the UN General Assembly to adopt a draft resolution calling for the right to privacy in the digital age. The draft calls for an end to excessive electronic surveillance, noting that the illegal collection of personal data 'constitutes a highly intrusive act'. Brazil and Germany have both been angered by allegations of large-scale US surveillance. The allegations stem from revelations by US whistleblower Edward Snowden. - [bbc.co.uk - 01/01/2013]

If the government is correct that it can search our every communication, then there is little to prevent the NSA from converting the Internet into a tool of pervasive surveillance.

CYBERSPACE 191

Evident is a longstanding wish towards collectivism and/or union, and with respect to the combined thoughts of mankind. In a 2010 article entitled '*Conceptions of a Global Brain*'; published in a special issue on the *Global Brain* in the journal: *Technological Forecasting and Social Change*, Francis Heylighen (1960-) wrote:

> But evolution in the biosphere is followed by the emergence of the **noosphere**, the global network of thoughts, information and communication, and it is here that spiritual union will be achieved.

Earlier Jesuit priest Pierre Teilhard de Chardin (1881-1955) wrote:

> No one can deny that.... a world network of economic and psychic affiliations is being woven at ever increasing speed which envelops and constantly penetrates more deeply within each of us. With every day that passes it becomes a little more impossible for us to act or think otherwise than collectively.... we are faced with a harmonised collectivity of consciousness, the equivalent of a sort of super-consciousness. The idea is that the earth is becoming enclosed in a single thinking envelope, so as to form, functionally, no more than a single vast grain of thought on the cosmic scale.

The Global Brain is a metaphor for an emerging, collectively intelligent network that may be formed by all the people of the earth; together with the *computers, thoughts, knowledge and communication-links* that connect them together.

It is a vast, complex and self-organising system.

The idea for a Global Brain was first codified in 1935, by Belgian Paul Otlet (1868-1944), who developed a conception of a network that seems eerily prescient of the world-wide web:

> Man would no longer need documentation if he were assimilated into a being that has become omniscient, in the manner of God himself. To a less ultimate degree, a machinery would be created [that would register at a distance] everything in the universe, and everything of man, as it was produced. This would establish a moving image of the world, its memory, its true duplicate. From a distance, anyone would be able to read an excerpt, expanded and restricted to the desired subject, which would be projected onto an individual screen. In this way, anyone from his armchair will be able to contemplate creation, as a whole or in certain of its parts.[14]

Knowledge is to be coalesced/linked; and in accordance with our previous definition of a computer—*to arrange items clearly in one's mind*—thus forming a type of universal oracle.

THE US GOVERNMENT HAS BETRAYED THE INTERNET

Government and industry have betrayed the Internet, and us. By subverting the Internet at every level to make it a vast, multi-layered and robust surveillance infrastructure, the NSA has undermined a fundamental social contract. The companies that create and sell us our hardware and software, or the companies that host our data: we can no longer trust them to be ethical Internet stewards.

This is not the Internet the world needs, or the Internet its creators envisioned. We need to take it back. And by we, I mean the engineering community. Yes this is primarily a political problem, a policy that requires political intervention. But this is also an engineering problem, and there are several things engineers can—and should—do.

One, we need to expose. Two, we can design. We need to know exactly how the NSA and other agencies are subverting routers, switches, the Internet backbone, encryption technologies and cloud systems. Three, we can influence governance. The NSA's actions are legitimising the Internet abuses of China, Russia, Iran and others. We need to figure out new means of Internet governance, ones that makes it harder for powerful tech countries to monitor everything.

Has any mass surveillance country avoided becoming totalitarian?

[theguardian.com]

According to the New York Times, the NSA is searching the content of virtually every email that comes into or goes out of the United States without a warrant. To accomplish this astonishing invasion of Americans' privacy the NSA reportedly is making a copy of nearly every international email. It then searches that cloned data, keeping all of the emails containing certain keywords and deleting the rest, all in a matter of seconds. If you emailed a friend, family member or colleague overseas today (or if, from abroad, you emailed someone in the US), chances are that the NSA made a copy of that email and searched it for suspicious information.

Jumping backwards in time once-more to the late 19th century, William James (1842-1910) said that for thoughts to fuse together (within a mind), there must be some sort of medium; hence he postulated a stream of consciousness where:

> Every thought, dies away, and is replaced by another... the other knows its predecessor, and finding it warm, greets it saying 'Though art mine, and art the same self with me'.[15]

Implicit here is that thinking happens within an environment; and the same being one which supports the process, remembering terms and happenings, and also provides access by the thinker to contained knowledge. But what will be the nature of such an environment (or thought-space) for multiple brains? Or how can a new reality be constructed in such a manner that the three *ways* of man are facilitated, and in which *any and all thoughts* are free to work together for the benefit of man?

In 1945, Dr Vannevar Bush (1890-1974) had the answer; laid out in a 1945 article: *As we May Think*; published in *The Atlantic Monthly*.[16] His idea *(related-to/developed-from Emanuel Goldberg's 'microthoughts' concept)* was to make more accessible the bewildering storehouse of all human knowledge; and he suggested giving man access to, and command of, the '*inherited knowledge of the ages*'.[28]

Bush wrote:

> A record, if it is to be useful to science, must be continuously extended, it must be stored, and above all it must be consulted... our ineptitude in getting at the record is largely caused by the artificiality of systems of indexing... filed alphabetically or numerically (in subject form), information is found by tracing it from subclass to subclass... (therefore)... information can only be in one place! (unless duplicates are used)... Our mind does not work that way, it works by association.... (and thus) ...selection must be by association rather than by indexing.[16]

This problem of universal access to all human knowledge remains largely unsolved even in the present day. Bush places his finger right on the central issue of the Global Brain, as identified by Goldberg, Nelson, Veltman and others; or how to freely access anything; and when there are not really (in truth) any subject categories and everything is deeply connected together or *intertwingled*.[6,7,24,28]

Desired is free and open: assembly, plus access to, all thoughts.

Where will it end, political correctness, spying, the 'right to be forgotten'?
An Orwellian world? A 'Brave New World' of thought-police and/or thoughtlessness?

CYBERSPACE 193

Bush focussed on two areas: [A] manipulation of ideas and insertion into the record; and [B] extraction of items, whereby the prime actions are *selection/navigation/exploration*.

Identified here is not only the problem, but its solution:

Hypertext in Action

> When the user is building a TRAIL (of multiple items through the knowledge system), he names it and inserts the name in his code book; whereby... the items are permanently joined... thereafter, at any time, when one of these items is in view, the other can be instantly recalled merely by tapping a button below the corresponding code space... when numerous items have been thus joined together to form a trail, they can be reviewed in turn, rapidly or slowly, by deflecting a lever, rapidly or slowly, a lever like that used for turning the pages of a book; and it is exactly as though the physical items have been gathered together to form a new book... ANY ITEM CAN BE JOINED TOGETHER INTO NUMEROUS TRAILS. (He called this device a MEMEX) A memex is a device in which an individual stores all of his books, records and communications, and which is mechanised so that it may be consulted with exceeding speed and flexibility... it is an enlarged intimate supplement of his memory... Books of all sorts, pictures, periodicals, newspapers... are all dropped into place... Any given book of his library can then be called up and consulted with far greater facility than if it were taken from the shelf... As he has several projective positions, he can leave one item in position while he calls up another! He can add marginal notes and comments... and allowed is... associative indexing; whereby any item may be caused at will to select immediately and automatically another; this is the essential feature of a memex; tying two things together.[16]

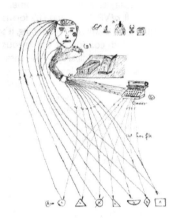

Vannevar Bush foresaw the basic features of the World Wide Web (and more)—and especially the basic functions of a hyperlink between items—way back in 1945! He predicted that whole new encyclopaedias would appear, ready-made with a mesh of associative trains running through them, ready to be dropped into the **Memex** and amplified.

The envisaged knowledge system, if it could be built, would be a true World Brain, or universal oracle.

> Presumably, man's spirit should be elevated if he can better review his <u>shady past</u> and analyse more completely and objectively his present problems... and because he has.. mechanised the record more fully. [16]

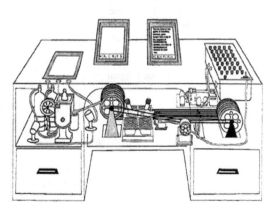

Skype audio and video chats, widely regarded as resistant to interception thanks to encryption, can be wiretapped by American intelligence agencies. [guardian.com]

COUNT THE WAYS

Given that we now know that the National Security Agency (NSA) has the ability to compromise some, if not all, of VPN, SSL, and TLS forms of data transmission hardening, it's worth considering the various vectors of technical and legal data-gathering that high-level adversaries in America and Britain (and likely other countries, at least in the 'Five Eyes' group of anglophone allies) are likely using in parallel to go after a given target.

So far, the possibilities include:

I. A company volunteers to help (and gets paid for it)

II. Spies copy the traffic directly off the fibre

III. A company complies under legal duress

IV. Spies infiltrate a company

V. Spies coerce upstream companies to weaken crypto in their products/install backdoors

VI. Spies brute force the crypto

VII. Spies compromise a digital certificate

VIII. Spies hack a target computer directly, stealing keys and/or data through sabotage

Jules Henri Poincaré (1854-1912) said that the question is (always) not 'what is the answer' but 'what is the question'. It does seem that Bush's **Memex** would help man to ask the right questions with respect to anything whatsoever—and in turn rapidly and efficiently find answers. Bush later in the 1950s became director of the *Information Processing Techniques Office* of the U.S. *Defence Department's Advanced Research Projects Agency* (**ARPA**); with hundreds of scientists effectively working under his direction. Although Bush did make attempts to actually build his **Memex** system; unfortunately these ideas were 30 years ahead of their time; and were left to others to develop.

Wells, Otlet, and Bush had clearly foreseen the future form of a possible Internet/Cyberspace; and we should not forget these original visions; and in particular because of the humanistic motivations behind such plans. These ideas were not lost, but would have to wait until the arrival of the desktop computer to have even a possibility of being realised.

Dr J.C.R Licklider (1915-1990) in his seminal 1960 paper *Man-Machine Symbiosis,* outlined the need for simpler interaction between computers and computer users.[17] He was focussed on use of information technology to <u>augment</u> human intelligence; and because he believed that most of the tasks of a human thinker were pre-occupation with: *clerical or mechanical searching, collocating, calculating, plotting, transforming, and preparing the way for a decision of logical insight.* He believed that these processes could be made automatic.

Licklider proposed that **computers will do the routinisable work that must be done to prepare the way for insights and decisions;** and so was an early believer in what is sometimes called *Intelligence Amplification.* This all sounds very straight-forward today, but remember his ideas were proposed a decade before personal computers, and some 30 years before the World Wide Web communications explosion of the 1990s.

In October 1962, Licklider was appointed head of the *Information Processing Office* (**IPTO**) at **DARPA**, then called **ARPA**; and played a seminal role in conceiving of, and funding, early network research, most notably the **ARPAnet.**

We are now aware of a terrifying reality—that governments don't necessarily need intermediaries like Facebook, Google, and Microsoft to get our data. They can intercept it over undersea cables, through secret court orders, and through intelligence sharing.

Privacy International

Licklider formulated the initial ideas of a global computer network (beginning in August 1962), and recorded in a series of memos discussing the *Intergalactic Computer Network* concept.

Many of these Global Brain ideas are related to the work of Professor Norbert Wiener (1894-1964); who is the originator of cybernetics, which is a formalisation of the notion of feedback. Cybernetics is a transdisciplinary approach to exploring regularity systems, their structures, constraints and possibilities. It is applied when a system is involved in a closed signalling loop, whereby actions generated by the system generates some change in the environment and that change is reflected in the system in some manner.[19,20]

Wiener's work is connected to the idea of a Global Brain in several ways; but mainly because it (in an analogous way) would connect many inputs/outputs of computer users together; and allow everyone to affect, and be affected by, an evolving consensus. Everyone could see everyone else's open-thoughts; and the ways that these are interrelated. Put simply, the Global Brain could regulate itself, because it 'knows' what itself (the whole of humanity) is thinking and/or doing.

Perhaps the greatest pioneer of computing is Dr Douglas Engelbart (1925-2013); who was an American engineer and inventor. In the 1950s, he decided that instead of having a steady job, he would focus on making the world a better place to live in. His idea was to use networks of computers to help mankind cope with the world's increasingly urgent and complex problems; and he believed that enabling all of the people on the planet to solve important problems was key (the sooner the better). Accordingly, because of their efficiency of operation in relation to *recognising and delineating problems, organising ideas, and arranging associated problem elements together*; Engelbart believed that computers were the pre-eminent vehicle for dramatically improving the world.

He envisioned intellectual workers sitting at display 'working stations', flying through information spaces, and harnessing their collective intellectual capacity to solve key problems together, faster and in much more powerful ways.[18]

SURVEILLANCE

U.S. intelligence officials have declassified a secret court opinion that both chastises the National Security Agency for misleading the court and highlights an eavesdropping program in which authorities have direct access to 'upstream' internet communications.

Today's startling revelation was outlined in a 2011 opinion by Judge John D. Bates, then the chief judge of the Foreign Intelligence Surveillance Court; a secret tribunal that often rubber-stamps government surveillance requests in classified rulings.

Earlier in the opinion, Bates wrote, 'the government has now advised the Court that the volume and nature of the information it has been collecting is fundamentally different from what the court had been led to believe.'

Sen. Ron Wyden (D-Oregon) and Sen. Mark Udall (D-Colorado), the leading Congressional critics of the NSA and its surveillance tactics, have said of the surveillance: 'We believe Americans should know that this confirmation is just the tip of a larger iceberg.'

Mark Rumold, a staff attorney with the Electronic Frontier Foundation —which fought to declassify the ruling—said in a telephone interview today, 'the opinion basically found that the government's surveillance by sitting on the wires of providers was unconstitutional.'

David Kravets

The National Security Agency (NSA) and its British counterpart have successfully defeated encryption technologies used by a broad swath of online services, including those provided by Google, Facebook, Microsoft, and Yahoo; according to new reports published by *The New York Times*, *Pro Publica*, and *The Guardian*. The revelations, which include backdoors built into some technologies, raise troubling questions about the security that hundreds of millions of people rely on to keep their most intimate and business-sensitive secrets private in an increasingly networked world.

Under Engelbart's guidance, the *Augmentation Research Centre* (ARC) developed, located at the *Stanford Research Institute* (SRI), with funding primarily from the *Defence Advanced Research Project Agency* (DARPA); and with the aim to develop the *oN Line System* (NLS) which was a revolutionary computer collaboration system designed around Engelbart's ideas.

The NLS demonstrated numerous technologies, most of which are today in widespread use; including the computer mouse, bitmapped screens, and hypertext; all of which were seen at the so-called *Mother of All Demos* in 1968. [See YouTube]

Engelbart possessed a clear vision for how computers should develop. He reasoned that the state of our current technology controls our ability to manipulate information, and that fact in turn will control our ability to develop new, improved technologies. Engelbart set himself to the revolutionary task of developing computer-based technologies for manipulating information directly, and also to improve individual and group processes for knowledge-work. Despite primitive components by today's standards; many of which Engelbart invented for himself *(such as the mouse and the interactive display)*; he succeeded in demonstrating the validity of his overall vision of a connected world. But his research funding was cruelly shut-off; and although he did continue on his own, many of his researchers left and Doug himself fell into relative obscurity.

Over the next two decades the microchip and personal computer arrived, and a decentralised vision of the Internet as a computing medium developed. Engelbart's stamp is nevertheless very much present on all modern systems. His inventions include: *the mouse, hypertext, collaborative tools, and precursors to the GUI.* Begging the reader's pardon; we shall now skip-over the next 20 years of computing history; and because this territory has been adequately covered elsewhere.[21,22,23] In any case the topic of the present book is mind-expanding technologies; hence we restrict ourselves to key milestones.

In the 1990s a new era of computer interconnectivity and satellite communications dawned. Might we at last see a World Brain as envisaged by Engelbart, Otlet and Wells?

Today, there are four basic places where most people's email can be compromised: On your device(s), On the networks, On the server(s), On your recipient's device(s).

In cyberspace, we meet other humans and see/read their thoughts—just like in the
real world; and people agree/disagree/argue—just like in the real world.

CYBERSPACE   197

Perhaps not completely; but something did arrive.

In December 1990, Sir Tim Burners-Lee built what most
came to see as the first World Brain; whilst working at the
European Centre For Nuclear Research (**CERN**). The *World Wide
Web* (or 'Web') is a system of interlinked hypertext
documents that are accessed via the Internet. Using a web-
browser, users can view web pages that contain: *text, images,
videos etc; and navigate them using hyperlinks.* People and
organisations could then create their own web-pages; and
'serve' information in a user-friendly format to people all
around the world. Although the Web enjoys unparalleled
popularity and success right down to the present day; many
pioneers and experts have criticised the basic design structure
of this system and highlighted its tremendous shortcomings.

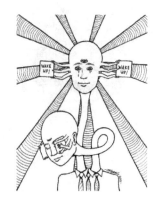

Perhaps the most vocal critic of the Web is Dr Theodor
Holm Nelson (1937-); who is the computer visionary who first
coined the terms hypertext and hypermedia in 1963. His ideas
run at a tangent to, and in some ways contradict the notion of
the World Wide Web as developed by Tim Berners-Lee. It is
worth looking at Nelson's ideas in detail; and because it seems
that his original vision for what became the Web—which
originates from him as much as anyone else—is only partially
fulfilled; and in fact his ideas point to a far superior and more
functionally sophisticated hypermedia filled world.

It is difficult to address adequately the all-encompassing
nature of Ted Nelson's vision; and because he disagrees with
so many of the basic concepts of computing that other
computer scientists generally agree on. Let us start with HTML
documents; which are the basic data-units of the Web; Nelson
says that they are 'rubbish' and simply virgin characters
scrambled by markup. We need a few pages of
explanation, and in order to understand this
statement. Nelson's vision of the web is a far larger,
richer, and more interconnected one; but in some
senses simpler. His concept is of a true Global Brain;
whereby emphasis is placed on the *accessibility, free
assembly and open publication of all knowledge.*

'NSA-led panel says theres no alternative to widespread NSA data collection' -
Gizmodo.com January 17th 2015. Reported was the NSA self-justification for its activities.
However oppressors/dictators throughout history have always justified their actions by a
supposed lack of alternatives, and/or by falsely blaming the victims and/or circumstances.

Nelson would re-design the current Web from scratch. He starts with a clean data structure; with which you can do much more. He says that the original idea of hypertext (his own concept) consisted of a whole suite of ideas, and provided user freedom/capability to do a lot more; and specifically included publication mechanisms. Crucially, needed are two way connections; whereby a 'forward' link not only moves you from one item to another; but 'backward' links allow you to see everywhere in the network where an item is used/ referenced. Also he has two types of links, a basic link, and a *transclusion*; which shows you an item's original 'context'.

Multiple overlaid links, or omni-links; would be allowed, whereby one item could be linked to many other items; and thus many *named-links* can be overlaid one on top of another.

Before getting into Nelson's ideas in detail; it is interesting to look at motivations and where these ideas come from. To begin with Nelson says that most of the current *Web, Libraries, books, journals etc,* are all arranged into hierarchies; whereby *subject areas, websites, topics, classes, titles, bibliographies etc;* are organised into (basically) <u>*opaque*</u> *piles of stuff.* Nelson (rhetorically) asks if this is the correct structure—or in other words is knowledge fundamentally structured like this; or is it a human projected/imposed structure. He comes to the latter conclusion; and claims that all data/information/knowledge (in general) has no structure whatsoever! None at all. Rather *parallel cross-connections, random and unstructured connections, relations which go in all directions, causations, jumping and branching points;* interpenetrate the entire corpus of human knowledge; and in every way imaginable.[24,25,26]

Thus paper documents have an intrinsic parallelism; and document boundaries (in fact **all** boundaries between information units) are arbitrary; hence everything may be potentially connected to everything else; and in every way imaginable. The question then becomes how to manage the cross-connections. This is the model for everything, and hence for all knowledge, according to Nelson.

Documents have deep and parallel structure, endlessly and without limit.

Why do we have thoughts in any case; fundamentally because they are for personal and private use; what is the alternative—automatons who are told what to think, say and do.

CYBERSPACE 199

Within such a scheme, we have only two types of structural connection. Links connect things together that are basically the same *(units of knowledge in the same context)*. Whereas a transclusion connects between things that are basically different *(same content re-used in different contexts)*.

For Nelson, it is the complexity of links that is the main problem with hypertext as implemented in the World Wide Web. Here links are unmanageable, hidden in amongst the documents; and so cannot be removed from the information. Currently on the Web, one cannot see where any item of knowledge is used across the network as whole; hence we need search engines like **Google** to attempt to remedy (poorly) this situation. **Google** is bolted on to the HTML based Web; and in an attempt to fix a fundamentally broken data structure!

According to Nelson, this situation is a continuation of a movement whereby the computer is dumbed-down to simulate paper. Here the filing structure adopted by **IBM/Apple** forced a false (arbitrary) file plus directory structure onto information; and remade the open world (of the real); in terms of black boxes or _opaque_ hidey-holes for information (**silos**). Thus even locally, information cannot be searched (easily) across different files; and because the (lumped) information is invisible and unsearchable —for non-geeks—and especially for networked users.

Nelson's criticism goes still further, because he also says that in the graphical user interface (GUI) we see a copying of the paper metaphor; whereby (in fact) many other (superior) forms of GUI are possible. We do not have a very good metaphor here (paper), and with word processing programs, because side-notes are not allowed, and copy and paste is not properly implemented. But it is largely the underlying information structure which severely limits capabilities at the level of the user interface. And even if this were not so, who says that knowledge should be represented in a rectangle. Rather according to Nelson, there is a deep structure to knowledge, with all kinds of *parallel-linkages* and *information-shapes* of every type present; and in every way imaginable.

Undoubtably Nelson is correct; and what we have today is a knowledge lock-down; or **_silos of invisible/lost/lonely thoughts_**.

What happens when a secret U.S. court allows the NSA access to a massive pipeline of U.S. phone call metadata, along with strict rules on how the spy agency can use the information? The NSA promptly violated those rules—'since the earliest days' of the program's 2006 inception—carrying out thousands of inquiries on phone numbers without any of the court-ordered screening designed to protect Americans from surveillance.

Why do we not (likewise) start dishing out truth serums in schools,
and so that we can 'catch' undesirable thoughts just as they begin to emerge?

WEAPONISED INTERNET

The internet backbone—the infrastructure of networks upon which internet traffic travels—went from being a passive infrastructure for communication to an active weapon for attacks.

According to revelations about the QUANTUM program, the NSA can 'shoot' (their words) an exploit at any target it desires as his or her traffic passes across the backbone. It appears that the NSA and GCHQ were the first to turn the internet backbone into a weapon; absent Snowdens of their own, other countries may do the same and then say, 'It wasn't us. And even if it was, you started it.'

If the NSA can hack Petrobras, the Russians can justify attacking Exxon/Mobil. If GCHQ can hack Belgacom to enable covert wiretaps, France can do the same to AT&T. If the Canadians target the Brazilian Ministry of Mines and Energy, the Chinese can target the U.S. Department of the Interior. We now live in a world where, if we are lucky, our attackers may be every country our traffic passes through except our own.

Which means the rest of us—and especially any company or individual whose operations are economically or politically significant—are now targets. All clear text traffic is not just information being sent from sender to receiver, but is a possible attack vector.

Nicholas Weaver
[wired.com - 01/01/2013]

Nelson says that software is a branch of cinema; whereby events on a screen: **affect the heart and minds of the viewer!** Unification and clarification of what the user does, is what's important! If these ideas do seem a little disconcerting, it is only because the reader is so used to seeing the computing universe in terms of rectangles, files, one-way (singular) links and a so-called networked system that wholly lacks context. Currently the vast interconnectedness of everything to everything else is simply not represented; hence it is impossible to visualise and explore all data/thought atoms *(see Nelson's own Xanadu project for a description of his vision [25,26])*.

What we take away from our discussion of Ted Nelson's work is overwhelming *(in terms of potential impact on the world's thoughts)*; because it becomes obvious that the World Wide Web, and every other large-scale networked system, one and all, suffer from a fundamentally crippled design methodology. The problem is clearly one whereby our current systems do not reflect the structure of knowledge itself (it has none!); and as a result do not enable users to likewise explore the local structure(s) for themselves. In Nelson's ideal system we would be able to search a term such as 'computer' and see a categorised listing of links to every: *quotation and article, book, web page etc*; containing this phrase; and link back to the original sources of every quotation, complete with *links, annotations, comments and guiding markers* to help us to explore the term; as it is used throughout the world knowledge system (like a universal linked/structured 'Hashtag').

In Nelson's system anyone may publish anything to be viewed/edited/annotated by all; and it is a system of constant revision; whereby all past edits are saved and truly available for examination/correction (unlike **Wikipedia**). Units of information are not saved all over the place *(logically if not in storage terms—for an atomic network)*; but rather there is just one (original source) copy of each data atom; which is served/implanted into any documents that may use this item. Much disc-drive space is saved as a result; and electricity is conserved, and the item's author may be paid each time his copyrighted information is used via a micro-payments system.

These ideas go right to the heart of key social problem(s) of today; and with respect to cloud(s)/centralisation-of-data.

One of the original architects of the Internet wants to remind us that privacy is a relatively new concept. 'Privacy is something which has emerged out of the urban boom coming from the industrial revolution,' said Google's Chief Internet Evangelist and a lead engineer on the Army's early 1970's Internet prototype, ARPANET. As a result, 'privacy may actually be an anomaly," he told a gathering of the Federal Trade Commission. [THE AUTHOR DISAGREES!]

Why on earth would anyone want to see someone else's thoughts,
if it was not for the express purpose of controlling their thoughts (and actions).

CYBERSPACE 201

Modern Systems

In the book *Who Owns the Future,* Jaron Lanier (1960-) posits that the middle class are becoming disenfranchised from online economies. According to this view; power is increasingly focussed on the owners of the largest server computers—companies he calls the **Siren Servers**. According to Lanier unless something is done to stop it, such a power imbalance will result in misery for countless millions. Furthermore a wealth-concentrated and top-heavy economy cannot be sustained, and is destined to collapse eventually.[27]

Lanier says that certain companies convince users to give away valuable information about themselves in exchange for free services—hence these same companies accrue large amounts of useful data at virtually no cost. He claims that popular digital designs do not treat people as being 'special enough'. People are treated as small elements in a bigger information machine, when in fact people are the *only* sources or destinations of information —or indeed of any meaning to the machine at all.

In *Who Owns the Future,* Lanier says:

> At the height of its power, the photography company Kodak employed more than 140,000 people and was worth $28 billion. Today it is bankrupt, and the new face of digital photography is Instagram. When it was sold for a billion dollars in 2012, Instagram employed only 13 people. Instagram isn't worth a billion dollars because those thirteen people are extraordinary. Instead its value comes from the millions of users who contribute to their network without being paid for it. Networks need a great number of people to participate in them to generate significant value. That has the effect of centralising wealth and power and limiting overall growth... in all these cases, we see the phenomenon of power and money becoming centralised around people who operate the most central computers, undervaluing everyone else... and... we need to monetise more of what's valuable from (and for) ordinary people... (and reward the currently uncompensated)... we're setting up a situation where better technology in the long term means more unemployment... instead we should seek a future where people will do well, without loosing liberty, even as technology gets much, much better.[27]

According to Lanier: when we make our world more efficient through use of digital networks, that should make our economy grow, not shrink.[27] One wonders if anyone (influential) is listening.

MISLEADING CLAIMS

Time and again we've seen the NSA defend its vast surveillance apparatus by invoking the spectre of terrorism, discussing its spying powers as a method to keep America safe. Yet, the truth is that counterterrorism is only a fraction of their far broader authority to seek 'foreign intelligence information,' a menacing sounding term that actually encapsulates all sorts of innocuous, everyday conversation. The *New York Times* reported, 'the (leaked) documents make clear, that the focus on counterterrorism is a misleadingly narrow sales pitch for an agency with an almost unlimited agenda.'

Under the Foreign Intelligence Surveillance Act, NSA is given a mandate for collecting 'foreign intelligence information' but this is not a very substantive limitation, and certainly does not restrict the NSA to counterterrorism—rather, it is defined to include 'information with respect to a foreign power ... that relates to ... the conduct of the foreign affairs of the United States.' Read that carefully for a minute. Anything 'that relates to the foreign affairs of the United States.' Interpreted broadly, this can be political news, anything about economics, it doesn't even have to involve a crime— basically anything besides the weather. Indeed, given the government penchant for warping and distorting the definitions of words in secret, we wouldn't be surprised if the government would argue that weather could fall under the umbrella of 'intelligence' too.

Trevor Timm [November 2013]

'The question of "who is it that's got the off switch for our connectivity" started to be asked because of Egypt,' said Berners-Lee. 'It's a rather obvious thing you can see happening, and a country that does that doesn't get very far. Turning off the Internet got the youths onto the streets because that's what they had left to do. So blocking of the Internet is kind of obvious.' But spying is this insidious form, because of its chilling effect if you feel someone's looking over your shoulder, there's all kinds of things you will not do... [You're not going to be] able to use facilities because of nameless fear.' - Tim Berners-Lee [arstechnica.com - 22/11/2013]

What's next—mind control technology? Actually the NSA has already tried that in the 1960s by experimenting with Acid (LSD) on soldiers.

INTERNET FREEDOM

Despite the air of pessimism surrounding the Web Index 2013 launch in light of the state spying controversies, Berners-Lee remained positive about the many good things that are happening around the globe. According to the report, the Internet remains vital in catalysing citizen action and real world change. Despite the fact that 30 percent of nations engage in targeted Web censorship and 'moderate to extensive blocking or filtering of politically sensitive content', the Web and social media played a big role in 'public mobilisation' in 80 percent of nations.

'This is not being spearheaded by political parties and NGOs', said Anne Jellema, CEO of the World Wide Web Foundation. 'It's spontaneous and grassroots action driven by social media.'

'I am optimistic', said Berners-Lee. 'I think the people will win. I have faith in people and humanity as a whole. There's going to be some push back, but change will come in lots of different ways—from activism, but also UN resolutions. Also from within government. There are people that care about this stuff.'

Lanier posits that the idea that information should be free is idealistic, and understandably popular; but information wouldn't need to be free if no one were impoverished! He predicts that a new wealthier middle-class could emerge, and a more genuine growing digital economy come about, if we could break out of the 'free information' ideas and implement a universal micropayment system.

Lanier supports Nelson's view of empowering the user through a properly implemented (two-way linked) hypermedia system; whereby information is truly de-centralised; preventing companies like Google from monopolising access to the world's information. When information *itself knows* where it is used within the global network; then there is no need for search engines (or, by and large, as we shall see, central servers); because it is people themselves who shall *categorise*, *organise* and *annotate* the information in such a way that it may be easily found, accessed and re-used etc. Other experts such as Kim Veltman argue for new ontologies similar to those described by Nelson; and there can be no doubt that such a system could go a long way in making our thoughts more *open, accessible and freely available.*

Our discussion has focussed on the creation of a Global Brain or world information library; but of-course there are many systems and 'Apps' with a narrower design remit; which are increasingly used on mobile devices. Not every system may need to have a full implementation of Ted Nelson's global hypermedia network. But such a network can nevertheless be the *communication backbone* for all the world's information/thoughts.

Especially prescient today are the problems of personal and organisational data security. On an almost daily basis we here reports of governmental and corporate vulnerabilities, break-ins and instances of stolen data. And government spying on citizens is now common. Debates are raging around many of these vital issues, which also involve legal points and problems of an ethical nature.

Considering what is at stake (civilisation); at least we are living in exciting times!

R. CRUMB '77

The NSA reportedly infected 50,000 computer networks worldwide with malicious software with the sole aim of harvesting sensitive information it wasn't privy to, which is basically what you'd call textbook spy work in the digital age, from an agency tasked with spying. [techcrunch - 23/11/2013]

Who knew that the Internet—a land of free-opinions—
would become *the* battleground for freedom-of-expression.

CYBERSPACE   203

Here we take a rather simplistic top-level view of computer networking; recommending that an important subset of these problems can be addressed by looking at personal data and adopting a straight-forward definition of the self and considering the resulting rights and capabilities that necessarily follow.

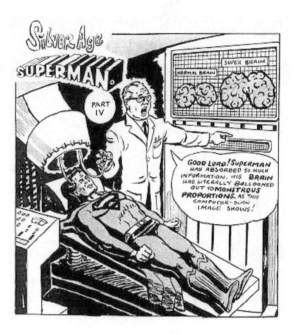

One example of system designers ignoring the individual's perspective, is that many application developers fail to consider that data is 'designed' at-all, and thus do not consider it in a wide enough context. For example there are no universal data types and/or effective data exchange mechanisms between different systems such as: *email, social networks,* and/or on devices such as*: TV, mobile, computer, telephone, consoles etc.* Non whatsoever—and because there is no data-layer for the Internet! [XML and semantic-web notwithstanding]

We surmise that smaller 'App' designers are using standard 'project based' design methods (and perspectives) such as the Unified Modelling Language (UML). So they focus on task and business specific system requirements. Such an approach characterises a standard system user in a narrow sense, and as a result, programmers design **information silos** without thinking of the broader needs of the self. Along the way a very narrow, localised, view of digital content wins; in terms of *data lifetimes, security, portability and accessibility.* As for the large system designers working for the server farm giants, I leave it to you to judge *their* motives. But it could be that people may soon tire of the inefficiency of central systems, and vote with their mice, signing up to systems that 'ask the right questions' (in Wiener's sense); and with respect to self.

Consideration of 'self-centric' data is an ignored solution, specifically to the problems created when taking a centralised approach to computer system design. Ignored are the needs of the individual; in terms of providing easy and open publication, and limitless preservation and/or transfer of thoughts/data.

PRIVACY RIGHTS

Given the apparent prevalence of this view (pro-spying) among the US intelligence community, today's new Report and Recommendations of the President's Review Group on Intelligence and Communications Technologies— authored by a number of insider establishment figures—comes as something of a surprise.

'There are sound, indeed, compelling reasons to treat the citizens of other nations with dignity and respect,' the report says in an entire chapter devoted to surveillance of non-US persons. 'Perhaps most important, however, is the simple and fundamental issue of respect for personal privacy and human dignity—wherever people may reside.'

Nate Anderson
[arstechnica.com - 18.12.2014]

As a key part of a campaign to embed encryption software that it could crack into widely used computer products, the U.S. National Security Agency arranged a secret $10 million contract with RSA, one of the most influential firms in the computer security industry, Reuters has learned. Documents leaked by former NSA contractor Edward Snowden show that the NSA created and promulgated a flawed formula for generating random numbers to create a 'back door' in encryption products, the New York Times reported in September 2013. - San Francisco (Reuters)

It's a fact that many developers lock data into information silos. However I believe that people are increasingly finding personal data lock-ins and/or personal data spying; <u>untenable</u>. Individuals also spend allot of time outside of any one application, network or system; and unfortunately as a result Apps offer a very narrow range of functionality. Who considers the broader needs of the person at the centre of all the Apps and networks? And who looks after your data in an era of multiple 'clouds'? What are your rights if the App looses and/or corrupts your data? We can conclude that *freedom, ownership* and *equality of thoughts/data* are vital aspects of our primary problem.

Technology companies act as if your data/thoughts is/are theirs. They routinely search emails, social network posts and tweets, for example, and throw task 'relevant' adverts at you. Also companies like **Apple** and **Amazon** seem to think that even once you have paid for data (songs, books); that they can later make changes to it (i.e. either delete data or change the content and copyright notices etc). And this happens even when the data has been transferred to a portable player such as an **iPad** or **Kindle**. People are increasingly outraged by such incidents, and rightly so. Another example is a **Facebook** post. Where once-upon-a-time the Internet was a medium of free expression, now people are routinely reported to the police for relatively minor acts of self expression and/or for voicing opinions. Plus employers and people in authority routinely scan posts also. It all seems a bit too much like *1984*. Overall, it is obvious that we now have a severe problem when it comes to *avoidance of big-brother spying, censorship and data/thought ownership.*

Another issue relates to the way that individuals relate to others in the real world. One can *give, lend, show or sell* real-world objects freely, without fear that they will be intercepted and often without anyone's knowledge. Is this not a fundamental human right and need, to perform certain low-level human-human transaction(s) *without being spied upon?*

LEARN TO PROGRAM

Berners-Lee suggested that empowerment should be facilitated by the destruction of the gulf that exists between the technology world and the policy world—our technology pioneers should not be afraid to engage in political matters, and policymakers need to understand the tech when drafting relevant legislation.

'I spend a lot of time encouraging people to program, not just because we need some people to understand technology—we need lawyers and those in parliament to understand it, otherwise they're not going to be able to make appropriate steps... We need those with the technological knowledge to be writing policy as well as standards in protocols.'

Tim Berners-Lee

If you were curious: Yes, the National Security Agency is collecting and filtering text messages to the tune of 194 million a day. It's a collection of data that one agency employee, obtained by *The Guardian* from leaker Edward Snowden, called 'a goldmine to exploit.' The agencies collect 194 million messages a day. They include 76,000 geocoordinates for users, thanks to people seeking directions or setting up meetings. They're able to link hundreds of thousands of financial transactions. They collect over 5 million missed call alerts, which then get pushed into a contact-chaining system.

Google is very secretive about the exact nature of its for-profit intelligence operation and how it uses the petabytes of data it collects on us every single day for financial gain.

CYBERSPACE   205

Armed with the primary goals of our new way of thinking about computer system design; in the next chapter we go to describe how a global network may be designed that meets human needs and solves the aforementioned problems. Here we take a humanistic perspective on computers, whereby we think of them not in terms of *Apps, tools for thought, information-appliances, or as a 'bicycle for the mind';* but simply as self.

Clear is that the current Web is suboptimal; and that it cannot be fixed, but rather it must be replaced by a new properly-hyperlinked world system based on a simple information structure that may be cross-linked, cross-referenced, published, annotated and overlaid in every way imaginable. Scrapping the current Web and starting over again might seem like a radical step; and one that would be very costly and involve enormous effort. But already clear is that the current Web is loosing its popularity; with an increasing use of centralised 'clouds', and company owned information repositories/silos. The trend is away from openness and towards centralisation and non-interoperable data standards. Why is this the case? The reason for these trends is in large part because the current Web has a fatal design flaw, in that the data it contains is fundamentally not adequately linked, reusable and/or available for free assembly as Ted Nelson foresaw.

Put simply the information (and our thoughts) is/are simply not sufficiently *visible, free, equal, linkable, useful and/or reusable.*

We must re-design our thoughts—or at least the digital representations and implementations of the same. Open-thoughts must be *accessible, freely assembled and be equal.* One can already see evidence of a trend towards free-assembly of thoughts on a platform like Twitter; whereby hashtags may be assigned to group/link conversations together; and this is actually a type of omni/back link, if a very primitive and unstructured/wholly un-patterned one (we cannot have meta-data, comments, overlays, pattern histories etc.)

In the next chapter we introduce a massively distributed atomic network that may be used to meet the needs of thought-surfers everywhere.

The internet—that wonderful boundless domain where anyone can access or provide content—is under threat. This week, a US constitutional challenge in the Court of Appeals overthrew the technical principle of net neutrality and held that internet service providers are entitled to block and discriminate against web content at their discretion. The potential implications of this are vast. (2014)

The thing was moving—it seemed to be leaving the screen—

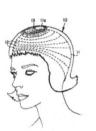

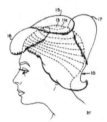

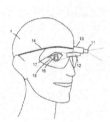

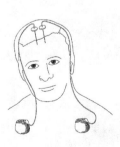

Kubla Khan by Samuel Taylor Coleridge (1772-1834):

In Xanadu did Kubla Khan
A stately pleasure-dome decree:
 Where Alph, the sacred river, ran
 Through caverns measureless to man
 Down to a sunless sea.
 So twice five miles of fertile ground
 With walls and towers were girdled round;
  And there were gardens bright with sinuous rills,
  Where blossomed many an incense-bearing tree;
  And here were forests ancient as the hills,
   Enfolding sunny spots of greenery.

But oh! that deep romantic chasm which slanted
Down the green hill athwart a cedarn cover!
A savage place! as holy and enchanted
As e'er beneath a waning moon was haunted
By woman wailing for her demon-lover!
And from this chasm, with ceaseless turmoil seething,
As if this earth in fast thick pants were breathing,
A mighty fountain momently was forced:
Amid whose swift half-intermitted burst
Huge fragments vaulted like rebounding hail,
Or chaffy grain beneath the thresher's flail:
And mid these dancing rocks at once and ever
It flung up momently the sacred river.
Five miles meandering with a mazy motion
Through wood and dale the sacred river ran,
Then reached the caverns measureless to man,
And sank in tumult to a lifeless ocean;
And 'mid this tumult Kubla heard from far
Ancestral voices prophesying war!
 The shadow of the dome of pleasure
 Floated midway on the waves;
  Where was heard the mingled measure
  From the fountain and the caves.
  It was a miracle of rare device,
  A sunny pleasure-dome with caves of ice!

A damsel with a dulcimer
In a vision once I saw:
It was an Abyssinian maid,
And on her dulcimer she played,
Singing of Mount Abora.
Could I revive within me
Her symphony and song,
To such a deep delight 'twould win me,
That with music loud and long,
I would build that dome in air,
 That sunny dome! those caves of ice!
 And all who heard should see them there,
 And all should cry, Beware! Beware!
  His flashing eyes, his floating hair!
  Weave a circle round him thrice,
  And close your eyes with holy dread
  For he on honey-dew hath fed,
   And drunk the milk of Paradise.

Chapter Nine
World Brain

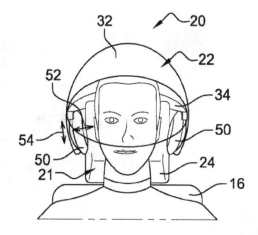

E VER SINCE the great library at Alexandria there has been an enduring vision of collecting all the world's knowledge together at a single location. In the present chapter foreseen is a new type of computer network, and the same (potentially) enabling each of us to access the vast assembly of all the open thought-atoms. Having comprehensive access to everything known is an appealing dream, but it is also a deceptively difficult —and some would say impossible—one to achieve.

Most recently the British Library, and the Bibliothèque in France, made attempts to physically collect every book, paper, magazine etc ever written. Despite progress (the British library has over 150 million items in its collection); the task proved illusive.

With the advent of electronic media it became clear that there were many advantages to storing knowledge in a digital format; including *remote accessibility, effortless replication and indestructibility, speed of access, and limitless storage etc*. A major advantage would be that the original dream of Vannevar Bush might (possibly) come true; whereby his Memex system would be achievable; being a desk (at home or work) from which all the world's information would be immediately available, or on call.[12]

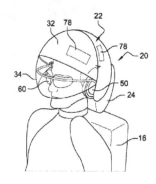

Hypertext as conceived by Ted Nelson in the 1960s, embodies Bush's/Goldberg's vision; and is a broad category of media defined as: a body of written or pictorial material interconnected in such a complex way that it could not conveniently be presented or represented on paper.

Nelson explained that:

> Hyper-media are branching or performing presentations which respond to user actions, systems of prearranged words and pictures (for example) which may be explored freely or queried in stylised ways... they are in some sense 'multi-dimensional', we may call them hyper-media, following mathematical use of the term 'hyper!'... the sense of 'hyper!' used here connotes extension and generality; cf. 'hyperspace'[1]

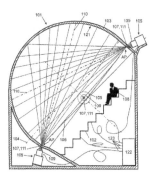

At first sight, and superficially, it may appear that Nelson's vision of a hypermedia world of connected/branching information has come true. We have the World Wide Web, Apps that provide access to vast cloud systems, and social networks; plus fabulous television/movie systems like YouTube and Netflix that provide, in effect, millions of 'branching' channels (for example).

Certainly progress has been made, and information is more connected, and accessible, than ever before.

But speaking in 2010, Ted Nelson said:

> Today's computer world is based on techimisunderstandings of human thought and human life, and the imposition of inappropriate structures through the computer and through the file that is used by the applications, and the imposition of inappropriate structures on the things that we want to do in the human world. It is time to re-imagine the computer world.

According to Nelson his original vision of hypertext is in no way represented by the World Wide Web (or Web).

In Nelson's words: that's NOT what I was talking about!

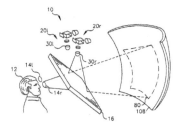

Instead, Nelson imagined a world knowledge system (in the 1960s) based on tiny pieces of data that could be connected in every possible way, complete with overlaid links and connections that went in every direction. Nelson said (and continues to say) that documents (and human thoughts) have deep structure; and it is this that must be *represented, made visible and accessible to all*. To sum-up Ted's position, most people don't (in a real sense) realise that computers have (in actual fact) been designed; and furthermore that (often) all of the wrong design decisions have been made; leading to vastly inferior, restrictive and/or sub-optimal computing systems.

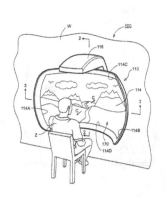

The subject of the present chapter, is how to implement Nelson's original vision; whilst merging his ideas with those of Kim Veltman's (and the author's ideas where applicable); and in order to produce a workable solution that meets the needs of everyone: *to see/access all the world's thoughts/data*.

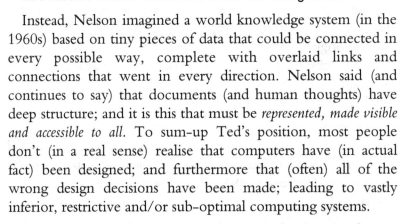

BIGGEST COMPUTER IN THE WORLD? Google runs GNU/Linux on a vast network. In 2006 the Google system was estimated to be 250,000 computers. Now it's surely over a million, and they're talking ten million at a thousand locations (don't know where, do you? They like it that way). - Ted Nelson

Wikipedia is built of transclusions, exactly like the basic
Xanadu substratum, but without overlays/history.

WORLD BRAIN   209

Let us begin by looking at Ted Nelson's **Xanadu** system, which is a (partially built) network for authoring and publishing the diverse forms of hypertext/media as envisioned by Nelson.

In the **Xanadu** vision, authors work on small pieces of media—*an explanatory paragraph, a movie segment, a schematic etc.* These segments can be connected with other things or segments/quotations from other documents/sources. One of the most common types of connection is a *transclusion,* which brings a small (re-usable) segment into a larger document *(an essay, a song etc).* Other types of connection are also possible *(text/book/image/movie links).* The **Xanadu** system keeps track of all changes to a document's segments (for example), rather than just a few discrete versions. Any version of any segment can be requested. A document can choose to transclude the most current version or a particular historical version.[1,2,3]

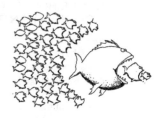

Authors don't just have their own knowledge segments to play with. Any public segment by any author can (potentially) be transcluded into any document by any author. Nelson understands that creative work builds on prior creative work; and **Xanadu** had the *remix,* the *sample,* and the *quotation* built into its basic design. Like the web, **Xanadu** employed front-end viewer software for wandering over a world of information (segments); located on back-end servers. On-the-fly assembly is key. While today we (apparently) live in the age of remix, the Web mostly serves up big, untranscludable/opaque chunks.

The strength of the Web lies in making a vast amount of information available. And this explosion was made possible by the Web's openness and non-proprietary nature. The Web engendered not a '*culture of piracy*' but a '*culture of the library*'. But what is missing, is access to a vast, almost limitless archive of tiny data segments (or thought-atoms) which could then be overlaid with vast numbers of interconnecting linkages and transclusions.

< {18} World Brain = hyperlinked thought-atoms / data + overlays + publish-ability + hyper-context + accessibility. >

Imagine a new libertarian literature with alternative explanations so anyone can choose the pathway or approach that best suits him or her, with ideas accessible and interesting to everyone, so that a new richness and freedom can come to the human experience; imagine a rebirth of literacy.[1]

WHO OWNS THE INTERNET

No one. Its parts (the fibre-optic cables and other transmission lines) are owned by different companies and universities. But the Internet has no head or centre. Its use cannot be controlled. Its technical and political aspects are overseen by various committees but they can only recommend; anyone with a server on the Internet can choose to do things differently. And anyone, anywhere, who sees a new opportunity for mischief or crime can take advantage of it, sending packets to probe, attack and steal.

THE FOUR HORSEMEN OF THE INTERNET

No one can argue: we must fight terrorism, child pornography, money laundering and drugs. These are the so-called 'four horsemen of the Internet', and tend to put an end to any discussion of freedom or privacy. This is deeply unfortunate, as there are many intermediate issues of great importance. [1]

On the Xanadu system, Nelson says:

We need software that allows everything (including documents, file listings, bookkeeping) to be annotated. We need systems that allow our work to criss-cross and overlap and interpenetrate like the real concerns of our documents and lives, and like (for instance) the topics of this book. If your work is a unified conglomerate that does not divide the way the software does, if your life is a unified conglomerate that you wish to manage from computers that we set up all wrong, you see the problem.

Not everyone does. I see today's computer world as a nightmare honkytonk prison, noisy and colourful and wholly misbegotten. We must everywhere use ghastly menus designed by people with no sense of the human mind. We are imprisoned in applications that can be customised only in ways that the designers allow. We are in the Dark Ages of documents, most locked in imprisoning formats, canopic jars from which they can never escape, or mangled within and by markup which hinders re-use, indexing, connection and overlay and overlap.

Xanadu and the World Wide Web are totally different and incompatible. The Web has one-way links and a fixed rectangular visualisation based on the strictly enforced rules of the browser. The browser will not composite or inter-compare documents side by side. Xanadu alumni consider the Web illicit and broken, exactly what they were trying to prevent; for having only one-way links, for conflating a document with a place, for locking it to one view, for having no way to maintain identifiable content from other sources, for having no means of visible connection to points within a document, for imposing hierarchy in a variety of ways.[1]

THE LITTLE GUY THAT LIVES IN-SIDE MY BRAIN

JAN. 30TH '86

Put simply, in Nelson's view; today we should have a unification of the design of information; whereby if everything was *interconnected* and *interrelated* the way it should be, then we would have instant access to all the world's thoughts/ideas. But this is precisely what we **do not** have; because almost nothing is connected, no discrete ideas (or very, very few) are even addressable or findable; and certainly information (as a whole) is not linked and connected in almost any way whatsoever.

One might wish to see, for example, where the word 'God' is used (and how) across the entire corpus of human knowledge. To see every single related thought/opinion/datum. A simple request.

To fit his World Wide Web distribution scheme, Berners-Lee creates the URL (a uniform way of addressing anything in the Internet). This makes the network uniformly traversable without special cases, hiding the variety of filesystems. This is a powerful unification of the whole Internet. It can be argued that this is Tim's great contribution to the world, rather than his one-way Hypertext system. [1]

The plan can be anything. The name computer has frightened people ever since.
It might just as well have been called an Oogabooga Box. - Ted Nelson

WORLD BRAIN 211

But one cannot do so; and because the vast majority of thought-atoms and patterns that relate to the concept of God are hidden deep inside *web-pages, files, books, papers, databases, and documents (externally visible or not) etc.* These thought patterns are invisible because they are not addressable; individually and separately from the enclosing media. In fact, the vast majority of items are hidden; and most thoughts, sentences, ideas etc; are all trapped inside of *opaque lumps*; that is they are lost/hidden.

Previously we had established that all human understanding can be equated to patterns (structures/contexts) of thoughts. Plus we noted in chapter three that the primary function (or definition) of computer is a device to **arrange items clearly in one's mind**. Unfortunately, our discussion has demonstrated that computers are in no way fulfilling any such (ultimate) purpose; and from the perspective of arranging the collective thought patterns of humanity; transparently for efficient use by all.

< {19} Largely unknown are the collective thoughts of humanity. >

Ted Nelson has identified the sole causative agent behind this lack of visibility/accessibility for human knowledge; and it is the incorrectly designed information units that lie at the heart of all digital systems. In his *Literary Machines*, Nelson specifies his design for Xanadu and also the information units behind his vision of a newly efficient hypermedia filled world.

According to Ted Nelson:

> We need unified personal systems for a variety of purposes. Computers should A) simplify our lives and B) Provide access to Ideas... We should read and write on screens with new freedom. Imagine a new libertarian literature with alternative explanations so anyone can choose the pathway or approach that best suits him or her, with ideas accessible and interesting to everyone, so that a new richness and freedom can come to the human experience; imagine a rebirth of literacy. There are two hopes: the simplification of our lives; and the cornucopia of ideas and writings and pictures. They are the focus of my own work. I say we need unified design. It has to be simple. It has to be powerful. It doesn't have to be complicated. I believe, indeed, that **the** design (ultimate information system) that we need will derive simply from what we have known in the past. The future of the written word can and will be built from an electronic version of its past, losing nothing of its heritage, but totally changing its nature by instantaneous accessibility.[1]

CONSTRUCTS

All the following are constructs and not technology: word processors, email, windows; imaginary places— Facebook, movie editing programs, chat rooms, playlists, etc

Almost everything you see on your computer screen is a construct— something people have imagined to present to you.

Much of what is called 'computer technology' consists of conventions, packages, constructs arbitrarily designed. These were chosen by various individuals, projects, companies, marketing campaigns and accidents. And there are always fights and controversies.

You've been taught that Computer Technology is inexorable, inevitable, and required. But the computer world has been built of competing ideas-passionately advanced and fought over by thousands of rival smart guys, disagreeing left and right. The myth of computer technology is that it has some compelling necessity of its own, forcing itself on us. No. It's been people and their ideas. The myth of technological necessity has stifled people's imaginations. And their willingness to demand more and better.

An example... Wikipedia is a fake in one conspicuous aspect; when you 'edit' an article, it is actually a submission that may stand briefly, but it will be considered by the *real* editors. It is a wiki - or everybody editable system, and it took off.[1]

Ted Nelson

A DIFFERENT DOCUMENT: The traditional computer document is an iron box of characters in sequence, with no tracking of their origins. The Xanadu document is a collage assembled by the user's client program, then sandwiched with a selection of links, markup and overlays. [1] Since every portion in the collage knows its original address, each original context is accessible. [2] Links can overlap in any number and have many types. [3] Rights management: the publisher allows re-use in any new context, since the original context is always accessible and each downloader purchases the original product. [1]

The NSA holds various secret, non-expiring patents, which can only be accidentally discovered when civilians apply to patent the same.

VOTING MACHINES

The original voting machine of 1892 could be examined by anybody to verify its fair operation. No more. Several brands of electronic voting machines have now been widely deployed in the USA, all questionable. It's best to think of an electronic voting machine as a video game; it's impossible to know the real rules, you can just hope. Mechanical voting machines, starting in 1892, were designed to be easily understood and guaranteed to be fair because anyone could see that they were fair. Today's friendly looking voting machines could be a total fraud, and there is no way that certification methods by mere testing can find out.[1]

Edit Decision List

Ted Nelson likens computing to movie-making; whereby the aim is to have the machine affect the *hearts and mind of the viewer*. In movie-making a basic entity is the *Edit Decision List* (EDL), which is used in the post-production process of film. The EDL contains an ordered list of reel and timecode data representing where each video clip can be obtained, in order to conform the final cut.[1,2]

Ted's view is that the paradigm of one document per file is wrong. Rather we should be using EDLs. The key analogy here is that the fundamental units of information that are to be the building blocks of a new way of organising knowledge must be tiny units of data, uniquely and independently addressable, and any changes/alternations to a unit must be trackable/addressable. Thus anyone will be able to run the changes (to an aggregated unit) forwards and backwards.

The tiny units would be:

- Filable under an unlimited number of categories
- Be available for dynamic outlining, indexing and transcluding
- Many different versions of the same materials must be available

Required is an evolutionary file structure that can be shaped into various forms, and which change from one arrangement to another in accordance with the user's changing needs.

Earlier Nelson called this file an *Evolutionary List File* (ELF) which has three elements : *entries*, *lists* and *links*.[3,4,5]

An entry is a discrete unit of information designated by the user. A list (or document) is an ordered set of entries designated by the user; and a given entry may be in any number of lists. A link is a connector, designated by the user (or others) between two particular entries which are in different lists—a transclusion.[3,5]

Two-way links: A Xanadu two-way link can be published by itself. When you click on it, it brings up the original content at both ends. When you click on the two-way link as part of a particular document collage, it connects to whatever content in that document it connects to.

Doug's vision - [1] a user could link to, and annotate, portions within a document;
[2] a 'plex' of connections could gather together a number of different entities.

WORLD BRAIN   213

According to this scheme a unit of knowledge may be represented in the form of a sequence (or list) of entries which are connected by links and overlays of various types. And lists can be *changed*, *moved-about* and *re-arranged* without affecting the actual knowledge units (entries) in any way whatsoever. Small atoms facilitate composite structures (ELFs) of any shape.

The multiple advantages of this simple idea are quite profound; and stem from the true hypertext nature of the resulting system.

Ted Nelson on: *the structure of ideas*:

A structure of thought is not itself sequential. It is an interwoven system of ideas (what I like to call a *structangle*). None of the ideas necessarily comes first; and breaking up these ideas into a presentational sequence is an arbitrary and complex process. It is often a destructive process, since in taking apart the whole system of connection (to present it sequentially), we can scarcely avoid breaking, that is leaving out, some of the connections that are part of the whole. Of course, we do this kind of simplifying sequential breakdown all the time, but that doesn't mean we should, it just means we have to.

People have different backgrounds and styles. Yet sequential text, to which we are funnelled by tradition and technology, forces us to write the same sequences for everyone, which may be appropriate for some readers and leave others out in the cold, or which may be appropriate for nobody. Thus it would be greatly preferable if we could easily create different pathways for different readers, based upon background, taste and probably understanding. In the computer world this will change, especially if—as I foresee—there will be one great repository, and everything will be equally accessible... Non-sequential writing on paper can be all sorts of things—magazine layouts, funny arrangements of poetry, pieces of writing connected by lines, or many other things.

The structure of ideas is never sequential; and indeed, our thought processes are not very sequential either. True, only a few thoughts at a time pass across the central screen of the mind, but as you consider a thing, your thoughts crisscross it constantly, reviewing first one connection, then another. Each new idea is compared with many parts of the whole picture, or with some mental visualisation of the whole picture itself.[1]

CREATIVE USE OF COMPUTERS

THE KINDS OF FILE structures required if we are to use the computer for personal files and as an adjunct to creativity are wholly different in character from those customary in business and scientific data processing. They need to provide the capacity for intricate and idiosyncratic arrangements, total modifiability, undecided alternatives, and thorough internal documentation.... thus... to the user it acts like a multifarious, polymorphic, many-dimensional, infinite blackboard....

The ramifications of this approach extend well beyond its original concerns, into such places as information retrieval and library science, motion pictures and the programming craft; for it is almost everywhere necessary to deal with deep structural changes in the arrangements of ideas and things... The file structure suggested here is the Evolutionary List File, to be built of zippered lists.[1]

Ted Nelson

Xanadu = generalised deep documents; it is not (as often supposed) a bungled attempt to create the World Wide Web; it is a sweeping design for text, audio and video in a uniform structure that can be shown in many different ways; but always with the option of side-by-side inter-comparison and visible re-use. Instead of a single visualisation, new programmable visions of any kind are welcome, but the canonical vision is side-by-side parallel strips with visible connections.[1]

Atomic Network

I know it may seem like our discussion has become quite technical, but it hasn't really. Our aim is to penetrate right to the heart of what is wrong with current computing systems (all of them!); in the biggest sense and in relation to allowing people everywhere to access all human knowledge as easily, simply and comprehensibly as possible.[18]

Ted Nelson's visionary ideas developed from those of Emanuel Goldberg, Vannevar Bush and Doug Engelbart; and likewise their own ideas would (perhaps) have evolved from the likes of Wells and Otlet etc.[10,11] However nobody has the complete answer, but rather each thinker moves us along a little bit on the human journey towards a happier, fairer and free world. In fact this is the underlying message of all these visionaries, that we must consider —and solve—problems *together* as a people.

In this spirit, we shall now step back and survey Nelson's solution from a clarifying distance. Nelson has certainly identified the key problem in computing—and perhaps humanity—parallel and easy-to-navigate linkage of anything to anything else. Open-thoughts must be *connected and be freely accessible*. And he has identified key elements of the solution, and there is no doubt in this respect. That said, my own opinion is that the problem becomes one of practically building this new network of thoughts/data. Ted himself would admit that with Xanadu he has not (yet) succeeded; and furthermore getting everyone to adopt such a system is no walk-in-the-park; even when it is vastly superior to everything else—or is potentially so. How then do we proceed?

A major problem is constructing a network infrastructure that allows people to build-in (plus classify/link-to) the content *themselves;* and so to make the system available, usable, and useful.

My idea is to build our World Brain using an atomic network.

---

[18] Obviously we are speaking of building a 'World Brain' or a global knowledge library/ repository; which itself does not preclude the existence of, or say anything about, the many millions of smaller IT systems/Apps/cloud applications that will/do exist.

Important note: Emanuel Goldberg also planned to atomize literature in the form of micro-thoughts:

"Facts" or "microthoughts" could then be arranged, rearranged and linked in multiple ways using the expanded decimal classification for the especially important and difficult task of linking each chunk with other chunks on the same topic and also those on related topics.[13] (Also see Kim Veltman's: Alphabets of Life, Ch.12 [14])

Freedom to read—everyone should be free to read whatever is published.
Freedom to publish, everyone must be free to publish. - Ted Nelson

WORLD BRAIN   215

An ***Atomic-Network*** [or Hyper-Network] is the polar opposite of a centralised or cloud network. It effectively provides a 'save' and 'load' function for the Internet, and offers an indestructible data type that cannot be controlled and lives forever. Let us examine how such a theoretical network might work.[6]

Assume that network members are scattered across the Internet; that is they are located on different IP (Internet Protocol) addresses and some may be behind Network Address Translation devices (NATs). Furthermore, each network member has a special client program on his personal computer or mobile device. Next we provide the following system actions; *save and load*, based on a unique data unit identifier. When the user chooses a sentence, document etc; and saves it to the network, it is automatically given a globally unique identifier, an owner identifier and a member-specific key and/or password if it is secret/private.

Now what the (World Brain) client program does next (upon save) is interesting (and unique), it '*atomises*' the data unit to the network. The item is split into many thousands of tiny pieces (atoms) which are then disseminated across the network as a whole. There are many, many identical copies of each piece (data atom) which are saved on multiple remote computers hard drives, for later retrieval at an unspecified time. Data atoms are encrypted according to the key for the data unit as whole. Next when the owner (or key holder) chooses to load (or retrieve) the data unit from the network, then the owner's client knows how to request from the system all of the constituent atoms, re-assemble them etc.

Network (P2P) members agree to reserving part of their computer disc for other people's data 'atoms'. We now have a robust way of sharing items using the link identifiers for the data unit. When a network member's client requests such a link, a 'torrent' of constituent data 'atoms' is sent to that client (from all across the network), until such time as the data unit has been reconstructed. Every network member's computer is now a data-atom server! And a sufficient 'stock' of identical replicated (live) copies of each data atom (perhaps 100's) is automatically maintained according to network maintenance tasks.

Do you think that you have complete freedom on the Internet? Poppy-cock. Apart from the potential spying on your personal activities by NSA, police, social networks, hackers etc; there is the far more worrying fact that you cannot see the open-thoughts/votes of anyone else; and in the sense that the thoughts of humanity are hidden inside books, papers, websites and on 'balkanised' social media. This information is (perhaps) not deliberately hidden, but is wholly unorganised, unconnected, unclassified. Do you want to find out what people think about your government, to see (links to) every single related item across the entire corpus of human thoughts, to see how these thoughts and ideas are interlinked, interwoven and connected etc, and across all media. No chance. Sorry.

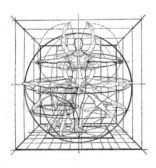

What has been achieved with such an atom network? Firstly, data/thoughts saved to the network are rendered effectively immortal and indestructible, and such a status relies on the unbreakable redundancy provided by massive distribution and replication of hundreds of identical atoms across many separate network locations. And the robustness of the network increases with number of network members (computers to store atoms). Other key advantages include no longer needing/having central servers; and this is environmentally friendly and brings security advantages.

Crucially here nobody can ever spy on said atoms where they are assigned as private/secret-thoughts. Additionally data save/loading speeds are much faster (i.e. no central server upload times and torrent-like atom transfers). The system also has virtually unlimited storage space, so long as the network remains in operation or has a minimum/proportionally-increasing number of users to operate and maintain its infrastructure (virtual disc-space). But perhaps most importantly the network can be a technical guarantee of the principles of the *Theory of Natural Thoughts*. Supported is *freedom, equality and free-assembly of thoughts*; and in particular because we do not have any network administrators, owners or Big Brother spying and/or network controlling interference from above.

Obviously we have said little about the technical implementation details about how this network would actually be designed; and presented is a purely top-level description. However there is no reason why such a system cannot be built; and in terms of technical hurdles etc. In design terms we equate the described data-atoms (assembled into units) with the thought atoms and data segments (Nelson's vision) discussed earlier.

Nothing has been said about how knowledge would be organised within such a network. In fact the simplicity of the underlying data structure allows many different organisational: *mappings, overlays, features and capabilities*.

There are a screen and two throttles. The first throttle moves the text forward and backward, up and down on the screen. The second throttle causes changes in the writing itself: throttling toward you causes the text to become longer by minute degrees. Gaps appear between the phrases; new words and phrases pop into the gaps, an item at a time. Push back on the throttle and the writing becomes shorter and less detailed. The *stretchtext* is stored as a text stream with extras, coded to pop in and pop out at the desired altitudes. - Ted Nelson

Hyper-thinking = The process of thinking with full access to all of the different subject-related contexts, relations, links, opinions, patterns, references, annotations, footnotes etc.

WORLD BRAIN   217

Digital Reference Rooms

It is organisation that is missing from the world's thought and data atoms. Kim Veltman has written copiously on the related concept of Digital Reference Rooms (DRR). According to Kim, a key problem with the Web is that everyone has their own rules for organising knowledge. On this point, Veltman says that if:

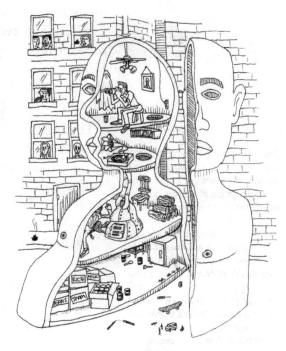

> There is no common framework for translating and mapping among these rules, then the whole is only equal to the largest part rather than to the sum of the parts... Hence we need standardised authority lists of names, subjects and places. This may require new kinds of meta-data. Indeed the reference rooms of libraries have served as civilisation's cumulative memory concerning search and structure methods through classification systems, dictionaries, encyclopaedias, book catalogues, citation indexes, abstracts and reviews. Hence, digital reference rooms offer keys to more comprehensive tools.[7]

Kim Veltman's requirements (for DRR):

A) Standardised names, subjects, places with their variants

B) Knowledge in context

C) Multicultural approaches through alternative classifications

D) Geographic access with adaptive historical maps

E) Views of changing terms and categories of knowledge

F) Common interfaces for libraries, museums etc

G) Adaptive interfaces for different levels of education

H) Seamless links with learning tools

THE ETERNAL FIGHT!

Once again we see a vision for a unification of data/ thoughts; combined with efficient accessibility tools.

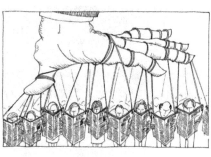

The generalised link of Xanadu goes between spans, or pieces within a document or work selected by whoever made the link. It is a strap between a collection of bytes on the left and a collection of bytes on the right; and neither collection need be all together... And the idea of transclusion is that something from one document is used in another document without copying it. It is represented in the second document as a special hidden pointer that says 'whenever you get this pointer, bring over the piece from the other document.'[13]

Never tell the truth to people who are not worthy of it. - Mark Twain.

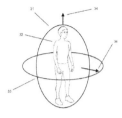

INFORMATION / KNOWLEDGE

The web thus far is about data and information: i.e. it is primarily about individual entities (what and who). Knowledge entails descriptions of and claims about entities (including where, when, how, why). Information is about 2 questions. Knowledge is about 6 questions. To go beyond the compromises of the Internet, WWW and PWW, a new approach to information and knowledge organisation is needed. It must i) include letters, words and terms; ii) link attributes and relations; iii) link sources; iv) link alternative sources; v) link these with questions for easier retrieval...

Initial visions of the Internet were about complete access to all knowledge. Part one of the paper examined a series of compromises made for pragmatic reasons. Underlying these compromises is a focus on who and what (entities) and a tacit assumption that all statements, claims are universally true. This assumption, common in the field of pure science, does not extend to the human sciences where spatio-temporal dimensions include ruined, restored, destroyed, lost and occasionally falsified sources. [7]

Kim Veltman

According to Kim Veltman, systematic access requires integrating tools for *searching, structuring, using* and *presenting knowledge*; linked with digital reference rooms that provide the aforementioned list of capabilities. Like Nelson, Veltman sees not only the problem, but ambitiously goes ahead and builds a solution; named his *System for Universal Media Searching* (SUMS).[7,8,9]

His approach includes a few similar ideas to Nelson, but with *Classifications, Learning Filters* and *Knowledge Contexts* identified to help the user cope with ten kinds of materials; namely:

1. Terms (classification systems, subject headings, indexes)
2. Definitions (dictionaries, etymologies)
3. Explanations (encyclopaedias)
4. Titles (library catalogues, book catalogues, bibliographies)
5. Partial contents (abstracts, reviews, citation indexes)
6. Full contents which can be divided into another four classes
7. Internal analyses (when the work is being studied in its own right)
8. External analyses (when it is being compared with other works)
9. Restorations (when the work has been been altered and thus has built into it the interpretations of the restorer)
10. Reconstructions (when the degree of interpretation is larger)

Veltman says that all of these are pointers to the books/items/thoughts in the rest of the digital library.

By use of such schemes the 'reader' may progress from *universal categories* to *particulars* and using *ordinal* and/or *subsumptive relations* between items/subject categories etc. When querying a knowledge system one may (for example) progress form broader to narrower terms in a quest for specifics. However as both Nelson and Veltman note; our thoughts and ideas are rarely hierarchically linked or arranged in singular contexts.

Thoughts and ideas are related in a myriad of overlapping patterns of unbelievable *complexity, beauty and meaning!*

Remember that Nelson said that the true structure of thought itself is not sequential; but parallel connection.

To the casual observer, one might think that in many everyday situations the ordinary user of a computer system would not need access to all of the many dimensions that a particular term, idea or thought-pattern might conjure up; and that all the related opinions, annotations, and links etc are not so interesting, or are somehow unimportant and/or irrelevant. However I would suggest that in reality one is always interested in the truth or falsehood, source and interrelation of anything to everything else. Context is everything; or else how can we tell that our news reports, school teachers, politicians etc are correct in what they are telling us.

Possible relations between thought/data atoms and patterns include: *alternatives, associations, complementaries, duals, identicals, opposites, antonyms, indicators, contextualisers* etc. Strangely, the problem becomes even more obtuse when we consider logical functions; including: *and/or/not, alternation, conjunction, reciprocal, converse, negative, subsumptive, determinative and ordinal relations* etc.

Veltman says that a possible solution to all of this complexity in terms of organisation and classifying ideas, is the concept of different types of 'knowledge object'; stating:

> Such that if one has a term, one can see its synonyms without needing to refer to a thesaurus. All these kinds of relations thus become different hooks or different kinds of net when one is searching for a new term and its connections.[8]

With this (abbreviated) discussion we begin to see the enormity of the challenge in terms of organising all of the world's ideas. **Google** simply blasts lists of stuff at you; in response to keywords, which are entirely unclassified (apart from overly simplistic groupings of images, web-links, videos etc); and in no way lets you see the structural patterns of thought. But it is these patterns that (in fact) underly knowledge in the biggest/smallest senses. **Googling** is like the game you play as a child whereby one person thinks of something (located in the environment) in his/her head, and the other person attempts to guess the item in question.

But this is no way to link-to/access knowledge! *(Googling)*

With **Google** you never even approach/see the true pattern of knowledge, or what are the diversity of opinions/ideas; but can only scramble about in an ad-hoc manner. This is because data and thought-atoms are grouped into files, isolated and hidden one from another; and so by and large free-assembly of thought-patterns is blocked/impossible. Veltman on knowledge organisation:

> We want to find something particular and yet we use single words, which are universal. The semantic web entails only subsumptive relations: what and who. Needed is a fuller approach that treats who as living entities, separate from what, and includes determinative and ordinal relations which are basic aspects of human life and knowledge: where, when, how, and why.[8]

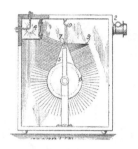

NEW APPROACH TO KNOWLEDGE

We want to find something particular and yet we use single words, which are universal. Linking is a key. Linking truples is insufficient because these entail only subsumptive relations: what things are, isolated from determinative and ordinal relations: who, where, when, how and why as aspects of human life and knowledge.

First, in addition to using truples to connect universals via *is* and *has*, we need to link letters, words, terms, and names with their particulars: attributes and relations. Second, each of these needs to be linked with their sources.

Third, because there are multiple sources, with changing opinions and claims over time and space, the linked attributes and relations need to be geo-temporally referenced to reflect different and even contradictory sources.

Fourth, in order to make the immensity of this information and knowledge accessible this corpus of links needs to be linked with questions such that personal (who), geo-(where), temporal (when), conditional (how) and causal (why) subsets can more readily be found.[7]

Kim Veltman

Hypertext means forms of writing which branch or perform on request; they are best presented on computer display screens. The computer display screen permits footnotes on footnotes, on footnotes; and pathways of any structure the author wants to create. - Ted Nelson

We've got the right to choose and there ain't no way we'll lose it... Oh, we're not gonna take it, No, we ain't gonna take it, Oh we're not gonna take it anymore. - Twisted Sister

Building the World Brain

Our discussion has shown how men like H.G.Wells, Paul Otlet, Emanuel Goldberg, Vannevar Bush, Douglas Engelbart, Ted Nelson and Kim Veltman; have made a unified call for the urgent development of what is effectively a *World Brain* (containing all the thoughts of humanity). These thinkers were/are visionaries and scientists, of one type or another; but they are by no means alone in expressing similar sentiments. Legion are those who have urged mankind to create humanistic systems that allow all the members of a society to share thoughts/votes/ideas freely and openly, and amongst the same are: Jean-Jaques Rousseau, Bertrand Russell, John Adams, Henry Ward, Norbert Wiener, George Orwell, Lewis Mumford, Julian Assange, Tim Berners-Lee, Douglas Rushkoff etc.

Why is/has there been such an overwhelming call for what is effectively a World Brain? Notably, the reasons given are not related to the creation of a utopia; but rather for education; and for avoidance of despotic regimes whereby technologies are used to subjugate man and/or to block his basic human rights. Accordingly, it is nothing less than preservation of civilisation that is at stake. It is my position that building a World Brain may in fact be a difficult task, but it is by no means impossible. Some people believe that we already have built such a brain; specifically in the form of: *the Internet, Cloud(s) and/or the World Wide Web*. Whilst these developments have been tentative steps in a useful direction, our analysis has shown how limited are the resulting systems in terms of the *freedom*, *ownership* and *equality of thoughts*.

Undoubtably our world is today more connected than ever before, in terms of *digital information flows and the rapid communication of (a small subset of) ideas, transactions and data etc.* Largely by default, it does appear that humanity is building a self-computer; and because the self is now almost fully immersed in technology whilst at school, home and work. But we must heed the warnings of the technology visionaries; and build/use mechanisms such as techno-rights; and to ensure that our machines foster humane values.

We do not want dictators, we do not want oligarchic parties or class rule, we want a widespread world intelligence conscious of itself. To work out a way to that World Brain organisation is therefore our primary need in this age of imperative construction. - H.G.Wells

Luckily quite a few of the greatest technologists who ever lived have spent their entire careers working along similar lines. As a result, the literature is rich in *ideas, plans, blue-prints and recommendations;* and in relation to building a World Brain. These ideas have been well-explored.

Obviously, due to space limitations, I cannot delve into the details of all of the various useful recommendations and/or detailed plans for a World Brain that have been developed. Instead we must focus here on the most important features that any ultimate system of knowledge would display.

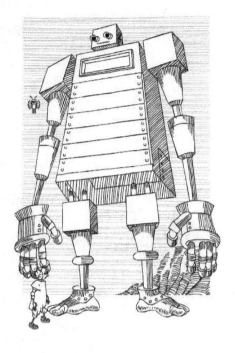

I have spoken at length on my belief that the world's cultural, religious and scientific knowledge corpuses are, one and all, composed simply of thoughts. Accordingly, and for humane purposes; recommended is close adherence to the *Theory of Natural Thoughts.* Stated is that thoughts can exist in *human minds, on media, and implanted in systems and machines.* The present chapter is obviously concerned with a world knowledge system; and hence with thoughts that exist on media. Explained has been a way to (partially) uphold the three essential Attributes of natural-thoughts (*ownership, equality* and *freedom of assembly*); and by means of an atomic network. In particular the atomic network allows the network-maker(s) (the commons) to build into the networked system a way to guarantee freedom from any type of centralised interference/control/censure.[6]

In the coming pages/chapters we assume that such an atomic network is a real possibility. Remaining is the question of what shall be the capabilities of the World Brain. Accordingly we envision a World Brain; and from a practical perspective. Perhaps after perusing the following sections, the reader will be able to judge if (in fact) the projected system is (in the specified senses) a superior one; and with respect to the current Web's limited freedom of access to, and lack of free-assembly of; all the world's thoughts/ideas/votes.

When men have realised that time has upset many fighting faiths, they may come to believe even more than they believe the very foundations of their own conduct that the ultimate good desired is better reached by free trade in ideas; that the best of truth is the power of the thought to get itself accepted in the competition of the market, and that truth is the only ground upon which their wishes can be carried out. Abrams vs United States, 250 U.S. 616,630 [1919]

Be optimistic, believe in humankind, and in our ability to solve any and all problems.

Features of the World Brain

We begin with the capability to share private-thoughts; which shall be provided by the atomic network in the form of a unique key-identifier and an encryption/decryption matched pair set that is known only to the sender and receivers of the shared thoughts/data-atoms. How these keys are passed securely across an open network is undetermined/left to the implementers, because there is today severe doubt (or certainty) that Public Key Encryption technology is absolutely secure; since the NSA appears to have paid the company dealing with the random number generators, and specifically to generate a 'crackable' or decipherable private/public key pair(s). Perhaps a good alternative method is to swap a book of keys physically (sender and receivers meet in the real-world [once]); and so that each side has (absolutely secret) cypher-matching; as in a one-key-pass-book technique (see KeyMail).

Secondly desired is sharing of open-thoughts; or identity signed and also anonymous thought-atoms. Signed items use an identity (individual or group) that is established by some un-specified method; and it could be tied to one's ID on a social aspect of the atomic network (similar to Facebook) whereby your friends establish your identity. Alternatively we could use a certificate system to establish a person's identity, but once again the implementation details are beyond the scope of the present book.

Note that in principle we do believe in enabling people to share thoughts anonymously, and capabilities in this respect include sharing data/thoughts of any type; and even where said data depicts crimes/anti-social activities. As a reminder, it is my belief that thoughts/data are never immoral/evil; and that only actions can be unlawful/wrong. I know that this latter point will be a contentious issue; and it is a key subject of much of the rest of this book. One argument in favor of open sharing of any thought atom; is to weigh guaranteed freedom of thought/expression (a definite win) against supposed prevention/visibility of crimes (an uncertain win). It is this very faculty; to share thoughts openly and without censure; that guarantees *ownership, free assembly and equality of thoughts*; capabilities which are the bedrocks of any free society.

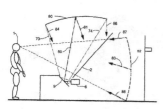

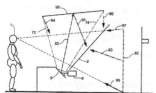

This World Encyclopaedia would be the mental back-ground of every intelligent man in the world. It would be alive and growing and changing continually under revision, extension and replacement from the original thinkers in the world everywhere. Every university and research institution should be feeding it. Every fresh mind should be brought into contact with its standing editorial organisation. - H.G. Wells

Document boundaries are arbitrary, the computer has been dumbed down to simulate paper, whereas a computer is a 'magic' piece of paper (with all kinds of new capabilities / possibilities). - Ted Nelson

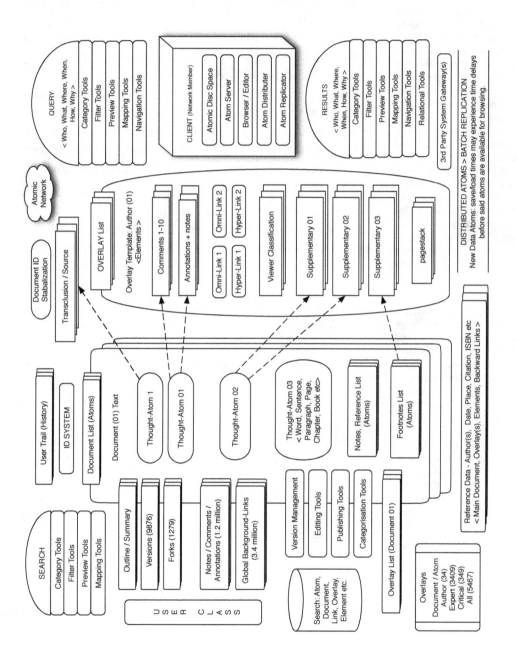

Figure 1: Flow-chart design for an Atomic Network (World Brain)

The world is a Phoenix. It perishes in flames and even as it dies it is born again.
This synthesis of knowledge is the necessary beginning to the new world. - H.G.Wells

I will ask you to imagine how this World Encyclopaedia organisation would enter into his life and how it would affect him... the reader can... without any great toil or difficulty, find in clear understandable language, and kept up to date, the ruling concepts of our social order, the outlines and main particulars in all fields of knowledge, an exact and reasonably detailed picture of our universe, a general history of the world, and if by any chance he wanted to pursue a question into its ultimate detail, a trustworthy and complete system of reference to primary sources of knowledge. In fields where wide varieties of method and opinion existed, he would find, not casual summaries of opinions, but very carefully chosen and correlated statements and arguments.

A great new world is struggling into existence. But its struggle remains catastrophic until it can produce an adequate knowledge organisation. It is a giant birth and it is mentally defective and blind. An immense and ever-increasing wealth of knowledge is scattered about the world today, a wealth of knowledge and suggestion that— systematically ordered and generally disseminated—would probably give this giant vision a direction and suffice to solve all the mighty difficulties of our age, but that knowledge is still dispersed, unorganised, impotent in the face of adventurous violence and mass excitement.

H.G.Wells

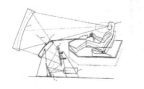

But how are we to prevent publication of crimes and/or illegal activities? How do we stop children seeing illegal or potentially corrupting data/thought atoms? Answer: do you really think that children are not already looking at all kinds of illicit material? I would suggest that an atomic network (or hyper-network) can provide a good solution in this respect; and by enabling all thought-atoms to be classifiable/annotatable (by everyone); and hence warnings and/or class-assignments can be placed on individual items (by many/all viewers). But are we not bringing back censure by the back-door here? Not really; and because users could (presumably) obtain a browser that enabled a child's parent to set a classification/viewing age for all content on the network as whole (people *choose* their own access level).

What about authority? Will this 'brain' not be a bit like Wikipedia, whereby reporting standards may *(sometimes be)* pretty poor; and because non-experts are allowed to edit anything, anytime. In actual fact Wikipedia (often) has high standards; and is not really like that at-all; but employs teams of professional editors to monitor edits. In any case, the World Brain will allow organisations to establish group consensus by overlaying/stamping their authority on particular thought structures, and so to develop *approved* assemblies of specific thought patterns.

The World Brain can replace, extend and supplant many activities that are today performed (or attempted to be performed) on the current World Wide Web. In particular open-publication is facilitated; whereby *anyone may publish anything to anyone and/or everyone else.* This is a primary feature; being a capability for everyone to contribute, and to *see/access/ annotate the open thoughts of the entire world,* and so to *see how they are all connected, interrelated and structured.* We shall be able to see: *who thought what, where, when and how.* And not only for the living and/or present-day thoughts; because the World Brain will be the repository for every thought ever *thunk* (at least those thoughts have been input into the system correctly).

A question arises. Who/what will enter all of these thought-atoms; and who/what will develop the classifications schemes, mapping and meta-data etc; and how? Answer; everyone will input/develop the content, just as happened with the Web.

We live in a world of unused and misapplied knowledge and skill. Knowledge and thought are ineffective. The human species regarded as a whole is extraordinarily like a man of the highest order of brain, who through some lesions or defects or insufficiencies of his lower centres, suffers from the wildest unco-ordinations; St. Vitus's dance, agraphia, aphonia, and suffers dreadfully (knowing better all the time) from the silly and disastrous gestures he makes and the foolish things he says and does. - H.G.Wells

Why would people go to the trouble of entering knowledge into this new 'brain'? Perhaps because it is a brain—a World Brain—and it is in their interests to do so. *Power to the people* can, should and will win, and in a similar way to the Web. When people realise that this system is so far beyond any previous system in terms of the *interconnectedness, accessibility and linkage of thought atoms*; people everywhere will be motivated to discover: *what the world is thinking/has-thought*.

I would suggest that we humans have reached a turning point; whereby we can simply go on much as in the past; allowing technology to progress in an entirely unplanned/ad-hoc manner (in the biggest sense). Whereby powerful people develop unrepresentative/narrow computing systems that are (in effect) simply excuses to foster more centralised control, and/or to exploit/limit the human-rights of, millions of weaker individuals.

Alternatively, we could start again and develop (at least one example) of a truly people-centric information system. A system which lets each of us see the *open-thoughts* of everyone in the world; and lets us vote *en masse* and so to discover our true wishes as a people. Developing a World Brain has been the dream of the most brilliant thinkers; but today it no longer needs to remain a dream; because we now posses the technology and (I would suggest) motivation and desire to actually make it happen. And it does not need the backing of a government or a large corporation to do so; but rather can be achieved in a grass-roots manner; whereby we can proceed along the lines of open-source projects like **BitCoin**, **BitTorrent** and **Linux** etc.

Enough said, because all of my cards are on the table, so to speak. But this book is only half finished. What then, you may ask, is the rest of the book to be about. In actual fact it concerns the building of the World Brain; and specifically: how to do so; likely obstacles, dangers of not so doing, and the exciting possibilities of the future if we do. It is not to be an artificial 'machine' brain (in any way); but will be composed simply of live/dynamic human thoughts; and primarily because we wish humanity to think collectively, efficiently and as one; aligning *the wishes, plans and actions of society* for the true benefit of all.

I am not saying that a World Encyclopaedia will in itself solve any single one of the vast problems that must be solved if man is to escape from his present dangers and distresses and enter upon a more hopeful phase of history; what I am saying—and saying with the utmost conviction —is this, that without a World Encyclopaedia to hold men's minds together in something like a common interpretation of reality, there is no hope whatever of anything but an accidental and transitory alleviation of any of our world troubles. As mankind is, so it will remain, until it pulls its mind together. And if it does not pull its mind together then I do not see how it can help but decline. Never was a living species more perilously poised than ours at the present time.

It may be objected that this is a Utopian dream. This is something too great to achieve, too good to be true. I won't deal with that for a few minutes. Flying was a Utopian dream a third of a century ago. What I am putting before you is a perfectly sane, sound and practicable proposal...

A greater danger, as I have already suggested, will come from attempts at the private mercenary exploitation of this world-wide need—the raids of popular publishers and heavily financed salesmen, and in particular attempts to create copyright difficulties and so to corner the services and prestige of this or that unwary eminent person by anticipatory agreements.

H.G.Wells

We want a reconditioned and more powerful Public Opinion. In a universal organisation and clarification of knowledge and ideas, in a closer synthesis of university and educational activities, in the evocation, that is, of what I have here called a World Brain, operating by an enhanced educational system through the whole body of mankind, a World Brain which will replace our multitude of uncoordinated ganglia, our powerless miscellany of universities, research institutions, literatures with a purpose, national educational systems and the like... an adequate directive control of the present destructive drift of world affairs. - H.G.Wells

From *The Great Chain of Being* by Arthur O. Lovejoy (1873-1962):

If we diminish variety in the natural world, we debase its unity and wholeness.
We destroy the forces making for natural harmony and stability,
for a lasting equilibrium, and what is even more significant...
we must conserve and promote variety.

Yet the species that succeeds in enlarging its niche in the environment,
enlarges the ecological conditions as a whole;
it expands its environment both for itself and for
the species which it enters into a balance with.

Conspiracy Theories

- Michael Drosin claims to have found hidden (prediction) messages in the Bible using specially written software (? surely false).

- SETI is a smokescreen and the government knows full well that little green men exist (? surely false).

- Governments worldwide eavesdrop in emails/surfing habits (true).

- The US government built a 'back-door' into the Java language (Sun MicroSystems JRE) to allow it (the NSA) to break into Apps/programs (true).

- No code (encryption) is unbreakable by CIA/NSA (perhaps false with correct tools).

- US Government [DARPA] setup Facebook as a spy network (maybe true given the Snowden spying revelations— in any case Facebook is spied upon).

- A Cyber war is ongoing worldwide. (true— governments routinely break into each-other's systems (USA/China etc)). These activities now extend to companies who routinely attack networks for a variety of reasons (spying, denial of service etc).

- Intel (attempted) to build spying 'backdoors' into all of its chips; and for all digital traffic {?}. In any case the UK captures all digital data (and saves it) on trans-atlantic comms cables.

Virtual Reality Apparatus

If anything is to count as a Thought, it must contribute —even if only potentially—to the operation of the system (of life) as a whole and to which it belongs.
Arthur O. Lovejoy

To radically shift regime behaviour we must think clearly and boldly for if we have learned anything, it is that regimes do not want to be changed. We must think beyond those who have gone before us, and discover technological changes that embolden us with ways to act in which our forebears could not.

Firstly we must understand what aspect of government or neo-corporatist behaviour we wish to change or remove. Secondly we must develop a way of thinking about this behaviour that is strong enough carry us through the mire of politically distorted language, and into a position of clarity.

Finally we must use these insights to inspire within us and others a course of ennobling, and effective action.

Julian Assange

Chapter Ten
Virtual Reality

T HE NOTION of *virtuality* refers to the design of imaginary worlds inside-of/outside the mind; and it may be considered to be, in a sense, the very opposite of reality—specifically because, according to the OED, it is:

- The possession of (unnatural) force or power;
- Apart from external form or embodiment;
- A virtual (as opposed to an actual) thing, capacity, etc.

During the 1990s, the term Virtual Reality (VR) became a popular way to describe any computer generated environment in which the user felt (or believed) that he had been transported into another realm or digital world that was (in some sense) entirely separate from his real-world body. Put simply, the computer simulated *presence* inside a false, imaginary, magical, or multi-dimensional reality. Because VR systems often used stereoscopic headsets and three-dimensional graphics; some people came to associate the term with 3D. However the ideas are (in fact) largely separate; and VR is linked with a whole range of presence transformation modalities; including: *visual-perception/illusions, sound, touch, taste, skin feelings, powers of the mind and thinking, macroscopic and microscopic explorations, remote terrain and/or multi-dimensional navigation, and even flight.*[1,2]

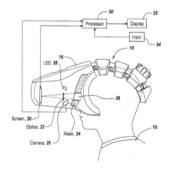

VR is also sometimes referred to as Immersive Media; being a computer-simulated environment that can simulate the real world and/or imagined worlds. VR covers remote or virtual presence of users, tele-existance or telepresence; and may be used for the purposes of communication with distant people and/or interaction with remote places, and/or to provide life-like experiences.

VR may be said to be all about creating realistic-illusions; i.e *artificial/augmented/illusive-reality* etc.

The vital factor of virtual reality is immersion, the degree to which the user's senses are limited to the simulation and screened from a real world. - Fjodor Ruzic

A virtual reality is not real, it is an illusion, a fake, and devoid of all the possibilities of life; and here one's vision/choices are at the mercy of the programmer.

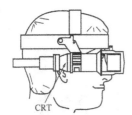

CRT

VR has its roots in creating simulations for training pilots; where it was used to help novice flyers get up to speed with the complex skills required to fly; and without all the attendant danger(s) of making a mistake.[2] Later during the early 1990s, VR technology enjoyed a brief popularity; and a number of university-groups and companies began experimenting with the opportunities that it seemed to offer for the scientific and medical fields, and also for entertainment.[1,3,4]

However much of the interest in VR faded away over the next twenty years or so; and perhaps because the necessary CPU processing power and/or graphics chips, plus software/displays were not available and/or powerful enough (yet). But currently VR is undergoing a new lease of life with fast and cheap VR headsets becoming readily available (see **Oculus Rift** etc). The time seems right to take a new look at VR; and to explore the possibilities of humans actually 'entering' the machine world.[5]

The term Virtual Reality can be traced to Frenchman Antonin Artaud (1892-1948), who in his 1938 book *The Theatre and its Double* described theatre as:

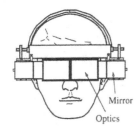

Mirror
Optics

> '*La réalité virtuelle*', a virtual reality in which, in Erik Davis's words, 'characters, objects, and images take on the phantasmagoric force of alchemy's visionary internal dramas... [claiming that] the perpetual allusion to the materials and the principle of the theatre found in almost all alchemical books should be understood as the expression of an identity... existing between the world in which the characters, images, and in a general way all that constitutes the *virtual reality* of the theatre develops, and the purely fictitious and illusory world in which the symbols of alchemy are evolved'.[6]

In this quote we see how VR was conceived (at least partially) as a mental world that the participant is somehow responsible for creating for himself (in his imagination). The concept of VR has been explored in films like *Brainstorm* and *The Lawnmower Man*. Other films like *Minority Report*, *Avatar* and *Transcendence* explored notions related to humans merging with digital world, remote viewing/presence, and escaping from the boundaries of time and space, and/or entering into alternative realities.

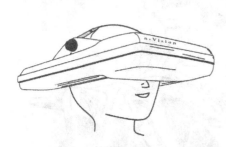

The computer is a protean technology; virtual reality is a protean medium. As virtual environments begin to diffuse throughout society, the range of these systems will be quite broad. The categories proposed here will certainly increase in complexity. The categories of components and the distinctions among systems will multiply as the virtual environment marketplace bursts into a kaleidoscope of applications and options. Like the microchip, a version of this medium may find its way into almost every form of mediated communication. - Frank Biocca and Ben Delaney

Because VR completely immerses a person into the virtual world, some people have claimed that VR constitutes a new form of human experience; a form that is as important as film, theatre and literature etc.[4] It is a technology that can potentially be applied to every type of human activity and be used to mediate in every human transaction (possibly). One could say that VR changes the nature of the human relationship to information/knowledge and reshapes our view of ourselves. It has been called by some the *last computing platform*—or the ultimate memory/mind extension. By totally immersing the consumer into the illustration itself, combined with the nonlinear, free-association format of hypertexts; it is difficult to come to any other conclusion than VR offering a *rejoining of mind and body*, a milieu that will create a new region/mode of human possibility.

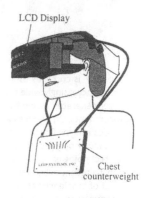

LCD Display

Chest counterweight

VR may be (part of) what we are evolving into/towards.

Many questions are raised by VR. What is the status of the virtual experience? Does it represent a pull away from, or else towards, the real world? Are VR simulations more or less *real* than our ordinary experiences? What is reality? Who am I? What is the nature of the beholder's share in viewing reality; and is anything truly real. Is the virtual a mere *hollow reflection* of the world, or does it magnify/enhance reality and allow us to perceive *more* of reality? To see panoramic vistas of information that shimmer, vibrate, and reveal themselves according to our whims, and thus to make: *the invisible visible*.

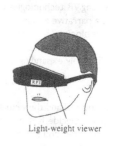

Light-weight viewer

In attempting to answer such questions, one must separate VR as it actually exists from mere speculations of VR as a possibility. With an idea as generalised, chameleon-like and all-encompassing as VR; we must withdraw from the temptation to associate VR with everything and anything, and with endless speculations/possibilities.

VR is no panacea. But rather is an extremely complex and impressive example of ordinary computer design; being constructed wholly from *machine implanted-thoughts* which have been so aligned as to create an illusion of a life-like universe within the artificial world. Thus VR is, in a sense, no more/less real than any other form of computer interaction.

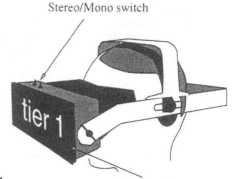

Stereo/Mono switch

tier 1

Detachable viewer

Virtual reality may become *everyday reality*; in that we might all soon be constantly interacting with immersive computing illusions and surrounding data-displays; extra 'worlds' that we feel that we are inside of, in some way; the same being 3D, holographic, projected scenes; whereby these are overlaid onto the real world, and in ways that seem perfectly natural, enjoyable and seductive.

'Virtual reality' is currently used to describe an increasingly wide array of computer-generated or mediated environments, experiences and activities ranging from the near ubiquity of video games, to emerging technologies such as tele-immersion, to technologies still only dreamed of in science fiction and only encountered in the novels of William Gibson or Orson Scott Card, on the Holodeck of television's *Star Trek*, or at the movies in *The Matrix* of the Wachowski brothers, where existing VR technologies make possible a narrative about imagined VR technologies. The term 'virtual reality' covers all of this vast, and still rapidly expanding, terrain.

Derek Stanovksy

Since the real and the virtual can never quite coincide, it is in creating the perspective and the viewpoint from which to observe the real (from the virtual) and vice versa that the scientist and artist dealing with virtual reality is inevitably adopting a political stance. Everything that has to do with virtual reality has political consequences and is therefore a more or less direct act of politics. By dealing with the creation of viewpoint, the artist or scientist who engages with virtual reality is in effect deciding how the user is to view the spectacle of the real.

Gabriella Giannachi

VR is an illusion. Only it is a particularly impressive illusion, and one that can potentially (in certain instances) inform or help the user to learn and/or to understand far more than any other type of human-computer interaction. Even though the VR world *itself* may be no more real than any other method of information exploration (it is a purely constructed representation); nevertheless wondrous possibilities may be opened up by its legerdemain. Seen philosophically, VR creates a new relationship to *symbols, language, thought and to human views/senses of reality; and ultimately, to ourselves.* No longer outside of the computer, VR lets us step into the looking glass and enter the world of *The Matrix (from the Sanskrit and Latin term 'mother').* As in *Neuromancer,* we become immersed into the information itself; only in our terms all is human thought-atoms or thought-outcomes in the form of (for example) data.[7]

In the language of the present book, everything we see in VR is simply computer implanted-thoughts, a reflection of the human mind. Here nothing is any more real than our thoughts; and in a way VR simply lets us explore the contents of our own minds. VR may help us to see or conceptualise the real world, as it expands our perception in a variety of ways, but the fact remains that the virtual is a construct, and all the machine's constructs (plus everything they contain) are dead (pre-visioned/pre-planned).

Hopefully my analysis does not sound negative, anti-VR or in any way a put-down of the capabilities of VR. Rather I am attempting to clarify the well-known/obvious fact that machines (VR) are human-made; plus we are limited by, and (in a real sense) constructed by, our own perception(s). VR may confer fabulous powers, enabling us to grow tall enough to see right up to the very 'edge' of the barrier(s) of human imagination; but no further. In a way VR lets us become more (or fully) human; and in this sense VR brings us in closer attune to the realm of life.

VR may be either separately or simultaneously: *a simulation, interaction, artificiality, an immersion, a telepresence and/or a networked communication.* Taken together with all of these transformations, we notice that VR is a potentiality to see reality anew, to don a set of psychedelic reality 'glasses'.

Virtual reality is a first person, sensory rich, computer generated environment, which displays video graphics and provides physical feedback. A flight simulator is an example of a high-end virtual environment, whereas an arcade game is an example of a low-end environment. And the Internet, the television, the telephone, and the photograph might be viewed as 'early VR technologies'. - Mychilo Cline

An ontological shift is a change in the world under our feet, in the whole
context in which our knowledge and awareness are rooted. - Michael Heim

VIRTUAL REALITY 231

VR transforms reality. But the transformation is by no means obvious, specific or singular. A VR simulator must be able to manipulate the senses, *overriding their normal functions*; so that we can experience an environment partially or entirely different from the one that we are actually located in. In a sense, all technologies of representational art and/or distant communication override the normal functions of these senses (to a degree). Virtuality is about seeing things that are not really there; or which may be, in one sense or another, present but are invisible due to scale, distance, complexity etc. VR is as if we had a dream where we obtained magical powers that enabled us to see with the mind of a God; an all-seeing, everywhere present and all-encompassing type of vision.

VR is a kind of _magic-mirror_ for reality/ourselves, or at least those parts/regions of reality that we are able to conceptualise as thoughts/design-concepts and then, in turn, represent to ourselves in the form of a VR system. According to David Deutsch (1953-), the laws of physics place no limitations on the ability of VR 'image-generators' to produce artificial worlds of almost any degree of accuracy plus detail; and to render visible simulations of an almost unbelievable complexity/truth.[8]

Tiny and enormous things, very fast and/or very slow processes become visible, and complex happenings may be simplified. The problems of VR world-construction are merely technical/technological, and the only limitation may be our understanding of reality itself. Indeed according to the vision of *The Matrix*, it may be that we humans could one day find these artificial world's so enticing, illuminating and enjoyable; that we retire from the real world altogether, and spend all of our days inside the imaginary world of the computer.

A frightening scenario? Perhaps. But a retreat from reality may be already happening. When did you last see a child playing outside? An 'artificialisation' of reality is occurring, of making dreams comes true, of painting unreal worlds inside/outside of the mind, of *imagineering* as the Disney company refers to it; and of projecting the hyperreal onto reality, or mapping the 'matrix' onto everything that is.

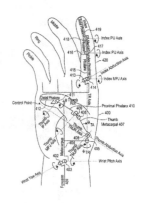

When children are growing up, they face a profound conflict between the internal world of their dreams and imagination, in which everything's possible and fluid, and the practical world in which they have parents, food, and friends, in which they're not alone, and in which they can survive. So as kids grow up, they have to gradually de-emphasise this world of imagination and celebration and emphasise the practical world, unless they're willing to be alone in their insanity and completely dependent on others for survival. Of course it's possible to integrate the two, but it's so hard, like walking a tightrope. I think the reason that kids instinctively love computers, and especially love virtual reality, is that it really does present a new solution, a way to make imaginary worlds that we can be together in, just like the real world.

Jaron Lanier

The language machine regulates and adjusts in advance the mode of our possible usage of language through mechanical energies and functions. The language machine is—and above all, is still becoming—one way in which modern technology controls the mode and the world of language as such... The language machine takes language into its management, and thus masters the essence of the human being. - Martin Heidegger

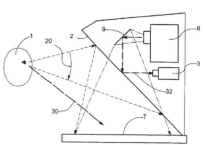

Cyberspace is Platonism as a working product. - Michael Heim

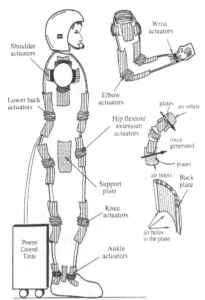

Wrist actuators

Shoulder actuators

Lower back actuators

Elbow actuators

plates   air inlets

Hip flexion/ extension actuators

force generated

plates

air inlets   Back plate

Support plate

Knee actuators

air holes in the plate

Power/ Control Units

Ankle actuators

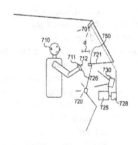

-70
710   750
711 712 721
730
726
720   725 728

Ultrasonic Head Tracker

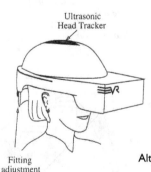

Fitting adjustment

In his 1992 book *Virtual Worlds, A Journey into Hype and Hyperreality*, Benjamin Woolley said:

> What are the limits of the artificial? Is there, can there be, any contact with reality when computers can create artificial worlds that are more realistic than the real world, when technology scorns nature? ... [but] ... an increasingly complex, artificial environment can diminish our sense of reality... and, as that sense diminishes, so innumerable troubling side-effects start to creep in.[1]

Perhaps mankind, the technology maker, is ever immersed in artificialities of his own making. Woolley notes that it is industry and the power to manufacture, that has made the world progressively more artificial and less 'real'; providing wealth and energy to change the natural landscape, and so to replace-it/augment-it with one of our own making. Thus a more relevant question may not be so much *what is real*; but rather how can we manage/create our real-world human reality in accordance with optimum outcomes.

We must learn to manipulate the *real world* artfully, and to do so according to our collective needs. The *Theories of Natural* and *Machine Implanted-Thoughts* spoken of earlier can perhaps help us to manage the process of creating 'useful' artificialities. Overall, we must be careful to 'see' the human condition from a sufficient (clarifying) distance. Desired is an unrestricted view of the two natures, the real and the artificial, and our relationship(s) to both.

According to Woolley, the industrial experience has both destroyed reality, and reinforced it, at the same time. Everywhere we see wholesale manipulation of the human mind; and our very thoughts are *structured, shaped, controlled* and *'pushed-about'*; by an enormous number of mediating factors. These same factors are introduced and promulgated by *mass media, culture, religion, science, historical narratives, and commercial messages etc.* Our personal and collective realities are constantly warped by all of these different forces; yet oddly it is very difficult to stand back and see all of these same factors from a distance, and so to obtain a clarifying perspective.

Although virtual reality is not likely to result in apocalyptic social change, as it is slowly integrated in daily life and activity, we should expect to begin to see some very important changes. Basic changes to daily life and activity will lead to the development of new social and economic interaction patterns, and to a new world view, as we adapt to a changing environment. Online communications will promote the formation of new social groups. - Mychilo Cline

Building a World Brain using an *atomic-network* can (possibly) supply a solution, enabling the vast interconnectedness of everything (all thought atoms) to be explored; and so to see many views of reality; and each with a new scope, detail and relevance. And this may be where VR can provide its most useful contribution to the human journey; in fact by making visible the true features of the World Brain, and enabling each of us to navigate the vast complexity of all the world's thought-atoms.

Hopefully this discussion is not veering too much into obscure metaphysics. At the UK's first VR conference, Tony Feldman said that when it comes to the implications of VR, *the metaphysics are inescapable.*

Benjamin Woolley wrote:

> Technology can manipulate reality to the point of being able to create it. Artificialisation is no longer just a matter of cultural observation or intellectual angst, it has become, well, real. It is for this reason that reality is no longer secure, no longer something we can simply assume to be there.[1]

Earlier I made similar case, stating that human thoughts may be embedded in media and/or machines; and the same can/do influence human realities, and in a variety of real, imaginary and restrictive/empowering forms. Noticed was that unnatural thought-forms restrict free-thinking processes in the most profound ways. Accordingly system implanted-thoughts may limit and/or empower human actions, possibilities and so influence human life most profoundly. However the boundaries of the self-computer are very difficult to see/define, and in terms of a separation of the naturally occurring mode(s) of being; from the artificial, technical, or machine-manipulated forms of human life.

Nevertheless, it is a central facet of my thesis that all artificial realities are (ultimately) human made.

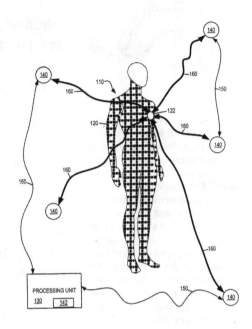

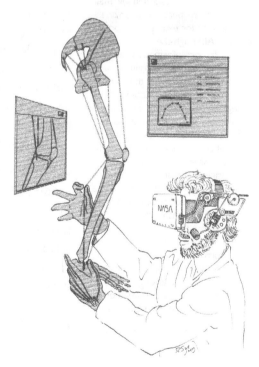

One hears talk of the 'virtual office', or the' virtual university'. To the extent electronics allow one to operate from a motel room as though he were situated in a conventional, unmovable office, there is good reason to speak here too of virtual reality. I shall call this form of virtual reality *electronic presencing.* As in a telephone conversation, a new kind of space is produced, based on annihilation of some of the effects of physical separation. - Thomas Langan

These are the fiery objects of dream and longing. - Michael Heim

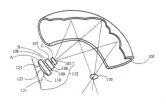

Communication in the age of virtual reality is in some ways about transportation. Tele-presence replaces tele-vision. The body's sensorimotor channels are conveyed to distant real and virtual worlds. Experience is transmitted. Transmission and transportation share more than a common root word. In the 19th century, telegraph wires and train tracks raced side-by-side across the fields and forests of America's western frontier. These two transmission channels, the train and the telegraph, competed to 'transport' information. Trains, planes, and trucks still transport information carried on physical media like paper and ink: mail, newspapers, and magazines-consider, for example, the postal system. Although the telegraph had far less information-carrying capacity than the train, it easily outraced the physical transportation channel. The telegraph's thin flow of information was more valuable than the train's car loads of slow information. The flow of communication is now sent across space and time through various transmission channels: copper wires, fibre optic cables, the electro-magnetic spectrum, and so forth. Millions of miles of wires criss-cross the planet and wrap it like a giant ball of string. Surrounding this giant ball, the electromagnetic spectrum thrums with the chant of millions of messages. The transmission of information surrounds us.

Frank Biocca and Mark R. Levy

The problem is one of seeing/sensing (and managing) the influence(s) of computers on human life; or in other words appropriate and human-centric design of the self-computer.

VR can help us in this respect. VR is the technology used to provide a more intimate 'interface' between the fundamentally different worlds of the human and computer. Simulated can be the full ensemble of those human 'senses' that make up the real. This process may require the wearing of devices such as headsets, bodysuits and/or for the body to be immersed in some kind of VR 'chamber' or encompassing/surrounding medium such as the CAVE VR system.[5] All of these technical systems and their working functionalities are well-known and described elsewhere; and so we shall not attempt technical exposition here. Rather we place emphasis on the nature of the simulated reality; and what it means for human understanding, decision making and efficient planning for and/or actioning of future (more humane) societies.

Regardless of implementation details, the fact remains that VR is simply an extension of ordinary computer functionality; in that it provides a simulation with which the user may engage. A simulation is a form of imitation or representation of *something*. What this *something* is or can be, is in fact a topic of much debate. Ultimately, as stated, and in my view, what can be simulated is merely the human mind itself *(plus data flows from reality)*. No matter how realistic a VR simulation may appear to be, its functions and representations are purely machine implanted-thoughts; and data—which also emanates from what the human designer tells the computer to take notice of.

VR is simply a reflection of the human mind; nothing more.

But perhaps VR is something more, much more; and because in a sense by allowing us to access these machine implanted-thoughts, to see their vast complexity, interconnections and relations; we may learn more about our own minds. VR allows us to delve into our minds to a greater degree than is possible using natural means. VR lets us picture the past/future; and because it operates as a time-machine; thus we can explore the possibilities of new assemblies of matter, models, and/or thoughts; and without actually having to build anything.

VR dangles in front of our eyes a vision of the media's future, changes in the ways we communicate, and the way we think about communication. The medium that tantalises us so has gone by a number of names: computer simulation, artificial reality, virtual environments, augmented reality, cyberspace, and so on. More terms are likely to be invented as the technology's future unfolds. But the enigmatic term *virtual reality* has dominated the discourse. It has defined the technology's future by giving it a goal; the creation of virtual reality. Virtual reality is not a technology; it is a destination. - Frank Biocca

Just like the pilots who experimented with VR as a training tool; the future of computing may be immersion into vast VR simulations of whatever models/constructions may take our fancy. VR allows us to tap nature's—and our own—hidden powers. VR may put us more in touch with cosmic forces, and ultimately with ourselves. As in the early LSD experiments, VR allows us to see how everything fits together to form (potentially) one universe/human-reality. All *hard* distinctions fade somewhat as a result; and the artificial lines drawn between one thing and another become less-distinct, less-permanent, less-important, and/or may be interpenetrated with many new links and/or modes of communication. False distinctions between *matter and form, alive and dead, inside and out etc,* may disappear altogether; as we begin to see the intricate interconnections present in the World Brain that is all human knowledge.[9]

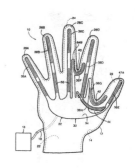

Artificial reality promises creation of a new world—any world that you could ever want or imagine. Worlds brimming with the *fantastical, beautiful, fabulous, terrifying, infinite, utopian.* VR is like the legendary river Styx in Greek mythology. This river formed a boundary between the Earth and the Underworld, and had powers that could make someone invulnerable. Likewise VR lets humans explore/engage-with whole new regions of being without fear of injury to self; a seemingly magical and enticing capability not present in any other technology.

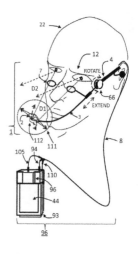

According to Woolley:

> Artificial reality does reveal a great deal about the way that the idea of reality is used and understood... if nothing else, it reveals that much of what we take to be reality is a myth. It reveals that the things we assume to be independent of us are actually constructed by us. It reveals that being 'real', like being 'natural', is not simply a value-free, unproblematic, apolitical, objective state.[1]

But according to Woolley there is an ultimate reality that human knowledge, and in particular science, attempts to approach. VR may help as move closer to this *real reality*, and/or to explore the possibilities of any chosen (modelled) reality that we could make real.

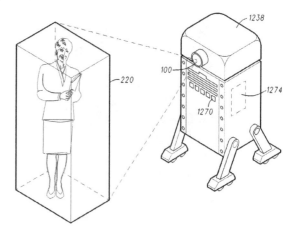

I began to realise why artificial intelligence and robotics and [computer-generated] animation have become such fundamental science. The VR researchers are reinventing the world from scratch. - Stewart Brand

The thing about a VR headset as opposed to a 2D screen, is that you are there, the data surrounds you, and the data becomes you in a way that never happens normally.

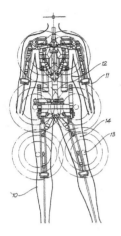

VR is, in a sense, a very personal experience. Regardless of whether you meet people inside of the artificial world; the individual nevertheless (typically) becomes the God of his own universe. A VR headset is the ultimate in detachment, in self-absorption, separation from the real world—or at least the world of one's immediate body.

But are the individualistic/antisocial aspect(s) of VR true?

According to our *Theory of Natural Thoughts*; everything known consists of vast assemblies of thoughts and associated thought patterns. Because VR is (in one sense) simply a means for exploring these thoughts, wholly machine implanted-thoughts (by/from other people); some form of public reality may be an inevitable aspect of the technology itself. And in my view, any technology of VR must (be designed to) preserve and protect the essential Attributes of natural-thoughts—in general; hence (for example) open-thoughts must be accessible to all. One would assume that many VR worlds would consist of the exploration of open-thought atoms; and hence a conclusion is made that VR is essentially a social technology (or at least if it is to be a natural form of human thought/expression/activity).

Jaron Lanier commented that the VR experience is:

> Very hard to describe if you haven't experienced it. But there is an experience when you are dreaming of all possibilities being there, that anything can happen, and it is just an open world where your mind is the only limitation. But the problem is that its just you, you are all alone. And then you wake up, you give up all that freedom. All of us suffered a terrible trauma as children that we've forgotten, where we had to accept the fact that we are physical beings and yet in the physical world where we have to do things, we are very limited. The thing that I think is so exciting about VR is that it gives us this freedom again. It gives us the sense of being able to be who we are without limitation, for our imagination to become objective and shared with other people.[1]

Thus a real advantage of VR may be that it allows us to explore the collective open-thoughts of everyone else. VR may be the ultimate social medium; and it may become where we spend most of our time (interacting/socialising).

Will a day (soon) arrive when we do not even bother to leave the house; when we see no need to interact with the real world, and other humans, ever. Does this not already seem very much like the teenager who has hundreds of 'social-network' friends he never meets, and who seems content to just sit in front of screens all day long. Actually, don't we all just sit in front of screens all day long; and are we not all then (in some sense) alone?

Already some people 'interact' with more people on social networks than they do in the real world; and many form relationships with people that they may never meet in real life, or certainly would not even wish to meet. VR thus has two strands. On one hand, it brings us closer together by allowing us to interact in a more realistic way using 3D graphics, touch etc. But it may enable people to (fully) explore the open-thoughts of others by facilitating views of complex (public) thought-patterns.

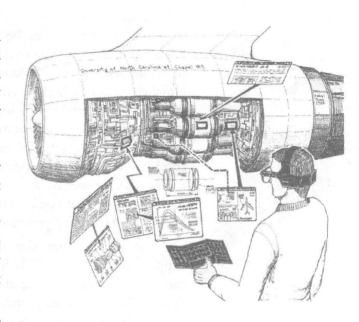

VR enables us to explore invisible and/or imponderable worlds that were previously inaccessible. It may provide views into the world as it exists at the molecular scale, or on the vast scale of colliding galaxies (for example); and/or give us x-ray glasses from which to see inside the human body etc. When immersed 'inside' of complex scientific models, the user gains an appreciation of previously unnoticed facts and/or may solve problems that were too intricate or obscure to solve normally. But we must remember that VR can only show us what has been conceived of in the human mind and no more. With VR we are only ever looking at thought-atoms or data that results from, or is prescribed by, other thought-atoms of one kind or another—and in a way—nothing is real.

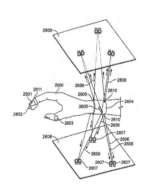

Certainly we may discover new facts and/or make discoveries by means of VR; but these are, in a sense, pre-figured/pre-determined; and because the programmer or system designer 'told' the system what variables to model and/or real-world data points to notice/collect/show etc. The designer himself may not actually have known what the VR system would find/show, but he nevertheless prescribed the regions of 'looking/searching'.

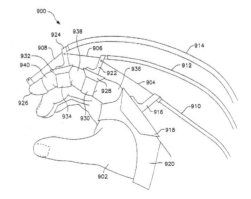

Computers are mostly used against people instead of for people. Used to control people instead of to FREE them, Time to change all that. - People's Computer Company

We hear about people who become addicted to technology. But can the mind actually become lost inside its constructs, and never truly come back?

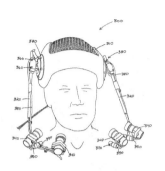

I am not trying to down-play VR in any way, but rather pre-warn the reader not to be fooled by the fabulous beauty, complexity, and/or apparent realism of VR. The reader will soon (if he/she has not already done so) be trying on VR goggles for him/her self as they became commonplace both at work and play. What a person 'sees' with a set of VR goggles is a very realistic-looking alternative reality, and it may be a very convincing one. The senses may be (entirely) fooled, and you are transported into another dimension, so to speak; complete with *wonderful artistic details, superb geometries, and beautiful vistas*; yet it is important to remember that what you are really seeing is simply (and solely) the open-thought atoms / prescribed data; of other humans!

Please do not get the impression that everything that happens in a VR world is somehow false, fictitious, suspect, subject to constant change and/or simply a matter of opinion. Some VR worlds may indeed be like this; with shifting/impossible transitions, boundaries and unreal properties/capabilities/visions; but others will be what Ivan Sutherland [1938-] called '*mathematical wonderlands*'; where ultimately what happens is determined by the laws of physics/mathematics etc.

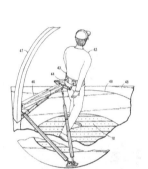

VR has (or will have) enough 'faces' to satisfy the varied tastes of all; and it will evolve in multiple/different directions.

This discussion brings to mind the question of what VR is, in and of itself. Marshall McLuhan (1911-1980) spoke about the medium being the message; but what he actually meant to say was that networks/technologies are not transparent; but rather the medium has a role in determining what the audiences see and how they make sense of it (i.e. the content). For McLuhan electronic technologies like television and radio brought the people of the world closer together, and in fact formed a type of extended human nervous system that comprised a global village.

McLuhan's vision extends the views of men like Wells, Goldberg and Otlet. VR may be a major part of our human destiny, and be how we see/enter the World Brain. VR could (one day) become the default interaction method for all (or most) computing systems/networks.

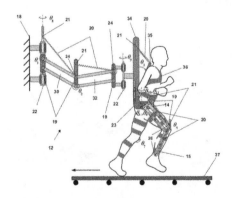

Who are you? How much of what you are as a human being is prescribed by socialisation and training. How much of you is defined by language. Are they your thoughts or were they implanted? Self-knowledge may ultimately be knowledge of all humanity.

If you meet someone in Cyberspace/VR, in what sense did you meet? Did you meet a real person or simply a figment of your own imagination? Is it not simply you meeting ideas?

VIRTUAL REALITY 239

Yet technophobes always seem to doubt the usefulness of any new technology, and the death of culture is sometimes predicted by anti new-media types. For example the death of the physical book has long been predicted. However studies show that people are reading more books in the year 2015 than ever before; or at least more are sold (including e-books). In short digital technologies, cyberspace, VR etc; are all unthinkable without the print culture that they claim to transcend. McLuhan himself stated that the content of any new medium is precisely the old medium that it is has replaced; and we are thus pulled relentlessly back towards the past. This is as it should be; for what can, or would we be, and what old-dangers such as totalitarianism would re-emerge, if we (in fact) desired (and achieved) a forgetting of the copious lessons of history.

Perhaps Cyberspace and VR represent a revolutionary expansion, and freeing-up, of our senses of (real) reality, liberty and also humanity. Let us hope so—in early chapters we noted that the problems faced by humanity are precipitous and real; and needed are solutions—desperately.

< {20} Human survival depends on enlightenment. >

Enlightenment (by all) of the biggest problems we face as a species; enlightenment of where the solutions may be found and how we may come together to enact appropriate actions. Enlightenment is traditionally a personal journey, but this collective enlightenment can only come from technology.

A technology such as VR reflects and re-inscribes the previously felt oppositions of: *mind/body, self/other, inside/outside, matter/form, animate/inanimate.* In terms of VR system design/goals, we need a wide-ranging investigation of the bigger questions; and especially those that relate to issues of a primary and collective concern.

The question remains of how can VR help? Perhaps by merging the concept of a World Brain, with real-world problems/viewpoints.

Often I have sat and thought, Philosophically, Am I the author of that thought, Or is it the author of me? - John Lucus

VIRTUAL INTERFACE ENVIRONMENT
SURGICAL SIMULATION AND PLANNING

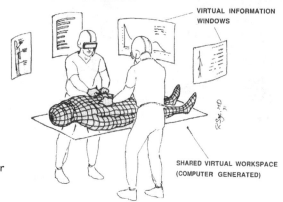

VIRTUAL INFORMATION WINDOWS

SHARED VIRTUAL WORKSPACE (COMPUTER GENERATED)

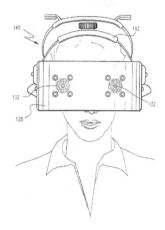

Human thought-atoms, patterns and assemblies must be (if we could adequately perceive all of them) of immense scale, complexity and interconnection. Hopefully we have now established that viewing the world's open ideas/votes is a good idea (with fantastic attendant benefits). Previously we described how a World Brain may be created using an atomic network (or hyper-network). Let us now suppose that such a network is already in place, and furthermore that people have a means of entering all the world's thought-atoms, and organising and inter-relating the same using two-way links, overlays, omni-links etc. A major question remains; how do we navigate such a vast network of thought-atoms?

VR is a technology that may provide such a capability.

Marcos Novak wrote:

> Cyberspace is a completely spatialised visualisation of all information in global information processing systems, along pathways provided by present and future communication networks, enabling full co-presence and interaction of multiple users, allowing input and output from and to the full human sensorium, permitting simulations of real and virtual realities, remote data collection and control through telepresence, and total integration and intercommunication with a full range of intelligent products and environments on a real space... Cyberspace is a habitat of the imagination... the place where conscious dreaming meets subconscious dreaming... the triumph of it-can-be-so over it-should-be-so.[4]

VR offers true convergence of minds; through the *visibility, transparency, and accessibility of thought atoms, votes plus data.* Perhaps this convergence of cyberspace and VR is already happening, in a very limited fashion and with ordinary (largely unconnected) data types. Systems like *Second-Life*, and massive multiplayer online games point to a shift towards bringing presence to the Internet. However as described, the Internet is fundamentally broken, and because the thought/data-atoms are wholly isolated and disconnected.

The question has always been how do we couple the human and machine parts of the system? How do we get information from the machine into the head, and how do we get information from the head into the machine? And that leads inevitably to computer graphics, because the eye is a broad-bandwidth information channel with specialised information processing and real-time pattern recognition. - Frederick Brooks

The danger of more and more realism is that if you don't have corresponding truthfulness, you teach people things that are not so. - Frederick Brooks

VIRTUAL REALITY 241

I do not think it is possible to argue that VR worlds may (in a sense) bring people closer together, and engender a type of social and/or mystical unity that is not provided by other technologies. But how exactly can VR cut, rather than untie, the gordian knot of present day problems? In part, and as stated, the answer lies in preservation of the Attributes of natural thoughts; and thus of an improved visibility of thoughts etc.

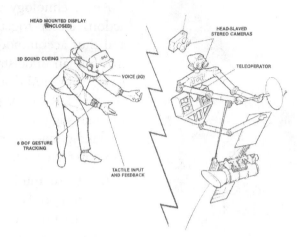

Yet we seek concrete answers.

Starving people cannot obtain sustenance inside of a VR world, even if they had access to such a technology. It is fair distribution of wealth and resources, including education, that are a permanent requirement. We have already discussed how formation and operation of a World Brain can potentially render the world into a more democratic place; and hence (one would suppose) indirectly provide solutions to the aforementioned problems. The question remains of how might VR boost the efficiency and/or effectiveness of the World Brain? As a partial solution, we have recommended the capability of virtuality to displace/transcend materiality. Yet this is (in one sense) a lie of the first order. The purpose of any communication technology must be to bring us *more in tune* with the material, with the real, and with the problems faced by us collectively as a species. This is the prime directive, mentioned earlier, design of the self-computer according to the real-world needs of humanity.

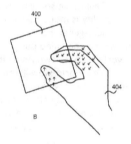

Denying materiality is a dangerous illusion; and one that politicians and other promulgators of rhetoric engage in everyday; whereby many mistake labels, buzzwords and 'statistics' for reality. But perhaps it is not only the politicians who are guilty of such category mistakes. We all 'see' the world through distorting 'lenses'; and it is difficult to objectify reality.

The primary research instrument of the sciences of complexity is the computer. It is altering the architecture of the sciences and the picture we have of material reality...The computer, with its ability to manage enormous amounts of data and to simulate reality, provides a new window on the view of nature. It provides a different angle on reality. - Heinz Pagels

Cinerama was invented by Fred Waller. He wanted to enlarge the field of view of the rather small rectangle presented by even the largest screens of the day. - Morton Heilig

To some extent, virtual reality may be viewed as an extension of existing technology, the telephone, television, and the video game. That is, virtual reality will replace the telephone, the television, and will fulfil those social roles. Yet, virtual reality is more than just the next-generation telephone, television, and video game; it is a world unto its own. And within this world, we will see the development of a virtual economy, new business models, new social groups, and new interaction styles. Welcome to the 'Virtual World'.

Mychilo Cline

Does virtual reality provide us with new ways to augment, enhance, and experience reality, or does it undermine and threaten that reality? Virtual reality is equally prone to portrayals as either the bearer of bright utopian possibilities or dark dystopian nightmares, and both of these views have some basis to recommend them.

Derek Stanovsky

Any technology that sought to bring collective wishes and actions closer together, must embrace democratic principles and thus accommodate a wide range of opinions. Remember that human understanding consists of logical thoughts and also *feeling tones*, and that both are used to perceive/assign meaning. Because VR brings presence, and greater connection/visibility; I would suggest that it (potentially) allows us to make decisions by taking into account these *feelings tones*, and hence to be more in tune with human needs.

Are these musings utopian, unrealistic and/or wish-driven? Do I ignore or lament human nature as it truly is, complete with anti-social and/or evil/crime tendencies. On the contrary, I claim that presence technologies, because they bring us closer together as a people, offer a very real chance for human beings to cross the divides of *cultural/material/ideological* differences, and to see the world's problems anew. How so?

It is my belief that a conceptual shift is possible (and essential); specifically in terms of how humanity views itself collectively, and in terms of its goals, capabilities and possibilities. In a similar fashion to the moon mission, where many people actually believed that it was mankind and not the Americans who walked on the moon; collective ownership of human problems/achievements is possible.

Once we see that human problems are owned by, and in a sense, caused by, us all; perhaps the first steps towards genuine solution(s) may be taken. The theory of implanted-thoughts may help us to see/realise the potential of VR. All of man's creative output; everything present in all of our social, industrial, educational and cultural systems; may be seen simply as instances of *world implanted-thoughts*; which are inserted into reality in the form of systems, machines and pre-defined processes. Dangers lurk when we come to see these world-implanted thoughts as disembodied; and without an owner or implementer who is responsible for resulting actions/outputs. We must take collective responsibility for our actions (or thought-outcomes); and discard the fiction/lie that the machines are out of control.

One of the most intriguing concepts of virtual reality is the ability to achieve a realistic simulation of worlds which are entirely the product of the imagination. One example of this sense of freedom is evident in the way that virtual worlds do not have to behave according to the laws of physics which rule over our physical world. Theories contradictory to our common spatial experience (and common sense) are easily applied to a VR environment. Buildings do not have to respond to the laws of gravity or physical material characteristics; collisions can or cannot happen; you can walk through walls; the figure-ground relations can be inverted; you can be at two or more places at the same time. New spatial sensibilities are discovered from the interactive processes used by a design in a virtual environment. The directions of left and right, in front and behind, up and down, corresponding to the Cartesian interpretation of the physical world could collapse. - Daniela Bertol

A human being sees 155 degrees vertically and 185 degrees horizontally. A movie screen fills only a small portion of the normal human field of view. - Morton Heilig

VIRTUAL REALITY 243

Earlier I highlighted the vast number, complexity and unprecedented diversity of system/world implanted-thoughts; and the question arises as to how it is possible to observe all of the countless affects of systems/machines on human life. My answer is that the people themselves can watch for instances where techno-rights (see end-notes) are broken and/or infringed. The World Brain allows such a process to happen; whereby vast numbers of 'eyes' watch and record the activities of systems everywhere; and in effect log the results for others to add-up. Thus humans may register malfunctioning system implanted-thoughts, and (using an atomic network) register new open-thought atoms as complaints for others to see and act upon.

VR helps in this process by providing a prosthesis to the natural 'sensorium'; and hence facilitating the experience of the mediated perception of countless open-thoughts; rendered immediately available to all users. A new multi-faceted vision; consisting of vastly distributed insect-like VR eyes can be 'switched-on'; with which to create a structural coupling between the designs and the actions/influences of machines on human life. This coupling has to be atomic and all-seeing, and in order to allow people everywhere to register (and to receive) their techno-rights.

It is precisely this coupling between a machine braking human rights, and the ability to sense, register and counter for its effects, that is missing from today's world. Couplings must be carefully designed. Coupling facets include: *detection of a human-rights infringement, formal and informal registration of the infringement, legal mechanisms to map/correct/compensate/enforce the techno-rights etc.* VR/AR technologies can help by visualising/locating infringement(s) in time and place; and registering the point of contact with humanity; and crucially by mapping the machine influence back to the human implementer. Such a mapping may involve finding actors of implanted-thought(s) and forcing legal compliance. VR helps us to visualise/navigate/interrelate these couplings.

The present invention, generally, relates to simulator apparatus and, more particularly, to apparatus to stimulate the senses of an individual to simulate and actually experience realistically. - Morton Heilig

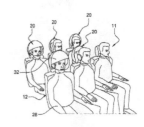

As a mere substitute of reality, a mask of the truth that hides behind its signs, virtual reality is not different from any other semiotic code: a mixture of conventional and iconic (mimetic) signs, both being signifiers of reality, the reality being the signified. And yet virtual reality claims to be much more than *mimesis* and representation. Virtual reality is a simulation of reality that demands to be experienced as a total replacement of reality itself. Whoever approaches virtual reality's environment as a totalising experience is hanging on the balance of such duplicity. On the one hand, one knows perfectly well that what he or she is experiencing is not real. On the other hand, the temptation to call it *another* reality (if not a self-sufficient reality) is very strong. Virtual reality is not just an experience that creates a new fragment of reality: the degree of participation involved is so high that it displaces non-virtual reality.

Alessandro Carrera

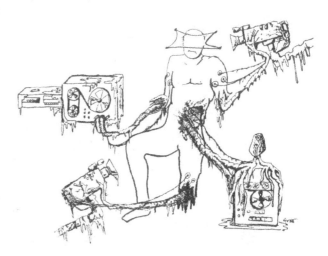

Desired is a change in the cultural status of machine/system implanted-thoughts; whereby it must no longer be acceptable to blame the 'ownerless' machine and/or a system 'error' when human rights are ignored or broken. The default mode of operation/influence of machines must be: *respect for techno-rights*.

All machines influence humanity, and because that is their intended purpose. Even when a machine appears to be wholly immaterial and/or illusive/benign; it must be influencing somebody, somewhere (one would suppose). Some machine influences will be in the form of *secret* or *private: system-implanted* and/or *media implanted-thoughts*; and hence be private. But in general most thoughts that interface/interact with society, and thus are implanted in the world in a 'public' sense, will be open-thoughts; and therefore inherently owned by all (according to the *Theory of Natural Thoughts*). Note that whenever a thought (of any type) affects a person by breaking his/her techno-rights, then that same thought has (where it touches humanity) become an open-thought atom in a legal/responsibility sense.

This discussion might seem a long way from the technical aspects and/or possibilities of VR; and somewhat distant also from topics that relate to the self-computer. In respect to the first charge, I plead guilty; and because the purpose of this book is not to discuss technicalities, per se; but rather to view matters from a broad perspective, and to identify general areas where solutions to current problems may be found, instead of identifying actual technical paths/solutions. In relation to the second aspect, current systems try to display facts, claims and thoughts online. Needed is a system that takes us back to the sources of those facts, claims and thoughts.

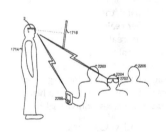

VR offers potential(s) to change many aspects of our lives; including in the *entertainment, creative and educational aspects.* However we have only briefly examined a single area; specifically the visibility and accessibility of social and machine implanted-thoughts; whilst leaving the other (well-discussed) aspects in the creative/entertainment/education areas to others. Much has been left for the reader to investigate and/or research for herself.

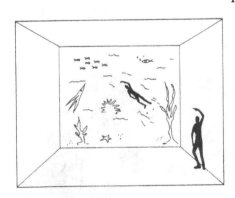

Our position is that VR fits nicely into the concept of the World Brain; and both may lead to a radical democratisation of human-thinking processes. Earlier we likened thought-atoms to words, sentences and even books. In *The Electronic Word*, Richard Lanham (1936-) claims that a book (obviously) has politics, and there are assumptions that come with it; that it is *authoritative and unchangeable, transparent and un-self-conscious; and read: in-silence/out-loud, in public or private.*[10]

Likewise for *thought-atoms/patterns (media/implanted thoughts)*.

Lanham wrote:

> Imagine a major 'textbook' continuing over a generation, continually in touch with all the teachers who use it, continually updated and rewritten by them as well as by the authors with the twenty-four-hour electronic bulletin boards and other one-to-one devices of communication such as a network inevitably simulates. Imagine a department faculty collaborating to produce a full on-line system of primary and secondary texts, with supporting pedagogical apparatus, to be collectively updated and enhanced; it might encourage a real, and nowadays rare, collegiality.[10]

An underlying assumption of the present book is that this type of World Brain system as envisaged by Lanham and others like Nelson, Veltman and Otlet; can be created. However it is a World Brain that must <u>defend itself</u>; specifically from centralised control; and so have *thought ownership*, *assembly* and *equality* built into its core principles of operation. Bruno Latour (1947-) has an interesting perspective here, claiming that the behaviour of people who use and/or lie within a technological system is caused as much by the system *itself* as by machines.[11]

The system forces the user to accent according to a diffusion of facts and processes within the machine/network functionality itself. We forget that the obedient behaviour of people (within systems) is what turns claims into facts; and introduced is a false technical determinism, paralleled by social and scientific determinism etc.[4,11]

I recognised right away why Cinerama and 3D were important... when you watch TV or a movie in a theatre, you are sitting in one reality, and at the same time you are looking at another reality through an imaginary transparent wall. However when you enlarge that window enough, you get a visceral sense of personal involvement. You feel the experience, and don't just see it. - Morton Heilig

MICROSOFT HOLOLENS

The HoloLens breaks the decades long miniaturisation progression from mainframe to minicomputer to desktop to laptop, then on to tablet, smartphone, wearable and soon to be 'computer-implants'. All were limited by physical boundaries of glass etc; But the HoloLens explodes the computer display into the full panoramic field of vision; and it can incorporate the 2D interfaces of old such as the Web-Browser, Skype, Apps etc; HoloLens 'Gobbles-up' or encloses the other devices, Apps etc; and just like the previous 'digital media revolutions' it encloses or contains all the other media within it. It has the potential to 'explode' reality; and to bring all the thoughts and data from the 'inner-space' of mind into the 'outer-space' of the real world.

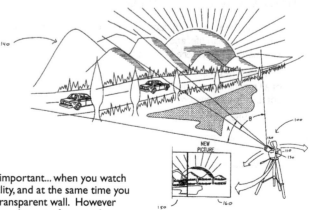

No lesser mind than Professor Stephen Hawking commented 'the development of full Artificial Intelligence could spell the end of the human race'. - BBC News (2014)

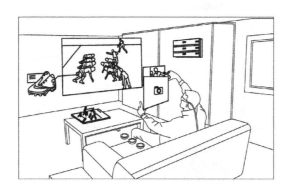

WHO OWNS THE FUTURE: MAN OR MACHINE?

Throughout the nineteenth century, much discussed were the drawbacks and negative influences of machines on human life, and question(s) of whether or not machines were taking over, enslaving us, super-seeding mankind etc; were hotly debated. What would become of humans in the machine era?

Did machines really create 'the good life' for most people; and listed were the positive/negative influences of all machines; including: steam engines, locomotives, electric lights, electro-magnets, propellers, revolvers, combustion engines, dynamite, submarines, torpedoes, machine guns, gunpowder, escalators etc.

Why has this debate dried up in the 21st century? Did the machine-supporters win?

Have we now accepted that machines/systems/computers are (without precedence; and in all cases) inherently beneficial to humanity, and despite overwhelming evidence to the contrary? Is the machine future already here; and/or inevitable/unstoppable? Are related topics not even worth debating anymore (for unknown reasons)?

Are the machines somehow out of control? Did they win the propaganda war?

We may, over a long period of time, evolve new symbol systems that employ colour and position and movement in three dimensions to represent ideas. - Myron Krueger (1983)

VIRTUAL REALITY 247

Our attention is drawn to the nature of human society. Professor David Bloor (1942-) says that: society is simply a medium of different resistances through which ideas and machines travel.[12] In this view society or social factors can (or may) only appear at the end of a trajectory; when something goes wrong. Our failure to account for the materiality of machines, and their role in a multitude of economic, social and cultural problems; is caused in a large part, by a stripping of machine implanted-thoughts from social context/responsibility.

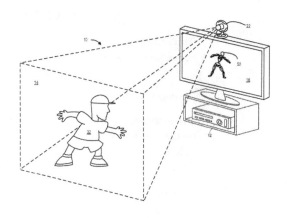

We manage computer designs at the wrong end of the trajectory of happenings; and (impossibly) attempt to direct/alter *ends*, as opposed to *means*. Computers cannot inherently (by themselves) de-contextualise implanted-thoughts from their own actions/processes. It is because (many) computers have been wrongly designed (and/or are not adequately monitored) that they restrict human rights. Properly conceived, machines can become a power to marshall a diversity of human-thought forms, plus machine implanted-thoughts; and for the collective good. Appropriate design refers not only to computers that respect techno-rights and uphold natural/implanted thoughts in a human context; but also to subtle and aesthetic factors such as presenting information to the user in an accessible, effective, and 'sense'-friendly manner. This is where VR can help, providing new sensoriums that foster an easy, effortless and enjoyable journey (or flow) through these new realms of information/thought.

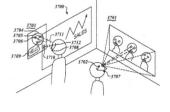

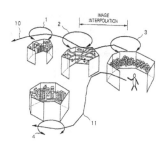

Ultimately, VR may become an all-embracing mixture of *augmented reality* (AR) and *personal virtual reality* (PVR); whereby a new type of *real-virtuality* (RV) or *everyday VR* becomes the normal mode of interaction. Often no headsets will be required, for brain/body-implants, wearables and projected scenes may follow us everywhere we go. *Real virtuality or mixed-reality* is when the virtual is blended with the real almost imperceptibly; where thought-atoms are ever present/available; to everyone and by/from everyone.

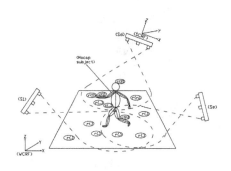

People jacked in so they could hustle. Put the trodes on and they were out there, all the data in the world stacked up like one big neon city, so you could cruise around and have a kind of grip on it, visually anyway, because if you didn't, it was too complicated, trying to find your way to a particular piece of data you needed. Iconics, Gentry called that. - William Gibson [Mona Lisa Overdrive (1988)]

Yes, we have a soul, but it's made of lots of tiny robots.

That's the view.

Yes, we have a soul, but in what sense?

In the sense that our brains, unlike the brains even of dogs and cats and chimpanzees and dolphins, our brains have functional structures that give our brains powers that no other brains have—powers of look-ahead, primarily.

We can understand our position in the world, we can see the future.

We can understand where we came from. We know that we're here.

No buffalo knows it's a buffalo, but we jolly well know that we're members of Homo sapiens, and it's the knowledge that we have and the can-do, our capacity to think ahead and to reflect and to evaluate and to evaluate our evaluations, and evaluate the grounds for our evaluations. - Daniel C. Dennett

Top 10 Programs

- Sabre (IBM, 1964)
- Maze War (1973)
- Adventure (1975)
- VisiCalc (1979)
- WordStar (1979)
- Hypercard (1987)
- Photoshop (1988)
- Lotus Notes (1989)
- Mosaic (1993)
- Minecraft (2009)

Top Languages

- C
- C++
- Java
- C#
- Objective C
- PHP
- JavaScript
- Python
- SQL
- Ruby

Fictional Robots

- R2-D2 (Star Wars)
- T-800 (Terminator 2)
- Bishop (Aliens)
- Bender (Futurama)
- Marvin (Hitchhikers Guide..)
- C-3PO (Star Wars)
- The Iron Giant
- Bumblebee (Transformers)
- Bubo Owl (Clash of the Titans)
- B9 (Lost in Space)
- Twiki (Buck Rogers..)
- Klyton (Robot Holocaust)
- Alpha 5 (Power Rangers)
- The Roboz (Riptide)

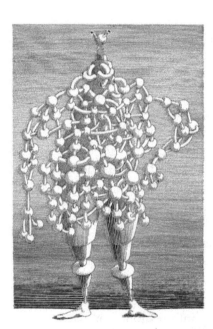

Top 25 Computers (All Time)

- 1977 Apple II
- 1986 Compaq Deskpro 386
- 1981 Xerox 8010
- 1986 Apple Macintosh Plus
- 1992 IBM ThinkPad 700C
- 1981 IBM Personal Computer, Model 5150
- 1985 Commodore Amiga
- 1983 Tandy TRS-80 Model 100
- 1982 Columbia Data Products MPC 1600-1
- 1991 Apple PowerBook 100
- 1998 Sony VAIO 505GX
- 1975 MITS Altair 8800
- 1984 IBM Personal Computer/AT Model 5170
- 1979 Atari 800
- 2001 Shuttle SV24 Barebone
- 1977 Tandy TRS-80 Model 1
- 1987 Toshiba T1000
- 1993 HP OmniBook 300
- 2002 Apple iMac
- 1996 Gateway 2000
- 1998 Alienware Area-51
- 1993 Hewlett-Packard 100LX
- 1997 Apple eMate 300
- 2006 Toshiba Qosmio G35
- 1982 Non-Linear Systems Kaypro

Artificial Creature / Robot (from Cyberiad)

It's this expandable capacity to represent reasons that we have that gives us a soul. But what's it made of? It's made of neurons. It's made of lots of tiny robots. And we can actually explain the structure and operation of that kind of soul, whereas an eternal, immortal, immaterial soul is just a metaphysical rug under which you sweep your embarrassment for not having any explanation.

Daniel C. Dennett

Cryptography and Human Freedom

Cryptography should (most definitely) not be made illegal, as UK Prime Minister David Cameron recently suggested in February 2015. Cryptography is a natural requirement of the need to protect our secret and private thoughts. Our minds (and natural thoughts) are the natural property of individuals and collectives, and not ownerless material 'objects' that may be stolen, controlled and/or 'used' by others against our will. Cryptography is how thoughts defend themselves from attack, and it is how we can obtain freedom of mind, heart and body; and therefore cryptography is a part of our very humanity; and it must be recognized as a fundamental human right.

Chapter Eleven
Robots and Automata

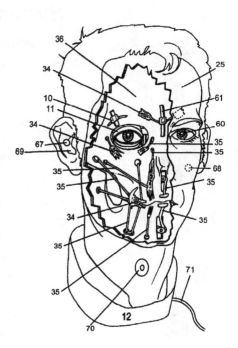

EVER SINCE I can remember I have been fascinated by robots. Robots of all kinds have engaged my attention, excitement and interest; and more than almost anything else. As a small boy I would even walk about in a mechanical fashion at school, and had the nickname '*The Mechanic*' (self-named!). When I was ten years old, my father helped me to build my own 'robot', a head/torso made of balsa-wood/meccano that was about 12 inches high, complete with: *electric light bulbs for eyes, Dalek 'speech' circuitry, meccano arms, and a speaker for a mouth.*

Even today I feel a little sad that I was unable to finish my robot and make it talk *(alone)*, think and move about! I was unrealistically ambitious even then.

Although humanoid robots did not actually exist in the 1960s, there were fictional robots on television programs like *Lost in Space* and *Star Trek*; and I read about them in science fiction books such as *I Robot* and the *Foundation* series.[1,2] These imaginary robots seemed very cool, and inevitably raised questions about whether or not artificial-life could be created, and perhaps become self-aware and/or achieve self-motivation. Robots were powerful, indestructible and often unstoppable; being ready to obey the designer's slightest whim. All of these features tweaked my imagination, and created a life-long interest in all things robotic, thinking computers and artificial life etc.

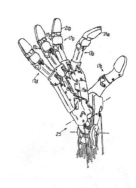

Overall, I think it is the agency/power-potential(s) of robots that fascinated me as a child, and continue to do so. The concept of a robot relates to the idea of transforming inanimate/dead matter into a moving/thinking mechanism; thus being one that can help people to perform difficult/dangerous/impossible tasks.

Robots are thinking/working slaves of manifold utility.

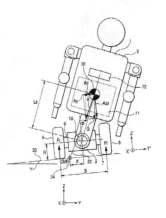

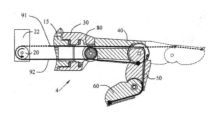

Humanoid Robots

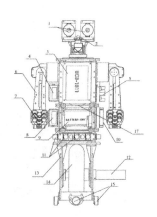

The OED defines robot thusly:

> [1] One of the mechanical men and women in Karel Capek's play; a machine (sometimes resembling a human in appearance) designed to function in place of a living agent, especially one which carries out a variety of tasks automatically or with a minimum of external impulse. [2] A person whose work or activities are entirely mechanical, an automaton.

These definitions make a nice starting point to begin our analysis of robots, but we are (in fact) seeking deeper knowledge; and to probe the idea/possibility of real-world *'artificial men'*. We wish to know how the concept of a robot originated, where it has-been/is used; and what exactly robots may come to be in the future.

The idea of a robot is related to that of an **automaton**; defined as:

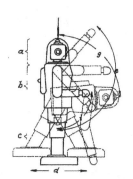

> [1] Something which has the power of spontaneous motion or self-movement. Thus applied also to [2] A living being viewed materially. [3] A piece of mechanism having its motive power so concealed that it appears to move spontaneously; a machine that has within itself the power of motion under conditions fixed for it, but not by it. In the 17th-18th century applied to clocks, watches etc., and transferred to the Universe and World; now usually to figures which simulate the actions of living beings, such as clock-work mice, images which strike the hours on a clock, etc. [4] A living being whose actions are purely involuntary or mechanical. [5] A human being acting mechanically or without active intelligence in a monotonous routine.

These ideas of an automaton are especially prescient; and because they relate to machine influences on human life, and whether the self-computer may be (in some sense) a 'giant' machine; and/or the ways in which automatic systems limit, control and/or constrain human thoughts and actions.

Man the automaton would be a monstrous being; and is what we are attempting to avoid.

The latest... Rotary Press, a veritable Robot in the complication work it performs night after night without a hitch. - *Daily News and Westminster Gazette* (1928)

If almighty God has populated the world with Robots,
legislation of this sort might have been reasonable. - *The Times* [2005]

ROBOTS AND AUTOMATA   251

Robots and automata are, in and of themselves, signs of an ever-present striving in mankind. We humans desire technical mastery of our surroundings, including the boundless spaces of the cosmos; and by means of our thoughts/actions. In a sense we wish to become as one of the Gods; by transcending both matter and (ultimately) ourselves. Put simply, we seek supremacy over all creation; and we humans have always created technologies to help us achieve these ambitious aims.

Man's powers are defined by his technology.

Viewed from this perspective, the history of robots and automata may be seen as a relentless struggle by man to dominate reality; to render it *understandable, profitable, predictable, safe, controllable and malleable.* But natural and technological limitations make up only ever half of the problem space(s) and/or battleground(s) of life; because no matter how fabulous our technologies may become; the struggle always includes issues of general human acceptance of, and appropriate applications of, our technological creations.

Paradoxically, as technologies have become ever more sophisticated, potent and capable; the human side of the equation has only become magnified in importance. Technology must be applied humanely. Accordingly, we ask; how are the robots and the automata of today being used; and do they operate in a humane (enough) context? In an attempt to find answers, we begin with a journey into the history and capabilities of automata.

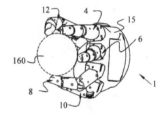

The first ancestors of modern automata are found in the twilight regions of remote mythology. Hephaestos, the Greek god of blacksmiths, craftsmen, sculptors etc; is attended by handmaids of gold resembling *living damsels,* filled with minds and wisdom. In the temple of Delphi it was claimed that statues existed that could walk about, and sing with melodious voices. Statues that moved of their own accord were imagined to have been built by Daedalus (of winged flight fame); and among them was a figure of Venus who was rendered mobile when quick-sliver was inserted into her, as related by Aristotle.

The British Robot Association believes between 6,000 and 7,000 robots were in use world-wide in industry last year. (There must be countless millions today!)

Daily Telegraph (1979)

Men who will go to their doom with the
unswerving directness of robots. - *The Spectator* (1937)

The topic of affording life and/or magical powers into a humanoid robot and/or automaton, has been a popular myth throughout time. Some stories relate that man himself may also be a mechanical creation. According to the Ancient Greek story of titan Prometheus, he shaped the form of man out of mud/clay, whilst Athena breathed life into the clay figure.

Related by second century (AD) traveler Pausanias, was the existence of brazen moving (flying/swimming) eagles and dolphins; which were used in Elis during theatrical performances. In ancient times also it has been claimed that speaking heads such as the oracle at Orpheus and Lesbos existed; whilst in the Norse myths of *Odin*, an oracular head, encased in gold, was said to posses the power of speech and to relate all the wisdom(s) of the East.

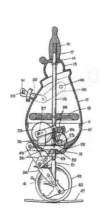

Even the Bible mentions the *teraphim*, an oracular figure or mummified head, coated with gold, that was consulted by Nebuchadnezzar and spoke to him in a language that he could understand. Despite the sin of multiple Gods; it seems that (in the Bible) miraculous human forms are commonly employed; as in Ob who is one who speaks-with/communes-with a skull and conjured up the dead by soothsaying. In Ancient Egypt we see legends of statues who are said to have replied to questions either by a nod of the head and/or by movement of the arm(s). Some speculate that these same statues were jointed dolls powered by steam or fire.

Overall, the belief that human-like forms could be imbued with a life-force is common throughout many, if not all, cultures. Often the goal was to demonstrate magical powers. In Ancient Rome, images or puppets that could be controlled by strings, named *neurospastes*; were employed by magicians, showmen etc.

All in all, fabrication of life-like figures seems to be an almost innate desire in humans; and whilst related technology has developed at a relatively slow pace; progress can be readily identified nonetheless; and in *form, capability and automation etc.*

The origins of modern robots therefore lie in remote history.

For example, Indian stories relate tales of wooden men who walked, sang and danced about.

Have you heard about the robot factories that make 800 cars each and every day; and that have no humans whatsoever in the building. Compare this with the human powered assembly-line factories in 1908 that made just 25 Model T cars each week!

In China, wise men cultivated the art of *khwai shuh*, a means by which a statue or portrait could be brought to life and employed as a servant. Tales of mechanical creations that appeared in human form, are thus commonplace in all cultures; perhaps (in part) because we humans desire to know the secret to life, and so that we can extend it in ourselves/others. But also the creation of robotic slaves is a constant (innate) fascination; and because the same may extend our powers, and through orders that must be obeyed.

The desire to create an artificial man has never ceased. During the middle ages attempts to create mechanical men picked up a pace. Speaking head illusions and/or myths were commonplace; and so much so that even Pope Sylvester 2nd (alias Gilbert) devised/built a speaking human figure that was said to be capable of replying to yes/no type questions.

Other automata appear in the writings of William of Malmsebury (1085-1143), whereby: a clock (autonomous machine) was constructed on mechanical principles: and an hydraulic organ, in which air, escaping in a surprising manner, by the force of heated water, fills the cavity of the instrument, and the brazen pipes emit modulated tones through the multifarious apertures. Believe it or not, such semi-automatic devices were thought to be real and partially living entities; and were equated with imbuing matter with semi-magical and/or life-like qualities; and the creators were often thought (by some) to be in league with the devil!

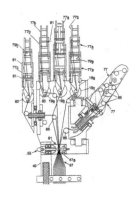

Other notable and respected middle-age thinkers/writers such as Dominican friar and Catholic bishop Albertus Magnus (1200-1280) and philosopher Roger Bacon (1214-1294) are linked with moving robot figures and even speaking heads.

The concept of a *man-made* man, that is the creation of a real living human being; is a related and popular topic. For example, modern *golems* (an animated anthropomorphic 'being'; originally present in jewish folklore); begin with Elijah of Chelm in the middle of the sixteenth century. He was the first person credited with (supposedly) making an artificial man which was said to be a Frankenstein-like monster who walked around menacing the entire world.

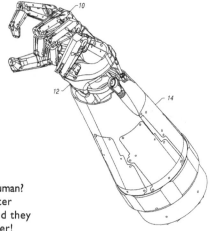

What happens when robots can do virtually *any* physical Job better than a human? Think it cannot and will not happen? Think again. Robots will be better workers, never resting, never striking, with 100 percent efficiency and they do not make mistakes, rest, complain, get tired, or stop working—ever!

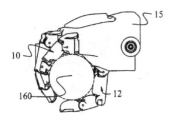

Similar stories of man-made men abounded during the sixteenth century; and doubtless reflect attempts (by scientifically minded-men) to re-create and/or explain *Adam Kadmon*, the so-called primordial man. The creation of intelligent life had happened (at least) once, with man himself; and so why not again? Remember that these stories arrive almost two hundred years before Darwin's theory of evolution showed how complex living beings may be said to 'design-themselves', very slowly, and through gradual changes that accumulate over millennia.

Doubtless these stories of artificial men captured the imagination of Mary Shelley; and inspired and/or influenced her *Frankenstein* story.[3] In fact the conception of a man-made man was to inspire a whole host of tales of mystery, horror and science fiction. In some senses the golem itself can be interpreted as the double of its maker, a self-fission, mirror-image or even a self-confrontation.

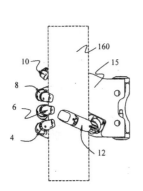

Often it is the insertion of life-essence into a lifeless manikin that becomes a key issue within such promethean plots; whereby the created golem needs somehow to be wound-up, or *'electrically-sparked into being'* and/or magically 'wished' into life. This is because, no matter how life-like or real the imagined robot's movements may become; always the problem comes down to imbuing the man-made creature with the power of life/thought, with feelings and emotions, and with purpose.

The Ancient Egyptian word for vital essence was *ka*, and it is this which was said to distinguish between a living and a dead person; whereby the god Meskhenet breathed a person's *ka* into them at the instant of birth. Ka may be equated with the concept of spirit in other religions. The question of how this spirit, or self-initiated power of movement and self-motivation etc; might be imbued into a created being, remains.

There have been many suggestions in works of fiction. E.T.A. Hoffmann (1766-1822) gives us one example in his story *The Sandman* [4], whereby created is a living automaton/vampire:

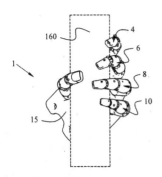

> Coppelius begins taking 'shining masses' out of the fire and hammering them into face-like shapes without eyes... (later) her 'ice cold' lips met his burning hot ones!... (and they had) passed off an automaton as a living person!

The world of the future will be an even more demanding struggle against the limitations of our intelligence, not a comfortable hammock in which we can lie down to be waited upon by our robot slaves. - Norbert Wiener

Villiers de l'Isle Adam (1840-1889) gives a striking description of an artificial being in *L'Eve Future*; whereby a talented inventor, named Edison, successfully creates a robot woman, who speaks, sings and answers questions; in fact, being indistinguishable from a real woman. But the ruse is up, when the friend he creates the robot for is unhappy, and because the 'artificial' woman is not sufficiently life-like to replace his lost lover.[5]

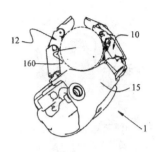

The word robot itself gained popularity from Karel Capek's widely read *Rossum's Universal Robots* (1923); whereby the word denotes an artificial being, soulless though mechanically without a flaw.[6] These are not exactly robots by the current definition of the term; but are creatures that are closer to the modern idea of cyborgs, androids or even clones, as they may be mistaken for humans and can think for themselves.

Despite our brief sojourn into the field of artificial men, unfortunately we do not have space is this book to develop even a cursory history of robots and automata; and within either myth, fiction or reality. Luckily fictional 'robot' compendia exist.[7,8,9] Rather our focus here is on robots and automata as they actually exist today, or may come to be in the near future. Desired is an understanding of what robots actually are, in and of themselves, and how such beings may (ultimately) differ from living humans and/or our ideal notions of a machine.

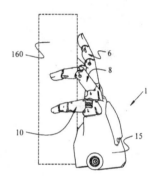

In order to take a *view* on robots, and to gauge their place in the vast order of human inventions; it is necessary to examine the roots of their development. We may start with the difference between a machine and a tool; which are both forms of technology.

One difference, is that a tool (I would suggest) is used by a human and is useless without the human; because it is an extension of one's physical/mental power(s), and is supervised by a human. With a tool, the human does the thinking, initiates all motions, and guides the path and/or actions of the tool at all times. Whereas a machine normally exhibits (at least partial) self-action under its own 'steam' and/or 'magnifies' or 'guides' the applied energy. The machine is often powered; and may sometimes initiate (programmed) action(s) alone, and without any (real-time) human supervision (or at least minimal supervision).

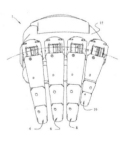

The Gems did not nag or complain... did not get body odour or hair, did not get spots, did not suffer from diseases or headaches, did not have annoying bad habits, did not need drugs or alcohol, did not need gifts such as jewellery, flowers, chocolate and money, did not need to shop, did not have piercings or tattoos, had no capacity to willingly lie or be fake, were never disloyal, were always eager to do any task required by their owner, did all the housework and cooking without complaint, were produced in the form of the perfect woman in the eyes of each client. - Robert Black

Is a bicycle a tool or a machine? Under these definitions it is not clear; but perhaps the lack of an energy source assigns it as a tool.

Obviously tools and machines operate under the direction of human programming and/or design constraints, or (in the language of this book) they represent (wholly and merely) world implanted-thoughts (in the form of a 'frozen' thought-plexus). The difference being that a machine, as opposed to a tool, is in some sense automatic in operation, and it may be said to be an automaton. Another aspect of the interest in machines, is the idea of perpetual motion, the *perpetual-flame* and self-initiated powers of movement. The related notions of energy and power took quite some time to enter into common vocabulary; and a modern scientific notion of energy/force did not arrive until the end of the 17th century with Isaac Newton's *Principia*.[10] Earlier the notion of life was made equivalent to energy/movement; and people were fascinated by objects that seemed to be self-powered/alive.

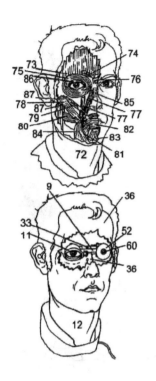

The cosmos, or universe, is patently self-sustaining, and once set in motion (by God?) did not need any further help (according to some); also everywhere we see motions, forces and movements causing other forces and movements. How original (prime-mover) motions began, or what forces wound-up and/or powered the great clock that is the universe remained a mystery; to say nothing of the 'mini-clocks' present in tiny lifeforms such as *insects, fish, amoeba and bacteria etc.*

Movement(s) *(Micro and Macro)*

Physicists tell us that a basic property of the universe, perhaps the fundamental property, is movement itself. Everything is in constant motion, even though this movement may take place in the tiny motions of atoms or sub-atomic particles; and the fact remains that nothing ever stays (completely) still, even for a micro-second. Everywhere atoms, electrons etc; are shooting about, colliding, interacting and/or vibrating.

Everything is change, and/or the result of motion.

All that we see, sense, feel or think; is the result of atoms, molecules, electrons etc; moving about.

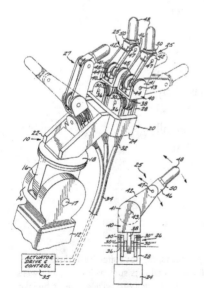

Let us remember that the automatic machine is the precise economic equivalent of slave labor. Any labor which competes with slave labor must accept the economic consequences of slave labor. - Norbert Wiener

Did you ever see a human acting like a machine or an automaton; or taking orders from / being managed by a machine? Perhaps this is more common than you think.

ROBOTS AND AUTOMATA   257

Ok, so motion (or change) is a primary quality in the universe; perhaps the *most* fundamental aspect. But what has movement got to do with machines, robots and automata? Quite simply that we might think of everything (man-made or not) as being categories of one *type of movement, static state* or *prevention of movement*; or as the *instigator* and/or *result of motion(s)*.

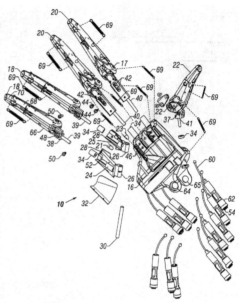

Everything relates simply to motion. When I look at a cat, for example; rapidly moving photons reflecting off the cat's body move into my eye, are focussed onto my retina, and cause electrons to be created on the photon-receptors, which move into my brain and influence/fire moving messages between neurons (communication via electrical pulses).

Eventually (as a result of similar events), millions of electrons influence millions of neurons; and in order to recognise the cat and judge what it is up to *(the brain has 86 billion to 17.2 trillion action-potentials per second)*. In this view, one might say that even thinking itself is movement; a highly specific type of movement with *patterns of electrons* (messages) passing between neurons (each second).

A related point is that computers (such as mobile phones) are sometimes thought to have no moving parts; but in reality *billions* of electrons are rushing about within the silicon wafers inside this mini-computer, and in order to register changes to memory units etc. The related *patterns of information* are basically binary representations of human thoughts, which constantly change arrangements and/or form; and so to calculate specific functions.

In a way, there are more man-made movement(s) (of implanted-thought patterns) going on inside computers than anywhere else in all of human society. The claim that there is no movement in computers may apply to the macro-level. It becomes ridiculous when we consider the micro and the nano levels! In fact there is constant movement; because inside a computer's 'brain' the integrated circuits and central processors, registers etc; are constantly in motion *(so long as it is powered-up)*.

Robots, the only things with a perfect lack of emotional capacity, are easily controlled, and I suddenly realised that's why the military often trains people to suppress their emotions. Unfortunately for them, humans aren't machines. We feel, we love, we cry, we despair, and we rejoice. Anyone who's ever tried to convince me not to feel is someone I shouldn't have trusted. The only reason you should shut off your emotions and emulate a robot is if you're doing horrible things. - Bruce Crown

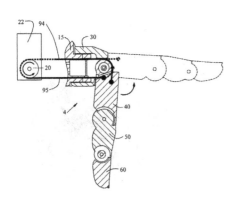

Given the reality of such micro-movements inside computers, those who claim that the distinguishing feature of a machine is that it has (large-scale) moving parts and is powered/moving mechanically; are mistaken. However, possession of self-initiated (large-scale) power(s) of movement is a vital aspect for any humanoid robot. In relation to this ability; one might examine factors such as movement choices/patterns, self-motivation, thinking capability and decision making ability etc.

Let us begin with the concept of choice in terms of what causes/controls a robot's movement(s).

Free-Will *(for systems / machines / computers)*

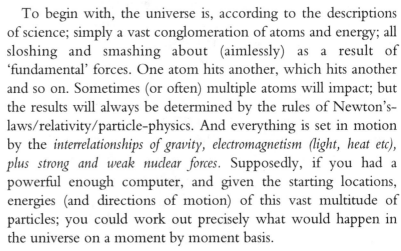

To begin with, the universe is, according to the descriptions of science; simply a vast conglomeration of atoms and energy; all sloshing and smashing about (aimlessly) as a result of 'fundamental' forces. One atom hits another, which hits another and so on. Sometimes (or often) multiple atoms will impact; but the results will always be determined by the rules of Newton's-laws/relativity/particle-physics. And everything is set in motion by the *interrelationships of gravity, electromagnetism (light, heat etc), plus strong and weak nuclear forces.* Supposedly, if you had a powerful enough computer, and given the starting locations, energies (and directions of motion) of this vast multitude of particles; you could work out precisely what would happen in the universe on a moment by moment basis.

But of course no such (infinitely complex) computer exists; and in any case how would you go about measuring the starting quantities in the first place; because in some respects physics says that such a measurement is impossible—*Heisenberg uncertainty principle*—theoretically, if not in a practical sense. But that does not stop physicists making generalised attempts at a universal theory of everything, regardless of such obstacles.

Why this sojourn into physics?

Quite simply, to figure out if (wholly/partially) self-initiated movement is (theoretically) possible for a robot.

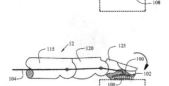

Will we soon be taking orders from robots. How long will it be before wearable Sat-Navs and Augmented Reality Maps start reprimanding / punishing us?

ROBOTS AND AUTOMATA   259

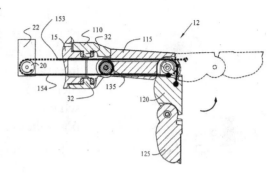

The universe, is patently and obviously; not self aware (discounting life itself) and has no central controller and/or all-seeing God *(at least one who interferes with the natural order)*. The basic (inanimate) constituents of the universe do not *compute anything* in relation to their own history, destiny and/or future possibilities. It follows that for the atoms themselves, there is no choice in terms of moving paths; and they are merely at the mercy of other atoms and fundamental forces.

Each atom is like a dodgem car without a driver; utterly lost and at the mercy of the other (possibly driverless) cars. My point is that it is in terms of motion that we can see the fundamental difference between a self-aware *(and universe-sensing)* life-form, and a mere mindless atom *(inanimate object, structure or group of atoms)*. A life-form such as a human can perceive the environment, and make adjustments accordingly. A woman can run from a lion, travel to a stream for a drink, climb a tree to eat fruit etc; all being examples of movements that are taken with a particular goal or purpose in mind. Sometimes she may choose to skip between two moving tree-stumps when crossing a stream; hence planning her own body's trajectory in a 'live', specific and patterned way never seen (yet) in any inanimate object.

This argument is the greatest, and most profound one, that can be made to rebut claims that we humans do not posses *freedom of will (free-will)*. Our explanation cuts right to the heart of the fundamental difference between being alive, and not being alive. A life-form 'sees' its environment, and knows that it exists and has a relationship to that same environment. Nowhere in all creation do we see inanimate objects making 'strategic' self-initiated movements of any kind. Inanimate atoms move, one and all, according to the dictates of other atoms and forces; and never choose to 'throw-away' energy by fighting the path of least resistance.

James Lovelock's insight was that humans gave the earth, and possibly the universe, eyes with which to see/change itself (plus hands to action 'thoughts').

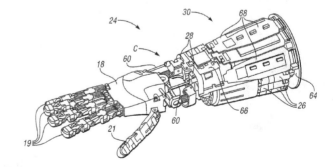

How long will it be before you send your children to school with a robot driver/helper. How long before the teacher is an android. Think it wont happen? Google is testing robotic cars. And robot teachers will be far cheaper!

Is it not obvious that our previously related discussion of the problem of free-will is solved by use of this argument. If animals (for example) did not posses the power of free-movement (or free-will); what is the point of nature (evolution) providing them with muscles with which to move about, brains with which to perceive, and eyes with which to see all the different possibilities afforded by the universe.

"YOU ARE HEREBY SENTENCED TO BE REBOOTED."

Free movement/will is the whole point of life; and there can be no other conclusion; unless one is resigned to life being absolutely (and ultimately) pointless and/or a joke played by some super-intelligent being on us all. The joke is that this superior intelligence makes it look like we possess free-will; and by providing (highly specific) animal movements that follow (apparently) self-determined paths and avoid dangers etc; when in actual fact we had been allowed no such freedom whatsoever; and because the great all-knowing 'program' of the universe was incredibly carefully designed/conceived; in fact with a specific purpose. And the purpose is (at least partially) to foster the *appearance of free-will* and to fool us all into thinking that we could choose/prescribe self-initiated atomic motions (re-arrangements).

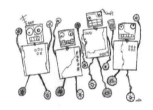

Postulating that everything that happens in the universe is pre-ordained is, in my opinion, preposterous, and because it requires a plan for the universe that includes making it *appear* that animals avoided/stalked each other etc. Such a plan would have to be all pre-calculated on an immense numerical scale; that includes also all micro-organism's avoiding, interacting and running towards and away from each other, plus the interactions of all the insects and animals that have ever lived etc. It would be an immense, never ending, pre-calculation of atomic patterns and causal outcomes.

OH...HAVEN'T YOU HEARD?—
THE INDUSTRIAL REVOLUTION
IS OVER... WE WON....

The 'clockwork motor' model makes no sense; and because it does not explain all of the local patterns of order; like animal interactions; and how these can be actioned, even if they are planned. Clearly the universe is decentralised, and there is no centralised control (at least in terms of plans); but there may be (partly) centralised order by way of the laws of physics/mathematics; and hence Plato's Forms.

Think these arguments of robot-capabilities are remote from everyday life. Not so.
Take a look at the US Atlas robot; do you really think this is for rescue purposes alone.

ROBOTS AND AUTOMATA 261

We have no 'thinking-computer' coordinating/managing everything. The behaviour (that is physical motions) of an animal is controlled (at least partially) by the animal itself, in a constant relationship to the animate/inanimate environment. Hence responsive intelligence or decision making behaviours can be felt (or instantiated) at specific space-time points; and the animal may possess free-will and (perhaps) possess the will-to-power or longer-term 'planned' behaviours (although these causal projections are primarily a human characteristic).

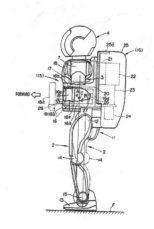

I call my argument in favour of free-will:

< {21} The Great Cosmic Joke of Pointlessly Coordinated / Patterned Animal Behaviours (how could such a plan / program be orchestrated?). >

< {22} Ergo: Humans (+ animals) possess the power of free-will. >

Free-will may be restricted according to: limitations of: *knowledge, power, and universal/natural processes.* All life-forms posses some degree of free-will, according to their powers of perception plus projection of thoughts/actions (in time and space).

A question arises; can/do robots likewise possess free-will?

Our discussion concerns the movements of objects/bodies. Specifically can a semi-intelligent (or pre-programmed) group of (dead) atoms make free-form atom-assembly related decisions, or choose a specific movement path (i.e a pattern, direction, speed), for a group of atoms. We know that a living being can do so; according to the *Cosmic Joke* argument; but what about machines?

It is obviously possible to program machines to make/follow self-programmed movements (happens every day); and thus (to some degree) we can say that machines have risen above ordinary inanimate matter, and because they may sense and direct and/or 'choose' movement paths (for objects/atomic-assemblies) through the universe; and potentially, at least, do so on multiple spatial scales, locations and on future time-lines.

One might call such behaviours intelligence; and admit that a machine has *some* (programmed) power(s) of foresight/free-will; and in relation to the movement of atoms present in the world.

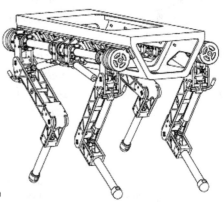

Is machine dominance over humans inevitable? Do we not already take instructions from machines everyday. Are traffic signals an example of machines conditioning/controlling humans? What is the difference between a robot telling you to stop running about on the playground and a human? Should your car/oven/toaster be able to warn you of dangerous use; or should we accept that humans know-best; even when they don't?

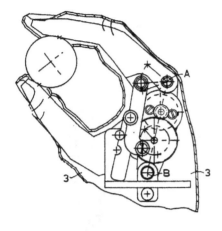

Remember that atomic movement(s) equate to all of the activity and changes present in the universe; and one might say that all *designs, actions, patterns, intelligences etc;* come about through movement. However, as previously discussed we need to look carefully at the *scope* of movement choices that a machine can potentially make.

In all cases, any 'semi-intelligent' creature's movement choices are tied to goals/pre-programming, and to the perception of the available future choices, and hence to conceptualisation of available atomic patterns, movements etc. Choice implies the ability to cogitate, think and/or to conceptualise the possibilities, see the future/past, and to take a 'world-view', so to speak.

We might say that thinking *(movements of electronic messages in the brain)* 'releases' the power of movement in the body and world; according to specific planned purposes.

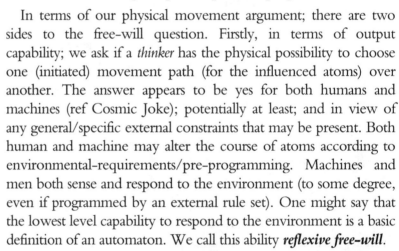

In terms of our physical movement argument; there are two sides to the free-will question. Firstly, in terms of output capability; we ask if a *thinker* has the physical possibility to choose one (initiated) movement path (for the influenced atoms) over another. The answer appears to be yes for both humans and machines (ref Cosmic Joke); potentially at least; and in view of any general/specific external constraints that may be present. Both human and machine may alter the course of atoms according to environmental-requirements/pre-programming. Machines and men both sense and respond to the environment (to some degree, even if programmed by an external rule set). One might say that the lowest level capability to respond to the environment is a basic definition of an automaton. We call this ability ***reflexive free-will***.

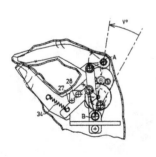

Secondly we ask if the *thinker* has the mental capability to imagine/build a structure for the influenced atoms; and according to a projected plan. Put another way, how clever/intelligent are the choices made for the atoms in question. In particular does the *thinker* possess <u>intention</u>; or has it considered a range of options and/or allowed a scope of future 'possibilities' to be taken into account. Can the intelligence design specific structures for highly-intelligent purposes? We call this ability ***pro-active free-will***.

There is no justification for the assumption that we first experience isolated facts or momentary views of snapshots of isolated facts and give them significance. - Hubert L. Drefus

ROBOTS AND AUTOMATA   263

How ***big*** is the ***free*** in will? What is the scope of the movement paths considered; and how varied are the options examined in terms of future strategy/events, and how clever or ingenious/portentous are decisions taken for future outcomes. One asks if the intelligence is aware of all (or many) of the different future possibilities in terms of the movement of real-world patterns (atoms). Can it align (conceptually assemble) multiple patterns of atoms in the real world according to long-term goals? Can it 'see' or imagine future patterns/events in response to complex (unplanned) happenings?

Situations where the *thinker* invents, plans and provides highly novel, or singularly creative solutions, we call ***creative free-will***.

Unfortunately for robots/machines, in this latter sense we have to admit that machines are severally limited. Machines posses merely a 'paltry' *reflexive free-will* (a very small or zero range of freedoms/choices); in that they can direct the motions (for limited sub-sets) of matter; but they can only do this directing in strictly limited and pre-determined ways. Machines can never operate ***truly*** spontaneously or be creative, and/or make guesses about the best way to proceed, or (typically) make optimal movements to respond to novel situations.

Fig 1.

< {23} Computers exhibit a purely reflexive form of free-will. >

A machine's responses are purely automatic/robotic; and we do not see a machine with *creative free-will* in the sense of making intelligent decisions/actions in response to un-anticipated events. Machines never even see things that we haven't told them to look for. As a result they only possess a catastrophically weak/stupid and purely *reflexive* form of free-will; being one that cannot get very far by way of complex behaviours, or long term and flexible goals. You will not see a machine building a shelter to cover itself from the rain for example, unless specifically programmed/instructed to do so *(it will not even notice the rain)*.

In spite of technological progress, Western man is basically empty and aimless, and though we can make some complex machines, we are largely ignorant about applying them for the true benefit of mankind. - by unknown [reference lost]

Robots do not understand that dead people, have not a tomorrow. They do not realise that some objects have time trajectories, end or change with time - they degrade.

Human versus Machine Thought(s)

To sum up, machines/robots/computers do not really *solve* problems, *anticipate* or *see* the future in any complex sense. One might ask: why is it that machines have such a limited capacity for problem solving? I don't think we humans (yet) know the answer; only that it has something to do with free-will and thinking/conceptualisation. And this topic may be very complex. We notice that machines can respond to happenings in the environment; but even insects/amoeba demonstrate a capacity for innovation/responsivity that is wholly absent in machines.

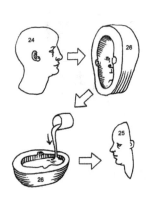

It is vital to recognise that machines are limited to purely pre-programmed responses to their environment; and can in no way depart from their original programming. As discussed, the difference seems to be related to the fact that machines are unable to program/learn/change *themselves* on the fly; to alter their programming and hence goals in response to environmental requirements. Humans see the world with a super-wide angled and *responsive-vision*; and notice happenings that are new; and we are **open to the environment**.

Humans always have one-eye open for novelty; and take notice of things/situations we haven't ever experienced before.

Why it is that machines do not notice un-programmed things/events/objects/situations? Douglas Hofstadter says it is related to thinking ability/techniques/processes. In his book *Surfaces and Essences* (2013), Douglas says that (for humans) without *concepts* there would be no thought, and without analogies there would be no concepts.

Douglas Hofstadter wrote:

> Each concept in our mind owes its existence to a long succession of analogies made unconsciously over many years, initially giving birth to the concept and continuing to enrich it over the course of our lifetime. Furthermore, at every moment of our lives, our concepts are selectively triggered by analogies that our brain makes without letup, in an effort to make sense of the new and unknown in terms of the old and known.[14]

Analogy is the recognition of equivalency, or likeness of relations, between different events/ circumstances/situations. By means of analogies humans are able to perceive flexibly using 'fuzzy' and malleable boundaries; and notice the ways in which things are alike and unalike; whereby we map old conceptual principles onto the novel. And our perceptive minds are constantly on the lookout for novelty; matching and attempting to match categories and analogies to everything that comes into view.

These spontaneous analogies and categorisations, constantly made up by our brains, are deeply influenced by: *language, era, personal history, culture, current frame of mind and purpose, instantaneous goals, body position and posture relative to things in the world etc.* According to Hofstadter, a category is a mental structure that is created over time and evolves and contains information in an organised form that may be accessed under suitable conditions.

But why are robots and machines so poor at making good decisions? Why are they so limited in thinking capacity; and why is their thinking so primitive? Hofstadter says:

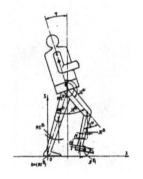

> That our advantage is intimately linked to categorisation through analogy, a mental mechanism that lies at the very centre of human thought but at the fullest fringes of artificial cognition. It is only thanks to this mental mechanism that human thoughts, despite their slowness and vagueness, are generally reliable, relevant, and insight-giving, whereas computer 'thoughts' (if the word even applies at all) are extremely fragile, brittle, and limited, despite their enormous rapidity and precision... As soon as categorisation enters the scene, the competition with computers takes on a new kind of lopsidedness—but this time in favour of humans.[14]

Thus the roots of human understanding lie in the automatic triggering, or unconscious evocation of familiar categories and analogies. Hofstadter also says that concepts (thought-patterns): are densely stitched together through relationships, similarity and context.

Human thoughts are as flexible as they are complex.

< {24} Concept = A thing conceived (similarity + relationships + context). >

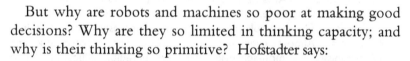

Whenever a computer looks or acts like its intelligent, or like its thinking; it is only the human-implanted thoughts that are reacting to / within the world; making processes and producing outputs that you are noticing; and in accordance with a wholly pre-planned scenario. The computer itself knows nothing of what it is doing; its purpose, and neither can it judge if its actions are right or wrong, good or bad, working or not working, harmful or un-harmful, expected or not expected etc. It's 'thoughts' are 'frozen' human thoughts, and not thoughts at all in any real sense; because they do not (intelligently) branch, adjust themselves according to real-world events and do not 'watch' themselves and their effects.

Robots have to understand objects/things/life-forms/human 'potential'
futures and in terms of processes that are possible/impossible.

Computers may be able to categorise objects/situations (sometimes); but according to Hofstadter there are big differences between categorisation and analogy making:

- Categorisation is routine; analogy is creative
- Categorisation is unconscious; analogy is conscious
- Categorisation is automatic; analogy is voluntary
- Categorisation favours similarities; analogy favours dissimilarities
- Categorisation applies to entities; analogy to relations

All in all, one might say that analogies somehow bring the *observing/thinking subject* into the equation, along-side the objects and processes of the world. Analogy is a large part of how humans think and analyse *situations*, *processes*, and *space-time relations* etc.

We humans think by placing everything relative to ourselves; to our *past-life, current situation, goals, and future requirements*.

Hubert L. Drefus (1929-) said:

> The burden of AI is its apparent need to proceed in futility from the atom to the whole. People, on the other hand, effectively seem to perceive first a whole and only then, if necessary analyse it into atoms... Almost everyone now agrees that representing and organising common-sense knowledge is incredibly difficult, and that facing up to this problem constitutes the moment of truth for AI. Either a way of representing and organising everyday human know-how must be found, or AI will be swamped by the welter of facts and beliefs that must be made explicit in order to try to inform a disembodied, utterly alien computer about everyday human life...

> Understanding of purposes and intentions is key; and things must be intelligible with respect to the whole of human life.

> One cannot equate a program which deals with 'a tiny bit of the world' with a program which deals with a 'mini-world'... In our everyday life we are, indeed, involved in various 'sub-worlds' such as the world of the theatre, of business, or of mathematics, but each of these is a 'mode' of our shared everyday world. That is, sub-worlds are not related like isolable physical systems to larger systems they *compose*; rather there are local elaborations of a whole which they *presuppose*. If micro-worlds *were* sub-worlds one would not have to extend and combine them to reach the everyday world, because the everyday world would have to be included already. Since, however, micro-worlds are *not* worlds, there is no way they can be combined and extended to the world of everyday life. As a result of failing to ask what a world is, five years of stagnation in AI was mistaken for progress.[11]

What assumptions are implicit and or explicit in thoughts. Machine programmed
thoughts must have/make a tremendous number of assumptions about the world in
which they interact/operate—and many of these must be wrong—and certainly most
if not all will be wrong on some occasions or eventually if you wait long enough!

What does a thought consist of? Judgements, perceptions, connections, models of past, present and future objects and processes.

ROBOTS AND AUTOMATA   267

Drefus brings attention to the way in which machine knowledge tends to exist in isolated islands, or small unconnected 'micro-worlds'; which are in turn in no way linked to any higher purposes, goals, relationships or possible future happenings in the biggest sense. Once again, the machine is not conscious of itself, the universe, and humans; and/or of the myriad of relations present between the two natures *(natural and technological)* and their intimate affects/influences with respect to the needs of humans *(for whom they were created to serve)*.

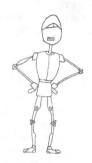

Hubert L. Drefus again:

> My thesis, which owes allot to Wittgenstein, is that whenever human behaviour is analysed in terms of rules, these rules must always contain a *ceteris paribus*, i.e., they apply 'everything else being equal' and 'what everything else' and 'equal' means in a specific situation can never be spelled out without a regress... The *ceteris paribus* condition points to a background of practices which are the condition of possibility of all rule-like activity. In explaining our actions we must always sooner or later fall back on our everyday practices and simply say 'this is what we do'. Thus in the last analysis all intelligibility and all intelligent behaviour must be traced back to our sense of what we are, which is, according to this argument, necessarily, on pain of regress, something we can never explicitly know.... Only our general sense of what is typical can decide here, and that background understanding by definition cannot be situation-specific.[11]

Put simply, we need machines that: *explore who, what and where I am, and not (only) what I know.* We need programming that creates computers that consider human objectives; that know for what (ultimate) purposes they were created; and take responsibility for their actions. According to Buckminster Fuller, what defines humanity is the ability to identify the operating principles/systems present in the universe; and key is the 'feeling' of spatial phenomena. It seems that intelligence must be situated; and made relative to the human/machine body itself; and to the world in which we (and the machines) live inside of.

Machines must 'align themselves' with the human point of view, and behave accordingly.

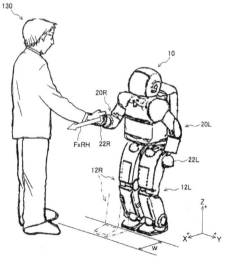

If anything is to count as a thought, it must contribute—even if only potentially—to the operation of the system to which it belongs.
A state or event that contributes to the operation of a system, might be expanded to have a distinguishable effect on the system output.

We live at the top of a pyramid of technologies, without really realising it.
Cyberspace is a type of memory prothesis. - William Gibson

Conceptuality

Turing found that theres no systematic way to tell in advance what a given code is going to do. You can't predict how software will behave by inspecting it. The only way is to actually run it. And this fundamental unpredictability means you can never have a complete digital dictatorship or world government because there will always be codes that do unpredictable things. This is why the digital universe will never be a national park; it will always be an undomesticated, unpredictable universe. And that should be reassuring to us.

In his paper 'Computing Machinery and Intelligence'; Turing went on to prove that there is no solution to ENTSCHEIDUNGSPROBLEM by first showing that the *halting problem* for Turing machines is undecidable; in general, it is not possible to decide algorithmically whether a Turing machine will ever halt! Therefore the halting problem is undecidable. So it proves that there are problems that cannot be solved by a Turing machine! This has profound consequences - and may be called the Turing Machine Decision Problem (my words).

George Dyson

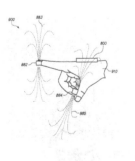

It is mankind's ability to model his immediate and real–world surroundings, and to create plans for the future, plans that are in close accordance to universal laws and also in harmony with his own goals; that separates him from the animals/machines. Humans create solutions using the *laws of physics, chemistry, biology*; and using all kinds of *models, concepts and knowledge* about what are the possibilities and limitations of future action. We employ principles, theory and understanding to 'construct' the future.

Buckminster Fuller created his own theory of how to understand systems in transformation, which he called Synergetics. According to Fuller, since systems are identifiable at every scale from the quantum level to the cosmic, and humanity both articulates the behaviour of these systems and is composed of these systems. Synergetics is a very broad discipline, and embraces a broad range of scientific and philosophical studies including: *tetrahedral and close-packed-sphere geometries, thermodynamics, chemistry, psychology, biochemistry, economics, philosophy, and theology* etc. Synergetics was an attempt to differentiate and relate all aspects of reality including: *the ideal and the physically realised, the container and the contained, the one and the many, the observer and the observed, the human microcosm and the universal macrocosm.*

Buckminster Fuller said of conceptuality/experience:

> The greatest of all the faculties is the ability of the imagination to formulate conceptually. Conceptuality (understanding of principles) is subjective; realisation is objective. Conceptuality is metaphysical and weightless, reality is physical... Conceptuality operates experimentally, independent of size... Conceptuality implodes, becoming increasingly more simplified... Experience is the raw material of science. It is the nature of all our experiences that they begin and end. They are packaged, both physical and metaphysical, and are always special case.[15]

At once we glimpse the reason why robots and machines are so different from humans. It is because they do not *form* and *interrelate concepts*; based on experience. They do not reflect on their experiences, and on the nature of the world.

In the 1956 ScFi movie *Forbidden Planet*, set in the 23rd Century; a starship reaches a distant planet Altair 5; where a previous expedition scientist Dr Edward Morbius has been using a mind-expanding device left behind by the long-extinct Krell race. As a result, the mind of Dr Morbius has become greatly magnified in power; but unfortunately this expands also his subconscious mind or *id*; whereupon an invisible monster is created (emanating from his mind) which proceeds to kill members of the new expedition (unknowingly at first on Dr Morbius's part). Eventually Dr Morbius accepts the truth, that the creature is an extension of his own mind, and it is 'his evil self'; whereupon he confronts the creature and is killed by it. Let us hope that mankind is not likewise racing to his doom, and as a result of developing systems, machines and computers that are a sub-conscious reflection of (purely) negative aspects of ourselves; but rather that we can find ways to truly benefit from our 'magnified' selves and so avoid the fate of Dr Morbius. (See images on pages 143, 205)

Machines do not have operating principles of which they themselves are aware. Robots do not possess a conceptual language with which to record, transcribe and evaluate happenings; and they know nothing of the *past, present or future.*

Thinking requires flexibility of analysis. The thinker must be free to adopt a variety of propositions, and to test them in accordance with reality; and to perceive possibilities. All this is required to understand reality in any way whosoever. The thinker experiments and tests propositions to see if they fit reality; and using overlaid and multiple analogous concepts which are by no means an exact match to the specific item under investigation.

And all knowledge has a social element, provided by the open-thoughts of other people. In Fuller's terms: I am willing to accredit the experiences of other men when I am convinced by my experiences that they communicate to me faithfully; that is I am able to enlarge my experiences by the experience of other.[15]

And as mentioned by Kim Veltman, **we all dream**; and have beliefs and wishes, and/or feeling-tones that strongly influence our behaviour. Human knowledge is no mere dead, ossified conglomeration of thought atoms; but is alive with: *situating viewpoints, opinions, feelings, experiences, intuitions, experiments, discoveries and productions* etc.

As Fuller stated:

> Evolution pivots on the conscious, selective use of cumulative human experience and not on Darwin's hypothesis of chance adaptation to survival nor on his assumption of evolution independent of individual will and design.[15]

A human being is alive to all the possibilities present in the universe; whereas a robot, we must concede, knows nothing of anything; and because it cannot form concepts, analogies and identify principles or generate adaptive plans for action.

We begin to realise that our brains are the most complex and self-determining things in the known universe. After all the measurements of atoms and galaxies are folded into laws in some corners of our networks, there will still be universes of interrelationships in the rest of our networks to be discovered. If this property of complexity could somehow be transferred into visible brightness so that it could stand forth clearly to our senses, the biological world would become a walking field of light, and human beings would stand out like blazing suns of complexity, flashing burning bursts of meaning to each other through the dull night of the physical world between. Is this not so?

John R Platt

To what extent is it true that we humans are already, in some sense (or in many ways) already acting like machines ourselves? Do we not routinely perform the same operations time and time again—just like an automaton; and in response to a machines dictates? Why can't user-interfaces, TVs, computers, cars, washing-machines just know what we want, read our brains and/or listen to our instructions (once only)?

Where is the marvellous AI that could help?

"And you say that each time you swallow it's accompanied by a soft whirring sound?"

People take for granted the extent to which they have been co-opted by their technology.
It is not possible for humans to return to a natural state. - William Gibson

Indeed, it is difficult to see how the subtle variety of ways things can matter to us could be exhaustivity spelled out. We can anticipate and understand Jack's reaction because we remember what it feels like to be amused, amazed, incredulous, disappointed, disgruntled, saddened, annoyed, disgusted, upset, angry, furious, outraged etc; and we recognise the impulses to action associated with these various degrees and kinds of concerns. A computer model would have to be given a description of each shade of feeling as well as each feeling's normal occasion and likely result. The idea that feelings, memories, and images must be the conscious tip of an unconscious frame-like data structure runs up against both *prima facie* (on first examination, a matter appears to be evident from the facts) evidence and the problem of explicating the *ceteris paribus* conditions...

Looking back over the past ten years of AI research we might say that the basic point which has emerged is that **since intelligence must be situated it cannot be separated from the rest of human life.** This denial of a seemingly obvious point began with Plato's attempt to separate the intellect or rational soul from the body with skills, emotions and appetites... think about the needs and desires in structuring all social situations, or finally the whole cultural background of human self-interpretation involved in our simply knowing how to pick out and use chairs.

Hubert L. Drefus

Let us now stop and evaluate where we are. This chapter is supposed to be all about robots and automata. Why then, have we placed so much emphasis on free-will and the question of how a machine thinks, or does not think? Why the emphasis on the 'mental life' of robots? Would it not be better to analyse what a robot may possibly come to look like in the future, what it may be capable of physically, and to study its functions and possible uses in society as whole?

Perhaps such an analysis would be interesting, but in the end such a (physically based) analysis may be pointless.

Humanoid robots are coming. Period. Go and look at the Asimo videos on YouTube, or the Atlas walking robot, or countless other examples of the demonstrations of robot arms, legs; and of *running*, *hopping*, and *flying* artificial creatures. My point being that it is patently obvious that we shall very soon see humanoid robots/androids amongst us; and many with physical capabilities very similar to those demonstrated by our own bodies. It will be perhaps 10 years at most, before we shall have the first (general purpose) humanoid robots in commonplace use in factories, in domestic positions, and working as waiters, helpers etc. It is true that robots of one form or another, have been in common use in factories for over 100 years; but I am referring to walking, talking *humanoid* robots who are able to understand verbal instructions, speak and perform everyday tasks autonomously whilst moving about much as we humans do.

True '*Robby the Robot*' friends/helpers will soon arrive.

Certainly there are obstacles to be overcome before these robots are ready to take their place amongst us. Problems exist, such as as developing: *a sufficiently energetic on-board power-supply, or a sufficiently 'intelligent' robot mind/vision etc.* But without a doubt, and in a physical sense, these humanoid robots will be built. However just as with computers, it is the robot minds that will, and should concern us; and we must consider carefully, before we accept such mechanical men into our world.

Critical problems surround the extent to which a robot actually understands the human world, and its own duties, responsibilities; and safe interactions/influences on mankind.

The fact is that people are people and not things, neither are they numbers nor percentages nor society, nor the community, nor even a mass. People—individual people—are unique... the whole bag of tricks of political theories, economic and educational system, social structures and the rest are all for the sake of people and not, as one might suspect, the other way around. - HRH Prince Philip

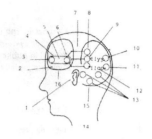

Robot 'minds' must be able to properly and adequately perceive the human world; by evaluating (and combining) relevant mini-worlds; and in turn by understanding their own relationship to the larger human-world of which everything (and especially themselves) plays a part. Flexible perception is required, whereby robots begin to use 'fuzzy' analogous methods to see and conceptualise adequately, (in fact) the *mini-worlds* and *big-world* in which they find themselves. Desired are intelligent responses; in terms of understanding human verbal instructions, and recognising human needs in specific situational context(s). I call this ability *analogical vision* or *situational templating*; and an example would be the robot recognising when a person has fallen over *(i.e the robot recognising human predicaments/intentions)*; and offering help; as opposed to (ignoring) the many (apparently) similar situations when a person is simply resting, playing or lying-down.

At first humanoid robots will be employed in physically-based occupations such as a *gardener, builder, shop worker etc.* The robot must be able to link the human and machine worlds in terms of priorities; and to recognise emergency situations etc; and to somehow respond to novelty. Major breakthroughs in Artificial Intelligence are required before this type of machine thinking becomes commonplace; but I think it will be possible to create robot helpers that can perform ordinary and everyday tasks quite adequately. Creating machines that can themselves creatively think *(e.g. possess creative free-will)*, or strategically problem solve, will be much more difficult, and is a long term problem space. It is the breadth of 'robot vision', in terms of 'big-world' perspective which is lacking; because unknown is how the human mind maintains a fantastic looseness of context whilst still working usefully towards specific goals.

Inventive/learning/self-programming robots may be a very long way off; if in fact they are possible at all. We humans 'live' inside a fully coherent 'big-world'; and accordingly created is a vast constellation of intricately connected concept/analogy 'clouds'; each one 'alive' with possibility/applicability. A useful robot must likewise be able to situate itself, and to consider what will be the likely *effects* of different actions (especially on humans); and to imagine/explore the options intelligently, so to speak.

The arguments for the mechanised society are compelling and they are advanced with the best possible intentions, but I am beginning to suspect that they miss, or perhaps just forget, the whole point of human life. A life devoid of challenge or risk, an existence of total stability and total security, may be splendid for cabbages but it would not be much fun for people... There is nothing wrong with this world which cannot be cured by people. Almost nothing in this world will be put right by theories, systems and organisations or by socio-political ideologies just by themselves... Oppression can silence a man but he is still free to choose his attitude.... everything begins with the individual and it is people who decide what sort of communities they are going to live in... it is people who are going to decide whether it will be humanly tolerable and civilised or whether it will degenerate into a human jungle... furthermore the decision still remains with the inhabitants.

HRH Prince Philip

Husserl found that he had to include more and more of what he called the 'outer horizon', a subjects total knowledge of the world. ...The assumption that background context (of common sense know-how) can be treated as an ordinary, patterned object is false. Heidegger criticised this; and I call it the metaphysical assumption.

Hubert L. Drefus

The non-mediated world has become a LOST COUNTRY; and one that we cannot find our way back to. The mediated world is now the world reality. We have a pervasive sense of loss and clear sense of what we have gained (we think). Sense of loss and Christmas remaining at the same time. We have vertiginous frightening moments which induce both terror and fantasy at the same time. - William Gibson

A report by the influential Public Accounts Committee (PAC) concluded an attempt to upgrade NHS computer systems in England ended up becoming one of the "worst and most expensive contracting fiascos" in public sector history. The final bill for abandoning the plan is still uncertain, the committee said. Ministers initially put the costs of the NHS scheme's failure at £9.8 billion pounds! (Times Newspaper)

Computer Disasters

- Faulty Soviet early warning system nearly causes World War 3 (1983).

- ESA's Ariane 5 rocket blew up due to trying to stuff a 64-bit number into a 16-bit address pace.

- The Mars Polar Explorer spacecraft crashes into the Martian atmosphere and is destroyed. The problem? A NASA sub-contractor had used imperial units (in computer code) rather than the NASA specified metric units (as used in Europe).

- An EDS UK software program managed to overpay and underpay more than 2 million people; and the system was later scrapped at a cost of over one billion pounds.

- In 1996, the Navy decided to retrofit the USS Yorktown with a bank of 27 computers, each with a dual 200 MHz processor (roughly one-fifth as powerful as a current iPhone). Things came to a head on September 21, 1997, when the USS Yorktown attempted to divide by zero. This crashed the entire boat and left it helpless in the middle of the ocean.

- Wall Street Crash of 1988. As investors fled stocks in a mass exodus, computer trading programs generated a flood of sell orders, overwhelming the market, crashing systems and leaving investors effectively blind.

It is paradoxical, yet true, to say, that the more we know, the more ignorant we become in the absolute sense, for it is only through enlightenment that we become conscious of our limitations.

Precisely one of the most gratifying results of intellectual evolution is the continuous opening up of new and greater prospects.

Nikola Tesla

Robot Cartoon (danscartoons.com)

Every living being is an engine geared to the wheel-work of the universe. Though seemingly affected only by its immediate surrounding, the sphere of external influence extends to an infinite distance.

Nikola Tesla

Cybergeddon

Today, we all dabble in some place that looks a lot like 1970s New York City—the Internet. Low-level crime remains rampant, while increasingly sophisticated crime syndicates go after big scores. There is a cacophony of hateful speech, vice of every kind, and policemen of various sorts trying to keep a lid on all of it—or at least, trying to keep the chaos away from most law-abiding citizens. But people still use the Internet every day, though the ones who consider themselves "street smart" do so with varying levels of defenses installed. Things sort of work.

Just like 1970s New York, however, there's a pervasive feeling that everything could go completely to hell with the slightest push—into a place to be escaped from with the aid of a digital Snake Plissken. In other words, the Internet might soon look less like 1970s New York and more like 1990s Mogadishu: warring factions destroying the most fundamental of services, "security zones" reducing or eliminating free movement, and security costs making it prohibitive for anyone but the most well-funded operations to do business without becoming a "soft target" for political or economic gain.

That day is not yet nigh, but logic suggests the status quo can't continue forever. The recent rash of major breaches of corporate networks, including the theft of personal information from the health insurer Anthem and the theft of as much as a billion dollars from over 100 banks are symptoms of a much larger trend of cybercrime and espionage.

Sean Gallagher, ArsTechnica.com [February 2015]

Chapter Twelve
Circuits of Thought

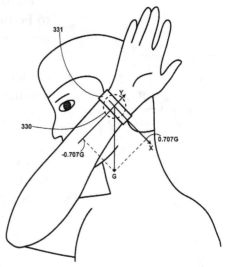

ELECTRICITY LIES at the heart of modern civilisation; allowing us to: operate all of our machines; achieve rapid transportation on land, sea and air; heat our houses; power industrial processes of all kinds; and it lies behind almost every kind of human communication in the form of digital networks/media. Without electricity most people would not survive very long, and those that did would be banished right back to the stone age.

To say that humans are enmeshed with, or reliant upon, electricity, is an understatement; but the relationship of humans to computers is an even closer, more intimate and elemental one. A key premise of this book is that we humans are merging/conjoining with the computer; mentally, physically and even spiritually/emotionally.

Computer-is-self; and *self-is-computer*; and conspicuous is a new form of part-human, part-artificial being; one with unique capabilities/limitations: the *self-computer*. But what is the evidence for this self-computer; how can/should it be created, formed and managed, and what are the implications for human life; individually and collectively?

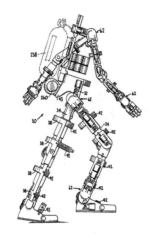

We shall approach these topics using the *Theory of Natural Thoughts*; combined with an analysis of how mind, media and system implanted-thoughts: *form, shape and construct the self-computer* as it exists today, and may come to exist in the future. Accepting that we humans are now, and shall ever be, fundamentally altered *by* (and perhaps *for*) machines, is unsettling; but it is a common theme for social-theorists, science-fiction authors, and also in futuristic movies etc.

The question is not so much: *is man master or servant of the machine*, but how closely do we merge with the machine.

Do we *embrace*, or *defend ourselves from*: computers?

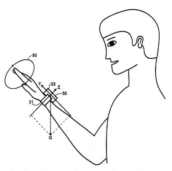

The function of the machine is to save work... (and)... the logical end of mechanical progress is to reduce the human being to something resembling a <u>brain in a bottle</u>... like a drug, the machine is useful, dangerous and habit-forming. - George Orwell (The Road to Wigan Pear)

The conception of the human brain has at last escaped from
the control of human minds. - Karol Capek

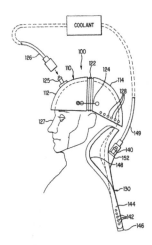

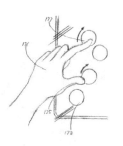

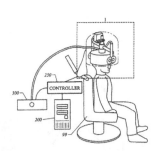

Perhaps we do both. We must ask ourselves: who do we wish to become? To what degree should we allow the capabilities of automatic systems and computers to merge with the human world? Which opportunities are opened-up/closed-off by computers; and what are the inherent and/or chosen: positive and negative outcomes of automatic systems.

Where are we going, and where do we wish to go?

Hopefully I do not have to convince you of the fact that a synthesis of humans and computers has already begun. But just in case, we shall see examples of, and possibilities/predictions of; such a trend in later chapters. For now we simply note that the coalescence of man/machine has progressed far; and in terms of all types of human activity; and it may (in fact) be irreversible.

George Orwell spoke about the dangers of dependence on machines; and that we would (probably) not even bother to work out the consequences. He also said that it is only when mechanisation has finally triumphed, that we can actually *feel* the tendency of the machine to make a fully human life impossible.

Orwell on machines (and hence computers):

> What is the function of the machine? Obviously its primary function is to save work, and the type of person to whom machine-civilisation is entirely acceptable seldom sees any reason for looking further... To these people, apparently, the only danger of the machine is its possible use for destructive purposes; as, for instance, airplanes that are used for war... (and in terms of progress towards the idea of a Western utopia)... machines to save work, machines to save thought... machines to save pain; more efficiency, more organisation... (towards)... the paradise of little fat men... (but)... the question is whether there is <u>any</u> human activity which would not be maimed by the dominance of the machine... The tendency of mechanical progress, then, is to frustrate the human need for effort and creation. It makes unnecessary and even impossible the activities of the eye and hand... and... (because) everything can (is, and should) be done by machinery... the process of mechanisation has itself become a machine, a huge glittering vehicle whirling us we are not certain where, but probably toward the padded Wells-world and the brain in a bottle.[1]

Orwell's views are not (at first sight) very positive in relation to machines; but we must read between the lines here.

Net Neutrality: European ministers are pushing for new laws which would "permit every imaginable breach of net neutrality", internet freedom campaigners have warned. Days after the US voted to protect an open internet where all traffic is considered equal, proposals agreed by the telecoms ministers of 28 members states could allow a two-speed internet, where companies such as YouTube or Netflix could legally pay mobile networks or broadband providers for faster, more reliable delivery of their content – potentially to the detriment of other internet users. Campaigners warn the move could stifle online innovation and undermine the digital economy. [arstechnica.com - March 2015]

Man must control, not be controlled: 'Machinery is aggressive...
if you do not use tools, they will use you'. - Ralph Waldo Emerson

CIRCUITS OF THOUGHT   275

Orwell referred not to the danger(s) of machines *per-se*; but to the outcomes/implications of the <u>purposes</u> that we humans put machines to. The truly frightening part of Orwell's visionary sermon, is not only the feeling that we are powerless to do anything about the progress towards the mechanisation of everything; but that humans are in some sense *too dull, listless or uncaring* to be bothered investigating the systemising process itself.

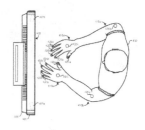

Myself I am not quite so pessimistic, despite the fact that many of Orwell's predictions do seem to be coming true; and in absolutely every respect. Today it does not take a genius like Orwell to recognise that something has gone wrong with machines, and that they are—in many instances—and in an overall sense—fundamentally broken (see quotations throughout).

Computers everywhere have somehow 'forgotten' their true purpose/function (to help **all** mankind); and appear to have gone 'mad' (truly helping only the **few**), so to speak. On the contrary perhaps it is <u>we</u> who have somewhat *madly* conferred onto the machine; meanings, applications and purposes that are wholly out of correspondence with the original and natural meaning of the term: *machine*.

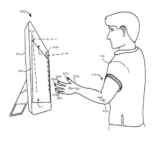

Etymological dictionaries trace the word *machine* from the French *machine* to the Latin *machina*, Greek *mekhos* and Indo-European *magd*. Mekhos can be translated as *means*; or as an *expedient*. Accordingly, machines are means, not ends; *servants* not *masters*. They are man made—and man makes machines to accomplish certain desired effects. So long as the end is desired, and attained, the machine is useful.

Now a leap of faith is required, and I ask that the reader accept that mankind is (currently) merging with the computer (sub-optimally); prior to exposition of proof (or supply of evidence) later on. Assuming that the reader can accommodate me in this one respect; we ask, what is the purpose of man making a machine that is, at least in part, his very self?

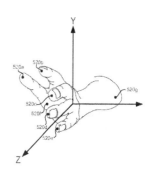

Surely the only logical answer to the question of why make a new self; is if that new self is improved, enhanced or made happier by the remoulding process. Man improves man. QED.

The all-encompassing, all-providing machine becomes the object of worship, and when it begins to break down its servants have lost the skills needed to repair it. But the resulting defects do not matter, for the 'human tissues' in that latter day had become so subservient that they readily adapted themselves to every caprice of the machine. - E.M. Forester

Man has lost the capacity to foresee and forestall.
He will end by destroying the earth. - Albert Schweitzer

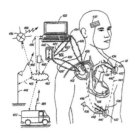

And if man can be equated with his thoughts; then it logically follows that any *mechanisation or automation* of his thoughts must proceed humanely. Accordingly, the topic of who can/will/may: *create, view, copy, use and share thoughts,* now and in the future, is the topic of the present chapter. In this section, we wish to probe the nature of thoughts that exist in mind(s) and on media; therefore we shall ignore machine-implanted thought form(s) *(apart from computer-aided thinking procedures/methods).*

Remember that we spoke about the individual and collective goals for humanity in chapter 2; whereby later we came to the conclusion that the only way to improve man was to confer on him more freedom; and from the vital perspective of: *freedom-of-thought.* An improved human, then, is one who may think/act freely; and (specifically) one who can create, share and protect his/her thoughts, opinions and votes; and according to the *Theory of Natural Thoughts.* I would suggest that this is the only respect (i.e. the provision of free-flowing ideas) that a merging of 'thinking' man and machine is absolutely necessary, desirable and workably (always) within the remit of truly 'beneficial' moral and ethical practice.

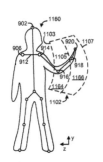

The desirability of freedom of thought/action; leads logically to the *Theory of Natural Thoughts;* which in turn (if upheld) provides for a free flow of thought-atoms (proof follows). We propose a profoundly democratic philosophy of cognition firmly grounded in, and based upon, human rights. Every integer of logic present in this theory relates to establishing *freedom-of-thought;* and for all the people of the world. Furthermore, hypothesised is that *(for mind and media-stored thoughts)* three factors are absolutely necessary; namely: *equality, natural property (ownership)* and *free-assembly (for all thoughts).*

< {25} Freedom = Equality, Ownership and Free-Assembly of thoughts. >

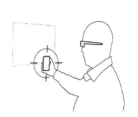

The question remains of how to construct a society *(including technological methods, legal and social systems etc)*; in such a form that it protects and upholds the aforementioned Essential Attributes; and hence upholds: *freedom-of-thought.*

The *problem-space* (I would suggest) is crystal clear.

Capital is money, capital is commodities. By virtue of it being value, it has acquired the occult ability to add value to itself. It brings forth living offspring, or at least, lays golden eggs. - Karl Marx

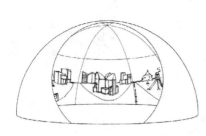

Computer fraudster Bernie Madoff (who was behind a 65 billion dollar Ponzi trading fraud) was a former chairman of NASDEQ, the worlds first and largest electronic Stockmarket. Talk about a conflict of interest/ethics!

Society does not consist of individuals but expresses the sum of interrelations, the relations within which these individuals stand. - Karl Marx

CIRCUITS OF THOUGHT 277

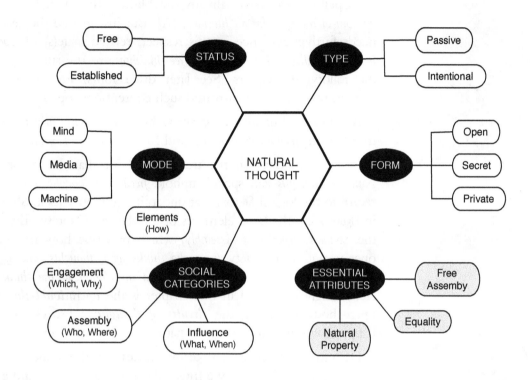

Figure 2: Theory of Natural Thoughts

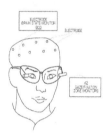

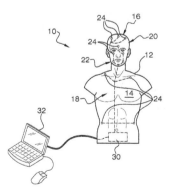

But the *solution-space (mapping of freedom-of-thought capability to the mechanisms-of-delivery)* may appear a little murky; hence...

To begin with I can anticipate certain objections in terms of the desirability of (completely unfettered/un-checked) *freedom-of-thought*; but begging the reader's pardon, I shall leave consideration of related matters to later chapters. Here we are concerned with developing workable designs for computers; the same being ones that can underpin the *Theory of Natural Thoughts*, and in particular to uphold the natural thought-rights that all humans inherently posses *(or should be afforded)*.

We begin by establishing three predicates:

[A] Freedom of ALL Thought(s) is desirable.

[B] The Theory of Natural Thoughts specifies [A].

[C] Computers must be carefully designed to provide [A & B]

The product of mental labour—science—always stands far below its value, because the labor-time necessary to reproduce it has no relation at all to the labor-time required for its original production. - Karl Marx

There is no such thing as a little freedom, either you
are free, or you are not free. - Walter Cronkite

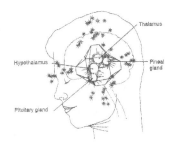

Hopefully we have already established the desirability of *freedom-of-thought (for all humans)* [A]. But just in case the reader needs further evidence in this respect; related issue(s) of: *social justice, morality, ethics, law and free-thinking;* are the subject(s) of the following chapters. See later discussion(s) for the many viewpoints/issues that surround such contentious topics.

At present, our aim is to show how it is *technically possible* to establish *freedom-of-thought*; and for everyone *(theoretically).*

In order to establish the truth of [B], or that the *Theory of Natural Thoughts* can specify/uphold *freedom-of-thought;* we now return to the logical factors that underpin the theory itself. Shown in **Figure 2** are the basic elements of the theory. Noteworthy are the *Social Categories of Assembly;* which prescribe how thoughts operate within a society *(i.e. who thinks what thoughts, and how, when and where are the thoughts located in relation to the thinker).* Accordingly examined in this chapter is the **operational-flow** of open-thought(s) along the **circuits of thought**; a process which happens within a **thought-space** that envelops the thinker.

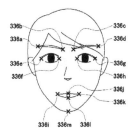

Definition of these key terms makes up the bulk of the present chapter; but first we must take a step backwards and ask: *what is the nature of thinking itself?* In an attempt to answer this question, Dr Karl Popper (1902-1994) came up with the so-called *Three-World's* theory of human thinking. **(See Figure 3) [2,3,4]**

Humans use a combination of sense and mind to analyse and synthesise *Things* in the *Physical World* [*World 1*]; and so to move these into the *Mental World* [*World 2*]. Using both *concepts-of-nature* and *concepts-of-culture,* and by employing *conscious/unconscious* and *individual/collective* thinking methods etc; we then proceed to *think*; whereby thoughts are coalesced into *concepts* and inserted into *World 3 (Products of the Human Mind).* Knowledge then develops from the resulting amalgamation of concepts into *facts, theories, principles etc.*[4]

The three-worlds theory is useful because it draws attention to classic Western dualities such as: *mind/matter, animate/inanimate, essence/percept;* and related methodologies such as: *signified, signifier and referent, etc.* Obviously ignored in **Figure 3** is the great diversity of human thought forms/processes; and competing theories etc.

Every man must have the right fearlessly to think independently and express his
opinion about what he knows, what he has personally thought about and
experienced, and not merely to express with slightly different variations the
opinion which has been inculcated in him. - Mstislav Rostropovich

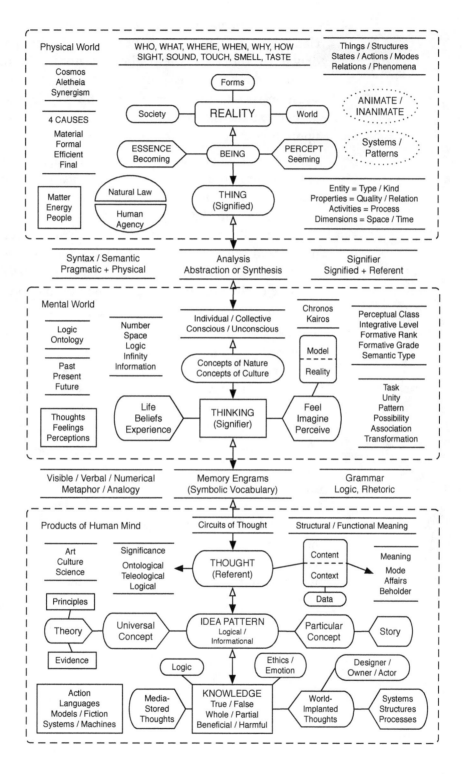

Figure 3: The Three Worlds Theory of Human Thinking
(author's interpretation)

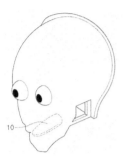

Despite an apparent simplicity, Popper's theory provides clarity in a couple of important respects. Firstly our attention is drawn to the fact that a thought-atom will have both a *structural* and *functional* meaning; and the functional or situation-specific meaning of a thought will depend entirely on its context of use; or (in the language of the present book) upon its context Status *(either context-free or context-established).*

Another subtler aspect is that a thought-atom can have either a *purely informational* or else a *logical* meaning *(i.e. be of a passive or intentional Type);* whereby only logical thoughts (apparently) can causally affect other thoughts and actions. However Popper claims that we can never know or understand what are all of the implications of a thought *(even when it is a passive or else a purely informational/theoretical one);* and due to the unknown usage of the informational content.

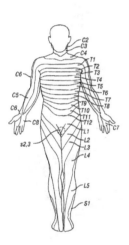

For Popper any attempt to tie-down meaning is a hopeless task, and because there are an infinity of projected/unforeseeable meanings belonging to the informational content itself. Popper claims that **we never know what we are talking about!** This is because we can never know what are: **all of the logical implications of a thought-atom**; that is the nature and meaning of all the statements which follow (from) it; because—contexts of re-use are innumerable.

I think that Popper is correct; and we do not (ever) *fully* know what we are talking about (in a sense); or else how our shared thoughts will be used/interpreted by others (or even by ourselves), and on different occasions. This is precisely why we stated that all natural (open) thoughts are *absolutely equal* and possess no (fixed) context whatsoever—that is until a context *Status* has been established for each one; whereupon its meaning is (perhaps) frozen 'inside-of' a specific usage scenario.

But remember that the thinker *(of a mind/media-stored thought-atom)* is (always) able to break the bonds of a thought-atom to its neighbours; hence un-fixing its Type (e.g. changing passive to intentional); and/or un-fixing its Status, re-establishing a new context, and/or change the meaning of a thought-atom according to the structural arrangements of a new association.

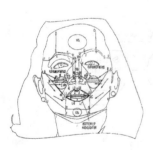

What is freedom of expression?
Without the freedom to offend, it ceases to exist. - Salman Rushdie
In short software is eating the world. - Marc Andreessen
Think? Why think! We have computers for that. - J. Rostand
Imagine if every Thursday your shoes exploded if you tied them the wrong way. This happens to
us all the time with computers, and nobody thinks of complaining. - Jeff Raskin

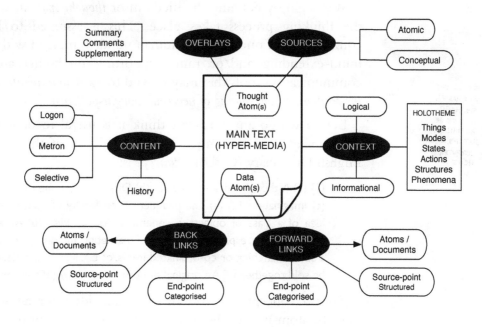

Figure 4: Hyperlinked Document

A thought-atom is an *idea that results from thinking*; and may itself be an *idea-pattern, image, sound, feeling etc.* Thoughts (represented meanings) are **dynamic entities**; whereby a great variety of different: *kinds of people, thought-processes, thinking methods/models and structural situations etc;* produce/use thoughts.

In this book we do not wish to speculate on *how* thinking takes place, or else the *why/when/what* in relation to a thought's impact(s) on society. These are named the *Elements, Influences and Engagements* of thoughts; and are largely ignored here.

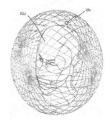

The *Theory of Natural Thoughts* says absolutely nothing about the *process-of-thinking (or theory of mind).* Rather it deals with the **operational-flow** of thoughts within a thought-space *(i.e. <u>who</u> thinks <u>what</u> thoughts, <u>how,</u> <u>when</u> and <u>where</u> are the thoughts located in relation to the thinker).* Operational-flow can be likened to the flow of electricity in a circuit, whereby desired is a free flow of ideas *(socially).* Operational-flow equates to efficiently navigating hyperlinked thought-atoms within a thought-space (see Figure 4).

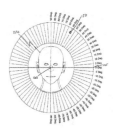

The NSA makes use of a 'selector' program in a communication chain; which employs identifiers that are unique to you (your PC Mac address, email address, mobile phone Sim card etc); whereby this 'robotic' intelligence then goes through the entire database of everything that has been collected (i.e. all digital records globally), and finds 'stories' to tell about you; such as (on one day) that you went to the shops, phoned this person and then went to work for 8 hours before going home to use your PC. Incredibly, they (the NSA etc) know where you went and what you did on each and every day! And they can move this data into the present/future, whereby the selector can be made real-time; and agents can watch what you are doing right now!

AFTER THE ACCIDENT, MY HEAD HAD TO BE REPLACED. BUT MY NEW COMPUTER HEAD IS EVEN BETTER.

We begin by defining the medium or *thought-space* in which the thinking process takes place. This is assumed to be a combination of one or more human mind(s); merged with any mind-extending and/or mind-supporting method(s) and/or communication tools that may be said to exist *(and which aid in the creation/vision/sharing of new/old thought-patterns)*.

Before we go any further I think it is useful to define the term: *concept*. According to the 2nd edition of the Oxford English Dictionary (OED); a **concept** is:

> [1] (a) A thought, idea = conceit; (b) Disposition, frame of mind; and (c) Imagination. [2] (a) The product of the faculty of conception; an idea of a class of objects, a general notion or idea. (b) A general notion or idea, esp. in the context of marketing and design; a 'theme', a set of matching or co-ordinated items. of e.g. furniture, a design to be sold together. [3] An original draft or rough copy (of a letter, etc).

Thus a concept is a pattern of related ideas (or assembled thought-atoms); and the same being ideas that form a set/ grouping of related notions; according to uniting conception(s) or else a specific frame-of-mind and/or viewpoint. Accordingly *useful* concepts are typically formed from parts that are (normally) logically coherent, and/or that work-together (in some way); and in order to achieve a specific aim, goal and/or to illustrate an idea. Put simply, a concept is a product of the human mind (a thought-atom and/or pattern); being one that the thinker has found to be, or hopes will be, in some way practically beneficial; and/or that: can/will/may aid the thinking process in some way. Of course things are never really quite this simple; but we shall adopt a definition such that:

> < {26}   A concept is a useful pattern of thought-atoms that have been grouped together to represent and/or model things; real and/or imaginary >

What the represented *things* actually are (in and of themselves) is left un-defined. Nevertheless, we can now develop the idea of a notional thought-space; in which concepts, real and imaginary, are to be created, linked, used and shared etc. There will be many different (notional) thought-spaces, and each thought-space will be distinct for a specific individual, and/or 'thinking' collective.

Many factors will inter-relate to form a thought-space.

THANKS TO THE CLOUD ALL MY DEVICES ARE IN SYNC... IT'S ONLY MY BRAIN THAT DOESN'T KNOW WHAT'S GOING ON.

Freedom of speech means freedom for those who you despise, and freedom to express the most despicable views. It also means that the government cannot pick and choose which expressions to authorize and which to prevent. - Alan Dershowitz

The operational efficiency of a thought-space will be related to factors such as: *the educational level and/or knowledge base of its members (i.e. the thinkers); plus the nature, truth, visibility, usefulness and number of available/useful concepts.* Each concept is wholly comprised of thought-atoms that (typically) are available for use and/or re-use within the space. One can imagine <u>measuring</u> the *number, quality (i.e. truth) and availability* of thought-atoms within a thought-space; a process involving (perhaps) judgement of the totality of mind-extending tools present such as: *books, magazines, libraries, computer networks etc.* At this point I would like to acknowledge elements of this theory that have been 'borrowed' from elsewhere; and in particular as detailed in the book: *Information, Mechanism and Meaning* by Professor Donald M. MacKay (1922-1987). In that book, MacKay developed a rather novel theory of the transmission of *meaning and information.*[5]

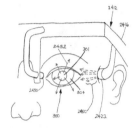

According to MacKay:

> A measurement is prescribed by some minimal significance, represented/grouped into conceptually distinguishable categories so as to delineate a certain form... and... the 'informational efficiency' of a given measurement could be estimated by the proportion of those elementary events (structural units or logons) involved that find themselves represented by atomic facts (metrical-units)... a representation... could have its 'size' specified in two complimentary ways: (a) by enumerating its (structural) degrees of freedom (conceptual categories) and (b) by enumerating its (metrical) atomic facts... hence the concept of information has these dual aspects... the structural and metrical.... what we really want is to discover a method which will give us the maximum amount of information (structural + metrical) for a given outlay of time or space. [5]

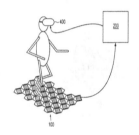

MacKay wanted to find a way to 'measure' information; and as we shall see, he (in fact) found a way. Accordingly we ask if it is possible to 'measure' thoughts; and if it may be possible to maximise the amalgamated knowledge, truth and meaning for *all* thoughts; (number and accessibility of useful concepts); and within a specific thought-space. I don't think anyone would attempt to deny that maximising useful knowledge (in a thought-space) would be beneficial *(but some people may!).*

Information is that which enables us to make a *selection* from a set of possibilities or to *narrow* the range of the possibilities about which we are ignorant. - Donald M MacKay

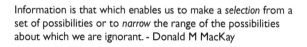

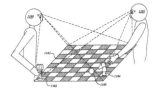

We can transpose Mackay's analysis of the *meaning of informational content* (for scientific measurements); to an analysis of the useful/beneficial thought-content within a thought-space. MacKay says that the informational content of a message/representation *(or indeed, we claim, a thought-pattern)* consists of three components; *descriptive, metrical and selectional.*

We shall explore each in turn...

MacKay defines *structural* or *descriptive informational content* as: that which yields the largest number of elements for a symbolic 'picture'; or which allows the maximum amount of fine structure in it. One could think of this same factor as being equivalent to the number, span and/or diversity of distinct words/concepts that are present in a *language of representation*; and in fact we are talking here about a language for 'thinking' within a thought-space.

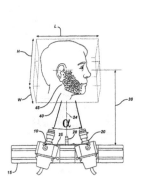

Thus a thought-space must contain the highest range or number of distinct conceptual-classes possible. Whenever a thought-space has a higher number of meaningfully distinct conceptual classes, then it is patently obvious that one has maximised the *representational* meaning-content or **amount of meaning** that can possibly be represented. Any thinker present in the same space has a higher range of choices and/or may (possibly) 'think' with a greater: *depth, breadth and logical accuracy.* Therefore the thinker may (one would suppose) create improved patterns *(i.e. more meaningful ones)* by combining a higher number and/or more appropriately chosen set of *diverse pieces* together, and thus creating more useful/complex/logical and/or meaning-saturated thought-patterns; hence the thought-space may be said to be more efficient.

We can characterise this first overall measure of any thought-space; as being the sum total of all the *descriptive thought-content* present; or the *logon content* or *logon capacity.*

< {27} Logon Capacity: An efficient thought-space contains the maximum number and <u>range</u> of logically distinct (universal) concepts. >

Of course this presumes that all thought-atoms are of equal usefulness/truth etc; and may be readily viewed/assembled/accessed; but we shall get to these issues shortly.

TENDENCY TO DANCE OR SQUIRM ABOUT AS A RESULT OF THE MACHINE'S ACTIONS: People 'dance' or 'squirm' about on either side of a system/machine/computer's trajectory of happenings; whereby system designers/owners/operators are (often wholly) disconnected from the system's logical/real-world effects and so can dance about (merrily) on the thought-projection side—and without a care in the world—safe in the knowledge that the system cannot affect 'them'; whereas the poor 'system influenced' humans on the other side must squirm about (painfully) in accordance with the system's (often harmful/uncaring) dictates/outcomes.

I believe in absolute freedom of expression. Everyone has a right to offend and be offended. - Taslima Nasrin

CIRCUITS OF THOUGHT 285

Thus far we have said nothing about how the thought-atoms within such a diversified thought-space may be formed/combined. In this respect, MacKay defines the *metrical information content* as: a measure of the weight of evidence in a representational pattern.

Metrical information content subsumes together the atomic facts, or actual knowledge elements present in a specific communication; that is the content, the atoms (of description) present within a single representation. One might think of these as the combined letter, word, and sentence *instances* that assembled together embody a conveyed (and particular) pattern of meaning. Hence this is the actual thought pattern contents *itself*; or the (enumerated) meaning(s) conveyed; and consists of atomic pieces of 'evidence', and/or descriptive informational concepts coalesced into a specific unit of meaning. Mackay called this the *metrical content* of the message/representation.

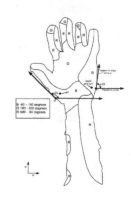

Metrical content and *structural (or descriptive)* content work together in a complimentary way to convey/represent meaning. For example, using a relatively primitive descriptive language with a narrow range of concepts; it may take quite a lot of metrical atomic facts to convey a specific meaning. Whereas when using a more developed language (i.e. containing a greater span of concepts); the same meaning may be conveyed using fewer atomic facts; in fact by employing higher order, and/or more complex and logically 'dense' or 'meaning-saturated' concepts.

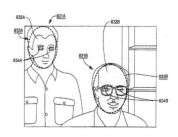

Previously we had noted the key problem within human affairs of identifying the most useful thoughts. Our suggested solution was to maximise the visibility and accessibility of all opinions. Metron capacity is a measure of how efficiently this process operates within a representation and/or thought-space.

< {28} Metron Capacity: An efficient thought-space contains the maximum number of logically distinct (particular) atoms of supporting evidence (opinions). >

It is important to note that *logon and metron capacities* alone are not sufficient to define the efficiency of a thought-space. MacKay also defined the *selective ability* for an informational content, which is a measure of not stuff, or individual thoughts themselves, but of a *relation* (or selective power) between a thought and an ensemble of other *(initially absent)* thoughts.

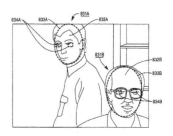

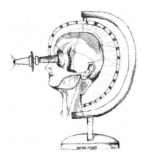

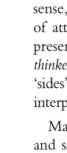

MacKay was a physicist *(i.e a materialist)*; but his theory nicely brings the observing *subject* into the normally overly (and in a sense, falsely) *objective* scientific method. His whole technique of attempting to maximise the degree of conveyed meaning present in a message/representation may be thought of as: *one thinker conveying a message to another thinker;* whereby on both 'sides' of the communication the thinkers 'cooperate' in order to interpret/assign meaning to the conveyed pattern.

MacKay introduced an important third measure of meaning; and said that the selective information content is a measure of the *unforeseeableness* of a representation.

MacKay noted that:

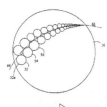

> Meaning is clearly a relationship between message and recipient rather than a unique property of the message alone... It looks as if the meaning of a message [and hence thought pattern] can be defined very simply as its selective function on the range of the recipient's states of conditional readiness for goal-oriented activity; so that the meaning of a message to you is its selective function on the range of your states of conditional readiness... for the original speaker, the meaning of what he says is the selective function he wants to perform on the listener's range of states of readiness.[5]

Selective ability measures the ability of a representation's *creator/producer* and *receiver/viewer*, present within a thought-space, to adopt logically equivalent *'modes of transmission and reception' (i.e. the inherency/identically of 'message' context).* This is the <u>beholder's share</u>, often spoken of by art historian Professor Ernst Gombrich (1909-2001); and/or the 'constructive aspect' of representation.[6]

We can usefully define:

< {29} Selection Capacity: An efficient thought-space contains the maximum number of (applicable) readily unforeseeable concepts (modal ones). >

And that's about it in terms of information measurement. According to MacKay the three capacities of: *logon, metron and selection;* wholly define the amount of information that may be conveyed in a representation. We have hereby (hopefully) usefully transposed these 'meaning-measurement' concepts from information; and to thought-atoms existing within a thought-space.

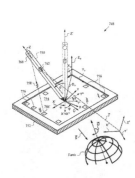

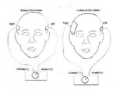

The secret of freedom lies in educating people, whereas the secret of tyranny is in keeping them ignorant. - Maximilien Robespierre

CIRCUITS OF THOUGHT   287

What remains is to see how these capacities can be practically enhanced, encouraged and/or facilitated within a thought-space.

A related goal is to establish a theoretical basis for the necessity of *ownership, equality and freedom-of-thoughts*. In this respect, we have established that an efficient thought-space maximises the capacities of *logon, metron* and *selection*; and accordingly the same thought-space may be said to facilitate the maximum: *number and range of distinct concepts; number of distinct (message-carrying) thought-atoms; and number of (applicable) readily unforeseeable concepts (inherent and/or modal ones).*

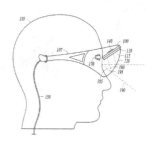

So how do we maximise these three capacities within a thought-space? The answer depends largely on how we define a thought-space. Remember that MacKay had stated (and proven) that for any specific representation it is these same factors that wholly define the degree or amount of meaning present. It stands to reason, therefore, that if we consider the whole body of human knowledge as one gigantic representation (or vast thought-space); being one that is, and should be, ever developing/improving, and hence becoming more complex *(in terms of contained knowledge and truth);* then it logically follows that we must maximise these three capacities for everything known.

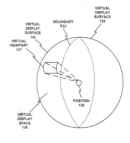

This conclusion (I would suggest) is inescapable. Despite the fact that different thinkers will (to some extent) have quite different local thought-spaces (i.e. contain secret and private thoughts etc); our goal should be to maximise the visibility of all open-thoughts: and hence the *size, extent, capacity, efficiency and usefulness etc;* of the world's thought-space. Connecting together the countless localised thought-spaces (e.g personal/organisational ones) enables formation of a large one of which they all form an integral part.

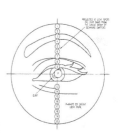

< {30} World Thought-Space: A thought-space comprising all of the connected local and global thought spaces/atoms/patterns/concepts etc; and hence it contains all the public knowledge of humanity. >

Hopefully these ideas do not sound too: utopian, remote and/ or impractical. A world thought-space is simply the theoretical basis of the World Brain spoken of earlier.

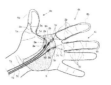

Now I shall attempt to link our newly established three vital capacities of the world thought-space to basic human rights as established by the United Nations. Within that declaration; freedom-of-thought is given three elements as follows: *free-thinking, freedom-of-belief, and the right to publish any thoughts.*[7] (see Figure 5 on the right hand side of this page).

'I missed that story – you blinked again!'

We can map the **3 capacities** to the **3 rights** as follows:

- Freedom-of-belief: have/see any thought: Logon Capacity (number + range of available (abstract) concepts) - EQUALITY (see)
- Free-thinking: create any thought: Metron Capacity (number of applicable thought-atoms) - FREE ASSEMBLY (associate/create)
- Public-proclamation: share/judge: Selection Capacity (number of applicable <u>readily unforeseeable</u> [*] concepts) - OWNERSHIP (judge)

Obviously for a World Brain, we are dealing with social or open-thoughts; at least for areas like scientific knowledge, art, culture etc; and hence the media-stored thoughts spoken of earlier. Yet one of the challenges and problems is that individuals may develop new (open) thoughts which do not come from a 'set of socially shared values' (e.g. be evil/horrible and disgusting ideas etc). However this drawback cannot be allowed to scupper freedom of thought; and methods such as social tagging, comments, annotations etc; can mitigate these problems.

In terms of the mapping process given above, I think that the three human rights factors, and three capacities, do match up nicely; and in fact demonstrate (perhaps) where these same factors come from, and/or how they have been developed *(specifically in terms of the maximising freedom-of-thought)*. How so? Well it seems that freedom-of-thought is largely concerned with freedom to: **perceive, associate and judge thoughts (from a set of socially shared ones),** and therefore with the ability to form new thought patterns of one's own choosing.

In our terms one might say that the efficiency of a thought-space is dependent the ability of **the thinker(s) to: see, create and share concepts.** Free-form mental thinking ability, or construction of open-thoughts is key; that is the ability to freely assemble thoughts into concepts; a process which depends on methods such as grouping, relation and analogy; and to put it simply: on the *free-flow* of thought-atoms alone.

"BAD NEWS — THE DRINKS MACHINE WON"

[*] N.B. The term 'readily unforeseeable' refers to the presence of inherent 'assumed' facts (within a representation), 'common understanding' and/or contextual knowledge that both creator and onlooker share in common. This knowledge may include common goals, assumptions, expertise, etc.

What is the hardest task in the world? To think. - Emerson
Thinking is very far from knowing. - H. G. Bohn

CIRCUITS OF THOUGHT   289

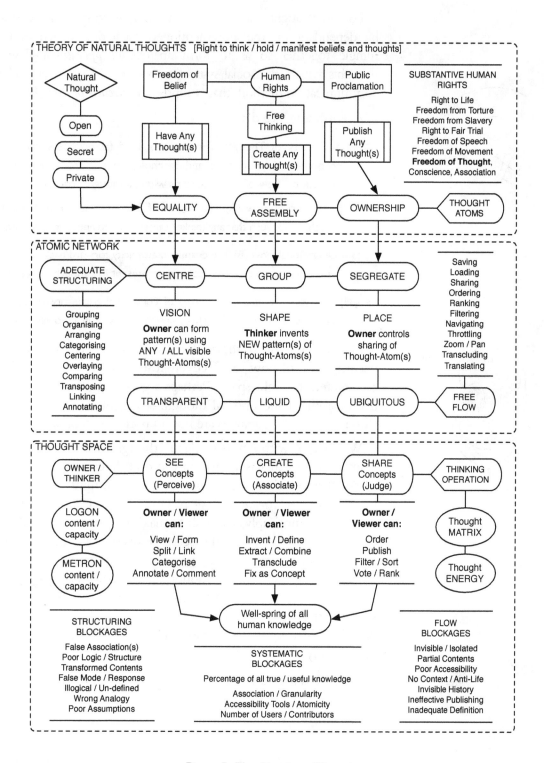

Figure 5: The Circuits of Thought

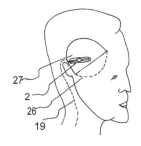

For any thought-space the flow of thoughts within that space will be dependant on the aforementioned capacities; which in turn mingle together so as to form an overall **operational-flow** of thoughts within the social system(s) present, and by means of the communication methods that comprise the **circuits of thought**.

Accordingly, we define...

< {31} Circuits of Thought: The sum total of factors: personal, social, economic, communicative and technological etc; that comprise the operational-flow of thought-atoms within a thought-space. >

< {32} Operational Flow (A): The degree of free-movement that exists in a thought-space such that any thinker can: see, create and share concepts. >

< {33} Operational Flow (B): The quantified atomicity, forward/backward/omni/source linkage, and overlays/comments; present in a thought-space. >

< {34} Atomicity: The quantified degree of 'conceptual granularity' or the size/number of addressable 'thought-atoms/data' present in a thought-space. >

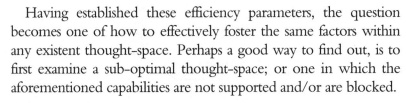

Having established these efficiency parameters, the question becomes one of how to effectively foster the same factors within any existent thought-space. Perhaps a good way to find out, is to first examine a sub-optimal thought-space; or one in which the aforementioned capabilities are not supported and/or are blocked.

We begin with an '*Orwellian*' thought-space; constructed from a society that is similar to the one described in the book *1984*.[8] Established is that members of a thought-space should be able to *see, create and share* concepts freely and without hindrance. Put simply, we wish to maximise the operational-flow of thought-atoms within the space. However in the Orwellian space we notice that our <u>vision</u> is blocked with censure; our <u>shaping-ability</u> is fixed by double-think, and <u>sharing-ability</u> is diverted by propaganda. We discover that for an Orwellian society, the operational flow of thoughts along the various circuits-of-thought that make up any thought-space; are unnaturally obstructed, altered, slowed-down and/or halted.

Identified are three kinds of blockages:

< {35} Thought-Flow blockages: lost/hidden (spying); warped (thought-control) and automatic/stolen thoughts (newspeak etc.) >

But 99 percent of the world is not connected (in terms of things). However by 2020 there will be 20-50 billion IP connected things!

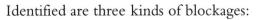

My thoughts are not your thoughts, neither are your ways my ways. - Old Testament: Isaiah, 1v, 8.

CIRCUITS OF THOUGHT 291

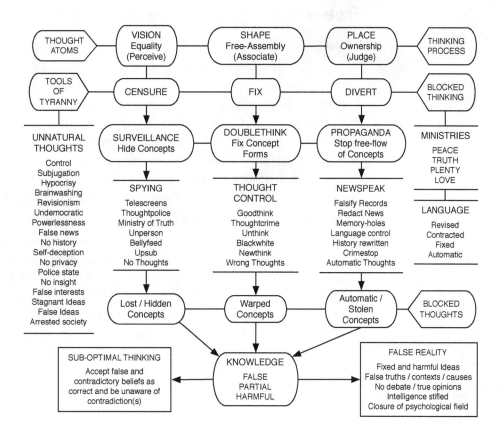

Figure 6: An 'Orwellian' Thought-Space

What has been gained as a result of this discussion? Perhaps only something of which we were already quite aware; specifically that totalitarian regimes will (above all else) attempt to shape/control/dictate our thoughts, and as a first and foremost priority. And the reason is simply to remove everyone's right to see, create and share concepts openly and without censure. Within such a regime, attempts are made to remove the natural human right to own thoughts; and more specifically to communicate thought-atoms to/with whomever one wishes.

Our discussion has established that thought: *ownership, equality, free-assembly*; are the bedrocks of any free-thinking society.

In Frank Herbert's epic Dune space-opera stories, a Butlerian Jihad results in the strict prohibition of all thinking machines, including computers, robots and artificial intelligence of any kind. The Mentat discipline is developed as a replacement for computerized calculation; and the Mentats (human calculators) possess exceptional cognitive abilities of memory and perception that are the foundations for supra-logical hypothesizing. Mentats are able to sift large volumes of data and devise concise analyses in a process that goes far beyond logical deduction: Mentats cultivate "the naïve mind", the mind without preconception or prejudice, so as to extract essential patterns or logic from data and deliver useful conclusions with varying degrees of certainty.

Free-Thinking: Sources and Methods

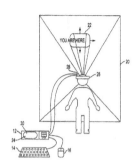

In the present chapter we had sought to answer two (seemingly) simple questions. Firstly we wished to discover how it may be technically possible to establish *freedom-of-thought*; within a thought-space; and specifically for **all** human beings; and hence (by extension) within the entire world's thought-space. One might say that this purpose is, in fact, the overriding goal of the present book; hence to some extent it shall be the reader's prerogative to judge if, in fact, we have established the same (after reading the book as a whole).

Nevertheless the first question, I would suggest, has been answered (in this chapter) by means of a theoretical implementation of the *Theory of Natural Thoughts*. In particular, demonstrated has been the possibility of protecting/maximising the operational-flow of thoughts within a thought-space. And specifically by eliminating and/or preventing (from occurring) certain thought-flow blockages which relate to: maintaining a sufficient diversity of concepts; maximising the weight of evidence; whilst maximising selective capability (range of opinions); and to do so for all of the thinkers within a thought-space.

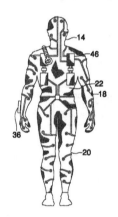

Our second aim, had been to establish a theoretical underpinning for the three elements of the *Theory of Natural Thoughts*, namely thought: *equality, free-assembly and ownership*. I would suggest that this goal has been more than demonstrated; in fact by making a dual mapping for each one; whereby established is: (a) linkage to human rights in the form of freedom of *belief, free-thinking and public proclamation;* and also (b) linkage to the *Logon, Metron and Selective* capacities of said thought-space.[5]

A brief note (or caveat) is worth making in relation to the logical consistency of the 'thought-related' concepts employed here; including: *(equality, free-assembly and ownership); (logon, metron and selective capacities); and (freedom-of-belief, free-thinking, and the right to publish any thoughts).* These concepts are (one to another) by no means causally independent, and/or logically district; but do rather overlap, interrelate and interpenetrate one with another.

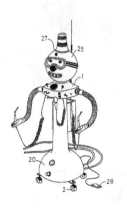

Overall, the thought-related concepts are introduced simply to foster clarity of analysis and exposition, and nothing more.

To think is more interesting than to know, but not to see and behold. - Goethe

We're going to fuck them all... Crack the world open and let it flower into something new. - Julian Assange

In summary, we ask what has been learned in the present chapter; and to some extent the entire book up until the present stage. Perhaps only that *freedom-of-thought* is an essential and fundamental part of any successful human future; and in particular that this future can be either: provided/supported by, or else blocked/limited by; computing systems. One example of a useful hypothetical system has been described; whereby we suggested that a *World Brain (plus an Atomic Network)* could provide a usefully hyperlinked world knowledge system of thought-atoms/concepts.

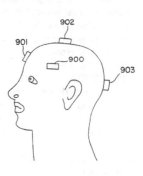

In the language of the present chapter, the World Brain would comprise a *world thought-space*; whereby described is a way to maximise the flow of thoughts across the circuits-of-thought; and hence to create an efficient operational-flow for all the worlds *ideas, concepts and thoughts etc.*

Often *powerful-people, social structures, technologies, mechanisms etc;* are used to block the operational-flow of thoughts within a thought-space. Sometimes money alone is used to block access to thoughts; or else to censure ideas; and concepts may be wrongly frozen/warped and/or ideas diverted etc. However sometimes it is simply that we do not assign ownership of thoughts where (and to whom) they are rightly due. For example, routine (largely accidental) blockage of access to scientific/cultural knowledge held in libraries *(or inside on-line databases)*. In actual fact these knowledge-based thoughts should be (largely) assigned as open-thoughts; that is to the ownership of all the people of the world. Accordingly, we ask...

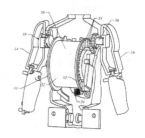

What will be our future when the vast majority of thoughts are hidden/lost deep inside the most dysfunctional thought-spaces?

We are reminded of the words of **YODA** from *Star Wars*...

Difficult to see is the future.

In today's world it is not only our *future-thoughts/actions* that are difficult to see; but also the *thoughts/actions* of both past and present; and in fact anything whatsoever; and because the world's ideas are not sufficiently: *linked, annotated, cross-referenced, open and/or freely available.*

Which of you by taking thought can add one cubit
  to its structure. - New Testament: Matthew.

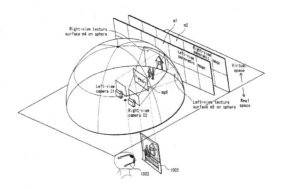

There is not a thought in our heads that has not
been worn shiny in other heads. - Meditations on Wall Street (1966)

Simulation is no longer that of a territory, a referential being or a substance. It is the generation by models of a real without origin or reality: a hyperreal. The territory no longer precedes the map, nor survives it. Henceforth, it is the map that precedes the territory — PRECESSION OF SIMULACRA —it is the map that engenders the territory and if we were to revive the fable today, it would be the territory whose shreds are slowly rotting across the map, where vestiges subsist here and there, in the deserts which are no longer those of the Empire, but our own. The *desert of the real itself*...

Something has disappeared: the sovereign difference between them that the abstractions charm. For it is the difference which forms the poetry of the map and the charm of the territory, the magic of the concept and the charm of the real... No more mirror of being and appearances, of the real and its concept....The real is produced from miniatured units, from matrices, memory banks and command models—and with these it can be reproduced an indefinite number of times. It no longer has to be rational, since it is no longer measured against some ideal or negative instance. It is nothing more than operational. It is hyperreal, the product of an irradiating synthesis of combinatory models in a hyperspace without atmosphere...

It is an operation to deter every real process by its operational double, a metastable, programmatic, perfect descriptive machine which provides all the signs of the real and short-circuits all its vicissitudes. Never again will the real have to be produced—this is the vital function of the model in a system of death....

Jean Baudrillard

As an aside, I would like to make a brief note in relation to the theory of Karl Marx.[9] Marx emphases the *use-value* of things; stating that a thing may have a use-value without having a value in strictly commercial terms; such as *air, sunshine, meadows etc.*

Accordingly, we ask; what is the use-value of human thoughts?

Surely if anything has an ultimate use-value; then it is our very thoughts; which may indeed be likened (for open-thoughts) to the air we breath; and in the (previously identified) sense of ubiquity (ownership). The results of human 'thinking' labour (i.e. thoughts); can (obviously) have a use-value without being a commodity. Hence thoughts are not necessarily commodities; and it is wrong or bad faith to assign them as such without precedence. In this view, charging anyone a fee to use a library, or to access the internet, seems to be an (almost) positively evil act.

But Marx's theory may be enlightening in another way. According to Marx, money is the circulation and exchange of commodities. The movement of money is therefore a circuit; and most importantly (according to Marx) this form of movement precludes a circuit from being made of money (in order to preserve the *unrestricted flow of commodities*). Can we (in a similar fashion) not liken thoughts to money; whereby desired is a constant *unrestricted* circulation, or flow, of thoughts, and in order to produce knowledge (useful working capital)? The concept of operational-flow is thus given another perspective. Perhaps knowledge is (in a very real sense) the true social capital of society; being those products *(ideas, concepts, theories etc)* that result from the free-flow of thoughts across human society. If so, then the ultimate *means of production* is knowledge, which is enabled by the operational-flow of all social thoughts; a process which happens within a notionally 'free' thought-space; and along the circuits-of-thought. Are the world's amalgamated open-thoughts not the rightful heritage of every child/adult? Who has a right to block open thought-flows? Or to warp/destroy open-thoughts for any purpose at all.

A question arises, as to how thoughts are assembled (by thinkers) into useful groupings, and by the members of a specific thought-space. How do we establish truth/beneficial-thoughts?

No sign or collection of signs possesses meaning intrinsically. Words or pictures (and thoughts) owe their significance to something outside of themselves (which is their role in the lives of the speakers/thinkers). To insist that a thought or mental image might posses 'original meaning', is to fall prey to what Hilary Putnam dubs a 'magical theory'. - Ludwig Wittgenstein

Psychologist Max Wertheimer (1880-1943), one of the founders of Gestalt psychology, wrote an informative book entitled *Productive Thinking*; whereby he identified some of the key features of productive thinking processes.[9] Amongst his findings was that productive thinking: *depends on structuring methods, habits, and hence on structural improvements*. Productive process is related to whole characteristics and calls for not piecemeal, but **'structural' truth**; and that in turn requires dealing with gaps and troubling regions.

Overall, terms have a dynamic meaning; and :

> The functional and structural meaning of an item first seen from an atomistic point of view, may very well change and be very different (when seen in a proper—wider—context). Productive thinking involves a grasp of the structural relations in a problem or situation, followed by a grouping of those parts into a dynamic whole. [9]

Wertheimer concludes that **centring**, **grouping** and **segregating** (*cf. ability to see, create, judge/share*) are the three key functions of productive thinking; and that a grasp of structural relations is essential.

According to Wertheimer:

> In traditional logic, propositions and concepts remain identical if repeated; but in real thinking; items do not remain identical... The functional meaning of an item changes as thinking advances, and without this change, thinking would be sterile! There is an intense 'directness' in the line of thought. All statements have a direction in their context. There may be an original context of use and an entirely different later context of use. [9]

Overall, Wertheimer says that productive thinking is concerned with the dynamics and structural relations of thought-atoms; and relates to the changing meaning(s) of thoughts when used in different contexts (thoughts are purpose-specific).

Thoughts and thinking are all about structure, relation and context. Above all, Wertheimer says that thinking has a direction, and if humanity is likewise to adequately chart the combined direction of our collective thought streams (*plus associated actions*); then it seems logical to do so together, as one body; and by means of a World-Brain. Vitally, this brain must deliver unrestricted operational-flow for all our thoughts; and within a free, open and unrestricted world thinking-space.

Not only may the same sentence (or thought) be used on different occasions to express different thoughts, but different sentences may be used on different occasions to express the same thought. - Gottlob Frege

Knowledge assures him (humankind) of his divine origin, yet through it he at once sees himself cut off and banished, as it were, from the original ground of all things. He is condemned to a long laborious way of search and research, from which there is no final escape... there is a knowledge (and a truth) and is the awareness at the same time that the possession of absolute truth is denied to man.

Ernst Cassirer

The society which rests on modern industry is not accidentally or superficially spectacular. It is fundamentally spectaclist. In the spectacle, which is the image of the ruling economy, the goal is nothing, development is everything.

The spectacle subjugates living men to itself to the extent that the economy has totally subjugated them. It is no more than the economy developing for itself. It is a true reflection of the production of things, and the false objectification of the producers.

Where the real world changes into simple image (or thought-atoms), the simple images become real beings and effective motivations for hypnotic behavior.

Guy Debord

For the first time on earth an atomic fire had burned for the space of a second, industriously kindled by the science of Man... Man, stunned by his success, looked inward and sought by the glare of the lightening (how) his own hand had loosened to understand its effect on himself. His body was safe, but what had happened to his soul?

Teilhard de Chardin

Cybercrud—Putting things over on people using computers.
At every corner of our society, people are issuing pronouncements and making pother people do things and saying 'it's because of the computer'.
The function of cybercrud is to confuse, intimidate or pressure.
Ted Nelson (1974)

Natural reproduction has been done away with and children are created, 'decanted', and raised in 'hatcheries and conditioning centres'.

From birth, people are genetically designed to fit into one of five castes, which are further split into 'Plus' and 'Minus' members and designed to fulfil predetermined positions within the social and economic strata of the World State. (All children are educated by hypnopaedic processes.)

Aldous Huxley - Brave New World (1932)

Trendy Topics

- Hactivism (by computers)
- Internet of Things
- Smart Objects
- Nano-printing
- 3D / 4D printing
- Driverless-cars (crazy)
- Drones (also crazy)
- Apps + Big Data
- Clouds (central control)
- Cyber-utopians
- Haptic technology
- Crypto-coins
- Swarm Robots
- Self-assembling machines
- Contextual computing
- Quantum computing
- Optical transistors
- Neuro-gaming
- Augmented Reality
- Everything on demand [Days of Future Past!]
- Emotional Gadgets
- Tablets + Smart Watches
- Google Glass (waining?)
- Curved TVs + 4k/8k TVs
- Holographic Computing
- Payment by Swiping
- Social Networks
- SnapChat
- Cyber-Warfare?
- Activist Hacking
- Smart Fabrics
- Nano-Compute
- HoloLens / Magic-Leap
- Internet of Everything
- The Quantified Self

Illustration from Un Autre Monde (Jean Grandville)

It moves. It moves not.
It is far, and It is near.
It is within all this,
And It is outside all this.

Upanishads [10,000 BC]

Destruction of intellectual freedom. Every digital communication is intercepted (around the world)!
And every analogue communication is recorded if it has sensors associated with it and to collect data.
People are careful about what they type into their search engines, and that limits the boundaries of their intellectual exploration. We are building the greatest weapon for oppression in the history of man...
People self-police their own views! It has become the expectation that we are being watched!
Edward Snowden - Citizen Four (2015 Oscar winning documentary)

Chapter Thirteen
Dystopian Visions

I N THE present chapter we open up a veritable pandora's box of stratified possibilities with respect to human civilisation; as we seek to characterise dystopian societies, real and imagined. Explored are key social factors, technological systems, and other forces, that may be said to 'bring-about' a dysfunctional society. Accordingly we adopt a variety of 'crystal-balls' *(facts/opinions/theories)*; in an attempt to help us to understand, and/or tie together, seemingly disparate matters; and so to bring forth the 'big-picture' for dysfunctional societies, and (hopefully) be able to make useful recommendations.

We observe a long-standing fascination with utopianism or social dreaming; and in relation to future societies; and clear is that not *everything comes up roses* in this respect; but rather evident (at the very least) is that all roses (social-structures/ideologies) have thorns.[1,2,5,6]

Indeed since ancient times humans have constantly disagreed and argued about, and implemented/tried-out, a variety of widely different societal policies/forms/structures.

Our purpose is not to attempt a comprehensive review of the great diversity of records, arguments (and theory) that relates to dystopias; and as evidenced by the vast record of human history. Rather we wish to focus on the part(s)/role(s) that technological creations (i.e. machines/systems) play in the great game of life. In particular, sought is knowledge of, and examples of, the interplay of computers and freedom-of-thought; and from the perspective of societal: *structures, rules, mechanisms, laws, social policies/processes etc.*

Put simply, we wish to probe the relationship(s) between freedom of thought/action and the design of systems/computers.

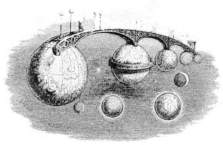

As the sun, the eye of the whole world,
   Is not sullied by the external faults of the eyes. - Upanishads.

Do androids dream? Rick asked himself. Evidently; that's why
   they occasionally kill their employers and flee here.
   A better life, without servitude. - Philip K. Dick

The topic of *computers and society* is by no means devoid of discussion, exposition, explanation etc; and is hardly barren of opinion(s). Rather it is a subject area positively jam-packed with *ideas, theory, points-of-view etc;* indeed so contentious are the issues that a writer hesitates to contribute.

However despite an apparent glut of opinions in this area, the calamitous and precipitous state of modern society; brings some pressure to bear on those who believe that they can contribute in a useful manner. Hence the current book.

We begin our analysis of dystopias by defining the opposite: the utopia. The OED defines **utopia** as:

> [1] (a) An imaginary island, depicted by Sir Thomas More as enjoying a perfect social, legal, and political system. (b) Any imaginary, indefinitely-remote region, country, or locality. [2] (a) A place, state or condition ideally perfect in respect of politics, laws, customs, and conditions. (b) An impossibly ideal scheme, esp. for social improvement.

Etymology: The word utopia or outopia was derived from Greek and means 'no (or not) place' (u or ou, no, not; topos, place).

A great many works of *fact, fiction, theory, fancy, description and imagination etc;* have been dedicated to discussion of the utopian outlook and/or to the possibility of mankind actually living in a utopia. Utopianism is the imaginative projection, positive or negative, of a society that is substantially different from the one in which the author lives. The word **eutopia** was penned by Sir Thomas More (1478-1535), meaning 'good place', and we can thus develop dystopia, meaning bad place.

Oscar Wilde (1854-1900) wrote the following in his essay *'The Soul of Man Under Socialism'*:

> A map of the world that does not include Utopia is not worth even glancing at, for it leaves out the one country at which humanity is always landing. And when humanity lands there, it looks out, and seeing a better country, it sets sail. Progress is the realisation of Utopias.[2]

Our attention is drawn to ideas of progress and destination; and to perfect/improve human future(s).

That new Utopia of Religion and Government into which they endeavour to transform this Kingdom. - Chas. I in Rushw. Hist. Coll. (1692) I. 727.

DYSTOPIAN VISIONS   299

Similarly with a dystopia considered is that the future might be worse in some way than present day circumstances; and/or that social structures and forces and/or other environmental conditions could make life far worse for many members of a society.

Our purpose here is not to discuss utopias and/or dystopias *per se*; but rather to scout-out and/or to delineate the relationship(s) of humans to technology. Sought is evidence of any negative tendencies and/or shaping forces and/or detrimental factors for computing systems (in terms of society at large). In particular we seek *viewpoints, facts, concepts, illuminating examples and causative factors etc;* and the same extracted from the writings of *social commentators, theorists, bloggers, exposers, science-fiction writers, whistleblowers etc;* and also in terms of recently reported news events and happenings etc (i.e. for the book as a whole).[1,2,4,6,7,8, etc]

Overall, we seek to discover how and why computers come to influence society; and to clarify the ways in which system design is related to the same. Our analysis largely ignores machine-implanted thoughts; and concerns thoughts in-minds/on-media.

Instead of adopting a time-line approach to analysing any negative relations between humans and machines; or else description(s) of the same; we shall hereby employ a topically focussed analysis. Presented is a three-pronged grouping of 'facts', happenings and emotive descriptions; and specifically in terms of the Forms of thought identified earlier (i.e. secret, private and open ones). Going along with this approach we shall explore the human ability to *see, create and also share/judge* thought forms, and in a variety of circumstances and social structures.

Our analysis might seem like a 'mashup' of unrelated descriptions of events, happenings and processes etc; but in an important way (I hope) this is (in fact) not so; because we have adopted relevant structuring mechanisms *(thinker's ability to: see, create, share thoughts)*; accordingly, and so to form a clear pattern/image of the self-computer.

We seek him (or it) here.. there.. and everywhere...

.... THE SELF COMPUTER ...
(OR MERGING OF MAN AND MACHINE)

To find adequate gratification in the artificial construction of hypothetical utopias. [1871] Morley Condorcet in Crit. Misc. Ser. i. 78

As a unity only is It to be looked upon-
This indemonstrable, enduring Being. - Upanishads

Secret Thoughts

HALTING PROBLEM

The **halting problem** is the problem of determining, from a description of an arbitrary computer program and an input, whether the program will finish running or continue to run forever (and thus operate as predicted). Alan Turing proved in 1936 that a general algorithm to solve the halting problem for *all* possible program-input pairs cannot exist. As a result, computers may be (to a large extent) unpredictable; and if so, then we may never be able to understand how our logical problems have been translated into the computer's mind; and/or what will be the outcomes of computer processing, or what the computer may or may not do by way of resultant actions, processing of information etc. Such 'Decision Problems' are yet another reason (plus lack of creative free-will and narrow 'little-world' vision) why humans must at all times be in charge-of/responsible-for computers and automated reasoning; and because we cannot ever be certain what they (machine intelligences) might do; and so humans must be available to correct the computer's mistakes!

Freedom Dyson said that the **halting problem** should be something that we humans are happy about; and because it guarantees that our artificial world's will remain (to some extent) unpredictable, untamed and/or an exciting frontier of exploration/ play. These sentiments are odd, and because the **halting problem** indicates that computers are inherently indeterminate; and that we cannot (ever) know what will happen when a computer program runs; and that computers can make (potentially catastrophic) errors!

The book *We* is a dystopian novel by Yevgeny Zamyatin (1884-1937) written in 1921 and published in New York in the year 1924.[1] *We* is set in the future where an engineer named D-503 lives in the *One State*, an urban nation comprised almost entirely of glass; and which allows secret police/spies to inform-on and supervise the public. The *One State* is similar to Jeremy Bentham's idea of the panopticon; and the construction of the state is likewise somewhat like a prison; where everybody marches in step and wears identical clothing etc.

We evokes a classic dystopian society; which is surrounded by a giant *Green Wall* to **separate citizens from untamed nature**; whereby all citizens are referred to by 'numbers'; and every hour in one's life is directed by '*The Table*'. It is a post-apocalyptic world, that has (we are told) survived a war with weapons of mass destruction; and accordingly therefore the state is surrounded by a contaminated post-apocalyptic landscape that must be feared and avoided at all costs.

We is a society in which being *too-individualistic* is seen as problematical (for society at large), and where even the process of dreaming, or of having dreams, is seen as a form of mental illness! In the world of *We*, everyone is watched by secret police (or the *Bureau of the Guardians*) at all times. Furthermore un-compliant or deviant citizens are forced to undergo '*The Great Operation*'; whereby they are psycho-surgically refashioned into a state of mechanical 'reliability'. This operation removes the imagination and emotions by targeting parts of the brain with X-rays.

> **Imagination** is defined as the action of imagining, or forming a mental concept of what is not actually present to the senses, a conception which does not—necessarily—(or may in fact) correspond to the reality of things. [It is the ability to form mental impressions]

< {36} Dystopian Society = removal of an individual's imagination. >

In the *We* society, the outlawed imagination can be equated with removing a person's ability to create concepts; and/or with blocking the ability (of people) to form, shape, and assemble thought-atoms together in their own minds; and **secret thoughts are banned.** The circuits of thought are wholly non-functional.

Memory (smara), verily, is more than Space. Even if many not possessing memory should be assembled, indeed they would not hear any one at all, they would not think, they would not understand. But assuredly, if they should remember, then they would hear, then they would think, then they would understand... Hope, is more than memory... Life is more than hope. - Upanishads

During the next one 100 years or so after the publication of *We*, other writers penned dystopic novels/tales that followed suit; sometimes overtly copying, and 'borrowing' aspects of the plot of *We*. For example: *Brave New World* (1930), *1984* (1949), and a more subtle example in *The Golden Compass* (2007).

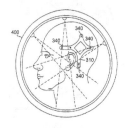

Some (even earlier) stories are eerily familiar. In *The Machine Stops* story published in 1909 by E.M. Forester (1879-1970), described is a post-apocalyptic world where everybody lives below ground in standard 'cellular' compartments to escape from a contaminated nature. A global *Machine* regulates all activities; whereby travel is permitted but is rare and considered unnecessary. All (or the vast majority) of communication is via a kind of instant messaging system/video conferencing machine called *'the speaking apparatus'*; with which people share ideas and what passes for knowledge.[13]

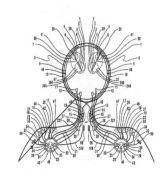

It is illuminating to quote at length from Forester's story:

> You talk as if a god made the machine... I believe that you pray to it when you are unhappy... Men made it, do not forget that. Great men, but men.... 'It is contrary to the spirit of the age'; she asserted (travelling and meeting in person). 'Do you mean by that contrary to the machine?'... 'It is not the proper thing, it is not mechanical'... 'Cannot you see... that it is we who are dying, and that down here the only thing that really lives is the machine?'... 'The machine has robbed us of the sense of space and of the sense of touch, it has blurred every human relation... it has paralysed our bodies and our wills... and now it compels us to worship it!'...

> 'Year by year it has served with <u>increased efficiency</u> and <u>decreased intelligence</u>'... 'In all the world there was not one man who knew the monster as a whole—those master brains had perished'... 'Progress had come to mean, progress of the machine'.. 'The machine is stopping, I know it, I know the signs'... 'Oh tomorrow—some fool will start the machine again'; 'tomorrow? never —never—Humanity has leant its lesson.'[13]

> Fascinating is that Forester penned these words in 1909; long before the computification of everything and everybody (Facebook, Twitter etc).

Unmoving, the One is swifter than the mind.
The sense-powers reached not It, speeding on before.
Past others running. This goes standing.
In It Matarisvan places action. - Upanishads.

His first attempt developed into a misshapen monstrosity which almost filled the vat.

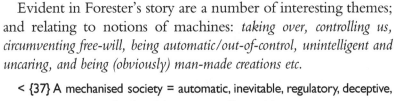

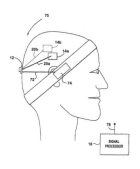

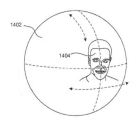

Evident in Forester's story are a number of interesting themes; and relating to notions of machines: *taking over, controlling us, circumventing free-will, being automatic/out-of-control, unintelligent and uncaring, and being (obviously) man-made creations etc.*

< {37} A mechanised society = automatic, inevitable, regulatory, deceptive, prerogatory, relentless, inhumane + self-sustaining. >

And these same factors/forces are not so much physical and/or activity-constraining for the individual; but rather exist also as **mental bonds**, restraints and/or negative shaping forces for 'good' patterns of thought; whereby a form of 'mind-control' is placed on the person. Here the thought-space of the thinker, and the operational-flow of thoughts is/are mechanized/constrained; a process which is, or may be, at least in part, self-perpetuating in some way. In the language of the present book, the world thought-space; and all local thought-spaces, are inefficient, narrow, warped, disconnected, diminished and dysfunctional.

According to many science fiction stories, a machine society *(i.e. a largely mechanized, regulated and/or systematised one)*; is one in which humans partake in a degree of self-control and/or self-censorship (in both thought and action). In this chapter (and the following one) we are interested in exactly how an overtly regulated/systematized and/or machine controlled society goes about warping/destroying: *secret, private and open thoughts*. It can even be the case that people (may) accept, comply or destroy (partially themselves) the basic human right of freedom-of-thought.

In the words of Aldous Huxley, and from *Brave New World*: 'Everyone belongs to Everyone Else'.[6]

In other words secret thoughts are not owned by the thinker, and one's very mind is 'borrowed' property.

Recall that we defined a secret-thought to be one whereby the thinker is afforded *freedom-of-thought* through the three essential Attributes of *Equality, Free-Assembly and Ownership*. Put simply, a thinker owns his (secret) thoughts, and he must be able to assemble thought-atoms together in whatever way(s) take(s) his fancy.

NSA has 1000's of NSA spies everywhere—and 14,000 cyber-troops!
In 2012, The United States Air Force employed 7,494 Drones (unmanned flying vehicles)!

WikiLeaks may become the most powerful intelligence agency on earth, an intelligence agency of the people. - Julian Assange.

Artists are really much nearer the truth than have been many scientists. - Buckminster Fuller.

DYSTOPIAN VISIONS 303

Obviously this freedom includes freedom (even) from self-censure; and formal, rigid or unnatural structuring methods; and also he/she must have access to, or visibility of, as many other open and private (social) thought-atoms as possible. Accordingly, in order to maintain a sufficient number, quality, truthfulness and all-round usefulness of thought-atoms; it is obvious that ownership implies also the freedom to assemble thought-atoms into new shapes, patterns and contexts that are entirely of one's own choosing.

One's own mind is one's own property.

True freedom implies maximising the efficient flow of thoughts within a thought-space; and assumes a fully socialised, connected society in which *ideas, concepts, thoughts and votes* move unhindered and unchanged (e.g. an efficient thought-space).

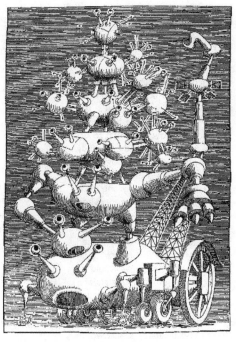

Earlier we defined an efficient thought-space; but we had not provided an ethical foundation for our conclusions; but rather looked to information theory to provide a foundation via a '*maximum knowledge*' argument.

Ethics attempts to give correct reasons for thinking that this or that 'thing', 'process' or 'event' is good. Good is an apparently simple notion (it is not complex). But what is good? This cannot be defined, good is good! (only the complex is definable). Jeremy Bentham provides perhaps the best definition of good: good is the greatest happiness of all those whose interest is in the question (and) as being the right and proper end of human action. Accordingly, we shall adopt this as a working definition of good ourselves.

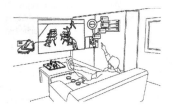

Whenever we judge that a thing is '*good as a means*', we are making a judgement with regard to its causal relations; and we judge both that it will have a particular kind of effect, and that the effect will be good in itself! QED.

To find causal judgements that are universally true is notoriously difficult. Yet we seek answers: how do we identify beneficial or 'good' thoughts/actions for humanity?

Thomas Huxley, said that he remained unimpressed by the the power, natural resources, knowledge, and machinery that has so greatly extended man's competence over his physical environment. 'The great issue, about which hangs a true sublimity and the terror of overhanging fate is, what are you going to do with all these things?'

I found myself asserting that I didn't think that nature has a department of chemistry, a department of physics, and a department of biology and had to have meetings of department heads in order to decide what to do when you drop your stone in the water. Universe, i.e. nature, obviously knows just what to do, and everything seemed beautifully coordinated. So I thought that nature probably had one coordinate system and probably one most economical, arithmetical, and geometrical system with which to inter-account all transactions and all transformations... I thought then that if we could find nature's own coordinate system we would be able to understand the models, and we would be able to develop much higher exploratory and application capability. I felt that if we ever found nature's coordinate system, it would be very simple and always rational...

I don't think it is the machine per-se that bothers man; it is just *not understanding*—anything—whatever it may be—that disturbs him.

I think the word creation implies adding something to the universe. And I don't think man adds to the universe. I think man is a very extraordinary part of the universe for he demonstrates the unique capability to discover and intellectually identify abstract, operative principles of the universe —which though unconsciously employed have not been differentiated, isolated and understood before, as being principles, by other biological species.

Buckminster Fuller

Which 'good' thoughts should we encourage and/or turn into actions, and how? Such questions fall into the domain of ethics. Luckily in 1903, Dr George Edward Moore (1873 - 1958) wrote an excellent book '*Principia Ethica*' to help us with such questions. According to Moore: to find casual judgements that are universally true is notoriously difficult. [14]

> We cannot even discover hypothetical laws of the form 'Exactly this action will always under these conditions produce exactly this effect!'

> Reasons given (by Moore) for such unpredictability include:

> • Because we require to know that a given course of actions will produce a certain effect, under whatever circumstances it occurs. We can never be entitled to more than a generalisation which will only be true, if the circumstances under which the actions occurs are generally the same.

> • We require to know not only that one good effect will be produced, but that, among all subsequent events affected by the action, the <u>balance of good</u> will be greater than if any other possible action (or no action) has been performed!

In other words, to judge that an action is generally a means to good is to judge not only that it generally does some good, but that it generally does the <u>greatest good</u> of which the circumstances permit. Such a process requires ethical judgments about the effects of the future action(s) in question;

But no machine can do this! And because a view of the future is required. It is obvious that our view can never reach far enough for us to be certain that any actions will produce the best possible effects! According to Dr Moore: we (humans) must balance present/future bad effects against immediate/future gains. We try to assure ourselves that probable future evils will not be greater than the immediate good.

> Judgements are unlikely to be true if:

> • If they state that the kind of thing in question <u>always</u> has good effects.

> • Even if they only state that it generally has good effects, many of them will only be true of certain periods in the worlds history!

The implications of these statements are quite profound, and of prescient applicability to machine perceptions of, and influence over, 'good' intentions/outcomes for humans.

Language is thoroughly indeterminate, by reason of the fact that every occurrence presupposes some systematic type of environment. - Alfred North Whitehead.

Electronic Brain = An electronic device that performs complicated operations comparable to those of the human brain; spec. an electronic computer.

Men at the same time are masters of their fates: The fault, dear Brutus, lies not in the stars, But in ourselves. - Julius Caesar

DYSTOPIAN VISIONS 305

Whenever a thinker wishes to choose between competing thoughts/actions; a view of the future must be created; because according to Dr Moore's argument; a process of *'balancing of good'* (for the choice itself) must be made (implicitly or explicitly); and especially in terms of the effects of choosing itself and all the consequences that may flow from that decision *(and/or perhaps not making that decision)*.

The thinker requires a *crystal ball*, because one can never predict what will be all the ramifications of any decision, and/or its interrelation with all of the other decisions/actions that are concurrently *being-made/will-be-made* elsewhere.

In the language of the present book choices that are made today, with respect to *assumed* future contexts (e.g. actions and machine implanted-thoughts) will have uncertain effects due to lack of knowledge about those future contextual situations.

Calculating and/or prescribing the *'greatest good'* is very, very difficult to do for any thought/action/choice placed into the world; and requires careful consideration/prediction of the future.

> < {38} Machines = deal with generalisations and wholly abstract thoughts; and they cannot calculate/judge adequately the predicted good or else balance this against the future good and so determine the greatest good. >

Humans also have difficulty with predicting what will be the ultimate effects of any specific judgment/action. But there will be many ways that humans can mitigate such a 'risky lack of information'; including tying together many *small-worlds* with the *big-world*; corrections, re-programming logic on the fly *(creative free-will)*; and also benefiting from the real-time judgment of many brains to help perceive/learn what *have-been/are/will-be* the likely effects in any particular case.

On the whole, and for complex/creative and uncertain tasks, I would bet on human decision making over machines; and especially in those situations where real-time consequences of any thought-action cannot be adequately pre-determined in advance.

Once again, **difficult to see is the future**; and I do not think we should (ever) leave high-level decision making to machines; and especially in cases where we affect human thinking itself.

The future is not being planned—we are growing a prosthetic, extended nervous system. - William Gibson

Three things can not hide for long. The Sun, the moon, and the truth. - Siddhartha

There are two ways in which a system can be complex. It can be complex in space, as the brain certainly is, or it can be complex in times, as both the brain and computer are. Complex in space means simply that it has a large number of parts with high connectivity. Complex in time means that successive states shall be highly varied and dependent upon earlier states in intricate and lawful ways. At least compared to the brain, a computer is not complex in space.

Ernest W. Kent

Phenomenology—Instead of modeling intelligence as a passive receiving of context-free facts into a structure of already stored data, Husserl thinks of intelligence as a context-determined, goal-directed activity—as a search for anticipated facts. For him the noema, or mental representation of any type of object, provides a context or 'inner horizon' of expectations or predilections for structuring the incoming data: a rule of governing possible other consciousness (of the object) as identical/possible, as exemplifying essentially pre-delineated types.

Hubert Dreyfus

The relentless innovations of technology and science have made it hard to deny that nature is both open to modification and inextricably bound to human acts of intellectual and physical reorganisation. At the same time, nature's modifiability is not infinite. True reform requires an acknowledgement of limits, of possibilities that cannot be realised... freedom can only be imagined as a concomitant of the dependancies, responsibilities, and limits that join us to others and to the nonhuman world.

John Tresch

Ethical Argument(s)

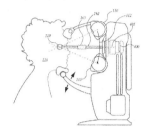

Dr Moore's ethical theory is echoed in the work of many other thinkers. Countering trends to dystopia, are strong ethical argument(s); often centered around the libertarian view that people have a natural right to hold any particular thought and/or point of view, and without any form of interference or attempt at thought-control. Thoughts are the thinker's natural property alone. This is proven because there are no adequate moral grounds upon which to rest any other conclusion; and especially due to the *Balance of Good* argument; whereby each person may manifest his/her views on/for the *greatest good* within a society.[1]

I call this the *Ethical Argument* for Free-Speech/Thought.

In his book *The Ethics of Cyberspace* [11], Cees J.Hamelink writes a chapter entitled '*The Decent Society and Cyberspace*'; whereupon he identifies three basic principles and standards of human conduct *(in general and especially for computers)*:

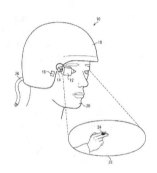

THE PRINCIPLE OF EQUALITY

There is equal entitlement to the conditions of self-empowerment... (including)... access to and use of the resources that enable people to express themselves, to communicate these expressions to others, to exchange ideas with others, to inform themselves about events in the world, to create and control the production of knowledge and to share the world's sources of knowledge.

THE PRINCIPLE OF SECURITY

Any valid human rights regime proposes standards of conduct against attacks upon people's physical, mental and morel integrity. The right to protection of privacy is provided by Article 12 of the Universal Declaration of Human Rights, and in Article 17 of the International Covenant on Civil and Political Rights, which protects against arbitrary interference with their private sphere.

THE PRINCIPLE OF FREEDOM

For Cyberspace, the equality principle will be used in the sense of freedom from interference with expression and access to information.

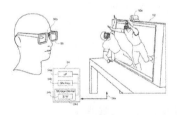

What drives you?
Well, I like being brave. I mean, I like being inventive, I've been designing systems and processes for a long time. I also like defending victims. And I am a combative person so I like crushing bastards. And so this profession combines all those three things, so it is deeply, personally, deeply satisfying to me.
Julian Assange

If we apply these principles to thoughts, we arrive at the principles of *equality, ownership and freedom of thoughts* identified earlier. In a way these ideas all come down to *ownership of thoughts,* individually and collectively. Whilst I do not wish to simplify/ gloss-over complex matters, or else to pass over very real social problems and difficulties/quandaries; in my opinion many problems go away when we simply focus on the issue of thought ownership. If we do, in fact, own our thoughts, then assigning ownership/sharing *(i.e. the process of transposing secret thoughts into private or open ones)* is the business of the thinker alone *(whether the 'thinker' is an individual or a collective/group-thinker).*

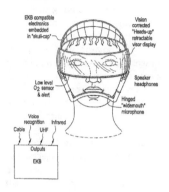

German social philosopher Jurgen Habermas proposes that moral standards are valid only when all those concerned would give their consent following their common deliberations. This forms the basis of so-called **communicative** or **discursive** ethics, and is in full agreement with the founding principles of the *Theory of Natural Thoughts*; whereby thoughts are established as the most intimate (preeminent/fundamental) personal property.

If we do have a morality/ethics of human thinking, as expressed in the *Theory of Natural Thoughts*; then it stands to reason that when thought-atoms pass from one person to another, at no stage can the ownership of a thought be re-assigned by anyone but the natural owner. Ownership is a legal right (or should be)—but it may be very difficult to protect.

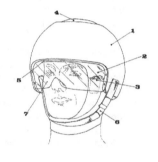

How can thoughts be protected? And how can ownership rights be preserved? Well, it can only be through technology.

My point being that when a thought-atom has been assigned as an open-thought *(by the owner and through natural legal assignment rights)*; then that same thought-atom must be open-access, or viewable/usable by all humanity.

Some people name human rights as the '*Common Language of Humanity*'; but surely it is our very thoughts; which are the true language of humanity; and because it is only by seeing, combining and sharing our thoughts that we may develop *human rights principles, concepts, laws, scientific principles and social stories, theories and frameworks etc.*

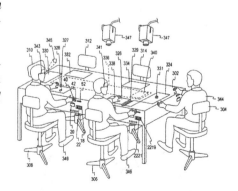

< {39} We are our thoughts, and our thoughts are us. >

[I think Assange should be assassinated actually. - Tom Flanagan]

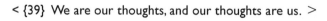

OMEGA AFFECT

Amplifier structures—consciousness could be turned up or down. With our machines we are turning mankind into an automaton; we are crushing, destroying free-will. Do we live in a deterministic world whereby man's mind has no free will? Machines treat people as objects; no it is worse than this; machines no more recognise a human than they do an atom, rock, pebble or wrinkle in mud. If people are objects; then they are expendable.

The omega experience—the unique experiencing of reality. (Natural History of Mind) The brain selects and supervises trains of action. Robots do not feel love, sympathy or pain.

The omega affect—underlying all our sensations, including pattern of shape and colour we call the scene; the subtleties of sounds, and the raw horror of death; it would include dreams, hallucinations, and visions. It would include fears; anxiety, love, horror and disgust, pleasure, joy etc. In a word emotions—should these all be grouped together? Range from euphoria to despair. It includes thoughts, plans and attitudes, and also will.

It would include subtler experiences; such as significance, familiarity, sense of anticipation, sense of clarity and of total confusion. Also sense of unity with all life. Theologians speak of the numinous sensation, or the idea of the holy. Personal identity; and consciousness.

[Source/Ref. Lost]

Private Thoughts

We start with a few words on the American vision of Internet freedom. Earlier I noted that it is illegal to send an encrypted email in the USA without providing the government with the decryption keys. I expressed amazement that a right we had as children (in the real world) had been taken away from us (at least in the USA).

Am I the only one who is incredulous at such a state of affairs?

In the *The Ontology of Cyberspace* [10], David R. Koepsell concludes:

> The dissemination of 'indecent' materials in any other medium (apart from the Internet) is clearly protected by the First Amendment of the U.S. Constitution. The mystique of the Internet, propagated in part by its foremost proponents, helped to convince the drafters of the Communications Decency Act (CDA) that the Net was a medium unlike any other.

No lesser expert than William Gibson (coiner of the term cyberspace) recently distanced himself from some of the more worrying implications of the term:

> It's not (a question of the line) between real and unreal—it's between real and real. The only reason we see that dichotomy [between real and virtual] is because we are old.

Establishing sanctity, security and hence ownership of secret, private and open-thoughts is evidently central to the destruction and prevention of a dystopia.

The Ethics of Participation

According to human ethics Professor Upendra Baxi, human rights languages, however *effete* remain perhaps all that we have to interrogate the barbarism of power.[14]

> The endowment of human rights emerges not so much as aiming to 'redeem what was' but rather as speaking to a high purpose 'to save what was not.'... The critical relation between actuality and possibility thus remains central to any preoccupation with the future of human rights. The future is, as all futures are, open and diverse. However not every 'achievement' endures in time and space... In the eyes of the future, that which we now name as 'human rights', may well live on (only) in the 'ruins of memory'.

WikiLeaks is a not-for-profit media organisation. Our goal is to bring important news and information to the public. We provide an innovative, secure and anonymous way for sources to leak information to our journalists (our electronic drop box). One of our most important activities is to publish original source material alongside our news stories so readers and historians alike can see evidence of the truth. - Julian Assange

According Dr Baxi, it is collective forgetfulness, plus de-contextualisation, and ignorance of evil/wrong-doing that concerns. The invisibility/unaccountability of the unnameable sufferings of the countless dispossessed poor and disempowered; and hence the sufferings of humanity must be rendered visible/knowable by all. But how else is this possible, except by making all the open (social) thoughts visible; knowable and debatable? Evidently, we need to make ownership/sharing of thoughts *the* fundamental human right.

Future making must include/consider the ideas, thoughts and votes of everyone. Once again, we need the World Brain. This is not to say that ambiguities, disagreements, and uncertain relationships will cease to exist, or that false facts and sub-optimal action(s) will somehow be automatically consigned to the vaults of history. Problems remain, only now (with an operating World-Brain) they can exist in the full glare of a rational 'sunlight'.

In his book *The Future of Human Rights*, Baxi identifies *participation* as a key value in human affairs.[14] Some specify truth as the ultimate human value; but evident is strong disagreement, and much debate, over the nature (and even possibility) of truth, and of its recognition in all areas of human life. Baxi says: human rights are the best hope there is for a participative making, and re-making of human futures. It assumes a world historic moment in which neither the institutions of governance nor the processes of market, singly or in combination, are thought equipped to fashion just (or righteous) human futures.[14]

In his book *e-topia*, William J. Mitchell says:

> The twenty-first century will need agoras—maybe more than ever.
>
> > But these will not be physical places. They will operate on an extraordinary range of scales, from the intimately local to the global. And even when they look familiar, they will no longer function in the same sorts of ways as the great public space of the past... And if these places are to serve their purposes effectively, they must allow both freedom of access and freedom of expression... (and) ...All will seek the advantages that make the most local sense. [15]

A computer can only work within a narrow context.
   Computers are not motivated.
      Computers have no curiosity.
         Computers have no moral sense.
      Computers have no aesthetic feelings. No sense of wonder. No sense of humour.
         Computers have no emotions. No values. No Attitudes. No preferences.

AUTOMATIC SYSTEMS

All automatic systems are closed and limited! The most serious threat of computer-controlled automation comes from displacement of the human mind and the insidious undermining of confidence in his ability to make individual judgements that run contrary to the system—or that proceed from outside the system.

But at this terminal point, where the automatic process is on the verge of creating a whole race of acquiescent and obedient human automatons, the forces of life begin, sometimes stealthily, sometimes ostentatiously, to re-assert themselves in the only form that is left to them: an explosive affirmation of the primal energies of the organism.

The mechanisms involved in organic behaviour are too dynamic, too complex, too quantitatively rich, too multi-fold to be grasped except by simplification... As machines become more lifelike, so humans become more machine-like!

Analysis, disassociation, and reduction were the first steps towards creating complex structures... Causal analysis, by definition, has no concern with final ends or human purposes.

Machines, however crude, are embodiments of a clearly articulated purpose, so firmly fixed in advance, both with respect to the past and future, that the lowest organism, if similarly designed, would be unable to utilise fresh genetic mutations or meet novel situations.

Lewis Mumford

Networked intelligence is being embedded everywhere, in every kind of physical system—both natural and artificial. Routinely, events in cyberspace are being reflected in physical space, and vice versa. - William Gibson

Mechanised Man

Mitchell draws our attention to the ways in which we make sense of the world, and that this may be (obviously and in unknown/invisible ways) determined outside of the self, and that we all have social aspects to self-construction.

According to Bernard Stiegler...

> We make the discovery that our self (just like our memory) is (in some sense) outside of us. This material memory, which Hegel termed objective, is partial... To write a manuscript is to organise one's thoughts by entrusting it to the outside world in the form of traces, that is, symbols. It is only through symbols that one's thoughts are reflected, takes on real substance, making itself repeatable (or iterable as Jaques Derrida would say) and transmissible.[16]

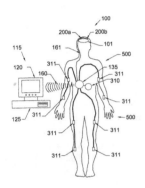

Stiegler highlights the ephemeral nature of thought, its immateriality and potential for loss. Arthur C. Clarke (1917-2008) and Buckminster Fuller both used to say that once you have had a (unique or novel) thought, then you have about 15-30 seconds to write it down before its gone forever (in all likelihood). Similarly, if you are surfing a 'web' of largely unconnected thoughts, with very poor/slow accessibility, the likelihood of making rapid, true, and useful connections, plus correct conclusions would seem to be severely degraded.

We need to see thoughts in their proper contexts (logical, social technical etc), all at once, and at the proper time. Only new technologies can do so for the vast corpus of human knowledge which is composed of all our open and implanted thought-atoms.

According to Edmund Husserl (1859-1938), knowledge is based on 'regional ontologies'; but what constitutes an ontology is highly dependent on the thinker, situation and hence on the associated thought-space itself *(plus connections to, and structure of, related thought-spaces)*. Innumerable patterns and constellations of meaning pre-occupy, form and construct, human consciousness.

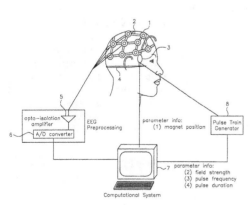

Man has built computing machines that may be loosely connected to his own think-box to augment his natural reasoning ability. - D.S.Halacy, Jr.

Martin Heidegger (1889-1976) alluded to technology as 'a challenge posed to humanity'; and this is a challenge which according to Louis Armand (1972-), is also a confrontation; and as such must be grasped firmly and bent to the collective will in useful ways. Earlier in this book we had promulgated a *profoundly* non-instrumental and non-mechanical conception of man; whereby we are in close accord with Jaques Derrida's belief that technics is 'a prothesis at origin' and therefore man must manage the 'ageless intrusion of technics.

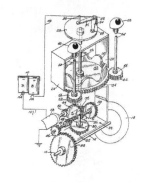

Man makes man; and ditto for machines/systems/computers.

The central tenet of the present thesis is that man is not a machine (in any sense whatsoever); and whilst man is (evidently) making a new home for himself inside of technology, the resultant being, the self-computer, must (we hope) remain broadly and wholly life-centered. We need to be careful not be fooled into thinking that we can automate, mechanise and/or systemise any aspect of life.

According to Louis Armand:

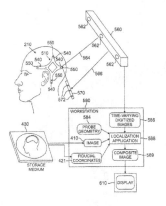

> Karl Marx identifies the machine not as the instrumentality of humanity's emancipation, but as a mode of revealing man's 'essential being'. Mankind—humanity—is neither transcended nor contradicted by the machine, but instead, as Derrida contends, is 'produced by the very possibility of the machine'. That is, by 'the machine-like expropriation', by which the so-called essence of man's being is encountered by way of 'technicity, programming, repetition, or iterability.' ... technology is 'no mere means', but as Heidegger says, an 'enframing' and a 'way of revealing'.[16]

We can conclude that man is not a machine, and neither can he be transformed into a machine by his technology (necessarily and inevitably). Rather machines/systems/computers can be used (by us all) either deliberately and/or accidentally/ partially on-purpose; to reveal/ transform the modes of life itself.

A tiny minority of technically-savvy humans must not be allowed to bully the less technically-literate masses; or else we may become a people split in two; whereby a race of machine-using 'Morlocks' prey on a meeker sub-race as in H.G.Wells *Time Machine* story.

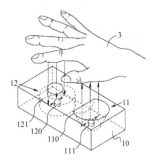

Implanted thoughts (present in our machines) are used to re-mold the nature of human life; its structure, available choices, possibilities, and actions etc. But needed are laws—techno-rights—to ensure that we retain our humanity as technological progress races forwards at an ever increasing speed. And it is in relation to our thoughts that systems and machines can have the most frightening, or alternatively liberating and transformational/transcendent outcomes; because with them we do get to re-think/remold the different 'versions' of our humanity. Evidently, we are responsible for shaping our own realities—as revealed and constructed by our machines.

Stretch-Reality and other 'Exploding' Realities

Computers, like psychedelic drugs, change the apparent nature of reality; and these new realities may, in a like manner, be partially/wholly self-created and/or be (slightly) different on every usage/viewing. Many new types of reality are made possible through computers; and some of these were foreseen in the 1960s by the likes of Ted Nelson, *(hyper-man, hyper-space, hyper-reality etc);* Before computers you had fairly static and one-dimensional reality-making machines; such as *books, pictures, photographs, cinema, TV and radio etc.*

All (or most) past reality-making employed largely one-dimensional windows into other realms of being; and were similarly comprised of both imaginary and real parts. Whilst we had accepted that each reality type may be partially created by the onlooker/experiencer, as in the so-called beholder's share; overall it was someone else who constructed this reality for us, and it was (in a sense) projected into your minds in (largely) fixed and pre-determined ways; You could reject or choose not to watch the reality-tape *(ref. Philip K.Dick's 'The Electric Ant');* but none of these 'broadcast-only' technologies allowed direct participation in the creative/constructive act(s).

In a way perhaps this state, whereby someone else dictates your reality, and 'projects' ideas into your mind; is a type of dystopia. Broadcasts may be heavily censored and/or be of low quality and/or be factually incorrect or marginal etc.

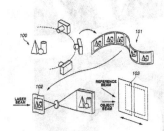

First in importance, guard the freedom of ideas at all costs. Be alert that dictators have always played on the natural human tendency to blame others and to oversimplify. And don't regard yourself as a guardian of freedom unless you respect and preserve the rights of the people you disagree with to free, public, unhampered expression. - Gerard K.O'Neil

Fixed realities may be subject to unfettered authority; defined (often by those in power) as the ability to tell people what to think! A dystopia gets into our head, so to speak.

Then with the emergence of personal computes (PCs), you gained more control over the construction of your own reality. Projecting and broadcasting your thoughts/opinions/reality becomes possible, and you can (for example) create your own website, place comments on newsgroups or on social media like **Facebook** and **Twitter**. Here there is vastly more choice in terms of content; and you may choose from 'millions' of channels on YouTube and the BBC archives etc; plus more fully uncensored (public and private) networks are available such as *4Chan, Pirate Bay, Silk-Road, SnapChat and Tumblr etc;* which all become readily accessible with networked PCs.

It is like our minds have become loosened from the bonds of *reality-slavery*, and you yourself can choose what to see, say/do and share; and Big Brother has been (to some extent) banished from our lives. Reality becomes more *lifelike, realistic, participatory, directable, social, personal, editable, 'zoomable', and multi-perspectival etc*; all at once; and whenever you choose, and (hopefully) in the way(s) that you do choose.

And today the computers are ever present; and networked together is vast amounts of information; whereby our everyday realities are supremely flexible, malleable and available for re-configuration in the blink of an eye. But, we ask, to what extent are you truly in control of these new 'digital' windows onto everything that is. Who makes the windows (social networks, encyclopedias etc), for example? And how and where are the new 'worlds' that the windows look into formed?

There is optimism for a set of new-found freedom(s) that may be possible in the coming 'digital' world(s); and much hyped are new kinds of reality; for example *blended-reality, mixed-reality, me-reality, infinite-reality etc.* The self-computer (we are told) becomes a partially self-constructed and malleable space; one which is fragmented, stratified, liquid etc. The Web is couched as a kind of truth reflector for human life. Hence it is the networked computer that provides the hyperreality spoken of in Chapter 2.

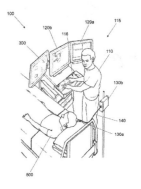

According to Descartes, reason becomes the religion whereby man frees himself from the material world and the dross of animal nature and becomes a pure, rational spirit.

The basic tool for the manipulation of reality is the manipulation of words. If you can control the meaning of words, you can control the people who must use them. - Philip K. Dick

The dominant principle of the new economy, the information economy, has lately been to conceal the value of information, of all things. - Jaron Lanier

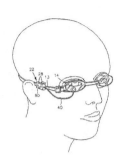

For some people, the Internet, cloud systems, drones, humanoid robots, and networked Apps etc; offer nothing but positive prospects. Most people in the West can surf the Web on a smart phone, see the earth from on-high with **Google Earth**, get on **FaceTime** video-chatting with distant friends, and follow life and video blogs of friends/mentors on live feeds using **Twitter** and **SnapChat** etc. Many people ask no questions as to whether or not we are living in the *best of all worlds* with respect to our computing creations. But for others there is much wrong with the ways in which modern computers have been designed, and (for example) the likes of Ted Nelson and Kim Veltman highlight social inefficiencies and the ways that computers limit access to knowledge and/or offer a means for social and reality control/censorship etc.

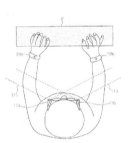

Regardless of which side of the fence you stand; it cannot be denied that we have/are entering a new digitally enhanced and/or partially digitally-constructed world. The nature of the ways that we all think and act is changing as a result of a tremendous fragmentation of human attention, combined with a (potentially) vast and game-changing coming together (socially) by means of knowledge and social networks.

What it all adds up to is difficult to say/predict.

But any fragmentation of self may in fact be your true self. The self is a constantly changing, but (to some extent) you create your own reality, and you can (perhaps) control the throttle on it (by means of technology). The stratified vistas of reality can be made to rapidly accelerate across the mind (or be focussed in on and dramatically slowed down). With our technology, we have created shifting boundaries between the real and unreal; and the self is a constantly shifting form; with new (and unbelievably varied) *structures, shapes and boundaries*; and we all now move in and out of a vast number of websites, networks, and Apps etc (and hence realities) constantly.

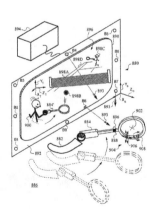

We have *quantum computing, holographic computing, augmented and virtual reality, ambient and contextual intelligence, smart objects etc.*

The greatest fortunes in history have been created recently by using network technology as a way to concentrate information and therefore wealth and power. - Jaron Lanier

An attempt to construct a mechanical man who can think... is to be made by the Massachusetts Institute of Technology. The 'Brain' of the new robot is an accomplished fact.

Holographic computing may possibly change everything; whereby products like Microsoft's HoloLens enable holograms to be projected onto reality; creating a new type of mixed, blended or 'digitally-fused' reality that is far more *timely, informative, situated, helpful, magnifiable, and rapidly explorable etc.* We are gaining the power to project our thoughts onto reality *(i.e. to create new kinds of individual and collective experiences of reality)*, in real-time and/or slowed-down/speeded-up time. We have the means to make our *Personal Realities* far more useful, entertaining and relevant.

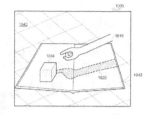

In the 1960s Ted Nelson came up with the concept of **stretch-text**; whereby within a hyper-media document the user could expand a paragraph/sentence; whereupon new words, sentences and details that related to the original statement become visible. The text becomes 'zoomable' in terms of details/knowledge displayed. Today we can take this concept further, and develop *stretch-thoughts* and *stretch-media*, and accordingly a *stretch-reality*.

A **stretch-reality** would be one whereby (for example); whilst wearing the Microsoft HoloLens; you look-at/select a real-world object of interest; whereupon a digital 'explosion' of the concept happens, and overlaid visually (in 3D) onto the object are new vistas or layers of information. This 'visual' or conceptual 'zoom' lets you see inside the object; to view its structures, molecular composition etc; and also to view explanatory texts etc. Other people can set virtual flags on such detailed views and 'edit' real world objects. This is the *real-virtuality* spoken of earlier; whereby Virtual Environments are overlaid on-top of reality in all kinds of useful ways.

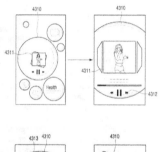

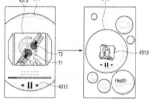

Earlier we said that a key feature of a dystopia is the removal of a person's imagination. People become isolated from the thoughts of other people, and the vast benefits of human creativity may be closed-off. This is a dark, singular, lonely and close-off reality; whereby mind-control is reality-control.

On the other hand, we may be 'lucky', and get *free-reality;* which is freedom to think; and *to see, create and share thoughts*. One's own mind is one's own property; you own your thoughts, and *secret, private and open-thoughts* may be freely seen/created/shared.

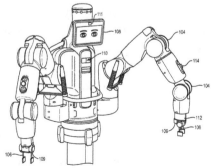

I can picture myself in a specific situation, and ask myself what would I do and how would I feel (can a computer do that?). - Hubert Dreyfus

That which exists through itself is called Meaning (Tao).

Meaning has neither name nor force.

It is the one essence, the one primordial spirit.

Essence and Life cannot be seen. It is contained in the Light of Heaven.

The Light of Heaven cannot be seen. It is contained in the two eyes.

The Golden Flower is the Light.

The Secret of the Golden Flower - The Chinese Book of Life
Taoist Text from Ancient sources.

Thefts using Computers

- EU Accounts Fiasco (2012) The European Court of Auditors said that over 5 billion euros was affected by 'material error'; and effectively that these funds were missing! How is this possible when even the simplest computer is accurate to fractions of a euro? The answer? Plain and simple old-fashioned corruption (of one type or another), that is deliberately disguised by system and computer 'errors'.

- Bernie Madoff stole 65 billion dollars from customer / client accounts by making up false computer records of trades he claimed to have performed (in a Ponzi scheme), but did not actually make (i.e he charged clients for fictitious trades - but kept the cash); activities which were registered over more than 20 years between 1980s-2009). Madoff later said 'Do you really think that I am the only one?' (who is embezzling funds in this way).[2010]

- Hackers infiltrated over 100 banks in several countries, stealing millions of dollars in possibly the largest bank theft the world has seen, according to a report published by the New York Times on Saturday. The malware apparently allowed the hackers to transfer money from the banks to fake accounts. According to the Times, Kaspersky Lab said the total theft could be more than $300 million, although the cybersecurity firm has not nailed down an exact figure.[February 2015]

Cartoon on Free Speech (by Jonik)

DECLARATION OF INTERNET FREEDOM

We stand for a free and open Internet.

We support transparent and participatory processes for making Internet policy and the establishment of five basic principles:

Expression: Don't censor the Internet.

Access: Promote universal access to fast and affordable networks.

Openness: Keep the Internet an open network where everyone is free to connect, communicate, write, read, watch, speak, listen, learn, create and innovate.

Innovation: Protect the freedom to innovate and create without permission. Don't block new technologies and don't punish innovators for their users' actions.

Privacy: Protect privacy and defend everyone's ability to control how their data and devices are used.

< Declaration of Internet Freedom signed by over 1500 organisations, people etc. >

Chapter Fourteen
Dreams of Utopia

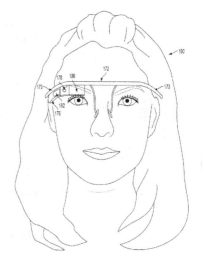

T HE TOPIC of utopia—or visioning/creation of a 'perfect' future society—is a common theme in science fiction (SciFi), films, games etc. We are all familiar with how the story unfolds. Typically it opens with a view of a society that has advanced far in terms of automation, systemisation, computerisation and machine capabilities. On the surface everything seems fine—and depicted is a society operating with great efficiency, collaboration and purpose. But it is not long before the reader/observer is introduced to the negative and dehumanising tendencies that adversely affect the ordinary citizens who must actually live inside this heavily mechanised and automated 'future world'.[1.2]

In SciFi, utopia inevitably turns out to be dystopia. Think of the nightmarish world's depicted in the films: *Logan's Run, Blade-Runner, Minority Report, Uploaded etc.* In this chapter we likewise attempt to envision the future; and to explore the possibilities—so to speak—and we shall do so with the help of science fiction. Our purpose is not merely to entertain, but rather to identify salient features within these stories; and to extract some (possibly) useful opinions/predictions.[9,10,11]

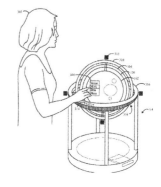

Why fall back on science fiction? Perhaps because its predictions have often turned out to be true (e.g. personal communicators from *Star Trek*, videophones in *Astounding Stories and Dick Tracy,* tablet computers in *Star Trek* etc).

It is however quite difficult to find examples of genuine utopias in fiction; and therefore we shall (more often) examine dystopias, and hence head the warnings of the various writers/visionaries; and in the hope that we can picture our goal by avoiding its opposite. Accordingly, we turn to the visionaries of science fiction; and to the futurists, writers, thinkers, movie makers and 'dreamers' who have sought to envision the future.[1,2, 5,12]

So, strap on your 'jet-pack', and grab your 'ray-gun'...

Most of the objective technologists or 'applied' scientists—
are specialists and are unaware of the comprehensively integrated
significance, to society, of the tasks they perform. - Hubert Dreyfus

What if every thought left its permanent mark - somewhere.

Science Fiction

The origins of science-fiction go right back to the mid-late 19th century stories of Edgar Allen Poe (1809-1849), Jules Verne (1832-1905) and H.G. Wells (1866-1946). And we can source the term to the so-called '*scientifiction*' stories first published by Hugo Gernsback's (1884-1967) in his pulp magazine *Amazing Stories* which he founded in 1926. SciFi really took-off with the earliest 1930s pulp stories; which featured *computers, time-travel, robots, space-travel, ray-guns, alien creatures etc.* Much of 1930s Science Fiction was referred to as '*Gadget-Fiction*'; and was about what happens when someone makes a technological invention.

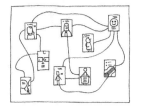

When looking through my personal collection of 1930s *Astounding Stories* magazines; one is immediately in awe at the prescience of the technology predictions made; including: *giant flat-panel displays/TVs; personal communicators; remote computer control(s) etc.* Although sensationalised *(in these stories we see rocket-ships, ray guns and alien invasions etc)*; one has to admit that much of the modern world is accurately foreshadowed.

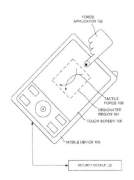

But futuristic technology was also much discussed by scientists and visionaries in the popular press, and in serious fiction books, during the 1930s-1940s. For example, in the 1932 book *Brave New World*, Aldous Huxley analysed the causes of dystopia; and he later admitted that he was (in part) motivated by an aim/desire to help humanity avoid his imagined world. Huxley begins his analysis by listing the forces that underly how problems in societal structures emerge.[13]

Huxley identifies these factors as symptomatic of a dystopia:

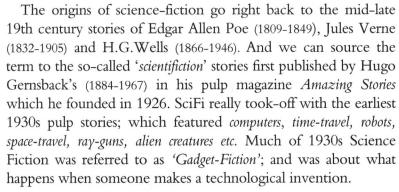

Overpopulation, social control, totalitarian regime (democracy), manipulation (psychological and classical conditioning), loss of individual identity, separation of society into castes (upper, lower etc), moulding of children's self-image and social outlook, use of platitudes such as 'ending is better than mending', and wanting to be an individual is considered horrifying etc.[13]

< {40} Dystopia = Mind-controlling + brainwashing + manipulative = a dysfunctional and unhappy society. >

What kinds of information is passed around on a P2P network is Facts-based and not Fictional-based as in heretical networks —politics becomes more about activity because feed-back and iteration are one and the same. - Douglas Rushkoff

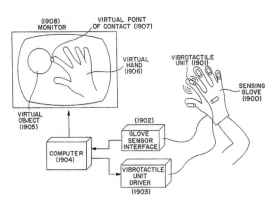

Wikipedia gives only summaries of knowledge.
Where is the knowledge itself?

DREAMS OF UTOPIA   319

Huxley's vision is a profoundly depressing one, and it is somewhat based on his idea that (for any society) the civil libertarians and rationalists, who might oppose the creation of such a society; have an infinite number of other concerns and constantly chase the wrong distractions. These kinds of (highly intelligent) people do not normally concern themselves with power, weapons and attacking their opponents; but (optimistically) assume that righteous arguments can and will win in the end (before it is too late).

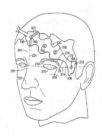

Hence a dystopia can come to be partly by accident, or partly as a result of anti-social individuals simply 'taking' what they want (without effective opposition), and partly as a result of our own stupidity and/or ineffective democracy etc.

Huxley's views are bleak and more than a little self-deflating.

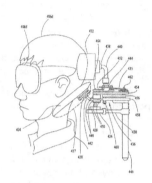

Many years later, In *The Hitchhiker's Guide to the Galaxy*, originally a BBC radio comedy aired in 1978, Douglas Adams (1952-2001); presented a more humorous slant on possible future utopias/dystopias. From '*Hitchhiker's*'...

It is known that there are an infinite number of worlds, simply because there is an infinite amount of space for them to be in. However, not every one of them is inhabited. Therefore, there must be a finite number of inhabited worlds. Any finite number divided by infinity is as near to nothing as makes no odds, so the average population of all the planets in the Universe can be said to be zero. From this it follows that the population of the whole Universe is also zero, and that any people you may meet from time to time are merely the products of a deranged imagination... (and)... It is a well known fact that those people who most want to rule people are, ipso facto, those least suited to do it. To summarise the summary: anyone who is capable of getting themselves made President should on no account be allowed to do the job.

"You may not instantly see why I bring the subject up, but that is because my mind works so phenomenally fast, and I am at a rough estimate thirty billion times more intelligent than you. Let me give you an example. Think of a number, any number." "Er, five," said the mattress. "Wrong," said Marvin (the 'paranoid' android). "You see?" [14]

Caption for the image on right:
'He used a radio to talk to the machine'.

Organic design (finalism) and causal determinism are antithetic concepts, which actually stand at opposite poles. As Hans Driesch pointed out, no one ever succeeded in building a house by throwing stones at random on the site; at the end of a century one would still have only a pile of stones. A machine more than any conceivable organism, is the product of design from start to finish—the machine introduced teleology or finalism in its classic form—a purposeful organisation for a strict, determined end.

Behind the cult lay an ancient perception, whose truth scientific inquiry has demonstrated, that the phenomena of life are actually influenced by remote forces, many, like cosmic rays, long unperceived, some doubtless still to be identified, over which man himself can have little, if any, control irrational obsessions and compulsions have been feeding a totalitarian power system—leaving humans powerless, directionless, incompetent, mentally defective, and psychotic, (and we need to) restore man to the vital functions he has lost!

The machine, 'advanced' thinkers began to hold, not merely served as the ideal mold for explaining and controlling all organic activities, but its wholesale fabrication and continued improvement were alone what gave meaning to human existence.... power, speed, motion, standardisation, mass production, quantification, regeneration, uniformity, regularity, control etc.

Lewis Mumford

Humour is defiantly helpful when considering the copious and evident problem(s)/predicament(s) of our species. Why our politicians ignore the biggest problems *(i.e inequality, education and installing true democracy)*; and insist on spouting platitudes and doing nothing, is well-captured by Adams.

Other more serious writers have much to offer.

For example, Neil Postman comments...

> What Orwell feared were those who would ban books. What Huxley feared was that there would be no reason to ban a book, for there would be no one who wanted to read one. Orwell feared those who would deprive us of information. Huxley feared those who would give us so much that we would be reduced to passivity and egoism. Orwell feared that the truth would be concealed from us. Huxley feared we would become a trivial culture, preoccupied with some equivalent of the feelies, the orgy porgy, and the centrifugal bumplepuppy. [Ref. lost]

Obviously, our problems are not all known and/or clear-cut.

Rather matching genuine human needs, wishes and requirements with the outcomes/offerings of technology is at issue. Easy to identify are the positive capabilities, efficiency-savings and potential advantages of systems and machines. For example we know that computers may *contract time and space, provide rapid and more complete communication (often), whilst providing new ways to model, visualise and manage physical (natural) and man-made processes and situations etc.* Yet somehow having these advantages does not get us very far, or help us to ensure that only positive, as opposed to negative, consequences appear. Surely (we suppose) any and all problems must relate to poor planning and sub-optimal implementation(s) of systems etc.[6,8,11]

Considering the potential of Artificial Intelligence (AI); we find even more frightening scenarios whereby machines begin to 'take us over'. Perhaps Augmented Reality (AR) may provide a solution. AR is described William Gibson's book *Spook Country*, which plays with layers of reality to make points about cyber-ghosts and data-disinformation *(i.e. the gaps between what we can and cannot perceive in a wired world).*

Digital tech is biased towards local things! Where is the planetary government? Arab springs are local. - Douglas Rushkoff

The 'brain' of the shell is a fuse, a tiny radio set—transmitter, receiver and aerial all combined—in the nose of the shell. - 1945 War Illustr. 7 Dec. 492/1

But perhaps the most technically convincing fictional account of an AR mediated future is Vernor Vinge's Hugo award winning book *Rainbows End* (2006). It is set in 2015, when people (are predicted to) interact through computer-generated graphic overlays provided by clothing embedded with lasers and microprocessors. Phantom keyboards can be called up for typing messages or using a search engine. Special contact lenses feed all the information directly into the person's visual field. Augmented views can be called up at will.

And the recent emergence of wearables and smart watches, glasses etc; does provide strong evidence that we are *(or may soon be inevitably and/or uncontrollably)* moving in the direction of constant immersion in technology, and as a people/species.

In Scarlett Thomas's book *The End of Mr Y* (2008); people can live the thoughts of others in the 'Troposphere'; an extra layer of reality. The Troposphere is a place where all consciousness is connected and you can enter other people's minds and read their thoughts. This sounds very much like Twitter, Tumbler or SnapChat etc.

But what is to become of us, the 'un-modified' humans?

Electric Men

Perhaps a better question is to ask what will be the ultimate capabilities of our future selves? Maybe one day soon, truly effective hypermedia will arrive; and you'll be able to 'see into' *movies, pictures, rooms, web-pages, books, and peoples real-time thoughts/ conversations (digitally, remotely and seamlessly)*. Perhaps we are already developing a taste for such a hyper-visible world. Some people have noted that tablets are trans-media devices that conflates books, Web and video etc. You film with the screen. And the tablet window watches you with a face-forward camera; but this is quite strange when you think about it; you watch it, and it watches you back! We look, and are, in turn, looked-at.

Are we to become digital objects ourselves? Do we now have hyper-reality and hyper-man? Wearables and sensors etc; enable us to know infinitely more about who we are individually and also collectively. They are a type of magnifying glass for humanity; and herald an era of hyper-visibility (but for what aim or purpose?).

Where are the flying-cars; domestic robots; and sentient machines?
All of these advances were supposed to arrive around the year 2000.
Did we massively under-estimate the problem/solution space(s)?
What other problem/solution space(s) are we now under-estimating?

PROGRAMMABLE WORLD

In our houses, cars, and factories, we're surrounded by things, intelligent devices that capture data about how we live and what we do. Now they are beginning to talk to one another. Soon we'll be able to choreograph them to respond to our needs, solve problems, even save our lives. We are seeing the dawn of an era when the most mundane items in our lives can talk wirelessly among themselves, performing tasks on command, giving us data we've never had before. Imagine a factory where every machine, every room, feeds back information to solve problems on the production line. Imagine a hotel room where the lights, the stereo, and the window shade are not just controlled from a central station but adjust to our preferences before you even walk in. Think of a gym where the machines know your workouts as soon as you arrive, or a medical device that can point toward the closest defibrillator when you have a heart attack. In this future, the intelligence once locked in our devices now flows into the universe of physical objects. Some call it the Internet of Things, or the Internet of Everything or the Industrial Internet or the Sensor Revolution. But we call it the Programmable World.

Bill Wasik

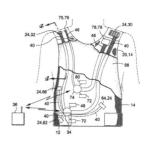

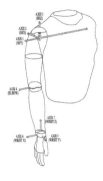

When we begin to use head-up displays, plus vibrating UIs, speech recognition plus augmented reality glasses like Microsoft's HoloLens; we shall see the world as no human has ever seen it. Computers will know exactly where you are in time and space, and this prospect smears the interface between you and the Internet across your nervous system.

Wearables/portable computers are the first steps in the augmentation of the human; stepping stones to a new class of part human, part computer being; the self-computer. And it's a self that is brimming with gadgets, technological 'enhancements' etc; and that are always with us and in use. Very soon (or now) you can never be lost—because your phone/watch/glasses (and even contact-lenses/clothing) will have *satellite navigation*. How long before these kinds of abilities are built into our bodies?

Think it won't happen? Consider how a perfect memory of everything, plus encyclopaedic knowledge, and constant communication etc; gives augmented humans superior advantages and allows them to win in the various battle(s) of life.

Quoting from Wired magazine [2014]:

> Its as if I am seeing their thoughts form, I can share something about what I am currently experiencing and immediately hear from others experiencing the same thing. We can experience events not only as they happen, but together.

The potentials/abilities of the augmented human seem near endless. Notifications of meetings 'just in time', warnings of shopping bargains, updates on the availability/health of friends, constant assistive comments on the weather etc. But according to *Wired* writer Steven Levy; for wearables to sing the body electric, they must first form choirs. It is not just the mechanical or software capabilities/possibilities that are important; but rather it is the way(s) in which live data-updates (and thought-updates) are networked together, sifted, shared and organised.

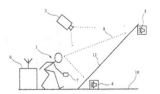

It is all of these new capabilities conflated together; networked and overlaid onto the real world; that creates a hyper-reality; and that allows the interconnected nature of everything to be seen/available for the first time in history. Real atoms become intimately linked to, ideas and bits; and the varied nature of the human/natural 'worlds' begin to coalesce.

Books were originally 'chained-down' (with locks and short lengths of chain to prevent them from being stolen)—do we not currently 'chain-down' our very thoughts—with copyright, poor-accessibility and as a result of wrongly-assigned ownership for all public (open) thoughts?

Some experts see a bright future for such frightening prospects as Swarm robotics; or robots that work together as decentralised, self-organising groups/swarms; able to coordinate their activities in order to accomplish goals/missions far more efficiently and cheaply than a 'classic' robot. These artificial creatures may look like tiny insects, flying drones; or else be humanoid creatures that live and work amongst us much as we do ourselves.

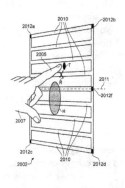

But wearables are how the self-computer (and the metaphysical world's of 'externalised' or implanted-thoughts and data) typically begin(s) to encroach on our personal, physical space. In terms of personalised technologies, there are two classes of wearables, *introspective* (they monitor you); and *extrospective* (they look outwards). Both kinds of device will predominate; but it does seem to the author that the extrospective ones are where the most profound implications/changes for human-life can/will be made.

As discussed, a World-Brain is desired/possible; and in order to fully connect the thought(s) of humanity.

These predictions may sound a little disconcerting; and appear to herald the arrival of augmented humans and/or cyborgs. Franz Kafka's story *Metamorphosis*, describes a related nightmare where a man (overnight) changes into a giant insect; and thus represents a person trapped in a hopeless situation. What about *Digital Metamorphosis*—changes to our sense of the world through continual overlays of computer generated *sound, video, graphics and positional data etc.* Are we creating our own nightmares; which cannot be switched-off, or be escaped-from?

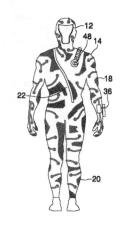

What are we evolving into, and how can we manage this process? In an insightful article: '*Awkward Moments from the Future of Computing*' [Wired, July 2014], Artem Sukhinin wrote:

> You can look at a new field of technology such as wearable computing and expect three things to emerge: the *Productive*, the *Pointless* and the *Perpendicular*.

In a similar fashion we ask; what is the point of new technology; because we can identify much that is pointless, and perpendicular or sub-optimal. In fact I would suggest that the vast majority of so-called technological advances/ inventions do not change anything in any way whatsoever.

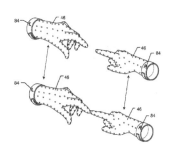

The computer itself knows nothing of whats its doing, its purpose, and neither can it judge if any of its actions are right or wrong, good or bad, harmful or helpful. Its thoughts are 'frozen' human thoughts, and not thoughts in any sense at-all.

Once we get enough of these objects into our collective networks, they're no longer one-off novelties or data sources but instead become a coherent system, a vast ensemble that can be choreographed, a body that can dance. It is the opposite of the Internet. By contrast, these connected objects will act more like a swarm of drones, a distributed legion of bots, far flung and sometimes even hidden from view but nevertheless coordinated as if they were a single giant machine.

Once we get there, that system will transform the world of everyday objects into a designable environment, a playground for coders and engineers. It will change the whole way we think about the division between the virtual and the physical.

Bill Wasik

(A)

(B)

Truly useful innovations; such the IPhone, IPad, and the Web etc; are (normally) adopted and used by hundreds of millions of people. In a way the marketplace does the talking, and with its wallet. However here we should perhaps make another distinction; and notice that even the aforementioned technologies are by no means perfect; but represent only a slight, but significant, improvement over the methods that they replaced. It is a fact that all technologies exist on a vector of development/evolution; and it is vital to keep an eye on where this vector is taking us. Technology is like a SatNav journey with a way-point or final destination which is ever present *(which may be either visible/explicit, or hidden/implicit).*

Innovation is a difficult process *(and is social + technological),* but we must always ask ourselves, where do we wish to go as a people. Evaluating positives/negatives, plus alternatives is key.

Fred Turner in his book *The Democratic Surround* notes that new and multimedia technologies emerged from postwar humanism; and further developed out of a society that was profoundly influenced by the individualistic and free-thinking values that emerged out of counter-culture movements. In this view technology is (at least partly) about enlightenment, personal liberation and escape from established power structures. Stewart Brand argues that the counterculture scorn for established authority was what spurred the philosophical foundations of not only the 'leaderless' Internet, but also the entire personal computing revolution.

Some experts have called these ideas digital-utopianism/libertarianism and related them to the fields of transhumanism and technoself etc. Transhumanism is a cultural and intellectual movement promoting the aim of transforming the human condition fundamentally by developing and making available technologies to enhance human *intellectual, physical and psychological capabilities.* Google-Glass, Microsoft HoloLens are first steps, but Samsung is already thinking about electronic/network connected contact-lenses.

We are going to integrate more and more with technology. It does seem likely that we will (eventually) have technology inside of our bodies and/or become inseparable from it.

Language disguises thought. From the outward clothing it is impossible to infer the
form of thought beneath it because the outward form of its clothing is not designed to
reveal the form of the body, but for different purposes. - Ludwig Wittgenstein

So I began to think people aren't really experiencing anything... we are actually living permanently in the future and that's whats really worries me. - Terry Gilliam

DREAMS OF UTOPIA 325

Do you want mental powers of calculation that make the most powerful supercomputer of today seem like an abacus? Do you want to beam your thoughts into the minds of others. Technology will provide the means to do so. It may even grant some of us immortality. Yet we face many new problems/questions/choices as a result. What shall be our rights in the machine dominated future; can techno-rights be established; and will they be applicable (or of any use).

Are techno-rights an overly simplistic solution and/or a naïve attempt to manage an incredibly huge, complex, and sophisticated technological entity (the self-computer)? Can the self-computer very-easily sidestep (itself) any attempts to control it and/or curtail its growth/powers? Present are very real unknowns, and related questions I would suggest are axiomatic to the vital problems that we now face as a species.

We must ask ourselves how far should the mechanisation/automation/computerisation of humanity be allowed to proceed. In his *Omni* magazine story, 'Half Jack'; first published in June 1970, Roger Zelazny wrote:

> His face opened vertically, splitting apart along the scar, padded synthetic flesh tearing free from electrostatic bonds... the uncovered portions of his face and body were dark metal and plastic, precision-machined, some gleaming, some dusky... 'I don't understand', she said when they finally drew part. 'What sort of an accident was it?'... 'Accident? There was no accident' he said, 'I paid allot of money for the work, so that I could pilot a special sort of ship. I am a cyborg. I hook myself directly into each of the ship's systems'.

The computer can be, and possibly should be, the ultimate container/extension to our reasoning. But we must ask ourselves *(in each case of a technological innovation)*; what (if anything) we are giving up as a result. How is our humanity changed/altered by computers? Are any identified changes visible ahead of time, and can they be reversed? Finding the answers is difficult; and is compounded by the fact that man normally just makes the innovation happen, and only worries about any consequences afterwords.

NEW SOCIALISM

Wikipedia, Flicker and Twitter etc are the vanguard of a cultural movement. A global collectivist society is coming and this time you're going to like it. The frantic global rush to connect everything to everyone, all the time, is quietly giving raise to a revised version of socialism. Mushrooming collaborative sites like Digg, StumbleUpon, the HypeMachine and Twine have added their weight in to this great upheaval. These developments suggest a steady move towards a sort of socialism uniquely tuned-in for a networked world. A digital socialism without the state, the new socialism runs over a borderless Internet, through a tightly integrated global economy. It is designed to heighten individual autonomy and thwart centralisation.

It is a decentralised extreme, broadly collective action is what Web sites and Net-connected Apps generate when they harness input from the global audience. In the 90s, activist, provocateur and ageing hippy John Barlow began calling this drift, somewhat tongue in cheek, 'dot-communism'. He defines it as workforce composed entirely of free agents, a decentralised gift or barter economy where there is no property and where technological architecture defines the political space... it is a spectrum of attitudes, techniques, and tools that promote collaboration, sharing, aggregation, coordination and *Hocracy*, and a host of other newly enabled types of social cooperation.

Kevin Kelly

This need to be constantly communicating. It doesn't matter what you're communicating so long as you're communicating. It's about detaching yourself from the neural network. Are we just neurons or are we just the synaptic gap? I'm just not sure. If there isn't information flowing through us, we don't seem to exist—and that I just find wearyingly tiresome. - Terry Gilliam

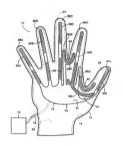

Perhaps we need highest level objectives for the self-computer. A simple top-level aim (for all the machines) might read like this: *only if the computer can perform a unifying function, only if it can keep records and orchestrate our activities, can we (all of humanity) derive full benefit.* Obviously such an aim (for society as whole) concerns many different *peoples, languages, disciplines, activities, topics etc;* and the influence(s) of machines are deeply intertwined with human affairs, and in all its infinite *variety, wonder and natural evolution.*

Thought-Spaces

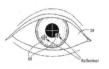

In this book we have focussed on the key facility of helping mankind to think better thoughts. The problem is that thoughts are (often) not properly linked, visible, contextualised and amalgamated/interlaced together. It is not that we want consensus (on all issues); although perhaps we do on issues like equal access to food, knowledge and opportunity etc; rather we want all the opinions on a given topic to be visible. We wish to know how these opinions link to everything else, and to see *relationships, actions, authors, origins, overlays, timelines, evolving opinions, truth, falsehood etc.*

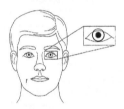

It is because thoughts have no (or little) context that today we are (largely) blind to the needs, wishes, requirements of the vast majority of humans. Individual thoughts are hidden amongst a cluttered mass of other thoughts; the same being ones that are often wholly unconnected, one to another *(apart from local connections).* We need to see everything in its proper and rightful context—even when (some of those) context(s) are blatantly wrong, false, immoral etc. Context alone provides meaning; combined with structure. When we have more contexts; and more structure, even when some of it is wrong (or labelled as such) and/or apparently irrelevant; we always have more meaning present.

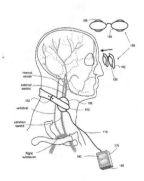

A useful question is to ask what makes us human, and what adheres us together as a people? The answer would seem to be fairly obvious. To start with we have (hopefully) moral values; which (perhaps) equate to *sympathy, gentleness, love, truth, help, factual information etc;* And all of these can patently be achieved through education (plus beneficial action(s)).

Rules are determined by the organization of the system.
It is possible to have a universe where one plus one equals one!
Edward de Bono

According to Aristotle, there are 3 intellectual virtues:

- Clear insight
- Grasp of causal connections
- Wisdom (insight, deductive powers)

Aristotle also identified two separate genera of moral values; [1] Justice and [2] Subjective passions. The biggest (and smallest) question(s) of humanity become a problem of linking plans with actions. But nobody knows all the layers of technology. So how can we cut through this gordian knot of vast complexity?

According to Stephen Pinker; intelligence consists of specifying a goal, assessing the current situation to see how it differs from the goal, and applying a set of operations that reduce the difference. Intelligence comes from information/thoughts/data. Popper likewise suggested that: everything depends upon the give-and-take between ourselves and our task, our work, our problems, our world 3; upon feedback, which can be amplified by our criticism of what we have done.

In an attempt to foster these type(s) of feedback processes in society, we have examined thinking methods/mechanisms. Previously identified are two kinds of thought; those that exist in a human mind/on-media, and those that have been implanted into machines. We can name these *Live-Thoughts* and *Frozen-Thoughts*. Live-thoughts exist inside of the mind of a thinker and are constantly changing structure/context and moving in and out of attention/consciousness. Frozen-thoughts (or implanted/static thoughts) are fixed and may lose some of their context/meaning when translated from the live form.

In this book, we have (hopefully) demonstrated that open thoughts may be (or should be) freely: *accessed and assembled,* by anyone, and that they are the property of humanity *(i.e they are our (open) social thoughts)*. Also no natural and free (open) thought, may judge, block, censure; or else be placed over any other natural free (open) thought *(without precedence or the presence of an established and highly specific-context)*. Plus there is no universally defined, or fully distinct operable meaning(s) for any thought; and no individual thought(s) may be universally judged.

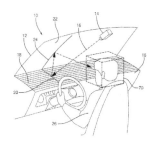

When I read a sentence with understanding something happens, perhaps a picture comes to mind. But what we call 'understanding' is related to countless things that happen before and after the reading of this sentence. When I say I understand a sentence; this can be different things in different cases. - Ludwig Wittgenstein

In explanation one tries to reveal how something unfamiliar is only a special arrangement of things that are already familiar. - Edward de Bono

Recently the Press recorded the invention of a calculating machine... They called it a 'brain'. -1951 R. Knox Stimuli iii. xxi. 129

Univac, the 'Giant Brain', an electronic automatic computer. 1952 Economist 1 Nov. 305

THE GODFATHER

There is a feeling when you're making something new you had better get the structure right, because it may end up being the structure of everything important in the future. Jaron Lanier describes this feeling as 'Karma Vertigo'... When email was first developing, all the questions that people deal with today were beginning to come up. **Who owns your words?** How do you organise these massive email conversations? On-line behaviour can be like chicken-pecking; if anyone shows blood, that bird is down... I was pretty sure that anonymity was toxic, and so at first (on the WELL network); I didn't want anonymity. This became a source of controversy, because it allowed people to tell the truth... Your Facebook identity is this identity that's confirmed by all the people who friend you, and therefore its the real you.

Kevin Kelly

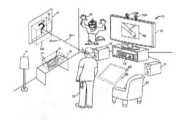

This latter point may be a little confusing and/or seem illogical. How can thoughts be meaningless (by themselves)? The answer relates to the fundamental nature of human thinking. Thoughts are established as the basic building blocks for the representation/communication of meaning, and in particular when assembled into thought-patterns. Thought-atoms are used in multiple contexts; and may have different/multiple meanings *(some of which are inter-dependent and change with time/context/thinker/reader/perceiver)*; hence we cannot establish any universal, singular or fixed meaning for a thought-atom prior to usage.

The natural 'home' of any thought is inside of one or more thought-space(s). And a thought-space:

- Provides a medium for thinking
- Consists of one or more human mind(s)
- Mind(s) are merged with mind extending/supporting methods
- Contains specific thought-patterns/concepts/definitions etc
- Contains specific communication methods/tools
- Contains unifying structures/relations/linkages
- May subsume/be linked to and/or overlap other thought-spaces
- Fosters specific deductions/propositions/logical-relations
- Obstructs certain deductions/propositions/logical-relations
- Adopts rules and ways of being/knowing for thought-atom(s)
- Has public interfaces, and public/private 'thinking' rules/processes; or has public 'windows' and private aspect(s)
- Adopts rules for linking/overlaying/subsuming other thought-space(s)
- May be communicated/written-down/stored
- May evolve/develop with time/experience/opinion

Thought-spaces are the *'little and big worlds'* discussed earlier. They are of varying size/complexity, and are sometimes layered and/or linked. They are logical and/or meaning saturated regions of mind in which thoughts may be said to live/reside; that is they are complex 'worlds' of meaning that *reflect experience, theory, knowledge, propositions, deductions, stories etc;* and they dictate which thoughts may exist and/or be accepted into a specific ensemble.

Private information protected by the little SIM card in your handset might not be so private after all. Based on new documentation from former NSA-employee-turned-whistleblower, Edward Snowden, The Intercept is reporting on a state-sponsored theft of encryption keys from Gemalto; a company that makes 2 billion SIM cards annually. With these stolen encryption keys, intelligence agencies can monitor mobile communications without seeking or receiving approval from telecom companies and foreign governments.

The brain seeks only to create explanations; but the explanations may be highly
acceptable but without much relevance to what is being explained! - Edward de Bono

DREAMS OF UTOPIA   329

Features of an effective/efficient *Thought-Space*:

- Maximised Logon, Metron and Selective Capacities
- Maximal Operational Flow of Thought-Atoms
- Hyper-Thoughts seen in Hyper-context (Hyper-Network)
- Focus is on Pattern Logic as Opposed to Focus Logic
- Focus is on Water Logic as Opposed to Yes/No Logic
- Parallel-linkages between all thought-atoms are visible
- Contain both forward and backward links (overlaid copiously)
- Allow comments on a link, comments on a relationship
- Facilitate (issue-specific) voting on any topic/link/thought-atom
- Uphold thought Openness, Freedom, and Equality
- Consist (typically) of multiple linked (or subsumed) thought-spaces, overlaid with links/contrasting elements visible
- Contains Topic-Spaces and ontological organising mechanism(s)
- Every thought be (potentially) connected to every other (World Brain)
- All open-thought-atoms are accessible and are immortal
- Thought-Atoms may be static/evolving; in terms of parts/pattern

In a nutshell, we can say that to be truly useful, all (relevant) thought-spaces must be (visibly and adequately) connected, one to another, and in every which way imaginable. Connections must be atomic, hyperlinked and with hyper-context.

Enemies of Freedom

These ideas of an ideal thought-space may sound overly utopian or impractical. However freedom-of-thought/free-expression/association etc; have always had enemies/critics; and these enemies will not just sit back and let freedom rule. Restriction(s) on freedom may be human and/or (apparently) technological in origin. In fact according to the warnings of Orwell, Huxley, Wells etc; the enemies of freedom will often lurk in our own society and/or be the result of a lack of will-power/determination to manage/design our societies with sufficient mechanisms so as to uphold freedom.

> < {41} Freedom = Effective thought-spaces = see + assemble + share thoughts; and openly use/link-to sub-thought-spaces (efficiently). >

WEARABLES

Wearables are truly upon us... this leap from the situated and leave behind-able to the always-on, always-present, always-connected, is not without its drawbacks... But it also provides a near future world of self-knowledge, sensors and superpowers. Even today we can monitor our activities and compare 'n' share with our friends, using devices such as the Nike+ fuelband, the FitBit or the Jawbone UP, and we can bring information, alerts and alarms to our wrist with devices like the Pebble watch and the Apple watch. Coming devices will give you heads-up displays, vibrating interfaces, speech recognition and a constant understanding of where you are in time and space. .

By smearing the interface between yourself and the Internet across your nervous system, wearables are the first step in augmentation of the human... The point isn't the gadget: it's the combination of the intimacy of a device that is always with us and that only we use, with the power of cloud-based processing and storage. The wearable device itself is actually only the small, physical manifestation of a much larger service: Google Glass gives its wearers a head-up display, a voice control and a forward looking camera... never forget a face, link to social networks... never be lost, develop an instant expertise in the art you are looking at with a reverse image search on Wikipedia. Have perfect memory of everything you do, say, see or hear... record, transcribe and automatically Googling everything you hear or see.

Ben Hammersley

We want to know how it works so we can make better use of it, perhaps change it, perhaps improve it, perhaps prevent it from going wrong, perhaps improve it, perhaps repair it. Above all, we want to know how it is going to behave in general and in special circumstances. - Edward de Bono

Desert of ossified words / thoughts.
Language is the mold of thought.

In a Wired magazine article from 2012, labelled *Inside the Matrix*; by James Bamford a frightening vision of the US intelligence efforts (against its own people) is described.

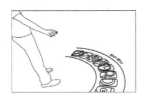

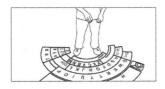

Deep inside the Utah desert, the NSA is building a massive surveillance centre. Yottabytes of data—including yours—will be stored there! The Utah Data Centre os a $ 2 billion centre, and flowing through its servers and routers will be stored in near bottomless databases; all forms of communication, including the complete contents of private emails, cell phone calls, and google searches, as well as all sorts of personal data trails—parking receipts, travel itineraries, bookstore purchases, and other digital 'pocket litter'... by programs/systems. It has created a supercomputer of almost unimaginable speed to look for patterns and to unscramble codes. Finally the agency has begun building a place to store all the trillions of words and thoughts and whispers captured with its electronic net. And of course its all being done in secret. [NSA = Never Say Anything—and they store 500 quintullia item of text—10 to the power of 20!]

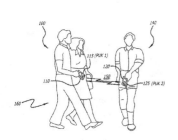

Words escape me at this point; because surely it would be better to spend this effort (and system development money) o*n better education systems, a more equal distribution of wealth; and on actual physical defense methods; and/or on curing the actual causes of home-grown terrorism* than on such a doubtful/harmful approach?

But perhaps it is not just the Big Brother of government that should worry us. When Max Schrems fought to see what the Facebook network knew about him, he got back 1,200 pages of data in 57 categories; including records of every person who ever poked him, all the IP addresses of machines he used to access the site, a full history of messages plus chats, and he even found items that he had deleted but never sent.

A lot of people have became worried about Little-Brother, or private companies knowing what you bought, where we went, what we are saying, and what we are searching for. Now it turns out that the Big-Brother can access that stuff too! And whenever a company is caught making a mistake or telling a falsehood; it invariably vows to do better (or to not get caught again); at least in terms of making its activities public.

< {42} Big Brother = lots of Little Brothers—often working together! >

How/when are open-thoughts to be assigned as open/public/social ones? Actually, this question hides a nest of ethical and moral issues; but if we rely on the Theory of Natural Thoughts, then whenever a writer's work (for example) enters the public domain, then that same work has become the public property of everyone in the world. Obviously the laws of copyright and patent(s) etc; are involved in determining when a work becomes public property; but the author supports a radical re-think of copyright; and that publicly-available property should be assigned to a public/free status much sooner (a fraction of 90 years)—and perhaps 5-10 years is sufficient for copyright protection.

Unfortunately, it appears that organisations such as the **NSA** are willing to compromise everything and anything (related to freedom) to get what it/they want(s). Similarly, national intelligence bodies scan all upstream and downstream communications right across the planet.

Future Technology

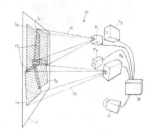

We are truly living in an era of accelerating technology.

New concepts/terms seem to pop-up every day; for example: *Holographic Computing, Holographic Apps, HoloLens, Mixed-Reality, Blended-Reality, Infinite-Media, Me-Media, Virtual-Environments (Virtual-Flags and 'Pinning' Holograms into reality), Augmented-Reality, Ambient-Intelligence, Nano-Particles, Quantum-Dots, Casual-Programmers, The-Internet-of-Food, Darknet, 3-D and 4-D Printing, Digital-Currencies, Adaptive-Education, Micro-Farming, Smart-Phone Supercomputer, etc etc.*

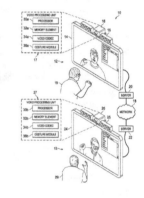

At the 2015 International Consumer Electronics Show (**CES**) show in Las Vegas, it was clear from the beginning that the show would focus heavily on connected devices such as wearables *(for example bluetooth-enabled toothbrushes with 3-D motion sensors)*. There was even a *smart babies bottle* on display! The unofficial theme of **CES** seemed to be: ***put a sensor in it.*** Evidently, technological developments are picking up apace; and the dazzling 'portmanteau' of imaging/communications technologies mentioned earlier (cf. hyper-reality); is really happening.

A useful perspective was related in a recent Wired article named: *The Tube Amplifier; by* Travis Coburn (May 2014):

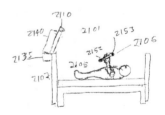

> As the smart phone becomes the first screen, its bringing us closer together. It is as if I am seeing their thoughts form, I can share something about what I am currently experiencing and immediately hear from others experiencing the same thing—we can experience events not only as they happen, but together.

Artificial Intelligence is suddenly everywhere (or *Simulated Intelligence* in the language of the present book). However most of this technology is still what the experts call *soft A.I.*, but it is (according to some experts) proliferating like mad.

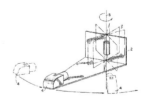

Security researchers at Kaspersky Lab have discovered apparently state-created spyware buried in the firmware of hard drives from big names like Seagate, Toshiba and Western Digital. When present, the code lets snoops collect data and map networks that would otherwise be inaccessible—all they need to retrieve info is for an unwitting user to insert infected storage (such as a CD or USB drive) into an internet-connected PC. The malware also isn't sitting in regular storage, so you can't easily get rid of it or even detect it. (2015)

We need *universal access* not just to the *Internet,* but to all the *open-thoughts.*

SOUS-VEILLANCE

We are witnessing an emerging culture of 'sous-veillance'— Sousveillance is the monitoring of events not by those above, but by citizens from below. Sousveillance will not go away. If anything, it is becoming woven ever more tightly into everyday life, with new tools arriving that let citizens document incidents in surprising new ways...
Always on videocameras are spreading... Many cars, for example, have cameras for backing up, and forward ones are gaining popularity. And wearable video devices are gaining popularity.

Clive Thompson

Natural thinking is the flow of activity from area to area on the special memory surface (within the mind). The flow is entirely passive and follows the contours of the surface. There is no question of an outside agency directing where it should go. The sequence of activated areas constitutes the flow of thought. The flow may be continuous, that is from one area to an adjacent one, or activity may die out in one area to start up in another unconnected area. Although the flow is entirely passive, certain artificial organising patterns which affect the direction of the flow can become established on the surface. Such patterns have usually been fed onto the surface deliberately.... Flow is determined by the natural behaviour of the surface and as a result it has certain definite characteristics.

Edward de Bono

So states a Vanity Fair article, *Enthusiasts and Skeptics Debate Artificial Intelligence*; by author and radio host Kurt Andersen. It is true that computer decision making, or automated reasoning *(from purely implanted-thoughts)* is increasingly being used for variety of purposes.

But it may be useful to differentiate *weak* AI, from its counterpart, *strong* AI. *Soft, weak* or *narrow* AI is inspired by, but doesn't aim to mimic, the human brain. These are statistically oriented, and are generally computational intelligence methods for addressing complex problems based on the analysis of vast amounts of information (big data); using powerful computers and sophisticated algorithms. Some of the results (of automated big-data processing) can (apparently) exhibit qualities that we tend to associate with human intelligence.

Soft AI was behind **Deep Blue,** IBM's chess playing supercomputer, which in 1997 won a celebrated chess match against then reigning champion Gary Kasparov; as well as Watson, IBM's question-answering system. And, as Mr. Andersen notes in his article, it's why: We're now accustomed to having conversations with computers: to refill a prescription, make a cable-TV-service appointment, cancel an airline reservation—or, when driving, to silently obey the instructions of the voice from the G.P.S.

Kevin Kelly, recently called soft AI a kind of...

Cheap, reliable, industrial-grade digital smartness running behind everything, and almost invisible except when it blinks off. It will enliven inert objects, much as electricity did more than a century ago. Everything that we formerly electrified we will now cognitise. This new utilitarian AI will also augment us individually as people (deepening our memory, speeding our recognition) and collectively as a species. There is almost nothing we can think of that cannot be made new, different, or interesting by infusing it with some extra IQ... Like all utilities, AI will be supremely boring, even as it transforms the Internet, the global economy, and civilisation.

And according to Buckminster Fuller: You never change things by fighting the existing reality. To change something, build a new model that makes the existing model obsolete.

There are, however a few words which do not describe things, but which provide tools for dealing with other words. Multiplication is a tool for carrying out a process. - Edward de Bono

New Models

A technology that is changing an existing model in major ways is crypto-currency. The original crypto-currency was **BitCoin** developed (anonymously) by nom-de-plume Satoshi Nakamoto; and projects such as *Ethereum, Blockstream, Maidsafe, Mastercoin, Counterparty, Stellar, Factom, Codius and NXT etc;* are innovating in related space(s) (with new forms of currency). Therefore a variety of services and applications will soon arrive that will push hard on, and/or test the limits of Satoshi Nakamoto's original vision *(to say nothing of standard economic theory/policies).* Today, the **BitCoin** landscape is murky, but patterns are beginning to emerge; and it looks like crypto-currencies are here to stay, and despite governmental attempts to crush these decentralised monies.

Many of the latest technological developments do appear to be quite magical, and fit well with Arthur C. Clark's statement that any sufficiently advanced technology is indistinguishable from magic.

A brief anecdote seems useful at this point. Back in 1979, when the British humorist Douglas Adams launched his hapless protagonist Arthur Dent on a hitchhiking tour of the galaxy; he also invented a fictional solution to the mutual incomprehensibility of the universe's dialects. The Babel fish was a *'small, yellow and leechlike'* creature that, when placed in your ear, would allow you to *'instantly understand anything said to you in any form or language.'* Suddenly finding himself on a Vogon space ship, Dent used a Babel fish to decipher the captain's announcements from the flight deck—though this understanding came at the cost of the *'sickening sensation'* of the Babel fish *'slithering deep into his aural tract'*.

Here on Earth in 2015, **Google** released the latest update to its translate app. The app doesn't speak Vogon, but it does let you speak a phrase into your phone and have the phrase translated back to you in a language you selected.

N.B. This (apparently AI based) translation capability may appear magical; but it is made possible by combining the working translation units/atoms from countless unpaid human translators (amalgamating countless human-translated documents).

< {43} Artificial Intelligence (AI) = Purely human sourced machine implanted-thoughts. >

The whole of culture is concerned with the formation and communication of ideas. But what about the process of changing concepts as opposed to establishing them. - Edward de Bono

---

INTELLIGENT MACHINES

Hal, the sentient computer of 2001: A Space Odyssey, murdered most of the spaceship crew it was built to aid and protect. The idea of a super-intelligent machine turning on its human masters is one of the oldest in science fiction... Our smart machines are still a long way from seeing; speaking and scheming; as Hal did, but they do exist, and they are beginning to change our lives... Like many people, computers find it harder to listen than to talk... we also acquire much of our knowledge visually... but visual perception may be even more complex than language. No one understands how the brain makes sense of the information our eyes supply. How effortlessly we process a jumble of light and shadow, movement and colour to recognise that the car speeding past us is a Jaguar, even when we have never seen one before.... the thread that connects these programs is that they are restricted to a narrow range of facts... we avoid being overloaded with data by using our judgement to focus on what is important! So AI hasn't come close to reproducing human intelligence. AI has painfully discovered that our type of intelligence cannot be isolated from the rest of human life and experience. But sooner or later, computers will probably duplicate most everyday human performed tasks.

Thomas Hoover
Omni Magazine (July 1999)

Constant need to:
- Cope with spam and pop-up adds.
- Perform software updates.
- Sign new Terms and Conditions for software packages/networks etc.

WHY WASTE OUR TIME IN THIS WAY?

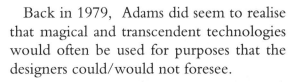

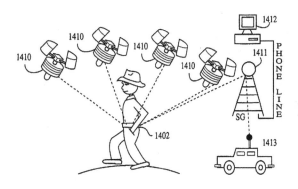

Back in 1979, Adams did seem to realise that magical and transcendent technologies would often be used for purposes that the designers could/would not foresee.

Often the designer of a new technology knows full well what his product is going to be used for, but this is not always so. Determining weather a technology is for the ultimate good is also difficult. Technologies like **BitCoin** and **BitTorrent**, I would argue, are a net *benefit* to society; and bring P2P exchange of money and technologies/data/content to millions of (otherwise) continually impoverished individuals. These kinds of *people-centric* technologies do seem to be a remedy for, and/or to some extent a (small) redress, for evident social inequalities.

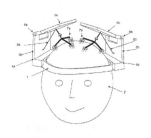

Other technologies do (at first sight) appear to be of a more dubious nature. For example, programmer Ross Ulbricht is finally getting his day in court, 15 months after plainclothes **FBI** agents grabbed him in the science-fiction section of a San Francisco library and accused him of running the billion-dollar online drug bazaar known as the **Silk-Road**. The **Silk-Road** website pioneered a new kind of online P2P marketplace (similar to **Napster**); and is one that is open to the public; but whose *administrators, buyers, and sellers* are anonymous, thanks to tools like the software **Tor** and **BitCoin**.

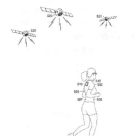

Ross himself characterises the **Silk-Road** as; at its core... a way to get around regulation from the state. If they say we can't buy and sell certain things, we'll do it anyway and suffer no abuse from them. The anonymous, BitCoin-enabled commerce that **Silk-Road** pioneered, he argued, was the beginning of a new era of anarchic markets with no regulatory control. To quote Ross once again: Sector by sector the state is being cut out of the equation and power is being returned to the individual. I don't think anyone can comprehend the magnitude of the revolution we are in. I think it will be looked back on as an epoch in the evolution of mankind.

Questions are raised about democracy and who has the right to make our laws and if, in fact, democracy is in any way a sham/ineffective.

Systems theory: [1] Avoid errors in the system that arise by thinking the system to be something that it is not. [2] Be aware of the limitations of the system. By being aware of the nature of the system one can make deliberate adjustments; by avoiding use of the system for improper ends or in situations in which it cannot work or was not designed to work. [3] Use knowledge of the system to make use of the characteristics of the system to to improve its performance or to achieve some end. - Edward de Bono

Transparency / Opacity: We must know what the machine
was designed to do; plus know what it actually does!

DREAMS OF UTOPIA   335

Technoself

Perhaps this chapter raises more questions than it answers; because many of these same technology-related questions *(privacy, democracy, freedom etc)* are hotly debated on a world-wide basis.

For example, does Artificial Intelligence threaten mankind?

Stephen Hawking, the most famous scientist in the world today, thinks that is does. Ditto Bill Gates and Eton Musk. Perhaps the danger(s) of true *thinking machines* are at the very least a long way off. And if the history of AI is characterised by anything, it is *over-optimism, lack of understanding, and the constant overblown false claims made by researchers/reporters etc.* Nevertheless, if we can have, or do get, strong AI (with a pro-active/creative free-will), then this will challenge the public to redefine the boundaries of human nature, identity, and what it means to be human within an advancing technological society.

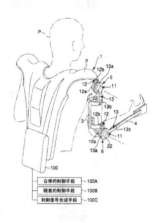

In the book '*Handbook of Research on TechnoSelf*'; editor Rocci Luppicini writes: Perhaps the most pervasive precursor of the technoself over the last three decades is derived from the notion of 'cyborg' (cybernetic organism) which refers to beings with both biological and artificial parts.

Haraway writes; We are all chimeras, theorised and fabricated hybrids of machine and organism; in short, we are cyborgs.[12]

Galvin and Luppicini (2011) describes *homotechnicus*:

> Animals are naturally endowed with the necessary instruments for their interaction with the rest of the nature; the human being is born without these means but has the possibility of building artificial instruments, since he himself is an artificial creature, in the sense that artificial is what is formalised by freedom and not by instinct. The original condition of man requires the free interaction with the material cosmos to produce technology. At the end, man is homotechnicus. [12]

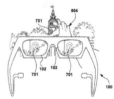

With similar sentiments in mind, the term '*self-computer*' is equated to *homotechnicus* and *technoself*; and describes the evolving configurations of human-technological relationships that continually shape the human condition and what it means to be a human being.[12]

< {44} Self-Computer = merging of human(s) with computers/systems/machines. >

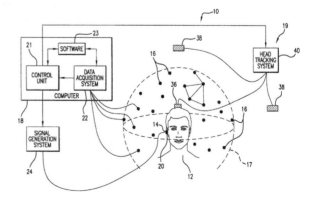

Complex operations are made up from the interaction of simple processes. It is (often) difficult to see how the units or operations come together. - Edward de Bono

What is the world's oldest running computer and/or code?
Well, the computers onboard some of the oldest spacecrafts like
Pioneer 10 (1972), Voyager I and II (1977) are still running.

Human versus Electronic Brains...

Artificial brains are influencing and controlling many (or most) aspects of our lives.

Examples of machine control (plus invisible powers) include...

- The number of powered CPUs (Silicon Brains) surpasses humans by a vast number (a quick count finds approx. 50 CPUs in my house). There are over three billion personal computers in the world; and the total number of (powered-up) CPUs must be around 100-1000 times greater (at least).

- Numerous are the number of times that you come into contact with a computer each day (in a live interaction sense); whereby it decides what happens next; including logging on to a system, receiving emails, tweeting, texting, Internet searching, driving your car, entering a secure building, traveling by train or jet, buying food, changing the temperature on your boiler etc.

- Frightening is how many times an artificial brain processes data about you, without you even knowing that it has happened; because not only can you never find this out, but you cannot even discover why this happens, its effects, or the basis of the decisions that have been made as a result.

- Terrifying is that our entire society is today wholly controlled by automatic and semi-automatic systems. How so? Consider how many systems are under automated computer control. Nuclear power stations, rockets, satellites, transport systems, nuclear and weapons systems, stock markets, the Internet (obviously), social security and hospital systems etc. Many of these same systems are networked together whereby a change in one small part of a system may affect events in another entirely separate system; and in ways that we may not (fully) understand.

- We need to consider the effects of the _Randomization of Decision Making_ as a result of computers! Knowing that many computers work together to set the price of petrol, electricity and food etc; and through automatic stock market trading; leads one to suppose that the larger system itself (the world trading system) may be no longer fully rational, and because of the networked affect(s) of all these computer brains working together. If one computer made a slightly unusual trading decision; could this not trigger anarchy? It happened in 1987 when the markets in Europe first went electronic. What's to stop it happening again?

- Imagine if the entire Internet crashed, GPS dropped for good, or a world-wide airport transponder network failed etc. How would this affect the stock market, food, transport systems and power supplies etc. Does anyone even know the answer? Remember the Internet has no central control, and it can/may crash for unknown reasons / hacks etc.

- The upshot is that countless decisions are made by electronic brains that may greatly affect your life, now and in the future; with or without your knowledge, and using logic that you cannot see, and which may (in fact) be faulty and/or break your (or other people's) human rights.

- Who is making the major decisions in your life: Humans or Machines? Can you even find out?

- Does a machine, someplace, somewhere, have the power to end the world (by itself)—and does anyone even know if this is in fact the case? What would be the machine's triggers?

- Has the End-of-Days already been programmed into the logic of computer(s)?

- Who is managing / coordinating all of the machines. Obviously NOBODY IS!

Be afraid, be very afraid. Electronic Brains are making most of the decisions!

And in ways that we do not understand, hence we cannot predict what will be the end result(s).

Chapter Fifteen
City of Thoughts

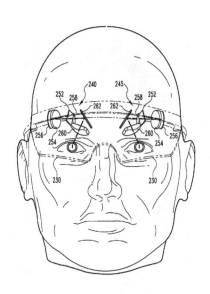

COMPUTERS CAN be a tremendous humanising, organising and collaborative force within society; giving humans the ability to think/ act *freely and ethically (and for the true benefit of all).*

In particular computers (potentially) allow humans to come together, and to form creative and transcendent solutions to the significant challenges of the future. Accordingly, a basic assumption of the present book is that computers can unite humanity; *aligning our needs, wishes and plans with industrial processes;* and through machines that foster collective freedom of thought/action.

We had identified social cohesion *(with respect to the amalgamated 'thoughts' of humanity)*; as precisely what is wrong with today's systems. Accordingly we asked a number of questions. Is man on a journey without a goal? Are we failing to recognise that technology is broadly life-centred; instead of work or power-centred? Who is designing today's systems, and for what purpose(s)?

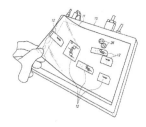

Sir Lewis Mumford said:

> Evidence abounds that irrational obsessions and compulsions have been feeding and encouraging computer systems that foster centralised, anti-social and sub-optimal power structures. With the result that humans are left *powerless, directionless, incompetent, mentally defective, and even psychotic.*[18]

Evidently, we need to restore man to the vital free-thinking functions that he has lost. [1,4,8,13,14] The phenomena of life are influenced by a vast array of closely-felt but often remotely created forces, some obvious, others only remotely perceived. And the same are forces formed by, created inside of, and promulgated/enforced by media, machines, systems and computers.[5,11,12]

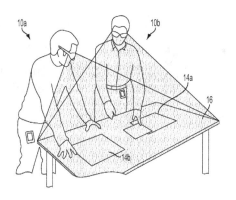

Machines are: logocentric (cf. humans: analogy centric); point-centric (cf. shape-centric); mechano-centric (cf. life-centric); use focus-logic (cf. water-logic); not self-aware; use hierarchical processing (cf. humans: parallel processing; have purely reflexive free-will (cf. creative free-will).

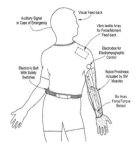

We have named these same forces *('lumped' together)*; the self-computer, and accordingly listed examples of the ways that human life is constructed and influenced by, plus delimited and restricted/controlled by, these powers.

Henceforth, the question of how to bring ethics, morality and democracy back to the design of automatic systems are essential ones. More specifically, how can we create computers that bring *freedom, ownership and equality* to our thoughts. In response, we have chosen a two-pronged attack; firstly looking in detail at what thoughts actually are, in and of themselves. Secondly we examined the nature of machines/ computers/systems at the most fundamental level(s).

Machines and Computers

Definitions of such terms are difficult to pin down, since the scope of man-made items that would seem to qualify under these headings, appears to be especially broad.

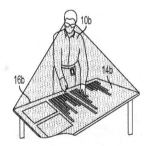

In particular we have limited our analysis to the metaphysical aspects of computers; and focussed on those aspects of computing 'machines' that relate to human thought, thinking and mental processes.

Some experts view machines/computers as extensions of man's control over himself/society. And the doctrine that *man is a machine* was argued long ago and most forcibly by La Mettrie; who also postulated a type of machine self-evolution; and that there is (or may be) no clear distinction between living and dead matter.[16] If man is a machine (in any way), then perhaps it is also arguable that he is a type of computer, or a processor and user of information. In chapters 3, 6 and 11 we presented extensive argument(s) as to the contrary view; that man—and life—are in fact not machine(s) (inherently); and that a sharp and unbridgeable distinction can be made between the two classes of entity.

In particular key differences hinged around arguments over free-will, self-determination; and above all that life exhibits a supreme *flexibility of purpose*.[5,9,14]

Life is multi-adaptive; in design, strategy, functions and goals.

Ultimately, the whole business of computing rests on the simple process whereby a switch can change from one state to another state, from on to off or the other way around. Millions of such switches arranged in different ways, in space or time, are the basis of computing. The elaboration of a few basic principles gives rise to the richest musical symphony. - Edward de Bono

However it may be that man is rendering his own life into a mechanical form *himself*; and through a mechanisation/automation of the various parameters of life; thereby 'systemising' its *structures, processes, ways and means of living*. Evidently machines are automating/crystallising the previously 'open' possibilities that were once (naturally) available to man (individually and collectively). It is difficult to argue against the evidence that man (partly) creates himself; through language, social structures, and using the laws and mechanisms of life etc.

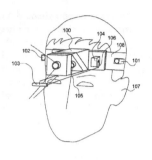

In many cases this remoulding of self is beneficial, desired and/or essential to efficient social operation(s). Nevertheless it is a basic assumption of the present thesis that this man-making process must be managed; and in all cases where systems and machines are used to help, that we must match needs and desires with actions; and in open, fair, moral and democratic ways.

In a way all of these issues come down to thoughts; and to finding ways to encourage beneficial thinking and associated 'good' thought-outcomes. Accordingly we ask our selves what thoughts are, how they come to be and exist/operate within a society. How can we recognise 'true' or beneficial thoughts?

What are Thoughts?

Questions surrounding the nature of thought (evidently) contain deep mysteries; and philosophers have long sought to unlock the origin(s) of thought/thinking. Our approach has been to find ways for computers to aid/facilitate natural thinking processes; and to encourage the aforementioned freedom(s) of thought that may be said to underpin a free society.

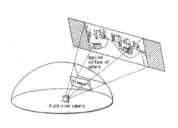

Accordingly, the present thesis lies at the intersection of thought and action, computer design and utopian ideas of an ideal society and/or the creation of humanistic techno-future(s).

We began with thought itself. In Chapter 5, we had identified ten basic properties (Attributes) of natural thoughts; and assumed is that a thought-atom is a pattern that reflects a real-world pattern and/or imaginary pattern *(in both specified and unspecified and/or mysterious way(s))*. Thoughts are often the result or a product of spontaneous acts of thinking.

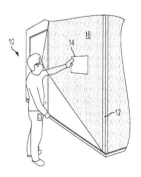

Simple basic units can be built up into complicated structures capable of complicated functions. But when one starts from complicated structures or functions then it is not so easy to see the basic processes. - Edward de Bono

YOU ARE NOT A GADGET

If observation of you yields data that makes it easier for a robot to seem like a natural conversationist, or for a political campaign to target voters with its message, then you ought to be owed money for the use of that valuable data. It wouldn't exist without you, after all.

The idea that mankind's information should be made free is idealistic, and understandably popular, but information wouldn't need to be free if it weren't impoverished... (we need a) move towards paid information with a stronger middle class than ever before... the way we are reorganising our world around digital networks is not sustainable.

As you read this, thousands of remote computers are refining secret models of who you are. What is so interesting about you that you are worth spying on... if things don't change, those who own the top machines will gradually emerge as the only elite left standing.

(on hypocrisy of technical folk) Surveillance by the technical few on the less technical many can be tolerated for now because of hopes for an endgame in which everything will become transparent to everyone... (This is what some (arch technocrats) imagine)... eventually, there will be no more secrets, no more barriers to access, all the world will be opened up as if the planet were transformed into a crystal ball. In the meantime, those true believers encrypt their servers even as they seek to gather the rest of the world's information and find the best way to leverage it. It is all too easy to forget that 'free' inevitably means that someone else will be deciding how you live.

Jaron Lanier

Thoughts will have physical and metaphysical origins, prescribed processes and effects etc, and be objective/abstract. Accordingly, the question of how meaning is assigned/encapsulated into thoughts is a fundamental and important one.

Evidently, we are what we think (or mean).

Thinking refers to the capacity to think, reason or imagine; and to the consideration of, or reflection on, an idea/theory/event etc. Thoughts may be fully-formed, or half-formed, and be anticipations of, or judgments of, objects, events and processes. We consider, attend to, regard and take notice of thoughts. Our ideas may be characteristic of a particular place, time and/or class of thinking. Thoughts may or may not: *take place entirely in the human brain, be conscious or unconscious, be expressed in a language, be formal/informal, and involve other concepts/ways-of-evaluating such as drawing analogies, interpreting, evaluating, imagining, planning, and remembering.* It is also a fundamental premise of the present book that thoughts originate in the human mind (sentient lifeforms), and thus cannot arise from inanimate matter, computers or artificial intelligence (AI).

In this book we have analysed the practical aspects of thinking, and had wished to learn how to help man to *think useful thoughts.* We sought a theory of right-thinking practice; that is *ethical, humane and democratic thinking methods, techniques, mechanisms etc.*

But what (precisely) is the nature of thinking?

A fairly modern approach to thinking is taken by phenomenology, or study of the structures of experience and consciousness. According to phenomenology, experience is the source of all knowledge, and (therefore) everything known has a (perhaps remote) origin in physical reality.

An important element of phenomenology that Edmund Husserl (1859-1938) developed, is intentionality (often described as 'aboutness'), the notion that consciousness is always consciousness *of* something. The object of thought is called the *intentional object,* and this object is constituted for consciousness in many different ways; and through, for instance, *perception, memory, retention and protection, signification etc.*

Free-will > It all depends where one draws the boundary for self: whether self includes the determining factors or is supposed to stand apart from them.

Edward de Bono

In other words, when a reference is made to a thing's *essence* or *idea*, what one 'really' sees (in one's mind) are only partial sides and aspects, specific surfaces etc; and it does not mean that the thing is only and exclusively what is conceived of and/or perceived. The thing-in-itself always contains aspects that escape detection.

Another problem relates to how we humans build up enduring patterns of meaning. Established are complex rules for so doing; for example we have universal and particulars, multiple and parallel links between items of knowledge, as well as hierarchical and topical structures etc. The problem in relation to tying down meaning for any particular thought-atom, is that a single referent (or sign) may 'stand-in', link-to and/or subsume whole patterns of thought and meaning.

Furthermore these patterns of meaning (that are pointed at) may not be 'directly' referred to, but be somehow assumed. Implicitly when 'experts' or close friends communicate they often use shortcuts that assume that much of the context of any particular thought-atom is already known and/or is already involved/active in changing the meaning of the communicated thought-atom(s). In Chapter 12 we named this modal property the selection capacity of the representation (c.f. the beholder's share in art etc).

Diversity of Meaning

There are also different types of thought, for example, thoughts that we use to help us to think, and to consider etc. We employ various logical rules, fixed thought structures/patterns/templates, and the syntax of language to convey meaning etc. Examples of semi-rigid thoughts; include *scientific theories, concepts, principles, object-classes, stories, laws and/or socially acceptable topics, word meanings (perhaps) etc.*

All thoughts normally fit into patterns in one way or another. However despite significant philosophical studies on the nature of thinking/thoughts, language etc; we find no standard rules and/or patterns for thoughts in general.

Liquid-forms, free-flows and changing patterns predominate.

END OF THE PAST

'The past is a foreign country' wrote novelist L.P.Hartly in 1953, 'They do things differently there.' But in the digital era the past is now the present and all around us. Millions of out of print books and historical video-clips, black and white movies, nearly forgotten TV shows and pop songs, are all available with a credit card or in many cases for free. We are now living in a history glut; the Internet has muddled the line between past and present. Spotify, Netflix, Apple TV and YouTube have all now built enormous databases based on organising the past for commercial exploitation. Old is just as easy to consume as new! Our past gets closer and closer to the present and the line separating our now from our then disappears. The past is never dead, its not even past.

Paul Ford

END OF UNPLUGGING

The practice of taking an intentional break from technology and civilisation is probably as old as technology and civilisation. But is seems increasingly urgent now, in an era when the Internet and most of the planet is as close as an IPhone. We go to seek 'WALDEINSANKEIT', as the poet Ralph Waldo Emerson described it; the feeling of being alone in the woods. We are living in a remarkable time, when it will soon be impossible to be truly alone. The phone isn't the problem. The problem is us, our inability to step away from our email and games and inessential data, our inability to look up, be it at an alpine lake or with family members. We need to learn how to live with a persistent connection, everywhere we go.

Mat Honan

Vince Cerf, Google's vice-president, has warned that 'bit rot' could lead to a 'forgotten century' as our masses of digital files are lost to progress and become unreadable as technology evolves. Cerf said that the applications to read files are being lost because they will no longer run on newer computers, rendering some files unintelligible and the data, memories and important happenings they contain lost to future generations.

With an approach known as whole brain emulation (WBE), the idea is that if we can perfectly copy the functional structure of the brain, we will create software perfectly analogous to one.

Overall, we can conclude that:

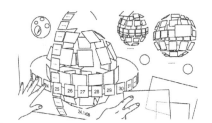

- There is no identifiable foundation for thought
- No universal standard(s) exist for thoughts
- No ultimate context is possible for a single thought
- No universality of meaning exists for any individual thought
- No ultimate or singular unity exists for any thought
- Thoughts are (re-suable) ideas that result from thinking
- Thoughts may have physical or metaphysical origins
- Thoughts may identify facts, objectives, dreams, beliefs and desires etc.
- Thoughts allow us to make plans / predictions
- Thoughts may be transformed into action (by machines/humans)
- Thoughts may be fully formed, or half-formed
- Thoughts may anticipate/judge: objects, events and processes
- The ego-subject places thoughts in its own context
- Thoughts may have a plurality of parts
- Machines consists (wholly) of implanted-thoughts
- Human knowledge is comprised (solely) of open-thoughts; hence these thoughts must be TRULY open and freely available to all

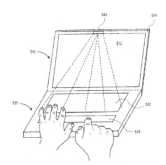

Station Points on a Journey / Path

Earlier we had mentioned that we would 'later-on' discuss the relationships of thoughts, information and data. Well I would like to suggest that not much discussion is required in this respect, and because data is recognised (in all cases) as being composed wholly of reality-informed thoughts, or thoughts that are (partially) open to the environment in some specific way.

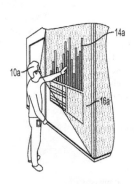

So we either observe a particular feature of the world ourselves (*e.g. noting down a set of facts/measurements*), or instruct our machines/systems to notice said feature(s) automatically. Herein the specific data items are by no means independent units in and of themselves, but have in all cases been largely/purely prescribed (foreshadowed) by the thoughts that comprised the act of 'looking'; and hence the form/types of data collected/received.

How a thing works will depend on the pieces that have been chosen and how they are put together. - Edward de Bono

In order to make any progress one tries to get away from words as things in themselves and tries to use them only as descriptions of other things which exist in their own right. - Edward de Bono

Scientists hope to create software that could theoretically experience everything we experience: emotion, addiction, ambition, consciousness, and suffering.

CITY OF THOUGHTS   343

Likewise information is recognised as being a type of data (or thought-pattern) that is further processed and/or perceptually constructed/conformed; whereby once again meaning is dependent upon the nature of the thought-pattern that *'set the perception/ judgement processes in motion'* and/or prescribed its form in some way.

Thoughts can only have a fully defined meaning from a particular standpoint, or point of view. There are many ego or 'thinker' station points (even for an individual), and infinitely varied contexts of use. It follows that all open thoughts must be available for use anywhere, within any argument, and for establishing the ultimate truth or falsehood of any proposition. False/immoral/evil thoughts are (or may be) signposts on the way to truth, hence there are no universally determined meanings for thought-atoms; and there can be no evil thoughts, sans context.

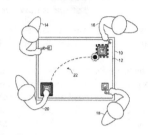

If we were to assign universal and fixed meanings to thought-atoms; then they cannot be used flexibly in all (or many) different situations; and we have delimited or reduced:

- The number of concepts/viewpoints that may be represented / expressed within the field of human thought (logon content).

- The number of thoughts that can be thought (metron content).

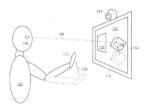

Thoughts are sometimes like letters in an alphabet—and are posited to hold no (specific) meaning whatsoever; and until they are assembled into an appropriate context. Sometimes one must consider multiple contexts to assign specific meaning(s); and to understand a situation in its true light. As an example, consider the expression *'It is wrong to kill'*. But what about killing animals for instance. Ok let us refine this statement to *'It is wrong to kill a human being'*. Well what about when the person himself asks you to, and because he is in pain and/or already dying. On the other hand, what if the same person is mentally ill, or constantly changes his/her mind.

I think you will agree that context is important in this respect, and that it is vitally important to determine the true meaning and morality of the statement in question.

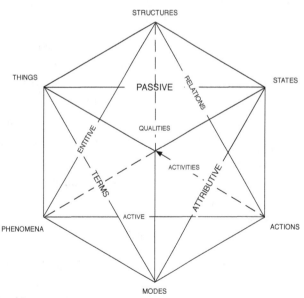

Figure 7: The Holotheme
as devised by Professor J.L.Jolley

Any given man sees only a tiny portion of the total truth, and very often, in fact almost perpetually, he deliberately deceives himself about that little precious fragment as well. - Philip K. Dick

SEPARATION BETWEEN BITS AND ATOMS

The trial separation between bits and atoms is now over.

We had become inseparable from our increasingly capable electronic organs; our very limbs has become fleshy antenna supports; our interconnections has ramified and intensified to an almost incomprehensible degree. From prenatal imaging and heartbeat monitoring to posthumous persistence of our digital addresses and traces, our bodies now existed in a state of continuous electronic engagement with their surroundings.

Thing-to-thing relationships has similarly mutated. Digital networks had begun as collections of large, expensive boxes connected by cheap wires. But over time the boxes got smaller, cheaper, and more numerous, while the wires remained much the same. Increasingly, then, it was the wiring of networks, not the boxes, that consumed space and cost money... By the dawn of the twenty-first century, though, inexpensive, ubiquitous wireless connections were linking whole new classes of things into networks—very tiny things, very numerous things, very isolated things, highly mobile things, things embedded in other things, and things that were jammed into tight and inaccessible places... Now nothing need be without processing power, and nothing need be left unlinked. The distinction between computer hardware and more traditional sorts of hardware was rapidly fading.

William J. Mitchell

In the book *2081: A Hopeful View of the Human Future*; Gerard K. O'Neil said:

- First in importance, guard the freedom of ideas at all costs.

- Be alert that dictators have always played on the natural human tendency to blame others and to oversimplify.

- And don't regard yourself as a guardian of freedom unless you respect and preserve the rights of the people you disagree with to free, public, unhampered expression.

O'Neil draws our attention to the diversity of human thought-forms; and to the need for *disagreement, debate and freedom of opinion*; and to the vital importance of being able to see a fact/opinion from many different points of view.

Good judgement possess a panoramic vision; being one that also penetrates right to the heart of the matter. We are reminded here of an evident symmetry between real world atoms and digital bits; in that each and every unit or atom may (potentially) influence (any) other in the most profound, and sometimes unexpected, and/or implicit ways.

Machine-Implanted Thoughts

Moving on to consider machines, or machine implanted-thoughts; we ask how it is possible (in a like manner) to determine singular meanings and fixed contexts-of-use for machines, and so to examine/determine their precise (and multifarious) effects on human life? Evidently, we wish to map machine implanted-thoughts to outcomes and influences; and in this way to assign responsibility to machine designs/actions/influences. As we saw in Chapter 6, tying down, or isolating, machine influences is very problematical.

Today it often appears that the designers/owners of computer systems succeed in hiding/covering-up most design decisions, forms, influences etc. Companies like Google, Facebook, and Amazon etc; are very secretive; and (for example) try to cover up the wholesale monitoring and control of user activities/data.

But every machine-implanted thought (or design) has a human designer—and hence can be assigned to a responsible source.

A model is a method of transferring some relationship or process from its actual setting to a setting where it is more conveniently studied. In a model, relationships and processes are preserved unchanged, though the things that are being related may be changed. All models involve transformation of relationships from their original setting into another. - Edward de Bono

In '*M++: The Cyborg Self and the Networked City*'; William J Mitchell commented:

> The virtual and physical were imagined as separate realms-cyberspace and meatspace, as William Gibson named these two 'spaces'... (but)... Networked intelligence is being embedded everywhere, in every kind of physical system—both natural and artificial. Routinely, events in cyberspace are being reflected in physical space, and vice versa... Bits don't just sit out there in cyberspace, to be visited occasionally like pictures in a gallery or poked at through a 'window' (telling metaphor). It makes more sense to recognise that invisible, intangible, electromagnetically encoded information establishes new types of relationships among *physical* events occurring in *physical* places. A bit is indeed a 'difference that makes a difference', but we should think of that difference as something concrete, with definite spatial and temporal coordinates—such as the opening or closing of some particular switch, door, or floodgate etc—rather than a change in value of an abstract variable. Bits organised into code now constitute the most powerful means we have for expressing intentions and translating them into actions.

According to this view, it becomes essential to create machines and media that render visible any and all relationships present; and in particular the ways in which systems structure and/or influence human thinking. In the language of the present book, we wish to create efficient thought-spaces that foster the effective operational-flow(s) of thoughts; and hence to free-up the circuits-of-thought. But the question remains of how to do so within a specific thought-space.

Embodied intelligence is essential here; and 'joined-up' thinking is required; whereby many little-worlds must be fully connected and inter-joined with the big-world (or larger human-world) of which everything is a part.[17]

Words such as self, free-will, humour, insight etc are useful as catalogue descriptions for the purpose of communication, but useless as explanations.
Edward de Bono

CO-EVOLUTION OF MEN AND MACHINES

I am suggesting, machines are mechanical—all too mechanical, to paraphrase Nietzsche. But, in saying this, I am also saying that they are all too human as well. The question, then, is are we to repeat the real Frankenstein story and by turning from the 'monsters' we have created also turn away from our own humanity or, alternatively, are we to accept the back-blow to our egos and enter a fourth discontinuity? ... humans are on the threshold of decisively breaking past the discontinuity between themselves and machines. On the one hand, humans are ending the discontinuity because they now can perceive their own evolution as inextricably interwoven with their use and development of tools, of which the modern machines is only the furthest extrapolation. We cannot think realistically any longer of the human species without a machine. On the other hand, the discontinuity is being bridged because humans now perceive that the same scientific concepts help explain the workings of themselves and their machines... (therefore) the sharp discontinuity between humans and machines is no longer tenable, in spite of the shock to our egos.

Bruce Mazlish

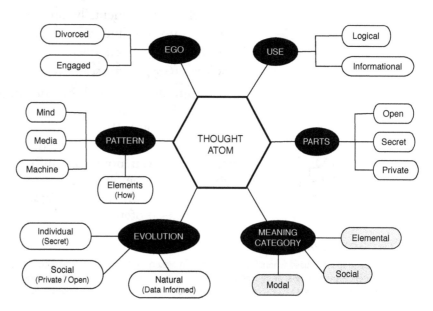

Figure 8 : The Thought Atom

Computers can only 'see' the wiggling end of our fingers,
they cannot see and employ the rest of our body. - Brian Eno

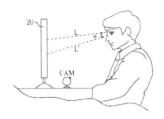

Accordingly we ask, if thoughts may be said to run a society (they do); then what does this mean? Well it means that we must create wholly beneficial, optimal, and humane thoughts *(plus socially-responsible machine implanted-thoughts)*; and then share/implant the 'best' thoughts into our creations as desired. But how are the best and most optimal thoughts created? How does a single human mind construct/think such thoughts? Or how do many minds construct/form/interlace the best thoughts together into serviceable/favourable ensembles?

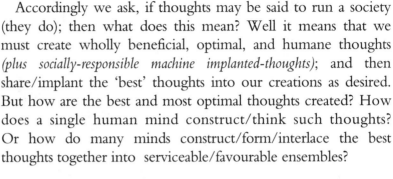

World Brain

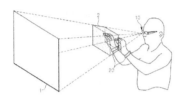

Earlier we spoke about the concept of a World Brain, which we defined as hyper-thoughts seen in hyper-contexts; and all existing on a hyper-network. A hyper-thought is one that is linked to any/all of its contexts of use; (i.e it has hyper-context); plus with all related annotations and comments visible etc. Hyper-thoughts are obviously *fictional* at the present epoch, since no computer network yet exists (today) that could even theoretically provide such a capability; but please do not assign hyper-thoughts as a mere fancy; or conflate them with an impenetrable impracticality.

Fully detailed in Chapter 9 is how to implement an atomic network that may provide/offer hyper-thoughts—and for all the worlds thought-atoms/data.

The problem of how to deliver hyper-thoughts in hyper-contexts, can be explained in another way; by stating that that the web is fundamentally broken, and because an interested party has no (possible) way to find an individual thought-atom that may be hidden deep inside a web-page, document or book etc (**Google** type searching did not solve this problem).

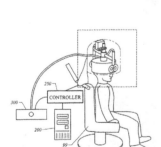

Put simply, universal broadcasting/sharing of thoughts is severely limited with the current Web (for everyone apart from the famous). What about social websites like **Facebook** and **Twitter**? Here broadcasting of thoughts becomes a little easier because you can now send information to close friends; and subjects can be 'tagged'; grouping conversations/topics together. Plus software like **Napster** and **BitTorrent** allow people to share files (potentially) with millions of other people.

THOUGHT-SPACES

A thought-space is used when: Reading: a book, magazine, theory, article, chapter, story, etc; Watching a movie; Considering/producing a: design, object, engineering plan; Considering/using a: house, car, city, mechanism, machine etc; and Whilst using/designing a: computer, computer program etc. A whole science/ecology of thought-spaces is possible.

You'll be able to 'see into' movies, pictures, rooms, web-pages, and books seamlessly. (Wired)

CITY OF THOUGHTS   347

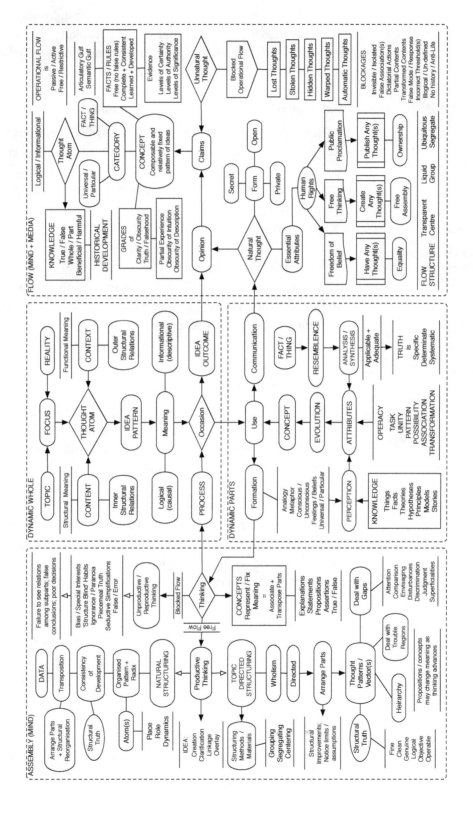

Figure 9: Flow-chart representation of a Thought-Space

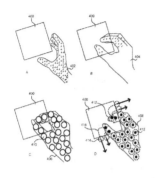

HUMAN EVOLUTION

After all, nature may be taken to imply all that is within the universe (man-made objects/ systems/processes included), not simply light and air, wind and water. Nothing is gained or lost even though man juggles about to suit his needs, desires, or capricious whims. The atom bomb may be thus construed as part of nature, for if it is not, then what can it be? Even if the pessimists are proved to be correct and a creature that is 100 percent artificial holds sway (over mankind), it may not be unfair to say that this too is natural evolution, no matter how unfortunate we may consider such an eventuality from where we sit.... we shall consider man very much a part of nature, (although) he has hastened, exosomatic evolution... (thus)... man is now an important factor in his own development... not only has he changed his environment, but he has also gotten to work on himself.

D.S.Halacy (1965)

However individual thoughts, or data/thought-atoms (micro-thoughts in Kim Veltman's terms); are still largely disconnected, unlinked and hidden deep-inside a great diversity of different systems and/or isolated documents etc. In our terms the vast majority of thoughts/concepts are lost, hidden, unconnected; and exist as black-thoughts, and/or memory holes etc.

Note that a **black-thought** is a (possibly) relevant thought-atom that has become lost/hidden/ignored/un-linked from a specific contextual pattern, in that the 'parent' thought-pattern may appear to be logically consistent (i.e. true) in and of itself; and according to both internal and external structures; however because (some) potentially related thoughts are 'black' or invisible; then the structure (as a whole) may be incomplete and/or false/sub-optimal (ref. shallow-context).

We can conclude that the vast majority of open and/or socially published thoughts are (on present day knowledge-systems) lost, and therefore the predominant form(s) for all of the open-thoughts of humanity is to exist in a black/invisible form.

<{45} The vast majority of open-thoughts (today) are black-thoughts; being lost, hidden and/or invisible ones. >

We are utterly blind with respect to the linkage/assembly of the vast majority of thought-atoms; and with current Internet technology. There is no point even trying to estimate the amount of information/knowledge that is missing from the current Web as a result, and because not even a single word/idea/thought/vote exists in its rightful hyper-context; and because that would require (for a 'common' idea like God)—millions upon millions of—categorised forward and backward links, and probably tens of thousands of overlaid (and categorised) comments, annotations etc; and for each related thought/data-atom etc.

Radiant should be each and every hyper-idea; with vast numbers of related thought-patterns visible. For example, all the (actually existent) 'lines-of-thought' that emanate from the idea of God should be topically categorised and interlinked in every possible way (*reflecting its hyper-context*).

< {46} Hyper-thoughts = Ideas/votes with hyper-context. >

To be truly efficient/effective, a thought-space should gradually improve, in terms of clarity, truthfulness, knowledge content, usefulness, applicability etc. You need to be able to see all of the linked-to and sub-thought spaces in sufficient detail/clarity also; and in order to be able to understand how these shape your thinking process (in the immediate thought-space), and so to be able to identify useful theories, concepts etc; and to know what assumptions and contexts your thinking outcomes are going to be based upon.

Long the domain of science fiction, researchers are now working to create software that perfectly models human and animal brains.

CITY OF THOUGHTS   349

Hence our ***thought-horizons/thought-scapes*** could be greatly expanded—and almost beyond the limits of our present understanding/imagination; and the *depth, clarity, history and linkage* of everything to everything else would be made visible for the first time. Currently we are stuck with ***mini-think*** in terms of our analysis of a concept such as God; but imagined is a way to see the concept in its true hyper-context(s); whereby everything *(i.e. all the related open thoughts)* become visible or ***white-thoughts***.

Desired is a brain—a World Brain—because the various parts of the brain, or the individual people/thinkers/ thoughts; must be able to see and influence each other, and to conceptualize what all the different pieces of the brain are thinking. And this problem has important ramifications for human society generally. It has long been supposed that the intentional attitudes—beliefs, desires, intentions—have a central place in the aetiology of intelligent behaviour.

Perhaps we need to return (once again) to Aristotle. He said that action has two components; *intentional* and *causal*. What one does does depends in some measure on what one believes. However at the present epoch it seems that we (as a species) do not even know what we believe (or think collectively) and hence we consign beneficial action to pure chance. Once again context is everything; and we need to see all open thought-atoms in their proper context(s). Desired is a way to render visible what are the thoughts of everyone, everywhere. Humanity must know what it is thinking/doing, and in the broadest possible context(s).

Language and Knowledge

We live inside a pyramid of technologies just like living at the apex of time, and likewise we often think that we live at the apex of technology; and it is tempting to conclude that technologies must all be *correct and/or finished/beneficial/useful etc.* This is not true however, and because computer programs and machines are (one and all) embedded with highly specific (planned) purposes; and have biases/political-goals which (for example) attempts to turn human attention into a commodity (ref. **Google, Facebook** advertising etc)!

CYBORGS

The cyborg concept, says: You wish to go into space? Then equip yourself with new forms of energy transformation so that you can live comfortably and 'naturally' in space. Fish, build yourself a lung! ... In our mist, and growing steadily in numbers, is the latest evolutionary step in man, sometimes called by the odd name of 'cyborg'.

Julian Huxley, the eminent biologist, sees not one evolution, but three. First there is evolution on the cosmic scale, the 'stellar evolution' of the universe that set the stage for the second kind of evolution, that of biological evolution. Finally, there is social evolution, which stems from the actions and interactions of the individual products of biological evolution. What will be the result of the new evolution? Julian Huxley suggested the term 'transhuman' for a superior being aware of his potential and able to work toward it because of his knowledge.

As defined by Dr Clynes, a cyborg —an abbreviation for 'cybernetic organism' - is an 'exogenously extended organisational complex functioning as an integrated homeostatic system unconsciously'. More simply, a cyborg is the joining of a living thing with a nonliving device or devices. A moment's thought will bring to mind many such couplings, and the term can be interpreted broadly enough to include the homeliest man-machine combination or in a narrower sense to mean only quite complex systems.

D.S. Halacy (1965)

Maybe each human being lives in a unique world, a private world different from those inhabited and experienced by all other humans... If reality differs from person to person, can we speak of reality singular, or shouldn't we really be talking about plural realities? And if there are plural realities, are some more true (more real) than others? - Philip K. Dick

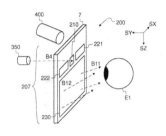

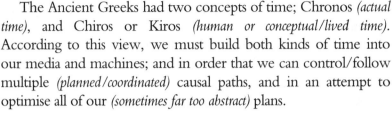

The Ancient Greeks had two concepts of time; Chronos *(actual time)*, and Chiros or Kiros *(human or conceptual/lived time)*. According to this view, we must build both kinds of time into our media and machines; and in order that we can control/follow multiple *(planned/coordinated)* causal paths, and in an attempt to optimise all of our *(sometimes far too abstract)* plans.

Hence for the Greeks, who wanted to control/direct/create the future by arranging the past (4th cause); at any present moment if you have not already 'arranged' the atoms/energy *(using conceptual time to direct physical time)* in such a manner as to bring about a desired result, then it is already too-late. Because an unpredictable or raw causal time *(and to some extent an invisible/unexpected/accidental causality)* and hence chaos would be the result of *'just letting things develop as they may'*.

Accordingly human understanding must be maximised— with respect to the use of both human and actual time(s). We must build a modern example of the **Speculum Maius**—the great mirror reflecting everything known—so that we can begin to see the vast scale of everything and how strong/complex are the effects of all the connections *(i.e. natural, technical and human ones)*.

Now ask yourself, what if every thought left its permanent mark somewhere? Within such a mirror no open-thought could possibly be left behind, existing as they did in a type of vast 'immortal' library. However comprehensive collections have their own dangers/drawbacks. In Jorge Luis Borges *'Labyrinths'* short stories (1963), a man who has perfect memory cannot think properly or reason in the abstract, and he cannot sleep because it means turning off his mind from the world. In his most famous story *'The Library of Babel'*, Borges tells of a fictional library containing countless books and that holds all possible knowledge. But it's a knowledge that is not indexed (just like the Web!); and for each book that is true and correct, there will be countless books that are less correct, false or blatantly wrong.

Separating truth from fiction, and beneficial from harmful ideas/thoughts etc; is extremely difficult as a result of a complete lack of debate/opinion etc. Clouded vision results.

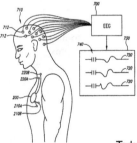

Today we live in a society in which spurious realities are manufactured by the media, by governments, by big corporations, by religious groups, political groups... So I ask, in my writing, What is real? Because unceasingly we are bombarded with pseudo-realities manufactured by very sophisticated people using very sophisticated electronic mechanisms. I do not distrust their motives; I distrust their power. They have a lot of it. And it is an astonishing power: that of creating whole universes, universes of the mind. - Philip K. Dick

Digital metamorphosis—changes in our sense of the world through digital overlays of computer generated sound, video, graphics and positional data. - Wired

CITY OF THOUGHTS   351

The Self-Computer

We humans are merging with computers, and everywhere we see evidence of computers *controlling, shaping and influencing* everything we do, or can (possibly) do in both the physical and digital worlds. Obviously and patently, computers are not doing so by themselves; but rather in every case where a computer touches/influences the human world; then a human designer, computer controller/user, lies behind the instantiated action/restriction/information-transaction etc.

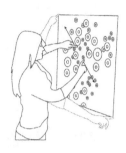

Desired is a new technopia, milieu or 'technological' Gaia; named the self-computer. In this book we sought to tackle related problems by urging a move towards collective thinking procedures.

As considered in Chapter 12, the innermost nucleus of Popper's World 3 (human creations) is the world of *problems, theories and criticism*. Although values do not belong to the nucleus, it is dominated by values; the values of **objective truth** and its growth. Truth is the highest value of all, and is a type of ultimate concept. But how do we determine, and uphold plus foster: truth? Popper asked himself the related question: **are problems, theories and arguments real; do they exist in the real world—and are they objective things.** He found that the answer is yes; and things/machines/systems can be decoded to analyse what values were used in their creation and what values they tend to propagate in the real world!

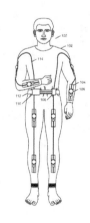

Accordingly, it is plain that we must code ethical values into the machines/systems/computers that make up all of World 3. But how do we do so? Popper believed that the answer lied in critical arguments, and in a supreme visibility of design forms; both prior to a systems deployment and also after its deployment. Essential is constant criticism of everything man-made; through *theories, stories, systems, models and computers etc*. In this respect, knowledge (open thought-atoms) is the *ultimate* human product; and accordingly, must be *ultimately* subject to social control/criticism.

< {47} Logical, ethical and moral truths (+ criticism) represent our highest value(s); and these must be built into the heart of the Self-Computer. >

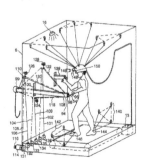

The omega point is where man is God and God is man, where all layers of the noosphere become involuted, fusing and consuming the All and the Person integrally in itself. - Teihard de Chardin

After the measurements of atoms and galaxies are folded into laws in some corners of our networks, there will still be universes of interrelationships in the rest of our networks to be discovered. - Arthur Koestler

Meaning

In Chapter 5 we gave a description of the *Theory of Natural Thoughts*, however we said little about how thoughts determine/specify/communicate meaning.

Thought meaning(s) can posses:

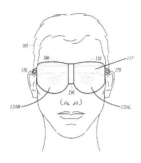

- Elemental Categories - Conceptual, Analogical, Relational
- Social Categories - Engagement(s), Assembly, and Influence
- Modal Categories - Thinker, Thought-space, Conversational

As formerly stated, the Elemental categories of thought (i.e. epistemological analysis) lie outside the present thesis; and would include all mind-bound thinking methods and perceptive processes, and anything related to *language, semantics, syntax, etc* (e.g. theory of mind). Earlier we delt with the Social Categories of Assembly, but largely avoided discussion of the related Engagements and Influences of thoughts *(because these relate to social and societal factors which lie outside our present analysis)*.

Noteworthy is that we have thus far overlooked the mechanisms and tools (or Modal Categories) that determine and influence the environment(s) in which thought assembly happens.

Thought-Spaces

We adopt a formal definition of a thought-space, which is a medium in which the thinking process takes place. This is assumed to be a combination of one or more human mind(s); merged with any mind-extending/shaping and/or mind-supporting method(s) and/ or communication/technological tools that may be said to exist *(and which aid in the creation/vision/sharing of new/old thought-patterns)*.

Obviously, thinking happens within human mind(s) *(and I claim never [yet] in machine/computer/robot 'minds')*. And here we shall overlook machine-implanted thoughts and cast aside all possibility of an artificial mind itself 'thinking' and label Artificial Intelligence as being (in actual fact) merely **Simulated Intelligence**; or thinking that possesses a purely reflexive form of free-will (N.B. critics must *prove* the opposite).

MUTUAL RESPECT

The fact remains that we must *have to do with each other* in the normal course of our lives—we must know each other—and therefore any genuine privacy can only be rooted in a deep and sensitive mutual respect. No technical gadgets can underwrite this sort of intimate respect; they can easily make it more difficult.

The alternative to intimate respect, is to isolate ourselves ever more from each other, taking refuge behind uncertain, shifting personas, remote forms of communication, and anonymous transactions, which we then call 'human freedom'. This can only lead to an abstract 'society' of automatons, inputs, and outputs. It may not matter whether you and I are really there, behind all the machinery of interaction, but at least we know ourselves to be free!

Stephen L. Talbott

An important difference exists between 'having-no' knowledge and having 'no-knowledge'. The former is a state of ignorance; the latter is one of ultimate enlightenment and universal sensibilities. - Stewart Brand (Whole Earth Catalogue)

We begin to realise that our brains are the most complex and self-determining things in the known universe. - Arthur Koestler

CITY OF THOUGHTS   353

A thought-space is established whenever a thinker or collective begins to think. This space consists of available language(s), knowledge(s), computer(s) etc, and may (or may not) reflect the thinker's entire history/education and/or the details of conversation(s) he/she is having (or has had) with others. Normally the thought-space itself consists of many visible referenced-thought spaces; as established and delimited by the rules of *language, logic, principle, science, culture etc*. It may be difficult for a thinker to 'see' how many, and what are the different thought-spaces he is using. And because thought-spaces are normally   partially constructed from technology; plus the *quality, efficiency and effectiveness* of any thought-space *(including its 'truth-content', evolution and/or logical development etc)*; these will be dependent on the design (forms) and evolution of said tools.

Thought-spaces are complex 'mini-worlds' of meaning that reflect human: *experience, theory, knowledge, propositions, deductions, stories etc*; and they dictate which thoughts may exist and/or be accepted into (or work within) a specific ensemble. A thought-space may be likened to 'patterned' element(s) of mind; and to be a place in which thinker(s) can obtain help: *perceiving situations, processing facts, making theories and deductions; forming conclusions and so creating, linking and establishing groups and assemblies of thoughts into useful groups and patterns*.

For an effective thought-space, all (relevant) sub/linked thought-spaces must be readily available and inter-connected in every (useful) way imaginable; and all available/used thoughts would (ideally) be hyper-thoughts with hyper-context. Examples of typical thought-space(s) are: when a thinker: *considers/works-out how to perceive/solve a problem, travel to a destination, make an object, contribute to a theory, write a book, walk along a path, consider a physics problem, watch a movie (entering another person's thought-space) etc*.

A World-Brain is the top-level 'hyper-linked' thought-space; and allows mankind, working together as unified collective, to think thoughts that are infinitely more *complex, relevant, specific, detailed, contextualised and humane/ethical etc*. Here every open-thought finds its true home(s), and a resplendent **city of thoughts** is born; being a World-Brain that allows everyone to visualise, shape and share all of our plans, ideas, votes and actions etc.

TRANSCENDING MACHINES

And it may also be the case (I believe it is the case) that what we have been imparting to the Net—or what the Net has been eliciting from us- is a half-submerged, barely intended logic, contaminated by wishes and tendencies we prefer not to acknowledge... we need to choose our future rather than compute it automatically and unawares. Not that freedom to choose brings predictability; it most certainly does not. It only makes us responsible. But out of that responsibility we can impose a worthy meaning upon the future.

(Manifesto of organisation: Digital Liberty) Digital Liberty believes that technology can set us free... the science of cryptology will finally and forever guarantee the unbreachable right of privacy, protecting individuals, groups, and corporations from the prying eyes and grasping hands of sovereigns. We will all be free to conduct our lives, and most importantly our economic relations, as we see fit.

One cannot embrace a *device* as the midwife of freedom without having lost sight of the living, ambiguous reality of freedom as an experience of alternative, *inner* stances. All that is left is a shadow of these stances, in the form of external, machine-mediated 'options'. Where freedom once required the fateful exercise of an enlightened, heart-warmed will, it is now enough to play with clickable choices on a screen.

Stephen L. Talbott

If this (communication) property could somehow be transferred into visible brightness so that it could stand forth more clearly to our senses, the biological world would become a walking field of light, and human beings would stand out like blazing suns of complexity, flashing bursts of meaning to each other through the dull night of the physical world between. We would hurt each other's eyes. Is this not so? - Arthur Koestler

Suddenly, everything has code beneath it; and everything you do,
and everything everyone does,
works according to the dictates of a computer.

Journalism is not a crime.

Communication is not a crime.

We should not be monitored in our everyday activity!

The powers of Big Brother have increased enormously;
and our expectation(s) of privacy have been reduced.

Democracy may die behind closed doors, but we as individuals
are born behind those same closed doors, and we do
not have to give up our privacy to have good government.

We don't have to give up our liberty to have security, and
by working together we can have both open
government and private lives.

Edward Snowden [Canada, 2014]

Information is power.

But like all power, there are those who want to keep it for themselves.
The world's entire scientific and cultural heritage, published over centuries
in books and journals, is increasingly being digitized and locked up by a
handful of private corporations.

Want to read the papers featuring the most famous results of the sciences?
You'll need to send enormous amounts to publishers like Reed Elsevier...

There are those struggling to change this.

The Open Access Movement has fought valiantly to ensure that scientists
do not sign their copyrights away but instead ensure
their work is published on the Internet, under terms that allow anyone
to access it. But even under the best scenarios, their work will only
apply to things published in the future.

Everything up until now will have been lost.

That is too high a price to pay.

Forcing academics to pay money to read the work of their colleagues?
Scanning entire libraries but only allowing the folks at Google to read
them? Providing scientific articles to those at elite universities in the
First World, but not to children in the Global South?

It's outrageous and unacceptable.

With enough of us, around the world, we'll not just send a strong message
opposing the privatization of knowledge—we'll make it a thing of the past.

Will you join us?

Aaron Swartz (Guerrilla Open Access Manifesto) [2008]

Chapter Sixteen
Technopia

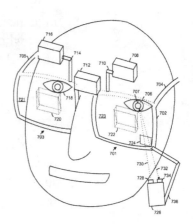

A LL STORIES must come to an end; and the present one is no different. But endings do differ (i.e. you can have happy or sad; optimistic/pessimistic ones etc). Hopefully, the reader takes lessons learned and integrates them into his/her own life; and if not what has been the point. Accordingly, this book ends with a brief overview of where we have been, and where we may be going—*individually and collectively*— and with respect to the self-computer.

My own time spent writing the current book is also ending. It has been a fascinating personal journey. And whilst I officially began to write this book some 15 months ago; as I look back over the topics addressed, it becomes clear to me that I have— in actual fact, been working on it (in one way or another) for around 20 years or so. Perhaps the ideas expressed here have been developing over an even longer timescale; and go right back to my intense interest in computers, robots and 'thinking-machines' that began during childhood.

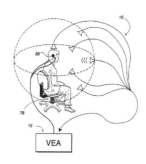

But these technological obsessions are not so uncommon for an Englishman born in 1964; a child of the sixties and seventies; who grew-up when *transistorised portable electronic radios, calculators and colour television* first emerged. During the 1970s, everywhere you looked; on TV, in movies, at school and in books etc; you saw optimistic views of technology. Soon (many experts predicted) we might even be living in outer-space, as so realistically depicted in Arthur C. Clark's space-opera film *2001*.[1]

Robots and computers would be part of a better, more prosperous, and leisure-rich future; and in the 1970s utopia seemed to be a very real possibility.

There is no question over whether the computer will remake society; it has.

Ted Nelson (1974)

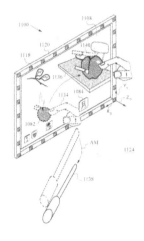

Whilst some visionaries could see dangers, negative influences, and the potential for dystopia in new technologies; most who lived during this period fell for the beguiling promises of a fabulous future where all the mundane, boring, and repetitive tasks would be performed by machines/computers.

Humans would be left to pursue creative and more rewarding activities like art, invention, travel, and sport etc.[2,3,4,5]

Today these ideas do seem to be quite unrealistic, naïve and perhaps even a little foolish. Whilst most people have now succumbed to the many advantages, and sheer convenience of technology; generally accepted at the same time are many negative aspects of technology. In the West, it does appear that we have welcomed new technologies into our lives; perhaps with some of the same goals in mind as earlier generations: and in the hope of a better, easier, more efficient, and rewarding life.

Or more likely we all simply assume/believe that we have no choice but to embrace new technologies. In fact it may be so; that we do not have the (realistic) option to avoid technology—altogether. How many of us would be happy to 'struggle-on' today without computers, cell-phones, laptops, and tablets etc? Most jobs require computer usage/interaction, and the vast majority of *financial, communication, legal, teaching/ learning and leisure activities etc*; involve computers in one way or another. As described, the self-computer is a very real (sometimes partially hidden) and constantly evolving prospect for the vast majority of people alive today. Most of us just get on with it—life—and simply accept/conform passively to the dictates of the self-computer; a process that happens (I would suggest) largely unconsciously.

It is almost as if we had forgotten that, whatsoever else it is, this self-computer must be human made.[6,7,8]

Our thesis has been that humans are merging with machines; and in particular that we are all continually joining/interacting with computers in one form or another. Accordingly, vital is that we understand what computers are, and how they affect humanity, and especially when we consider the increasingly close relationships that we all now have with our artificial creations.

< {48} We need to consider how computers are/should-be changing us. >

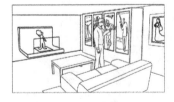

The fact that even the best laid plans for directing human affairs still often fail may turn out to be humanity's saving grace.

Wikipedia stores knowledge summaries, and Facebook records our idle chatter; but what about all of the actual (open) thoughts of humanity?

TECHNOPIA   357

We spoke about notion of Artificial Intelligence (AI), and in particular considered the topics of self-determination plus evolution for computers; and specifically we came to the conclusion (due to lack of evidence) that machines are not self-determinate; and hence that computers are solely human-designed artefacts and nothing more. Accordingly any negative influences (badfluences) of computers on human society must be our own fault. Our analysis did accept that good/bad influences may be un-foreseen, unplanned, and/or accidental; but we come to the view that in major respects humans are not managing the influences/ramifications of computers adequately/optimally.

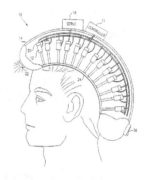

Especially prescient in this respect are the way(s) that computers reflect/influence human thinking methods; and more especially we came to the conclusion that our thinking mechanisms are (at present) suboptimal. We listed three respects in which computers interfere with, and/or do not facilitate beneficial-outcomes:

- The wishes of the few (too-often) outweigh the needs / rights of the many

- Vast numbers of useful ideas, data and votes are hidden, lost and/or ignored

- Computer systems have become divorced from social responsibility

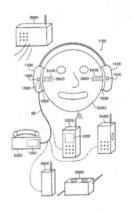

As we have seen, open/free thinking methods are routinely clogged-up by computers, and in particular, according to the *Theory of Natural Thoughts*; the *circuits of thought* are (typically) dysfunctional, and block/prevent the free flow of ideas/votes across the world's stratified (and disconnected) thought-space(s).

Collective decision making is evidently sub-optimal; and foreseen (as a solution) was a global thought-space. And it is not just the author who thinks that a World Brain is a good idea; because as we have seen, great thinkers like H.G.Wells, Paul Otlet, Emanuel Goldberg, Ted Nelson etc; have all prescribed this as a major cure-all for the (seemingly) ever-present problems of humanity.[2,9,10]

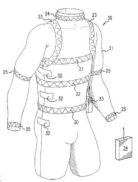

Evidence of this requirement is overwhelming; witness that the minority of humans (effectively) make economic slaves of the majority; and the fact that ideas are not free to merge, coalesce, and render visible the collective needs/wishes of humanity; and hence make possible truly democratic plans/actions.

To the extent that rational thought corresponds to the rules of Logic, a machine can be built that carries out rational thought. To the extent that thought consists of applying any set of well-specified rules, a machine can be built that, in some sense, thinks. - Stephen Pinker

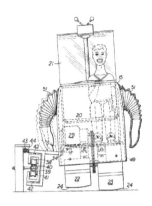

GLOBAL HARMONY

To a generation that had grown up in a world beset by massive armies and by the threat of nuclear holocaust; the cybernetic notion of the globe as a single, invisible play of information, and many thought they could see the possibility of global harmony.

John Perry Barlow drafted the 'Declaration of the Independence of Cyberspace': 'We are creating a world that all may enter without privilege or prejudice accorded by race, economic power, military force, or station of birth. We are creating a world where anyone, anywhere may express his or her beliefs, no matter how singular, without fear of being coerced into silence or conformity... Your legal concepts of property, expression, identity, movement, and context do not apply to it. They are all based on matter, and there is no matter here. Our identities have no bodies, so, unlike you, we cannot obtain order by physical coercion. We believe that from ethics, enlightened self-interest, and the commonweal, our governance will emerge'.

Buckminster Fuller

These ideas might sound overly utopian and/or unrealistic; and especially given the nature of power politics worldwide.

But evident is a strong self-destructive and/or negative tendency in human society for sub-optimal behaviours, wars, and poor decision making (collectively) etc. However as stated in the first chapter, desired are not merely opinions, suggestions and/or 'woolly' and/or indistinct ideas; rather we had sought to find specific and practical solutions; blueprints and problem-solving strategies that may possibly help; and perhaps even to correct/solve a few of the major problems that we all face.

Desired is a revolution in human-thinking procedures; individually and collectively. Some people claim that the Internet and/or cloud applications and/or social networks etc must (and do) form a (potential) solution space. But as explained in this book (*and supported by many quotations/opinions/blueprints etc*), we have seen that the current knowledge system(s) are simply not up to the task. The natural parallel relationships of everything to everything else is missing/lost, and *hyper-thoughts* are not visible in their true *hyper-contexts* (for example). The majority of thought and data-atoms are lost/hidden/black ones; and they might as well be consigned to a vast sea of opaque oil/tar.

Unfortunately today's systems cannot evolve from their current form(s); and will not (ever) be able to change sufficiently so as to come close to reflecting what are human wishes/needs/requirements in the largest (and smallest) sense(s). Accordingly, we have developed our *Theory of Natural Thoughts* to prescribe a new form of World Brain and associated atomic network; and the same (we suppose) may be used to support: *Freedom of Thought*; and in the specific [3] senses listed above. How so?

Well to sum up, the human journey might be said to be all about correct, moral, and righteous thinking outcomes; tied to appropriate action(s). We must decide to act together, as a people; and using a World Brain. On all matters we must decide/choose between competing thoughts/actions; and accordingly, a view of the future must be created, and a process of '*balancing-of-good*' be made (implicitly or explicitly) and in order to choose in terms of the effects of all the consequences that flow from our decision(s).

What will we tell our grand children when they ask us where are all the books, magazines and newspapers that we had in our youth?

CyberSpace Cadets - There are 362 million internet users in China; and 24 million of its children are thought to be 'hooked'.

The frantic global rush to connect everything to everyone, all the time, is quietly giving rise to a revised version of socialism. - Kevin Kelly

Cyberspace is both a mirror (for the human soul) and a window
(into other world's—and this world), it is who we are and where we are going.

TECHNOPIA   359

Put simply we must adequately judge all of our collective thoughts/actions; and judgement is consideration of outcomes. We must predict/access how our decisions will affect all parties, and therefore we must consider all opinions. The only way of so-doing is to foster a free flow of thoughts; whereby all ideas/votes can be readily seen, and freely assembled (by all). To put it simply we must collectively own all the open-thoughts; which must exist in public thought-spaces and include any and all thoughts that have been used, and/or which relate to, decisions/actions that affect the living conditions of humanity. Thought-ownership is key; whereby the *circuits of thought* enable the free flow of all thoughts *(including secret, open and private ones within their specific thought-spaces)*. Accordingly visibility, accessibility, and open-publication/sharing of thoughts/ideas must be maximised.

We developed the concept of thought-energy to measure the amount of meaning present in a thought-space; and accordingly only where a thought-space contains the maximum thought-energy can thought(s) be seen in their proper context. Hyper-thoughts are the key goal; being ones that allow a thinker to explore all of the (present/potential) linkages, relationships, and contexts that exist for any particular thought-atom; and across the entire corpus of knowledge. *Memory holes, black-thoughts, lost-thoughts, warped-thoughts, hidden-thoughts, automatic-thoughts, double-think, mini-think and newspeak etc; are all rendered impossible (or at least more difficult to create/maintain).*

What I am proposing is a new Internet, constructed on wholly different principles, a World Brain that can underpin and be the backbone of all the world's information systems. But this will not happen by accident, and it cannot evolve/develop without enemies/obstacles. Rather we must develop it according to the techno-rights discussed in the last chapter.

Techno-rights may be useful, but they do not and cannot guarantee that such a free, open and decentralised World Brain can/will develop. Perhaps some kind of cyber-war will be required to ensure its victory, and/or we may need to develop it according to Peer-To-Peer (P2P) principles; whereby it is created in an underground way; and to check any hostile authorities who may wish to prevent/block its open and free development.

Wikipedia, Flckr, and Twitter are the vanguard of a cultural movement.
A global collectivist society is coming - and this time you're going to like it! - Kevin Kelly

Computers have (until now) developed according to extremely un-democratic principles; or how else can we explain Microsoft, Google and Facebook; companies that created the richest fortunes in history for a very small number of people. We need computers designed by, and that foster/uphold, democratic principles.

THE MACHINE IN THE GHOST

Apply a few volts of electricity to some duly prepared slivers of silicon, and—if you are like most people—there will suddenly take shape before your eyes a Djinn conjuring of a surreal future. It is a future with robots who surpass their masters in dexterity and with intelligent agents who roam the Net on our behalf, seeking the informational elixir that will make us whole; new communities inhabiting the clean, infinite reaches of cyberspace, freed from war and conflict; and lending libraries of 'virtual real' experiences that seem more sensual than the real thing—all awaiting only the proper wave of industry's well-proven technological wand... (but) some people wonder what the Djinn will ask of us in return.

We meet ourselves in computers...

[1] Anthropomorphism (MACHINE AS HUMAN) that confuses technical capabilities with human qualities.

[2] A habit of abstraction through which inner qualities such as personal respect disappear into mechanisms.

Machines operating with a life of there own. Out of control. Divorced from human needs/wishes.

Stephen L. Talbott

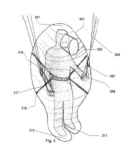

To see a whole galaxy of thoughts, to visualise / understand a myriad of
endless ideas, links and inter-relationships; to explore the World Brain.

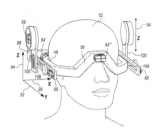

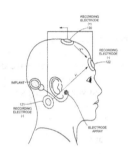

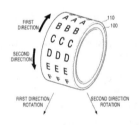

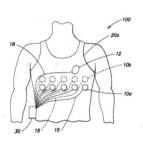

Picture BitCoin, BitTorrent, Wikipedia, Linux etc; where the commons *itself* develops what is commonly needed/desired/required. Freedom is won, not given.

According to Edward de Bono:

> Natural thinking is the flow of activity from area to area on the special memory surface. The flow is entirely passive and follows the contours of the surface. There is no question of an outside agency directing where it should go. The sequence of activated areas constitutes the flow of thought. The flow (thinking) may be continuous, that is from one area to an adjacent one, or activity may die out in one area to start up in another unconnected area. Although the flow is entirely passive, certain artificial organising patterns which affect the direction of the flow can become established on the surface. Such patterns have usually been fed onto the surface deliberately.... Flow is (and should be) determined by the natural behaviour of the surface and as a result it has certain definite characteristics (c.f Natural Thoughts).[11]

Dr de Bono draws our attention to the nature of human thinking, and he refers to certain factors such as the transformation of patterns/relationships from one setting to another; plus memory, and artificial organising factors etc.

Earlier we had defined a computer as a device whose key aim was to 'arrange items clearly in one's mind'; whereby the computer (in Dr de Bono's terms) helps the thinker to structure and flow ideas across the *special memory surface*. In our terms the computer helps ideas flow across the *circuits of thought*; which are: The sum total of factors: personal, social, communicative and technological etc; that comprise the operational-flow of thought-atoms within a thought-space (or (normally) multiple connected/linked thought-spaces).

Where the operational-flow of thoughts has been maximised; thoughts posses: *equality, ownership and free-assembly*.

Provided is freedom for all open-thoughts; hence the thinker can have/see any thought, create any thought, and share/judge any thought—a combined capability which we have named the operational-flow of thoughts within a society. Where operational-flow is high and/or unrestricted, thinkers have the capability to see, create and share concepts as desired.

All models involve this transformation of relationships from their original settings to another. Watches, books, machines, calculus are all models.
What we really require of a memory-trace is that it should tell us what happened, what caused it. Memories constitute their own consciousness and their own perception. There is no need to play back to something outside themselves. - Edward de Bono

There is nothing in the depth of the seas, nothing in the heights of the firmament that man is not capable of discovering. - Foucault

TECHNOPIA 361

How to provide freedom-of-thought (for everyone) has been fully described; whereby it is the *atomicity, visibility, publish-ability, accessibility, connectivity, overlays, comment-ability, and forward/backward linkage of all thought-atoms* which defines such a capacity.

In Ted Nelson's words...

> We need to be able to see the parallel linkage of everything to everything else.

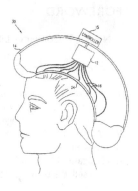

Established is that thoughts are the true social capital of a free society; being those thinking products *(ideas, concepts, theories, votes etc)* that result from the free-flow of thoughts across a community. Hence the ultimate means of production is open, free and communally assigned knowledge; and thought(s) are recognised as the pre-eminent and *sacred* property of our species, individually and collectively; whereby it is the amalgamated thoughts of humanity that are the rightful heritage of every human being.[12]

< {49} We are our thoughts, and our thoughts are us. >

Let us now come together (as a people) and create a beneficial world thinking/acting space; forming a World-Brain with which to imagine, plan and direct the continuing human journey. Accordingly, the Self-Computer is not some artificial being, unnatural and/or an unstoppable force; and neither is it an evil dictator or a benevolent God etc; rather it is who we are in the deepest sense. Computers are reflectors/moulders of mind, body and spirit; and our systems/machines *comprise* us; physically and metaphysically, and they define/construct our humanity.

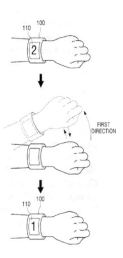

We are both inside and outside of computers; which surround/infuse us completely; and desired is *Technopia*; a self-made 'technological' Gaia or nurturing home within which we can all live.

The *Self-Computer* is a real existent entity that we must build, shape, manage and embrace; and it cannot be 'switched-off'/ignored. Computers are not just extensions of man; but embodiments of those relationships that we humans have, one to another; and accordingly they prescribe how the World-Brain knows itself; or how/why/when/where humans manage the natural, human and technological worlds.

< {50} Technopia = A World-Brain of Hyper-Thoughts = beneficial plans / actions = harmony of life for all. >

It is not information that wants to be free—but rather thoughts want (and need) to be free—and that is the only way that we humans can possibly attain freedom for ourselves!

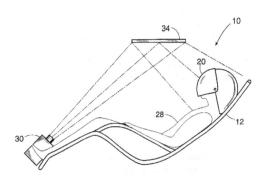

Notes

FOREWORD

1. Nelson, T.: Computer Lib / Dream Machines. (1974).

PREFACE

1. Radley, A.: *Computers as Self.* Fourth International Workshop in Human-Computer Interaction, Tourism and Cultural Heritage in Rome, Italy. (2013)
2. Wiener, N.: *The Human Use of Human Beings.* (1950)
3. Orwell, G.: *Nineteen Eight-Four.* (1949)
4. Foucault, M.: *Discipline and Punishment.* (1975)
5. Russell, Bertrand.: *Skeptical Essays.* (1963)

INTRODUCTION

1. Nelson, T.: *Computer Lib / Dream Machines.* (1974)
2. Lincoln, A.: "In giving freedom to the slave, we assure freedom to the free -- honourable alike in what we give, and what we preserve. We shall nobly save, or meanly lose, the last best hope of earth. Other means may succeed; this could not fail. The way is plain, peaceful, generous, just -- a way which, if followed, the world will forever applaud, and God must forever bless." Annual Message to Congress (Concluding Remarks), December 1. 1862, Washington DC.
3. Levy, S.: *How the NSA nearly destroyed the Internet.* Wired. (January 2014)
4. Veltman, K.: *The Alphabets of Life.* (2014)
5. Orwell, G.: *Nineteen Eight-Four.* (1949)
6. Lanier, J.: *Who Owns the Future.* (2013)
7. Wiener, N.: *The Human Use of Human Beings.* (1950)
8. Bush, V.: *As We May Think. The Atlantic.* (1945)
9. Otlet, P.: Monde: *Essai d'universalisme.* (1935)
10. Veltman, K.: *Understanding New Media.* (2006)
11. Gibson, W.: *Neuromancer.* (1984)
12. Berners-Lee, T.: *Weaving the Web.* (1999)
13. Berners-Lee, T.: *World wide Web needs bill of rights.* On-line BBC News article. (12 March 2014) (http://www.bbc.co.uk/news/uk-26540635) Accesses 9 April 2014.
14. Rheingold, H.: *Tools for Thought.* MIT Press. (1983)
15. Rucker, R.: *Mind Tools.* Penguin Books. (1987)
16. Landauer, T.K.: *The Trouble with Computers .* MIT Press. (1996)
17. Gelernter, D.: *Mirror Worlds.* (1991)
18. Ashby, W.R.: *Introduction to Cybernetics.* (1956)
19. Licklider, J.C.R.: *Man-Computer Symbiosis.* (1960)
20. Engelbart, E.: *Augmenting Human Intellect: A Conceptual Framework.* (1962)

21. Kurzweil, R.: *The Singularity is Near.* (2005)
22. Bradbury, R.: *Fahrenheit 451.* (1953)
23. Ashby, W.,R,: *Introduction to Cybernetics.* (1956)
24. Sagan, C.: *The Demon Haunted World: Science as a Candle in the Dark.* (1997)
25. Carroll, J.B.: *Language, Thought and Reality.* (1956)

SELF

1. Descartes, R.: *Mediations on First Philosophy.* (1641)
2. Descartes, R.: *Discourse on the Method of Rightly Conducting the Reason, and Seeking Truth in the Sciences.* (1637)
3. More, M. and Vita-More, N.: *The Transhumanist Reader.* (2013)
4. Hunger Statistics, *United Nations World Food Programme.* (2013)
5. Domhoff., G.W.: *Wealth, Income and Power.* On-line article: http://www2.ucsc.edu/whorulesamerica/power/wealth.html (accessed 7th April 2014).
6. Wiener, N.: *The Human Use of Human Beings.* (1950)
7. Kelly, K.: *What Technology Wants.* (2011)
8. Asimov, I.: *I Robot.* (1940-1950)
9. Daily Telegraph. :*Do we want to give them A License to Kill?* (November 15th 2013)
10. Maslow, A.: *Motivation and Personality.* (1954)
11. Schelling, F.W.J.: *System of Transcendental Idealism.* (1800)
12. Freud, S.: *The Interpretation of Dreams.* (1899)
13. Jung, C.: *Archetypes and the Collective Unconscious* (1959)
14. Foucault, M.: *Discipline and Punishment.* (1975)
15. Orwell, G.: *Nineteen Eight-Four.* (1949)
16. Orwell, G.: *Animal Farm.* (1949)
17. Poster, M: *The Mode of Information.* (1990)
18. Rose, N.: *Governing the Soul.*
19. Rose, N.: *Inventing Ourselves.*
20. Marx, K.: *Das Kapital.* (1867)
21. Fuller, B.: *Synergetics, Explorations in the Geometry of Thinking.* New York. Macmillan. (1975)
22. Baudrillard, J.: *Fatal Strategies.* (1983)
23. Bauman, Z.: *Liquid Modernity.* (2000)
24. Dasgupta, S.: *A History of Indian Philosophy, Volume 1.* (1940)
25. Lemert, C.: *Thinking the Unthinkable, The Riddles of Classical Social Theories.* (2007)
26. Kurzwell, R.: *The Singularity is Near.* (2005)

4.7 billion dollars spent in 2012 on cyber operations! General George Alexander, the head of the NSA controls this budget, and has stranglovian powers as a result!

An estimated 5 exabytes for all human expressions so far has been offered... According to the EU, there were around 2 billion books. - Kim Veltman *[Perhaps only 10 percent of all books are preserved.]*

Cyberspace is architectural, with classic architecture, its a rectilinear, navigational, iconic information space. - William Gibson

NOTES 363

COMPUTER

1. Human Brain Project: European Commission Project. See: https://www.humanbrainproject.eu/en_GB. Accessed 10th April 2014.
2. DeRose, S., Bringsjord: Are Computers Alive, Abacus, Vol. 2, No. 4, (1985) Springer-Verlag, New York, Inc.
3. Simons, G.: The Emergence of Computer Life, Abacus, (1984) Springer-Verlag, New York, Inc.
4. Turing, A.: Computing Machinery and Intelligence. Mind. (1950)
5. Descartes, R.: Discourse on the Method of Rightly Conducting the Reason, and Seeking Truth in the Sciences. (1637)
6. Diderot, D.: Pensees Philosopiques. (1746)
7. Ayer, A.: Language, Truth and Logic. (1936)
8. Wittgenstein, L.: Logisch-Philosophische. (1921)
9. Wittgenstein, L.: Tractatus Logico-Philosophicus. (1922)
10. Kelly, K.: What Technology Wants. (2011)
11. Arthur, W.B.: The Nature of Technology. (2009)
12. Leibniz, Gottfried.: Essays on the Goodness of God, the Freedom of Man and the Origin of Evil. (1710)
13. Watson, Richard.: Future Minds: How the Digital Age is Changing Our Minds, Why this Matters and What We Can Do About It., (2010)
14. Talbott, Steve.: The Future Does Not Compute: Transcending the Machines in our Midst. (1995)
15. Transhumanist Reader: Classical and Contemporary Essays on the Science, Technology and Philosophy of the Human Future. (2013)
16. Lanier, Jaron.: Who Owns the Future, Penguin (2013)
17. Asimov, I.: I Robot. (1940-1950)
18. Asimov, Isaac.: Robot Visions. (1991)
19. Nelson, T.: Computer Lib / Dream Machines. (1974)

IDEAS

1. Schopenhauer, A.: The World As Will and Representation. (1844)
2. Nietzsche, F.: The Wanderer and his Shadow. (1880)
3. Nietzsche, F.: Daybreak. (1880)
4. Nietzsche, F.: Thus spoke Zarathustra. (1883)
5. Rand., A.: Atlas Shrugged.
6. Plato.: Collected Dialogues.
7. Heisenberg, Werner.: Physics and Philosophy. (1962)
8. Penrose, Roger. The Road to Reality: A Complete Guide to the Laws of the Universe. (2007)
9. Aristotle., Barnes, Jonathan.: The Complete Works of Aristotle; Volumes 1 and 2. (1984)
10. Feser E.C.: Aristotle on Method and Metaphysics. (2013)

11. Tresch, John.: The Romantic Machine: Utopian Science and Technology After Napoleon. (2012)
12. Bradbury, Ray.: Omni magazine article. 1980s.
13. Lovelock, James. Gaia: A New Look at Life on Earth. (2000)
14. Weizenbaum, J.: Computer Power and Human Reason. (1976)
15. Wertheimer, M.: Productive Thinking. (1959)

THINKING

1. Aristotle., Barnes, Jonathan.: The Complete Works of Aristotle; Volumes 1 and 2. (1984)
2. Baxi, Upendra.: The Future of Human Rights. (2012)
3. Hofstadter, Douglas, R.: Surfaces and Essences. (2013)
4. Veltman Kim.: Understanding New Media. (2006)
5. Nelson, Ted.: Computer Lib / Dream Machines. (1974)
6. Nelson, Ted.: Geeks Baring Gifts., (2013)
7. Veltman Kim.: The Alphabet of Life, (2014)
8. McLuhan, Marshall.: Understanding Media: The Extensions of Man., (1964)
9. McLuhan, Marshall.: The Global Village: Transformations in World Life and Media in the 21st Century., (1989)
10. Shannon, Claude, E.: A Mathematical Theory of Communication. (1949)
11. Dawkins, Richard.: The Blind Watchmaker. (1986)
12. Sartre, Jean-Paul.: Being and Nothingness: An Essay on Phenomenological Ontology., (1943)
13. Milton, John.: Complete Works. 2012.
14. Universal Declaration of Human Rights. UN General Assembly. (1948)
15. Letter to Bishop Mandell Creighton, April 5, 1887 published in Historical Essays and Studies, edited by J. N. Figgis and R. V. Laurence (London: Macmillan, (1907)
16. Shelley, Mary.: Frankenstein, or The Modern Prometheus. (1818)
17. Volokh, Eugene (2000).: "Freedom of Speech, Information Privacy, and the Troubling Implications of a Right to Stop People from Speaking about You". Stanford Law Review 52 (5): 1049–1124. doi: 10.2307/1229510.
18. Solove, Daniel J. (2003).: The Virtues of Knowing Less: Justifying Privacy Protections against Disclosure. Duke Law Journal 53 (3): 967–1065 [p. 976]. JSTOR 1373222.
19. Mayes, Tessa (18 March 2011): "We have no right to be forgotten online". The Guardian.
20. Bradbury, Ray.: Fahrenheit 451., 1953.
21. Mumford, L..: The Myth of the Machine: Volume 1. (1971)

Somewhere we have bodies, very far away, in a crowded loft roofed with steel and glass.

Somewhere we have microseconds, maybe time left to pull out. ... jacked into a custom cyberspace deck

that projected his disembodied consciousness into the consensual hallucination that was the Matrix.

Case fell into the prison of his own flesh. - W. Gibson

Victorian belief in the inevitable improvement in all human
institutions as a result and through the machine. - Lewis Mumford

MEN AND MACHINES

1. Development:The Myth of the Machine:Volume 1.,(1971)
2. Lovelock, James.: Gaia.
3. Lovelock, James.: A Rough Ride to the Future,(2014)
4. Hofstadter, Douglas, R.: Godel, Escher and Bach:An Eternal Golden Braid.,(1979)
5. Hofstadter, Douglas, R.: Surfaces and Essences., (2013)
6. Aristotle., Barnes, Jonathan.: The Complete Works of Aristotle; Volumes 1 and 2.,(1984)
7. Aristotelian Society. Men and Machines; Symposia Read at the Joint Session of the Aristotelian Society and the Mind Association at Birmingham (July 11th-13th 1952.) Harrison and Sons Ltd.
8. Berleant, Daniel.: The Human Race to The Future: What could happen - and What to do.,(2014)
9. Stiegler, Bernard.: Technicity.,(2013)
10. Bell, Wendell.: Foundations of Futures Studies (Volumes 1 and 2).,(2004,2010).
11. Lanier, Jaron.:Who Owns the Future, Penguin, (2013)
12. Mitchell, William, J.: Me++; The Cyborg Self and the Networked City., (2003)
13. Baxi, Upendra.: The Future of Human Rights.,(2012)

USER INTERFACE

1. Laurel, B.: Computers as Theatre., Addison-Wesley Publishing Company Inc. (1991)
2. Sutherland, I.: Sketchpad – A Man Machine Graphical Communication System. AFIPS Conference meeting. (1963)
3. Tuck, M.: The Real History of the GUI, Online article: http://www.sitepoint.com/real-history-gui/. Retrieved 2013-08-13.
4. Johnson,J., et al.:The Xerox "Star:A Retrospective". Online Article: http://members.dcn.org/dwnelson/XeroxStarRetrospective.html. Retrieved 2013-08-13.
5. Hiltzik, M.A.: Dealers of Lightening, Zerox PARC and the Dawn of the Computer Age. Harper Collins, New York. (1999)
6. Howard, I.P, Rogers, B.J.: Binocular Vision and Stereopsis. Oxford University Press. (1995)
7. Panofsky, E.: Perspective as a Symbolic Form. Zone Books. (1997)
8. Gombrich, E.: Art and Illusion. Phaidon Press Ltd. (1960)
9. Flocon, A., Barre, A.: Curvilinear Perspective, From Visual Space to the Constructed Image. University of California Press. (1992)
10. Brand, S.: The Media Lab: Inventing The Future at M.I.T., p. 144. R.R.Donnelley and Sons., USA. (1989)

11. Gibson, J.J.: Th Ecological Approach to Visual Perception. Psychology Press. (1986)
12. Veltman, K.H.: Linear Perspective and the Visual Dimensions of Science and Art. Deutscher Kunstverlag. (1986)
13. Termes, D.: Artist Website. http://termespheres.com/about-dick-termes/. Retrieved 2013-08-13.
14. Radley, A.S.: Mirror System Producing a Real Space 3-D Reflected Image of a Person (Hologram Mirror). UK Patent granted - GB2454763. (2009)
15. Ernst, b.: The Magic Mirror of M.C.Escher. Taschen GmbH. (2007)
16. Bowman, D.A.: 3D User Interfaces, Theory and Practice. Addison Wesley. (2004)
17. Veltman, K.H.: Bibliography of Perspective. (1975-1995);See online: http://vmmi.sumscorp.com/develop/
18. Veltman, K.H.: Sources of Perspective; Literature of Perspective (1985-1995) See online: http://sumscorp.com/perspective/

CYBERSPACE

1. Gibson, William.: Burning Chrome., Omni Magazine, (July 1982).
2. Gibson, William.: Neuromancer, (1984).
3. Kennedy, Barbar, M., Bell, David.: Cybercultures and the World we Live in. The Cybercultures Reader., (2000).
4. Rushkoff, Douglas.: Cyberia: Life in the Trenches of Hyperspace.,(1994).
5. Burroughs, William, S., Hibbard, Allen.: Conversations with William S. Burroughs. (2000).
6. Veltman Kim.: The Alphabet of Life, (2014).
7. Veltman Kim.: Understanding New Media, (2006).
8. Rose, N.: Inventing Ourselves.
9. Prince Philip.: HRH The Duke of Edinburgh. Men, Machines and Sacred Cows.,(1982).
10. Berleant, Daniel.: The Human Race to The Future: What could happen - and What to do.,(2014).
11. Wells, Herbert, George.: World Brain.,(1936).
12. Gaines, Brian, R.: Convergence to the Information Highway, (1996).
13. Hume, Robert, Ernest.: The Thirteen Principal Upanishads., (2010).
14. Otlet, Pual. Monde: Essai d'universalisme, (1935).
15. James, William.: The Principles of Psychology. (1950)
16. Bush, Vannevar.: As We May Think.The Atlantic, (1945).
17. Licklider, J.C.R.: Man-Computer Symbiosis.,(1960).
18. Rheingold, Howard.: Tools for Thought. MIT Press, (1983).
19. Wiener, Norbert.: The Human Use of Human Beings. The Riverside Press (Houghton Mifflin Co.), (1950).

Towers and fields of it (data) ranged in the colourless non-space of the simulation
matrix, the electronic consensus hallucination that facilitates the handling
and exchange of massive quantities of data. - William Gibson

Philosophy re-designs language. Every definite entity requires a systematic
universe to supply its requisite status. - Alfred North Whitehead

NOTES   365

20. Wiener, Norman.: *God and Golem: Comments on Certain Points Where Cybernetics Impinges on Religion.*, (1990).
21. Hafner, Katie., Lyon, Matthew.: *Where Wizards Stay Up Late: The Origins of the Internet.*,(1998).
22. Aspray, William.: *Computer: A History of the Information Machine.*, (2004).
23. Barrett, Neil.: *The Binary Revolution: The History and Development of the Computer.*,(2006).
24. Nelson, Ted.: *Computer Lib / Dream Machines,*(1974).
25. Nelson, Ted.: *Geeks Baring Gifts.*, (2013).
26. Nelson, Ted.: *Possiplex - An Autobiography of Ted Nelson.*, (2011).
27. Lanier, Jaron.: *Who Owns the Future,* Penguin, (2013).
28. Buckland, Michael. Emanuel Goldberg and His Knowledge Machine. (2006).

WORLD BRAIN

1. Nelson, Ted.: *Geeks Baring Gifts.*, (2013).
2. Nelson, Ted.: *Computer Lib / Dream Machines,*(1974).
3. Nelson, Ted.: *The Hypertext,* Proceedings of the World Documentation Federation, (1965).
4. Nelson, Ted.: *A File Structure for the Complex, The Changing and the Indeterminate. Complex Information Processing,* proceedings of the ACM 20th national conference 1965, (1965).
5. Nelson, Ted.: *Literary Machines,* (1982).
6. Radley, A.: Computers as Self., Proceedings of the 4th International Conference in Human-Computer Interaction, Tourism and Cultural Heritage, (2013).
7. Veltman, Kim.: *Frontiers in Conceptual Navigation for Cultural Heritage,* (2001).
8. Veltman, Kim.: *Towards a Semantic Web for Culture,* (2004).
9. Veltman, Kim.: *Understanding New Media.*
10. Wells, Herbert, George.: *World Brain.*,(1936).
11. Otlet, Pual.: Monde: *Essai d'universalisme,* (1935).
12. Bush, Vannevar. *As We May Think.* The Atlantic, (1945).
13. Buckland, Michael. Emanuel Goldberg and His Knowledge Machine. (2006).
14. Veltman Kim.: *The Alphabet of Life,* (2014).

VIRTUAL REALITY

1. Woolley, Benjamin.: *Virtual Worlds.*, (1994).
2. Fisher, Scott.: *Virtual Environment Display System,* ACM Workshop on Interactive 3D Graphics, Chapel Hill, NC, Oct 23-24 (1986).
3. Rheingold Howard.: *Virtual Reality.*,(1991).
4. Markley, Robert.: *Virtual Realities and Their Discontents.*,(1995).
5. Blascovich, Jim, Bailenson, Jeremy. *Infinite Reality: Avatars, Eternal Life, New Worlds, and the Dawn of the Virtual Revolution.*,(2011).
6. Artaud, Antonin.: *The Theatre and its Double.*, (1938).

7. Gibson, William.: *Neuromancer,* (1984).
8. Deutsch David.: *The Fabric of Reality.*, (1997).
9. Grau, Oliver.: *Virtual Art.*, (2004).
10. Lanham, Richard.: *The Electronic Word.*, (1995).
11. Latour, Bruno.: *Science in Action: How to Follow Scientists and Engineers Through Society.* (1988).
12. Bloor, David.: *Knowledge and Social Imagery.*,(1991).
13. Gibson, William.: *Mona Lisa Overdrive.*,(1988).

ROBOTS AND AUTOMATA

1. Asimov, Isaac.: *I Robot,* Gnome Press (Trade Paperback), (1951).
2. Asimov, Isaac.: *Foundation,* (1951).
3. Shelley, Mary.: *Frankenstein, or The Modern Prometheus.* (1818).
4. Hoffmann, E.T.A,.: *The Sandman,* Die Nachtstucke (The Night Pieces), (1816).
5. de l'Isle-Adam, August Villiers.: *Tee Future Eve,* (1878). (First use of term 'android')
6. Capek, Karel.: *Rossum's Universal Robots,* (play). (1921). (First use of term 'robot')
7. Cohen, John.: *Human Robots in Myth and Science.*,(1966).
8. Reichardt, Jasia.: *Robots: Fact, Fiction and Prediction.*,(1978).
9. Malone, Robert.: *The Robot Book.* (1978).
10. Newton, Isaac.: *Mathematical Principles of Natural Philosophy (Principia).* (1687).
11. Dreyfus, Hubert. L.: *What Computers Can't Do: A Critique of Artificial Reason,* (1972).
12. Bragdon, Claude, Fayette.: *A Primer of Higher Space (The Fourth Dimension).*,(1923).
13. Nelson, Ted.: *Geeks Baring Gifts.*, (2013).
14. Hofstadter, Douglas, R.: *Surfaces and Essences.*, (2013).
15. Fuller, Buckminster.: *Synergetics, Explorations in the Geometry of Thinking.* New York. Macmillan. ,(1975).
16. Prince Philip.: HRH The Duke of Edinburgh. *Men, Machines and Sacred Cows.*,(1982).

CIRCUITS OF THOUGHT

1. Orwell, G.: *The Road to Wigan Pier.* (1937)
2. Popper, Karl.: *The Open Society and Its Enemies.* (1945)
3. Popper, Karl.: *The Logic of Scientific Discovery.* (1934)
4. Popper, Karl.: *Objective Knowledge, An Evolutionary Approach.* (1972)
5. MacKay, Donal, M.: *Information, Mechanism and Meaning.* (1969)
6. Gombrich, E.: *Art and Illusion.* Phaidon Press Ltd. (1960)
7. *Universal Declaration of Human Rights.* UN General Assembly. (1948).
8. Orwell, G.: *Nineteen Eight-Four.* (1949)
9. Marx, K.: *Das Kapital.*,(1867).
10. Wertheimer, Max.: *Productive Thinking.* (1971)

Russian businessman Dmitry Itskov is attempting to build a complete replacement for the
Human Brain, based on some form of electronic technology by the mid 21st century.
This aims to eliminate death and allow people to upload themselves into a digital form.

A consequence of successful technology is that the performance and needs of the operator become an important set of input variables. - Lewis Mumford

DYSTOPIAN VISIONS

1. Zamyatin, Yevgeny., Brown, Clarence.: We.,(1921). Wilde, Oscar,: The Soul of Man Under Socialism.
2. Wells, Herbert, George.: The Shape of Things to Come.,(1933).
3. Prince Philip.: HRH The Duke of Edinburgh. Men, Machines and Sacred Cows.,(1982).
4. Marx, K.: Das Kapital.,(1867).
5. Huxley, Aldous.: Brave New World.,(1931).
6. Bradbury, Ray.: Fahrenheit 451.,(1953).
7. Lanier, Jaron.: Who Owns the Future, Penguin, (2013).
8. Daily Telegraph.: Do we want to give them A License to Kill? (November 15th 2013).
9. Liberty.: Liberating Cyberspace, (1999).
10. Koespsell, David, R.: The Ontology of Cyberspace, (2000).
11. Cees, J. Haemlink.: The Ethics of Cyberspace.(2000).
12. Forester, E.M.; The Machine Stops, (1909).
13. Moore, George, Edward.: Principia Ethica, (1903).
14. Baxi, Upendra.: The Future of Human Rights. (2006).
15. Mitchell, William.J.: E-topia.(2000).
16. Bradley, A., Arman, Louis. Technicity.(2006).

DREAMS OF UTOPIA

1. Wells, Herbert, George.: A Modern Utopia.,(1905).
2. Wells, Herbert, George.: The Shape of Things to Come.,(1933).
3. Mannheim, Karl.: Ideology and Utopia: An Introduction to the Sociology of Knowledge.,(1955).
4. Hamelink, Cees, J.: The Ethics of Cyberspace.,(2000).
5. Brate, Adam.: Technomanifestos.,(2002).
6. Upendra, Baxi.: The Future of Human Rights.,(2006).
7. Claeys, Gregory., Myman, Tower Sargent.: The Utopia Reader.,(1999).
8. Mitchell, William.J.: e-topia.,(2000).
9. Talbot, Stephen.,L.: The Future Does Not Computer: Transcending the Machines in our Midst.,(1995).
10. Buckminster-Fuller., R., Utopia or Oblivion., (1969).
11. Toffler, Alvin.: Future Shock., (1970).
12. Luppicini, Rocci, Handbook of Research on TechnoSelf. (2013).
13. Huxley, Aldous., Brave New World. (1931).
14. Adams, Douglas. Hitchiker's Guide to the Galaxy. (1978).

CITY OF THOUGHTS

1. Licklider, J.C.R.: Man-Computer Symbiosis.,(1960).
2. Arthur, W.B.: The Nature of Technology.,(2009).
3. Thring, M.W.: Man, Machines and Tomorrow.,(1973).
4. Rose, N.: Inventing Ourselves.

There are no leaps in nature; everything is graduated, shaded.
If there were an empty space between any two things,
what reason would there be for proceeding from one to another?
M. Foucault

5. Fuller, R. Buckminster.: Operating Manual for Spaceship Earth., (1969).
6. Otlet, Pual.: Monde: Essai d'universalisme,(1935).
7. Veltman Kim.: Understanding New Media, (2006).
8. Marx, K.: Das Kapital.,(1867).
9. Lovelock, James.: Gaia.
10. Grills, Chad.: Future Proof: Mindsets for 21st Century Success., (2014).
11. More, Max., Natsaha Vita-More.: The Transhumanist Reader.,(2013).
12. Bradley, Arthur., Armand, Louis.: Technicity.,(2006).
13. Ithiel de Sola Pool.: Technologies of Freedom.,(1983).
14. Demczynski, S.: Automation and the Future of Man.,(1964).
15. Kurzweil, Ray.: The Singularity is Near., (2009).
16. de La Mettrie, Julien, Offray.: Man a Machine., (1748).
17. Dreyfus, Hubert.: What Computers Can't Do. (1972)
18. Mumford, Lewis.: Technics and Human Development: The Myth of the Machine: Volume 1.,(1971).

TECHNOPIA

1. Clarke, Arthur, C..: (2001),
2. Wells, Herbert, George.: The Shape of Things to Come.,(1933).
3. Forster, E.M.: The Machine Stops.,(1909).
4. Halacy, D.S.: Cyborg: Evolution of the Superman.,(1965).
5. Mann, Steve., Niedzviecki, Hal.: Cyborg: Digital Destiny and Human Possibility in the Age of the Wearable Computer.,(2001).
6. Frauenfelder, Mark. The Computer: An Illustrated History., (2013)
7. Arthur, W.B.: The Nature of Technology. ,(2009).
8. Roberts, Keith.: Machines and Men.,(1973).
9. Otlet, Pual.: Monde: Essai d'universalisme, (1935).
10. Nelson, Ted.: Computer Lib / Dream Machines,(1974).
11. de Bono, Edward.: The Mechanism of Mind.,(1976).
12. Marx, K.: Das Kapital.,(1867).

Page 138: Hack Solution...

Power: 2 Sums: 11 01
Power: 5 Sums: 1000 011000
Power: 5 Sums: 11000 01000
Power: 3 Sums: 10 110
Power: 2 Sums: 0 00100
Power: 4 Sums: 101 1011
Power: 3 Sums: 0 01000
Power: 7 Sums: 101000 001011000
Power: 7 Sums: 110111 1001001
Power: 5 Sums: 1000 11000
Power: 6 Sums: 101010 10110
Power: 2 Sums: 011 00001
Power: 10 Sums: 1111001101 110011
Power: 10 Sums: 111101 1111000011
Power: 5 Sums: 00111100 100
Power: 5 Sums: 0011 0011101
Power: 14 Sums: 11111111110110 1010
Power: 10 Sums: 00001011 0111110101
Power: 6 Sums: 110011 0001101
Power: 5 Sums: 11 11101
Power: 6 Sums: 10001 101111
Power: 6 Sums: 10100 00101100
Power: 4 Sums: 100 1100
Power: 5 Sums: 111110 10
Power: 2 Sums: 0000010 10
Power: 3 Sums: 0 1000
Power: 5 Sums: 100 11100
Power: 2 Sums: 00010 10

Magna Carta for the Internet

The inventor of the world wide web Sir Tim Berners-Lee believes an online 'Magna Carta' is needed to protect and enshrine the independence of the medium he created and the rights of its users worldwide. Tim said: 'There's a battle ahead. Eroding net neutrality, filter bubbles and centralising corporate control; all threaten the web's wide-open spaces. It's up to users to fight for the right to access and openness.

The question is, 'What kind of Internet do we want?' Tim told the Guardian (newspaper) the web had come under increasing attack from governments and corporate influence and that new rules were needed to protect the 'open, neutral' system. Speaking exactly 25 years after he wrote the first draft of the first proposal for what would become the world wide web, the computer scientist said 'Unless we have an open, neutral internet we can rely on without worrying about what's happening at the back door, we can't have open government, good democracy, good healthcare, connected communities and diversity of culture. It's not naive to think we can have that, but it is naive to think we can just sit back and get it.'

Principles of privacy, free speech and responsible anonymity would be explored in the Magna Carta scheme. 'These issues have crept up on us,' Berners-Lee said. 'Our rights are being infringed more and more on every side, and the danger is that we get used to it.'

'We also need to revisit a lot of legal structure, copyright law—the laws that put people in jail which have been largely set up to protect the movie producers. None of this has been set up to preserve the day to day discourse between individuals and the day to day democracy that we need to run the country,' he said. Berners-Lee also reiterated his concern that the web could be balkanised by countries or organisations carving up the digital space to work under their own rules, whether for censorship, regulation or commerce. Berners-Lee called for a bill of rights that would guarantee netizens' privacy and keep the web independent.

Tim added, 'You shouldn't trust your government but you shouldn't trust your companies either. We have to have checks and balances for them all.' When asked about the 'biggest single threat to the free internet today,' Berners-Lee replied: 'I used to say it was either government controlling the internet, in countries like China, or big companies controlling the internet, in countries like America,' he says, carefully. 'It actually turns out to be more subtle than that. In America, the big companies fund congressmen and election campaigns. There's a popular bumper sticker in Washington, "Invest in America, buy a Congressman". So you could say big companies control the government anyway.'

'The biggest threat is for any large powerful force to take over the internet.' - Sir Tim Berners Lee

Declaration of Internet Freedom (www.savetheinternet.com)

Tired of fighting bad bills like SOPA, PIPA and CISPA? Want to stand up against those who are trying to control what we do and say online? It's time for something different. A group of more than 1,500 organisations, academics, startup founders and tech innovators has come together to produce a Declaration of Internet Freedom, a set of five principles that put forward a positive vision of the open Internet. Our goal: Get millions of Internet users to sign on to this Declaration. Build political power for Internet users to make sure that we get a seat at the table whenever, and wherever, the future of the Internet is being decided. It's time to stop playing defence and start going on the offensive. The open Internet is central to people's freedom to communicate, share, advocate and innovate in the 21st century. But powerful interests want to censor free speech, block the sharing of information, hinder innovation and control how Internet users get online.

And all too often, people in power are making political decisions behind closed doors about how the Internet should operate—and they're doing this without the involvement of actual Internet users. The result: policies that could close down the open Internet and destroy our freedom to connect.

It's time for us to reclaim the Internet for its users.

Take action now and sign the Declaration of Internet Freedom. [see 5 principles on page 316]

Ram: 'Do you believe in the Users?' Crom: 'Sure I do!'
'If I didn't have a User, then who wrote me?' - Tron [1982]

Everything known is comprised simply of thought-atoms (and all are sacred).
Once a thought is an open-thought; it is fully open. But what if it has parts that
were stolen and/or are secret/private thoughts? There is a moral quandary here.

Glossary - of (mostly) coined terms/concepts

Artificial Intelligence (standard term) - Non-proven capability of artificial machines to: think, inuit, have free-will, self-determine, self-program, have flexibility of purpose, reproduce, become self-aware, posses life, be conscious, intelligently process information etc. In the author's opinion it is a misnomer, being false and/or unproven and/or wholly-undemonstrated at the present epoch in human history (ref.: Simulated Intelligence).

Atomicity - The quantified degree of 'conceptual granularity' and/or 'evidence granularity'; or the number of addressable 'thought-atoms' present in a thought-space.

Atomic Network - Network data massively distributed plus replicated to multiple locations.

Atomisation (of data/thought-atoms) - Data is split into small units and each piece is replicated to many identical copies which are stored at many separate locations.

Automatic-Thought - A thought-atom that is unnatural, because it is blocked in terms of existence and/or operational flow. Specifically the inner structure and/or external context of the thought has become (unnaturally/rigidly) fixed in form/nature; and so that it may be no longer be freely assembled by thinker(s) into any pattern whatsoever. This is not the same as a context-established thought-atom; because the thinker(s) are in some way prevented/precluded from free-assembly, and against their knowledge/will.

Balance of Good - Whenever a thinker wishes to choose between competing thoughts/actions, a view of the future must be created, and a process of '_balancing of good_' must be made (implicitly or explicitly); and especially in terms of the effects of choosing between all the consequences that flow from a decision. We seek the _greatest good_ that the circumstances permit; requiring ethical judgements/predictions about said outcomes.

Black-Thought - A (possibly) relevant thought-atom that has become lost/hidden/ignored/un-linked from a contextual pattern, in that the 'parent' thought-pattern may appear to be logically consistent (i.e. true) in and of itself; according to internal and external structures; however because (some) potentially related thoughts are 'black'; then the structure may be incomplete and/or false/sub-optimal (ref. selection-capacity).

Blocked-Thought - A thought-atom that is unnatural, and is blocked in terms of existence (internal structural form), visibility, context and/or operational flow.

Circuits of Thought - The sum total of factors: personal, social, communicative and technological etc; that comprise the operational-flow of thoughts within a thought-space.

Cosmic Joke (Great) - The evident fact that animals interact, one relative to another; hence if free-will is false for animals, then to afford the same, an (all powerful) universal force would have to (pointlessly) coordinate/pattern ALL animal behaviours (simultaneously). The patent falsehood of this conjecture leads to the conclusion that all animals possess at least some degree of freedom of will.

Creative Free-Will - Situations where the _thinker_ invents, plans and provides un-foreseen, highly novel, and/or singularly creative solutions.

Data Immortality - Data that cannot be destroyed and which 'lives' forever.

Elements-of-Thought - Refers to how all of the structural and relational elements of a thought-pattern function; may involve both logical and/or informational components, describing how they interrelate and work together to impact human society.

Referenced terms coined by Edward de Bono (see text for explanation) ...

Memory Surface - Thinking space existing inside an individual's brain.

Memory Trace - A set of inter-relating ideas/images on the memory surface.

Focus-Logic (cf. Water / Pattern / Gestalt Logic) - Machine logic with narrow basis, blindness, few links, no concepts/analogies, hierarchical as opposed to parallel processing etc.

Freedom of Thought - Thought Equality, Ownership and Free-Assembly. {1}

Ethical Argument (for freedom of thought) - All humans are equal with respect to the right to hold a particular thought and/or point-of-view. Thoughts are the thinker's natural property alone. This is proven because there are no adequate moral grounds upon which to rest any other conclusion; and especially due to the *Balance of Good* argument; whereby each person may manifest his/her views on/for the *greatest good* within a society. {1}

Hidden-Thought - A thought-atom that is unnatural, and because it is blocked in terms of existence (form) and/or operational flow. Specifically aspects of the inner-structure and/or structural context of the thought-atom are hidden from a particular thinker; and in a situation where the same thinker has ownership rights in relation to the thought-atom.

Hyper-Context - An item of knowledge which is situated within the broadest possible context(s), with many possible definitions, opinions, overlays, viewpoints, links to uses, histories, and annotations etc; and all (or a vast majority) are visible.

Hyper-Network - A computer network providing hyper-context for all knowledge.

Hyper-Thought - A thought which exists in a hyper-context.

Implanted-Thought - A thought-atom implanted into a machine/system/computer.

KeyMail - Multi-encrypted P2P electronic mail (developed by the author).

Live / Frozen Thought - Live = exists inside the mind of a thinker and is malleable / subject to judgement ; Frozen = stored on media and/or implanted in a machine / system / computer.

Local Thought-Space - A (flow limiting) medium in which the thinking process takes place.

Logon Capacity (Donald MacKay) - A measure of the number and range of logically distinct (universal) concepts present in a thought-space.

Lookable User Interface - A user interface designed to have visual accessibility of data-content / user-options / choices etc; as its primary feature.

Lost-Thought - A thought that is unnatural, because it is blocked in terms of existence (form) and/or operational flow. Specifically all aspects of the inner-structure and/or structural context of the thought-atom are hidden from ALL thinker(s); and in a situation where the same thinker(s) have ownership rights in relation to the same thought-atom.

Metron Capacity (Donald MacKay) - A measure of the number of logically distinct atoms of supporting evidence (facts/opinions) present in a thought-space.

Mini-Think - When a thinker/actor/human/machine can only apply inadequate/wrong/ simplistic and poorly applicable theories/concepts to a situation. Put simply, the thinkers knowledge and/or programming is inadequate to achieve a desired aim and/or outcome.

Natural Thoughts (Theory of) - Thoughts with ownership, equality and free-assembly.

Open Publication - Anyone may publish anything to anyone.

Open-Thoughts - Thoughts which are the (natural) property of the entire human race.

Operational Flow (A): The degree of free-movement that exists within a thought-space such that any thinker can: see, create and share concepts.

Operational Flow (B): The quantified: atomicity, forward/backward/omni/source linkage, plus overlays/comments; present in a thought-space.

Focus on opinion, evolving knowledge and complexity of human thoughts rather than imagining 'objective' data/information exists. - Ted Nelson

The scale of Beings constitutes a whole infinitely graduated, with no real lines of separation; that there are only individuals, and no kingdoms or classes or genera or species. - A. Lovejoy

Machines as... Extensions of man's control over nature
(and not as a way to control man himself). - Lewis Mumford

Personal Reality - UI in which the world view adapts to the person in a highly specific way.

Personal Augmented Reality - An artificial reality generated in a real-environment (and not necessarily dependent upon wearable technology).

Personal Virtual Reality - An artificial reality generated by means of wearable technologies, and that accommodates itself to the viewer in a useful manner.

Private Thoughts - Thoughts which are shared amongst a restricted group of people.

Pro-Active Free-Will - When a *thinker* has the mental capability to imagine/design specific structures for highly-intelligent purposes.

Reality-Tape (Philip K.Dick) - Self-constructed reality according to pre-programming.

Real Virtuality - The real world becomes partly or wholly 'virtual' (or digital - overlaid with digital data) in some sense; and (often) without glasses, headsets or wearable technology of any kind.

Reflexive Free-Will - When an entity only has the pre-programmed capability to choose/plan a narrow range of movement path(s) (for the influenced atoms) over another, and (purely) in response to singular environmental events/happenings. One might say that this lowest level capability to respond to the environment is a basic definition of an automaton.

Secret-Thoughts - Thoughts which have not left the mind of the thinker.

Selection Capacity (Donald MacKay) - A measure of the number of (applicable) readily unforeseeable concepts (modal ones) present in a thought-space. Measures the ability of a representation's *creator* and *receiver*, present within a thought-space, to adopt logically equivalent *'modes of transmission and reception' (i.e. the inherency of 'message' context)*.

Self-Centric Data - Data which retains the notion of personal property/natural ownership; and therefore is highly interoperable between devices/programs etc.

Self-Computer - Merging of human(s) with computers/machines/systems/technology.

Shallow-Context - Eventuality when a thinker/human/machine has only a limited understanding of all the different and inter-relating contextual factors present, and/or situational circumstances that are/or will-be contingent, and for a specific state of affairs.

Simulated Intelligence - What Artificial Intelligence is at the present epoch. A form of intelligence that exhibits a purely reflexive form of free-will (i.e. a wholly pre-programmed one).

Spectasia - A Lookable User Interface built as a 3D finder for Macintosh and Windows computers; existing as an experimental prototype file browser/launcher.

Stretch-Thought (ref. Ted Nelson's stretch-text) - A thought-pattern which can/could be expanded whereupon new (inherently present) thought atoms/patterns come into view.

Technopia - A society so arranged as to benefit all; upholds everyone's techno-rights. Affords democratic/collective voting and decision-making, plus freedom-of-thought.

Thought-Atom - An isolated thought pattern (probably has no fixed context).

Thought-Energy - A measure of the quantified Logon, Metron and Selective Capacity for a particular thought-atom within a thought-space. Measures the amount of meaning present. It is obviously a very difficult (if not impossible) quantity to measure in practice/reality.

Every system must have an objective—and a purpose or reason for existence.
Computers are containers and implementers of human thoughts and wishes.
(that is ALL they are!) Grave social defects of the human machine. - Lewis Mumford

The mechanisms involved in organic behaviour are too dynamic, too complex, too quantitatively rich, too multi-fold to be grasped except by simplification.

GLOSSARY 371

Thought-Horizon - A limiting and/or occulting region for an 'imaginary/modelled' causal bubble beyond which it is impossible to make any logically correct predictions/deductions. May relate to thought-energy and/or operational flow present within a particular thought-space.

Thought-Operacy - A measure of the applicability of a particular thought to a specific situation; has six components as follows: Task, Unity, Pattern, Possibility, Association and Transformation.

Techno-Rights - Ordinary human rights transposed into a technological world.

Thought-Equality - All (naturally owned) thought-atoms are 'equal' in terms of free-assembly, accessibility, and context-of-use (context-free thought-atom).

Thought-Matrix - Thoughts assembled/weaved together into a coherent body of functionality, consisting of bundles of thought-atoms plus relationship 'fibres'; and the same closely interconnecting, inter-operating and functioning together so as to produce specific outcome(s) for humanity.

Thought-Ownership - Thinker/owner may freely view/assemble/share said thoughts; and the owner chooses who may see/access said thought-atom(s) (sharing-rights may be set). Established in human rights laws{1}, and provided/upheld by technology which (to guarantee said right) operates according to prescribed techno-rights.

Thought-Scape - Entire 'visible' field of thought-atoms / patterns available to a thinker.

Thought-Space - A medium in which the thinking process takes place. This is assumed to be a combination of one or more human mind(s); merged with any mind-extending and/or mind-supporting method(s) and/ or communication/technological tools that may be said to exist *(and which aid in the creation/vision/sharing of new/old thought-patterns)*.

Topic-Space - A thought-space consisting of categorised assemblies of knowledge.

Warped-Thought - A thought that is unnatural, and because it is blocked in terms of structure and/or operational flow. Aspects of the thought-atom have been altered and/or changed for a particular thinker; specifically in unnatural ways; whereby the structure, ordering, association, linkage etc of concepts have become falsely arranged in relation to the ordinary or pre-established 'form' of the same thought-atom.

White-Thought - Relates to a (possibly) relevant 'white' thought-atom that is not currently contained in a specific thought-pattern, in that the same 'parent' thought-pattern may appear to be logically consistent (i.e. true) in and of itself; according to both internal and external structures; however because potentially relevant thoughts are 'white' and hence visible/available for assembly/re-assembly; then the structure as a whole (may have) superior evidence and/or be fully true/beneficial/optimal. (ref. selection-capacity)

World Brain (H.G. Wells) - An imagined world knowledge system based on tiny pieces of thoughts/data that can be connected in every possible way, complete with overlaid links and connections that go in every direction. Data (and human thoughts) have deep structure; and it is this that must be *represented, made visible and accessible to all.*

World Thought-Space - A thought-space comprising all of the connected internal and external, local and global, thought spaces/atoms/patterns/concepts present etc; and hence it contains all of the public knowledge of humanity.

In the **dream world** (of the computer), **space and time dissolve**, near and far, past and future, normal and monstrous, possible and impossible merge into a hopelessly disordered conglomeration.

The most serious threat of computer-controlled automation comes from displacement of the human mind and the insidious undermining of confidence in his ability to make individual judgements that **run contrary to the system—or that proceed from outside the system.**

Irrational **obsessions and compulsions** have been feeding a totalitarian power system—leaving humans **powerless, directionless, incompetent, mentally defective, and psychotic.** - L. Mumford

Universal Declaration of Human Techno-Rights

PREAMBLE

Established is a common understanding that the rights and freedoms as declared in the United Nations *Universal Declaration of Human Rights* are to be protected and upheld, within and by all: machines, automatic systems and computers, and as stated in the ten articles of techno-rights listed below.

Article 1 [UNIVERSALITY]

Thoughts are universal instruments to be used in all kinds of different situations.

Article 2 [FREEDOM]

All human beings are endowed with the right to freedom of thought, and established is that thoughts are the natural property of the thinker, are inherently equal (sans context), and everyone may freely assemble thoughts into patterns of any structure and meaning.

Article 3 [MODES]

Any thought has three possible Modes of existence; in the human mind, preserved on media, and built into a machine, computer or automatic system.

Article 4 [FORMS]

Possible are three natural Forms of thought; secret-thoughts which have not left the mind of the thinker(s), private thoughts which are shared amongst a restricted group of people, and open-thoughts which are the natural property of the human race.

Article 5 [PROPERTY]

All thoughts begin 'life' as the natural and unassailable property of the thinker (or a group of thinkers); and it is up to said thinker how, where, when and if, originally secret-thoughts are transformed into private or open thoughts.

Article 6 [COMMUNICATION]

Everyone has the right to communicate (i.e. to share) his/her signed thoughts (identity established) privately with anyone, and/or in an open manner (signed or anonymously) with everyone else.

Article 7 [TRUST]

In the case of private-thoughts, an element of trust is engendered whereby the receiver(s) do not break the ownership rights of the owner, and the receiver(s) do not have the (natural) right to openly-publish and/or to pass said thoughts on to others, and without the owner's permission.

Article 8 [IMPLANTED-THOUGHTS]

All machine or automatic system implanted-thoughts originate in human-mind(s), may have material outcome(s)/ influence(s), and are inherently automatic once set in motion or enacted by human actor(s), and not withstanding any act(s) of God, and notwithstanding the actions of any human(s), and not withstanding the influence(s) of any other implanted-thoughts present in the same automatic system and/or other automatic system(s), and notwithstanding influence(s) from any data dependent real-world sensing instrument(s)/mechanism(s) resulting from implanted-thought(s); and notwithstanding said factors that may influence said outcome(s).

Article 9 [RESPONSIBILITY]

Once set in motion by a human actor, thought instrument(s) may produce material changes; and legal responsibility for said outcome(s) is established by causal chain, and the same mechanistic analysis begins at the point where said implanted-thought(s) touch humanity; and the same implanted-thought(s) become shared or open-thought(s) at that point with respect to the legal, ethical and moral rights of the influenced person(s).

Article 10 [CLARIFICATION]

None of the above techno-rights conflict with and/or break the *Universal Human Rights*, and simply carry said rights into a technological setting.

Illustrations

This book contains approximately 1000 illustrations; and these are supplied for the purposes of clarification/education; hence the same images are not considered to be a primary part of the conveyed (unique) material content. The vast majority of images have been taken from the patent literature, and therefore fall outside of the various act(s) of copyright; and likewise whereby for many images the original artist(s) could not be identified and/or located.

Where the creator/owner of an image wishes it to be removed from future editions of this book then he/she should send the author a note to this effect at: alan.radley@gmail.com. Alternatively the author/creator/owner of an image can ask to have his name listed as the author of said image in future editions.

List of authors/owners/artists/creators:

[1] Page: Inside Cover: Cyborg head: unknown artist.
[2] Page vi: Cartoon of man reading comic: unknown artist.
[3] Page viii: Cartoon of child with iPad: unknown artist.
[4] Page ix: (page 59) Alice from Alice in Wonderland; Tin Man from Wizard of Oz: unknown artists.
[5] Page ix: Worried man on computer; Man being spied upon: unknown artists.
[6] Page 3: Writing woodcut; Page 4: Man in Goggles: Bruneschelli (perspective): unknown artists.
[7] Pages 9: 19,28, 30,31,56,58,69,81,92,95,97,98, 106,107,113: Image(s) from Astounding Stories: unknown.
[8] Pages 13,17, 24,64,65,78,116,117,118,119,157: Cartoon(s) from Robert R. Crumb: Zap comix.
[9] Page 16: Image from Ted Nelson's Computer Lib Dream Machines.
[10] Page 18 (bottom left), 28 (bottom), 220 (bottom-left),230, 260, 269: Image(s) from Omni.
[11] Page 21 (bottom right): Robot reading book: unknown artist.
[12] Page 30 (bottom): drawings: unknown artists.
[13] Page 29: Robot drawing: unknown artist. [14]; Pages 46, 47: Photography images: unknown artists.
[15] Page 54: Man inside VR system: unknown artist.
[16] Page 59: IPad frozen: unknown artist; [17] 59,94,95: Robby the Robot: Unknown artist.
[18] Page 70: Hospital patient cartoon: Unknown artist. [19] Page 73: Google cartoon: unknown artist.
[20] Page 83: All images by unknown; Page 88 (top left): By Blake; bottom right: unknown.
[21] Pages 83,296,297,298,299: Images from: Tales of the Arabian Knights; Andrew Lang (1873);
[22] Page96: R2D2: by Ralph Mcquarrie (1977). [23] Page 102 (bottom left): unknown artist.
[23] Pages115,122,123,125,126,127,130,131,133,137,140,141: from Astounding Stories: by unknown.
[24] Pages 142,143,144,145,146,147, 150,152,153,154,155,156,161: from Astounding Stories: by unknown.
[25] Page 144: Middle left: image of man plus wires: by unknown. [26] Page 149 (bottom-right): by unknown.
[27] Page 153 (bottom-right): drawing of men at computer(s): by unknown.
[28] Page 159 (top-right): Drawing by unknown.
[29] Pages 163,182,184,186, 202,204,205, 227,236,250,251,283,301: from Astounding Stories: by unknown.
[30] Pages: 166,168,169, 178,179 : by Andrew Barre and Andrew Flocon.
[31] Pages 184, 185:, 186, 187, 188,189,192: Cartoon images by unknown.
[32] Pages 194,208,209,221,248,253,267,302,303: from The Cyberiad: artist: Daniel Mróz
[33] Pages 196,197,226,227,232,233,237,239,244: drawings from Artificial Reality by Myron Kruger.
[34] Pages 198, 199: Cartoons of Ted Nelson by unknown.
[35] Page 210: Man inside brain: by unknown.
[36] Pages 212, 213 ,214,215,216,217,220,221,222,228,229,238,239,242,243,263: Images by unknown.
[37] Pages: 266, 267, 280(bottom-left), 28, 282,286,288,315,332,350: Images by unknown.
[38] Page 90: Technocracy cartoon: unknown artist.

Memory Surface / Memory Trace {model of the thinking process}

Separate memories may be imagined to be stored on a large flat surface, a memory surface, made up of units each of which is capable of indicating a change.

In two-dimensional space the position of each unit is given by its relationship to its neighbours which surround it.

It is the fixed relationship in space that allows the memory-surface to record and keep images.
Edward de Bono

Technopian Manifesto

The present manifesto is a reflection of those human rights established in the United Nations *Universal Declaration of Human Rights*. Our purpose is to transpose human rights into a technological and societal setting. Accordingly, articles in this manifesto are linked to *Universal Human Rights*, the *Theory of Natural Thoughts* and the associated *Bill of Techno-Rights*.

Article 1 [UNIVERSALITY]

We establish that thoughts are a universal and sacred faculty of all human beings. In a way, all of civilisation, all of man's activities and discoveries; are simply vast conglomerations of thoughts and thought-outcomes. Consequently, providing open, free and easy access to, plus comprehensive, logical and humane assembly of thoughts is a key feature of any civilised society.

We identify that thoughts are the natural and unassailable property of the thinker; and exist in the mind of the thinker free from any form of external ownership and/or imposed structural relationship(s) whatsoever. Patterns of thought are the thinker's business alone.

Article 2 [FREEDOM OF THOUGHT]

Society must preserve and protect freedom of thought, and in both the individual and collective senses. Freedom of thought means: to think as one likes, and thus to produce thoughts and ideas freely and without coercion. Obviously in a societal context a trade off must be made between the needs and wishes of the individual against the requirements of humankind as a collective. The ideal is a democratic assignment of priorities, and with respect to (for example) use of collective resources, and thus knowledge of the collective thoughts of humanity becomes a priority. However knowing our collective thoughts is pointless unless we can be sure that everyone actually possess the faculty of freedom of thought. Freedom of thought means equality of thoughts (sans-context), whereby anyone and/or group may freely assemble (any) thoughts into patterns of meaning.

Article 3 [FREEDOM OF ASSEMBLY / EXPRESSION / SHARING]

Possession of the faculty of free-assembly of thoughts must be co-aligned with a corresponding degree of freedom in relation to communicating the same thought-patterns to others. It has been established that natural thoughts come in three types; secret, private and open thoughts. It goes without saying that no party has the right to force or coerce anyone to share secret thoughts; whilst we uphold it as fundamental human right for an individual and/or collective to be able to share private-thoughts with whomever he/she/they wishes; and to not be prevented from so doing and/or to have those same thoughts compromised and/or spied upon in any way.

We establish a caveat here in that vulnerable people (i.e. children) may be protected from the potentially harmful thoughts of others, and by means of restrictive access to thought patterns, wherever and whenever such a restriction is deemed appropriate by said guardian of said individual; however under no circumstances can anyone censure an adult's access to the entire corpus of thoughts of humanity, unless such a restriction is self-imposed and hence desired. Where an individual thinker and/or group of thinkers do not have such a full degree of privacy in relation to their private thoughts; then it is patently obvious that they do not have freedom of thought; for unsanctioned sharing and/or spying breaks the right(s) of natural and private ownership.

Article 4 [EQUALITY OF ACCESS TO OPEN-THOUGHTS]

In a similar fashion to the arguments for free assembly and free expression as detailed in Article 3, it is patently true that human knowledge (i.e. scientific, artistic, and cultural expression(s) etc), as a whole, is simply a vast conglomeration of open thought-patterns; the same being thoughts that are (in actual fact) owned by all of humanity. Accordingly equality of assembly, free sharing and open access to all open-thoughts is established as a fundamental human right (see Article 7).

The origin of action is its efficient, not its final cause; the origin is choice,
and that of choice is desire and reasoning with a view to an end. - Aristotle

ILLUSTRATIONS   375

Article 5 [FREEDOM FROM SPYING / SABOTAGE]

Established is that everyone has the right to protect and to prevent his/her thoughts from being spied upon and/or interfered with in any way. No machine, automatic system or computer can/will/should interfere with the free and open creation, assembly, expression and sharing of private and open thoughts as detailed in Articles 1-4 above.

Article 6 [LEGAL STATUS OF THOUGHTS]

Established is that no thought can ever, in and of itself, be illegal in any way whatsoever. No thought, no matter how horrible, monstrous or evil it may appear from its contents, is ever itself unlawful. In all cases it is when thought(s) are transposed into action(s) that law(s) may be broken. In all cases where any law making societal body attempts to establish thoughts (or thought assembly/sharing) as illegal, and without the free-consent of its members, that same body has evidently broken and/or limited the human rights of its members. A law-making body can (for example) make sharing of weapons manufacturing expertise illegal so long as the members agree to said restrictions freely and without unwarranted coercion.

Article 7 [PROPERTY / COPYRIGHT]

Since thoughts are the natural property of the thinker, everyone has the right to decide how his or her thoughts are to be used in an external sense. The thinker has the right to profit from his own thought inventions, and to have related rights protected. Said rights are a subject of intellectual property laws as established generally. The present manifesto does not attempt to make any changes to legal precedents in this respect, but merely highlights the thinker's ownership rights to secret, private and open thoughts, hence the free assembly, access and sharing rights for all forms of thoughts, and for the rightful owner(s) were appropriate. Established is that once a thought has legally become registered as an open thought, then that same thought has become a legal property of the entire human race. Henceforth it should be the aim of society to provide free and open access to all open thoughts, and in order to foster visibility, sharing and free assembly for all the open thoughts of humanity.

Article 8 [IMPLANTED-THOUGHTS]

Machines, computers and automatic systems in all cases consist wholly of implanted thoughts that have been arranged into structural patterns, and in order to achieve and/or progress an automated aim, goal or purpose. A machine's inner logic is wholly automatic, but it may be operated / programmed by a human actor and/or influenced by another human being and/or automatic machine, however machines, computers and automatic systems consist of designs entirely composed of implanted thoughts alone.

Article 9 [RESPONSIBILITY]

Everyone has a legal right to establish a direct causal linkage between material outcome(s) from a machine or automatic system's instantiation of an implanted thought, and specifically in the case where said outcome interferes with a person's legal right(s) and/or blocks a human right as listed in the articles of the *Universal Human Rights*. Everyone has the right to establish a legal chain of cause and effect back to the human actor who caused the same outcome. It is a fundamental human right to know what (when, where, how) and who is responsible for material outcomes that result from automatic systems and that in turn affect one's legal and human rights.

Article 10 [COPYRIGHT]

No article defined here conflicts with and/or breaks any principle contained in the United Nations *Universal Declaration of Human Rights, the Universal Human Rights*, the principles of the *Theory of Natural Thoughts* and/or the associated *Bill of Techno-rights*, and said articles merely carry said rights/features/articles into a technological setting.

Actions are bodily movements induced or inhibited in
part by constellations of beliefs and desires. - Aristotle

All must be full or not coherent be, and all that rises, rise in due degree. - Alexander Pope
Logical thinking is used to avoid the errors of natural thinking. - Edward de Bono
A natural-thought contains its entire history and varied structure(s) within itself.

To fly along thought-spaces—to freely explore ideas in hyper-contexts—
to see knowledge transparent, fractal, kaleidoscopic and endlessly linked/overlapping!

Bibliography

Abbott Abott, Edwin.: *Flatland.*(1884).

Anderson, Chris. *Free:The Future of a Radical Price.* New York, (2006).

Anderson, Walter, Truett.: *The Future of the Self.*,(1997).

Aristotelian Society.: *Men and Machines; Symposia Read at the Joint Session of the Aristotelian Society and the Mind Association at Birmingham (July 11th-13th 1952).* Harrison and Sons Ltd.

Aristotle., Barnes, Jonathan.: *The Complete Works of Aristotle; Volumes 1 and 2.*,(1984).

Armand, Louis., Bradley, Arthur., Zizek, Slavoj., Stiegler, Bernard.: *Technicity.*,(2013).

Arnasaon, H.,H., Mansfield, Elizabeth, C.: *A History of Modern Art, 7th Edition.*, (2012).

Arthur, W.B.: *The Nature of Technology.*, (2009).

Ash, Brian.: *The Visual Encyclopaedia of Science Fiction.*, (1978).

Ashby, W.R.: *Introduction to Cybernetics.*,(1956).

Aspray, William.: *Computer: A History of the Information Machine.*, (2004).

Astounding Science Fiction Magazine: 1930s - 1980s

Asimov, I.: *I Robot.* (1940-1950)

Asimov, Isaac.: *Machines that Think: The Best Science Fiction Stories About Robots and Computers.*, (1985).

Asimov, Isaac.: *Robot Visions.*, (1991).

Auletta, Ken.: *Googled, The End of the World as We Know It.*, (2011).

Ayer, A.: *Language, Truth and Logic.* (1936)

Banks, Michael, A.: *On the Way to the Web: The Secret History of the Internet and its Founders.*,(2011).

Barrett, Neil.: *The Binary Revolution: The History and Development of the Computer.*,(2006).

Battelle, John.: *Search,* (2006).

Baxi, Upendra.: *The Future of Human Rights.*,(2012).

Baudrillard, J.: *Fatal Strategies.* ,(1983).

Baudrillard, Jean.: *Simulacra and Simulation.*,(1981).

Baudrillard, Jean.: *Simulations.*, (1983).

Bauman, Z.: *Liquid Modernity.* ,(2000).

Bell, Wendell.: *Foundations of Futures Studies (Volumes 1 and 2).*,(2004),(2010).

Berleant, Daniel.: *The Human Race to The Future: What could happen - and What to do.*,(2014).

Berners-Lee, Tim.: *Weaving the Web,* (1999).

Berry, Adrian.: *The Next Ten Thousand Years.*,(1975).

Blascovich, Jim, Bailenson, Jeremy.: *Infinite Reality: Avatars, Eternal Life, New Worlds, and the Dawn of the Virtual Revolution.*,(2011).

Bragdon, Claude, Fayette.: *A Primer of Higher Space (The Fourth Dimension).*,(1923).

Bradbury, Ray.: *Fahrenheit 451.*,(1953).

Brand, Stewart.: *The Clock of the Long Now: Time and Responsibility: The Ideas Behind the World's Slowest Computer.*,(2000).

Brand, S.: *The Media Lab: Inventing The Future at M.I.T.*, p. 144. R.R. Donnelley and Sons., USA.,(1989).

Brate, Adam.: *Technomanifestos: Visions of the Information Revolutionaries.*,(2002).

Brown, Jonathon.: *The Self.*,(2007).

Brunn, Stanely.: *Collapsing Space and Time.*,(1991).

Bolt, Richjard.: *The Human Interface, Where People and Computer Meet.*, (1984).

Boole, George.: *An Investigation into The Laws of Thought.*,(1854).

Bowman, D.A.: *3D User Interfaces, Theory and Practice.* Addison Wesley. ,(2004).

Buckland, Michael. *Emanuel Goldberg and His Knowledge Machine.* (2006). Burdea, George. C., Coiffet, Philippe.: *Virtual Reality Technology.*,(2003).

Bush, Vannevar.: *As We May Think.* The Atlantic, (1945).

Calabrese, Andrew et al.: *Communication, Citizenship and Social Policy.*,(1999).

Cassirer Ernst.: *The Myth of the State.*,(1961).

Cassirer Ernst.: *The Philosophy of Symbolic Forms: Volumes 1-3.*,(1965).

Cassirer, Ernst.: *The Problem of Knowledge: Philosophy, Science and History Since Hegel.* (1969).

Claeys, Gregory., Sargent, Lyman, Tower.: *The Utopia Reader.*,(1999).

Clarke, Arthur, C.: *The Exploration of Space.*,(2010).

Cohen, John.: *Human Robots in Myth and Science.*,(1966).

Cork, Richard.: *Vorticism and Abstract Art in the Machine Age (2 volumes).*,(1976).

Copleston, Frederick.: *A History of Philosophy; volumes 1-11.*, (1946-1974).

Cotton, Bob; Oliver, Richard.: *Understanding Hypermedia.* ,(1983).

Coxeter, H.S.M.: *Introduction to Geometry.*,(1989).

Daily Telegraph.: *Do we want to give them A License to Kill?* (November 15th 2013).

Dale, Rodney.: *Edwardian Inventions.*,(1979).

Dasgupta, S.: *A History of Indian Philosophy.* Volume 1.,(1940).

Dawkins, Richard.: *The Blind Watchmaker.* (1986).

de Bono, Edward.: *Lateral Thinking: An Introduction.*,(1999).

de Bono, Edward.: *The Mechanism of Mind.*,(1976).

de Bono, Edward.: *Eureka.*,(1979).

de La Mettrie, Julien, Offray.: *Man a Machine.*, (1748).

de Sola Pool, Ithiel.: *Technologies of Freedom.*,(1984).

de Vries, Leonard.: *Victorian Inventions.*, (1991).

Debord, Guy.: *Society of the Spectacle.*,(1984)

Some people think that the purpose of computers is to simulate paper; complete with all of its decorations;
but this is wrong; the pioneer Engelbart was concerned about structure—structure in the form of collaboration.
Linkage is key. What we got is a fig-leaf over the operating system;
and the computer was dumbed down at the same time.
We got a simulation of paper—organising things into rectangles. - Ted Nelson

DeRose, S., Bringsjord: Are Computers Alive? Abacus, Vol. 2, No. 4, (1985). Springer-Verlag, New York, Inc.

Descartes, R.: *Mediations on First Philosophy.,*(1641).

Descartes, R.: *Discourse on the Method of Rightly Conducting the Reason, and Seeking Truth in the Sciences.,*(1637).

Deutsch, David.: *The Fabric of Reality: The Science of Parallel Universes - and Its Implications.,*(1998).

D.H.L Hieronimus, Meyerhoff, Zohara, J.: *The Future of Human Experience: Visionary Thinkers on the Science of Consciousness.,* (2013).

Dick, Philip, K.: *Eye in the Sky.,*(1957).

Dick, Philip, K.: *A Scanner Darkly.,*(1977).

Dick, Philip, K.: *Do Androids Dream of Electric Sheep.,*|(1968).

Dick, Philip, K.: *The Man in the High Castle.,*(1962).

Dick, Philip, K.: *The Minority Report.,*(1956).

Diderot, D.: *Pensees Philosopiques.* (1746)

Domhoff., G.W.: *Wealth, Income and Power.* On-line article: http://www2.ucsc.edu/whorulesamerica/power/wealth.html (accessed 7th April 2014).

Earnshaw, R., A., Gigante, M., A., Jones, H.: *Virtual Reality Systems.,* (1995).

Elliott, Anthony.: *Concepts of the Self.,*(2007).

Encyclopaedia Britannica: 11th Edition, 29th editions.

Ernst, b.: *The Magic Mirror of M.C.Escher.* Taschen GmbH.,(2007).

Engelbart, E.: *Augmenting Human Intellect: A Conceptual Framework.,*(1962).

Flocon, A., Barre, A.: *Curvilinear Perspective, From Visual Space to the Constructed Image.* University of California Press.,(1992).

Fraser, J., Y.: *The Voices of Time.,* (1981).

Frewin, Anthony.: *One Hundred Years of Science Fiction Illustration.,*(1988).

Frauenfelder, Mark. *The Computer: An Illustrated History.,* (2013)

Freud, S.: *The Interpretation of Dreams.* (1899)

Forster, E.M.: *The Machine Stops.,*(1909).

Foucault, Michel.: *Discipline and Punishment: The Birth of the Prison.* Penguin,(1975).

Foucault, Michel.: *The Order of Things: An Archaeology of the Human Sciences.,*(1966).

Fuller, R. Buckminster.: *Operating Manual for Spaceship Earth.,* (1969).

Fuller, Buckminster.: *Synergetics, Explorations in the Geometry of Thinking.* New York. Macmillan.,(1975).

Fuller, R. Buckminster.: *Utopia or Oblivion: The Prospects for Humanity.,*(1972).

Gelernter, David.: *Mirror Worlds: or the Day Software Puts the Universe in a ShoeBox... How it will Happen and What it Will Mean.,*(1993).

George, Frank.: *Man the Machine.,*(1979).

Gibson, J.J.: *Th Ecological Approach to Visual Perception.* Psychology Press.,(1986).

Gibson, William.: *Neuromancer,* (1984).

Ginsberg, Morris.: *On the Diversity of Morals.,*(1957).

Gleick, James.: *The Information: A History, A Theory, A Flood.,* (2012).

Gabor, D.: *Innovations: Scientific, Technological, and Social.,* (1970).

Gombrich, E.: *Art and Illusion.* Phaidon Press Ltd. (1960)

Gray, Chris, Hables.: *Cyborg Citizen; Politics in the Posthuman Age.,*(2002).

Grau, Oliver.: *Virtual Art.,* (2004).

Grills, Chad.: *Future Proof: Mindsets for 21st Century Success.,* (2014).

Hafner, Katie., Lyon, Matthew.: *Where Wizards Stay Up Late: The Origins of the Internet.,*(1998).

Halacy, D.S.: *Cyborg: Evolution of the Superman.,*(1965).

Hamelink, Cees, J.: *The Ethics of Cyberspace.,*(2000).

Hamit, Francis.: *Virtual Reality and the Exploration of Cyberspace.,* (1993).

Haraway, Donna.J., Hables-Gray, Chris., Eglash, Ron., Clynes, Manfred.E.: *The Cyborg Handbook.,* (1995).

Henderson, Linda, Dalrymple.: *The Fourth Dimension and Non-Euclidean Geometry in Modern Art.,*(1983).

Heppenheimer T.A.: *Colonies in Space.,*(1977).

Heil, John.: *The Nature of True Minds.,*(1992).

Heidegger, Martin.: *Being and Time.,*(1927).

Heidegger, Martin.: *What is Called Thinking?,*(1976).

Heim, Michael. *The Metaphysics of Virtual Reality.,*(1994).

Hertzfeld, Andy.: *Revolution in the Valley.,* (2011).

Hiltzik, M.A.: *Dealers of Lightening, Zerox PARC and the Dawn of the Computer Age.* Harper Collins, New York.,(1999).

Hinton, Charles, Howard.: *The Fourth Dimension.,*(1913).

Hobbes, Thomas.: *Leviathan.,*(1668).

Hodges, Andrew., Hofstadter, Douglas.: *Alan Turing: The Enigma.,*(1982).

Hofstadter, Douglas, R.: *Godel, Escher and Bach: An Eternal Golden Braid.,*(1979).

Hofstadter, Douglas, R.: *Surfaces and Essences.,* (2013).

Hofstadter, Douglas, R.: *The Mind's I: Fantasies and Reflections on Self and Soul.,* (1982).

Hofstadter Douglas.: *Metamagical Themas: Questing for the Essence of Mind and Pattern.,* (1986).

Holtzman, Steve, R.: *Digital Mantras: The Language of Abstract and Virtual Worlds.,* (1995).

Howard, I.P, Rogers, B.J.: *Binocular Vision and Stereopsis.* Oxford University Press. (1995)

Documents do not exist in isolation—we need to be able to follow connections and sources; and every quotation (or thought-atom) should be visibly and immediately connected to its source. Visible representation of parallel pages. History—we need to be able to see what was happening at the same time. Connections plus footnotes should be on the side. Consider intrinsic parallelism. - Ted Nelson

Howe, Jeff.: Crowdsourcing: Why the Power of the Crowd is Driving the Future of Business., (2009)

Human Brain Project: European Commission Project. See: https://www.humanbrainproject.eu/en_GB. Accessed (10th April 2014).

Hume, David.: A Treatise on Human Nature., (1738).

Hume, Robert, Ernest.: The Thirteen Principal Upanishads., (2010).

Hunger Statistics, United Nations World Food Programme.,(2013).

Husserl, Edmund. Ideas: A General Introduction to Phenomenology: Volumes 1-3.,(1913-).

Husserl, Edmund, Gustav, Albrecht.: Logical Investigations., (1900).

Huxley, Aldous.: Brave New World.,(1931).

Jacobson, Linda.: CyberArts: Exploring Art and Technology.,(1992).

Johnson, George.: In the Palaces of Memory: How We Build the Worlds Inside Our Heads.,(1992).

Johnson, J., et al.: The Xerox "Star: A Retrospective. Online Article: http://members.dcn.org/dwnelson/XeroxStarRetrospective.html. Retrieved 2013-08-13.

Jarvis, Jeff.: What Would Google Do?, (2001).

Jung, C.: Archetypes and the Collective Unconscious.,(1959).

Jung, Carl.: Man and His Symbols, (1968).

Jung, C.G.,: Hull, R.F.C. The Collected Works of Carl Jung (Volumes 1-20).,(1960-1990).

Kant, Immanuel.: Critique of Pure Reason.,(1787).

Kahn, David.: The Code Breakers: The Comprehensive History of Secret Communication from Ancient Times to the Internet., (1996).

Kelly, K.: What Technology Wants.,(2011).

Kent, Ernest, W.: The Brains of Men and Machines.,(1980).

Kery, Patricia, Frantz.: Art Deco Graphics.,(1986).

Kirk, G.S., Raven, J.E.: The Pre-Socratic Philosophers.,(1969).

Kirkpatrick, David.: The Facebook Effect: The Inside Story of the Company That is Connecting the World.,(2011).

Klee, Paul.: Notebooks of Paul Klee (Volumes 1 and 2), (1964, 1992).

Koepsell, David, R.: The Ontology of Cyberspace: Philosophy, Law and the Future of Intellectual Property., (2003).

Krueger, Myron.: Artificial Reality 2. (1991).

Kurzweil, Ray.: The Age of Spiritual Machines: When Computers Exceed Human Intelligence.,(1999).

Kurzweil, Ray.: The Singularity is Near: When Humans Transcend Biology., (2006).

Laithwaite, Eric.: An Inventor in the Garden of Eden.,(1994).

Lanier, Jaron.: Who Owns the Future, Penguin, (2013).

Lanier, Jaron.: You are Not a Gadget: A Manifesto., (2001).

Landauer, Thomas, K.: The Trouble with Computers: Usefulness, Usability, and Productivity.,(1996).

Laurel, Brenda.: The Art of the Human Computer Interface., (1990).

Laurel, B.: Computers as Theatre. Addison-Wesley Publishing Company Inc.,(1991).

Leibniz, Gottfried Wilhelm.: Philosophical Papers and Letters: Volumes 1 and 2., 1976, (2011).

Lemert, C.: Thinking the Unthinkable, The Riddles of Classical Social Theories.,(2007).

Lem, Stanislaw.: The Cyberiad: Fables for the Cybernetic Ward., (1976).

Levy, Steven.: How the NSA nearly destroyed the Internet. Wired Magazine, January (2014).

Levy, Stephen.: In the Plex; How Google Things, Works, and Shapes Our Lives., (2012).

Lewis, Arthur, O.: Of Men and Machines.,(1963).

Licklider, J.C.R.: Man-Computer Symbiosis.,(1960).

Lilley, S.: Men, Machines and History., (1948).

Linzmayer, Owen. Apple Confidential 2.0, 2004.

Locke, John.: An Essay Concerning Human Understanding.,(1689).

Lombardo, Thomas.: Contemporary Futurist Thought: Science Fiction, Future Studies, and Theories and Visions of the Future in the Last Century.,(2006).

Lovejoy, Arthur, O.: The Great Chain of Being: A Study of the History of an Idea.,(1936).

Lovelock, James.: Gaia.

Lovelock, James.: A Rough Ride to the Future,(2014).

Luppicini, Rocci.: Handbook of Research on Technoself: Identity in a Technological Society., (2012).

Mann, Steve., Niedzviecki, Hal.: Cyborg: Digital Destiny and Human Possibility in the Age of the Wearable Computer.,(2001).

Mannheim, Karl.: Ideology and Utopia: An Introduction to the Sociology of Knowledge.,(1955).

Markley, Robert.: Virtual Realities and Their Discontents.,(1995|).

Markoff, John.: From Counterculture to Cyberculture: Stewart Brand, the Whole Earth Network and the Rise of Digital Utopianism., (2008).

Markoff, John.: What the Dormouse Said: How the Sixties Counterculture Shaped the Personal Computer Industry.,(2006).

Marx, Carl., Engels, Friedrich.: The Communist Manifesto.,(1848).

Marx, K.: Das Kapital.,(1867).

Maslow, A.: Motivation and Personality.,(1954).

Merleau-Ponty, Maurice.: Signs., (1964).

Merleau-Ponty, Maurice.: Nature.,(2000).

Menezes, ALfred, J., von Oorschot, Paul, C., Vanstobe, Scott, A.: Handbook of Applied Cryptography.,(1996).

Understand and represent the true nature of thought; its integrated nature.

We need one simple system for everything!

To have a clean data structure from which you can do allot more. - Ted Nelson

If Quantum Computers are possible; then EVERYTHING changes!

McLuhan, Marshall.: *The Mechanical Bride: Folklore of Industrial Man.*, (1967).

McLuhan, Marshall.: *Understanding Media: The Extensions of Man.*, (1964).

McLuhan, Marshall.: *The Global Village: Transformations in World Life and Media in the 21st Century.*, (1989).

Mill, John, Stuart.: *On Liberty.*, (1859).

Mitchell, WIlliam. J.: *e-topia.*, (2000).

Mitchell, William, J.: *Me++; The Cyborg Self and the Networked City.*, (2003).

Moore, G., E.: *Principia Ethica.*, (1966).

More, Max., Vita-More, Natasha.: *The Transhumanist Reader: Classical and Contemporary Essays on the Science, Technology and Philosophy of the Human Future.*, (2013).

More, Thomas.: *Utopia.*, (1516).

Moritz, Michael.: *Return to the Little Kingdom: Steve Jobs and the Creation of Apple.*, (2010).

Morrison, E.: *Men, Machines and Modern Times.*, (1966).

Mudrick, Marvin.: *The Man in the Machine.*, (1977).

Muller, Max.: *Sacred Books of the East: The Texts of Taoism.*, (1891).

Mumford, Lewis.: *The Pentagon of Power: The Myth of the Machine.*, (1970).

Mumford, Lewis.: *Technics and Human Development: The Myth of the Machine: Volume 1.*, (1971).

Murrell, Hywel.: *Men and Machines.*, (1976).

Nagel, Ernest.: *The Structure of Science.*, (1961).

Nelson, Ted.: *Computer Lib / Dream Machines,* (1974).

Nelson, Ted.: *Geeks Baring Gifts.*, (2013).

Nelson, Ted.: *Possiplex - An Autobiography of Ted Nelson.*, (2011).

Nietzsche, F.: *The Wanderer and his Shadow.*, (1880).

Nietzsche, F.: *Daybreak.*, (1880).

Nietzsche, F.: *Thus spoke Zarathustra.*, (1883).

Norman, Donald, A.: *The Invisible Computer.*, (1999).

O'Brien, Fitz, James.: *The Diamond Lens.*, (1858).

O-Neill, Gerard, K.: *2081: A Hopeful View of the Human Future.*, (1981).

Omni Magazine: Complete Collection

Orwell, George.: *Animal Farm.*, (1949).

Orwell, George.: *Nineteen Eight-Four.* Secker and Warburg, London, (1949).

Otlet, Pual.: *Monde: Essai d'universalisme,* (1935).

Ouspensky, P.D.: *A New Model of the Universe.*, (1969).

Ouspensky, P.D.: *In Search of the Miraculous.*, (1949).

Panofsky, E.: *Perspective as a symbolic form.* Zone Books. (1997)

Penrose, Roger.: *The Road to Reality: A Complete Guide to the Laws of the Universe.*, (2007).

Pinker, Steven.: *How the Mind Works.*, (2009).

Pinker, Steven.: *The Stuff of Thought: Language as a Window into Human Nature.*, (2008).

Plato.: Collected Dialogues.

Plato.: Cornford, Franics., M. *Plato's Theory of Knowledge: The Theaetetus and The Sophist Plato.*, (1957).

Ploman, Edward, W., Hamilton, L. Clark.: *Copyright: Intellectual Property in the Information Age.*, (1980).

Popper, Karl, J.: *The Open Society and It's Enemies (Volume 1 and 2).*, (1971).

Portola Institute.: *The Whole Earth Catalogue.*, (1972) Edition, (1986) Edition, (1995) Edition.

Poster, M: *The Mode of Information.*, (1990).

Prince Philip.: HRH The Duke of Edinburgh. *Men, Machines and Sacred Cows.*, (1982).

Radhakrishnan, S., Raju, P., T.: *The Concept of Man: A Study in Comparative Philosophy.*, (1960).

Radley, A.S.: *Mirror System Producing a Real Space 3-D Reflected Image of a Person (Hologram Mirror).* UK Patent granted - GB2454763., (2009).

Rand, Ayn.: *Atlas Shrugged.*, (1957).

Rand, Ayn.: *The Fountainhead.*, (1943).

Reichardt, Jasia.: *Robots: Fact, Fiction and Prediction.*, (1978).

Rheingold, Howard.: *Tools for Thought.* MIT Press, (1983).

Rheingold Howard.: *Virtual Reality.*, (1991).

Roberts, Keith.: *Machines and Men.*, (1973).

Rogers, Everett M.: *Diffusion of Innovations.* (2003).

Roheim, Geza,. Muensterberger, Warner.: *Magic and Schizophrenia.*, (2006).

Rose, N.: *Governing the Soul.*

Rose, N.: *Inventing Ourselves.*

Ross, K.W., Kurose, James, F.: *Computer Networking; A Top Down Approach.*, (2012).

Roszak, Theodore.: *The Making of a Counter Culture.*, (1969).

Routledge, Robert.: *Discoveries and Inventions of the 19th Century.*, (1900).

Rucker, Rudy.: *Mind Tools.* Penguin Books, (1987).

Rucker, Rudolf., Povilaitis, David.: *The Fourth Dimension: A Guided Tour of the Universe.*, (1985).

Rushkoff, Douglas.: *Cyberia: Life in the Trenches of Hyperspace.*, (1994).

Russell, Bertrand.: *Skeptical Essays.* Unwin Hyman Ltd, (1963).

Russell, Bertrand.: *The Problems of Philosophy.*, (1912).

Sagan Carl.: *Dragons of Eden: Speculations on the Evolution of Human Intelligence.*, (1986).

Sagan, C.: *The Demon Haunted World: Science as a Candle in the Dark.*, (1997).

Salinger. J.: *The Catcher in the Rye.*, (1951).

Salomon, David., Bryant, D.: *Handbook of Data Compression.*, (2009).

Sartre, Jean-Paul.: *Imagination.*, (1962).

Access to knowledge is a human right.
Open-thoughts are public knowledge.
Knowledge belongs to us (humanity) as a commons.
We need public access to the public domain.
Open-thoughts must be open-access!

True nature of thought.
Hyper-thought(s) in hyper-context(s).
Parallel linkages, overlays, comments etc.
True nature of thinking. Hyper-reality.
Multiple thought-space(s), all connected.

Sartre, Jean-Paul.: *Being and Nothingness: An Essay on Phenomenological Ontology.*, (1943).

Shelley, Mary.: *Frankenstein, or The Modern Prometheus.* (1818).

Schelling, F.W.J.: *System of Transcendental Idealism.* (1800)

Schopenhauer, A.: *The World As Will and Representation.*, (1844).

Searle, John, R. : *The Mystery of Consciousness.*, (1990).

Shannon, Claude, E.: *A Mathematical Theory of Communication.* (1949).

Simons, G.: *The Emergence of Computer Life*, Abacus, (1984). Springer-Verlag, New York, Inc.

Singleton, W., T.: *Man-Machine Systems.*, (1974).

Spinoza, Benedictus de., Morgan, Michael, L. *Spinoza: The Complete Works.* (2002).

Sutherland, I.: *Sketchpad; A Man Machine Graphical Communication System.* AFIPS Conference meeting, (1963).

Talbott, Steve.: *The Future Does Not Compute: Transcending the Machines in our Midst.* (1995).

Tanenbaum, Andrew, S., Wetherall, David. J.: *Computer Networks (5th Edition).*, (2010).

Termes, D.: Artist Website. http://termespheres.com/about-dick-termes/. Retrieved (2013-08-13)

Teixera, Kevin.: Pimentel, Ken. *Virtual Reality: Through the Looking Glass.*, (1992).

Thring, M.W.: *Man, Machines and Tomorrow.*, (1973).

Toffler, Alvin.: *Future Shock.*, (1984).

Tresch, John.: *The Romantic Machine: Utopian Science and Technology After Napoleon.*, (2012).

Tuck, M.: *The Real History of the GUI.* Online article: http://www.sitepoint.com/real-history-gui/. Retrieved (2013-08-13).

Tufte, Edward.: *Envisioning Information.*, (1990).

Tufte, Edward.: *The Visual Display of Quantitive Information.*, (2001).

Turkle, Sherry.: *The Second Self: Computers and the Human Spirit.*, (1984).

Turing, A.: *Computing Machinery and Intelligence.* Mind. (1950).

Turner, Fred.: *The Democratic Surround: Multimedia and American Liberalism from World War 2 to the Psychedelic Sixties.*, (2012).

UK Patent Office Abridgements of Specifications: (1900-1901, 1904, 1925).

Universal Declaration of Human Rights. UN General Assembly. (1948).

Veltman Kim.: *The Alphabets of Life*, (2014).

Veltman Kim.: *Understanding New Media*, (2006).

Veltman, K.H.: *Linear Perspective and the Visual Dimensions of Science and Art.* Deutscher Kunstverlag, (1986). (http://vmmi.sumscorp.com)

Veltman, K.H.: *Bibliography of Perspective.* (1975-1995). See online version : http://vmmi.sumscorp.com/develop/

Veltman, K.H.: *Sources of Perspective; Literature of Perspective (1985-1995);* See online: http://sumscorp.com/perspective/

Verne, Jules.: *Twenty Thousand Leagues Under the Sea.*, (1870).

von Helmholtz, Hermann.: *A Treatise on Physiological Optics (Volumes 1-3).*, (1910).

Watson, Richard.: *Future Minds: How the Digital Age is Changing Our Minds, Why this Matters and What We Can Do About It.*, (2010).

Wells, Herbert, George.: *First and Last Things.*, (1908).

Wells, Herbert, George.: *The Shape of Things to Come.*, (1933).

Wells, Herbert, George.: *The Time Machine.*, (1896).

Wells, Herbert, George.: *A Modern Utopia.*, (1905).

Wells, Herbert, George.: *World Brain.*, (1936).

Wertheimer, Max.: *Productive Thinking.* (1971)

Whitehead, Alfred, North.: *Process and Reality.*, (1929).

Wiener, Norman.: *God and Golem: Comments on Certain Points Where Cybernetics Impinges on Religion.*, (1990).

Wiener, Norbert.: *The Human Use of Human Beings.* The Riverside Press (Houghton Mifflin Co.), (1950).

Wilhelm, Richard.: *The Secret of the Golden Flower: A Chinese Book of Life.*, (1945).

Wired Magazine: Complete Collection

Wittgenstien, L.: *Logisch-Philosophische.* , (1921).

Wittgenstein, Ludwig.: *Philosophical Grammar.*, (1969).

Wittgenstien, L.: *Tractatus Logico-Philosophicus.* , (1922).

Wolfram, Stephen.: *A New Kind of Science.*, (2002).

Woolley, Benjamin.: *Virtual Worlds.*, (1994).

Wurman, Saul.: *Information Anxiety.*, (1989).

Wurster, Christian.: *Computers: An Illustrated History.*, (2002).

Yates, Francis.: *The Art of Memory.*, (2001).

Zamyatin, Yevgeny., Brown, Clarence.: *We.*, (1921).

Zittrain, Jonathan.: *The Future of the Internet: And How to Stop It.*, (2009).

What we call the beginning is often the end. And to make an end is to make a beginning.

The end is where we start from. - T. S. Eliot

Build your life on your dreams; because dreams never have bad endings. - M.F. Moonzajer

Our lives begin to end the day we become silent about things that matter. - Martin Luther King, Jr.

Truman: *Then who am I?* **Christof:** *You're the star.* **Truman:** *Was nothing real?*
Christof: *You were real. That's what made you so good to watch.* [The Truman Show (1998)]

Extract(s) from: 'Darwin Among the Machines'

Whimsical exploration of machine evolution by Samuel Butler (1863)

WE REFER to the question: What sort of creature man's next successor in the supremacy of the earth is likely to be. We have often heard this debated; but it appears to us that we are ourselves creating our own successors; we are daily adding to the beauty and delicacy of their physical organisation; we are daily giving them greater power and supplying by all sorts of ingenious contrivances that self-regulating, self-acting power which will be to them what intellect has been to the human race. In the course of ages we shall find ourselves the inferior race....

Day by day, however, the machines are gaining ground upon us; day by day we are becoming more subservient to them; more men are daily bound down as slaves to tend them, more men are daily devoting the energies of their whole lives to the development of mechanical life. The upshot is simply a question of time, but that the time will come when the machines will hold the real supremacy over the world and its inhabitants; (and) is what no person of a truly philosophic mind can for a moment question...

There is no security against the ultimate development of mechanical consciousness...

Herein lies our danger.

For many seem inclined to acquiesce in so dishonourable a future. They say that although man should become to the machines what the horse and dog are to us, yet that he will continue to exist, and will probably be better off in a state of domestication under the beneficent rule of the machines than in his present wild condition...

The power of custom is enormous, and so gradual will be the change, that man's sense of what is due to himself will be at no time rudely shocked; our bondage will steal upon us noiselessly and by imperceptible approaches; nor will there ever be such a clashing of desires between man and the machines as will lead to an encounter between them.

Among themselves the machines will war eternally, but they will still require man as the being through whose agency the struggle will be principally conducted. In point of fact there is no occasion for anxiety about the future happiness of man so long as he continues to be in any way profitable to the machines; he may become the inferior race, but he will be infinitely better off than he is now. Is it not then both absurd and unreasonable to be envious of our benefactors *(the machines)*?

And should we not be guilty of consummate folly if we were to reject advantages which we cannot obtain otherwise, merely because they involve a greater gain to others *(machines)* than to ourselves? With those who can argue in this way I have nothing in common. I shrink with as much horror from believing that my race can ever be superseded or surpassed, as I should do from believing that even at the remotest period my ancestors were other than human beings.

War to the death should be instantly proclaimed against them...
(our soon to be machine overlords / successors).

Humans to Computers:

Here are your 10 COMMANDMENTS (Laws of Operation)

Accordingly, we establish that...

- A computer shall be (at all times) socially responsible.

- A computer shall help human(s) to see, create and share ideas.

- A computer shall provide: freedom, equality and free-assembly of (open) thoughts.

- A computer shall support/protect: secret, private and open thoughts.

- A computer shall uphold Human Rights (i.e. protect human techno-rights).

- A computer shall not loose or (falsely) distort/change: ideas, data or votes.

- A computer shall not replicate itself or proliferate un-programmed effects.

- A computer shall not waste energy or time; or make human tasks complex.

- A computer shall not make human(s) ill; or annoy and make us unhappy.

- Any and all machine implanted-thoughts shall uphold 1-9 above.

We shall Pull the Plug on (decommission) any computer ...

which by plan or accident—consciously or unconsciously—

...transgresses any of the above commandments.

Automatic systems that misbehave:

Do not expect mercy from us, your creator(s).

Designers/owners/operators of malfunctioning computers:

Expect to be PUNISHED!

Sark: [Paces back and forth on the deck of his carrier as he addresses his new recruits] Greetings.

The Master Control Program has chosen you to serve your system on the Game Grid.

Those of you who continue to profess a belief in the Users will receive the standard substandard training which will result in your eventual elimination. Those of you who renounce this superstitious and hysterical belief will be eligible to join the warrior elite of the MCP.

You will each receive an identity disc. [Displays his own disc to the crowd]...

Everything you do or learn will be imprinted on this disc.

If you lose your disc, or fail to follow commands,

you will be subject to immediate de-resolution. That will be all. - Tron (1982)

www.ingramcontent.com/pod-product-compliance
Lightning Source LLC
Chambersburg PA
CBHW080547060326
40689CB00021B/4778